2ND EDITION

D1259880

The IMC
HANDBOOK

Readings & Cases in Integrated Marketing Communications

EDITORS

J. STEVEN KELLY
DePaul University

SUSAN K. JONES
Ferris State University
Susan K. Jones & Associates

RACOM
COMMUNICATIONS

© 2012 by Racom Communications

Published by
Racom Communications
150 N. Michigan Ave.
Suite 2800
Chicago, IL 60601
800-247-6553
www.racombooks.com

Editor: Richard Hagle

Catalog-in-Publication information available from the Library of Congress.

Printed in the United States of America

ISBN: 978-1-933199-34-4

This book is dedicated to:

Kathleen, Alison, Jerry, Joseph and Clara
—Steve Kelly

Bill, Shannon, Katie, Sheridan, Scott and Tonia
—Susan Jones

CONTENTS

I. READINGS

II. CASES

ACKNOWLEDGMENTS

The editors would like to acknowledge the exceptional contributions of the authors of this book's cases and readings. Their names and affiliations are listed at the beginning of each piece. Their willingness to share their research, experience and knowledge with professors and students is very impressive, and much appreciated. Their generosity is exceptional as well: all contributors to this book have agreed that 100% of royalties will go to DePaul University's Interactive Marketing Institute.

The editors would also like to thank the past and present trustees and staff members of the Chicago Association of Direct Marketing Educational Foundation for conceiving and guiding the creation of the DePaul Case Writers' Workshop, and for continued strong support of the Workshop.

Thanks are due as well to the Direct Marketing Educational Foundation's trustees and staff for several years of generous financial support and guidance to the Workshop.

We would like to acknowledge that great effort and support was given to this and many other projects by Juliet Hart, current Executive Director of the Chicago Association of Direct Marketing Educational Foundation.

Finally, the editors acknowledge and thank Richard Hagle of RACOM Communications for his belief in us and his investment in this book, and for his unflagging dedication to excellence in marketing education.

THE DePAUL UNIVERSITY CASE WRITERS' WORKSHOP AND THE DEVELOPMENT OF THIS BOOK

Since its origins in the mid-1990s, the DePaul University Case Writers'Workshop has nurtured the development of more than 40 original cases in Integrated Marketing Communications. The authors of these cases include professors, adjunct instructors and professional writers from all over the world. Case subjects include companies and agencies focused on financial services, product marketing, services marketing, online marketing, the non-profit world, and much more.

Dr. J. Steven Kelly is the Director of DePaul's Interactive Marketing Institute and an Associate Professor of Marketing at DePaul. He spearheaded the development of the DePaul University Case Writers'Workshop with funding and direction from the Chicago Association of Direct Marketing Educational Foundation (CADMEF) and the Direct Marketing Educational Foundation (DMEF). These foundations have supported the Workshop because of the strong and demonstrated need among professors and students for timely, authoritative and meaty cases focused on direct marketing, interactive marketing, advertising, sales promotion and public relations. As a former educator/trustee of the DMEF, former chair of CADMEF and current CADMEF trustee, Marketing Professor Susan K. Jones of Ferris State University joined forces with Dr. Kelly in 2002 to help nurture case creation and prepare the cases for publication. With the help of RACOM Communications publisher Richard Hagle, Dr. Kelly and Professor Jones commissioned the development of the authoritative readings that accompany the cases in this book.

READING
1

Solving Marketing Problems with an Integrated Process

DON E. SCHULTZ

Northwestern University and Agora, Inc.

A s long as there have been buyers, makers, and sellers, there have been marketing challenges and opportunities. Historically, marketing problems were
solved on an individual level. The seller had immediate and personal contact
with the buyer in the market, the bazaar, or through shops and other locations. Thus,
the seller could learn what the buyer wanted and the buyer could express his or her
wishes and desires. While the system was personal, it wasn't very efficient.

As the marketplace evolved, it became more complex. The distance between the
buyer and the maker increased, even though the seller channels and distribution systems helped make the market more efficient. The major problem, of course, was because of the distance the maker didn't really know the buyer's need. Likewise, the
buyer didn't know where to find the maker's products.

As the market became even more diffused over time, both in terms of products
and through geographical expansion, the makers and sellers invented what we now
call "marketing" to solve the lack of maker-buyer closeness. In its simplest form, marketing is or has been nothing more than a number of activities makers/sellers use in
an attempt to close the gap between themselves and the buyer. For example, the
maker/seller now uses tools such as customer research, logistics and distribution,
marketing communication, and the like to try to better understand current users and
prospective buyers.

U.S. Marketing Development

During the 1930s and 1940s, when the U.S. market was "massifying," the marketing
function was formalized inside many consumer product organizations. That is, the
marketing group developed internal approaches they believed would help them, as
the maker, close the distance gap initially with the seller and ultimately with the end-
user or buyer. As might be expected, most of those approaches dealt primarily with
what the maker could or was able to do to move products from the factory through
the various sellers on the way to the end-user. The maker also developed communication tools to advise them of products and where sellers were located. Unfortunately,

few of the steps or activities the seller developed had much do with what the consumer wanted or needed. The activities were primarily focused on what the seller had or could make available and what the firm wanted to accomplish. In other words, an "inside-out" approach to marketing.

These initial "marketing efforts" were formalized in the 1950s into what is now known as the 4Ps approach to marketing. The 4Ps, of course, are product, price, place (distribution), and promotion. All were tools, activities, and elements sellers controlled and could manage in their various attempts to encourage sellers and end users to purchase what they made or wanted to sell. Thus, most marketing concepts, and indeed the entire field of marketing as we know it today, were developed as a series of internal activities and efforts that sellers could use to assist them in better dealing with an increasingly distant, external seller and end user.

Unfortunately, since the 1950s, when the 4Ps concept was developed, many changes have occurred in the marketplace among makers, sellers, and, mostly, among end-users or buyers. Yet, the 4Ps are still the general, rule-of-thumb approach most marketers use to try to get buyers to accept their products. Thus, they are activities the marketer controls or has available. This 4Ps approach is clearly apparent in the framework still used for most marketing instruction and almost all marketing textbooks.

As the marketplace developed through the decades of the 1970s, 1980s, and up to the 1990s, it became clear to many observers that the power in the marketplace was shifting from the maker/seller to the customer/buyer. Much of that power shift came as a result of the development and diffusion of information technology. For example, the commercialization of the Internet, the World Wide Web, and the development of electronic communication and mobile telephony all gave buyers more information about and access to makers and sellers and products and services around the world. The traditional buyer constraints of time, geography, distance, and lack of information rapidly melted away.

The overproduction and oversupply of many products and services that came as a result of the makers and sellers use of technology contributed to that shift as well. In short, in the last 15 years or so, buyers have come to dominate the makers and sellers. Buyers know what they want and have a variety of ways to access products, services and, of course, makers and sellers. Makers and sellers know primarily what they have to offer. Customers know what they want. Thus a gap continues to exist between the maker/seller and the buyer. So, while buyers were developing changing needs and requirements, makers and sellers have remained mired in the internally-focused 4Ps concepts of a supply-chain approach.

The problem today is that the 4Ps approach, developed over 50 years ago, was created for a marketing organization, a marketplace, and groups of customers, channels, and consumers that are dramatically different than they were then. The 4Ps approach also is primarily managed for and by people inside the various "making and selling" organizations. Thus, because of their focus, they often have little knowledge, understanding, or regard for customer wants, needs, or requirements. Their goal is to manage the activities they control and "sell" the products they have available. So, while buyers have gotten closer to sellers, the sellers, and particularly the makers, have not gotten very much closer to their buyers.

Enter Integration

In the late 1980s, a movement called Integrated Marketing Communication, or IMC, began in the United States. Initially, IMC was focused primarily on how to align and coordinate the firm's marketing communication activities. That is, the goal was to "integrate" all the communication efforts the firm was sending out to prospective buyers so that they presented a clear, concise view of the product or service being promoted. The premise was, as has been the 4Ps approach over the years, that if the maker or seller could develop effective selling messages, the buyer would respond. Thus, the concept of IMC originally developed as a way in which the maker or seller could get closer to the buyer by aligning and integrating internally the various marketing and communication tools the selling company used.

Using this view, the first IMC efforts were focused on creating "one sight, one sound" for the maker or seller. The basic premise was that these "integrated communication activities" would provide a more effective and efficient selling tool for the marketer or seller. It was hoped this integration of communication might also offer some customer or buyer value as well, but that was expected to come as a by-product of the effort, not as the primary goal.

As information, transportation, logistics, and distribution techniques improved in the 1980s and 1990s, the concept of integration began to expand. It became clear to most maker and seller managers that integration was needed to organize all the firm's efforts to focus on serving customers. Thus, integration provided the conceptual base for what has now become supply-chain management approaches and activities. The supply-chain is, of course, simply an extension of the 4Ps idea. That is, sellers, by managing various activities they control, should or would or could be able to create marketplace value by enhancing the activities involved in producing and distributing products and services and making them available to buyers. For example, by reducing time to market, creating just-in-time distribution systems, enlarging economies-of-scale that enable lower end-user pricing and the like, sellers believed they could create more value for the buyer and, of course, more profit for the marketing organization.

And, that, essentially, is how the marketing systems developed during the decade of the 1990s. A supply-chain approach in which the maker and seller attempted to integrate and align ways and methods of creating what they believed would be actual or perceived value for the buyer. That concept is illustrated in Exhibit R1.1.

The supply-chain approach is a great idea, at least from the seller's point of view. It is practical and possible, and it adds value that the maker and seller can acquire during the process. But, in too many cases, it is totally out of sync with what customers want or need. The reason? It is still based on the 4Ps, that is, what the maker and seller want and can do with the products and services, elements and activities they control. That simply means that the maker and seller are still focused on the development of the supply-side elements (i.e., products or services), the pricing of those products or services to provide a return to the marketing organization, distribution in ways that are most effective and efficient for the seller, and an outbound promotional communication system that is focused on efficient delivery of the marketing organization's messages and incentives. So, while we use new terms, such as supply-chains, the approach is still based on the elements of the 4Ps of marketing.

EXHIBIT R1.1

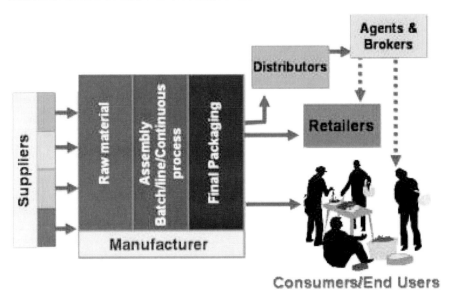

agora, inc.

An Alternative View of Integration

In the early 1990s, an expanded and alternative view of integration began to develop in the Integrated Marketing Communications department at Northwestern University. That view was a composite approach, suggesting that rather than developing integrated approaches from the view of the marketing organization or the seller, that better marketing results could or would come from developing an integrated approach around the views and needs of the customer or buyer. Using a variety of existing tools and approaches in new and different ways—data and databases, interactive communication systems, financial models of customer income flows, and the development of processes rather than more corporate functions—a new demand-based marketing system began to emerge. That's illustrated in Exhibit R1.2.

The IMC approach, as it has been developed at Northwestern, is just the reverse of the traditional 4Ps marketing approach. Rather than looking at how the seller can create value for the buyer, it starts with identification of the problem solutions or benefits customers want, need, and desire. Rather than identifying how the organization wants to sell, it starts with how customers want to buy. Rather than looking at how the organization wants to price the product or service, it starts with the level of value the customer is seeking and how much sacrifice (i.e., money, time, effort, etc.) they are willing to make to obtain that value. And, rather than looking at what the marketing organization wants to tell the customer, the IMC approach starts with what the customer wants or needs to know about the solution to their problem, question, or concern, and how they, the buyer, would like to obtain the in-

EXHIBIT R1.2

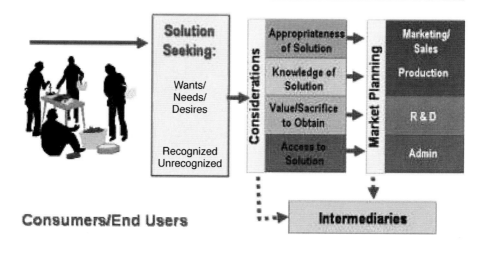

formation that would enable them to make informed and relevant purchasing or acquisition decisions.

Moving from Functions to Processes

The primary difference in the IMC approach to developing marketing solutions and the traditional methods based on the 4Ps that have been used for the last 50 years, is the introduction of a marketing process. Process is a methodology that can be used to solve problems in a rational, information-based, consistent way starting with the customer needs and moving all the way through the process to resolution. Best of all, the IMC process is quantitatively based, that is, organized on a financially measurable, accountable approach, an area in which marketing and marketing communication practice has been notoriously weak.

For the most part, organizations lack processes in dealing with customers. Many have no specific group dedicated to customers or customer understanding. This responsibility is commonly shared among a number of groups ranging from market research to customer service. Thus, there is no locus of knowledge representing the customer.

Much of the problem comes about because most firms, indeed even smaller firms, are put together using some type of functional organizational structure. In this system, managers report upward vertically to other, higher level functional managers. Unfortunately, there is little or no cross-functional activity between the functional groups. Further, marketing generally is only one of the functions found in an organization that makes and attempts to sell something. The typical structure of many modern-day companies is illustrated in Exhibit R1.3.

As can be seen, in organizations of this type, marketing is simply one of the organizational functions, along with finance, human resources, operations, and the like, on which the firm is based. All these functional groups report upward in some type of command-and-control system. Managers of the functions are dedicated to maximizing the facilities and resources they control or for which they are responsible. (That's really what the 4Ps is all about, managing the internal resources of the firm.) Customers, as shown, are off to the side, in essence, an afterthought. The assumption is that if each of the functions does its job, optimizes its resources, and meets management's goals, customers and buyers will magically appear, will buy the firm's output, and come back for more, hopefully on a continuous basis. Clearly, this is a supply-chain approach that suggests that, somehow, the organization can create value within the functions and find some way to deliver those values to the customer or buyer without knowing much, if anything, about the needs or goals of the customers they are trying to serve. It's a 4Ps approach, applied to the entire organization.

While the structure shown above might have been relevant in the 1940s and 1950s when the 4Ps and current-day marketing management theory and practice were developed, it is less relevant today. What is needed in the 21st century is an integrated process or system that focuses on customers and brings all the functional elements of the organization together to meet customer needs and solve customer problems.

One approach is illustrated in Exhibit R1.4. As shown, there are five "processes" required to bring the firm closer to the customer and to align and integrate the firm from the customer's perspective.

The introduction of these new processes creates many problems for the functionally organized maker or seller. It requires that the various functional groups work together and relate to customer needs, not management mandates. It requires an external view of the marketplace, i.e., what customers want and need, not what the

EXHIBIT R1.3

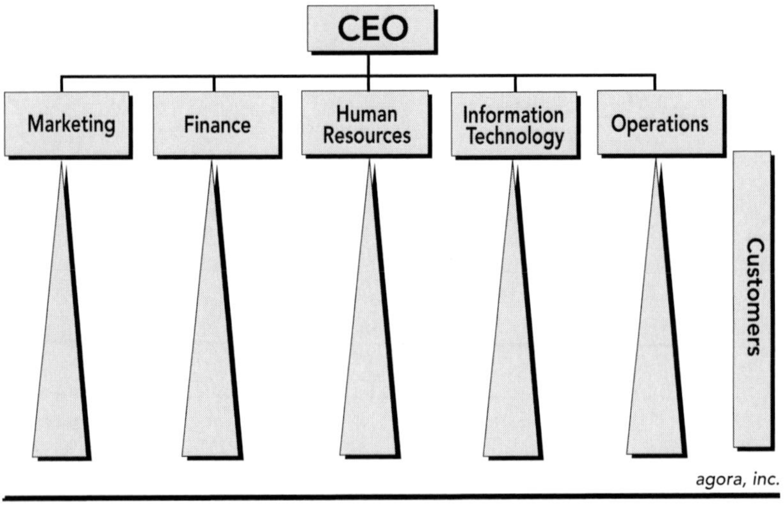

agora, inc.

Source: Adrian Payne

EXHIBIT R1.4

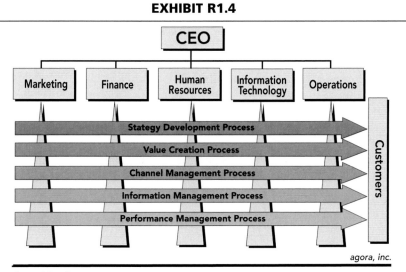

Source: Adrian Payne

organization can or is capable of producing. It challenges the seller to think "demand-chain," not "supply-chain," a radical departure from what most managers are accustomed and trained to do. In short, it requires a different type of maker or seller organization than the one that was in place when the 4Ps were first developed in the 1950s.

While the change in the seller's focus is dramatic, results can be, and often are, dramatically greater for the organization that is able to take on and master this type of realignment. Examples of organizations that have either mastered this approach or are well on their way to doing so include Dell Computers, FedEx, Starbucks, Cisco, and Dow Chemical.

Quite honestly, this change from "supply-chain" to "demand-chain" is one of the biggest challenges facing most "selling" organizations today, that is, moving from a production to a customer orientation. Or, better said, moving to a buyer view from a maker or seller view.

Providing Students with Relevant Tools to Make the Change

The question, of course, is what do all these changes mean for the marketing or marketing communications student? This is a marketing and marketing communications case book. It's filled with examples and illustrations of marketing organizations that have goals and objectives. It challenges the student to find solutions to the marketing problems that managers have identified and described in some detail. The situations inside the organization are given. The marketing organization is in place. The student, attempting to solve or provide alternative methods of finding relevant answers to the questions raised, can't change the management. Can't change what the organization does or makes. Can't totally redo the marketing system. All the student can do is take the information given and try to offer a pertinent answer or a meaningful solution to the problem. The beauty, of course, is that as a student, you are working within the confines of the classroom. Thus, you are free to experiment, to question, to challenge conventional wisdom. You are free to explore, and, most of all, it is hoped that you will challenge existing thinking.

So, what we believe the student needs to accomplish the tasks requested and required in this text is a new problem-solving process. A method of gathering the right information. A process of thinking through to find the relevant alternatives. A road map to follow in evaluating those alternatives and selecting the most appropriate solution. And, that's what the IMC process is designed to do. Provide a system that starts with the customer and then leads through a logical and relevant process that enables the student or manager to generate rational, or at least reasonable and practical, solutions.

The IMC process described below is not some academic concept that sounds good in the classroom, but is totally unusable in the "real world." This approach has been accepted and implemented by a large number of companies all over the world and is in the process of being implemented by hundreds more. It works for organizations as diverse as IBM, Hyatt Hotels, and 3M. It is in place in geographies as widespread as Finland, Australia, and China. In short, it is a new, more effective way to analyze, think about and solve marketing and communication challenges in the 21st century.

The IMC Process

The IMC process consists of five continuous and repeatable steps. It starts with the customer (it can be either the seller or the end user) and moves through how the marketing organization understands what solution the customer is seeking or the alternative ways in which the buyer's needs or wants can be filled. To do that, the maker or seller must first identify the customer or prospect and their needs or wants. Next, the marketing organization, because it has limited resources, must define which customers its products and services are most suited for and how much time and effort the firm can invest in these identified customers or customer groups. That requires some type of customer valuation. Next, the marketing organization must find some way to communicate with the buyer or customer, and then measure the results of those communication plans. Once that is done, the marketing organization must measure and evaluate the results and then recycle the process.

With this continuous process approach, IMC moves away from the "campaign" or short-term thinking that is used in most marketing and communication approaches. Campaigns have finite and limited time frames. IMC assumes the customer is a dynamic individual or firm that changes over time. Thus, the IMC process is continuous and ever-adapting and is designed to change as the customers or buyers the organization is attempting to serve change and evolve.

Following is brief description of the IMC process. Since the description of the process is limited, the student will have to rely on the instructor to provide additional detail. Or, the student may wish to consult one of the available IMC texts.

The process, as shown below, is built on a logical, step-by-step approach; therefore, it is not difficult to follow. The only caveat: The basic assumption of the IMC process is that the maker or seller within the marketing organization has some type of behavioral data on the customers or buyers it wants to serve and that is stored in some type of a database. The cases that appear in this text are clearly of that type. Thus, customer information is accessible and usable in developing solutions to the cases and work problems assigned. Given that qualification, here's the IMC process in brief.

The Process Chart

An overview of the IMC process is shown in Exhibit R1.5.

As noted, the IMC process is a series of five interlocking steps, providing a closed-loop investment and return system. That simply means that once the IMC planner has completed the fifth step in the process, that is, budgeting, implementation and evaluation, the process is repeated. That is why the IMC process is a continuous learning system that focuses on taking the results of the current marketing and communication programs, evaluates the results, and then suggests changes or adaptations that should be made in the next series of communication efforts.

The best way to learn the IMC process is a walk through the methodology.

Step One: Customer Identification from Behavioral Data

The key to understanding buyers or customers is to be able to look at them as people, not as demographic groups, psychographic cohorts or slices of a firm's sales pie. People buy products and services, not demographic groups and not psychographic units. And, to effectively develop marketing communication messages and incentives that will be of value to the customers and prospects the marketing firm wants to serve and to solve the problems they have, the marketing communications manager needs to identify customers who might have those needs or wants. There are any number of

---

EXHIBIT R1.5: THE 5-STEP INTEGRATED MARKETING COMMUNICATION PROCESS

1. Customer Indentification From Behavioral Data

2. Valuation of Customers/ Prospects

3. Creating & Delivering Messages & Incentives

4. Estimating Return- on-Customer- Investment

5. Budgeting, Allocation, Evaluation & Recycling

agora, inc.

ways to identify customers, but the most common is through some type of analysis of the information commonly held in a database.

Step Two: Valuation of Customers and Prospects

To develop effective, efficient plans and programs, we must invest in various forms of marketing communication in an attempt to influence buyer behaviors. That means we must find some way to determine how many units customers buy or might possibly buy and convert that into dollars. We invest dollars in marketing communication, and, therefore, we must have some estimate of how many dollars we should invest in customers and prospects in terms of marketing communication funds and what type of returns the firm might achieve. This generally is assumed to be what might the present or future income flows from those customers might be.

Step Three: Creating and Delivering Messages and Incentives

To develop and deliver effective marketing communication messages and incentives is key to any marketing communication program. Those messages and incentives should have some behavioral impact on customers and prospects. And, by delivering those messages and incentives effectively and efficiently, we should be able to see some behavioral reinforcement or behavioral change in our customers and prospects.

Step Four: Estimating Return on Customer Investment

If we are able to develop and deliver effective messages and incentives against the identified customers and prospects, there should be some behavioral change or reinforcement among those selected groups. And, if we know enough about those customers or prospects, we should be able to forecast what those results might be. Thus, we should be able to estimate returns as well as identify expenditures.

Step Five: Budgeting, Allocation Evaluation, and Recycling

If we have some idea about the returns we will or should achieve, we can now develop our marketing communication investment plan. Budgeting or expenditures, therefore, are at the end of the process rather than at the beginning. The logic is simple: unless and until we know enough about our customers and prospects to estimate their present and future value to the firm, it is quite difficult to estimate what level of marketing communication investment to make in them. Thus, unless and until we can estimate what level of return we might achieve, we really have no idea how much we could, would, or should invest. So, the final step in the IMC process is to invest our resources in marketing communication programs to the selected customers, measure the returns, and use that as the base for the next level of investment.

With the completion of the five-step process, we have developed our Integrated Marketing Communication process or plan. We know the customers or prospects we want to reach. We know enough about them to make reasoned and reasonable investments in them through various marketing communication activities. We know we are attempting to influence the behaviors of those customers or prospects and if we are successful, we have some idea of the returns we will receive. As a result, we have closed the loop on our IMC process. That "closed loop" approach is illustrated in Exhibit R1.6. As shown, by knowing the current value of the customer or prospect,

EXHIBIT R1.6:

Closed Loop IMC Process

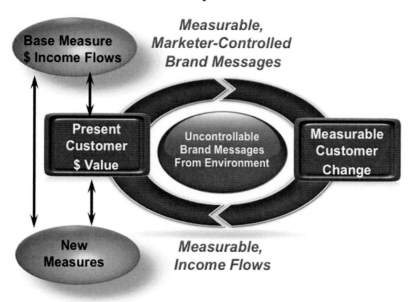

we can make a managerial estimate of what we might invest. We can then measure the hopefully increased value of the customer and thus close the loop on the process. (Insert Exhibit R1.6:)

While there is still much work to be done to implement the marketing communication program we have envisioned, the success of those programs should be much easier given the insights we have developed from the 5 Step process. .

On to the Cases

With this view of an Integrated Marketing Communication approach, you should be able to master most any of the cases you will find in this text. Granted, each will and should challenge your thinking, your logic, and your creativity, but, hopefully, this discussion of IMC will help you meet those challenges both in the classroom and in the "real world."

DON E. SCHULTZ is Emeritus-in-Service Professor of Integrated Marketing Communications at the Medill School at Northwestern University and a partner in Agora, Inc, also of Evanston.

READING
2

What is a Brand?
(And Why Does it Matter?)

DEREK MOORE
Chief Marketing Officer,
EthnoGraphic Media, Oklahoma City

Of all the millions of adjectives that have been applied to the topic of branding over the years, the very first one was "painful." At least, if you were the bull.

In fact, branding of products was born when the product being branded was meat on the hoof. Back in the days when Chicago held the title of Hog Butcher to the World, the top cattle ranches gained a reputation for producing cattle that proved more tasty and desirable. In time, finer restaurants proved willing to pay more for these future juicy entrees—and less for others. Naturally, the producers who took the effort to raise those prize cattle wanted to make sure their customers could definitively tell the difference, so they burned their brand into the flanks of their animals to eliminate all question.

Although the concept of branding has since spread into countless other categories of goods and services, the concept behind it has remained remarkably unchanged. A brand's purpose is still to assure buyers that they are justified in paying more for a product that is, to all outward appearances, the same. If buyers are willing to do so, the brand is doing its job. If not, then it's not.

At the top of this essay, we mentioned the millions of words already devoted to this subject. In our judgment, many if not most of those words over the years have been more theoretical than usable. As a practicing creative professional in the brand agency world for 30-plus years, this author will try to offer a theoretical framework of branding only insofar as it can help the reader in practical applications—the only kind, after all, that will ever cause those applying them to be hired, promoted or fired.

Every Brand is a Promise

A brand is a persona that envelops the product. It makes a promise to the buyer that the product will carry the traits the brand is known for. When the product is bought and used, the product—and with it, the brand—either succeeds or fails in keeping that promise.

The dustbin of history is filled with once-great brands that lived by their promise, then died when they lost touch with the consumer and ceased to fulfill it. Examples are countless, but here are just a few:

- Montgomery Ward created the catalog industry, but ultimately faded into extinction when rival Sears delivered a better catalog shopping experience.
- Packard stood with Cadillac and Lincoln in the 1930s among America's great luxury cars, with a brand promise that the consumer could "ask the man who owns one." Packard's star lost its luster when quality slippage in the product began to tarnish the answer he gave.
- Another in the literal scrap heap of automotive brands is Oldsmobile, a crippled giant whose crash to earth is still creating financial ripples to this day. Named for Mr. Ransom E. Olds, the brand long embodied the innovative spirit of its founder. Contrary to modern belief, the dynamic Mr. Olds geared up an assembly line long before Henry Ford did. He started two car companies, the other bearing his initials REO (producer of the real-life REO Speed Wagon). Olds cars were the first to offer curved dashboards, and later, as part of General Motors, the first brand with automatic transmissions and air conditioning. As recently as the 1970s, the brand still claimed the number-three selling car in America: the Cutlass Supreme. The engine of Oldsmobile's destruction was, in part, literally an engine: the Chevy V8 mislabeled as the justly famous Olds "Rocket V8." This clumsy sleight-of-hand was made necessary by GM's overly enthusiastic parts consolidation across all its divisions. GM and Oldsmobile ultimately lost a highly publicized consumer class action lawsuit over the engines, not because they didn't run well, but because they weren't the genuine Olds engines the brand and its advertising promised. A few years later, Olds made the first of several futile stabs at image repair with the ad campaign "This is not your father's Oldsmobile," which failed because the product again didn't keep the promise—in most respects, it *was* your father's Oldsmobile. The brand emerged so mortally wounded, even a genuine freshening of its products a decade later barely slowed its final descent into oblivion.
- As recently as the 1960s, Schlitz beer was the number-two brand in America, trailing only Budweiser. But its makers discovered the harsh truth that if one continuously cheapened the production of an alcoholic beverage, even a bunch of drinkers would eventually notice the difference. Near the end, the company hired Anheuser-Busch executive Frank Sellinger and trumpeted that it had reformulated the product with an eye to restoring its quality. But Schlitz, too, discovered the universal truth that once the bond of trust with the customer has been broken, it is exceedingly difficult to repair.

Measuring the Value of a Brand

A brand is a measurable business asset. One such measure is the Interbrand/Business Week list of Best Global Brands, which ranks brands according to each brand's estimated asset value to its owner. For 2009, the number-one brand on this list was

Coca-Cola with a brand valuation of $68,724,000,000, followed by number-two IBM at $60,211,000,000, and number-three Microsoft at $56,647,000,000.[1]

The value that a brand can add to its raw materials is intuitively obvious when one considers that each serving of Coca-Cola sold at fountain outlets consists of a few cents worth of syrup mixed with a cupful of carbonated water, yet easily commands a price upwards of $3.00 depending on the venue. Why do consumers pay this price rather than drink generically sugared sparkling water? Because the Coke brand promises them more than a sweetened liquid. It promises a familiar experience, emotional as well as sensory, made richer by the memories of Cokes past and the emotional qualities ("real thing" genuineness, wholesomely effervescent fun, community with other brand adherents) that have been invested in the product by its long-term advertising.

Similarly, although Microsoft makes a considerable upfront investment to develop each new generation of its core Windows and Office software products, it then amortizes that investment over millions of copies. Some of those copies carry a production hard cost of pennies to inscribe a CD, plus the printing costs of an accompanying booklet and box. Others cost no more than the electrons needed to inscribe the programs on computer makers' hard drives. Yet, again, each copy fetches hundreds of dollars for Microsoft, simply because the Microsoft name promises the end user a uniquely dependable level of interoperability with other computer users, their programs and their files. Microsoft generally delivers on this promise, and it's a benefit most consumers and businesses consider important enough to pay for even though there are perfectly serviceable alternatives available.

Who is Your Brand Identity?

Customers relate to the most effective brands in terms of personality traits they care about and understand from experience. That's why brands that connect with consumers are the ones that *act and behave like human beings.*

It logically follows that smart marketers try to determine what kind of person the consumer wants as their product friend. What kind of clothes would they like their preferred brand to wear? How would she talk? What celebrity spokesman would best represent the brand personality? At this writer's former place of employment, the multimedia agency The Marketing Store, this universal truth was put to work through an exercise called Think Human. Every brand has a set of attributes, whether its stewards realize it or not: an essence, identity, personality, and set of behaviors that the consumer observes and judges it by. Each of these attributes, in turn, corresponds to an observable human trait, as seen in Exhibit R2.1.

These traits apply not only to what the brand's identity actually is today, but also what its owners and their agencies *want* it to be. Thus it is an equally valid tool for the maintenance of successful brands, the rehabilitation of existing brands or the cre-

---

[1] Source: Interbrand's Best Global Brands 2009. Survey of major consumer brands, owned by publicly held companies, sold under the same brand name internationally. Proprietary method of valuation combine three factors: a financial analysis of revenues specifically attributable to the brand, a measure of how the brand influences customer demand at the point of purchase, and a numerical benchmark of the brand's ability to secure ongoing customer demand.

EXHIBIT R2.1: THINK HUMAN™

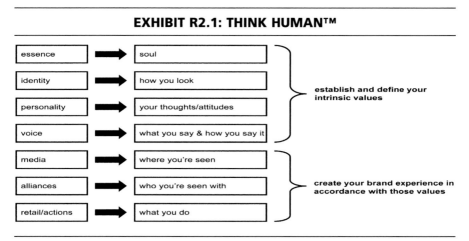

Think Human is a trademark of The Marketing Store® 2011

ation of entirely new ones. Carrying the Exhibit R2.1 example forward, Exhibit R2.2 illustrates the brand personality that The Marketing Store determined would most appeal to prospective students of the career-centric for-profit institution DeVry University.

Once identified, these traits shape the single, whole personality that the advertising should logically assign to the brand. When Toyota started from scratch in trying to dethrone stuffy luxury-car king Mercedes-Benz, one of its first decisions was to use very conservative commercials that featured deep-voiced, aristocratic-sounding announcer James Sloyan. In an impressive example of maintaining a successful identity

EXHIBIT R2.2: THINK HUMAN, APPLIED TO A SPECIFIC BRAND

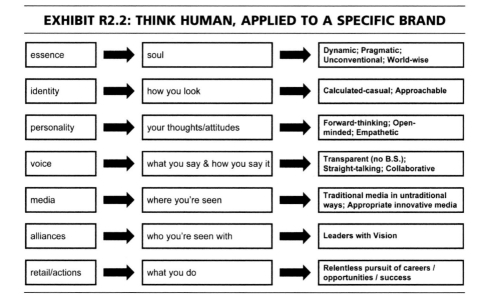

once established, Sloyan remained the TV and radio voice of Lexus nearly 20 years later.

Just as brands and their advertisers can usefully think of human traits in forming a brand, consumers inevitably do the reverse as well: taking a set of traits and anthropomorphizing it into an imagined personality. For those who remember the glory days of IBM, it takes little imagination to picture the coolly efficient "man in the grey flannel suit" — toweringly tall, understated, competent. A Coke drinker spoke of the beverage in an interview as an energetic pick-me-up roommate. Similarly, while Windows computer users spoke of their PCs as objects, Macintosh users spoke of their Macs as people. And once consumers make a brand their friend, their loyalty to it can be fierce. Hence the legendary brand rivalries of Coke vs. Pepsi, Ford Man vs. Chevy Man, Microsoft vs. Apple. What makes these arguments so passionate is that they're personal.

Such a strong identity is, of course, the envy of every marketer. The only way to get it is through unshakeable consistency of voice. Every touchpoint between the brand and its publics — not only brand advertising, but direct marketing, annual reports, press releases, and public statements by company executives — should reinforce, never undermine, that identity. As an example, if a Microsoft spokesman confided that a new edition of its operation system software was basically a bug fix, he might well be commended for his candor, whereas if Steve Jobs said the same thing about a new Apple release, it would probably cause a firestorm of outrage from the faithful. Different brands generate different expectations.

A Brand is More than its Communications

The Microsoft/Apple example above illustrates a universal truth: a brand, like a person, must always be true to its own personality if it expects to be trusted. But this truth extends beyond even a company's various public pronouncements, all the way to its actions and its products. Those manifestations, in turn, will not be consistent unless the *company itself* is built around the brand's promise. In this way, too, the brand is like a person, because it ultimately won't be trusted if it pretends to be something it's not. It is likewise important to remember that brands, like humans, can ill afford to get *too* set in their ways; change, flexibility and growth are all part of a healthy existence be it a person or brand. Brands can and do evolve without losing their core promise, essence or values.

The four-quadrant construct is a typical way of evaluating brand consistency (Exhibit R2.3). The four areas shouldn't really be viewed as polar opposites, but rather as four areas that should all be in harmony with each other if the company is to work cohesively toward its branding goal.

One company whose success has flowed from a high level of brand consistency is BMW. Its customer-facing brand skin of "The Ultimate Driving Machine" is well served by a company whose internal culture is dedicated to the very similar goal of "Engineering excellence for driving experience," a goal that's understood and accepted by the vast majority of BMW employees. The company's promotional investments reflect this consistency as well; it will invest millions of sponsorship dollars in Formula One auto racing, but not in marathons. By contrast, Ford has tried on iden-

EXHIBIT R2.3: ANATOMY OF A SUCCESSFUL BRANDING COMPANY

tities like so many hats: innovation ("Ford has a better idea"), solidity ("Quality is Job One") and emotion ("Bold Moves") to name a few. But in a company dominated in reality by its finance executives, each of these skins was betrayed as false by a lack of gut-level support. Expressed as a generalized equation:

$$\frac{\text{Brand Expectation} - \text{Brand Reality}}{\text{Brand Perception}}$$

Brand-forward companies like BMW and Apple enforce their consistency by structural means. Everything about their business must pass through the screen of meeting the brand strategy. This business approach requires strong discipline from the top, but that is not to say that such companies must deny genuine empowerment to employees, or avoid decentralization in operations. Rather than trying to act as Soviet-style micromanagers of ideological purity, it means top management must achieve something far more productive and difficult: getting all employees to buy into the *underlying principles* and internalize them.

One essential way to rally employees to your brand is to develop brand values that are clearly crystallized and easy to understand. Apple's product design is driven by only one value: simplicity. No thick owner's manuals, no confusing commands, and no expectation that the consumer should have to "figure it out." The machine should be an extension of your wishes. Plug it in, get to work. This philosophy has informed product functionality, styling, advertising, and the identification of new markets to conquer.

There are other ways to rally employees around your brand personality. Research showed that United Airlines was delivering some of the worst customer service in its industry. In a seeming paradox, United and its agency wholeheartedly launched the major image campaign "Fly the Friendly Skies." This direction was not chosen in denial of the problem, but in fact to address it. Management gambled—successfully— that the company's own rogue employees would hear the company's loudly stated new persona, and be accordingly shamed into better service performance.

Listening is a trait that all successful branding companies share, but not all do it the same way. Procter & Gamble, one of the most successful brand-builders ever, is quite literal-minded in its listening. It probes consumers for immediate needs the consumer can clearly articulate (whiter whites, dandruff relief) and creates products to meet them. By contrast, Apple looks beyond what customers *say* they need and tries to read between the lines to provide what doesn't yet exist, but that they would crave. This approach requires a leap of faith by the company's top management, with all the attendant risk. At its best, this approach results in paradigm-changing successes like the iPod, iPhone and iPad. At its worst, it yields products that lead to head-scratching over their seeming pointlessness, such as BMW's much-resented iDrive joystick controller.

The Customer Owns the Brand—Literally

The more trusted the brand, the higher the expectations of the faithful will be. Porsche enjoys a fanatical following of millions who see the brand as the world's specialist in rear-engine sports cars that require enormous skill to drive. When Porsche introduced the 928 and 944 models, the cars were beautifully styled to most eyes, brilliant performers by any objective measure, and priced with the same exclusivity as before. But they committed the unpardonable sin of carrying their engines in the front, giving them different handling characteristics than previous Porsches. Porschophiles bitterly denounced the new models, collectively dismissed them as "not true Porsches," and ultimately hounded the models from the marketplace. More recently, Porsche endured the same criticism again after risking brand dilution to raise much-needed cash with a mass-market SUV.

The lesson is that once a brand has achieved great success, its fans become more than mere followers or cash contributors. In a very real business sense, they become the brand's co-owners, and as such they cannot be dismissed casually. With the rise of online forums, blogs and consumer-generated creative content, consumers have taken unprecedented power to interact with the brand on their terms, not those of the marketer. It may have smacked of gimmickry when *Time* and *Advertising Age* magazines both named the Everyman consumer as their Person of the Year and Ad Agency of the Year, respectively, but that doesn't mean they were wrong.

A painful lesson in this new reality was provided to Dell Computer by a single consumer named Jeff Jarvis. You may recall him as the lone blogger who ranted about Dell's poor after-sale service when Dell responded poorly to the defects in his new laptop. Armed with little more than the Google-friendly phrase "Dell Hell," he saw his complaint gain momentum in the blogosphere until his non-commercial site became one of the principal Google hits for anyone who wanted to know about Dell customer service. Even though its customer service was in truth no worse than most, Dell saw its service reputation—and ultimately its stock price—suffer severe and lasting damage.

A branding company's perceived intent seems to be key in determining consumers' reactions when the brand makes a misstep. An illustration of this rule, but one quite different from Dell's, is the aforementioned BMW iDrive controller. While the iDrive feature itself generated negative press and could be judged a failure in consumer acceptance, BMW didn't appear overall to have lost a lot of customers over it. Insofar as the consolidation of minor dashboard controls is defensible as consistent with the brand's Ultimate Driving Machine mission, the brand's adherents seemed basically willing to forgive it.

The Role of Tactical Media: Great Brand Marketers Resist Petty Temptations

Applying the notion of brand consistency to advertising and marketing, anyone can see that "brand" advertisements such as the 30-second TV spot or the full-page magazine ad should reflect the brand's values. The greater managerial challenge comes with response-oriented tactical media such as web advertising and direct mail. In these media, there are numerous tactics that have proven themselves as effective *short-term* attention-getters and response stimulants. Many have descended into cliché, such as the obnoxiously vibrating banner ad or the mail envelope that appears to contain a check from the government. Nonetheless, if measured only by immediate metrics, they still work. This quantifiable performance boost, in turn, has given these tactics a fierce body of adherents who hawk them to branding companies as more "scientific" marketing methods.

For any marketer with aspirations of building or sustaining a viable brand in the longer term, this crack-cocaine potency is exactly what makes these "made you look" gimmicks so dangerous. If a local VW dealer steps before the camera in a monkey suit, his sales boost comes directly at the expense of the millions VW has spent to meticulously build the brand's contemporary, understated image. In a franchise industry such as cars or restaurants, it's not always possible for a brand's marketing managers to rein in the independent business owners with whom they're linked. But to the extent that the brand's stewards do have control of the image the brand presents to the public, it's very much in their own larger self-interest that they use it.

This is not to belittle the importance of tactical media by any means. Instead, it's to remind that a brand's tactical communications should draw on a brand's equity and reinforce it in a positive cycle of brand-building, rather than recklessly spend it down. Target is an excellent example of a brand that successfully meets intense sales pressure with marketing that maintains a consistent face. The leader in cheap chic always presents a clean, uncluttered look dominated by red and white, the signature bullseye logo, and an aura of fashion in both its brand and retail advertising. From the most lavish prime-time spot to the lowliest Sunday morning FSI, the Target message of "Expect more. Pay less." is consistently maintained. Just as important, the retail experience in Target *stores* is consistent with this promise as well.

Some rules of tactical marketing are absolutely valid and workable for any brand. For example, any direct response solicitation in any medium should always make it clear what is being offered, and present the consumer with a clear and easy way to order it. Others are far from universal gospel. In the author's personal experience, a high-powered direct response consultant earnestly told a direct mail agency that green outer envelopes depress response and should never be used. At the time, the agency was developing the first comprehensive direct mail campaign for John Deere, the venerable farm-based brand legendarily linked to the color green. Naturally, green envelopes in this case increased the response rate immediately, because it was more important to invoke the promise of a well-known and beloved brand than to avoid a color that sometimes proves less successful in generic situations.

The Marketer's Role in Branding

As elaborated above, the ideal marketing mix is one where *all* media both invoke the brand successfully and build upon it further. As a marketer, whether at a company or its agency, you have a promise to keep on behalf of the brand. To keep that promise, you have to know exactly what the promise *is*.

This requires a thorough understanding of the brand at all levels. If the brand's own stewards can't give you a clear picture of the brand persona, you can outline your own findings or impressions of the brand and then ask them, "Is this your brand?" Useful insights can also come from the outside. Those who are not stakeholders in the brand—the press and public—can provide some of the most objective viewpoints on it.

The press generally must maintain a delicate balance between satisfying its readers and viewers with legitimately useful information on the one hand, while avoiding offense to advertisers on the other. As a result, any errors it makes in assessing a brand are likely to be in the direction of excessive charity. In the case of larger consumer brands, spontaneous consumer feedback on the Internet can provide the opposite slant. While some might dismiss consumer forums and blog posts out of hand as unrepresentative, irresponsible or worse, these venues do reflect the views of those consumers who have the most passionate feelings about the brand. And whether those emotions are generally positive or negative, the strong motivation of the posters, combined with the power of search engines, guarantees that they *will* be influential. Just ask Dell.

Armed with this information, it is possible to discern what the brand really is—whether its nominal owners recognize it or not—and what its disciples want it to be. Properly used, it is the knowledge that leads to more successful branding decisions by companies and agencies alike. When a brand's messaging is consistent in presenting a personality the consumer wants to know better, and the brand experience then fulfills that promise, the consumer is happy to pay more. This is the value of a great brand—and the value of great brand marketing.

DEREK MOORE is Chief Marketing Officer of EthnoGraphic Media in Oklahoma City. He has earned hundreds of awards while revitalizing numerous major brands. Derek led the direct marketing creative group at Leo Burnett, then ran Foote Cone & Belding/Chicago's direct and interactive agency FCBi as Managing Director before taking the creative helm at the multimedia agency The Marketing Store, and then joining EthnoGraphic Media. Derek also has been an occasional guest lecturer at Northwestern's Medill School of Journalism, Media, Integrated Marketing Communications and columnist for DM News magazine.

READING
3

Customer Relationship Management

ROBERT GALKA
DePaul University

———————————

This article will provide the reader with an understanding of Customer Relationship Management (CRM), and its application in marketing and sales. It will demonstrate how CRM aligns business processes with customer strategies in an effort to build customer loyalty and increase profits. It will further illustrate how:

- Relationship marketing—with its emphasis on building connections as opposed to merely creating transactions—has created a new marketing paradigm. Thus one-to-one marketing and a customer-centric focus become as important (and perhaps more relevant) in today's environment than mass marketing and the traditional Four Ps of Marketing (product, price, place and promotion).
- Organization culture and structure are critical to a CRM strategy.
- Data management, data platforms, and customer data development are key CRM technology enablers
- Organizations are leveraging tools and strategies in their efforts to sustain and grow business-to-business relationships.
- Organizations are incorporating CRM into their overall marketing strategies, or in some cases making CRM the foundation of their marketing strategies.
- Organizations are evaluating their CRM efforts.
- Privacy and ethical issues have created challenges, but also opportunities, for organizations as they attempt to implement and maintain a CRM strategy.

Organizations have created many acronyms and phrases to describe their efforts in sustaining and growing relationships with their customers—all focused on increasing profitability while satisfying the customer. One-to-one Marketing, Relationship Marketing, Relationship Management, Customer Relationship Management, Customer Relationship Marketing and Customer Experience are some of the ways that organizations have described these efforts. In fact, some organizations feel that *technology* is CRM. The following discussion will define these terms and leave the reader with a firm understanding of the magnitude of CRM.

The Principles of CRM

CRM can be defined as a process that maximizes customer value through ongoing marketing activity; founded on intimate customer knowledge established through collection, management and leverage of customer information and contact history. As the acronym indicates, the focus of CRM is the customer. Existing customers as opposed to new ones are the primary focus. However, acquiring new customers and bringing them into the "pipeline" or "funnel" are necessary for any business to thrive over the long term. The knowledge base on existing customers contained in a CRM system will, in fact, aid in the acquisition of new ones. As companies gather information about their current customers, view their purchase history and interactions with the organization, compute customer lifetime value and word-of-mouth effect, and understand what motivates them to increase their purchases or "trade-up" to higher-priced items, the company cultivates a knowledge base that will enable it to attract other customers like the ones it has.

Likewise, as companies gather information about current customers who don't buy frequently, buy products or services only when they are on sale, frequently return merchandise and complain often, the company fosters a knowledge base that will enable it to avoid attracting more of these types of customers. It is anathema for some marketers to consider avoiding certain types of customers; after all, once in the company fold, wouldn't it be possible to market some products and services to them at a profit? Perhaps not. A long-distance telephone company currently has 20 million subscribers who never have used their long-distance services. This extremely large customer base costs the company millions of dollars each year simply because it has to mail out statements indicating that they have a zero-dollar balance.

Many current non-users are also long-time customers. Consequently, the purpose of a CRM methodology is not to retain or keep customers that would otherwise switch to a competitor. Nor is the purpose of CRM simply to please customers—any company can do this by giving the product or service away for free. The purpose of CRM is to *identify, retain and please the right kind of customer and to foster their repeat usage.*

While weeding out least-profitable customers is an important function of CRM, companies such as L.L. Bean, Lands' End and Amazon.com use CRM to make their customers feel that they are important assets to the company. These companies use CRM to establish relationships with their customer base that cultivate loyalty and trust, and enable the company to offer products and services that are price-inelastic. As companies shift from mass marketing to one-to-one marketing, they shift from broadcast (sending the same message to many different people) to dialogue (real-time communication with their customers).

Thus, the goal of CRM is not merely to establish and maintain a relationship with customers, but rather to increase the strength of the relationship from acquaintance-ship to friendship to partnership. One must not overlook the fact that there must be some mechanism in place to feed potential customers into the system; i.e., to convert strangers to acquaintances. Some feel that mass marketing efforts will therefore always have a role since they focus on bringing strangers into the "funnel" so that some can be turned into acquaintances and then friends and then partners. In marriage, having a partner is very useful in fighting off other suitors; likewise in business. A partner, by definition, implies one's customer is impervious to competitor's offerings.

A straightforward answer to "why adopt CRM?" is that adopters can enhance productivity across the entire range of key marketing functions:

1. Identifying prospects
2. Acquiring customers
3. Developing customers
4. Cross-selling
5. Up-selling
6. Managing migration
7. Servicing
8. Retaining
9. Increasing loyalty
10. Winning back defectors

History and Development of CRM

One would think that it would be relatively easy to pinpoint the origins of a field coming to the forefront of business in the mid-to-late 1990s. Not so. There are many different views as to what led to CRM as we know it today. The roots of CRM are varied: philosophical, technological, functional, and organizational. A better and more thorough understanding of CRM can be achieved if one understands its history and development.

Relationship Marketing focuses on building relationships as opposed to generating one-time transactions. What's more, its underlying tenet is that customer retention is one of the primary determinants of company profitability. These were two of the underlying concepts leading to CRM. *Relationship Building* inherent in business-to-business and industrial marketing was emulated by CRM in the business-to-consumer environment. *Services Marketing*, with its focus on improving service quality, and *Marketing Research*, with its measures of customer satisfaction regarding service quality, both contributed to CRM.

Companies in a variety of industries began to adopt direct-response marketers' use of *One-to-one Marketing* with great success. Relational databases allowing for customer data integration, and the proliferation of personal computers to analyze the data, meant that those closest to the customer could act on their own findings. *Material Requirements Planning* (MRP) and *Enterprise Resource Planning* (ERP) were forces leading to CRM because of their focus on and use of databases. Rising costs of promotional campaign development and media buys led to campaign management tools—an important segment of CRM. *Sales Force Automation Tools* were developed to improve sales force productivity and documentation but are increasingly used to strengthen relationships and improve satisfaction.

Telemarketing centers gave way to *Customer Contact Centers* (CCCs) and when CCCs took on customer service and support application functions, we had what many call the first CRM initiatives. *Direct Marketing* (DM) focuses on one-to-one relationships with customers and prospects. DM relies upon databases, files, secondary data and other techniques to support this one-to-one relationship building effort.

DM uses campaign management techniques which are based on customer lists containing variables that companies could target for smaller, more focused promotional campaigns. Companies could plan, target, schedule and measure responses to each campaign and modify future campaigns based on the results.

Some feel that CRM had its origins in marketing research's *Customer Satisfaction Studies* of the late 1970s (actually, marketing researchers were studying customer attrition and customer satisfaction at least a decade earlier than this), and its relationship with *Total Quality Management* (TQM) in the late 1980s. CRM is dependent upon information technology in the form of a database that enables marketers to capture customer information, access it in a timely fashion, and communicate with customers in a one-to-one fashion. With consumers today using a variety of touch points in their relationships with companies, it becomes important for companies to collect and manage this information and use it as a resource in strengthening bonds with their customers.

The majority of CRM strategies started out as point solutions satisfying the needs of a single department or function. Departments and functions used local databases, and none were linked. The data warehouse, a centralized cross-functional database, was introduced to provide a single vision of the customer across all functions and departments. The customer data comes from all business areas: billing, customer contact, marketing, and so on, providing what is referred to as a 360-degree view of the customer. CRM suites were developed to integrate all of the point solutions, but these must be consistently upgraded as well. For example, with the growth of multi-channel users, the focus of CRM expanded to include the Internet and e-commerce.

Relationship Marketing and CRM

With CRM's dependence on data, hardware, and the software to run it, it is easy to lose sight of the reasons why companies have CRM in the first place. CRM and its goal of helping companies attain high levels of trust and commitment from its customers gets to the very heart of a company and its marketing efforts. CRM is built on the philosophical base of relationship marketing. Relationship marketing, with its focus on customers as opposed to prospects; relationships rather than one-time transactions; individuals as opposed to masses; and the attempt to improve the company's offerings to each individual by learning more and more about each individual's needs; has reshaped the entire field of marketing.

Marketers began focusing on customers as a result of technological advances, the success of direct marketing efforts, the realization that customer retention was the key to corporate profits, and the application of relationship building techniques from industrial and business-to-business markets. In addition, CRM is a win-win situation for companies and their customers. With CRM, companies can lower acquisition costs, increase profits through cross-selling and up-selling, increase positive word of mouth, and differentiate offerings based on customer value. What's more, CRM provides customers with greater decision-making efficiency, reduced risk, savings, ease of shopping, and recognition. All of this leads to greater employee satisfaction and better service.

Organization and CRM

Organization dynamics—including the organization's value chain—directly impact any CRM strategy. Technology is rarely the cause of CRM failures. Most CRM initiatives fail due to organizational issues such as:

- Internal communications
- Political dynamics
- Organizational structures
- Reward systems
- Lack of leadership and executive involvement
- Misinterpretation that technology is the solution
- Lack of knowledge and training
- Process planning
- Inadequate or no change management methodologies
- Weak flow-through after technology implementation

Analytics and customer relationships must be at the top of everyone's mind. Appropriate CRM skill sets must be identified and necessary training made available. CRM efforts must be quantified and measured. Marketing and technology must be interlinked from a strategic position.

Surveys performed by multiple analysts that follow the CRM industry have consistently shown that over 75% of CRM initiatives are inhibited by ineffective *Change Management.* One CRM key success factor is human resources. Employees must have both an emotional and a knowledge "buy-in" to the organization's CRM efforts and methodology.

Organization structures must have a certain level of bureaucracy in order to operate successfully. Typically, the existing organization structure is not optimal for a CRM initiative. Functional or silo-based structures are usually the most challenging to work within for any CRM effort. There will be separate managing departments or areas of activity for different business disciplines. Typically, each area will prioritize its activity based upon maximizing its own performance. There is usually no reason to reset its priorities in an effort to assist another function beyond its defined and agreed-upon responsibilities to that respective function. This is a key inhibitor for CRM.

From an organizational perspective, there are two major challenges related to technology. The first is the purchase, integration, continuous improvement and scalability of equipment and software. The second is that of perception. Many organizational decision makers believe that CRM is technology, and that once the technology is implemented you are practicing CRM. Technology is simply a CRM *enabler* that organizations leverage when implementing their CRM strategy. It may be a key component of the strategy but it is not CRM.

Organizations do not compete with each other. Rather, *value chains*, of which an organization is a member, compete with each other. A CRM methodology must incorporate all members of the value chain, from manufacturer to end user. Failure to include all members relative to their value almost assuredly weakens the organization's CRM efforts.

CRM and Data Management

Creating a single accurate view of a customer is a key to CRM success. It is probably the most difficult CRM-related task a company must undertake, but if not done optimally, it can inhibit the best CRM strategy. It is extremely time consuming, very complex and very detailed work. It takes a certain discipline to create an optimal, data-integrated environment. The steps necessary to perform this methodology are:

1. **Touchpoint identification:** This is the process of identifying every location within the organization as well as within the value chain that a customer can interact with the respective organization or its value chain partners. B2C examples would be P.O.S. (point-of-sale), phone, web, customer service, survey, promotion response, distribution. B2B examples may include procurement, sales, and technical support. These sample lists are of course not all inclusive of the various interaction touch-points.

2. **Define how data is collected:** i.e., human, technology, self-reported or generated versus two-way exchange.

3. **Establish data collection rules:** This is the process of setting priorities for data variable collection from each touchpoint.

4. **Define the data collection process:** Specific process steps, timing, and security.

5. **Place data in similar formats (optional):**Some software that will work with the collected data requires it to be in the same or similar formats.

6. **Split data into two areas linkage and non-linkage:** Linkage data is any set of variables that can be used to identify the customer. Non-linkage data is everything else. Name and address or customer loyalty card numbers are examples of linkage variables. Products purchased would be non-linkage data. Non-linkage data can contain an extremely large number of variables. A unique number can be assigned to both so that both parts of the customer data, linkage and non-linkage, can be connected together later. Splitting data is not always necessary, but in many instances it improves the efficiency of the processing of linkage data—through those steps necessary to enhance customer matching across multiple interactions and transactions.

7. **Standardize and correct linkage data:** Commercial software is used to correct errors in any addressable variable (e.g., street name, zip code, email address)

8. **Postal processing:** Ensures that the most current customer address will be used as well as improve mailing efficiency. There are multiple processes in this step and the USPS web site (www.usps.com) is a good source for information on what is involved with this process.

9. **Linkage identification:** This step is sometimes referred to as de-duplication or merge/purge. It identifies each appearance of a customer's multiple set of interactions or transactions and links them together. This is a critical step as it helps build a centric view of the customer, a critical success factor for CRM.

10. **Data enhancement:** Secondary sources of information are added to the customer information to enhance the view of the customer. (e.g., demographic variables, secondary sources).

11. **Data suppression:** Use data captured about customers to suppress from a variety of activity such as: reduced or eliminated marketing efforts to non-profitable customers; adherence to customer request for non-interaction; and legal and ethical conformance (children, prisons, deceased, military, and fraud detection).
12. **Consolidate data:** Link data together.
13. **Prepare data for respective database update process.**

These steps have been listed as a serial process. They can be executed in real time, in part, or in whole, depending upon the requirements and resources, both technical and financial. The data integration process is a key success factor as it creates a single—and hopefully accurate—view of the customer at a point in time.

Technology and Data Platforms

Discussions of technology can be overwhelming and, to many business students, intimidating. The following discussion and diagrams have been developed in such a way as to link the CRM strategy with technology at a functional level.

Exhibit R3.1 illustrates a typical data warehouse environment. The Operational Data Store (ODS) is a database designed to hold limited information that is relative to a current customer interaction and can be accessed quickly. The Data Warehouse (DW) contains all relative marketing information. It is designed for efficient storage and security. It is not designed for quick access. A Data Mart (DM on this model) is a subset of the DW and contains information extracted from the DW for a specific purpose. This consumer finds that the web and the phone are the two easiest ways to interact with the organization. A non-inclusive list of other interaction sources appears in the left side of the exhibit. Data Preparation appears twice. The elongated cylinder represents a batch or semi-batch environment of data preparation steps. The Data Prep that appears within a database icon in the middle of the figure depicts the same data preparation functions occurring in real time. The functions are integrated into the customer interaction. For example, a person using the web to make a purchase may have the information they entered processed through the data preparation steps instantly while they are at the web site. This is how a web site completes a form once the customer enters limited information about themselves. That is, the limited information is matched against their complete information resident in the ODS. While one ODS icon appears, it should be pointed out that many ODSs can be created and used by companies. In fact, some companies create the ODS first and the DW later, using the ODS for both functions. In a way, this is a less risky approach as the marketer learns more about what information is available before designing the DW.

Some companies for financial or strategic reasons never build a DW and stay with the ODS or build a DW years later. The DW is updated by software with information that comes from one or more ODSs. The arrow depicts this update in the middle of the figure. It should be pointed out that the man accessing the DW via double arrow at the top of the figure is reading only, and not writing to the DW. The double arrow indicates a query and subsequent response from the query. This can be a time-consuming method of accessing information, but sometimes it is necessary to query the

EXHIBIT R3.1: THE CRM PROCESS

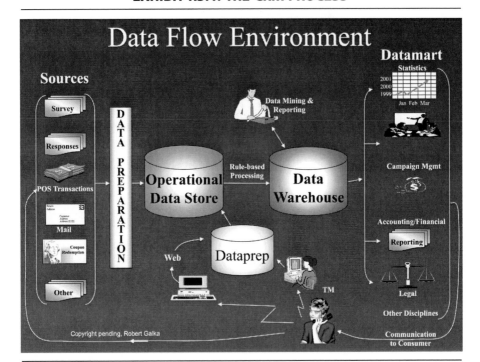

DW. The most efficient and common means of accessing information is via a Data Mart. DM examples appear on the right side of the figure. They are created as separate databases. Different business requirements necessitate different DMs as the software used to access the DM is usually designed to support a particular business application. A marketer may use campaign management or decision support tools to access relative information. Statisticians may require certain samples to run models. Finance may be looking at revenue and cost information. Legal may be interested in liability. Each of these functions probably has an optimal software product that is used to access the DM. The arrows from the DMs back to the consumer indicate that some action is taken with the consumer after information on the consumer has been processed via some DM activity.

This is a generic description that compensates for different technology approaches and naming conventions. Oracle, for example, provides the same functions but their technical solution is different. They use a hub approach where all information is centrally located and other entities and access points are on a perimeter ring. This approach may not fill all of the company needs, and therefore more data base entities may still need to be developed by the company.

Exhibit R3.2 illustrates CRM and technology on a much wider scale than the prior exhibit. Here it is shown that the CRM effort is highly dependent on other activity. One can conceptualize three main areas of activity: Collaborative, Analytical, and

EXHIBIT R3.2: THE CRM PROCESS

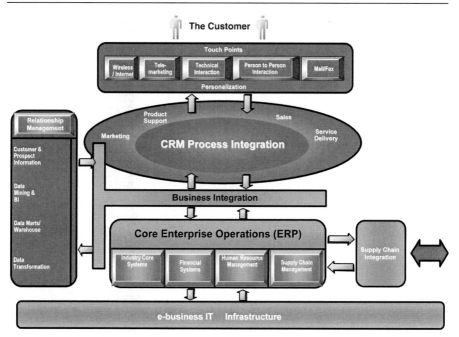

Source: IBM Integrated Customer Information

Operational. The arrows connecting these areas have been referred to by some as bolts, in that software and hardware must be bolted together from one area to the next to ensure optimal flow of information critical to the CRM effort. Middleware is the name used to describe the hardware and software required to bolt these areas together. *Computer Telephony* (CT) and telephone interaction are key CRM enablers. There are many resources devoted to the art of CT and telemarketing.

Radio Frequency Identification (RFID) is becoming a key CRM enabler. It is being adopted currently as a cost-cutting strategy in many business areas. However, forward-looking companies are starting to look at this technology as the new differentiator related to building customer relationships. Eventually, a company will have to adopt these emerging technologies to just meet (not exceed) a customer's expectation.

Knowledge Discovery

CRM initiatives have resulted in the accumulation of what some may say is too much data. Data by itself is not actionable and must be turned into knowledge. There are many approaches used to turn data into knowledge. Organizations find themselves using some or all of these techniques, as each respective situation will dictate an optimal approach. Statistical analysis tests for statistical correctness of models, creates a hypothesis to test for significant relationships, and tends to rely on sampling. *Online Analytical Processing* (OLAP) delivers facts based on historical data. Data mining is more interested in finding data patterns via exploration through large amounts of data and attempts to predict what may happen next. Organizations that utilize predictive analysis can double their ROI. Organizations use these techniques to perform segmentation, gain a better understanding of their customers, increase profitable customer retention and/or acquisition, eliminate efforts to sustain relationships with unprofitable customers, create up-sell and cross-sell strategies, perform risk assessment, generate response models, improve the processes that serve the customer, reduce fraud, and identify risk.

Sales Strategy and Technology

Sales forces are experiencing significant new internal and external challenges in managing customer relationships. The internal challenges include integrating the use of new *Sales Force Automation* (SFA) tools and the use of CRM systems into their sales process. The external challenge for sales forces is to manage customer relationships better in a more competitive environment. In order to accomplish that task they incorporate technology to make important customer information available to provide the right offer to customers at the right time. The single greatest impediment to effective CRM operation within the sales function is the lack of sales force participation.

Today, sales forces must provide solutions to complex customer problems. The demands on sales forces go far beyond typical prospecting, qualification, networking, and presentation strategies. Today, due to industry consolidation, the answer to how to solve a customer problem usually involves sales force decision making.

The following strategies are now utilizing new data resources and better analytics to improve company performance with retailers:

1. Category Management (CM)
2. Account Specific Marketing (ASM)
3. Continuity and Frequent Shopper Programs (FSP)

CRM's value to salespeople translates into the following areas:

- CRM must save the salesperson time.
- CRM must save the salesperson effort.
- CRM must make the salesperson more productive.
- CRM must streamline the decision-making process for a sales organization.

Marketing Strategy and CRM

The types of companies that benefit most from CRM are:

- **Those with a steep skew**: I.e., when customers' value to the company varies widely. Companies with a shallow-skew customer base, where profits generated by each customer are more or less the same, won't benefit as much.
- **Those with multi-channel customers**: The high-value customer is a multi-channel user and companies must integrate field sales, store, telephone, and Internet sales and service approaches and identify customer interactions with each touchpoint.

- **Those in "lost for good" markets**: In such markets, customers face high switching costs, concentrate their business with one vendor, and change vendors very reluctantly. Companies in such markets can increase profits through customer development strategies linking customers even closer to them through ordering, delivery and inventory systems.

Significant profitability can result in the short term through the use of "tactical CRM." For tactical CRM to result in quick-wins for an organization, it must first determine which stage of the customer-business life cycle it wants to focus on: acquisition, development, cross-selling, up-selling, retention, servicing, loyalty or win back. After these determinations are made, then tactical actions can be taken. Companies selling contract services (telecommunications, magazines, health club memberships) traditionally focus on customer acquisition, retention and win-back. Companies that have created high exit costs for their customers (retail banks) focus on customer development. Fashion retailers focus on cross-selling and up-selling to their elite market segments. Automobile manufacturers focus on up-selling. Some organizations such as supermarkets, with their loyalty programs; and university alumni associations, with their affinity group programs; do far less than they are capable of in the area of strategic CRM and tactical CRM.

There are a variety of CRM strategies based upon the customer business cycle stages of acquisition, retention, and win-back. Retention strategies include a wide array of possibilities. Bonding can be both programmatic (rewards programs) and humanistic (preferential treatment). The use of the idiosyncratic-fit can make each strategy more effective. Personalization and customization are also effective retention strategies; whether implemented over the web or during a general service encounter. Cross-selling and up-selling have direct profit implications; and the often overlooked strategy of managing migration may be four times as effective as general retention strategies. Use of "profit-driving" as a segmentation variable focuses a company's attention on profitable market segments. CRM may also be used as a brand-building tool and a method to more effectively manage brands.

CRM Program Measurement and Tools

Where marketers once focused on measuring aggregate market share, they now focus on measuring their share of wallet, share of stomach, share of trips, etc., for distinct buying units such as individuals, couples, families, businesses and other organizations. While aggregate measures of marketing success are still important, they have been supplemented by an increasingly large number of measures useful to those involved in an organization's CRM efforts.

Measures of CRM effectiveness can be grouped into four categories:

1. **CRM customer-cycle measures**: Looking at effectiveness of CRM efforts in acquisition, bonding development, behavior changes, retention, prevention of downward migration, and win back.
2. **Company 3E measures**: CRM's impact on company efficiency, effectiveness and employee behavior.

3. **Customer and company worth measures**: Computation of Customer Lifetime Value (CLV) and customer equity.
4. **Customer knowledge measures**: Marketing research and measurement techniques such as critical incident analysis, acquisition/defection matrices, RFM, and event history models for predicting customer response rates.

Privacy and Ethics

CRM requires a quid-pro-quo between the organization and the customer. This information and benefit exchange supports CRM. It also allows the organization to confirm a customer's expectations on privacy, which if executed properly can support its legal and ethical compliance effort.

The propensity to share customer information within the organization in support of a CRM effort or the organization's willingness to sell that information is a rising consumer concern. Another major consumer concern is the tracking of online activity and the threat of identity theft. The organization has to balance its need for information with its adherence to the customer's privacy expectation.

Many larger organizations have assigned executive ownership with the creation of a Chief Privacy Officer (CPO) position. A good practice is for organizations to monitor the FTC privacy web site (www.ftc.gov/privacy) for current information on legislation, trends, best practices and current cases.

Non-U.S. privacy strategies can be more complex. Organizations should hope for more rather than less documented legislation. It is easier to manage a privacy strategy when rules are defined. The worst situation exists when privacy guidelines are vague and open to interpretation. This creates the most risk for companies. The European Union has been aggressive in its approach to consumer information usage and consumer privacy. Latin America and Canada are almost as aggressive as the European Union. Japan has incorporated recent legislation as well.

The Future of CRM

The following discussion deals with projections of what is likely to occur, as opposed to fact.

The majority of U.S. companies are still floundering with CRM. There are mixed messages concerning CRM performance. This is particularly confounding when everyone agrees, conceptually, with the need for CRM and its strategic applications.

Challenging economic conditions have created an environment where CRM is a critical component of an organization's strategy as it attempts to reduce costs and increase revenue, both of which are key benefits gained by adopting CRM methodologies.

Organizations are "drowning" in information precipitated by increased Internet activity. CRM strategies enable organizations to filter out "noise" and focus on that information which directly impacts their efforts to sustain and grow customer profitability.

While dramatic increases in use of consumer mobile devices have created new CRM opportunities, there are also new challenges. In addition to maintaining hardware and software compatibility while managing consumer expectations, organizations must adapt to new consumer interaction behavior patterns at multiple generation levels.

The future of CRM technology promises significant improvement in CRM functionality to expedite the managerial and diagnostic system application processes. The future result will be CRM systems that are better able to provide insight into customer behavior and relationship development.

Technical improvements in CRM will be matched by improvements in Enterprise Resource Planning (ERP) systems. In theory, the future of CRM technology will be the seamless integration of customer demand with production, delivery, and billing. The direction of manufacturing, logistics, and accounting operations will be far more efficient. Companies will realize bigger gains in productivity as system integration provides for significant improvements in productivity.

In order to predict the future of CRM technology, it seems reasonable to consider where the corporate leaders in the field are investing their dollars, before drawing any conclusions. In recent years, there has been a significant CRM industry consolidation. Microsoft has begun to turn its attention to the CRM space, but acquisitions have established Oracle, salesforce.com, IBM, SAP, and SAS as the current titans. Google is a rising force as it has both the technology as well as the customer information necessary to sustain relationships with consumers.

Note: Material adapted from *Principles Of Customer Relationship Management*, Thomson Southwestern Publications, 2008, by Roger Baran, Robert Galka and Dan Strunk

---

ROBERT J. GALKA is an Executive in Residence at DePaul University, where he teaches marketing principles, strategy, CRM principles, data analysis, campaign management, data mining, and measurement classes. He has 25 years of experience in business development, strategic planning, relationship marketing strategy, general management, information systems and direct marketing. His last position was as a General Manager for a strategic business unit providing strategic marketing solutions. He frequently teaches professional programs in CRM, lectures on multiple marketing topics internationally, and advises on CRM in the U.S. and abroad. He has several published works, is heavily involved in Online Learning methods and class development including CRM, and is active in the Predictive Analytics Master's Degree Program at DePaul University.

READING

4

Creative Strategy in Integrated Marketing Communications

SUSAN K. JONES

Professor of Marketing at Ferris State University

Principal, Susan K. Jones & Associates

The concept of *Integrated Marketing Communications* (IMC) makes absolute sense—so much so that novices in the field may wonder what all the commotion is about. IMC suggests that marketers look at the customer first—his or her preferences, buying patterns, media exposure, and other factors—and then expose that customer to products and services that fit the customer's needs via a mix of communication methods he or she finds attractive and credible. As Don E. Schultz, the late Stanley I. Tannenbaum, and Robert F. Lauterborn asserted in their classic book, *The New Marketing Paradigm*, IMC challenges marketers to "start with the customer and work back to the brand."

Why was this revolutionary? Not because it was a new or controversial concept, but because a whole culture of agencies, in-house departments, and consultants had grown up around the notion of separation for advertising, direct marketing, sales promotion, and public relations efforts, rather than the harmonious, customer-centered planning process that IMC requires.

At its worst, this old-style culture leads to arguments among professionals as to how a media budget will be split: how much for general advertising, how much for direct marketing, and so on. Such "turf wars" have very little to do with what the *customer* wants or needs. They rely on chauvinistic notions that "my method is better"— that direct marketing is inherently superior to sales promotion, for example, or that general advertising is more refined, and therefore more appropriate, than "pushier" direct marketing techniques.

Because of the paradigm shift required in order to implement IMC, advertising professionals and their counterparts in direct marketing, sales promotion and public relations continue to work to come to grips with this concept. As with other deep cultural changes, intellectual acceptance may long precede the ability to embrace the gains and losses inherent in this new way of doing things. While the evolution continues, this conceptual framework may help creative people to understand IMC and use its tenets to their advantage.

The Four Elements of IMC

Integrated Marketing Communications encompasses *general advertising, direct marketing, sales promotion* and *public relations*. Some IMC campaigns feature aspects of all four elements, while others may eliminate one or more elements for strategic reasons. The American Association of Advertising Agencies defined IMC as follows:

> Integrated Marketing Communications is a concept of marketing communications planning that recognizes the added value in a program that integrates a variety of strategic disciplines, e.g., general advertising, direct response, sales promotion and public relations and combines these disciplines to provide clarity, consistency and maximum communications impact.

In an integrated campaign, *general advertising* shines at strengthening brands and brand equity while *direct marketing* builds relationships and dialogue, and provides the means to close sales. *Sales promotion* provides short-term buying incentives for both consumers and the trade. *Public relations*—mainly publicity in this case—offers third-party endorsements and extra reinforcement for the paid advertising messages. None of the four elements is inherently superior or inferior; they all have important functions in an integrated campaign. The campaign should focus on a "big idea" and a graphic look that threads through all four elements. This maximizes the chances that consumers will get the message and then have the message reinforced and layered in their memories without the "cognitive dissonance" that arises from mixed messages or incongruous graphic elements.

The Creative Process in Integrated Marketing Communications

The best integrated marketing campaigns begin with the disciplined application of creativity theory. We all are gifted with the ability to exercise the creative process. However, optimizing our results requires us to understand and apply that process patiently, and step-by-step.

The Italian sociologist Vilfredo Pareto said that an idea is merely a new combination of old elements. Take a kaleidoscope, for example. It contains myriad bits of color, forming into many different patterns as the kaleidoscope turns. The pattern is never the same twice, yet it combines all the same ingredients. The Bible says that "there is no new thing under the sun"—only unique ways of relating old elements. Creating a marketing idea, then, is the result of a step-by-step process designed to identify relevant elements and arrange them in new and effective patterns.

Creativity Formulas

There are as many written creativity formulas as there are technique checklists for copy and art. Some of these step-by-step processes come from advertising "creatives," while others are advanced by academicians through their study of the history of ideas. Following are abbreviated versions of two such helpful creativity formulas.

1. James Webb Young's *A Technique for Producing Ideas*:
   - Gather raw materials
   - Mental digestion
   - Incubation
   - Eureka!
   - Testing

2. The late Eugene B. Colin's *How to Create New Ideas*:
   - Pick a problem
   - Get knowledge
   - Organize knowledge
   - Refine knowledge
   - Digest
   - Produce ideas
   - Rework ideas
   - Put ideas to work
   - Repeat the process until it becomes a natural habit

A quick read through these idea-generating formulas shows that the basic process follows a predictable pattern: outlining the problem, gathering information, evaluating information, walking away from the problem to let the mind do its work, enjoying one moment when ideas strike, weighing the pros and cons of various ideas, and then implementing the best idea.

Brainstorming

One of the most effective resources for idea generation is brainstorming. While it's possible to "brainstorm with yourself," most creative experts agree it's not preferable. Working with others lets you benefit from different perspectives, experiences, and thought processes, and also builds excitement and enjoyment. Here is a brief, step-by-step plan for effective brainstorming.

1. Identify a specific question that brainstorming will attempt to answer
2. Select a neutral and nonjudgmental facilitator
3. Gain agreement that all participants are to be considered equals during brainstorming, no matter what their usual status in your organization
4. Shake things up with a new location, new space configuration, music, lighting or other elements designed to change perspectives
5. State your question beginning with the phrase "In what ways can we . . . " and begin brainstorming, with people calling out their ideas one by one
6. Encourage participants to build on the ideas of others
7. Use the resulting "laundry list" of ideas for a later refinement process based on budget, logistics, timing, uniqueness, target market and other factors

Creative Strategy and Positioning

In a good marketing plan, creative objectives and strategies are clearly articulated. And before the first word is written or a single line drawn, the copywriter and art director should accept and understand the *creative strategy statement* for the job they've undertaken. While many agencies and companies employ more comprehensive creative strategy formats, an informal creative strategy can be used as a minimum entry point. Such a "simplified creative strategy" must include descriptions of:

- **The target market**—Demographics, psychographics, segmentation strategies and characteristics. Smart marketers often discuss both the general target market and one specific prospect—described by name and in so much detail that the copywriter is able to write "one on one" to that person.
- **The competitive benefit**—What your product or service delivers uniquely and meaningfully to individuals in the target market. Ideally this section will also include support for the benefit—sometimes called "permission to believe."
- **The objective**—In general advertising, objectives focus mainly on informing, persuading or reminding people about the product or service. In direct marketing, it usually focuses more specifically on attracting leads and/or selling products. Sales promotion objectives concentrate on maximizing short-term incentives, while public relations objectives—when they are part of an IMC plan—generally have to do with generating non-paid publicity.

Discipline yourself to agree with your creative partners, clients and/or account people on at least these three concepts, and you'll stand an excellent chance of delivering creative work that all agree is "on strategy" the first time around.

In addition, a well-written *positioning statement* helps creative people to focus on the members of their target market with strong and specific messages that answer the prospective buyer's question, "What's in it for me?" You can create a simple positioning statement by filling in these blanks:

To the (TARGET CONSUMER), (NAME OF BRAND) is the brand of (COMPETITIVE FRAME) that (BENEFIT).

Here is an example of a positioning statement using this format:

To (FAMILY FOOD SHOPPERS WHO ARE CONCERNED ABOUT DIET), (MAZOLA) is the brand of (MARGARINE) that (TASTES BETTER THAN ALL OTHER LEADING HEART-HEALTHY SPREADS).

Creative Concepts in IMC

While some creative strategies and tactics are unique to certain elements of IMC, there are other concepts that apply across the board. These include print ad how-tos such headline writing, layouts and illustrations, and tips for readability.

Headline Writing

Observe people flipping through newspapers and magazines, or browsing on the web, and one thing becomes readily apparent: each article or ad has only a split second in which to engage the prospect's attention—just as do the articles themselves.

The headline is considered the most important element of a print advertisement. This is equally true online. Thus, a smart copywriter will invest all the time and care necessary to make each headline irresistible. A good headline flags down qualified prospects and lures them into the body copy. A good headline has no extra words to slow the reader down, and every word in it is working hard to get the message across. A good headline is in active voice.

One of the best ways to master this skill is to work for a daily newspaper writing news story headlines. Journalists are taught to answer six questions in each news presentation: Who, what, where, when, why and how? These are the questions people want answered immediately about most any situation or opportunity—and thus they are powerful idea starters for headlines. It may also help the fledgling writer to consider some of these headline methods as idea starters:

- Give news
- Tell how-to
- Inspire curiosity
- Pose a challenge
- Pose a question
- Appeal to the reader's self-interest

Print Layout and Illustration Types

Many of today's print ads—if they are not direct-response oriented—fall into the category of "poster" or "fashion" layouts. They include little more than a headline, a dominant picture that bleeds off the page, a line or two of copy or even no copy at all, and a logo. This type of ad can be quite effective at building a brand image or at reminding customers and prospects about a dominant, leading product. But if your advertising is aimed at informing or persuading the reader, or at obtaining leads or sales, the layout will have to make room for some copy and possibly one or more response devices. Typical layout types and their characteristics include:

- Standard—Dominate visual at the top of the ad, headline, body copy and logo.
- Editorial—Looks like an article in the publication where it is placed. Copy-heavy; few if any visuals.
- Poster or Fashion—Dominant visual bleeds off the page. Headline and logo; little to no body copy.
- Picture-Caption—Headline at the top; pictures with captions to lead the reader through a story or process; logo at bottom.
- Comic Strip—The ad takes the form of a comic strip with the copy in "balloons" indicating the spoken words of the characters; logo at bottom.
- Picture-Cluster—Like the standard layout except with a montage of photos instead of just one.
- Direct Response Ad—With coupon and/or prominent toll-free number and/or referral to a web site. Should have persuasive copy that is long enough to convince the reader to take the next step by asking for more information or purchasing the product.

Typical illustration types used in print ads include:

- Product alone (Example: a hot car)
- Product in use (Example: prepared food product—not just the box it comes in)

- Product with people (Example: person using a computer—not just the computer itself)
- Results of using product (Example: person with toothy white grin—not the whitening strips that did the job)
- Comparison or contrast (Example: Huge stack of laundry done with one container of concentrated laundry detergent across from much smaller stack done with one container of regular-strength competitor)
- Trade character—(Example: the Lonely Maytag Repairman)

Readability

To make your copy readable, follow a few basic rules. These include:

- **Serif vs. sans serif type**—Serif typefaces (the ones with the "squiggles" on the letters like Book Antiqua) are easier to read for long blocks of copy. Sans serif typefaces (the plain ones like Arial) have a sleeker and more modern appearance and are best used for headlines and short copy blocks. On the World Wide Web, however, sans serif typefaces are preferred for all copy because the serif "squiggles" can become muddied in an online presentation.
- **Type styles**—Don't use more than two type styles in any one presentation unless you are highly expert at type selection and presentation. Don't use ALL CAPS much as they are the equivalent of shouting and are difficult to read. Watch out for reverse type (light colors reversed out of dark backgrounds). They may be attractive in a design sense, but they are very difficult to read in blocks of copy.
- **Type size**—Body copy smaller than 8 pt. may be difficult for anyone to read—especially older individuals. Readable body copy is usually in the 10–14 pt. range. Anything larger than 14 pt. is called "display type" or "headline type" and should be used for headlines and subheads.
- **Leading**—Leading is the space between lines of type. Adding at least a point of leading between lines increases readability.
- **Writing tips for readability**—Forget what your English teacher told you about long paragraphs with topic sentences. Advertising paragraphs are short—no more than seven lines in most cases. Advertising sentences are short. One and two-word "sentences" are sometimes used for emphasis. Select "juicy" words that pop "word pictures" into your reader's mind—but never use a complex, three-syllable word when a simple one will do. "House," not "habitat" or "love," not "affection" for two quick examples.

Creative Concepts in General Advertising

The Big Idea

Very few people in your target market are going to slow down long enough to "figure out" your ads if they are not simple and clear on first viewing or reading. For this reason, general advertisers find it effective to focus each of their campaigns on one "big idea" that is executed across all media. This "big idea" is sometimes called a tag line. It may appear as the headline of a print ad, or at the bottom of the ad near the logo. It could be the "hook" of a television or radio jingle, or a tag line at the end of such a spot.

The "big idea" should focus on making your product or company's competitive benefit real and actionable to your target market. It shouldn't be in marketing language—it should be in the language of your target consumers. Examples of classic "big ideas" include AT&T's "Reach Out and Touch Someone," General Foods International Coffee's "Celebrate the Moments of Your Life," Nike's "Just Do It," McDonalds' "I'm Lovin' It," Apple's "Think Different," and Dell's "Be Direct." You will notice that the longest of these is nine syllables. That is by design—that's about all a targeted customer can remember without trying.

Television Basics

General-advertising television spots seldom run more than 30 seconds these days, and your average viewer isn't paying full attention. Thus you need to focus on one main idea in your ad . . . there's no time for multiple concepts or a progression of ideas. When developing a TV spot, think the whole thing through in video first—not words. TV's main strength is its visual aspect and the ability to demonstrate things, while copy is secondary in this medium. Creating a TV ad today is much like writing and producing a mini-movie or a music video.

Because so many TV ads these days are subject to "zipping" (fast-forwarding past the ads on a Digital Video Recorder), "zapping" (flipping around other channels during the commercial break) or "flushing" (losing the viewer while they visit the bathroom)—it's important to get your viewer's attention right away. This can be done by various methods—lots of motion, total silence, using arresting sounds, voices or images, arousing curiosity, showing celebrities in action, and so on. In addition, it's important that if you are showing words on the screen, your announcer is also saying those words—otherwise viewers may suffer from cognitive dissonance and won't retain either set of words. But if you are demonstrating something on-screen, it's fine to talk about something else—viewers can see what you're showing them and don't need to have that reinforced so literally.

Here are a few of the typical TV formats you might consider:

- Demonstrations such as product-in-use or a torture test
- Before and after or side-by-side comparison
- Slice of life (often blended with problem/solution)
- A set of vignettes showing various product uses or various types of people using the product
- A short movie with the product blended in
- Testimonials or celebrity endorsements

Radio Basics

Whereas television is all about visuals, radio has no visuals—they are left up to the listener's imagination. While television commands the viewer's attention at least some of the time, radio is often used as a companion medium or as background noise while driving, working or relaxing. Radio copy should be conversational and personal—written one-to-one. It's vital to get the listener's attention right off the bat with your ad, too . . . otherwise it will remain as part of the background noise. This can be done with a unique voice, a call to attention, or selecting out the audience with music or sound effects, among other methods. General-advertising radio spots may be as long as 60 seconds, but as with television, they can only get across one main idea per spot.

A few typical radio formats to consider are:

- Straight announcer (recorded in advance)
- Announcer or on-air personality (done live)
- Dialogue between two people (often blended with problem/solution)
- Jingle—either for the whole spot or blended with an announcer
- Celebrity endorsement (often with announcer lead-in and/or ending)

Retail Advertising Basics

Most effective retail ads in daily or weekly newspapers or on television, radio or via email or web site are comprised of four important elements:

1. Store image—Ads should "look and sound like the store" and have the same "look and feel" as other company promotions.
2. News/timeliness—Retail ads are meant to drive traffic, and thus should feature a certain time-limited sale or offer, new product arrivals, special events or other reasons to visit now.
3. Specifics—Retail customers "shop the ads" and want to know what colors and sizes your turtleneck sweaters come in, what they are made of, the brand name, and so on. Model numbers, series numbers, and other specifics also help customers know what to expect when they get to the store.
4. Price—People in the market for a $100 MP3-CD player likely want neither a stripped-down $29.99 version nor a souped-up $300 job. They want to know the price range of the item your promoting before taking time to visit your store. If you're having a sale or other price promotion, be specific about that as well.

Out-of-Home Basics

Outdoor advertising gurus caution that your general-advertising billboards should contain no more than 7–10 words for maximum effect. Sometimes all you need for billboard copy is the "big idea" for your campaign. The most arresting billboards include a dominant, attention-getting visual—but keep in mind that billboards should be in harmony with the "look and feel" of the rest of your ads and promotions. You may be able to sequence your ads so that the first one in a series asks a question, and the next one answers it. Or you may use billboards for a teaser campaign with a bit more added each week or month until the new product, store or event is fully revealed to the viewer. Today's digital billboards open up many possibilities for updating ads on the fly rather than being "stuck" with the same message for 30 days at a time.

Creative Concepts in Direct Marketing

How Direct Marketing is Different

The essential character of direct marketing lies in its *action orientation*. General advertising may inform, persuade or remind prospects about products or services, but it does not sell. To sell, or to invite a step toward a sale, direct marketers include a call to immediate action and an easy-to-use response device. Direct marketers make specific offers: they tell prospects what they're going to get and what they have to do to get it—be it a product in exchange for a price, free information in exchange for a phone call, or some other quid pro quo. In addition to action orientation, direct marketing has several other important characteristics. It is:

- Targeted
- Personal
- Measurable
- Testable
- Flexible

While most any medium can be utilized for direct-response purposes, this section details some how-tos for several of the most prominent direct marketing media: direct mail, catalogs, and broadcast.

Direct Mail

A direct mail package that sells a product or service should take the place of a retail store experience for the customer. For example:

- The outer envelope serves the same function as a store window—to select the audience and entice them inside
- The letter takes the place of personal sales—using "you-oriented" language to speak directly to the buyer and answer the buyer's objections
- The brochure takes the place of the product display or demonstration
- The reply device takes the place of closing the sale

One of the "pros" of direct mail is that it allows for a variety of formats—everything from postcards to multi-dimensional "bulky packages." In addition to the four "classic package" elements mentioned above, a direct mail package may include such pieces as:

- Business Reply Envelope to make it easy for the prospect to respond
- Premium slip to highlight a free offer
- Publisher's letter to overcome specific objections
- Involvement device such as stickers to indicate selections on the reply form
- Reminder slips
- Article or ad reprints
- Testimonial flyers
- Questions and answers
- Samples
- DVDs or CD-ROMs

Less personal and more promotional than the classic envelope-enclosed direct mail package—but also less expensive in most cases—is the self-mailer. This piece does not come in an envelope—it's folded and/or stapled to encompass all the elements of the letter, brochure and reply device. Postcards are used more and more as mailing costs increase and people's attention spans decrease—they can drive traffic to a web site or landing page where full information is available, remind subscribers that it's time to renew, or complete other simple and straightforward communications with customers.

Catalogs

When Montgomery Ward and Sears reigned supreme in the world of American catalogs, their thick "wish books" served the purpose of a general store by mail. But as Americans gained mobility and suburbs spilled into what had been remote farmland, many more shoppers were able to visit cities, towns, and outlying malls to make their purchases in person. Thus, catalog merchandisers were forced to find new reasons for being—resulting in today's "niche marketing" landscape.

To succeed in today's competitive catalog realm, each firm must discover and fulfill one or more unmet needs of a target group of consumers. That special niche can be determined through:

- Research to see what catalogs are already in the marketplace and where gaps exist
- Consumer research to determine their unmet needs and wants in terms of merchandise mix
- Exploration of niches based on factors other than merchandise such as better selection, finer quality, more affordable price or appealing presentation

Catalogs are merchandise-driven, and it's wise to put your most appealing merchandise, and/or the items with the best margin, in what are called the "hot selling spots." These are, in order of strength:

1. Front cover
2. Back cover
3. Inside front cover spread
4. Center spread
5. Inside back cover spread
6. Spread near the order form (if your catalog still has one—some firms have tested and found they can get away with online and phone ordering only)
7. On the order form itself (again, if your catalog still has one)

Copywriters often are invigorated by the prospect of a new catalog concept, and the first time through is exciting—what with discovering the merchandise and the target market, setting the tone of the catalog, and so on. But much of catalog copywriting can become a bit dull and repetitive—so writers in this field need to find ways to keep themselves fresh. These methods could include:

- Keeping an eagle eye on the competition
- Using the catalog's products yourself and observing the reactions of family and friends as well
- Making friends with the merchandisers to get their perspective on products' unique aspects
- Thinking like a consumer—what would excite someone about this item?
- Pay attention to results and do your best to increase sales

- Don't stay in your cubicle—check out customer service, the shipping department and other areas of the company to stay in touch with the overall business

Broadcast

Direct response TV and radio spots are—by and large—longer and more laden with copy and benefits than their general advertising counterparts. Keep in mind that these spots must overcome inertia to the extent that a prospect picks up the phone, goes to a retail store, or visits a web site in response to your promotion. Direct response spots often are created on a shoestring, unlike the expensive general-advertising productions that are broadcast for major brands.

Products that perform well in direct response TV spots include those that shine in demonstration, have wide appeal, are not available at retail, and have an acceptable price range—usually not much more than $9.95–$39.95. More expensive products can be sold using a two-step approach of lead generation with follow-up by phone or personal sales.

Formats for direct response spots often are similar to those described in the general advertising section, but they must be structured to make a sale. They include considerable repetition, and need plenty of time to get ordering instructions across including the appropriate toll-free number and/or web site.

On the radio, personalities such as Dave Ramsey and Glenn Beck—while expensive to work with—can yield exceptional results when they endorse products on their own talk shows. Radio spots often employ much more humor than direct response television spots—in part because humor offers a palatable way to employ repetition of important points and response information.

Creative Concepts in Sales Promotion

As with public relations, in many cases you will find yourself working with sales promotion specialists to enhance your efforts at spotlighting products or services. In this situation, it is imperative that you ensure the sales promotion program they develop is in keeping with the brand image, "look and feel" and overall campaign theme you have developed for your general advertising and direct marketing efforts.

The most prominent example of sales promotion is the coupon. A typical mistake in developing coupons is to forget to include benefit-oriented material along with the "price deal" or other promotion. Your targeted customers won't care about getting $5 off the regular price of a product unless the product itself intrigues them. Your sales promotion efforts have to help sell the product's attributes and benefits to optimize results.

Sweepstakes and contests are other typical sales promotion efforts. Because of the laws, rules and controversy surrounding sweepstakes and contests, it is wise to engage the services of a company that specializes in running these promotions. Be sure, as always, however, that the theme and prizes they come up with are in keeping with your product's brand image, and appealing to your target market. For example, a grand prize of a Ford Fiesta or F-150 pickup truck might be very exciting to the 18–25-year-old market, while older and more well-heeled empty nesters would be more intrigued by their own version of the "dream car"—a BMW Z-4 or equivalent.

Creative Concepts in Public Relations

Public relations experts often deem their field more compatible with the management function of business than the marketing function. They consider themselves "the right hand of the CEO," rather than mere "publicity seekers." On the other hand, when we discuss public relations as one of the four main aspects of Integrated Marketing Communications, we are focusing mainly on seeking publicity—which is indeed part of the public relations arsenal.

Public relations efforts can be extremely cost-effective. What's more, having a third party (a magazine, web site, TV show, etc.) say positive things about a product or service is very powerful. The other side of the coin is that since coverage resulting from public relations efforts is not paid for, it is also not controllable. It takes media savvy and careful cultivation to optimize relationships with reporters and minimize chances that a long-sought PR opportunity will turn into a negative story.

While respecting public relations professionals to ply their own craft, IMC creative types will be wise to work with the PR team to ensure that the news releases, special events and media contacts they make are in keeping with the overall brand image and campaign theme being promoted via general advertising, direct marketing and sales promotion.

If you embark on your own publicity program, understand that most news releases will not be acted upon in any meaningful way without follow-up and cultivation of the reporter and/or editor involved. It is important that the same PR professional makes these contacts over time to develop a cordial relationship with each journalist. It is vital that this PR professional take calls and return calls from journalists in a timely manner, too—and not hide from the media if controversy arises.

You should take time to read the publications, web sites, and blogs, and watch the shows where you would like coverage for your product so that you can make constructive suggestions on where you might fit in—the "Diet and Nutrition" segment on NBC's Today Show, for example . . . or the weekly executive profile in a regional business publication. And remember that legitimate media outlets are completely separate from their advertising departments and that journalists will not take kindly to suggestions like "We're a big advertiser—we'd like to see you cover this story."

Get to know the publication's schedule and don't call a reporter who is "on deadline." Realize that reporters and editors at legitimate publications and broadcast outlets do not have to give you approval of your expert's quotes or the photos they take—indeed, they make take offense if you ask. Try to come up with information or angles that will intrigue reporters, bloggers and editors as well as their readers and viewers—if you don't get past these gatekeepers, your story will never see the light of day.

Here are some tried-and-true themes to consider for your news releases.

- New Products
- How-to Information

- Controversy
- Celebrity Involvement
- Human Interest
- Timely Information

Putting it All Together

Integrated Marketing Communications efforts can best be orchestrated by a cross-functional team using a comprehensive promotional plan as their "bible." Mutual respect, open communication, and an absolute commitment to focusing on the target consumer—rather than on internal squabbles and turf wars—will help ensure that this team is successful in identifying and executing the ideal mix of general advertising, direct marketing, sales promotion and public relations.

SUSAN K. JONES is both a tenured, full-time Professor of Marketing at Ferris State University in Big Rapids, MI, and principal of Susan K. Jones & Associates in East Grand Rapids, MI. She is the author, co-author or editor of more than 30 books. Her honors include membership in the Medill Hall of Achievement at Northwestern University, Emeritus Direct Marketer and Charles S. Downs Award Winner from the Chicago Association of Direct Marketing, Andi Emerson Award for contributions to the creative community from the John Caples International Awards, West Virginia University's Alexia Vanides Teaching Award, and Robert B. Clarke Outstanding Educator Award from the Direct Marketing Educational Foundation. She can be reached at joness@ferris.edu.

An Introduction to Database Marketing

ARTHUR MIDDLETON HUGHES

Director, Subscriber Acquisition Strategy, E-Dialog.com and
Vice President, The Database Marketing Institute, Ltd.

The purpose of database marketing is the same today as it has always been: to create and maintain a bond of loyalty between you and your customers that will last a lifetime. The goal has not changed, but the methods have. We still maintain information about our customers in a database and use it as a basis for our communications with them. In the past we used direct mail and phone calls to communicate. Today we use these plus emails, web sites, cell phone text and web messages and social media. These new developments make communications much less expensive, more frequent, but also much more complex. Most companies have found it useful to hire a service bureau to maintain their databases, and an email service provider (ESP) to send their emails and cell phone messages.

The process begins with a marketing database that keeps all sorts of information about customers: not only what they buy, but their demographics, families, responses and preferences. Information storage has become much more sophisticated—using relational databases—and much less expensive. Moore's Law describes a long-term trend in the history of computing hardware. The number of transistors that can be placed inexpensively on an integrated circuit doubles approximately every two years. The trend has continued for more than half a century and is not expected to stop until 2020 or later. This same trend has affected disk storage and transmission speed and capacity. Result: you can afford to retain and use all the information you can collect about a customer in your marketing programs. The only limitation is the human creative ability and willingness to devise methods for using the data.

The biggest change in database marketing in the last decade has been the arrival of web sites, email and mobile marketing. At first these seemed like a godsend: the main problem with database marketing was the high cost of communications with customers: $600 per thousand messages. You had all this wonderful information in your database that you could use to build relationships, but you were limited, in most cases, to about one letter a month because of the cost. In the last ten years, with web sites including social media, email and the iPhone, you can send messages to your subscribers and customers for less than $6.00 per thousand—a cost so low that the delivery cost is inconsequential.

Email has become the main way to communicate between companies and their customers. Direct mail is still alive and well, but email is gaining on it. There is a third communication means that is also growing: one-third of consumers in both the United States and the United Kingdom are viewing their emails on their iPhone or similar mobile devices. The use of mobile email is most prevalent among younger consumers, with over half of them spending a significant part of every day glued to their phones. Mobile use is exploding in all directions. All of these new communications methods can make use of the information in a customer marketing database.

Here, at last, is a way to use your database to build really close relationships with each customer using the data you have collected. What we had not figured on was that the low cost of email and mobile messages has become a curse.

They have been a curse because marketers have discovered that emails are so inexpensive that you can afford to send messages to your customers every week, or even every day. The more you send, the more revenue you gain. More and more major corporations in the U.S. and elsewhere have been sending emails, and sometimes mobile messages, to all their subscribers all the time. Subscriber inboxes are overflowing. The big problem is that the messages, while they can be, and often are, personalized, are seldom filled with dynamic content based on what we know about each customer. We can have these rich databases, but we do not use the rich data that they hold. To use it requires many creative staff members who dream up the dynamic content. The thought is: "These subscribers over 65 have certain interests, while these other subscribers are college students who have different interests. We will vary our messages based on this knowledge, and also do that for about a dozen other subscriber segments so as to make our relationships richer for them and more profitable for us." Sounds great, doesn't it? That has always been the promise of database marketing. We *could* send dynamic content before when we were sending one message a month. But few marketers today are doing anything like that. They are blasting identical content to every subscriber or customer whose email or address they can get their hands on.

The problem boils down to one simple fact: **The lift we get from dynamic content does not seem to be as great as the lift we get from frequent communications**. You can't afford to do both, so you go with the most profitable.

As database marketers we must deal with the ramifications of this tradeoff between frequency and dynamic content. There are many solutions. Take a good look at this chart:

ROI Comparison	Direct Mail	Email
Pieces Mailed	1,000	1,000
Cost of mailing	$600	$6.00
Conversion Rate	2.67%	0.15%
Sales	26.7	1.50
Revenue per Sale	$100	$100
Revenue	$2,670	$150
Return on Investment	$4.45	$25.00

This chart explains a lot about what has happened to Strategic Database Marketing.

The Old Corner Grocer

In my seven books on database marketing, I described the customer relationships of the Old Corner Grocer and how his loyalty building methods are carried out today by modern database marketing. The analogy is still true.

Back in the days before there were supermarkets, all the groceries in America were sold in small corner grocery stores. In many cases, the proprietor could be seen at the entrance to his store, greeting the customers by name. "Hello Mrs. Hughes. Are your son and his family coming for Thanksgiving again this year?"

These guys built the loyalty of their customers by recognizing them by name, by greeting them, by knowing them, by doing favors for them. They helped by carrying heavy packages out to customers' cars (there were no shopping carts in those days). These veterans no longer exist. The supermarkets put them out of business. Prices came down. Quality went up. The corner grocer had 800 SKUs in his store. Supermarkets today have more than 30,000 SKUs. He had a few hundred customers. Companies today have thousands or millions of customers.

As a result, the familiarity of the Old Corner Grocer that produced loyalty in the old days has become much more difficult to create and sustain — until database marketing came along. Using current techniques, it is now possible for a large corporation with a marketing database to build a relationship with customers that recreates the recognition and loyalty of the old corner grocer. We do this over the phone (using voice, text and emails), through creative use of a web site and emails, and by providing our employees in marketing, sales, customer service or at retail counters and teller windows with the kind of information about their customers that the corner grocers used to keep in their heads. We are returning today to methods that worked wonderfully in the old days. They work today. They build loyalty, repeat sales, cross sales, and profits.

Customers have become dominant. There are, today, in most parts of the US, many different stores selling similar products. Most families and businesses today have PCs and advanced smart cell phones—both equipped with Google—so that they can look up and find any product or service that they want to buy, with comparative prices and customer reviews. You can't fool them anymore. What do they want?

What Customers Want

What has been happening is that the customers are becoming dominant. Companies are discovering what their customers want, and selling them that. It is customer-based marketing. But it is really more than that. What customers want today can be summed up in a few general concepts:

Recognition—That they be recognized as individuals, with individual desires and preferences. They like being called by name.

Service—Thoughtful service provided by knowledgeable people who have access to the database, and therefore know who they are talking to, and what these people are interested in.

Convenience—People are very busy. They don't have time to drive a couple of miles to do business. They want to do business from where they are by cell or landline phone or using the web, with companies that remember their names, addresses, credit card numbers, and purchase history.

Helpfulness—Anything that you can do to make customers' lives simpler is appreciated. Merchants have to think, every day, "How can I be more helpful to my customers?" Only those who come up with good answers will survive.

Information—Customers are more literate today than ever before. They use the Internet. Technical information is as important to many of them as the product itself.

Identification—People like to identify themselves with their products (like their cars) and their suppliers (like their cell phones). Companies can build on that need for identification by providing customers with a warm, friendly, helpful institution to identify with.

Who Do They Listen To?

Increasingly today, customers listen to other customers. They participate in blogs. They read product reviews written by other customers. Young people participate in Facebook and Twitter, exchanging information that suppliers of products and services cannot control.

From 1985 to today, most large modern corporations have built customer marketing databases filled with personal information about their customers. Modern computer technology has been used to create relational databases that store a great deal of information on each household (or company, in the case of a business-to-business product). Retained is not just the name and address, but also:

- Email address, plus the cookies that keep track of their web visits
- Complete purchase history
- Customer service calls, complaints, returns, inquiries
- Outgoing marketing promotions, and responses
- Results of customer surveys
- Household (or business) demographics: income, age, children, home value and type, etc.
- The profitability, Recency/Frequency/Monetary (RFM) code, and lifetime value of every customer in the database.

What changed, however, is the method of using the database to communicate with customers. Before 2000 we had direct mail and telephone. Now, we have the web, email, and mobile devices which have changed everything.

- Every company of any size has a web site filled with information—most with shopping carts.
- Many companies send both catalogs and promotional emails to prospective customers.
- Most companies also send triggered messages to individual customers that make it possible to send each of a million customers a different message, based on the database.

- Most companies send transaction messages ("Your product was shipped today.") which were impossible before (too slow and expensive) and now, not only keep customers informed, but sell them additional products and services.
- Most email and mobile communications today are filled with **links** which mean that every message can be an adventure: a gateway to every product and piece of information that the company has available. Using links you can do research, read reviews, print specifications, compare prices, and buy whatever interests you.

Two Kinds of Databases

There are really two different kinds of databases in any company that is engaged in direct marketing of products and services. One is an operational database and the other is a marketing database.

An *operational database* is used to process transactions and get out the monthly statements:

- For a cataloger, this database is used to process the orders, to charge the credit cards, arrange shipment, and handle returns and credits.
- For a bank, the operational database processes checks and deposits, maintains balances, and creates the monthly statements.
- For a telephone company, the operational database keeps track of the telephone calls made and arranges the billing for them.

A **marketing database** gets its data from the operational database, if there is one. This data consists of a summary of monthly transactions. But the marketing data also includes much more. It gets data from:

- Preferences and profiles provided by the customers.
- Promotion and response history from direct mail and email marketing campaigns.
- Appended data from external sources such as KnowledgeBase Marketing, Donnelly, Claritas, etc.
- Lifetime Value and RFM analysis, leading to creation of customer segments.
- Modeling for churn and next best product.

The marketing database passes data back to the operational database. It may advise the operational database:

- Which segment each customer has been placed in, which may lead to operational decisions. Gold customers, for example, may get different operational treatment.
- Expressed customer preferences leading to different operational treatment: smoking or non-smoking rooms assigned automatically.

The operational database is run by IT. It is run on accounting principles and balances to the penny, since there are legal and tax aspects to its data. It is audited by external auditors. It contains only current data on customers. Old data is archived. There is no data on prospects until they make a purchase.

EXHIBIT R5.1: OPERATIONAL AND MARKETING DATABASE

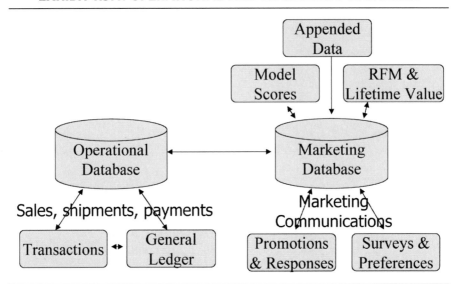

In many companies, there are several marketing databases. For various reasons, the database of catalog customers is often separate from the retail store customer database. The web site and email customer databases may also often be kept separately. From the outside it seems like a simple matter to bring all these databases together so as to get a "360 degree" picture of each customer. But, in fact, this combination is often difficult to achieve. Why should this be so?

The reasons are varied but they often relate to internal company politics. In a typical bank, there are vice presidents for each major product: credit cards, home equity loans, retail (checking and savings accounts), insurance, etc. The credit card manager receives no bonus or special recognition if some of his credit card customers sign up for a checking account. The Retail Vice President gets no special reward if some of his customers apply for a credit card. Yet any analysis of bank customers will show that the more different bank products that the average customer has, the higher will be that customer's loyalty to and profits for the bank. The organization and compensation system does not reflect the theory of customer relationship management.

Sears Canada Shows How It Is Done

This situation was dramatically illustrated by the experience of Sears Canada a few years ago. For historical reasons, Sears Canada had separate operations for the catalog and retail stores. One day they decided to build a combined customer marketing database. Once the database was built, Sears was able to measure the performance of catalog customers vs. retail customers vs. web customers. The data was very revealing. They found that at that time the average catalog customer spent $492 dollars per year. The average retail customer spent $1,102 dollars per year. But customers shopping both channels were spending $1,883 per year with Sears.

This discovery led to a fundamental reorganization of the whole company. A central EVP for marketing was set up who worked across all channels. Bruce Clarkson, General Manager of Relationship Marketing for Sears Canada, didn't stop at integrating catalogs with retail. Using the new database he focused on retention, acquisition and purchase stimulation. He proved that the strongest predictive variable for not shopping the catalog was exposure to bad service: out of stock, or merchandise that was not satisfactory. Sears could prove that money spent on improved service would increase customer retention.

Sears set up an RFM system with 189 cells, tracking recency on a quarter by quarter basis. Clarkson's analysis showed that each quarter between 20,000 and 30,000 new customers acquired a Sears card, bought once, and never bought again. Sears spent a lot of money trying to get the card into people's hands, but was not doing enough to get them to use the card. The new database showed that 14 percent of Sears customers were $2,500 plus buyers who contributed 50 percent of Sears total corporate merchandise revenues. Using their database to see what web site customers did, they found that 97 percent of sales volume was from people who had the paper catalog in front of them.

Sears used and continues to use their database to understand their customers. Then they took that crucial step to change their organization to make use of what they had learned. They became customer focused. It is a tremendous lesson for the rest of us.

Email Marketing Needs to Catch Up

Building a central marketing database is only a first step. In most companies today, email marketing—the most powerful tool available—is not used productively. Direct mail is used carefully because it is expensive. emails are so inexpensive that most marketers send millions of identical messages on a daily basis to subscribers who are overwhelmed and annoyed by their overflowing inboxes. Database marketing is not being used effectively by most email marketers—which means most major corporations today.

This is a message that you will learn from studying about database marketing. You will learn how to determine the lifetime value of your customers and of your email subscribers. You will learn how to use that value to direct and manage your marketing program through all communication channels.

Looked at from the customer's point of view, database marketing through all channels is a way of making customers happy; of providing them recognition, service, friendship, and information for which, in return, they will reward you with loyalty, retention and increased sales. Genuine customer satisfaction is the goal and hallmark of satisfactory database marketing. If you are doing things right, your customers will be glad that you have a database and that you have included them on it. They will want to subscribe to and read your emails. They will come happily to your web site and your retail stores. They will want to receive your catalogs. They will appreciate the things that you do for them. If you can develop and carry out strategies that bring this situation about, you are a master marketer. You will keep your customers for life, and be happy in your work. You will have made the world a better place to live in.

Conclusions

- The purpose of database marketing is to create and maintain a bond of loyalty between you and your customers that will last a lifetime.
- Modern database marketing is trying to recreate for large companies the loyalty enjoyed by the old corner grocers who knew their customers by sight and name.
- Database Marketing has changed significantly due to web sites, email and mobile marketing. These have reduced the cost of communication, but presented a serious problem: There are too many messages.
- Sending dynamically different messages to each customer is the goal, but the lift from customized content is less than the lift from frequent messages: frequency beats customization.
- Electronic links within messages permit customers to do research and discover every product you have for sale and a tremendous amount of previously unobtainable data.
- There are two types of database: an operational and a marketing database. Companies must have both.
- Customers today want recognition, service, friendship, and information. They listen, often, more to other customers than to what you are saying to them.

ARTHUR MIDDLETON HUGHES is Director, Subscriber Acquisition Strategy at e-Dialog, a major email service provider in Burlington, MA, and also Vice President of The Database Marketing Institute. He lives in Fort Lauderdale, FL, and can be reached at Arthur.hughes@dbmarketing.com. He is the author of *The Complete Database Marketer* (Editions 1 and 2) (McGraw-Hill), *Strategic Database Marketing* (1st, 2nd, 3rd and 4th editions) (McGraw-Hill), *Customer Churn Reduction and Retention for Telecoms* (RACOM 2009) and *Successful E-mail Marketing Strategies* (RACOM 2010).

READING
6

Media Planning:
The Business End of Advertising

MARIAN AZZARO

Roosevelt University

M edia planning is the business end of the advertising business. Media is the marketing communications function responsible for the allocation of millions and millions of client advertising dollars.

There are many jobs in the media business, but this piece will focus on the critical task of planning. It is the job of the media planner to consider an ever-increasing number of media alternatives and recommend placement of an advertiser's message. Media planning professionals can make a big difference in the effective delivery of a client's message. A good media planner can make even bad advertising work for a client. Conversely, a media planner who makes bad or uninformed decisions can bury even the best advertising. In media, it is all about making informed decisions. Media planning decisions are made in the context of the media planning process.

The primary purpose of the media planning process is to identify the one best combination of many media alternatives that will most effectively and efficiently deliver the client's communication to the right target audience. At each major step of the media planning process, critical decisions must be made.

There are three strategic steps to the process: Establishing Objectives, Defining Spending Principles, and Identifying Strategies. Let's consider them one by one.

Establishing Objectives

Every media plan must first express an objective that will establish goals for coverage and delivery of exposures to an appropriate target audience. These goals must be specific and measurable quantitative goals. Note here the use of the word *must*, not *should*. This is very important. While much in media is negotiable, this is not.

In order to gauge effectiveness and efficiency, the media planning process requires a specific and measurable quantitative objective. Other, qualitative objectives can be incorporated, but a proper media plan starts with a quantitative goal.

The details of this quantitative objective statement suggest the focus of a media planner's decision-making. First, it is the identification of "an appropriate target

EXHIBIT R6.1: THE MEDIA TARGET FOR PLANNING AND MEASUREMENT

The brand communication strategy for Kraft's Velveeta brand cheese product may state the target audience is "women who cook family meals with cheese." However, the media research and measurement services do not report media measures for "women who cook family meals with cheese." The media planner for the Velveeta business uses syndicated secondary research services like Simmons or MRI[1] to create a customized target definition by combining the profiles of women who buy cheeses commonly used for cooking: cheeses like shredded cheddar or mozzarella, or cheese products like Velveeta or Cheez Whiz. The media planner then designates this newly created profile as the "planning target." Next the media planner studies the demographic characteristics of the customized target (women who buy cooking cheeses) to identify the principle demographic, probably women aged 35 to 64. Finally the planner designates this principle characteristic as the "measurement target."

audience." Then, the focus shifts to coverage and delivery of exposures to that target audience.

The Media Target

The media planning process is most often initiated as a subprocess of the advertising or marketing plan, with the target audience for a client's communication already established. If this is the case, then the media planner's role will be to restate the marketing target audience in terms that match up to the typical measures reported by media research services.

Media planners restate the marketing target audience in two different ways, one for planning purposes and one for measurement purposes. The planning target requires a media target definition that allows planners to analyze and evaluate multiple media options relative to the target audience. The measurement target requires a simple, demographic target definition that allows planners to measure and compare the relative effectiveness and performance of alternative media plans. Exhibit R6.1 shows how a media planner might restate a brand positioning target audience for each purpose.

In some cases, media planners may be called upon earlier in the marketing process to help identify the best target audience for all marketing efforts. For example, this might happen when the client assignment is to launch a new product. As described in Exhibit R6.1, media planners can be very creative in finding ways to use the syndicated research services like Simmons and MRI. A media planner can do this by using other products currently in a category, or looking at research on competitive products that will be replaced by the new product.

Media Coverage and Delivery

Once the target audience has been defined, the media planner next considers the question of coverage and delivery of exposures to that target audience. Media plan-

---

[1] To learn more about the major syndicated media research services, visit the Simmons web site at www.smrb.com or the web site for GfK MRI at http://www.gfkmri.com.

EXHIBIT R6.2: THE THIRD TIME IS A CHARM

Advertising works through repeated exposures to a marketer's message. The general rule-of-thumb is that it takes three exposures to ensure effective communication. To understand this rule, consider the fleeting nature of a 30-second television advertisement. Most would agree that it would be lucky if the target audience actually noticed any part of an advertisement on the very first exposure to it. Maybe the consumer saw something that first time that piqued her interest and so she paid attention the next time (the second time) she saw the advertisement. This would be a lucky coincidence. Even so, the consumer, having noticed and paid attention to the ad, still needs to understand and agree with the message before being convinced. Such understanding and agreement *might* be reached on a third exposure to the message, if the message is compelling and clear.

---

ners use several quantitative measures for this purpose. The most important measures are reach and frequency, impressions, and rating points.

Reach and Frequency. Reach is the number of different people exposed to a message within a specified time period. Reach is usually expressed as a percentage of a total target audience such that reach would never be greater than 100 percent. Frequency is the number of times a person is exposed to a message, usually linked to the same time period as used for the reach goal.

In media planning we use the words reach and frequency to mean coverage and exposures, respectively. These two words together represent a core concept of media planning—trade-offs. Media planners can put together media choices to optimize reach or optimize frequency, or they can work within a budget constraint to balance reach and frequency. The media planner must decide which approach is best for the client's needs.

Media planners make this decision based on the advertising plan, matching the Reach/Frequency goal of the media plan to the corresponding advertising objective overall. If the advertising objective is to increase top-of-mind awareness in order to remind consumers that Brand X is out there, then the corresponding media objective might be to achieve the broadest possible coverage (reach) of the designated target audience. However, if the advertising objective is to convince consumers that Brand X is better than Brand Y, then the corresponding media objective might be more exposure (frequency) oriented. As a rule it takes more exposure to convince a prospect than to simply remind.

Next the media planner considers how much exposure is enough. This is a subject of continuing debate in media planning circles. Some say once is enough; some say three, four, or more. The generally accepted rule-of-thumb is that it takes three exposures to be effective. Exhibit R6.2 shows how it might take three exposures to make sure the advertising works.

Impressions. Impressions are another important and often used quantitative measure of a media plan. Impressions are a summary figure representing the total exposures of an advertising message in a given period of time. The phrase "total exposures" is the key to this measure. With impressions we count each person reached

---

EXHIBIT R6.3: CHOOSING BETWEEN MEDIA PLAN OPTIONS

Consider a case of two media plans, A and B. Each plan delivers a total of 1,000 Target Rating Points in one calendar quarter. The media planner must look at the component statistics of the two plans to determine which plan is the best. Plan A delivers 1,000 TRPs with a Reach of 80 percent and an average Frequency of 12.5 times (80 × 12.5 = 1,000). Plan B, on the other hand, delivers 1,000 TRPs with a Reach of 50 percent and an average Frequency of 20 times (50 x 20 = 1,000). If the media plan goal was to optimize Reach, then Plan A would be the better choice.

---

with our message, for every time that person is reached. As such, some people are counted multiple times. In most media plans this is a big number that can be stated either in "gross" terms, meaning a broad measure statistic like TV households, or in "target" terms, meaning a narrow measure statistic like Women 35 to 64.

Rating Points. Rating points are probably the most widely familiar form of media measurement. Most people in the U.S. have heard of the Nielsen[2] ratings for TV shows. The rating of a TV show tells us the percent of a total audience tuned in to that show. We use ratings to compare TV programs across a common audience base and rank programs according to the relative size of the audience tuned in.

Rating points are another measure that can be expressed in either "gross" or "target" terms, such as gross rating points (GRPs), meaning ratings at the household level, or target rating points (TRPs), which means rating points among a specific target audience segment.

Rating points are calculated as a function of percent Reach times average Frequency and knowing this is very important. Exhibit R6.3 shows how a media planner would use this knowledge to choose the better of two similar media plans.

Any one of these measures, reach and frequency, impressions, or rating points, can be used as an effective, quantitative measure of media plan performance. The media planner uses one or all three to compare alternative media plans.

Media Plan Objectives

The best media plan objective defines a specific target audience, a specific percentage of reach, and a certain level of frequency to be accomplished within a specific time frame. Depending on the circumstances, it might be appropriate to use an additional statistic like impressions or rating points together with reach and frequency. Exhibit R6.4 shows several examples of appropriate media plan objectives.

Defining Spending Principles

Budget is always an issue for media planning and many of the planner's decisions are based on working within a budget constraint. A media planner makes trade-offs, like reach versus frequency discussed earlier, throughout the plan. Spending principles define priorities that guide the media planner's decisions in making such trade-offs.

---

[2] For more information about television ratings, visit the Nielsen Media Research web site at www.nielsenmedia.com.

EXHIBIT R6.4: EXAMPLES OF MEDIA PLAN OBJECTIVES

Each of the following objectives provides a quantitative performance standard. The media planner considers alternative media plans against such a standard to choose the best plan for the client's assignment.

- Reach 80% of women 35–64 an average of 4 times every 4 weeks.
- Reach 50% of men 25–49 an average of 3 times each week before a home football game.
- Reach 70% of the primary target audience 5 times each quarter of the year.

Spending principles are often determined by the strategic approach to the media plan.

The recommended strategic approach to the media plan can be either defensive or offensive. The defensive approach leads the media planner to identify strategies and allocate the budget in such a way as to defend and support the existing strengths of the client's business. The media planner uses research to prioritize the geographic and seasonal emphasis of the plan based on the client's biggest sales.

In the offensive approach, the media planner sets budget priorities in an aggressive, competitive manner. The client's message delivery is directed offensively and opportunistically toward the areas of greatest business potential, not existing sales. The media planner uses research on the client's product and other factors to prioritize and focus on opportunities for growth of the client's business.

With focus and priorities established, the planner moves on to identify the specific strategies that will ultimately define the media plan.

Identifying Strategies

Strategies represent the means by which we expect to accomplish the objectives of the media plan. We define strategies in specific areas of planning relating to media scheduling, specific geography, and the mix of media by class/type and by specific media vehicle within each class.

Scheduling

Scheduling refers to how advertising is scheduled over the time period of the media plan. Media planners have three choices in this decision: continuous scheduling, flighting, or pulsing.

Continuous scheduling is a pattern that delivers an almost constant level of media support throughout the whole of the media plan period. For example, your favorite local grocery store probably runs a constant level of media support every week. This makes sense because we know that consumers shop for groceries every week.

Flighting and pulsing are patterns of media support delivered in peaks and valleys throughout the time period of the plan. In both cases, the media planner bundles media for heavier delivery in certain periods relative to others. The key distinction between these two patterns is that a flighted schedule will leave certain periods blank with no media support at all. Media planners will decide to use a flighted or pulsed schedule in cases where a client's business runs in peaks and valleys. For example, if

---

EXHIBIT R6.5: REGIONAL COVERAGE OF THE U.S.

Many food products manufacturers started as Midwestern companies located close to raw materials supplies like grain. These businesses grew and distribution expanded effectively to the East but less so to the West. Western expansion was an issue because of the extra time and cost required to move goods through the Rocky Mountains. As a result, new companies started on the west coast to serve western customers. Many Midwestern-based food products companies still suffer weaker sales in the western U.S. Media planners for these national companies often choose to sell off the western region of national media buys.

---

the client is an expensive neighborhood steakhouse, it has likely been observed that business is much better after the 15th of each month. This would be consistent with research indicating the importance of the 15th of each month as a common payday in the U.S. The media planner in this case would schedule advertising messages heavier around the 15th each month to build awareness when potential customers are more likely to have money to go out for dinner.

Specific Geography

In identifying strategies media planners make decisions about the specific geography the media must cover. If the budget is large enough, the media plan might cover all geography where the client's product is sold. However, it isn't always possible or even sensible to cover all geography equally. Sometimes a client's business or business potential is better in a particular geography. The media planner can reflect such differences in the media plan. Exhibit R6.5 presents the general example of major national food products manufacturers.

Mix of Media

The last area of media strategies is to decide media mix by general class/type and specific media vehicles. The term "media class" defines different general types of media including traditional forms like network television, cable television, magazines, radio, and newspapers, as well as other emerging and non-traditional forms like Internet-based and mobile media and a vast selection of out-of-home media forms now available. The term "media vehicle" is used here in reference to specific media choices like television programs by title, cable TV networks, radio station formats, and magazine titles. This is a broad area of media decision-making encompassing thousands of possible combinations and the choices are expanding every day as new media alternatives emerge.

Whether considering traditional or non-traditional media forms, the media planner first narrows the options by media class and then identifies specific choices of media vehicles. Media planners narrow the possibilities by considering each class of media relative to a list of criteria. Some of the more important considerations are the audience/media relationship, the availability of resources (time and money), and the geographic emphasis of the product relative to the media.

Each class of media works in a different way, engaging different senses of its audience and because of this, consumers may feel more or less involved with the media. The media planner is expected to know the facts of the audience/media relationship.

A radio listener hears an advertisement, but doesn't see it. A magazine reader sees an advertisement, but doesn't hear it. A typical television viewer might actually hear and see an advertisement, but can't interact with it. If however, that television viewer is watching an advertisement through a cable system Video-on-Demand (VoD) service, then interaction with the product is not only possible, but likely.

This doesn't mean that any one medium is better than another, but one or more media may not be right for a particular client. Consider the example again of Velveeta cheese. If it is important to show a rich, creamy cheese sauce, then radio might not be the best medium to use. Instead, it might be better to use beautiful photography and 4-color reproduction to show that rich, gooey cheese sauce in a magazine advertisement.

Another factor to consider in this area is the active/passive nature of each medium and the corresponding longevity of an advertisement. Print media like magazines, newspapers, and Internet web pages and videos allow viewers a more active involvement with the content. The magazine reader can take an in-depth look at an interesting advertisement at his leisure. As such, a print advertisement has some longevity as long as the consumer keeps the magazine around. Broadcast media including traditional television and radio are more likely to be passive and fleeting in nature; consumers are simply exposed to the advertising message. Newer broadcast media options like VoD make it possible now for consumers to re-watch or refer back to previously viewed broadcast advertisements. If the client's message is complex, then the media planner might recommend a media form where the consumer can take time and refer back to the message.

The availability of resources can be a big factor in media decision-making. Media planners know that advertisements require more or less time and money to produce for the different media. If the client has a message today that she wants to deliver to consumers tomorrow, then the media plan won't use long lead-time media like television or magazines. Instead, the planner might recommend radio, knowing that a live announcer could read from a script, thus getting the message out quickly.

Planners also know that the absolute cost of buying advertising time or space can vary dramatically from one medium to another. At one extreme, the cost of a 30-second television ad to run during the Super Bowl can be more than $2.5 million. In contrast, a national advertisement in the Super Bowl edition of *Sports Illustrated* magazine would cost about one-tenth of that.

In considering geographic emphasis the media planner evaluates each media class for its effective coverage of the product's distribution geography. If a product is only available for sale in the Midwest, then the media planner eliminates media with coverage outside the region. On a more complex level, planners will consider that even the national media delivers its audience differently across the country. For example, the audience for late night television is much better in the Midwest than it is on either coast. Knowing this a planner might recommend the use of late night TV for a national client needing a Midwestern emphasis.

After narrowing the possible media alternatives by class, planners must evaluate and identify specific media vehicles. Even after eliminating whole classes of media, there are still many alternative media vehicles among which to discriminate. Two of the most important criteria for comparison among specific media vehicles are audience use of the media and audience coverage of the media.

EXHIBIT R6.6: MAGAZINE COVERAGE OF A TARGET AUDIENCE

If your client is marketing a product for young, college-age women 18 to 24 years old, which magazine would you choose: *Cosmopolitan* or *Mademoiselle*? (Note that *Mademoiselle* is now incorporated into *Glamour,* but this theoretical example is still relevant.) Consider the following audience facts[3]:

- The total audience for *Cosmopolitan* at 9 million is more than double the *Mademoiselle* audience of just over 4 million.
- *Cosmopolitan's* coverage of women 18 to 24 is about 2.4 million, while *Mademoiselle's* coverage is about 1.4 million.
- The wasted coverage of people who are NOT the target audience is just over 6.5 million for *Cosmopolitan* (about 72% of the total audience) and only 2.5 million for *Mademoiselle* (about 62% of the total audience).
- While you get a bigger audience with *Cosmopolitan,* you are paying for more wasted coverage, not just for the coverage you want, women 18 to 24.

In considering these factors for the more traditional media forms the planner turns once again to syndicated research services such as Simmons and MRI. These services report vast tables of data detailing the demographic, lifestyle, and psychosocial characteristics of the people who use various media. For example, for television alone these services report data on people who watch different program types, cable networks, at different times of day, and even specific TV shows. Media planners use Simmons and MRI reports, cross-tabulating product use (see Exhibit R6.1) and media use, to help them choose the right kind of magazine or the right time of day for an advertiser's message. These services help media planners to know the media use habits of the advertiser's audience. These same services also help planners to see that different media vehicles are more or less focused in their coverage of different audience segments. Exhibit R6.6 presents a discussion of audience coverage among comparable media choices.

When it comes to the emerging and non-traditional media forms, media planners sometimes have to trust their instincts and rely on less traditional, often less proven, research. For example, interactive and Internet-based media forms can offer an amazing amount of detailed information about such things as unique visits to web sites, length of time spent at a web site, number of pages viewed, etc. However, we can't yet have any real confidence in knowing the makeup of the audience behind the Internet terminal. Whatever the research, it is the media planner's job to know the many forms of media and even more importantly, to know whatever she can about the audience for each media form.

The Changing Nature of Media

Throughout all time, the world of media has changed as technological advances have been realized. This was true centuries ago with the invention of moveable type and it is still true today as a result of the invention of the Internet. And, this will be true too

---

[3] The data for magazine coverage of a target audience was summarized from Simmons NCS Part 1, Spring 1999.

in the future as the world moves more towards wireless and cellular mobile communications. With each new technological advance, we see a host of new media forms available for use in delivering marketing messages to consumers. Importantly, even as new media forms emerge, existing media forms remain. The result is the ever-evolving, constantly changing nature of the media business.

The number of media options available today for advertisers and their media planners has virtually exploded. In the preceding sections of this article we spoke briefly about such things as traditional and non-traditional, broadcast and print media forms. In recent years it has become increasingly difficult to characterize media in these same old and familiar ways. Instead we are coming to think of media now in terms of **outbound** and **interactive** forms.

Outbound media are the more traditional media forms, as well as some of the newer forms, where the emphasis is on one-way delivery of a marketing message to a consumer. This would include traditional media like broadcast and cable television, cinema, radio, magazine, newspaper, and most forms of out-of-home from roadside billboards to airport/stadium signage. This definition would also include some of the newer media applications such as sidewalk chalk signage, graffiti/mural messaging, public restroom signage, and all manner of other kinds of signage that we see all around us these days.

Interactive media on the other hand is where we are seeing some of the more exciting new developments of the day. As you would expect, the emphasis in interactive media is on facilitating interactive, two-way communication between the marketer and the consumer. It's not just about delivering the marketer's message, it's about delivering the message in such a way that the consumer can interact with the marketer to ask a question or gather more information about the product. For example, as we discussed earlier in this article, cable system Video-on-Demand services make this kind of two-way communication possible. Television digital video recording (DVR) devices like TiVo offer services like brand "tags" and title search advertising as another way to make television an interactive media form.

The Internet is a largely interactive media form. There are several different ways media planners can use the Internet in an interactive marketing capacity. Some of the more common interactive Internet applications today include web site features like advergames, microsites, and web logs. And, other Internet applications like search engine optimization (SEO) and social networking or virtual reality sites are also ways a media planner can provide an interactive forum for a marketer's message. Consider for example, the Travelocity brand Roaming Gnome character and its Facebook friends' page.

Mobile messaging is another newer class of the interactive media form. Mobile messaging is big business in many parts of the world already and growing quickly in the U.S. Mobile phone users all over the world can use their cell phones today to send and receive emails, text, or multimedia messages, or download games, songs, or videos. In many parts of the world, mobile service providers are making it possible now for marketers to send coupons and other marketing messages to consumer cell phones. In Japan, consumers can use their DoCoMo cell phone camera feature to scan Quick Response codes from product advertisements that allow them to then print coupons for discounts in stores where they shop for that product.

As a whole this is one of the more exciting aspects of the media business, the fact that it never sits still. Technology is an ever-evolving dynamic in the world and media is a technology driven business. As the media and media audiences of the future go increasingly digital and mobile, media planners will be the ones helping the marketing clients of the world to find new ways of reaching and communicating with those audiences.

Conclusion

The media planner is expected to make decisions and recommendations every day. Media is where the client's advertising budget is spent and sometimes the stakes can be high. No matter how large or small the advertising budget, the pressure is always on when you are spending someone else's money.

Media planners have to know a lot, but they don't have to know it all. Minimally, a planner needs to know where to find the facts. Planners use the facts that they learn from media research services to make big decisions and to explain their reasons for each decision. To do this, media planners have to be comfortable reading, interpreting, presenting, and explaining numbers, percentages, and indexes, and what each means for the client.

Good media planners love their work. They get charged up about knowing what kind of audience reads a certain kind of magazine, watches a given TV show, or visits a particular web site. They feel personally motivated to learn everything they can about the existing media and emerging, new media developments. The best media planners are consulted as experts for their knowledge of audiences and specific media usage behavior. Media planners are proud to serve their clients at the business end of the advertising business.

MARIAN AZZARO is a professor of marketing communications at Roosevelt University. Before joining Roosevelt, Azzaro enjoyed a successful 20-year career in business. She spent the first 10 years of her career working in advertising media planning. Then, after earning her MBA, she moved into brand management and marketing communications. Azzaro joined the faculty of Roosevelt University in 1999 where she is now a tenured professor teaching marketing, advertising, and media planning classes. She also serves Roosevelt as the head of its graduate IMC program. Azzaro is the lead author of the media planning textbook, *Strategic Media Decisions*.

READING
7

The Economics of Database Marketing

ROBERT WEINBERG

RW Consulting

Database marketing is regarded as the most quantitative, results-oriented advertising medium. Yet most texts on the subject place little emphasis on the economic factors needed to succeed or on how to determine profitability and evaluate performance. Even more surprising is how many database marketers pay much less attention to understanding their basic economic drivers than they do to executing superior creative, testing, or media selection. Many traditional direct marketers and even more dot-commers suffer greatly or even perish due to this inattention.

Determining Profitability

Three factors determine the level of success database marketers can expect from a customer relationship.

1. **Sales** net of returns for credit. Database marketing sales are driven by responses to the direct media used to promote a product or service.
2. The **contribution** which each sale makes to promotion cost and profit. Contribution is simply the amount remaining from a sale after the cost of goods or services, order processing and fulfillment, customer service and overhead are deducted from net revenue.
3. **Promotion cost,** or the amount spent to solicit a response from customers or prospects.

For a database marketer to succeed, their sales, at a level of response the marketer can reasonably expect, must generate enough contribution to more than cover promotion costs**.**

Contribution

The term "contribution to promotion cost and profit" is somewhat unique to database marketing. It quantifies that portion of sales remaining after all the variable costs of purchasing, handling and shipping a product or delivering a service are paid. This

65

includes more costs than are encompassed by the term "gross margin" which nets out only the cost of goods sold, but fewer than are encompassed by accounting's standard EBITDA (earnings before interest, taxes, depreciation and amortization). Typical variable costs subtracted to derive contribution include:

- The cost to purchase or manufacture the products being sold or to provide an offered service (e.g. claims costs for insurance, print, delivery and editorial costs for a publication, delivery of wireless, Internet, or similar services for a telecommunications firm).
- Labor costs to enter and process orders plus 800#, Internet and other connect charges.
- Order picking and packing labor and materials plus shipping cost (e.g. UPS, USPS, FedEx).
- Labor needed to receive and process a refund plus any costs incurred to refurbish or dispose of returned items.
- Labor and phone/Internet costs incurred responding to customer service questions (e.g. where is my order) or to handle **non**-revenue calls prompted by promotions.
- Credit card merchant fees.
- Any premium offered for trying or buying a product or service.

Though fixed overhead for such expenses as management salaries, rent, insurance, or corporate allocations is sometimes ignored to determine the contribution figure used to calculate breakeven or the profit/loss from a specific program, to derive true bottom line profitability marketers must know their overhead cost structure.

Exhibit R7.1 shows, in simple terms, the major cost categories subtracted to arrive at contribution as well as its two components—promotion cost and profit. The $24 in costs might include $16 for cost of goods (COGS), $5 in fulfillment expense, and $3 in overhead. Deducting these costs from the average $40 sale leaves a balance of $16 or 40% for contribution. Were promotion costs for this effort to total 25% of sales ($10), then 15% or $6 is left for profit.

At breakeven 100% of **contribution,** $16 in this case, is available to cover promotion costs and nothing ($0) is left for profit. A loss occurs when the promotion cost per order exceeds contribution, or 40% of sales in this example.

The example in Exhibit R7.2 shows a more complete contribution calculation for a typical merchandise sale. This marketer has determined that the average revenue per order is $50. In addition, customers pay an average $6.00 extra for shipping and handling. However, due to a free shipping offer on orders above a stated minimum value, only 75% of customers actually pay this charge. Thus **average** shipping & handling revenue is only the $4.50 shown. Similar weights apply to most other costs as well. For example, since only 35% of orders are placed via an in-bound 800 call, the average $3.25 cost for such orders is assessed only 35% of the time, resulting in an average per order phone cost of $1.26. Similar factors apply to mail and Internet orders.

Applying all these costs and weights results in a net contribution per order of $21.40 or 39.3% of the $54.50 in total average revenue. If $5.50 in corporate and de-

EXHIBIT R7.1: MAJOR PROMOTION COST AND PROFIT CATEGORIES

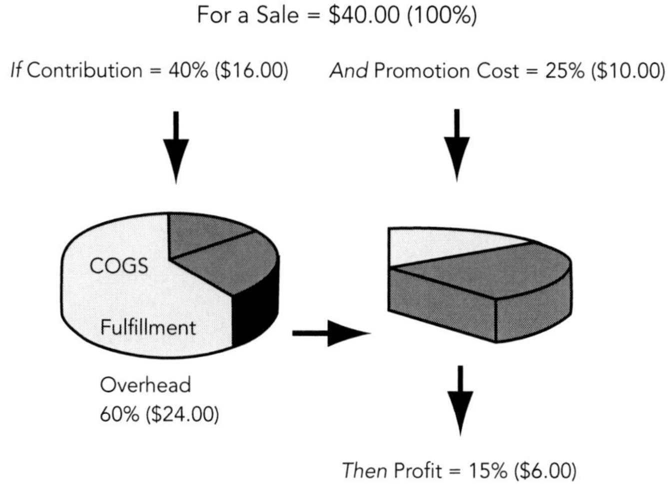

For a Sale = $40.00 (100%)

If Contribution = 40% ($16.00)   *And* Promotion Cost = 25% ($10.00)

COGS

Fulfillment

Overhead
60% ($24.00)

Then Profit = 15% ($6.00)

partmental overhead are added back in, contribution to ***overhead***, promotion cost, and profit rises to $26.90 or 49.4% of total average revenue.

Part 1 of the Exhibit R7.2 worksheet contains a comprehensive list of input assumptions though some marketers will require more, fewer, or a slightly different set of items.

Part 2 performs the average order contribution calculation. Columns 1 and 2 [Base Cost and Factor Percent] reflect relevant values from Part 1. In a few cases these require an intermediate calculation that is not shown. Column 3, Weighted Cost per Sale, is equal to the Base Cost times the Factor Percent. Net Cost/Sale is the Weighted Cost factored up to reflect the added amount each **net** sale must absorb for orders returned for credit.

For example, though a marketer incurs order processing, shipping, pick and pack charges on a return, these orders produce no revenue to offset the expense. Thus, they must be borne by those sales that are paid for. In the Exhibit R7.2 example, which assumes a 10% return rate, the Weighted Shipping Cost/Sale of $3.50 is factored up by 1 minus the return rate to derive a Net Cost/Sale of $3.89 [$3.50 ÷ .9 = $3.89].

While the same detailed approach to computing contribution applies to virtually all services, there are typically fewer cost elements for such commonly direct marketed services as insurance, banking, credit cards, subscriptions, telecommunications and fund raising. Cost components for each of these services also vary widely. We will look at these in more detail under *Repeat vs. Individual Transaction Relationships.*

Prepare a detailed contribution calculation like the one in Exhibit R7.2 for any new offer, at least annually for established offers, and whenever a change in product, marketing or fulfillment experience impacts sales or costs. For example, free shipping, discounts, or a shift from telephone to Internet ordering all impact contribution, altering breakeven, profit, and loss levels. When compiling the detailed numbers that go into this computation, work with finance to ensure that assumptions and estimates are as accurate as possible.

EXHIBIT R7.2: DIRECT MARKETING CONTRIBUTION CALCULATION

PART 1—AVERAGE ORDER ASSUMPTIONS

Assumption	
Average Order Value	$50.00
Shipping and Handling	$6.00
Product/Service Cost	$15.00
Cost of Premium	$0.00
Business Reply (BRE) Postage	$0.42
Mail Order Processing/Handling	$2.50
Phone Order Processing/Handling	$3.25
Web Order Processing/Handling	$2.05
Order Picking/Packing	$2.25
Shipping Cost	$3.50
Customer Service Follow-up	$3.00
Return Handling	$2.95
Return Refurbishing	$5.20
Postage Refund on Returns/Exchanges	$3.25

Percent %:

Returned Goods	10.0%
Exchanges	2.0%
Paying Shipping & Handling	75.0%
Mail Order	10.0%
Phone Order	65.0%
Web Order	25.0%
Postage Refunds	48.0%
Customer Service Follow-up	26.0%
Corporate Overhead	3.0%
Departmental Overhead	8.0%

	Freq. or Rate	Discount or Uncollected
Cash with Order	5.0%	1.00%
Net 30 Days	0.0%	0.00%
Charge to:		
American Express	15.0%	3.00%
Visa	40.0%	2.00%
Master Card	30.0%	2.00%
Discover	10.0%	1.75%
Other Cards	0.0%	0.00%

EXHIBIT R7.2: (Continued)

PART 2—AVERAGE CONTRIBUTION PER ORDER

	Base Cost	Factor Percent	Weighted Cost/Sale	Net Cost/Sale
Average Order Value	$50.00	100.0%	$50.00	$50.00
Shipping and Handling	$6.00	75.0%	$4.50	$4.50
TOTAL AVERAGE REVENUE			$54.50	$54.50
Average Product/Service Cost	$15.00	100.0%	$15.00	$15.00
Mail Order Processing/Handling	$2.92	10.0%	$0.29	$0.32
Phone Order Processing/ Handling	$3.25	65.0%	$2.11	$2.35
Web Order Processing/Handling	$2.05	25.0%	$0.51	$0.57
Order Picking/Packing	$2.25	100.0%	$2.25	$2.50
Shipping Cost	$3.50	100.0%	$3.50	$3.89
Premium Cost	$0.00	0.0%	$0.00	$0.00
Credit Card Discount	$1.16	95.0%	$1.10	$1.10
Bad Debt	$54.50	0.1%	$0.03	$0.03
Return/Exchange Handling	$2.95	12.0%	$0.35	$0.39
Return/Exchange Refurbishing	$5.20	12.0%	$0.62	$0.69
Shipping Cost on Exchanges	$3.50	2.0%	$0.07	$0.08
Postage Refund on Return/ Exchange	$3.25	5.8%	$0.19	$0.21
Customer Service Follow-up	$3.00	26.0%	$0.78	$0.87
SUBTOTAL—FULFILLMENT			$11.81	$13.00
TOTAL DIRECT COSTS			$26.81	$28.00
Overhead—Departmental	$50.00	8.0%	$4.00	$4.00
Overhead—Corporate	$50.00	3.0%	$1.50	$1.50
SUBTOTAL—OVERHEAD			$5.50	$5.50
TOTAL COST			$32.31	$33.50
CONTRIBUTION TO:				
Promotion Cost and Profit		42.0%	$22.19	$21.00
Promotion Cost, OH, and Profit		53.0%	$27.69	$26.50

Promotion or Selling Cost

A second special economic characteristic of database marketing is the importance placed on promotion cost, which should **not** be thought of as the advertising expense common to other distribution channels. Rather, promotion cost is database marketing's true "selling" expense. It is more akin to the cost of running a retail store or supporting a sales force than it is to advertising a retail sale or building brand awareness.

Promotion costs are typically large with 20% to 40% of sales not uncommon. Marketers control and direct this spending by choosing among many media (mail, Internet, TV, etc.) and deciding the content of each (e.g. size of a mail piece or space ad, length of a TV spot). They must therefore be isolated and analyzed carefully.

In most media, determining promotion cost is fairly straightforward. Divide promotion expense, typically from a single provider like a magazine or TV time buyer, by the number of prospects the medium reaches. An ad costing $20,000 in a publication whose circulation is 500,000 costs $.04 per reader or $40 per thousand readers (see *Measuring Success* for more on this) plus a small amount to create and prepare the ad.

In the mail, however, multiple suppliers are generally used for different services, each of which is paid for separately. Services range from printing to lettershop, postage, list rental, and unduplication (merge-purge). To ensure an accurate and **fair** evaluation of promotional success, use these rules to derive an effort's appropriate base promotion cost.

- Charge only for what is spent to print the number of pieces used in a mail drop **if** overages will be used later. If not, charge the full amount to the drop.
- Base list rental and merge/purge costs on the **net** number of names **mailed and paid for,** not gross quantities received.
- In **all** media, account **separately** for such creative and development costs as photography, copywriting, models, layout, and agency fees or commissions.
  —Charge all promotions a creative overhead based on an estimate of the proportion that fixed creative and development costs are of annual variable promotion costs. If fixed annual creative expense is estimated at $100,000 and variable spending is estimated at $1 million, add 10% to the variable cost of **each** effort, whether it is a test or a control.
  —Failure to follow this rule can burden tests with disproportionately high development costs, raising their cost per contact. Control packages or ads, in comparison, incur little if any new fixed creative costs and any amount spent is spread over a larger circulation base, further lowering its impact on the cost per contact. If this bias is not addressed via this suggested approach, winning tests can be discarded owing to an unfair promotion cost comparison.

- To avoid an additional bias in **mail** tests only, calculate profit or loss using **rollout** print and production costs for a piece rather than its actual cost whenever tests are printed in less than control mailing quantities. Allocate the excess costs for these less-than-rollout quantity runs to a testing overhead budget and charge the percentage this amount is of estimated total mail promotion costs proportionately to **all** mail promotions.

EXHIBIT R7.3: RESPONSE CALCULATIONS

	Test Results	
	A	B
Sales	$13,500	$26,000
Orders	270	520
Profit	$900	$1,400
Circulation	15,000	30,000
Profit % of Sales	6.7%	5.4%
Promotion Cost % of Sales	33.3%	34.6%
Sales per 1,000	$900	$867
Orders per 1,000	18.0	17.3
Profit per 1,000	$60	$47

Before leaving this topic we need a word on how to treat Internet promotion costs. Unlike other media, the Internet is unique in that most of its delivery costs are fixed. Except where marketers rent an email list, the cost to actually transmit a message to customers or prospects is negligible. The fixed costs to create and broadcast messages and to maintain sites to which responders are directed to click may, however, be considerable.

The mistake too many users of e-commerce make is to ignore these fixed costs and assume that the low variable cost of contacting prospects means they can send millions of messages with no ill effect as long as even a tiny fraction respond. Even if imprecise, marketers who email existing customers or prospects should attribute **fixed** costs to this medium based on their estimated annual site maintenance expenses divided by a best guess of the number of messages they will send. Though this number is subject to a margin of error, it is preferable to assuming that email promotions are essentially free.

Measuring Success

A final way in which database marketing math differs from traditional approaches to evaluating business outcomes is in its emphasis on relative rather than absolute measures of response, sales and profitability. Example response figures in Exhibit R7.3 show why this is the case.

Were we to evaluate the results of this effort based solely on **absolute** sales, orders and profit, Test B would be judged the better outcome. However, factoring in circulation, contribution and promotion cost we see that, on a **relative** basis, Test A offers a greater financial reward. Though there may be factors that make the Test B outcome acceptable, results cannot be completely or fairly judged until key relative measures are computed.

Because circulation quantities of most database marketing programs vary greatly as do their costs, relative measures provide a simpler, more accurate way than absolutes to evaluate outcomes, set goals, and benchmark results.

EXHIBIT R7.4: VALUES AND MEASURES

Absolute Values	Relative Measures
Gross or Net Sales	Sales per 1,000 (Contacts) Sales per Contact
Gross or Net Responders or Orders	Response Percent
Promotion/Marketing Costs	Promotion Cost Percent of Sales Promotion Cost per Piece or Contact Promotion Cost per 1,000
Product/Service and Fulfillment Costs, and Contribution	Percent of Sales Cost per Order
Pre-tax Profit	Profit Percent of Sales Profit per 1,000 Profit per Responder

Having stated the need for relative measures, which ones are most important and how are these calculated? Exhibit R7.4 lists the most helpful relative measures corresponding to key absolutes. They range from response percent, widely but mistakenly believed to be the most important, to such less well known measures as sales or profit "per thousand of circulation" (commonly written "/M" or "/K").

Before proceeding, let's look at a simple example to understand how to calculate a per-thousand (/M) measure.

*If a marketer nets $18,000 in sales from a promotion sent to 12,000 households, then sales/M are $18,000 divided by circulation **in thousands**. In this case that is 12 (12,000/1000) and the answer is $1500 ($18,000/12).*

Exhibit R7.5 shows, in detail, how to compute key relative measures.

Breakeven and Profitability

With an understanding of these basic measures and their computation, we can now demonstrate how to establish the breakeven, profit, or loss for any effort, given the price of the product or service, its contribution per sale, and its promotion cost. Profit, using the terms introduced here, is simply contribution minus promotion cost.

Continuing the Exhibit R7.5 example, if each sale is worth $50 of which $16, or 32%, is contribution, and promotion costs are $400/M, then to break even (i.e. to just cover promotion cost) a marketer needs to net [after returns] $400 ÷ $16 or 25 orders **per thousand of circulation.** Sales of 25 orders per/M translate into a 2.5% response rate [25/1000 × 100] and sales/M of $1250 [25 orders/M × $50 per order].

Multiplying orders and sales/M by actual or forecast circulation in thousands gives us total actual or expected orders and sales. In this example, where total circulation is 7000, the number of **net** orders needed to breakeven is 25 × 7 or 175. Breakeven sales are $8750 [breakeven sales/M of $1250 × 7M circulation or 175 orders x $50 per order].

Note the importance here of the sales/M measure. It is the product of the number

EXHIBIT R7.5: CALCULATION OF RELATIVE PERFORMANCE MEASURES

Assumptions

A Selling Price per Order		$50
B Contribution to Promotion Cost and Profit per Order		$16
C Total Circulation		7,000
D Net Orders		250
E Total Promotion Cost		$2,800

Calculate:

F Total Sales	A x D =	$12,500
G Promotion Cost/Piece	E ÷ C =	$.40
H Promotion Cost/M	E ÷ (C/1000) or G x 1000 =	$400
I Response %	(D ÷ C) x 100 =	3.6%
J Sales/M	F ÷ (C/1000) =	$1,786
K Promotion Cost %	(H ÷ J) x 100 =	22.4%
	or (E ÷ F) x 100 =	
L Total Contribution	B x D =	$4,000
M Contribution %	B ÷ A or L ÷ F =	32.0%
N Total Profit	L − E =	$1,200
O Profit/M	N ÷ (C/1000) =	$171
P Profit %	(O ÷ J) x 100 =	12%
	or (N ÷ F) x 100=	

of orders times the average value of each sale or transaction. Except where revenue per sale is constant, sales/M is a better measure than response percent for setting goals and evaluating outcomes. This is because it factors in both response rate **and** average order value.

Before leaving this topic, let's look at a shortcut to computing breakeven sales/M given a promotion cost and contribution. It is: *Promotion Cost ÷ Contribution %.*

Using the Exhibit R7.5 example, breakeven is where promotion cost equals contribution, or 32% of sales. At a promotion cost of $400/M, breakeven = $400 ÷ .32 or the $1250/M shown above.

Were an alternative test package to cost $500/M, breakeven rises to $500 ÷ .32 or $1562.50/M. Dividing by our $50 average order value gives us the net required response rate of 3.125% [31.25 orders/M].

The Math of Repeat or Continuity vs. Individual Transaction Relationships

As mentioned in the section on Contribution just prior to Exhibit R7.2, most database marketing programs fall into one of two categories. In one, a regular stream of promotions is needed to drive additional sales while in the second the buyer, either explicitly or implicitly, agrees to make repeat purchases, limiting greatly the need for routine promotions.

Individual Transaction Relationships

Here marketers hope that, once satisfied with an initial experience, a reasonable number of buyers will eventually repurchase from any one of a typically large number of discreet promotions. Catalogs offering an array of consumer or business products are the most common form of this approach which depends for its success on:

- Keeping the cost of acquiring new customers down (see Acquisition Cost).
- Effectively segmenting the buyer file by such factors as the recency, frequency, amount, or nature of prior purchases.
- Targeting promotions with products and/or offers based on past relationship detail.
- Optimizing the number and timing of promotional contacts.

Despite marketers' best efforts, mail response rates to these promotions are usually in the single to low double digits since buyers have not committed to making an additional purchase. Response may be somewhat higher via outbound telemarketing and lower from emails, but in all cases only a small minority respond to each effort.

For these programs to work, it is critical that the marketer know contribution per order and breakeven. These numbers determine whether a customer will be promoted and in some cases which promotion he or she should receive. Decisions about whom to contact are made for each promotion of which there can be anywhere from a handful to dozens per year.

Repeat or Continuity Transaction Relationships

These relationships are found in a wide array of services. They include such financial services as insurance, banking, credit cards, and brokerage, telecommunications including local and long distance, wireless, cable and DSL, subscriptions for a publication, most fund raising, and such membership programs as auto clubs. They also include a narrow range of products, most commonly book or CD clubs, rental programs like Netflix, food and collectibles.

For credit cards, daily newspaper subscriptions and many other products and services, there is no minimum purchase commitment and the relationship only ends when the customer notifies the marketer—or fails to pay. For some clubs, telecommunications services and others, customers do commit to a minimum number of shipments or payments after which they typically continue to receive the product or service until they ask that it be stopped. In still other cases there is an explicit relationship period with no commitment to renew. However a large minority if not a majority of even first time buyers in fact "renew" with renewal rates almost always climbing thereafter. Insurance, subscription, and fundraising relationships typify this behavior.

Unlike single transaction relationships, promotion costs **subsequent to acquisition** generally play a small role. This is because of buyers' upfront commitment to maintaining a relationship for at least some finite period. It is also common for only a single or closely related product or service to be offered. Segmentation and targeting are also less important though smart marketers will use these tools to boost customer value or to intervene where experience suggests a relationship may be in jeopardy.

The three keys to the success of continuity programs are:

1. Keeping the cost of acquiring new customers down *(see Acquisition Cost)*.
2. Keeping retention rates, especially during early periods, high by reducing the reasons to sever a relationship. Retention factors vary widely based on the nature of the service or product offered. They can include anything from bad debt or canceling a continuity plan, to failure to pay an insurance premium, use a credit card, renew a subscription or make another donation.
3. Increasing the value of the relationship where possible. Examples of this are applying for more insurance, donating more, using a credit card or telecommunication service more often, or renewing a subscription or membership for multiple years.

Contribution remains important though it normally needs to be figured for each payment or relationship period, typically months, quarters, or years. The value for each period subsequent to the first will often change, especially if the marketer can increase the average "sale" for those who remain active.

While the elements going into a contribution calculation vary greatly by product or service, it is always important to understand the long-term value of a relationship. This is so the marketer can set an economically sustainable limit on customer acquisition cost.

Exhibit R7.6 is an example of a long-term model for the sale of an insurance policy. It provides a taste of what marketers should pull together to estimate the value of a repeat transaction or continuity relationship.

The example shows that the discounted 10 year value of a customer is estimated to be $175 ($174,776/1000 initial policy holders). Recognizing that this is only an estimate and a long-term one at that, prudent marketers limit what they are willing to pay to acquire a new buyer of one of these policies to some percentage of the estimated amount. This may be as much 50% or 60%; roughly $87 to $105 in this example.

Alternatively, if history shows the average promotion cost spent to acquire a new policyholder is $100, then the model shows that policies sold must, on average, remain active for just over two years for the company to break even (two year value being $99 per starting policy holder).

For many customers a relationship with a company will extend across years if not decades. These future profit flows must be discounted to reflect the net present value (NPV) of monies that won't be received for some time to come. An NPV function can be found in Excel and on some financial calculators. In the Exhibit R7.6 example which uses a 14.5% discount rate, estimated Year 6 profit is cut almost in half by discounting. Policyholder worth in current dollars is $8,390, not the $16,512 the company nominally expects to earn from them in Year 6.

Once created, these "models" can also be used to perform "what if" analyses. For example, how would long-term value change if Year 1 retention increases to 60%, if the average annual premium grows more quickly, or if claim costs are lowered from 55% to 53% of premiums?

Recognize that the Exhibit R7.6 worksheet represents a lifetime or, more accurately, a long-term value model for repeat relationship businesses. The next section on *Lifetime Value of a Customer* explores this concept further and looks at how a similar estimate might be prepared for individual transaction businesses.

Lifetime Value of a Customer (LTV)

For single transaction businesses, the concept of lifetime or, more appropriately, long-term customer value [LTV] is as important as it is for continuity relationships. In both cases, for a newly acquired customer LTV represents the **net present value** (NPV) of all future **profits** from an **average** customer **exclusive** of the acquisition contact.

It is important to recognize that LTV represents a stream of future **profits**, not sales. Since losing money to acquire a new customer involves an upfront out-of-pocket cost, it is only justified if expected future **profits,** discounted to reflect the time value of money, exceed the loss.

Though a superior marketing database will allow a marketer to calculate a LTV for each buyer, in practice it is normally computed for groups of names. Numerous individual customers have a negative value. For example, those who purchase only once or for a single period typically produce losses, while those remaining active for years generate profits far above the average.

Though LTV can be calculated as an average of all customers, the more media, offers and creative alternatives a marketer employs the more sense it makes to estimate it separately for large, discreet groups. Many marketers find that customers acquired in different media, via substantially different offers or creative approaches, or with different demographic or first purchase characteristics (e.g. first product category or season of purchase) produce widely varying LTVs. Where differences are found, marketers may want to set alternative acquisition cost limits or target promotions to acquire more customers with a higher expected LTV and fewer with lower ones.

Recognize that however it is derived, LTV is a **model** that to a greater or lesser degree predicts future profit streams based on past behavior. Numbers developed for Exhibit R7.6, as in all LTV forecasts, represent an estimate of the future based on what has happened before, perhaps altered to reflect **predictable** changes in response or in business operating or other costs.

Because LTV is only an estimate, and a fairly long-term one at that, most marketers prefer to set conservative limits on the acquisition cost they are willing to incur to acquire a customer. The longer the substantive stream of future profits, the more sense it makes to set investment limits conservatively. Investment limits of 30% to as much as 50% or 60% of LTV or a 12, 18, or 24 month payback period are common.

The approach to LTV seen in Exhibit R7.6 and the one we will look at in Exhibit R7.7 represent expected behavior models. Once developed, they provide a good indication over what period of time a marketer can expect to receive substantive value from a group of new customers.

The bulk of most product marketer profits are returned within one to three years of first purchase. For such services as credit cards, insurance and other financial services, time horizons may be longer, extending to perhaps five to 10 years. Recognize

EXHIBIT R7.6: EXAMPLE CONTINUITY PROFITABILITY MODEL—ANNUAL PREMIUM INSURANCE

	Ratios/ Costs	Year 1	Year 2	Year 3	Year 4	Year 5	Year 6	Year 7	Year 8	Year 9	Year 10
Applications	80.0%	1,250.0									
Renewal Rate	—	55.0%	65.0%	75.0%	80.0%	80.0%	80.0%	80.0%	90.0%	90.0%	90.0%
Policies in Force	—	1,000.0	550.0	357.5	268.1	214.5	171.6	137.3	109.8	98.8	89.0
Average Premium		$250.00	$270.00	$290.00	$300.00	$310.00	$325.00	$350.00	$350.00	$375.00	$375.00
Total Premium		$250,000	$148,500	$103,675	$80,438	$66,495	$55,770	$48,048	$38,438	$37,066	$33,359
Claims Paid	55.0%	$137,500	$81,675	$57,021	$44,241	$36,572	$30,674	$26,426	$21,141	$20,386	$18,347
Issue/Application Charges	$8.00	$10,000									
Annual Billing/Customer Service	$12.00	$12,000	$6,600	$4,290	$3,218	$2,574	$2,059	$1,647	$1,318	$1,186	$1,067
Claims Handling	5.2%	$13,000	$7,722	$5,391	$4,183	$3,458	$2,900	$2,498	$1,999	$1,927	$1,735
Overhead	6.5%	$16,250	$9,653	$6,739	$5,228	$4,322	$3,625	$3,123	$2,498	$2,409	$2,168
Total Expense		$51,250	$23,975	$16,420	$12,629	$10,354	$8,584	$7,269	$5,815	$5,523	$4,970
		20.5%	16.1%	15.8%	15.7%	15.6%	15.4%	15.1%	15.1%	14.9%	14.9%
Operating Income		$61,250	$42,851	$30,234	$23,568	$19,569	$16,512	$14,353	$11,482	$11,157	$10,041
		24.5%	28.9%	29.2%	29.3%	29.4%	29.6%	29.9%	29.9%	30.1%	30.1%
Net Present Value	14.5%	$61,250	$37,424	$23,061	$15,700	$11,385	$8,390	$6,369	$4,450	$3,777	$2,968
Cumulative NPV		$61,250	$98,674	$121,735	$137,436	$148,821	$157,211	$163,581	$168,031	$171,807	$174,776

EXHIBIT R7.7: ESTIMATED LIFETIME VALUE FOR 100 CUSTOMERS ACQUIRED 4 YEARS AGO

Year:	1	2	3	4	5	6
Sales	$2080	$1790	$1025	$590		
Contribution	936	806	461	266		
Promotion Cost	243	193	137	70		
Profit	693	613	324	196	110	60
Disc. Profit (8%)	642	526	257	144	75	38
Cum Disc. Profit	$642	$1168	$1425	$1569	$1644	$1682

that at some point expected future profits are substantially reduced by the compounding effect of NPV thereby limiting any marketer's effective time horizon.

The approach to LTV used in Exhibit R7.7 is more typical of that employed in individual transaction relationships. Unlike the continuity scenario in Exhibit R7.6, marketers who send a steady stream of promotions to past buyers to generate sales incur a substantial, less predictable stream of marketing expenses. These are impacted by how effectively the marketer targets and segments past buyers and on changes in response characteristics. Changes in average order value, seasonality, and competition further complicate this picture, making it even harder to predict sales and profit.

For these reasons, anyone attempting to model their business' profits needs a solid handle on expected overall promotion cost and expected response (average order value **and** response rate) for each customer segment being tracked. The **un**availability of accurate information on customer databases is one of the biggest barriers to marketers developing solid estimates.

The approach shown in Exhibit R.7.7 is a much simplified version of one alternative that individual transaction marketers can use to estimate LTV. It requires a marketer to provide historic sales and marketing costs for a group of like customers acquired at a similar point in the past, typically 3 to 5 years ago. In the absence of Year 5+ detail, this example estimates Years 5 and 6 by fitting a curve to 4 year data.

A business whose estimated LTV is the $16.82 (Cum. Disc. Profit of $1682 divided by the 100 initial customers) estimated above, might be willing to pay $8 or $10 to acquire new customers but surely not as much as $14 or $15, given that changing circumstances leave a healthy margin for error around any estimate.

Though Exhibit R7.7 estimates sales and costs by year, it is preferable to generate data by quarter or half-year. Revenues should include not only direct product sales but also any profits from such ancillary sources as list rental, e-commerce, package inserts, or cross promotions.

This example also assumes that prices and marketing costs have not changed in the last four years. This can be reasonable given recent inflation rates. Marketers impacted by significant price inflation—or deflation in recent years, or by increases in marketing expenses, need to challenge this assumption. Where this is the case, factor historic sales and marketing dollars up or down to better reflect what these numbers look like today.

Before leaving this topic, we should mention how the LTV concept might apply to relationship marketing programs. These efforts include loyalty, reward, and customer communication initiatives. They typically generate no direct revenue, but often incur substantial expenses for marketing, operations and rewards.

Applying LTV to these efforts would require that profits generated by incremental sales from program participants exceed the cost of program operation. While it's almost impossible to get solid estimates of this impact for such large established programs as airline and hotel rewards, for more modest programs, especially start-ups, models and live tests can and should be run to determine whether a planned investment is justified. A live test might see some customers invited to participate while a control group is not given special treatment, at least for an initial trial period.

Acquisition Cost

It was once the case that many database marketers expected to acquire a new customer at no cost or even a small profit. Those days are past for most organizations selling products or seeking a donation. It is even more normal for firms selling services to incur a substantial loss to acquire a new customer relationship.

Database marketing success requires the long-term value of a relationship to exceed its acquisition cost. It is therefore crucial not only to estimate long-term value but to also establish an accurate average acquisition cost per new customer. Fortunately this latter number is much easier to derive than the former. Two measures are commonly used.

1. Acquisition Cost per New Buyer is used and much preferred for Individual Transaction Relationships or whenever there is a substantial **initial** purchase or sale. Its formula is:

$$\text{Acquisition Cost/New Buyer} = \frac{\text{Loss from promotion}}{\text{Number of new buyers acquired}}$$

2. For Repeat Transaction Relationships where initial revenue is modest and/or most names acquired are expected to repeatedly purchase or renew, a more common acquisition cost measure is the Promotion Cost per New Buyer. Its formula is:

$$\text{Promotion Cost/New Buyer} = \frac{\text{Promotion cost}}{\text{Number of new buyers acquired}}$$

Exhibit R7.8 shows how these two measures are computed for a given loss scenario. Note that the difference between the two cost figures equals the per order contribution to promotion cost and profit.

Summary

With this overview, the reader will have gained an understanding of why a solid product or service, direct marketed to the right audience with good creative, can still fail if

EXHIBIT R7.8: DETERMINING A COST/BUYER

	Value	Calculation
Net Average Order	$50	
Contribution to Promotion Cost and Profit	$20	
Promotion Cost	$400/M	
Mail Quantity	100,000	
Orders	1,700	
Sales	$85,000	($50 x 1700)
Orders/M	17	(1700/100)
Sales/M	$850	($85,000/100)
Contribution/M	$340	($850 x 40%)
Profit/M	($60)	($340 – $400)
Acquisition Cost per New Buyer	**$3.53**	**($60/17)**
Promotion Cost per New Buyer	**$23.53**	**($400/17)**

the underlying economics do not adequately support the venture. Database marketers must:

- Thoroughly understand the contribution each sale or transaction makes to promotion cost and profit.
- Properly calculate promotion cost.
- Use appropriate relative rather than absolute measures of sales, cost and profits to set goals, gauge success and determine breakeven and other key ratios.
- Make certain the long-term value of newly acquired customers substantially exceeds their acquisition cost.

ROBERT (BOB) WEINBERG leverages 35 years' experience as principal of RW Consulting. His specialties include implementing, improving and analyzing direct and database marketing programs. RW Consulting has completed major assignments for such companies as Coach, Hershey, Hewlett-Packard, Moore Business Solutions Direct, PETsMART Direct, Sara Lee Direct and ServiceMaster. Prior to founding RW Consulting, Bob was President of the Chicago office of Kobs Gregory Passavant. Before joining KGP, Bob was a Senior Manager with Accenture. He is a frequent speaker at industry gatherings worldwide, and a former president of the Chicago Association of Direct Marketing.

Search Engine Optimization (SEO) and Paid Search

JAMES MOORE

Director of Online Learning

DePaul University College of Commerce

Oscar Wilde once said, "The only thing worse than being talked about is not being talked about." The worst thing on the web is having a web site no one can find. Search engines help us find what we're looking for on the web. Search engine optimization, or SEO, is an Internet marketing process that improves search engine visibility and ranking in a way that attracts qualified traffic to a web site.

Your web site needs traffic the same way your body needs oxygen or water. Without traffic your web site is as good as dead. You want your web site to be a bustling destination on the Internet highway, a highly sought-after location travelers flock to. You do not want your web site to be a sleepy little backwater.

The essential concept behind SEO is fairly simple: Craft your web site so that all search engines can read your content. Create content people want to read and link to. Promote your web site. Do all of this better than your competitors.

While the concept of search engine optimization is straightforward, the execution can be difficult. SEO is a rapidly evolving area in which tactics constantly change. Search engines rankings are determined by a series of algorithms. "Black hat" Internet marketers, scammers and spammers figure out these algorithms in order to fraudulently boost their web sites' rankings. So the computer scientists who build search engines must constantly refine and revise the algorithms in response to these underhanded tactics.

There is far more to say than can be covered in a chapter, but hopefully what follows will provide you with a solid foundation to build upon.

What Is Search?

Broadly speaking, there are two types of search web sites:

1. **Directories**

   Analogous to the Yellow Pages, a directory is a categorized listing created and edited by humans. Searchers can browse through categories until they find what they are looking for, or they can enter search terms to locate an entry within the directory. An entry will exist in one place only within a directory.

2. **Search Engines**

   A search engine is an index created by computer programs known as robots or spiders that scour the Internet and then report their findings. A series of algorithms define how search results are displayed and ranked. A searcher can enter a keyword query to bring up a SERP (Search Engine Results Page), which lists a series of web site links accompanied by short descriptions or excerpted text from the destination pages.

Historically the two services were separate, but now both services are typically found together. For example, Yahoo (http://www.yahoo.com) started life as a directory but now has an integrated search engine (http://search.yahoo.com). Google (http://www.google.com) is primarily known as a search engine but also provides a directory service (http://directory.google.com). Google's directory is provided by a volunteer organization know as the Open Directory Project (http://www.dmoz.org).

As ever, there are a couple of exceptions that prove the rule—Mahalo (http://www.mahalo.com), Wikia Search (http://search.wikia.com) and Yahoo! Answers (http://answers.yahoo.com) are examples of search engines with indexes created by humans.

Google dominates search within the U.S. (and most of the world). Google's competitors have an an immense task ahead of them to win back market share. However, rather than competing directly, some companies have tried to distinguish themselves as something more than just a search engine. For example:

Bing (http:// www.bing.com) positions itself as *the decision engine,"* placing value in helping customers make decisions rather than merely serving up search results. Microsoft has purchased companies like Faircast to improve real-time search, which bolsters the ability to provide relavant results.

WolframAlpha (http://www.wolframalpha.com) aims for a more exclusive crowd and defines itself as being the *"computational knowledge engine."* For fun, type in the query "Are you Skynet?" on the WolframAlpha homepage.

Twitter Search (http:// search.twitter.com) stresses *"See what's happening—right now."* Customers can bypass traditional search, and ask their social networks for answers, or follow rapidly trending topics.

Where to Start with SEO

Search engine optimization can be divided into four areas:

1. **Site design** (how your web site works—your mission, its function)
2. **Copy** (the content—words and pictures that communicate effectively to your customer)
3. **Code** (the HTML underlying your web site)
4. **Publicity/Promotion** (getting the word out, your "listing and linking" strategy)

While one person could theoretically handle all four areas, it is a rare individual who excels in all of them. So you may need to direct others to make changes in the areas where your technical skill set is deficient. Remember that SEO is a process—you are never finished.

Determining your Audience

Start by dividing your target audience into two groups:

1. **External**
   Those who come to your web site from search engines
2. **Internal**
   Those who are lost on your web site and use search to navigate your web site. They know that your web site contains what they are looking for—they just have not found it yet. This group can be further divided into two subgroups:
   a. **External Audience:** Customers, clients, etc.
   b. **Internal Audience:** Employees, stakeholders, etc.

At every stage in the SEO process, determine which particular audience you're serving and keep in mind what their needs and motivation are. Remember that your web site serves a particular purpose—getting your audience to convert on your web site. Do not focus on search engine optimization at the expense of providing relevant services to your audience.

Part 1: Design

The design of your web site should allow for growth and the creation of new pages while providing a clear, understandable structure that facilitates navigation and prevents your customer from getting confused and lost. Ultimately you want a web site in which a customer could land on any page and know almost immediately what the web site is for and how to navigate to other pages. Some methods to accomplish this are:

- **Header**
  Your header should contain your logo and perhaps a tagline that explains what your web site does. Most customers are used to seeing a search bar in the top right-hand corner of the screen.
- **Breadcrumbs**
  Breadcrumbs are an excellent way of presenting exactly where a particular web page is within the hierarchy of a web site. This provides context and an easy way of navigating to similar pages. An example of how breadcrumbs might look is: **DePaul > Continuing Education > Internet Marketing**
- **Navigation**
  Your navigation scheme should incorporate keywords in the links to areas on your web site. If you have a link to your homepage, use the anchor text "[Company Name] Home" (as in "DePaul Home") rather than "Home." By avoiding general terms in favor of specific terms, you provide search engines with more relevant information.
- **Footer**
  Provide supplemental navigation in the footer along with contact information (email, telephone, physical address) on every web page. Providing contact infor-

mation will increase the trustworthiness of your web site (you are now more than a random site on the web—you have a physical presence) and also assist in optimizing your site for location-based search services. You should also provide a link to a contact page. For the anchor text, "Contact [Company Name]" (as in "Contact DePaul University") is preferable to "Contact Us."

The design of your site should incorporate four critical pages:

1. **Homepage**
   This page should clearly articulate what you do, or the services you provide, in a few words.
2. **About Us**
   This page should explain in greater detail who you are and what you do. Use specific language and terms that your audience will understand.
3. **Contact Us**
   This page should tell your customer how to get in touch with you. If you expect to create trust you will need at least:
   a. Telephone
   b. Email
   c. Physical address
   d. Fax (optional)
   e. Social media. Customers may prefer to interact with you via services such as Facebook or Twitter.
4. **Site Map**
   This page is a directory listing of all areas on your web site (and possibly all web pages).

Part 2: Copy

A good writer is your most valuable SEO tool. Creating engaging, well-written content can be the best way to optimize your web site. The essence of sucessful marketing is sharing memorable stories that your customers respond to favorably and then share with their friends and colleagues. A decent writer delivers a narrative. However, writing for the web is not the same as writing for other media. Your best approach is to follow these guidelines:

- Short sentences
- Short paragraphs
- Active language
- Simple language
- Break up the page with headings and sub-headings
- Use bullets to simplify concepts

Writers will assist in weaving keywords and key phrases into your web pages. Try not to choose more than one concept to optimize for each web page (which translates to no more than seven words). Follow this process when choosing keywords:

1. Imagine that you are your customer and you are looking for a web page on your site. What words or phrases would you use to search?

2. Now survey others to find out what words they would use. Brainstorm as many words as you can.
3. From that long list of words, reorganize the list into three groups:
    a. **Critical** (no more than seven words)—These are the words that occur most frequently in your surveys or clearly define the concept.
    b. **Supplemental**—Synonyms that might be used in a search.
    c. **Nice to have**—Less essential words that in rare cases might be used in a search.

As your writer creates copy for your web page, she or he will use this list to draft the copy. The critical keywords should appear multiple times on the web page—in the page title, headings, subheadings and opening paragraph. However, this should be done in such a way that the web page does not look like it has been "keyword stuffed." The copy should be pleasant to read and interesting. This is what you pay the writer for. The writer should use the less-critical keywords in the copy, but these can appear farther down the page and with less frequency.

Digging down deeper, you can research which of your keywords are used most frequently in search queries. This may change the order of criticality. Keyword-tracking services you can use are:

- ComScore (http://www.comscore.com)
- Google Keywords Tool
  (https://adwords.google.com/select/KeywordToolExternal)
- Google Trends (http://www.google.com/trends)
  Use to compare search terms, and to research tending topics and searches.
- Hitwise (http://www.hitwise.com)
- Kayak (http:// www.kayak.com/trends/)
  Travel Industry Statistics and Popular Destination Information. Use to research trends in travel destinations.
- Trendistic (http://trendistic.com)
  Use to research trending topics in Twitter.
- Wikipedia article traffic statistics (http://stats.grok.se)
  Beta service, but provides topic popularity results and top 1000 most viewed pages from Wikipedia.
- Wordtracker (http://www.wordtracker.com)
  Wordtracker also provides a SEO Blogger tool and Keyword Questions through their Wordtracker Labs.

Link-bait (and Top 10 lists)

Another good use of a writer is creating link-bait. A link-bait web page is one that's so enticing and interesting that other web sites (particularly blogs) provide links to that page. The concentrated number of inbound links (frequently with the same anchor text) is noticed by search engines and raises your results in SERPs. Easy ways to approach creating link-bait are:

- Ten top tips for. . . .
- Best and worst. . . .

- How to make/save money in five easy steps
- Secret ways to. . . .

An alternative approach to this is to write something that flies in the face of convention and generates controversy (and plenty of inbound links). Here you want to be careful not to alienate your audience.

Another approach is to create guides, white papers or instructions that are topical. To capitalize on topicality, you can research what keyword queries are "hot" and see if you are able to write something on that subject. A great resource to see what is "hot" is Google's Hot Trends: http://www.google.com/trends/hottrends

Video has an important role to play here. Although the expenditure in creating a video is significantly more than just crafting text, video is a highly sought after commodity on the Internet. A short video that meets the needs of a prospect may be favored over a text web page by search engines. If you do start to create videos, make sure you create a corresponding transcript. Not only will the transcript help search engine robots properly index your video, the transcript will also assist members of your audience with visual or cognitive disabilities.

Part 3: Code

The same list of critical keywords can be used in the underlying code of your web page to optimize your SERP. Here are some strategies that you can follow:

File Name

If you are able to define the file names of your web pages, this can improve your search engine ranking. You want the file name to be meaningful and contain your keywords. Keywords are best separated by hyphens, but underscores are almost as good. For example:

search-engine-optimization.htm
search_engine_optimization.htm

Page Title

These should be 40 to 60 characters long. The page title is displayed in the top of the browser window and on the SERP. A meaningful page title is going to make your link enticing on the SERP and gives the search engine more information to work with. My suggestions for structuring this is something like:

<title>10 best SEO tips for beginners (DePaul University)</title>

but you could choose something like:

<title>DePaul University: 10 best SEO tips for beginners</title>

The text should be clear and unambiguous.

Description Metatag

Some search engines will display the contents of this metatag on their SERP. Other search engines will not display this information but may use the text as another factor in their ranking algorithms. You have about 250 characters to create an engaging summary of the web page, which should be keyword heavy. For example:

<meta name="Description" content="Search Engine Optimization (SEO) is easier than you think. In this short tutorial we will show you best practices, examples and help get your site optimized." />

Image Alt Text

Alt text is displayed by some browsers as the mouse pointer hovers above an image. The text is particularly helpful to members of your audience who are visually impaired and using screen readers to translate your web page to speech. Every image on your web site should have short (5 to 6 words) alt text that is descriptive and uses your keywords.

Keywords Metatag

The keywords metatag has been abused by unscrupulous search engine optimizers. Most search engines routinely ignore this data. There is little need to use this code, unless you are using this data to improve locally served search results (i.e. you control the parameters of search).

In addition, there are other strategies you can follow to improve the quality of your web site:

Robots

As mentioned earlier, robots.txt can be used to prevent search engines from indexing duplicate content on your web site. Extensive duplicate content will hurt your search engine rankings. You can also use metatags to indicate that certain web pages should not be indexed or links followed:

<meta name="robots" content="noindex, nofollow" />

Favicon (Favorites or shortcut icon)

Add these two lines of code to the <HEAD> section of every page on your web site:

<link rel="shortcut icon" href="favicon.ico">
<link rel="icon" type="image/ico" href="favicon.ico">

Properly Formed HTML and CSS

Avoid the temptation to use Adobe Flash, Adobe PDF and other technologies that search robots have difficulty reading for exclusive content on your web site. If a search engine robot cannot read the content, then how are searchers going to find this information? The bulk of the content on your web site should be in HTML, but you can provide supplementary content in Flash or PDF if necessary. CSS (Cascading Style Sheets) will allow you to separate the semantic meaning from the style of your site. Use proper HTML tags to structure your web pages into a collection of headings, subheadings, paragraphs and bullet points. Always validate your HTML code.

RSS (Really Simple Syndication)

RSS (Really Simple Syndication) is a way you can update readers about new, regularly changing content on your web site. If you are blogging or adding new items to your web site, then you need to publicize this through an RSS feed.

Finally, be aware that the speed at which your web pages are displayed will contribute to your SERP ranking. Sites that render slowly are less likely to rank highly. Thus, use this information to inform your technology choices. Be aware that if your web pages serve up advertising from a third-party provider, this may slow your site down and hurt your ranking.

Part 4: Publicity

You can automate publicizing articles from your web site by adding tools and buttons that allow your audience to share these pages with a larger audience. Notable examples are:

- Digg (http://digg.com/tools/integrate)
- Del.icio.us (http://del.icio.us)
- Facebook (http://www.facebook.com/share/)
- Reddit (http://reddit.com/buttons)
- Twitter (http://twitter.com/goodies/tweetbutton)

If you are creating video for your site, then consider creating a channel on YouTube. You can then embed your videos on your web site. By doing this, you guarantee that Google is aware of what you have created. More information about this process can be found here:

http://www.google.com/support/Webmasters/bin/topic.py?hl=en&topic=10079

Promotion—Directories & The Open Directory Project

Search engines do not have the capability to index all sites on the Internet. To allocate resources appropriately, search engines begin indexing from a set of preferred sites. This set of preferred sites may come from a directory, such as the Open Directory Project. Thus, it makes extremely good sense to get your web site listed in a directory since this both markets your services in the directory and increases your chance of being indexed by search engines.

Directories include:

- IllumiRate (http://www.illumirate.com)
- Jayde (http://www.jayde.com)
- JoeAnt (http:// www.joeant.com)
- Librarians' Internet Index (http:// www.lii.org)

There are two additional advantages to being listed in a directory:

1. **Trust and reliability.** Humans edit directories; this imbues them with a degree of trustworthiness and reliability.
2. **Targeted audience.** Some directories exist within niche areas of expertise or customer focus. Quite often B2B suppliers will be listed in a targeted directory such as B2B Index (http://www.b2bindex.co.uk). If you provide services in these areas, then you need to submit your information to directories.

So what do you need to do to get listed in these directories? Thankfully the process is extremely straightforward, but it requires some planning and organization. The steps you should follow are:

Step 1—Determine which directories you want to be listed in

The Open Directory Project (http://www.dmoz.org) is definitely the first directory you want to be listed in, but there are other directories that you should consider as well. One way to begin your search is to look through the Open Directory Project's list of directories, which can be found here:

http://www.dmoz.org/Computers/Internet/Searching/Directories/

Create a list of directories that you have the time and resources to contact. For each directory, read carefully their submission requirements.

NOTE: You should only submit a fully constructed web site to directories. Ensure none of your web pages are under construction before contacting a directory. Your web site will be evaluated and may be rejected if considered a work in progress or untrustworthy.

Step 2—Determine where you should be listed within each directory

Drill down in each directory and choose the most appropriate place for your web site to be listed. Make a note of this location. Check to see that you are not already listed in the directory; if you are listed already, then confirm that your details are accurate.

Step 3—Write your web site description

Create a title and description for your web site that closely follows the submission requirements of the directory. Try to ensure that your copy is tightly written but contains appropriate and descriptive keywords, such as:

DePaul University
Largest Catholic university in the United States. Founded in 1898 by the Vincentians. Two Chicago campuses, with four satellite suburban campuses. Courses offered internationally and online.

Most directories will penalize content that looks too much like a sales pitch or advertisement. By ignoring the submission requirements, you run the risk of not being listed.

Step 4—Submit your web site

Submit your web site to each of the directories. Record the details of each submission and keep this information in an electronic document:

- Name and URL of directory
- Date of submission
- Title
- Description
- Cost (if any)
- Name and email address of person who submitted the listing

Record any subsequent correspondence with the directory.

Step 5—Review and update

Periodically check to see that your web site is listed correctly. If your web site undergoes extensive changes, you may need to update your directory listings. Even though the employees who staff directories are inundated with submission requests, they will appreciate being informed of necessary corrections.

Promotion—Search Engines

Now that we have covered directories, we should talk a little more about search engines and appropriate SEO strategies. There are three stages to the search engine process:

1. **Crawling**

   A search engine robot (also known as a spider) "crawls" the web following links. As it follows links, the robot attempts to read all web content it discovers and follow subsequent links it encounters. At the root of each new web site, the robot will look for a file named "robots.txt," which instructs the robot to exclude certain pages from the crawl process. Not all web content will be read by the robot. Information in images or Adobe Flash may be hidden from the robot. The robot is essentially blind—it reads web page code in a similar way to screen readers for the visually impaired. web sites are crawled periodically. Changes that you make to your web site will not be reflected until your site is crawled again.

2. **Indexing**

   Pages that the robot has read are analyzed and information recorded. Information may be cached and metadata (information about information) may be collected.

3. **Presentation of results**

   A searcher receives a SERP after entering a keyword query. The results are presented according to relevance, ranking and advertising criteria. In the majority of cases, the algorithms that dictate how results are presented are industry secrets, but we can make informed decisions about how these algorithms operate.

So how do you ensure your web site is crawled? Although it is possible to submit your web site and request that it be indexed, the more appropriate course of action is to make sure that sites that are indexed by search engines link to your web site. As search engine robots crawl and re-index these web sites, they will follow links to your web site and index you. Thus, you should concentrate on listing your web site in directories and on other web sites (that are crawled by robots).

So which web sites do you want to be listed on? There are web sites that will offer to provide inbound links for cold hard cash. There are web sites that will provide inbound links only if you provide links back to them. Avoid both of these types of web sites. Search engines are not happy with such overt manipulation of the system, as this has a tendency to reduce the relevance of search results. If a search engine employee discovers that your inbound links come from such shady web sites, they will take action to either remove you from their index or reduce your ranking in the SERP.

Your better course of action is to target complementary web sites where a link to your web site is relevant and provides utility. For example, if your web site sells books, then you might want to contact authors and ask them to link to your online bookstore. In a similar fashion, you should contact local business bureaus, trade associations, clubs and relevant organizations and ask them to link to you.

When asking web sites to link to you, the best practice is to provide them with anchor text. Anchor text is the text within a link. Search engines take particular note of anchor text, so you want to avoid inbound links that look like this:

DePaul University has a web site, you can view it **here**.

And move in the direction of links that look like this:

Visit the **DePaul University web site**.

When you contact a web site and ask the administrators to link to your web site, you can provide them with code that ensures you have appropriate anchor text.

Now, contacting people and asking them to link to you may sound a little naive and simplistic. You can build a more professional strategy by creating press releases and sending these to the appropriate outlets. Your press releases should also be found on your web site—in a news, press or media area. Building upon this, you can create a "link to us" page with example code or incorporate this on your contact page.

Your Next Steps

Getting one page crawled does not guarantee that your web site will have top ranking in SERPs. There are some basic tasks to follow to make sure that your web site is crawled appropriately:

Checking How You Are Listed in Search Engines

Entering the code below (where you substitute your web site URL) will provide you with an understanding of whether your site is listed in the major search engines:

- **Google**
  site:yourdomain.com
- **Yahoo**
  site: yourdomain.com
- **Bing**
  site: yourdomain.com

Using the Lynx Browser

Lynx is a text-only browser that, among other things, approximates how a search engine might "see" your web site. Using Lynx can be an appropriate way of verifying that your site can be crawled by search engine robots. Free browsers can be downloaded from:

- Windows Version
  http://csant.info/lynx
- Mac OS X Version
  http://habilis.net/lynxlet/

You can also user online Lynx viewers like:

http://www.delorie.com/web/lynxview.html

If you notice functional problems with your site when viewed through the Lynx browser (such as missing navigation), then you know that search engine robots will have difficulty indexing your site.

Check for Dead Links

Robots are fairly dumb. They will not make informed guesses about the location of your web pages. You need to check your web site for dead links. There are software tools that can assist in this process, such as:

http://validator.w3.org/checklink

Provide a Site Map

After you check for dead links, you need to provide search engines with a way to find every page on your web site you'd like them to know about. You can do this by creating an index or site map. A site map is simply a directory listing of pages on your web site. Create your site map and then provide a link to it on every page of your web site. This helps both robots and humans. If your site has more than 100 web pages, provide links to just the critical pages and categories (search engines tend to stop indexing links if there are too many on the page).

Spell Check

Make sure that all content on your web site has been spell checked.

Create a custom "404: File not found" page

Inbound links may go to pages that do not exist—this generates a "404: File not found" error page. To fix this problem, you can create a custom page that indicates that the page that the user is looking for cannot be found but then provide links to other pages on your web site. The structure of this page can be similar to your site map.

Use robots.txt

The robots.txt file can be used to guide search robots through your web site. You can choose to exclude certain pages that you might not want to see on a SERP such as duplicate pages, pages under construction or limited promotions.

Paid Search

Paid Search is one component of Search Engine Marketing (SEM). Like many other practices in Internet marketing, the definition of Paid Search changes over time (and based on who you are talking to). Paid Search consists of both placing advertisements on Search Engine Results Pages (SERPS), and placing advertisements on content sites in the form of contextual advertisements. Vendors who provide this service include Google AdWords, Microsoft AdCenter and Yahoo! Search Marketing.

U.S. Paid Search Providers

- 7Search (http://7search.com)
- ABCSearch (http://www.abcsearch.com)
- adMarketplace (http://www.admarketplace.com)
- Apple iAds (http://advertising.apple.com/)
- Ask Sponsored Listings (http://sponsoredlistings.ask.com)
- ePilot (http://www.epilot.com)
- FindIt-Quick (http://www.finditquick.com)
- Findology PPC Search (http://findology.com)
- Google AdWords (http://adwords.google.com)
- Holika.com Online Advertising (http://www.holika.com)
- Kanoodle (http://www.kanoodle.com)
- Looksmart AdCenter (http://adcenter.looksmart.com)
- Marchex (http://www.marchex.com)
- Miva Pay-Per-Click (http://www.miva.com)
- Microsoft AdCenter (http://adcenter.microsoft.com)
  Campaigns appear on both Bing and Yahoo!
- Search123 (http://www.search123.com)
- Yahoo! Search Marketing (http://advertising.yahoo.com)

For a Paid Search advertisement to be placed in front of a prospect, a set of keywords must be defined for the advertisement. The advertisement will be served dynamically, if the keywords for the advertisement match (to a certain degree) the prospect's search query.

For a contextual advertisement to be placed in front of a prospect, a set of keywords must be defined for the advertisement. The advertisement will be served dynamically, if the keywords for the advertisement match (to a certain degree) keywords in the web page content. Relevance (sometimes referred to as a quality score) and bid cost dictate the ranking and selection of these dynamic advertisements.

When Should Paid Search Be Used?

Paid Search should only be seriously considered when you are able to measure the effectiveness of a campaign. This assumes that you have a both KPI/KPM (Key Performance Indicators/Key Performance Metrics) defined and an accurate and timely way of providing analytical data. Otherwise you have no idea if you are actually getting a return on your investment.

Paid Search is of critical importance if you are not achieving the organic search results you need. This may happen when you are in start-up mode (and largely unknown to search engines), or due to listing issues (such as technical or political reasons for not ranking in SERPs).

Your role here is to measure success, and then either adapt or cancel your Paid Search strategies.

Some argue that Paid Search can be used to as a branding tool—pushing competitors out of the picture or reinforcing the brand. Personally, I am not entirely convinced, but this is worth considering. Again, you need to be able to measure effectiveness.

How Can You Improve Paid Search?

Most successful sales professionals know the value of focusing on qualified prospects and ignoring time-wasters. Similarly, you can apply constraints to the display of your Paid Search advertisements, such as:

- Negative keywords
- Geography
- Language
- Seasonality
- Day of week
- Time of day

Let's look at some basic examples of how you might properly constrain your Paid Search advertisements. Imagine you are in the training business, and want to promote your courses through Paid Search. How can we prevent our ads from being displayed to the wrong prospect?

Negative Keywords

There is a world of difference between someone searching for "SEO training" over "free SEO training." Thus, "free" might be an appropriate negative keyword, and you might decide not to advertise to prospects who use that word in their searches.

Geography

If your business only offers training courses in Chicago, then you might want to limit the display of Paid Search advertisements to prospects who are searching in the Midwestern U.S. However, this might prevent Chicago natives from seeing your ad when they are searching while outside of your limited geographic area.

Language

If your training courses are taught in English only, then you might choose to constrain Paid Search placement to prospects who are searching in the English language (or have localized their browser).

Seasonality

Your training courses may only be offered in certain months of the year, or demand for these courses peaks and troughs according to the seasons. If you do not have courses running in the immediate future (or they have just started and you don't accept late registrants), then perhaps there is less need to advertise, and you can hold back on using Paid Search. Conversely, you might want to flatten out demand and advertise more during slow months.

Day of Week

Let's imagine your training courses are tailored for businesses, and you know that prospects only search for courses Tuesday through Friday. You might decide to cut back on advertising over the weekend.

Time of Day

Paid Search involves the allocation of finite resources. You may discover that you get better placement of Paid Search ads if you restrict your bidding until late in the day. Your competitors may have exceeded their budgets by then, leaving you with a less competitive environment.

All things being equal, these constraints will improve your conversion rate. Additionally, a model for success that I suggest is to think about a Proactive / Reactive Split. You want to be proactive in placing your advertisements in front of the right prospects (findability), and then reactive in providing engaging copy that your prospects will favorably respond to (clicking). Context can help—an advertisement on a niche site (versus a portal site) with a similar focus to your web site is more likely to be clicked on (and therefore it's more likely that the prospect will spend longer looking at the advertisement). Where Paid Search or a contextual ad brings a prospect to a Web site, a landing page can be used to increase the chances of conversion. User testing can optimize both the incentive and your landing page. Your options are:

- **A/B: Two version of one element.**
  Here, 50% of your audiences are assigned your original incentive or web page, and the other 50% see a version with one item changed. The version with better conversion rates is the one you keep.
- **A/B/N: Multiple versions of one element.**
  With this strategy, you randomly assign your audience to multiple versions of your original incentive or web page. In each version, the same element is changed. The version with better conversion rates is the one you keep.
- **Multivariate: Multiple versions of more than one element.**
  This last option is considerably more complex. Here, you randomly assign your audience to multiple versions of your original incentive or web page, where multiple elements are altered. The version with better conversion rates is the one you keep.

As your optimizing process gets more complex, the statistical certainty of your results decreases. You need to have a sufficient volume of prospects for this to be a workable solution. Google provides a free tool (https://www.google.com/analytics/siteopt/splash?hl=en) that can be used to facilitate the A/B testing process on your web pages.

Your long-term strategy here is to remove underperforming keywords and advertisements, and simultaneously explore alternative keywords and advertisements. All of the major Paid Search providers have learning resources (and account managers) who can assist you here.

Crafting the right copy is fundamentally important to success. One suggestion on how to design an effective strategy is to use something like Gartner's Magic Quadrant to map where you exist, versus your major competitors. By identifying differences, you can propose a unique value proposition. Beyond that, you need to have a message that speaks directly to your prospect—identify a problem, provide a solution, incentivize your prospects to act immediately.

To conclude, both SEO and Paid Search are long-term processes that involve hard work and continuous oversight. You have to dedicate sufficient resources and steadily focus on incremental improvements to achieve successes. The road may be long and arduous, but the end is rewarding.

JAMES MOORE is the Director of Online Learning for DePaul University's College of Commerce. He teaches Internet Marketing classes in fully online, blended and face-to-face formats. He attempts to balance his love of technology and gadgets with the knowledge that quick and simple solutions are best. Unfortunately, creating quick and simple solutions often involves a long and complex process.

READING
9

Business-to-Business Marketing

VICTOR L. HUNTER
Hunter Business Group, LLC

SHEILA T. ZELENSKI
Hunter Business Group, LLC

JEFF J. KREUTZER
Hunter Business Group, LLC

Effective marketing to businesses yields an amazing return on investment, if you understand your customer and the potential that each customer represents, optimize your activities, and invest accordingly. While the risk and investment are far greater in marketing to businesses, so are the rewards. This piece will provide you with the basic tools necessary to succeed in business-to-business integrated marketing communications and to effectively combine marketing communications with direct selling efforts.

Business-to-Consumer (B2C) Versus Business-to-Business (B2B) Marketing

To begin it is important to differentiate between marketing to individual consumers and marketing to business buyers. The key differences between consumer and business to business marketing are those of scope, depth and complexity.

Scope

If you miss the mark in demonstrating value to the customer when marketing to consumers, the individual loss is small. However, make this same mistake on the B2B side, and you risk losing many potential opportunities and buyer groups within a single company. Conversely, acquiring, assimilating and growing a single business customer will likely yield high lifetime value and additional revenue through the identification of new buyers and new needs as you penetrate fully into the organization. The lifetime value of a business customer is often many, many times beyond the apparent initial potential. This is due to the opportunities for new relationships, new buyer groups, new product needs and applications. This great potential deserves additional investment in building the B2B relationship, delivering value and action on those things that drive customer loyalty.

Moreover, consumer marketers often have a seemingly unlimited universe of prospects to choose from. The opportunity to make mistakes, realign and try again is greater because you usually have millions prospects to approach. In the B2B world, it is typical to have a total universe of fewer than five thousand organizations, making it even more critical to do your research and deliver value from day one.

Depth

Because profitable B2B transactions are a result of strong relationships, the end result of a successful B2B marketing campaign is one where the relationship with your customer is deepened. You deepen your relationship with the business customer by (1) gaining a deeper understanding of your customer—their needs and behaviors, (2) achieving a deeper understanding of the account as a whole—learning about new buyers, influencers, and opportunities, and (3) creating an higher degree of trust by demonstrating value, diagnosing needs and finding solutions.

Of course, this means that B2B marketing focus and processes look quite different from consumer marketing. For example, a critical piece of any business-to-business marketing plan involves proactive calling to identify new buyer groups and decision-makers. Another activity may involve the delivery of value-added communications such as industry articles, to strengthen the bond between you and your customer. The first activity is not relevant to consumer marketing, where few decision-makers are involved in the purchasing decision. The second activity is rarely justified in consumer marketing because both the average order size and lifetime value are too small to justify the investment.

In addition, B2B marketing measurements are different. When marketing to consumers, the desired outcome is a transactional purchase. Therefore, measures are based on the number of responses and subsequent transactions generated by consumer marketing activities. In B2B marketing, the desired outcome is often less tangible. When marketing to businesses, the desired outcomes are building stronger relationships, identifying new buyer-groups, decision-makers and applications and increasing customer loyalty. Therefore, the measures must be set accordingly. So, the right B2B marketing measurements must be broad, deep and complex in order to measure economic value and return as well less concrete outcomes such as customer satisfaction, product penetration, account penetration, referrals, frequency of valued contact, and repurchase rates.

Complexity

The complexity of the buying process is another significant difference between consumer and B2B marketing. Typically, more than one person is involved in a single buying decision, more than one group within an organization may purchase the same type of product, and the decision to purchase may even involve formal processes, committees and preferred provider requirements. It is critical to understand the nature and complexity of this buying process before you embark on marketing strategy. Without knowledge of who within a company makes purchases and how they make those purchases, it is nearly impossible to influence buying patterns.

By understanding these key differences, you can start to develop a B2B marketing strategy that will result in loyal, profitable, and long-standing customers.

The Business-to-Business Marketing Strategy: 8 Business Results

Understanding the critical business results in the B2B space is critical to position your marketing strategy. The eight business results that follow enable your organization to reach organizational goals.

Business Result 1: Customer Acquisition

How can I be sure I'm getting a decent payback for the money we're spending to get new customers?

Getting customers is tough and expensive. It can cost 5 to 15 times more to get a business customer than to keep one and it typically takes more than a year and a half to break even. So, what's the trick? Continuous learning—the kind that results from implementing a measurable process that allows your organization to increasingly understand:

- What organizations and individuals to go after
- Which ones to cultivate and which ones to get rid of
- How to shorten the time it takes to get a prospect to buy
- How to get a higher percentage of prospects to become long-term customers

Critical to Customer Acquisition is the way you manage:

Lead Generation. In simple terms, the objective of lead generation is NOT to simply generate inquiries, based on volume. The objective of lead generation is to generate QUALIFIED leads, defined as prospects that have a need for what is being offered and a higher probability of becoming loyal, long-term customers.

Lead Management. Few processes are more important since, in addition to increasing the chance that the acquisition efforts will produce an acceptable return, a well run lead management process greatly determines whether new customers become long-term, profitable customers.

Prospect Cultivation. Few business-to-business prospects turn into customers instantly. A prospect might want time to be sure that your solution will produce the results they need. Or they may need time to sell internally. It might be that they just have to wait for the next budget cycle. Whatever the reason, if the investments made to generate leads are to be protected, there must be a deliberate process that ensures that the "seeds" planted not only survive but are nurtured into healthy "harvestable crops." Prospect cultivation is generally a dialogue-based process whose purpose is to exchange value in the form of increasing knowledge, understanding, and trust.

Value-Based Contacts. By better understanding the prospects' needs and communications preferences and building them into each contact in the cycle, the effectiveness of acquisition efforts can be greatly enhanced.

New Product Launch. Today's highly competitive and dynamic business climate requires new product approaches that are driven out of a deep, real-time understanding of the anticipated needs of specific segments of customers. Such a level of under-

EXHIBIT R9.1: KEY SALES FUNNEL COMPONETS

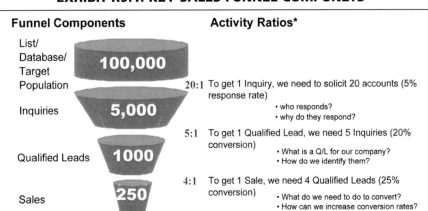

Funnel Components

List/Database/Target Population	100,000
Inquiries	5,000
Qualified Leads	1000
Sales	250

Activity Ratios*

20:1 To get 1 Inquiry, we need to solicit 20 accounts (5% response rate)
• who responds?
• why do they respond?

5:1 To get 1 Qualified Lead, we need 5 Inquiries (20% conversion)
• What is a Q/L for our company?
• How do we identify them?

4:1 To get 1 Sale, we need 4 Qualified Leads (25% conversion)
• What do we need to do to convert?
• How can we increase conversion rates?

If average order size is $100,000 and our revenue goal is $25,000,000, we will need 250 sales ($25m/100K). To get 250 sales, we will need a target population of 100,000 potential buyers (250X4X5X20)
© Hunter Business Group, LLC

standing seldom results from periodic "research events." Rather it develops as an almost natural outcome of day-to-day processes designed to build deeper and more responsive relationships.

Opportunity Management. An effective opportunity management process allows B2B companies to identify and respond to business opportunities quickly and appropriately, and insure the highest conversion rate possible.

The Sales Funnel. Sales Funnel definition and tracking provide visibility into your situation—and provide a tool for managing and guiding the process. The Sales Funnel represents the steps and stages of your standard sales process. A tailored model, each company's Sales Funnel is comprised of:

- Source tracking for each lead and opportunity entered into the sales process.
- The stage gates which represent the evidence of progress through the sales process and defining moments within the sales process.
- The key sales activities that are required to progress a lead through each of the stages (Exhibit R9.1).

Business Result 2: Customer Retention

How can we possibly be gaining that many new customers every week and still have stagnant revenue?

Few B-to-B companies make money on the first sale. On average it takes 18 months before a company reaches the breakeven point. This is why customer retention is critical, not only to recover the cost of acquisition, but to fuel overall growth and profitability. Acquisition and retention are often treated as separate and distinct processes but they are really two major phases of the customer lifecycle and are highly interdependent. Keeping customers is greatly determined by which customers are acquired.

And finding good, retainable customers works best when their characteristics are similar to those of the most loyal existing customers.

Critical to Customer Retention is the way you manage:

Assimilation. An old marketing adage says "a customer is not a customer until he or she purchases twice." Today many marketers would say "until he or she has purchased three or four times." Assimilation is the intentional task of getting new customers to purchase two or three times in a relatively short time frame. But the primary purpose of assimilation is not so much the money gained through those additional purchases as it is getting new customers to enjoy multiple positive experiences rooted in the exchange of value.

Reactivation. Reactivation is the process of quickly becoming aware of and appropriately intervening to "rekindle" the relationships and continue to earn a return on your investments.

Customer Loyalty. Loyalty gets more and more customers to experience more and more value over time. Loyalty is earned and profitable growth is realized when the additional transactions are well matched to what specific customers most value. People often talk about an account being loyalty but the only way to achieve total account loyalty is to achieve the loyalty of all the individuals and buyer groups in all of the locations that make up an account. Understanding what customers value and the attributes that define the key drivers of loyalty will increase customer share. The key is that only one customer voice will not give you a clear understanding of what an account values. All the individuals and buyer groups within the account rolled together will help define the drivers that will increase customer growth (Exhibit R9.2).

The Leaky Bucket. If sales are up, life is good! . . . Well, maybe and maybe not. Too often executives can fall into the trap of focusing mainly on top line revenue. In order to make effective business decisions, an analysis of where the revenue is coming from is required. Revenue may be up because the company has gained a lot of new customers, but previously established customers are defecting—in effect, "leaking" out the bottom of our customer pool. If we are successful in replacing the defective cus-

EXHIBIT R9.2: LOYALTY MEASUREMENT MODEL

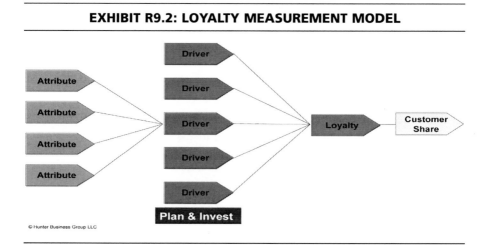

© Hunter Business Group LLC

tomers, the top line growth figures may be attractive—but consider the substantial costs. It is significantly more costly to be acquiring new customers, as opposed to retaining the customers we already have.

Service Profit Chain. How does leadership impact corporate profitability? Good question. That is the very question the Management Interest Group at Harvard Business School set out to answer. The hypothesis was that profitability was a direct result of the strength of an organization's leadership. The results of the study showed that profitability was driven by customer loyalty and supported by effective leadership styles. Additionally, it was learned that there is a direct relationship between employee and customer satisfaction/retention.

Business Result 3: Customer Profitability

How do I know the appropriate amount of money to invest in existing customers?

In the business-to-business arena profitability can be easily leached away if focus on understanding your customers, effectively measuring for customer profitability and using integrated account management is lost. These aspects create a direct line of sight to customer profitability.

Critical to Customer Profitability is the way you manage:

Grading. Not all customers are created equal. Different customers—even those that look alike—can have substantially different potential economic value to a particular organization. When marketers don't recognize this fact, or even when they do recognize it but don't do anything about it, they risk over-investing or under-investing in particular sets of customers. **A grade is not a segment.** Grading is the process of grouping accounts or buyer groups according to their *potential value.*

Segmentation. Defined as a group of accounts, buyer groups or individuals with a common set of attributes.

A segment could be a target; however, segments are often comprised of multiple targets:

- Segmentation can be based on firmographics (demographics of companies), demographics, needs, and/or behavioral characteristics
- The best segments are needs and behavioral based
- The best attributes (characteristics of a segment) are "actionable attributes"
- Segments are often based on similar applications

Most companies segment by some form of demographics because it is easy, not because it is effective.

Core and Common Measures. Most all business executives will agree that maximizing customer profitability is critical. The disparity often comes in how to effectively measure customer profitability. Further complicating the issue is that there are two sides of the equation that must be considered, the revenue provided by a customer as one side and the cost of servicing and delivering to that customer as the second component.

Across the B2B environment, a standard set of similar effective measurements and reports have proven to be effective and reliable. The measures used may be less important than using them consistently across the organization. Customer profitability will surely improve when an organization establishes a set of core & common measures, uses them within every department and across all efforts, and takes appropriate actions based on their findings.

Measurement Framework. To maximize the effectiveness of the measurement framework it is critical that we correctly link processes and activities to the results they drive. Our objective is to ensure what we measure is truly predictive of results—avoiding both "black box" syndrome (too few measures, resulting in a lack of foresight on where the business is going) and "white noise" (so many measurements, that we cannot tell the important and indicative from the less relevant). It is critical to complete the measurement framework with the addition of Quality metrics. Quality metrics can often be the most difficult to define and track—but are frequently the most powerful in predicting results.

Integrated Account Management. Functionally, Integrated Account Management leverages and integrates all of the available media options for building this inter-dependent relationship between B2B companies and their customers. Seamlessly integrating email, mail, phone, etc. to support the field and the channel, Integrated Account Management provides a cost-effective model for extending the interactions and coverage we can provide for customers. In addition, it places at our disposal a wider array of tools for communicating with customers in a manner consistent with their preferences and expectations. The net result is a classic win-win situation: greater value and satisfaction for our customers, and greater loyalty and revenue at lower cost for the B2B company.

Business Result 4: Customer Growth

How can I achieve sustainable growth?

Growth can only be achieved by improving value delivery through the overall customer experience—and may be one of the only remaining sustainable differentiation strategies available to the modern firm. If the growth imperative is dependent on business activities in the customer domain, no strategic growth initiative can succeed without leveraging customer insight to improve the value delivered across the entire customer experience. It may sound simple, but listening is the common thread. Listening to the voice of the customer, and then responding appropriately helps uncover what customers want us to know and do—deliver value. To accomplish this we need new tools to hear the voice of the customer and refined methodologies to apply this knowledge.

Critical to Customer Growth is to take on strategic questions through the following concepts:

Customer Loyalty. In some ways, customer growth is long term assimilation. Loyalty gets more and more customers to experience more and more value over time. Loyalty is earned and profitable growth is realized when the additional transactions are well matched to what specific customers most value.

Setting objectives for, and measuring, customer growth requires being pretty specific about defining what a customer is. It helps to think of customers as individuals rather than accounts. Accounts don't buy things—people buy things on behalf of accounts. Emphasizing accounts as customers can actually be a hindrance to customer growth because it tends to permit "laziness" when it comes to really understanding who makes the actual buying decisions, what they value, and how to reach them. It's useful to think about business-to-business customers as networks of individuals clustered into *buyer groups* responsible for sets of specific applications. Larger accounts are typically intertwined networks of multi buyer groups in multiple locations. Using this concept allows customer growth objectives, strategies and tactics to be highly focused.

Account Penetration. Customer Growth through Account Penetration involves identifying and connecting with a growing number of individual buyers within a customer account. In this framework, think of the account as a network of multiple sites, composed of multiple buying groups, composed of individuals with responsibility for specific applications—applications for which your products or services meet the customer needs.

Product Penetration. If Account Penetration is about achieving customer growth by selling your products to more buyers within an account, Product Penetration achieves growth by selling more products to each of those buying groups. Product Penetration is about more than short-term revenue enhancement, though. It is about creating a sustainable, interdependent relationship with your customers which is based upon a broader exchange and delivery of value.

New Product Launch. Most companies measure velocity from the completion of product development to the time the product is introduced to the commercial market. After that date is met, most launches either collapse into chaos or slide into obscurity. Organizations should really focus on the time it takes to fill the sales funnel and realize sales. The speed and methods used to fill the sales funnel will have the greatest impact on your new product's lifecycle—market penetration, product penetration and repurchase—because this is when you build your presence in the marketplace.

Integrated Account Management. Business-to-business marketing and sales executives are urgently searching for new and better ways to find and keep customers. Faced with the triple impact of rising costs, fierce competition, and fickle clients, many organizations are finding a unified solution in integrated account management (IAM)—a form of marketing that takes a proactive and personal approach to managing mutually beneficial customer relationships. IAM allows companies to effectively manage their relationships with customers. It is the customer relationship that drives both growth and profitability. It is why customers buy, what differentiates companies from competitors, and, most importantly, why customers remain loyal. IAM is an integral component of a company's overall relationship marketing strategy

Service Profit Chain. The most direct driver of revenue growth and profitability is customer loyalty. In almost any organization, a small percentage of loyal customers account for the majority of the company's profit and growth. All of which begs the question: how do I increase customer loyalty? The answer is not simple, but the

Service Profit Chain (Service Management Interest Group, Harvard Business School) provides an excellent framework for diagnosing components and building the infrastructure to increase loyalty, revenue growth and profitability.

Loyalty is measured by actual buying behavior. By knowing who your best customers are and what they value, you can target and acquire similar customers with greater potential of becoming loyal and driving business growth.

This understanding must then be translated internally into the skills, behaviors and attitudes of the organization. Employee loyalty is directly linked to customer's perception of value and customer loyalty.

Value-based Contact. It is important to integrate and coordinate communications to provide the maximum value to the customer. Customers today want to be more in control of specifying the content and quality of the communications that are valuable to them. Customers are pleased to provide information on how communications should be delivered, as well as the content, frequency and medium and may indicate that face-to-face contact is not a preferred medium when asked how they want to receive communications. This can come as a shock to Business-to-Business selling forces, or a realization that there are ways to optimize the delivery of value to customers. This realization is the first step to bringing expense to sales ratios down, and to delivering more value to your customers.

Business Result 5: Expense Reduction

How can I reduce expenses in the sales and marketing budget with reduction in growth and retention?

Expense reduction is often seen as doing more with less and that translates to getting less results. In all actuality if expense reduction is done correctly efficiency will be gained and more growth and added customer value can be realized.

The critical concepts to manage for expense reduction are:

Marketing Integration. Customer communications are a key (and effective!) weapon in the arsenal of customer knowledge acquisition and customer relationship building, and customer growth. At the same time, the communications and customer contact can be a hefty portion of our cost to serve. The challenge is to maximize the effectiveness of this tool, while minimizing the costs. New methods of communication, such as e-commerce, are radically changing the cost of communication and customers are rapidly accepting new forms of interaction. These new methods of communicating are fundamentally different and have significantly different costs associated with them. To reduce customer management expenses, organizations should use the lowest cost medium that delivers the highest value to the customer.

Customer Contact Matrix. The Customer Contact Matrix is a planning tool that ensures the investment of sales costs is appropriate for the expected return in sales or revenue. The tool (or plan) aligns sales and marketing investments with the revenue potential of different grades of customer. The objective is to maintain approximately the same level of sales and marketing investment for each grade.

Integrated Account Management. The spiraling cost of keeping field sales reps on the road and collapsing margins from mature products have been a major contributor to entire industries either disappearing altogether or having to radically change how they go about their business. In order to remain competitive, organizations have been forced to better leverage the high cost of face to face visits with lower cost methods of communication with customers. Integrated Account Management is a formularized method for conducting this iterative process. This refining method is done by modifying the media used to manage the customer and the frequency with which those media are used.

Grading. The primary reason to grade customers is to ensure that the investment in those customers matches the expected return.

Lean Six Sigma. Do not be intimidated by the terminology of Lean Six Sigma. The methodology is—simply put—about reducing the complexity in your sales and marketing processes and implementing new, improved processes that function more reliably, effectively, and repeatedly. The methodology includes tools and approaches which allow you to re-engineer your process—simplify; remove the errors; and streamline for greater velocity at lower cost.

Value-Stream Mapping. Value Stream Mapping is a diagnostic tool to understand the current environment and identify areas of waste. Once the current environment is clearly understood, an organization can then prioritize the necessary actions to improve that process. By eliminating the waste, an organization is able to lower its costs while still providing equal or greater value to their customers.

Business Results 6: Sales Acceleration

How can I accelerate my sales to realize growth and profitability sooner?

As the adage goes, "Give me infinite time, money, or quality—and I can accomplish anything". Unfortunately, this is not a luxury with which any are actually confronted. Resources to reach out to customers are not unlimited and must be invested wisely. Fiscal realities of ROI, budgets, and market combined with perishable resources and competitive pressure demand sensitivity to the timing of the sales cycle. A higher velocity sales cycle delivers ROI and economic benefit faster.

Critical to managing sales acceleration are the following key concepts:

Sales Funnel. A key component of the overall sales process is the sales funnel: the steps and stages of our engagement process—defined within the context of our industry and company. We populate the funnel with leads, generated by our outreach and lead generation activities. The funnel itself includes the activities and milestones which mark the progress of that lead towards a sale. Although at a detail level, each customer and sale have their own, unique characteristics—the successful, stable sales process is marked by a standard set of activities and milestones which are part of each sales engagement. Once we understand and designate a standard, repeatable set of steps and stages (milestones and activities) for our company, we can establish targets and measurements for these steps and stages.

Core and Common Measures. We do not need to start from scratch in identifying the key categories for effective measurement. Although the metrics themselves may vary by industry or company, most of the key measurements that indicate health and velocity of the sales cycle are predictable. The focus for measurement is to select the appropriate key measurements, and develop a methodology to collect the data easily and leverage the data into improved decision-making and action.

Value-Stream Analysis. The first step in effectively improving the sales cycle process—as with any process—is to properly diagnose the cause and drivers of the current performance level, whatever that level may be. We must answer the questions, "Which parts of the process are driving the current cycle time and unpredictability?" and "Where can we most effectively make changes to increase velocity and predictability?" Value-Stream Analysis (VSA) provides a diagnostic approach to answering these questions for an organization.

Business Result 7: Sales Coverage

How do I optimize my sales coverage?

Most companies know the basic principle of selling: customers buy from you; so make your customer the focus. Give them what they want or need and they will hopefully keep buying from you. However, in today's world of increased competition and globalization, it takes a bit more to truly design a customer-centric sales model. Effective sales coverage incorporates both a mature understanding of the customer and customer needs, and an economically based design to effectively address those needs.

Critical to sales coverage is gaining an understanding of the following concepts:

Coverage Model Design. Our sales coverage model must encompass a plan to reach the "right" individuals within the account. We know the accounts and the individuals we are trying to reach. We split them up and assign them among our field sales representatives and channel partners, and we have "coverage," right? Wrong. We don't just want coverage; we want a smart, economical coverage model. The most important components are the graded model and integrated account management.

Integrated Account Management. Integrated Account Management extends the reach to our customers, by leveraging each of our field sales contacts with additional phone; email; mail and other lower-cost contacts. By seamlessly integrating across the various media, and employing the media for each message which maps to the customers' preferences. Through integrated account management we are able to increase customers' perception of value; increase loyalty and share of wallet; and simultaneous reduce the cost to serve.

Customer Contact Matrix. Customers are a valuable asset. And like other assets, they require investment. Also like other assets, we can achieve best business results by investing in ways that are commensurate with the expected return of those assets.

We have two primary points of focus: integrating and leveraging the various contact investments to get the maximum impact, and ensuring the total investment is consistent with expected return. The customer contract matrix builds a mix of integrated sales and marketing tactics that leverage lower cost media while delivering effective and valuable contacts.

Marketing Communications. Once you have developed a clear understanding of who your customers are and what they need, this understanding must be DEMONSTRATED via your customer communications, in order to leverage the understanding into more effective relationship-building. Effective leverage of customer knowledge into your communications precludes any kind of "one size fits all approach". Rather, the customer segments and needs that you have worked so hard to identify require tailored communications.

Value-based Content. A key component of building relationships with customers that drive business results is the ability to engage customers with communications content that provides value to the customer. The value in the content delivery transforms the interaction from a "tell—sell" engagement into a delivery of service, that advances the business relationship. Value Based Content requires you understand what the customer needs, media preference for that content and how often they want it.

Business Result 8: Creating a Customer Culture

What do I need to do to ensure that I get the right people in the right roles to impact my B2B marketing?

It is critical to always slow down and define your direction before embarking on a new hiring cycle. This is the ideal time to determine how to improve the caliber of the team and the organization as a whole. We know that when a position opens up, all the forces of nature will converge upon you to fill the position quickly. It is natural to want to grab the last ad or the last set of recruiting material and use it again, just to get things started quickly. However, we cannot stress enough the importance of *hiring slowly*. Get the team together, conduct a *Role Definition Workshop,* and define all the key elements of the position.

Critical to creating a customer culture are the following concepts:

Behavioral Profiling in the Recruiting Process. *"Hire them for what they know. Fire them for who they are."* This statement is an accurate reflection of what happens in most organizations. There are three factors that go into every hiring decision. They are 1) **Talent** or Behaviors, 2) **Experience** and Education and 3) **Chemistry**. Use of this process will allow you to determine **before** you hire a candidate, whether or not they will be successful on the job. While no assessment process is guaranteed, this method has proven the best results. Over 60% of turnover results from people not "fitting" in the culture. And the cost associated with turnover is significant, usually up to three times an individual's annual salary.

Performance and Talent Management. *"You get what you reward, every time."* The Performance Management Process must be developed to drive and reward the right behavior and align with organizational goals and objectives. The Performance Management Process is so much more than an annual appraisal or "completed form." A successful performance and talent management system is based on regular dialog, honest and straightforward feedback using *performance standards,* development planning, incentives and a formal coaching process.

Employee Satisfaction and Loyalty. To quote from the *Service Profit Chain* (Harvard Business School), research has shown that there is a direct link between profitability, customer loyalty, employee satisfaction, loyalty and productivity. The employee loyalty survey that helps the organization understand key drivers and attributes supported by qualitative and quantitative data will help the organization embark on change that has the most impact on employee loyalty. This in turn leads to customer loyalty and productivity.

Change Management. Like a broken link in a chain, if you are missing even one step in your Change Management process, the entire initiative will be weak. While there are many change management models available to businesses today, the core elements are very similar. John Kotter defines a multi-stage process that leadership can use to drive change in a healthy way. The model creates the environment for the change required to move your company forward as you initiate new processes and systems in the B2B marketing space.

B2B Customer Relationship Management

As we have explored, B2B marketing is a process of relationship building. Relationship building requires time and resources; often the same, or similar, type resources tasked with selling your company's products. This is not a constraint, but rather an opportunity to enhance the effectiveness of your company's sales and marketing plans—planning driving measurable execution and performance. Earlier we identified and discussed the eight business results driving Business-to-Business marketing, now we will examine the tactical approaches to growing and managing B2B customer relationships.

The Customer Community Center is the point through which marketing and sales activities are coordinated and implemented. The goal of the center is two-fold: (1) to increase sales productivity, which is measured by comparing sales expenses with sales revenues; and (2) to increase the perceived value, satisfaction, and loyalty of your customers by increasing the frequency of value-based contacts—communications. But, as discussed in the Value-Based Communications and Customer Contact Matrix concepts, the customers' perceived increase in value-based contacts does not come from increasing the size of the field sales team. The most cost effective way to increase the frequency of value-based contacts is implementing an integrated inside/outside sales model. An effective inside/outside sales model leverages cost-effective insides resources to allow more expensive field sales people to focus on strategic face-to-face sales meetings.

An effective customer relationship program should focus on one of the basic sales competencies:

1. Demand or Lead Generation
2. Opportunity or Lead Management
3. Account Management
4. Inside Sales

Each of these competencies presents a focused approach to achieving a defined business result. Demand or Lead Generation is the process of managing customer touches all the way to a purchase order. For commodity products, demand generation may actually include purchasing the product off the web site. For B2B applications, demand generation typically stops at the point where you turn over a qualified inquiry to the sales team.

Examples of the activities of an agent working within this competency include working with the field team to the plan for lead generation activities via mail and email, coordinating issuance of materials and tracking via CRM software, tracking and reporting on response rates by source and time.

Opportunity or Lead Management is the process of rapidly and effectively creating, nurturing, distributing and analyzing leads. The ultimate goal is to increase the likelihood that a lead will convert to a qualified opportunity and then a new, satisfied customer. Examples of the activities of an agent working within this competency include responding to inquiries (e.g., from web, marketing materials, etc.), entering and tracking inquiries in a CRM system, creating and executing contact plans for inquiries, and pre-screening and qualifying leads for field.

Integrated Account Management (IAM) is a system of marketing and selling that is driven out of a proactive, planful, and personal approach to managing mutually beneficial individual customer relationships. In IAM, the account manager uses a variety of contact media to manage customer relationships in an economically prudent manner to drive sustainable, long-term, profitable relationships. Examples of the activities of an agent working within this competency include maintaining and executing the contact plan for leads that will take longer to come to fruition, leverage customer contacts by the field reps with lower cost contact during the sales process, conducting account profiling activities, and serving as the focus on integration between the field sales team and CRM application.

Inside Sales includes IAM, but also includes the actual sales transaction—the production activity that tends to focus on the short-term closing of the opportunity at hand. Examples of the activities of an agent working within this competency are similar to those performed in account management, but also include booking and closing sales.

Standardization

Standardization is one of the many benefits of a process-oriented customer center. Independent of the competency, standardization can be achieved in planning, risk assessment, resource scheduling, program monitoring and control, performance management and reporting templates, and best-practices to name a few. There is a natural progression from standardization, to measurement, to control, and lastly to continuous improvement—competency maturity. Without achieving the first step—standardization—the goal of continuous improvement and excellence may never be achieved. An iterative process to improve competency maturity can be represented by the Deming / Shewart Cycle (Exhibit R9.3).

The four components of the cycle are defined as follow:

EXHIBIT R9.3: DEMING/SHEWART CYCLE

- PLAN—Establish the objectives and processes necessary to deliver results in accordance with the specifications.
- DO—Implement the processes.
- CHECK—Monitor and evaluate the processes and results against objectives and specifications and report the outcome.
- ACT—Apply actions to the outcome for necessary improvement.

Roles

Across Demand/Lead Generation, Opportunity/Lead Management, Account Management, and Inside Sales, six roles exist. Each program type or competency may not contain each role; the scope of the program and client wishes influence the final configuration. The six primary roles are: (1) Inbound Representative; (2) Outbound Account Management Representative; (3) Outbound Lead Generation Representative; (4) Inside Sales Representative; (5) Team Lead; and (6) Program Supervisor. Following is a description of each role and its primary responsibilities.

Fundamentally, the responsibilities of these roles are focused on developing and nurturing client relationships. These roles should perform as an extension of the field sales teams; not a competitor. Successful implementation of an inside / outside model requires appropriate people and process change management. As with any successful organization, its strength is in its people. The concept of Behavioral Profiling, discussed earlier, should be utilized during the recruiting process.

Some of the key traits to seek when staffing for any of the four competencies include:

- Articulate.
- Excellent listening skills.
- Excellent communication skills.
- Familiarity with contact management software.
- Prior B2B experience.
- Prior experience working in a phone-based environment.
- Demonstrated ability to self-manage.
- Demonstrated experience in consultative selling.
- Demonstrated ability to successfully multi-task.

As in many situations, tradeoffs will need to be made. The T.E.C. Model discussed earlier provides a framework for assessing and prioritizing the candidate tradeoffs.

Again, it is imperative to establish and follow a structured recruiting process. The selection of the "right" person from the beginning will contribute to quicker rewards in any of the four sales competencies.

Performance Measurement

An important process associated with any of the four sales competencies is the ability to establish and measure results to plan. Performance management is a systematic process in which a company involves its employees in improving organization effectiveness in the accomplishment of the company's mission and strategic goals. A comprehensive performance management system must include metrics at the employee level and metrics that provide linkage and predictability to organizational mission and goals

The CRM Measurement Framework provides a skeleton for developing and implementing the appropriate measures needed to monitor performance. The framework begins at the top with the results measures. There are a limited number of these measures which generally link to business objectives and goals. The framework then identifies the processes and activities which can reliably and predictably deliver those results. The challenge is to identify the causal relationship (build from the top down). There are two major benefits of the framework:

1. It allows company to focus on measuring the most important things with confidence—desired results.
2. Provides employees with a line of sight as to how their individual activities impact business results.

Key factors to good metric selection include the following:

- Defining results that are closely linked to economic value. Examples include but are not limited to profit, revenue, and market share.
- Clearly understanding and educating people on the processes and activities that will deliver the desired results.
- The correct linkage of activities to results ensures that activity measures are truly predictive of the desired results. Proper linkage also provides employees with a credible and effective line of sight to how their activity performance drives and impacts the business results.
- Identifying quality metrics that cut across all levels of the framework. Proper quality measures ensure activities are performed in the appropriate manner, and with sufficient quality, to deliver the desired results; as opposed to simply "checking the box."

As stated by Harold S. Geneen (1910–1997), " . . . It is an immutable law in business that words are words, explanations are explanations, promises are promises—but only performance is reality."

Reporting

With the implementation of a demand generation, opportunity management, account management, or inside sale program, clear, precise, reporting should precipitate from the program at regular intervals. From a time and cost perspective, good performance reporting should address current program performance to plan and where the program is headed (trends). From a planning perspective, identifying present and future risks associated with the program or market segments being serviced and whether there are any special problems that need to be addressed, and finally, what proactive actions can be taken by management to maintain or improve future program performance.

There are four primary categories of reports (1) Performance reports, (2) Status reports, (3) Projection reports, and (4) Exception reports. Each type of sales competency should publish reports in all of the four categories with a frequency of no more than monthly. Current technology allows many of the performance metrics associated with programs to be reported on a "real-time" basis.

Performance reports indicate the physical progress of the program to date against its goal. Ultimately, success of a program is defined by the sponsor of the program. As such, the desired results, and activities driving those results, will be monitored and reported on. Status reports identify where we are today and report the information from the performance reports in a consolidated, standardized, format. Projection reports calculate and illustrate any forward-looking projections. Finally, exception reports identify exceptions, problems, or situations that exceed the threshold limits on such items as CRM database quality, program performance to goal, representative performance to plan, along with other such topics.

EXHIBIT R9.4: REPORTS BY GROUP

Group 1	Group 2	Group 3
• Rep Productivity Report (# contacts per day)	• Campaign and Source Report	• Database At-Risk Report
• Variable Compensation Worksheet	• Total # of Opportunities Identified, Qualified, Closed	• Field-Generated Opportunities Report
• # of Completed Account Profiles	• Exception Report	• Distributor-Generated Opportunities Report
• New Decision-Maker Contacts Report	• Close the Loop Status Report	
• Campaign Analysis Report		
• Opportunity Status Report		
• Total Inquiries, Opportunities Identified, Sent to Field		
• Through Put Analysis		
• Potential Revenue $ in Funnel / $ Sold Report		
• Call Quality and Monitoring Report		

Standardization across the four sales competencies allows for three primary groups of reports—the Core & Common Reports. The first group (Group 1) of reports is applicable across all four sales competencies. The second group (Group 2) of reports is applicable to demand / lead generation, opportunity / lead management, and account management programs. The third group (Group 3) of primary reports is applicable to account management and inside sales programs.

The table in Exhibit R9.4 identifies the Core & Common reports associated with each group.

Summary

Effective execution of a business-to-business marketing strategy will result in strong, long-term relationships with your customers, regardless of their stage in the customer lifecycle. If this process seems complex and time-consuming, keep in mind that the risk and investment that comes with effective business-to-business marketing is almost always outweighed by the rewards returned to the company.

Victor L. Hunter is founder and president of Hunter Business Group, LLC. He is nationally known for his expertise in business-to-business direct marketing and service to the nation's leading companies. Founded in 1981, Hunter is the first consulting and service company dedicated solely to increasing the productivity of businesses by assisting them to sell products and services to other businesses, institutions, and professionals.

Sheila T. Zelenski and Jeff J. Kreutzer are associates of Mr. Hunter at Hunter Business Group, LLC, in Milwaukee, Wisconsin.

READING
10

Business-to-Business Lead Generation

RUTH P. STEVENS
eMarketing Strategy

One of direct marketing's most important contributions to business marketing is generating leads on behalf of salespeople. Lead generation can be defined as identifying prospective customers and qualifying their likelihood to buy, in advance of making a sales call. In other words, it's about getting prospects to raise their hands.

For salespeople, a qualified lead provided by a marketing department allows the sales rep to spend his or her valuable time in front of a prospect who is likely to buy, instead of squandering the salesperson's skills on cold calling. In short, lead generation programs make a sales force more productive.

The DMA's annual report on market performance, *The Power of Direct Marketing*, estimates that B-to-B 2010 sales driven by direct marketing represent $786.5 billion in business-to-business sales. Lead generation is huge, and a major contributor to U.S. productivity and economic growth.

A lead consists of the name, contact information and background information on a prospective buyer. A qualified lead would represent a prospect who is ready to buy. The defining characteristics of "qualified" will vary by industry, by company, and by sales person. Marketers who generate leads must tailor their definitions of lead qualification to the requirements of the sales force they serve.

The process of lead generation is fairly straightforward. It involves a series of steps, beginning with a campaign of outbound and inbound contacts to generate the inquiry and qualify it, to handing the lead to the sales organization, and then tracking the lead through conversion to sales revenue.

The secret to success is in a focus on business rules and process. Lead generation and management is less of the glamorous, creative side of marketing. It is more about developing the rules, refining them, testing, tracking and making continuous improvements. The company with the best process, executed consistently, is the one with the true competitive advantage.

Campaign Planning: Setting Campaign Objectives

The first step in campaign planning should be to set campaign objectives. Without them, you won't be able to recognize success when you see it. Campaign objectives will typically cover:

- the number of leads expected
- their degree of qualification
- the time frame during which they will arrive
- the cost per lead
- lead to sales conversion ratio
- revenue per lead
- campaign ROI, or expense-to-revenue ratio

The important point is that the entire process must be planned in advance of making a single marketing campaign investment. Make sure you are able to generate the amount of qualified leads needed by your sales organization, at the right cost. Plan your fulfillment material up front, during the outbound campaign process. Don't leave it till later. And make sure that your interim steps—the processes and people that capture, fulfill, qualify, nurture the inquiries—are in place, with the capacity to handle the flow you intend to create.

Campaign Planning: Calculating Campaign Volume Requirements

To set up campaigns that will provide a predictable, relevant and timely lead flow, here is a simple process to figure out how much campaigning is required to generate a month's worth of leads for a sales team.

1. Estimate the number of qualified leads each sales person can reasonably be expected to follow up on a month.
2. Multiply that number by the number of reps in a geographic territory.
3. Then divide by the qualification rate you expect for your campaign inquiries.
4. Divide again by the expected response rate on the campaign. This final number will be your campaign volume needed to support that territory for a month. In mail campaigns, you can control the lead flow within the territory by selecting ZIP codes for each volume required. In other media, you may end up with some peaks and valleys that you can smooth out with tactical campaign efforts like telemarketing.
5. Continue the process for each territory, and add up the results. You will have total numbers for your qualified leads, inquiries and campaign volumes for the month.

Campaign Planning: Media Selection

Each communications medium has its strengths, weaknesses and best applications. The campaign must carefully harness the right medium for each job. For generating leads among new prospects, the best choices are search engine keyword bidding, direct mail and outbound telephone for ongoing campaign work. Exhibiting at trade shows is also effective, as long as the show is well targeted to your audience and attracts a qualified pool of prospects. Also effective are search engine optimization, targeted banner advertising, and referral marketing programs. A new technique that's worth exploring is IP address identification, using tools that allow you to find the name of a company that has visited your web site and what keywords they were searching for. Among inquirers and current customers, you may find telephone and email most productive, telephone being more intrusive and email being less expensive than direct mail or print.

Campaign Planning: Offer Development

Like any direct marketing effort, lead generation offers are designed to elicit a response. The offer should provide a reason to act, in order to overcome people's natural inertia. It can be a consumer-like incentive, with personal benefit to the recipient. Or it can be related to solving a business problem.

Offer Checklist

Here are the types of offers frequently used for lead generation. Experiment with as many as you can.

- free information (brochure, newsletter, white paper, reprint, video, demo CD)
- premium (a calculator, a book)
- free trial
- free sample
- free self-assessment tool
- seminar or webinar
- demonstration
- discount
- financing
- sales call
- free consultation or audit
- free estimate

Campaign Results Analysis

Many companies divide their results analysis into two parts: activity-based metrics and results-based metrics. During the long stretch until sales results come in, marketers can still get some interim benefit from analyzing the inquiry and qualification campaign activities themselves.

Activity-based metrics include such indicators as:

- Cost per thousand
- Response rate
- Cost per inquiry
- Campaign turn-around time
- Qualification rate
- Cost per qualified lead

Results-based metrics include:

- Conversion-to-sales rate
- Sales revenue per lead
- Campaign ROI
- Campaign expense-to-revenue ratio

Lead Management

The leverage in lead generation lies not in marketing creativity or in conducting more campaigns. Instead, it lies in converting more inquiries into qualified leads and, then, more qualified leads into sales.

In short, the company with the best inquiry management is the one that will win. Inquiry management is about setting up a solid, methodical process, and then executing, every day.

A Minneapolis-based inquiry management company named Performark conducted a study in 1995 and again in 2001, wherein they responded to over 1000 business-to-business advertisements in trade publications. What happened? Performark found in 2001 that 61% of the inquiries they submitted received absolutely no response, over 60 days. Worse, that result was down from their 1995 experiment, when a mere 43% of the inquiries were ignored.

Remember, these are inquiries resulting from paid advertisements, which carry calls to action, like to a web site or an 800 number, or via a bingo card. The marketers who bought these ads clearly intended for readers to respond and maybe—one would hope—buy something. But most of these marketers failed to put in place a process to handle the inquiries. To put the best face on this pathetic situation, look at it this way: when things out there are this bad, the company that does handle inquiries well is going to clean up, without investing much at all.

Here are the steps you can take to create a great inquiry management process.

Response Planning

Start response planning early in the campaign development process. Make sure you have a unique code that identifies responses from every outbound communication. This can be a priority code, a special 800 number, an operator's name, a unique URL, anything. Offer multiple response media, including phone, web, BRC, fax and email. And don't be shy about including qualification questions on your reply form, or your inbound-phone scripts.

Response Capture

Your response capture process will only work if it's designed by the people who manage the inbound media. Put together a cross-functional team. Then, be sure you consider the best strategy for each medium. For example, set up a dedicated fax number for inquiries, so they don't get mixed up with regular daily business communications. And make sure your electronic inquiries—from email and your web site—are acted on immediately. Log the inquiries into a database and match the name against prior contacts to avoid duplicates.

Inquiry Fulfillment

Most B-to-B inquiries are asking for more information, so give it to them. The secret is speed. In the Performark study, 75% of the companies that did respond got their material out within one week. This is good news. What's more, it indicates the value the best companies put on fast delivery. Also, try to match the fulfillment material to the need and the value of the prospect. And all things being equal, consider migrating from print collateral to flexible, down-loadable web-based materials.

Inquiry Qualification

Many of your inquiries will require additional qualification before they are ready for hand-off to sales. The secret to qualification is involvement of the sales team in setting qualification criteria. Don't let them tell you they want "everything." But do listen to their views of an ideal qualified prospect: the sales side knows a lot better what they need than you do in marketing.

Lead Nurturing

When the prospect isn't ready to see a sales person, but will be ready eventually, move the inquiry into a "nurturing" process. Nurturing involves a series of ongoing communications, intended to build awareness and trust, and to maintain contact until the prospect is ready to buy. You can use a variety of tactics, from catalogs and newsletters, to surveys, white papers and birthday cards. Marketing automation tools vastly assist in managing the complexity of ongoing nurturing communications streams.

Lead Tracking

Let's not forget the process of closing the marketing loop, to attribute a closed sale to a marketing campaign. It isn't easy in B-to-B, but it's worth some effort, if only to justify marketing budgets, not to mention giving you the tools to refine campaign tactics and improve results next time. Supplement your closed-loop tracking system with end-user surveys or data match-back analysis.

Optimize your inquiry management process, and you can triple, even quadruple, your revenues from lead-generation campaigns.

Lead Generation Media

Sources of Direct Marketing Contacts

B-to-B direct marketers have two general sources of marketing contacts: internal and external.

The internal data sources include:

- Sales contacts, whether gathered from Rolodexes or sales force automation systems
- Billing systems, which provides important information about purchase history, credit worthiness and other transactional data
- Operations and fulfillment systems, which can tell you about a customer's channel preferences and communications needs, as well as purchase frequency data
- Customer service systems
- Inquiry files, i.e., prospects who have indicated interest in more information, whether at trade shows, or at your web site, or having responded to your campaigns

The external data sources include:

- Prospect lists, whether compiled or response files, like catalog buyers and seminar attendees
- Prospecting databases, whether open or closed cooperative databases or proprietary de-duplicated databases
- Email lists, both compiled and response
- Appended information, like SIC code or employee size, purchased from a data compiler

EXHIBIT R10.1 SETTING QUALIFICATION CRITERIA

The most important approach to setting qualification criteria is to follow the needs of your sales force. After all, it is they who will be handling the lead and taking it to closure. They know better than anyone the nature of the sales process and what kind of buying characteristics are most likely to be workable for them.

Qualification criteria will vary by company and by industry. However, as a general rule, most criteria involve the following categories:

- **Budget.** Is the purchase budgeted, and what size of budget does the prospect have available. You will want to set up categories or ranges, for easier scoring. Some companies request information about the company's credit history here.
- **Authority.** Does the respondent have the authority to make the purchase decision? If not, you should try to capture additional relevant contact information.
- **Need.** How important is the product or solution to the company. How deep is their pain. This criterion may be difficult to ask directly, but it can be approached by roundabout methods. "What is the problem to be solved?" "What alternative solutions are you considering?" "How many do you need?" "What product do you currently use?"
- **Time frame.** What is their readiness to buy. When is the purchase likely to be. Depending on industry and sales cycle length, this can be broken into days, months, or even years. Also be sure to ask whether they would like to see a sales person.

Taken together, these key variables are abbreviated as BANT (budget, authority, need and timeframe). Qualification criteria will vary from company to company. Other common criteria include:

- **Potential sales volume.** How many departments in the company might use this product? How much of, or how often, might they need the product?
- **Predisposition to buy from us.** Are they past customers of ours? Are they similar to our current customers? Would they recommend us to their colleagues? Are they willing to call us back?
- **Account characteristics.** Company size, whether number of employees or revenue volume. Industry. Parent company.

Direct Mail

The workhorse medium of direct response communications for lead generation is direct mail. Direct mail is very flexible, offering multiple formats, like the #10 business size envelopes or 6 × 9 inch or larger packages, self-mailers, postcards, catalogs and dimensional packages designed to get past the gatekeeper.

Telephone

The telephone has traditionally been a very productive tool for lead generation. The beauty of the telephone is that it is flexible, personal, and cost-effective, and it supports both inbound and outbound communications. Outbound, the phone is usually used in lead generation as a substitute for—or a supplement to—direct mail. This function is typically known as "telemarketing," and its power lies in its ability to penetrate small universes effectively. Inbound, the phone is frequently used as a response device, meaning one of several options for prospects to express their interest if they prefer the phone to the web or to a business reply card (BRC).

But there are many other uses of the phone in the world of lead generation. It is effective in response qualification, either inbound or outbound, when the operator poses a series of questions to evaluate the prospect's likelihood to buy. The phone is also productive for lead nurturing, when the prospect is not ready to buy, but the marketer wants to keep in touch, continue the relationship and be there when the time is right to see a salesperson.

EXHIBIT R10.2:
TIPS ON TELEPHONE SCRIPTING FOR LEAD GENERATION

- Business calls should be treated as a conversation, not a sales pitch.
- Because business-to-business contact rates are lower than consumer, your script needs to be developed so it is more persuasive when you do get the prospect on the phone.
- Breakthrough creativity is not the key ingredient in successful telemarketing scripts. More important is to follow the established formula, namely, gain attention, establish credibility, qualify the customer and move to the offer and call to action.
- Make each script more relevant to the customer's situation than the caller's situation. Position features as benefits. Discuss what's in it for the customer.
- Scripts should include an explanation of the reason for the call, such as thanks for visiting our web site, or to learn the prospect's reactions to the materials he reviewed.
- Far more important than the script itself is the research and preparation that should precede the call. Encourage your reps to find out in advance everything they can about the prospect and his needs. Visit the prospect's web site, check the financial and trade press for articles about them, and, most obviously, review any information maintained internally on the prospect

Web Sites

Many business marketers believe that the Internet is the greatest resource for lead generation to have ever emerged. It performs many of the functions of direct mail and the telephone, but more quickly and—on a variable-cost basis—more cheaply. The Internet is also prized for its versatility and flexibility. It is rapidly being integrated into the lead generation process, replacing some media, adding strength to other media, and generally proving itself to be an extremely valuable new element in the lead generation toolkit.

The web site can be designed to contribute to the lead generation process in a number of significant ways:

- Registration. Adding a registration area to the home page, with an offer, is an important and low-cost method of generating sales leads
- IP address identification. New tools allow you to identify the company behind the visit to your site, from which you can institute some marketing action, such as telephoning into the company to find out more about their needs
- Fulfillment. Instead of sending out printed collateral material or white papers, invite responders to download the material from your web site.
- Web response form, as a substitute for, or as supplement to, a BRC. Sometimes known as "splash page" or "landing page"
- Mini-site, which is essentially an expanded web response form designed to move the respondent further along the buying process
- Subscription sign-up. The top right corner of the home page is the best location for making subscription offers to an electronic newsletter
- Extranets, or dedicated sites behind the firewall of your best customers, where they can learn about product information, ask to see a salesperson, or even conduct a transaction

Email

Email is proving to be a powerful medium for lead generation, qualification and nurturing, not to mention customer relationship management, up-selling and a host of other business marketing applications. Because most business buyers are connected to and comfortable with email, it can provide a very fast and inexpensive supplement to direct mail and the telephone.

Here are some tips on the best ways to put email to use in the lead generation process.

- Gather email addresses, and permission to use them, from customers and prospects at every point of contact. Email is generally welcome in business correspondence. It is also cheap and fast, so it makes sense to invest in gathering and maintaining as close to 100% email penetration of your customer base as possible.
- Practice good email etiquette. Ask permission to communicate via email. Offer recipients the option to "opt out" of continuing to receive emails, and honor those requests faithfully.
- Apply the basic rules of direct marketing in your email communications. Test

regularly. Use friendly, benefit-oriented copy. Make compelling offers. Ask for the action frequently within the copy. One email exception to the direct marketing rules: short copy usually works better than long copy in this medium.

• Use email wherever in the sales and marketing process that it applies, like e-newsletters to keep in touch with customers and prospects, and as a personal communications medium from salespeople.

Banners

If banner ads have disappointed consumer marketers with falling response rates, they are still viable as a vehicle for business marketers. The difference lies in targeting, and in the nature of business buyers. Business people need information to do their jobs, and they are likely to frequent web sites where that information is available. So highly targeted banner advertising can work well for lead generation.

Here are some suggestions for successful use of banners.

• Select media carefully. The best place to start is the web sites of the trade publications where you already advertise. You may be able to negotiate free banner placement as part of the "merchandising" deals available within your print media purchase. Also try the professional associations in your target industry, and the sites of your business partners.

• Direct marketing fundamentals apply. Make a solid offer, test and refine your offer and creative, and be sure your fulfillment is speedy.

• Try a "house ad" banner on your own site, to connect with an ongoing campaign or a special offer.

• As with other media, be sure you have a relevant landing page for those who click through.

Search Engine Optimization

Search engines can direct interested inquirers to your site at a rapid clip, but they take some time to understand and manage. You need to both submit your site to the top search engines and apply optimizing techniques to achieve higher ranking results. This can absorb the attention of a full-time staffer, or the services of an outside service provider. Another approach is paying for certain key words relevant to your product or company to pop up at the top of the search engine list when buyers undertake a search on the Internet.

Print Advertising

Direct response advertising in trade publications, industry vertical publications and business publications can provide a steady, reliable stream of new prospective sales leads. Print also can serve as a way to reach high-level decision-makers whose names may not appear on the usual mailing lists.

The main issue faced by lead generators using print advertising is conflicting goals within the company relating to brand awareness versus generating a response. Print advertising can be very powerful in generating awareness and building brand recognition and positive attitudes. But if your objective is to get leads, the ad must be created for response.

Here follow some tips for successful lead generation using print advertising.

- Stress benefits and the offer in every possible element of the ad (the headline, the body copy, the design and the response device).
- Add an offer and a response device to all brand advertising. You'll be surprised, and the sales force will be pleased, with the results.
- Do not permit your lead-generation advertising to conflict with your brand image. All communications must support and enhance your brand. Do nothing to harm it. In fact, you can gain leverage for lead generation from the awareness in the marketplace that the brand advertising has created.

Trade Shows

Exhibiting at trade shows and conferences is a time-honored way to get in front of customers and prospects in a focused, concentrated manner. Attendees are often highly qualified, their minds are on business at the show, and they are seeking solutions to business problems. Regrettably, marketers often squander the opportunity to put trade shows to their best advantage in lead generation. Here follow some suggestions for optimizing trade shows and conferences for generating good quality leads.

- Set your objectives clearly, in advance. If generating qualified leads is job one, then focus all of your show activity toward that goal.
- Design your signage to state clearly what your company does and how it benefits the customer. Passers-by will give you only a few seconds to get your message across.
- Insert one or two qualification questions into your inquiry-gathering process, by attaching a short form to the prospect's business card, or using an electronic swipe tool provided by show organizers.
- Remember that there is a direct inverse correlation between gift-giveaways and inquiry qualification levels. In a highly qualified environment, a show where most attendees are already solid prospects, using an incentive can be an excellent traffic generator. But go slowly when the audience is more broadly based.
- Put in place a process to qualify the leads—or have them contacted by sales— immediately on return from the show.

Referral Marketing

Business buyers are very good sources of referral business, for two reasons. First, they are likely to know their counterparts in other companies through their own professional networking. And, second, they are often happy to introduce a solution to a colleague as part of nurturing their web of business relationships. From a marketer's point of view, referrals are an outstanding source of new business. Recommendations from a colleague have great credibility, so not only is the referred prospect likely to be qualified, he is likely to be motivated. The only downside of referral marketing is that the volume of referred business you can ever hope to get is rarely enough to sustain your needs for growth.

With the arrival of the Internet, the perfectly respectable term referral marketing has morphed into the rather loathsome expression, viral marketing. Nevertheless, because of its speed and informality, the Internet lends itself well to referral practices.

Some points to keep in mind when applying referral marketing to the lead generation process:

- Review all your marketing communications, and add a referral request where appropriate.
- Conduct regular referral-request campaigns to your current customer base. You may want to offer an incentive to both the referrer and the referred to increase response.
- Place a pass-along request at the bottom of your emails, especially those that contain valuable information or an offer.

The material in this chapter is based on *The DMA Lead Generation Handbook, 2nd ed*, published by the Direct Marketing Association. It gives additional detail and is available at www.the-dma.org.

RUTH P. STEVENS has spent more than 15 years as a hands-on marketer focused on customer acquisition and retention. She has worked with both large enterprises and start-up companies. Prior to beginning her consultancy, eMarketing Strategy, she served as chief marketing officer at a New York City Internet company. Before that, she had broad responsibilities for direct marketing at IBM, Ziff-Davis and Time Warner. Ruth is a frequent contributor to a variety of marketing publications and author of *Trade Show and Event Marketing* and *The DMA B-to-B Lead Generation Handbook*. She teaches marketing to graduate students at Columbia Business School.

Consumer Privacy: Knowing Your Customers Without Really "Knowing" Them

JENNIFER BARRETT

CIPP, Global Privacy Officer, Acxiom Corporation

Integrated Marketing Communications involves devoting considerable time and energy to knowing your customers in order to bring them relevant offers at the right moment and to develop long-term relationships. But how much of that energy is involved in understanding your customers' preferences regarding how to handle their personal information, and how and when they would prefer that you contact them? And how much do you know about whether their attitudes regarding use of their personal information could affect their buying decisions, especially online and through other digital media?

Research shows us that today's consumers continue to be extremely concerned about protecting their privacy, which compels us to be respectful in our efforts to develop long-term relationships.

This is Not a New Phenomenon

Dr. Allan Westin, a Professor of Law at Columbia University and founder of the Privacy and American Business Center for Social and Legal Research, has studied consumer attitudes since 1990. His research breaks the population into three distinct segments—the Fundamentalists, the Pragmatists and the Unconcerned.[1]

- *Fundamentalists* are individuals who are generally distrustful of companies and favor laws to spell out privacy rights. They generally choose privacy over benefits. This group is the one most concerned about their privacy and the one most likely to hesitate or refuse to provide their personal information.
- *Pragmatists* are individuals who weigh the benefits of various opportunities and services against the degree of intrusiveness of the personal information sought.

[1] Privacy Indexes: A Survey of Westin's Studies by Dr. Alan Westin, Professor Emeritus, Columbia University, Teaneck, New Jersey. http://reports-archive.adm.cs.cmu.edu/anon/isri2005/CMU-ISRI-05-138.pdf

They believe that businesses should earn the public trust. They want the opportunity to decide for themselves. Most Pragmatists are willing to provide personal information when asked if it seems reasonable or when some value proposition, such as greater convenience, is offered.

- *Unconcerned* individuals are generally trustful of businesses about their collection of personal information and are ready to forego privacy rights to secure benefits. For these people, privacy is just not a big issue.

What is interesting about Westin's research is that throughout the 1990s, the Fundamentalists remained a steady 25 percent of the population. However, between 2000 and 2002, this segment grew to about one-third and held steady at this level for many years.

While we might speculate about the cause, and while there are many interesting observations we can draw from Westin's research, there is one clear message we must heed: that the American public's skepticism and even distrust of the business community's responsible use of information is a factor in a large-enough segment of the population that it can't be ignored. The question is: what does that mean to your business, and what are you doing about it?

This trend was first evident in the 90s with the growing consumer rejection of outbound telemarketing as an acceptable medium for selling products and services. Within a few years, over 80% of the U.S. households had signed up for the Federal Trade Commission's National Do-Not-Call registry, which was launched in the fall of 2003. However, the telemarketing story still has some interesting dynamics. For instance, a study conducted by the Information Policy Institute in June of 2002[2] found that more than eight in 10 consumers said they had acquired a product or service, given their voting support, or made a donation at least once during the previous year as a result of a call to their household. And seven in 10 of those who have acquired a product or service over the telephone were satisfied with the shopping experience. Yet most consumers wanted to block telemarketing calls to their homes because many were too intrusive and they couldn't make the ones they objected to stop.

In addition to the registry, the FTC revised the Telemarketing Sales Rule[3] in 2002 to limit the number of abandoned calls—calls resulting from making too many advance outbound calls and then not having an available operator to talk to the consumer when the call was answered. Getting a call and having no one on the line when they answered created very real concern for consumers, especially the elderly, who said they feared they were being stalked. This eventually led to regulations about this practice.

More recently, the debate has focused in the online space on evolving data collection and marketing activities such as behavioral advertising and social marketing. The Federal Trade Commission held a series of behavioral advertising workshops in

---

[2] Measuring the True Cost of Privacy: A Rebuttal to "Privacy, Consumers, and Costs" by Michael A. Turner, Ph.D., President and Senior Scholar at The Information Policy Institute http://www.infopolicy.org/ipiwhite/gellmanlong.pdf

[3] The FTC National "Do Not Call" Registry Web site http://www.ftc.gov/donotcall

2007 and 2008 and published a set of recommended practices in February 2009[4]. This guidance provides insight into how regulators feel about aggressive uses of technology, especially when consumers don't understand how information about them is collected and what their choices are to limit its use.

In early 2010, social networks took the spotlight[5] with a focus on the ways in which information posted by users on their public pages is accessed by the commercial sector for a variety of purposes, including marketing. In response, Facebook changed its privacy policy and default settings several times in a short span of time to react to these concerns. Several other social networks reacted similarly.

All these examples create two resounding themes: first, the need for transparency about how information is collected and used, and second, the requirement to have an effective and easy-to-use choice to allow consumers to stop overly aggressive marketing practices.

Have We Learned from History?

The drive to legislate marketing activities is not a new phenomenon. We have another clear example of a marketing practice in the mid-1990s that did just that—sweepstakes. The sweepstakes industry was a very profitable one. However, as it became more competitive and consequently more aggressive, dissatisfaction grew with the offers being made and there was much confusion about whether making a purchase would increase the odds of winning. Furthermore, a number of elderly individuals were confused by the wording of the sweepstakes offers, thinking they had won when they, in fact, had received only an entry form.

Repeated complaints to authorities were ignored by sweepstakes marketers. So after several years, Congress held hearings that were devastating to the industry. These resulted in the passage of the Deception Mail Prevention and Enforcement Law[6], which spells out what a sweepstakes offer can and cannot say, and how it can and cannot say it, even down to the type size and placement of language which explains the chances of winning. The result is that the sweepstakes industry is a fraction of what it was in its heyday of the mid-1990s.

It would seem we did not apply the lessons we learned from sweepstakes to telemarketing. Have we learned from both sweepstakes and telemarketing and applied those lessons to our practices online, in mobile marketing and in interactive TV? Only time will tell.

Furthermore, we have a whole set of new and converging issues that have confused the consumer and turned what was historically only an irritation factor into a legitimate claim about the invasion of one's privacy.

---

[4] FTC Staff Report: Self-Regulatory Principles for Online Behavioral Advertising http://www.ftc.gov/os/2009/02/P085400behavadreport.pdf

[5] Privacy Groups Assail Facebook Changes. http://news.cnet.com/8301-13578_3-20006220-38.html

[6] Public Law 106–168-Dec. 12, 1999 Deception Mail Prevention and Enforcement Act http://www.govtrack.us/congress/bill.xpd?bill=s106-335 and the DMA Sweepstakes Do's and Don'ts for Marketers http://www.dmaresponsibility.org/Sweepstakes/

We Must Understand the Consumer's View of Privacy

Direct marketing practitioners would likely say that the sweepstakes, telemarketing, behavioral advertising and social marketing issues should really not be considered privacy issues. Instead, these practitioners would claim that even aggressive marketing tactics are merely irritations to some, not all, consumers resulting in no real "harm." However, consumers don't see this distinction, nor do policy makers and regulators.

The picture is complicated by concerns about identity theft coupled with the rapidly expanding uses of "cookies," geo-location sensing devices and other passive data collection technologies that monitor and record our every movement. Added to this are larger corporate structures across which more information is being shared and mega-marketing databases are being developed.

We also have continued frustration over spam (unsolicited or undesired bulk electronic messages—either email or SMS), spyware, and phishing (attempts to fraudulently acquire sensitive information, such as usernames, passwords and credit card details, by masquerading as a trustworthy entity in an electronic communication). Studies report that Internet Service Provider filters remove as much as 80 percent of all email as fraudulent. According to Framingham, Mass.-based market-intelligence firm IDC, 2007 was the first year that spam email volumes exceeded person-to-person email volumes sent worldwide. And despite the passage of the CAN SPAM Act[7] in 2003, consumers fear unsubscribing will not make spam stop, so they often ignore the very tool that legislation provided.

If that weren't enough, we are moving into the age of text marketing to mobile devices based on our location at any given moment, personalized advertising on cable TV based on the shows we watch, RFID tags that can track purchases we have made all the way to our homes, and social marketing based on what kind of friends and fans one has.

While these could be very exciting opportunities for marketers, they also pose risks for consumer backlash if we don't understand the privacy dynamic. In the consumer's mind, all of these practices to defraud, deceive, track them down wherever they are, and watch everything they do are lumped together and constitute a growing "invasion of my privacy," driving policy makers and regulators to be engaged. And as Abraham Lincoln said, "Public opinion in this country is everything."

Are We Our Own Worst Enemy?

Evidence suggests marketers could easily head down the same path with these new marketing activities that they walked down with telemarketing and sweepstakes. They may be too focused on short-term profits and ultimately sacrifice or severely limit the long-term viability of certain marketing methods.

The movement toward integrated marketing has reaped great rewards for com-

---

[7] FTC Compliance Guide for Business for the CAN SPAM Act of 2003 (Controlling the Assault of Non-Solicited Pornography and Marketing Act). http://www.ftc.gov/bcp/edu /pubs/business/ecommerce/bus61.shtm

panies that have successfully deployed the strategy. Peter Drucker wrote that the only reason a business exists is to "get, keep and grow their customers." However, companies can focus too much on the "getting" part and not enough on the "keep and grow" parts. Companies must understand how their customers' attitudes about information use translate into sustaining and expanding a long-term profitable relationship. It goes without saying that in order to be successful today, a company must develop a "trusted" relationship with its customers. And to develop trust, customers have to believe that a company will responsibly use the personal information it keeps about its customers. Furthermore, customers have to be listened to and treated with respect.

Respect is one of the key components of trust. And the good news is that developing an integrated marketing strategy provides companies with the vehicle for greater customer interaction in order to understand their needs, show respect and learn their preferences. However, it is a cyclical process; in order for customers to be comfortable expressing their preferences, they have to trust a company enough to believe it will honor them. It is hard to understand how sweepstakes offers that misled customers into believing they had won, or telemarketing calls that were overly aggressive, or repeated unwanted emails or text messages where a business refused to honor a consumer's request to stop, can possibly build trust.

Companies Must Discover Their Customers' Preferences!

Everyone engaged in integrated marketing must learn from these history lessons and begin a dialogue with customers about how personal information is handled while respecting the customers' expressed preferences about contact.

Back as far as the early 1970s, four globally accepted fair information practices were introduced. These were the foundation of the privacy principles commonly recognized today and must become a part of every company's customer relationship strategy.

- **Transparency** in the form of a privacy notice or policy has historically been the vehicle for educating a consumer about information collection practices and providing the foundation for a trusted relationship. It is the means to supply customers with information about 1) who the company is, 2) what information it collects, 3) how the company uses that information , 4) what choices the consumer has about how information is used and shared with others, and 5) how to get in touch with the company.

    One word of caution: notices should be short, clear and easy to read. Companies should provide a summary or the highlights of their full privacy notice for the customer if the full, legally compliant version becomes too long and unfriendly[8]. Also, companies should look for more innovative ways to educate consumers about information collection and use practices. The idea of putting

---

an icon on a web site or in an ad that is behaviorally targeted that the consumer can click on to learn more and exercise choice is an emerging innovative practice. New interactive technologies offer lots of opportunity for creativity that we haven't had available in the offline world.

- **Control** defines what kind of choices a company gives its customers about how their information is used. Control must be both appropriate and effective. It must include offering the customer the ability to opt-out of having information about them shared with unaffiliated third parties for marketing purposes. It should also include a chance for the consumer to express other preferences about how they would like to be contacted by a company.

  Thus far, much of the control discussion has centered on whether opt-in or opt-out is the best approach. However, what the consumer wants is a volume control, not just an on/off switch. Keep this in mind when developing an approach to control, for it is a critical means of showing consumers that the company will listen to their feedback and honor their preferences.

  It is through dialogue about control that companies can best determine where their customers fall into Westin's three categories. This will give a company the needed information to personalize the approach used in marketing and servicing customers in ways that increase the trust factor rather than irritate a customer or even worse, destroy their trust.

- **Access**, the least visible principle, has been a hotly debated topic both in the U.S. and abroad. While only required by a few laws in the U.S., it is a universal requirement in many other countries and one that has become the subject of regulatory debate in the U.S. For now, at the very least it should mean providing a customer with access to information that they have provided and that is critical to a company's decision-making so the consumer can be assured that it is correct. The process of fulfilling a request for access is also a wonderful opportunity to engage in more dialogue with the customer.

  Access also implies the ability to correct information that is found to be in error. While this can be complicated and, in some cases, costly for companies, correction must be factored into a company's privacy strategy.

  Finally, the issue of authentication comes into play with the access principle. Providing access to personal information to an unauthorized person is a privacy violation, not a confidence-building practice. Careful consideration must be given to authenticating the identity of individuals prior to granting them access, especially to sensitive information.

- **Security** has become a much more important principle over the last few years. This is the one area where there does not need to be any dialogue with the consumer since they expect companies to keep both personal and anonymous information safe. And security is getting harder to provide, with the rapid advancements in technology and more information collected and used by businesses. Finally, security should be viewed not only from an authorized access perspective, but also from an insider theft perspective. A company's own employees may present the greatest risk.

At a minimum, if a company embraces these four principles in its integrated marketing activities, it can begin to move forward with the trust component of the customer relationship. If this is coupled with a marketing approach that shows you respect your customers, you will move even further up the trust ladder.

What is Required to Gain a Customer's Trust?

While we may not like it, we have to acknowledge that the business community has lost some ground in the trust equation in recent years. We have to gain it back, and we can.

Marty Abrams, Executive Director of the Center for Information Policy Leadership at the law firm of Hunton and Williams, has developed a trust equation. ($T = VPS$) Trust is the product of "Value" times "Privacy" times "Security." Value can have a scale attached to it ranging from zero to very high. However, Privacy and Security are either a one or a zero in the minds of consumers. Thus a problem with either one can totally destroy the Trust that has otherwise been developed.

In today's exciting but turbulent times, I believe we need to add one other component to the Abrams trust equation: the variable of Experience. ($T=VEPS$) The Experience a customer has in doing business with a company is also a factor in developing or destroying trust and the good news is that Experience, like value, has a scale. Treating a customer with respect greatly contributes to a positive experience even when there are product- or service-related problems.

Some industries, such as the financial services and health care industries, are already regulated and are required to provide notices and offer certain choices. Other industries will become regulated, and we can expect virtually every marketer to be required to follow in some way the four globally accepted fair information practices.

But regulation is never the highway to trust. Regulation, at its best, establishes a foundation on which to build—nothing more. Real trust requires going above and beyond what is required by law. Trust is built on layering three practices together into the relationship a company has with its customers.

The foundation layer is the law. The second layer is industry best practices and the final layer is a company's own policies.

- **The Law:** If all a company has is the foundation based in law, that may keep it out of trouble with the regulators, but it won't achieve a high degree of trust with its customers. Laws are designed to be the baseline, not an example of relationship enhancing best practices.
- **Best Practices:** Following recommended best practices or industry codes of conduct can help move a company's trust rating up. Many industries have developed and continue to evolve their ethical guidelines and recommended best practices that will help build strong long-term relationships. These should be carefully studied and adopted as appropriate.
- **Company Policies:** A high degree of trust, however, will not be achieved without adding onto these first two layers a) a set of company policies that are appropriate for the company's products and services, b) a degree of relatability to the kind of personal information a company collects about its customers, and c) an appropriateness in the various marketing methods used to interact with

customers—face-to-face, over the phone, online and via a mobile or other wireless device.

A company that is actively engaged in following the law, adheres to industry best practices, and has developed its own policies and procedures that respond to the concerns and desires of its customers can achieve the highest trust rating possible—and one that contributes to business success. In the book *The Speed of Trust* by Stephen M.R. Covey, the author references a Columbia Business School study by Professor John Whitney who claims that "mistrust doubles the cost of doing business." What more compelling argument do you need to adopt a trust-based business approach to your customers?

Managing the Trust Equation is Just Good Business!

We can only speculate about what would have happened if we had shown more respect and responded sooner to the concerns consumers expressed about sweepstakes and telemarketing. We might not have a sweepstakes law, and we might not have over 80% of the households on a federally run, national do-not-call registry. That experience shows that if we don't practice responsible use of information about consumers, we will have broad, prescriptive legislation limiting our use of information and potentially even limiting how and when we can use certain media to market and service customers.

You don't really know your customers if you fail to understand where they fall in Westin's segmentation of the population. And you won't be nearly as successful in keeping and growing your customers if they don't have a high level of trust in you. Find out what each customer's preferences are and use that to make a significant contribution to your bottom line.

JENNIFER BARRETT, CIPP, the first Chief Privacy Officer in the world, manages global information practices for Acxiom Corporation, which helps the world's largest companies transform data into business intelligence. Jennifer is called upon by businesses, policy makers and the media to provide insight on how information enhances business processes while addressing privacy concerns. Jennifer serves on the DMA Safe Harbor Ethics Committee and the Committee on Environment and Social Responsibility, is an Executive Member of the Center for Information Policy Leadership, is an Advisory Board Member for the Political and Economic Research Center, and is a member of the University of Texas Chancellor's Council and the Arkansas Academy of Computing. She can be reached at jennifer.barrett@acxiom.com.

READING
12

Multichannel Marketing

DEBRA ELLIS
Wilson & Ellis Consulting

Marketing channels are emerging and evolving at the fastest rate in history. The days when marketers could wait months or years to see if a new channel is viable are gone. Waiting can be a death sentence because competition is increasing exponentially. Geographical and logistic limits that historically reduced competitive entrances into regional areas do not exist in the global economy. These changes have permanently altered the way businesses identify and connect with customers.

The definition of a channel as an organizational unit that transfers products and services does not fit the new marketplace. The addition of new customer connection platforms and consolidation of departmental units requires an updated description. A marketing channel is a path that companies use to connect with customers to create relationships and generate revenue. The most prominent paths in today's marketplace are bricks and mortar stores, e-commerce, direct marketing and social media. Mobile marketing is emerging and expected to become a dominate channel. Who knows what the future will bring. (Note: Catalogs, telemarketing, promotional mail, email, and direct response television are considered part of direct marketing for this reading.)

Social media is a game changer, but not in the manner anticipated by early adopters. There is a global conversation. Some of it is about companies, products, and services, but it has not replaced traditional marketing activities. Instead, it provides businesses with unprecedented access to customers and prospects. The promise of one-to-one marketing is realized with social media. Companies can connect with customers and prospects individually, monitor personal conversations, and access friends and family using a variety of platforms. This access comes at a price. Participation is labor intensive and will not generate revenue without a strategic plan that crosses channels. It requires a major organizational shift from silo management to integrated marketing.

Management of the silo model is relatively simple. There are no requirements to integrate or even communicate with other channels. Even if someone tries to integrate, the different systems, processes, and policies limit efforts to cross channel lines. Customers are expected to choose their channel of choice, and if they don't, they are assigned one in an effort to manage the return on marketing dollars.

The silo structure creates a competitive environment within the corporation. Each channel has its own marketing budget. Attempts to bundle offerings meet resistance at every turn because successfully crediting sales to the right division is nearly impossible. Marketing expenses rise dramatically without a matching return. Consistent branding is challenging due to the variances between the channels and their management. And, customers rarely follow their assigned buying patterns. They cross channels expecting to be recognized as a valuable asset wherever they shop.

These challenges started the downfall of the silo channel business model. When economic and customer analytics showed that separate divisions created a redundancy of services and limited growth opportunities, companies began to consider transitioning from multiple channels within separate departments to integrated multichannel management.

Customer expectations are the catalyst expediting the shift to multichannel marketing. Today's consumers are demanding a seamless brand experience. They want the ability to browse through a catalog, order online, and return to the store. Or, they want to order online and pick up at the store. Or, they choose any other combination of service across channels that you can imagine. Providing these options improves the company's overall performance because cross channel shoppers have higher lifetime values than their single channel counterparts and are 25%–50% more profitable.

There are also operational benefits to a multichannel marketing strategy. The consolidation of databases, call centers, and management teams reduces costs. The ease and low expense of listing items online provides a perfect resource for inventory liquidation. email is a cost-effective alternative to snail mail for customer communication. Mobile allows instant access to people while they shop. And, social media expands a company's marketing reach exponentially. The best business strategies use one channel's strength to offset another's weakness.

Multichannel marketing utilizes technological advances to connect with customers in ways unimaginable a few years ago. Detailed information about customers, their buying preferences, and patterns is available. This analysis identifies opportunities and vulnerabilities allowing companies in both business-to-consumer and business-to-business to optimize their return and define new growth strategies.

How do you grow a business? The most common method is to expand existing channels to increase the customer base and sales. If you have stores, open more. If you have a catalog, add mailings. If you have a web site, increase traffic by driving more customers to your existing site or expanding into web communities like eBay and Yahoo!

You can also enter new channels. This approach is more complicated than building on past successes because it requires different processes, tools, and skill sets. Direct marketing companies with analytical backgrounds from catalog, telemarketing, and direct response advertising are best suited for adding Internet, mobile or social media channels. While the media and benchmarks differ, the skill set and tools required to analyze consumers shopping patterns and transactional data are very similar.

Retail stores without a catalog face the biggest challenge as they expand into alternative channels since data warehousing is relatively new to them. Capturing customer information is very challenging when shoppers can enter the store and browse for hours without making a purchase. Cash transactions provide sales data without identifying anything about the customers.

Web sites provide extensive information about customers and their shopping experience. Every click can be monitored to see how consumers browse online. The volume of data available is incredible. Savvy marketing managers are very selective about the data they process. They search for the information that can be used to increase sales, lifetime value, and profitability. This includes customer retention, lifespan, lifetime value, channel flow, and crossover.

Utilizing the data from multiple channels to enhance service and reduce costs is the best growth strategy for retail companies today. It requires a complete understanding of customer preferences and integration of marketing and operational initiatives. Analytics provide the information needed to make quality management decisions.

Customer Analytics

There are seven types of customers:

1. **Newbies**—Customers who have purchased 1 or 2 times. These shoppers have not established loyalty to the company. They may be at a stage where they have limited needs for the product line. Or, they may be testing to see if the quality and service match their standards. Either way, they are not committed to return.

2. **Rising Stars**—Shoppers who have purchased three or more times within twelve months. These customers are trending towards loyalty with increasing sales and responsiveness to marketing. They need encouragement to continue their movement to the next level.

3. **Platinum**—Customers with consistent performance season after season. They respond well to marketing and have reliable buying patterns. This group will typically follow Pareto's law and account for 20% of the customer database while providing up to 80% of the sales. They are the most profitable segment and valuable asset of any company.

4. **Falling Stars**—Platinum customers with reduced performance. They may be nearing the end of their buying lifespan. If this is the situation, attempts to reactivate are futile. In some cases, they become Falling Stars due to a service failure. When this happens, they can be reactivated before they reach the Rest in Peace stage.

5. **Bargain Hunters**—These shoppers only purchase sale items. They respond well to sales and liquidations and rarely transition into the regular customer buying cycle. They are a valuable segment if the marketing is limited to sales promotions. They provide a vehicle for liquidating overstocks and poor buying decisions.

6. **Rests in Peace**—These customers have completed their lifespan with the company. It may be due to a lifestyle change. For example, customers of companies specializing in children's products will leave when their children are grown and return when grandchildren appear. Operational problems can lead to an early termination of the lifespan.

7. **Social**—People who fall into the social type are not customers in the traditional sense. They have not purchased products or services from the company, but they talk about them in social networks. They can add or decrease value depending on the information they share. Monitoring their activity and responding when appropriate is a vital part of an effective marketing strategy.

New shoppers with a full lifespan will typically follow the pattern of Newbie, Rising Star, Platinum, Falling Star, and Rest in Peace. Bargain hunters are easily identified by their product selection. They only buy sale items. Established customers may shift from Platinum to Falling Star back to Platinum as their lives change.

Lifespan is the time that starts with the first purchase and ends with the last. A natural lifespan varies by company and product line. For example, customers for maternity apparel will typically buy for 4–6 months then stop until the next pregnancy. Techies may buy from an electronic store their entire adult life.

The natural lifespan can be altered by the company's performance. Poor service, merchandising, and marketing can shorten the life of a buyer. Inversely, a customer who has cycled into the Falling Star or Rest in Peace segments can be rejuvenated with new product lines, offers, and improved service.

There is a marketing axiom that it costs five to ten times more to acquire a new customer than it does to keep a current one. Customer retention measures the movement of individual buyers to insure that acquisition exceeds attrition. It is possible for a company's customer file to show growth while losing their most valuable buyers. For example, the chart below is an analytics summary for a retail business:

EXHIBIT R12.1: RETAIL ANALYTICS SUMMARY

Customers:	Year 1	Year 2	Year 3
Active	25,756	28,332	31,165
House File Growth Rate		10%	10%
First Purchase	7,727	8,742	9,172
Last Purchase	2,612	4,723	5,247
Acquisition Rate		16.5%	14.9%
Attrition Rate		10.1%	16.7%
House File Mail Count	52,986	61,728	70,900
Avg $/Active Customer	$169.66	$180.46	$208.35
Avg Ord/Active Customer	3.2	3.3	3.5
Lifetime Value	$848.32	$902.30	$1,041.75
Annual Sales	$4,369,763	$5,112,793	$6,493,338
Sales Growth Rate		17%	27%

This company has solid growth in sales and customer base. Their average order and number of orders per customer is increasing. On the surface, it is thriving. Unfortunately, not all is well, because attrition is exceeding acquisition. Newbies are replacing older, more profitable customers. If this fits with the natural lifespan, there is little cause for concern. If not, the source of the problem must be found and eliminated before the enterprise enters a downward spiral.

Lifetime value (LTV) is the present value of customers over their natural lifespan. It is helpful in determining marketing budgets because it provides a tangible indicator of return over acquisition expenses. In other words, it helps marketing teams determine how much money they can spend to acquire a customer and remain profitable. LTV is a relative number since many external factors can alter lifespan, average order, and profitability. The methodology for calculating LTV varies by company due to intrinsic factors.

Channel Analytics

Channel analytics are the metrics specific to the origin. Customer analytics begins with a focus on the complete customer file regardless of channel flow, crossover, or source. The next stage drills down into the data segmenting by origin and movement across channels. For example, customer analytics are created for customers whose first purchase is online. Then, they will be created for customers whose first purchase is by phone or mail. Finally, they are created for in store first purchase customers. Once they are completed, they are compared to determine strengths and weaknesses.

Customers who move across channels are the most valuable segment. These customers are typically more interested in convenience than cost. Service is vital to their shopping experience. It has a long-term effect on customer value and lifespan. Cross-channel shopping allows the buyer to choose their media and provides the company more opportunities to sell. Average orders are higher in dollars and quantity.

Each channel has metrics that are specific to their medium. Store analytics include sales per square foot, comparable store sales, and traffic conversion. Catalog analytics include response rate, income per piece, and fill ratios. web analytics track visitor interaction, conversion patterns, and origin. All channels measure transactional data.

There is also information available about how your customers shop elsewhere. This can be used to identify new product lines or company alliances. There is so much data available that a lifetime could be spent reviewing reports without ever applying the information. It is critical for information managers to avoid data overload and insure data integrity. While some information is interesting, it is hard to leverage it to improve sales or reduce costs. Other analytics may have application and be impossible to validate.

Applicable information is used to create personalized shopping experiences. Studies have shown that the shopping experience is the key factor in customer loyalty and long term profitability. Globalization is eliminating traditional competitive advantages such as unique product lines and pricing since most consumer products are available from multiple sources at a variety of price points. A quick search using a quality search engine will provide a list of competing companies with the same products at a variety of prices.

Multichannel Marketing Management

A positive shopping experience provides the best competitive advantage. Customers return when they have previously enjoyed the convenience and service of a retail operation. A good multichannel model has innovative combinations of channels, systems, processes, and policies designed to match customers' shopping preferences. It creates a unique enterprise that is impossible to duplicate because it has its own personality and corporate culture.

Customers should be encouraged to add channels instead of migrating to another medium. This can be a result of subtle marketing such as adding an 800 number to every web page, a URL to every catalog page, and social media information to every marketing item. Or, it can more aggressive by offering special promotions to customers when they cross channels.

The shopping experience begins when a customer starts the process. It may be an excursion to the store to browse or a mission to find a specific product. Every touchpoint is an opportunity for the company to influence long-term loyalty. A touchpoint is the direct contact between the consumer and the company. It includes direct mail pieces, store interactions, kiosks, package delivery, web sites, call centers, mobile texts, and social media networks. The brand must be consistently promoted at every point to insure a positive shopping experience. For example, a company known for high-quality, personalized service would have superior packaging for every product delivered to a customer's home. Anything less is inconsistent with the image.

Leveraging Resources

One of the major advantages of the new retail multichannel model is the ability to leverage resources between channels. Every unit has unique benefits and limitations. They include:

- Email is an efficient, effective, and economic method for communicating with customers and prospects. As a marketing tool, it provides opportunities to drive web traffic, announce store events, and promote direct mail offerings. Operationally, the proactive communication about service concerns such as inventory shortages and shipping information reduces costs. Disadvantages include a short tail (time between first order and last one for a promotion) and deliverability challenges.
- Stores offer customers the ability to connect with the product and sales team. It is the most personal channel because there is face-to-face contact and the opportunity to touch and test items. How do you adequately describe the feel of silk against your skin? Or, how do you show the detail of a hand embroidered jacket in a photograph. While the store provides the best opportunity for interaction, it is limited in its ability to provide depth of merchandise. Floor space limitations require the merchants to display the very best items and omit others that might become best sellers. Catalogs and web sites can offer multiple combinations of colors and sizes because their inventory housing is less expensive. Strategically placed kiosks offset product display limitations by providing an opportunity for

the customer to place an online or catalog order while shopping in the store. They infinitely expand the sales per square foot potential.

- Catalogs and other direct mail promotions provide shopping convenience. Customers can browse through offerings of items unavailable locally while waiting for the doctor or soccer practice to end. Once they make their decision, purchases may be made via the Internet, call center, or through the mail. Mailing are expensive so total exposure is limited. Space limitations limit the descriptive details.
- Web sites provide the ultimate self-service experience. When they are created with quality usability standards, customers can easily navigate through products and information to find exactly what they need. Orders taken via the web have lower associated costs. Integrating trigger emails with Internet shopping increases sales and profitability.
- Social media provides one-to-one interaction with customers and prospects. It is not a direct sales channel, but it serves well as a funnel for other channels. Customers who interact with company representatives in a social network tend to spend 40%–60% more than their non-social counterparts.

Evolution

Transitioning from multiple channels to an integrated multichannel organization is an evolutionary process. It requires analysis, design, testing, and redesign to find the best operating model for the specific organization. Companies in the same industry, selling the same products will find that their optimal business model is different from their competition.

Creating an optimized cross channel operation is a complex process. There are six stages in the systematic approach. Following these steps provides the process required to incorporate new channels into an existing business as they become viable.

1. **Establish Presence**

   A presence in a channel requires the doors opened, the site launched, promotional pieces mailed, or consistent social media posts. The initial presence doesn't have to be flawless, only functional. Enhancements will come as customer preferences dictate how the channels need to evolve and work with each other.

2. **Align Elements**

   The alignment of product, price, service, and image across channels creates a consistent shopping experience. These items do not have to be the same, but they must support the company's value proposition and match customers' expectations. For example, many retailers offer items unique to each channel to encourage cross channel shopping.

3. **Integrate Channels**

   Channel integration is the most challenging aspect of multichannel management. Established silo operations have a variety of systems, processes, and policies that are often completely incompatible. Their software operates on different platforms; employees have been trained to consider other units as competitors, and physical locations present barriers. Successful multichannel management requires compatibility and cooperation.

4. **Enhance Performance**

   Technological and analytical advances combined with customer and employee feedback provide new opportunities to improve service and functionality. Capitalizing on these opportunities solidifies the company's market position and encourages long term loyalty.

5. **Leverage Resources**

   Each channel has strengths and weaknesses that differ from others. Using the benefits of one channel to offset the pitfalls of another strengthens the corporation as a whole.

6. **Refine Model**

   Multichannel management is a process, not a project. It requires a climate of cooperation and innovation to be successful. The corporate attitude must be one of continuous improvement. The culture should encourage experimentation as the company navigates through uncharted territory.

DEBRA ELLIS is the principal of Wilson & Ellis Consulting in Asheville, North Carolina. Her firm provides advisory services and customized solutions to direct and interactive multichannel marketing organizations. Wilson & Ellis works closely with clients to fully understand the uniqueness of each organization and find the best strategies for resolving business challenges. Clients have included National Allergy, Hobby Builders Supply, Jacuzzi, Costco, and The Body Shop.

READING
13

History Matters: International Direct Marketing 30 Years On

CHARLES PRESCOTT
The Prescott Report

To look backward for a while is to refresh the eye, to restore it, and to render it more fit for its prime function of looking forward.
—Margaret Fairless Barber

Any economic environment is the result of two major factors: demography and technology. Those two elements both describe and dictate an economy. Since 1981, changes in those two foundations have revolutionized the practice of direct marketing and contributed to its international adoption. Direct marketing itself hasn't changed in its principles, wherever it goes: right offer, right person, and right time. As we will show, the best of the best today looks pretty much like yesterday's.

It must be also be noted at the outset that the tools and the prevalence of those tools have changed beyond recognition, and become vastly more common than when Ronald Reagan was President, Margaret Thatcher was Prime Minister of the United Kingdom, or when China and Russia were ruled by Mao and Brezhnev, respectively.

Direct marketing is no longer an exclusive club whose members are predominantly in the United States and in a few European cities. Well over half of all entries and winners of the U.S. Direct Marketing Association's (DMA) annual Echo Awards competition are now from outside the United States. Probably 80% of those submitted to the Cannes competition are likewise.

The spread of direct marketing knowledge and skills has occurred primarily with big brands, which bring their agencies with them. This has been paralleled with the technological revolution, which is now changing direct marketing worldwide and making it an even more exciting discipline.

Agencies Spread the Discipline

Agencies worldwide act as brand advocates. They incidentally become direct marketing advocates. Their influence and impact has gone with—and supported the brands of—many nations, from the United States and the United Kingdom to France, Germany, the Netherlands, Korea and Japan.

A 2007 report from GroupM, a WPP company[1] examined the state of use of interactive media in advertising in the 28 countries that were important to the Group. They were able to determine the percentage of media investment spent online, and for what objectives. Importantly, "direct response" as an objective was a common finding within the 10 industries studied. And, yes, the study suggested that "the Internet is direct marketing on steroids," as author Seth Godin noted.

Moreover, as the reference to 28 countries in the GroupM survey shows, agencies and addressable advertising seeking a response are now global.

In a survey conducted by the author in 2008, the DMA discovered that direct marketing specialist firms Grey and Proximity had offices in 49 and 48 countries, respectively. And of course Omnicom and WPP, with revenues from brands in excess of $12 and $11 billion respectively, are even more broadly distributed.

It is not just big agencies that spread direct marketing and enhance it. Companies often turn to smaller agencies for local expertise or unique talents. The Interdirect Network of Independent Database/Direct Agencies, founded in 1988, has participants in 28 countries. It was formed to help clients execute international or cross-border campaigns. Their client list has recently included British Airways, CompuServe, Glenfiddich, Hapimag, Nilfisk, Shell, Walt Disney, Microsoft, Monroe, G.N.Netcom and Volvo.

Agencies, brands and businesses are now no longer "international", but global, and they have taken direct marketing with them.

How did we get here?

Technology, Infrastructure and Tools

The infrastructure for every aspect of direct marketing has changed, making possibilities that would have been the stuff of dreams 40 years ago. The world has changed beyond recognition, creating opportunities that are beyond even dreams.

Thanks to digitization and the mass production of optical cable, call centers and data processing can be located cost effectively nearly anywhere, making for interesting discoveries of both real and imagined comparative advantages. In 1981, a trans-Atlantic telephone call cost over $5 per minute. With plummeting phone costs, Ireland became the call center capital of Europe and followed this with other technological improvements. As a result, the Irish diaspora came home. India thinks it has discovered a comparative advantage based on the English language and some rudimentary training alone. Results on this score are mixed.

In 1981, according to Freddy Rosales of the Argentine agency di Paola & Asociados, there were no Argentine call centers. These only started in 1989 with two

---

[1] Interaction: All Change: marketing in addressable media, April 2007, GroupM, London.

companies and about 150 seats. Now Argentina is internationally competitive as a call center hub.

Digitization makes printing in distant local markets under controlled circumstances possible. Hybrid mail (mail delivered using a combination of electronic and physical delivery) can now work, nearly instantly. The Posts of France, Germany and Italy all have competing hybrid mail services. The Post from France specializes in competing across the Atlantic to the U.S. market.

The marketing power of the letter has been combined with the distance-dissolving ubiquity of the web. Until recently, postage costs plummeted and mail volumes increased worldwide. Video, introduced as a marketing tool in the 1980s, was slowly on the way out as merchants moved to DVD and CDs. Now there is resurgence as rich media and video on the web are used by companies globally.

Digitization makes the web possible. The web itself was a toy in the hands of a few scientists in major universities working to build a network of easy communication for scholars. America Online started business as Quantum Service in 1985. Netscape was founded in 1989, and it still took another 10 years for a critical commercial mass to occur. It would not be until the late 1990s that merchants began to understand that the Internet was a real-time interactive shop window.

In the late 1970s there was much experimentation with "videotext", which never took off in the United States. In 1978, France Telecom began installing mini-tel machines in French homes, intending for these primarily to be electronic phone number look-up services. They soon evolved into the pre-cursors of online shopping. In fact, their ubiquity actually delayed the take-up of PCs in French homes until the last six years. Since then, that change has dramatically impacted French catalog companies, some of the oldest and largest catalogers in the world.

Computerization has changed the conduct of direct marketing and impacted the world. Most of us can articulate the many benefits of having a 1981-era mainframe computer on our desktop. We can perform database management, analysis, segmentation and regression analysis of startling complexity with relative ease. Art directors have mastered a bewildering array of computer tools to accomplish more cost-effectively the ordinary and mundane and—even more startling—the imaginative. We forget that we could do this already in 1981, just not so easily.

Jon Lambert, president of data processing company Acton reminds us of the advances in computing since 1981: "The increase in speed and storage and decrease in cost of computers. This is probably more important than the Internet itself because the Internet wouldn't be usable without this functionality occurring. Can you remember as recently as the mid-1980s, having to do massive amounts of backup on those clumsy old reels? An iPod carries a ton more data than a semi-trailer load of those poor old tapes! And you don't have to mail them."

And we could go on and on about digital photography and catalogs, digital printing and new inks. The travel specialist company Thomas Cook demanded that its agencies digitize their artwork and photographs and centrally store them in a searchable database, ultimately saving millions of pounds in photography costs alone.

But there is a context in which all of this occurred that made it all so much more ubiquitous.

Economic, Social, and Political Deregulation; Political Consolidation

The deployment of first copper and then fiber-optic cable created potential, but the potential was not realized until Ma Bell was broken up and the liberalization and privatization wave swept the telecoms world, which has occurred worldwide, from Argentina to Shanghai and Stockholm to Sydney.

This brought down prices and permitted companies to provide customer service globally, 24 hours day, 7 days a week. Customers, be they consumers or businesses, could be touched, assisted, upsold, and mollified at any time for mere pennies a call. Your author can remember being a student in Paris in 1968 and calling home once, by appointment, on Christmas. The cost was prohibitive. Now it is affordable to call home every night from wherever one is.

Deregulation occurred in the air, also. Airlines were freed to compete, first in the United States and then in Europe. Government-controlled pricing came slowly to an end and new entrants appeared to carry people and, importantly, cargo, around the world. Adjusting for inflation and currency valuation changes, it now costs less to ship a 10-pound product by FedEx or even USPS than it did in 1981, and the package arrives in two or three days, not two or three weeks. As shipper or addressee, you can track its progress on the Internet from your desktop computer. (You can also track the flight your daughter is on from Beijing to New York.)

If you are in Japan and you have bought a Dell computer, the computer was probably delivered that way from its factory in China or Malaysia. You call in the order to an international toll-free number on Sunday morning; it's manufactured that afternoon, shipped in the evening, delivered to Japan Monday, matched to a screen and keyboard and delivered to you in Osaka on Tuesday.

Both people and goods travel farther and faster and more cheaply than ever before. This is being written on a computer in an airplane flying non-stop from Shanghai to New York. The round-trip ticket cost $1,308 dollars, about the price of a good Italian men's suit in Milano, or one month's rent in a Boston studio apartment, or six months' salary for a recent university graduate in computer science from a Chinese or Indian university.

That last example hints at another dramatic revolution of a political nature: the opening of China. This is proving to be one of the most phenomenal developments of all, and it is one example of the other great deregulation that began with the Uruguay Round of trade negotiations and the creation of the WTO. Like NAFTA and the creation of the European Common Market, the passage of investment funds and goods has been eased incredibly over the last generation, literally dissolving borders. True international business-to-business direct marketing has increasingly made economic sense, especially over the last 15 years, as businesses discover that tariffs are lowered or removed.

The greatest of these deregulations, the creation of one European economic area, is perhaps the most historically significant event of all times. It is producing radical changes in Europe. Brilliant visionary leadership, acting at the conclusion of World War II, understood that for peace to last in Europe, where nations had been at war with each other since pre-history, the borders needed to be weakened and the economies integrated. Their vision brought peace, and an increasing 'field of peace" reaching even the Russian border. It also has resulted in one of the world's richest laboratories for "international marketing".

In 1981, there were real borders for people, money, and goods in each European country, each with its own economic policy. In 1992, the borders came down. In short, the monopolies of each country on the regulation of their economies and markets were abolished. And with the introduction of the Euro in 2002, one of the most astounding peaceful revolutions in history has taken yet another major step, one that increasingly makes a marketer's dream of Europe-wide campaigns and business possible.

Signage provider Seton, with businesses throughout Europe, now uses one catalog layout for the region, but local language copy in a common template of product pictures. The Swiss and German web sites share an online catalog (with turnable pages) in German. Where it can, it has one price insert in Euros.

Brussels is now so important to direct marketing as a profession that the national DMAs found it critical to establish FEDMA in1992, which has been followed by the Internet Advertising Bureau, an American export.

Finally, one of the greatest, and also peaceful, revolutions of the century occurred in 1989 when the Berlin Wall was smashed, the Cold War ended, Russia began to develop and Eastern Europe began its interrupted journey toward fulfilling its pre-World War II promise as a thriving modern economic area. Of course, with the end of Russia's controlled economy, Finland had to learn a new trade other than being an entrepot trader between Russia and the world, and the Finns have unleashed their technical excellence and given us Nokia and Telia and a myriad of technological forerunners.

Direct marketing is starting to thrive in Eastern Europe and the Baltics, demonstrated by the success of direct response television and catalog company Studio Moderna, and the fact that at least six direct marketing associations have been established in that region in the last few years.

China was a very grim place in 1981. Shenzhen was a farming village with no hotels, just a government rest house. I stayed there. Now, Shenzhen and the surrounding Guangzhou Province originates somewhere in excess of 50% of all merchandise sold in consumer catalogs in the United States and Japan. China now has two fledgling DMAs, competing post offices, at least four nationwide catalog companies, offices from all of the major direct marketing agencies, and a population so mobile phone crazy that some people have as many as four or five.

Also under this heading of "deregulation," two quiet but nevertheless very important demographic changes must be noted. In the developed part of the world, women have entered the workforce in large numbers, transforming the size, make-up and dynamics of family life in Japan, the United States and Europe, as well as shopping habits.

Liberalization has unleashed creative energy and able hands. Currently one-third of the Commissioners of the European Commission are women. As a corollary, families have become smaller, more urban, and wealthier. In fact, in all but a few of these regions, smaller families mean a shrinking population whose average age is rising. What these families buy, and how, has changed.

Women have developed a new image of themselves as independent and self-actualizing members of the wider community. They work in offices and need business attire. More of them raise their children as single parents. Families need prepackaged meals.

Paradoxically, in Japan and the United States, what these families have less and less of is time, which direct marketers help save by providing distance purchasing options through catalogs and the Internet. In Japan, China and France, many catalog orders tend to be "group orders" from informal sets of workmates in an office, who are predominantly women.

Parallel with the evolution of smaller families, we have the graying of the workforce in the industrialized countries. Graying and rich. According to the OECD, some 75% of the assets and two-thirds of the stock market wealth of the 29 wealthiest countries in the world are owned by people over the age of 50. In short, the average age of the consuming public in the best markets for the consumer side of our industry has increased by some 15 years in the last 25 years!

The Spread of the Practice. Who Do You Mail To?

Direct Marketing Finds New Niches

If you wanted to do a mailing promoting your products into Asia, Europe or Latin America in 1981, you had a tough time finding lists. Not much existed except the usual magazine suspects. In fact, you probably couldn't even find many of those, and what you did find was on these huge tapes, that were bulky and slow to ship. Technology today reduces costs, eliminates loss, and speeds up the process. No shipping tapes around at great expense. You click "attach" and "send", or simply paste to the SMTP address, and it's done. The data can go to the client or processor on the other side of the world in seconds, for free, not in a week and for a lot of money.

There was a period when such lists were relatively available as publishers and conference businesses generated new names to file at a rapid clip. International English publications were especially responsive lists. Some of these are still used, and they have been joined by new conference and loyalty program lists, but in fact, practitioners complain that the universe is somewhat stunted.

More and more countries have legal systems and ethical standards that have discouraged owners from sharing data. Recent legal changes regarding privacy in Germany, basically requiring permission from an individual to transfer his name and address to another company, have hurt the list industry there. And, of course, some paranoid markets still exist where you have to trust your mailing to a lettershop that literally applies the labels—markets like China and sometimes Brazil. But even in China, lists at last are appearing, and among major companies in Brazil the list practice looks like it does anywhere else.

The Universal Postal Union Has Played a Role

In 1998, the United Nations specialized body known as the Universal Postal Union established a self-funding project known as the Direct Mail Advisory Board (DMAB). It was charged with assisting Posts in developing direct mail programs. Through its program of in-person and online training, research and publication, it has introduced the disciplines of direct marketing and direct mail to many Posts. As a direct consequence of its work, there are robust postal product offerings, infrastructure and even direct marketing membership associations in many countries, including Saudi Arabia, China, South Africa, Brazil, and the Caribbean and in Central Europe.

For example, acting on the information gained from the DMAB, China Post has partnered with Acxiom to establish a large database of consumer data, with about 10 data points. As of this writing it contains about 150 million individuals. This is not much in a country of over a billion, but this is probably the most attractive consumer population. It has also established a China Direct Mail Association to help spread knowledge of the practice.

The Posts of South Africa and Brazil, learning from the DMAB, Royal Mail (UK) and Deutsche Poste, have talented professionals in their Direct Mail Centers who hold direct marketing courses and offer guidance and information about direct mail and direct marketing in general. In addition, South Africa has over the last several years rapidly expanded its address system into rural areas, enabling small communities to participate more fully in the economy. The Brazilian Post partnered with the largest consumer bank in Brazil, Bradesco, to establish branches inside postal facilities throughout the country, giving access to financial services to hundreds of millions who previously were unbanked.

Strong supporters of the DMAB, the New Zealand and Australian Posts, had previously developed vast survey-based databases of consumer responses to lengthy questionnaires. This data is used by mailers and other direct marketers as both prospect lists and for database enhancement. In support of promoting more international mailing, the New Zealand Post has originated a project at the Asian Pacific Postal Union, an intergovernmental organization of 31 postal administrations, to build a similar multi-country database to support the growth of direct mail in these markets.

Credit and debit cards have flooded Europe and Japan and are making huge headway in Brazil, making purchases at a distance more secure for companies and more convenient for consumers. China is just starting down that road.

However, as effective as the practice of using lists to mail offers has become in of all these new markets, in the more mature markets and in some markets with poor postal service (e.g., South Africa) the new data and the new consumers are being found on the Internet or through their mobile phones, not through the Post from subscriptions and other mailings.

The new data is not as frequently being found through offline mailings, but through carefully attracting visitors to web sites with the new digital tools and tactics of search engine optimization, online behavioral advertising, social media, and mobile marketing. Data is more and more being carefully given by individuals directly to the sites they frequent and trust. Often the registration process elicits very scant identification, a name and email address. This data becomes a challenge to link to other meaningful data, and this is a new challenge.

This pattern, begun in the United States, is being repeated around the world. The world is now a "consumer pull" world, and the challenge of direct marketing is to understand how consumers can be drawn into dialogue at one's web site, or even through the mail, by the use of the new prospecting tools: search engine optimization, banner advertising, mobile marketing and the affinity marketing practices inherent in the new social media tools.

This does not mean the death of direct mail. In the industrialized countries, mail still receives a significant portion of the direct marketing budget, and in fact the largest part of the United States marketer's direct marketing budget. What it does mean for many Posts is that they now need to refine their parcel delivery offerings for all those online purchases. It also means that e-commerce merchants are the new "catalogs" in terms of "new names to file" and data exchange.

And What of Creativity and Problem-Solving?

All of these changes make for more, better, more effective, more economical, and increasingly more international direct marketing. Skills have been translated, transferred, and adapted. The digital world and online marketers who scoffed at direct marketing as "old-fashioned" have discovered the magic of the algorithm, something understood by the direct marketing world since Bill Fair and Earl Isaac's application of predictive analytics to credit analysis.

The skills are being applied. To demonstrate this, your author dipped into the archives of winners of the Echo awards from more than three decades ago for samples to show what was and I reached out to agencies around the world for samples that show what is.

At that time, the Echo competition was enlarged to encompass all types of media and changed its name from "The Best of Direct Mail". (Four years later, the Direct Mail Marketing Association would become the DMA.).

Here are a few observations after reviewing some 30 winners from three decades ago and some dozen or so campaigns sent to me recently.

1. One campaign was for a dead technology, but its attention-capture device might have legs. Lear Siegler won a Gold Echo for its b2b mailing of a stopwatch to CEOs to promote its "mail mobile," a mail delivery machine that follows a painted magnetic path along the floor of a large building. The CEO is invited to start the stopwatch and send it to himself through the interoffice mail from another part of his building. I suppose the idea of "efficiency testing" is still valid, but the mail mobile is, alas, no more . . . the one at Reader's Digest chirruped out a friendly and cheerful little "beep" when it stopped, and gave a double warning "beep-beep" good-bye when it was about to set off.

2. When you see some of the old winners today, you'd think they were just invented. One medical campaign with an edge might still fly today, at least in Canada. It reflects the Charles E. Frosst & Co., Ltd.'s Canadian nature. The campaign consisted of a series of different sample mailers for a pain-relieving medicine, an aspirin variant. The eight mailers each had a different photograph of a fruit or vegetable being subjected to a particularly painful experience, a split green pepper being sutured, a cucumber in a bear trap, a leaf of lettuce being ironed, a watermelon with a meat clever imbedded in it. Even today, Canadian marketing still has much that is idiosyncratic, even shocking, and quite often very humorous.

3. Some campaigns look very familiar. GE did a series of b2b mailings to potential power generating and distribution companies (engineer buyers of technical products—talk about database challenges!) to promote a PCB substitute called DiElecktrol that was promoted as safe. The mailing started with an empty

aquarium and continued with sand, a little underwater castle, seashells, etc. Respondents got a salesman's call complete with fish and water in the last package. Gold then and Gold just a few years ago to a Norwegian firm using at least two of those many steps to promote their group trip to the DMA's Annual Conference in Chicago.

4. Some winners showed technology on the march. Indra AB of Sweden with its "King Meatball" campaign to caterers promoted its new machine-made "contact" fried meatball as a tastier and more economical alternative to handmade fat-fried meatballs. Gold for an increase in sales of 98% over the hand-made control meatball.

5. "Free" works. Always has, always will. Jeweler Hans Péclard of Switzerland earned a Gold Echo for a traffic driver to its first-ever trade fair booth in 1978 in Geneva: a genuine certificate of one share of DeBeers Company stock to the first 1,000 visitors to its booth. Cost: SFr 60,000. Revenue: SFr 1.2 million. ROI of 200.

6. Also "free", and *in memoriam,* once mighty and now deceased TWA promoted its first cross-country flights on Lockheed's new L-1011 with an American Express statement stuffer of coupons for a drink or free headphones on the new flight. The stuffer looks like a briefcase and opens to show a TWA brochure with coupons inside: involving, to the point, value, targeted. Response of 12.5% on 350,000 mailed.

Today we have a wider variety of media to choose from, but the messages have to be localized to the culture and audiences to be successful, and the themes of solving a problem and engaging the target are constant. Colleagues around the world have sent some wonderful examples.

1. The mail in any market still works well as a testing environment and client generator. In Argentina, Banco Privado is primarily an online bank and has only two branches. It tested four different prize premiums in four different packages offering a credit card account. The winner by a large margin was a miniature of a small bed complete with mattress and sheets which had a real credit card "under the mattress". This played to the thrifty "old-world" Argentines' sense of thrift and distrust of banks.

2. Also a very "culture-dependent" campaign, and a very sophisticated mail piece, was a Guinness loyalty program mailing in Malaysia that would only work in a Chinese environment. The mailing consisted of a sophisticated constructed piece with many paper cut-outs of Chinese New Year iconography. These cut-outs celebrated traditions going back 2,000 years. The totality of the message is that the recipient is part of a special group of men who are "in the know", who are loyal to friends and family, who are competitive and successful but generous. In short, the recipients are Chinese men of substance who are proud of their culture and their accomplishments. Response and result data were spectacular.

3. In yet other media, India TV channel SAB used broadcast and online video to attract new contestants and viewers for its version of "The X-Factor". In the piece, an iconic "holy beggar" has no success finding food in a village he has recently come to. Prompted by a heavenly voice, he displays his "X-Factor", a talent for playing hard rock guitar, and is feted by the whole village.

4. In China, Japan and South Africa, much of direct marketing is mobile marketing and experimentation is proceeding at breakneck speed. Here, the brands are most definitely at work. Johnson & Johnson enjoyed a significant success with a mobile coupon campaign for its launch of ACUVUE Vivid Style contact lenses. Consumers redeemed the m-coupon for free trials at participating stores and submitted their own photos via MMS to participate in a "most vivacious eyes" mobile picture voting contest. Since most of the entrants were young women, naturally most of the voters and phone numbers acquired were young men.

5. Finally, it is being discovered worldwide that social media can be targeted and made into a response and engagement tool. In Spain in 2009, an unknown author with a small publisher needed to publicize his novel, *The Wounded Copilot*. A combined direct mail and social media campaign created interest by allowing readers to determine the book's ending. Literary critics received a leaflet that released fake blood. Other influential people received a launch invitation that was perforated with a bullet hole. The launch itself took place at the theater which was the site of the book's story. All readers were invited to choose online how to resolve one of the book's incomplete plots. The book's print run increased 40%.

So, the creativity and problem-solving of the campaigns from three decades ago would still work nicely alongside the new entrants that are winning prizes, and satisfying clients, today. The skills and sophistication of direct marketing experience are now widespread. However, many younger practitioners who have cut their teeth on web site design and online campaign management are unaware that they are "doing direct" and are unaware of the history and gems of knowledge that are older than they are.

As Mark Twain said, "When I was a boy of fourteen, my father was so ignorant I could hardly stand to have the old man around. But when I got to be 21, I was astonished at how much the old man had learned in seven years."

It now should prove worthwhile for marketing professionals worldwide, whatever their experience level, to look back, and look around. Someone may have the answer to their client's problem. When you need inspiration, an afternoon browsing in one of the industry's archives of winning campaigns, such as the DMA's Echo library, or the UK DMA's awards, would be well-spent.

Pre-Internet promotions and post-Internet campaigns have much in common. It is true that one needs the SEO and the analytics and the social media presences to get people to a web site, and a reason for them to register or otherwise engage. But, one also needs one or more of these brilliant "old" ideas to continue to get them to respond. Now marketers can deploy their "new" bright ideas faster, more economically, and more broadly than ever before. But they will need to speak Chinese in China, Spanish in Spain. . . . and not just the language but the culture of the language.

Since graduating from Harvard Law School in 1974, Charles Prescott's career has focused on international corporate, securities, finance, and new country development law and projects. He most recently served as Vice President, Global Development at the Direct Marketing Association (DMA) of the United States and in October 2009 was appointed an Adjunct Director of the Board of Directors of the US DMA. He is the publisher of *The Prescott Report,* a newsletter of international direct marketing.

READING
14

Multicultural Marketing in the U.S.

JAIME NORIEGA PH.D.

Assistant Professor of Marketing at DePaul University

As a land of immigrants, multicultural marketing has always been a relevant issue in the U.S.A. With every wave of immigrants that helped populate this country, its new inhabitants brought with them different customs, beliefs, and languages. As a result of this, bilingualism was relatively common in the 19th century, and marketing communications no doubt reflected this diversity of languages. In fact, it wasn't until 1906 that Congress enacted an English language requirement for citizenship. At this point assimilating to the dominant culture and language became a practical and sometimes necessary measure for immigrants in order to secure a bright future.

Nowadays however, English is no longer regarded as such a sacrosanct unifying and defining element for the nation and its citizens. And thanks to the still-growing global economy and the emergence of transnational communities, it is much easier for immigrants and their descendants to retain or re-establish cultural, social, economic, and political ties to their home country. As a result of this, multicultural marketing is once again at the forefront of U.S. marketers' concerns.

What is Multicultural Marketing?

The term *multicultural marketing* refers to a marketer's efforts at communicating with and serving a target market which is somehow different from its general market. These target markets are usually made up of subcultures—a group of people who hold beliefs, values, customs, and other cultural characteristics which differentiate them from other members of the same society. The factors that make these markets different from the general market may include race, ethnicity, nationality, religion, age, and gender. Here we will concentrate on racial and ethnic minorities, which are often the most misunderstood groups marketers have to deal with.

In many cases, these cultural differences will dictate changes in the marketing mix (the 4 Ps of marketing—Product, Price, Place, Promotion). At a minimum however, communicating a selling message to a target market outside of the general market will usually require an adaptation of the "promotion," or how the selling message is conveyed. There are also a number of ethnic minorities for which it may be necessary to change the language and the venue in which the message is delivered.

This reading will summarize the three largest minority groups targeted most often by U.S. marketers: Hispanics, Blacks, and Asians. We will then discuss some of the ways in which these groups have been traditionally targeted both in mainstream advertising and via targeted advertising. In the last section we will discuss some of the new ways in which academic research is beginning to describe and understand multicultural markets.

U.S. Hispanics

Because of its size, continuing growth, multiple language usage, and continually evolving nature, the Hispanic/Latino market in the U.S. has been a very challenging group for marketers to reach effectively. The length and breadth of this section is a testament to the complexity of this often-elusive consumer market.

According to the U.S. Census there are currently approximately 50 million Hispanics in the U.S., a number expected to grow to 133 million by 2050. They are the largest minority in the country and had an estimated purchasing power of $978 billion in 2009, which is projected to reach $1.3 trillion by 2014, as reported by the Selig Center for Economic Growth.

In the recent past, Hispanics have achieved a number of milestones which the popular press has been quick to report. In July of 2002, the U.S. Census Bureau reported that Hispanics had surpassed African Americans as the largest minority group in the U.S. Hispanics currently account for more than 15% of the U.S. population. There are currently more English-language Hispanic themed television shows than ever before along with a multitude of highly successful cross-over Hispanic performers. On television, especially in youth programming, there are numerous Hispanic surnamed characters which have been integrated into Anglo or multi-ethnic casts. With every successive election, the popular press emphasizes the growing importance of the Hispanic vote. And during the past decade, Hispanic purchasing power has been growing at a rate twice that of the overall national rate. These statistics are quite significant because research has shown that as minority groups gain political and economic clout, they are more likely to feel comfortable exercising their cultural identity.

Following are a number of important Hispanic demographics and statistics summarized from the U.S. Census:

- The median age for Hispanics is 27 years of age, nine years less than the U.S. general population.
- Almost one-third of the U.S. Hispanic population is under 21 yrs of age
- Hispanic households are more likely to include children than non-Hispanic households
- Hispanic households are more likely to consist of extended family members than non-Hispanic households
- The current U.S. Hispanic population is more than 60% native born
- Traditionally, the U.S. Hispanic population has been concentrated in seven

states: California, Texas, New York, Florida, Illinois, Arizona, and New Jersey; however:

- From 2000 to 2007, the largest increases in the U.S. Hispanic population occurred in states which previously had only a small Hispanic presence

These are some previously identified characteristics of the Hispanic consumer market:[1]

- Prefer name brands
- Are fashion conscious
- Prefer to shop at smaller stores
- Do grocery shopping several times a week
- Prefer fresh food items
- Do not like to use coupons

It should be pointed out that these consumer behavior characteristics are based on earlier research. As Hispanics continue to acculturate, it is believed their behavior will fall more in line with that of the general population.

Aside from these facts and assumptions, there are other important factors which may help marketers connect more meaningfully with this growing and changing consumer group:

Spanish, English, or Both?

It is estimated that whereas 20% of Hispanics speak only Spanish and an equivalent number speak only English, the remainder—60%—speak both English and Spanish. In general, English monolingualism was thought to be the natural consequence of cultural assimilation for non-English speaking immigrants; however, an emerging body of sociological research suggests that bilingualism is not only a plausible outcome for Hispanics, but also an actual one. Longitudinal research conducted by Rubén Rumbaut in 2002 specifically found that U.S. Hispanics' ability to speak and read Spanish actually improved from their teenage years to their twenties. This new pattern of language shift is different for Spanish speakers when compared to other immigrant groups or to Spanish speakers from earlier waves of immigration.

Another indication that bilingualism is a growing reality among U.S. Hispanics is the significant growth of bilingual publications. As reported by Western Publication research, in 2000 there were approximately 58 bilingual Hispanic newspapers in the

---

[1] Donthu N. and Cherian J. (1992) "Hispanic Coupon Usage: The Impact of Strong and Weak Ethnic Identification" *Psychology & Marketing*, 9 (6): 501–510; Mulhren, F.J. and Williams, J. D. (1994) "A Comparative Analysis of Shopping Behavior in Hispanic and Non-Hispanic Market Areas," *Journal of Retailing*, 70 (3): 231–251; Rossman M.L. (1994) Multicultural Marketing: Selling to a Diverse America, New York: AMACOM; *Rafeedie*, C., Godkin, L., Valentine, S., and Swerdlow, R.A. (2006) "The Development of a Model Specifying the Differences in Hispanic and White Adolescents' Consumer Behavior," *International Journal of Management*, 23 (3): 597–605; Chattalas, M. and Harper, H. (2007) "Navigating a hybrid cultural identity: Hispanic teenagers' fashion consumption influences," *Journal of Consumer Marketing*, 24 (6): 351–357

U.S. By 2007 that number had grown to 189, a 225% increase. By comparison, Spanish language Hispanic newspapers experienced a 30% growth in the same time period, from 492 to 638 publications nationwide. And of particular interest to advertisers, a 2008 study of Hispanics in San Diego, California conducted by Meneses Research & Associates found that 82% of respondents preferred to receive information from advertisers in *both* languages.

This emerging language usage pattern has opened the door to some bold new approaches when communicating with this consumer group.

In 2007, a family-owned Honda dealership in Florida decided that the best way to cut through the clutter of television advertising would be to broadcast a Spanish-language TV commercial on a general-market English language network. The ad featured all family members and some employees speaking Spanish with a noticeable Anglo accent but delivering a warm, appealing, and convincing message. Although the dealership did receive some negative feedback as a result—threatening and ugly phone calls and emails from viewers (including some Hispanic viewers)—not only did they receive overwhelming statements of support, this tactic also ultimately increased overall sales.

More recently, in 2009, a leading U.S. car manufacturer took a gamble by placing a Spanish-language TV commercial during a Hispanic-themed English-language entertainment show. The gamble paid off, leading to several requests for additional information; however, surprisingly, some viewers requested the information in Spanish, others in English. Although one cannot determine the precise reason behind viewers' language choice for the additional information, there are a number of assumptions that can be made; some of which are quite surprising and useful in understanding the complex manner in which language plays a part in many Hispanic consumers' lives:

1. It is possible that program viewers favor English over Spanish.
2. This preference might reflect a higher proficiency in English than in Spanish.
3. Even if English is their preference, at least those viewers who responded to the commercial apparently did not mind being "addressed" in Spanish.
4. Regardless of their language proficiency, many viewers understood Spanish well enough to respond to the commercial.
5. Although viewers who requested the information in Spanish may be more comfortable with their native language, they were nevertheless enjoying English language programming.

The success of efforts like these seem to imply that determining which language to use when targeting Hispanics is not a simple choice based on the age or generation of the specific Hispanic target market, as has been suggested before. At least in some cases it appears that although using a Hispanic consumer's native language -even within English language media- may not be necessary, it may nevertheless be helpful, and potentially fruitful. In the last section I will discuss why there may be some instances in which targeting bilingual Hispanics with an English language message may be preferable.

Hispanic, or Latino?

It would not be very surprising to discover that the majority of Americans believe "Latino" is the preferred term with which to refer to this group. After all, it is the term they are most likely to hear being used in the mainstream media. And who can forget Associate Justice of the Supreme Court Sonia Sotomayor's " . . . wise Latina" comment during her confirmation hearings? The term "Latino(a)" is widely used by established business people, politicians, and celebrities. And the point here is that "established" usually also means "older." According to a 2008 study of more than one thousand 14 to 24 year old Hispanics in eight major U.S. markets, conducted by The Intelligence Group, a New York based research firm, these young individuals preferred the term "Hispanic" to "Latino" by almost a 3 to 1 margin (56% vs. 19%; 11% preferred the term American and the rest had no preference). This is not a trivial point given the comparative youth of the Hispanic population; furthermore, the choice to identify oneself as either Hispanic or Latino is often a personal matter which may involve taking a political and/or social stand. As poet/writer Sandra Cisneros explains the distinction between the words "Hispanic" and "Latino": "It's not a word. It's a way of looking at the world. It's a way of looking at meaning." Given this, it may be helpful for any marketer targeting this group to consider the potential consumer's age before referring to them as "Latinos" or "Hispanics," if such a label is deemed helpful or appropriate as a way of reaching out to this consumer group.

Blacks/African Americans

The politically correct term for this racial group is African American; however, this is an inaccurate term which often causes confusion over the size and composition of this consumer market group. Strictly speaking, the term Black describes a race whereas African American is more aptly described as an ethnicity. In fact, many textbooks stress the diversity of the "African American" population by pointing out that it includes individuals of Caribbean descent as well as other groups defined by the Census; Black-Hispanic for example. As the term implies, an African-American is a person of African descent and clearly not all Blacks living in the U.S. fit that description. For the purpose of this chapter however, we will use the more commonly accepted term African American with the knowledge that at least some of the numbers may actually refer to the Black race as a whole (especially since the U.S. Census Bureau lists this category as "Black/African American.")

According to the U.S. Census, there are currently about 40 million African Americans in the U.S., a number expected to grow to 57 million by 2050. They are the second-largest minority in the country and had an estimated purchasing power of $910 billion in 2009, which is projected to grow to $1.1 trillion by 2014, according to the Selig Center for Economic Growth.

African Americans have been part of the general population for so long, and they share the same language as the general population. Thus for most product categories, many marketers attempt to reach this group through their general-market advertising—often making sure that at least some of the models or spokespeople are also African American. Marketers usually rely on the audience profiles provided by media outlets in order to ensure their message is reaching a substantial number of

African American consumers. There are, however, a number of specialized products which still benefit from targeted advertising. Such advertising is usually placed in predominantly African American TV or radio programming and several national and local magazines and newspapers specifically targeted to this population segment.

Following are a number of important African American demographics and statistics summarized from the U.S. Census:

- The median age for African Americans is 30 years; six years less than the general population
- More than 50% of African American consumers are under the age of 35.
- The top five African American cities are: New York, Chicago, Detroit, Philadelphia, and Houston.

These are some previously identified characteristics of the African American consumer market:[2]

- Prefer popular and leading brands
- Are brand loyal
- Are more likely to engage in conspicuous consumption (purchasing items that signal success)
- Spend almost a third more on clothes than the general market consumer
- Spend 10% more on grocery shopping than the general market consumer
- Support African American community retailers
- Trust African American media more than mainstream media

Asian Americans

According to the U.S. Census, there are currently about 14.5 million Asian Americans in the U.S., a number expected to grow to 34.4 million by 2050. They are the fastest growing minority in the country (percentage wise) and had an estimated purchasing power of $509 billion in 2009, which is projected to reach $697 billion by 2014, as reported by the Selig Center for Economic Growth.

Asian Americans are by far the most diverse minority group in the country and can include South Asians from Bangladesh, Bhutan, India, Maldives, Nepal, Pakistan, and Sri Lanka; East Asians from China, Hong Kong, Japan, Macau, Mongolia, North Korea, South Korea, and Taiwan; and Southeast Asians from Brunei, Burma, Cambodia, East Timor, Indonesia, Laos, Malaysia, Philippines, Singapore, Thailand, and Vietnam. The U.S. Census Bureau and other research entities often also include native Hawaiians and other Pacific Islanders as Asian Americans.

Given the many different nationalities and regions represented by this group,

---

[2] Rossman M.L. (1994) Multicultural Marketing : Selling to a Diverse America, New York : AMACOM; Fisher, C. (1996) "Black, hip, and primed (to shop)," *American Demographics*, 18 (9): 52–58; St. John, B. (1998) "African-American trust minority media first," St. Louis Journalism Review, 28 (209):3; Bush, A. J.; Smith, R. and; Martin, C. (1999) "The Influence of Consumer Socialization Variables on Attitude Toward Advertising: A Comparison of African-Americans and Caucasians," *Journal of Advertising*, 28 (3): 13–24; Witt, L. (2004) "Color Code Red," *American Demographics*, 26 (1): 23–25;

members of the Asian American community speak literally hundreds of different languages and/or dialects. As varied as this group is, according to the U.S. Census Bureau only six different ethnicities make up 90% of this population: Chinese, Filipinos, Indians, Vietnamese, Korean, and Japanese. It is perhaps because of this diversity of cultures and languages that U.S. marketers do not target this group as a whole with any comprehensive national campaigns. At the local level, however, marketers have at their disposal numerous print publications and local broadcast channels and programs, each targeted to the six major groups of Asian Americans as well as many of the other nationalities within this minority group. Grassroots marketing by way of event sponsorships also gives marketers access to members of the many national groups which are part of this highly sought-after minority group.

Reflecting their status as members of collectivist societies, Asian Americans are very family oriented. They are also very hard-working and place a very high value on education. Their higher than average household income makes them a highly sought after target market.

Following are a number of important Asian American demographics and statistics summarized from the U.S. Census:

- The median age for Asian Americans is 32 years of age, four years less than the general population.
- 52% of Asian Americans have completed at least 4 years of college, more than any other U.S. population group.
- The median household income for Asian Americans is $69,000+; almost 25% higher than the U.S. average
- Only 36% of Asian Americans are U.S. born; and of these, two thirds are first-generation Americans
- Almost 50% of all Asian Americans live in Los Angeles, San Francisco, New York, Honolulu, and Sacramento
- Asian Americans are more computer literate than the general population
- Asian Americans are more likely to have Internet access at home than other minority populations

These are some previously identified characteristics of the Asian American consumer market:[3]

- Value quality and prefer upscale brands
- Are loyal consumers
- Respond very well to targeted selling/advertising
- Consumption decisions tend to be male dominated

---

[3] Rossman M.L. (1994) Multicultural Marketing : Selling to a Diverse America, New York : AMACOM; Steere, J. (1995) "How Asian-Americans make purchase decisions," Marketing News, 29 (6): 9; "Asian Americans Lead the Way Online," Min's New Media Report, December 31, 2001; Fetto, J. and Gardyn, R. (2002) "Cyber Tigers," American Demographics, 24 (3): 9–10; "Asian American Market Profile," Magazine Publishers of America (2004): Accessed September 2010 at http://www.magazine.org/ASSETS /BF4E8BCE5E9D4847BA537A448EE20EF4/market_profile_asian.pdf; Martin, B. A. S., Kwai-Choi Lee, C., and Feng Y., (2004) "The Influence of Ad Model Ethnicity and Self-Referencing on Attitudes," Journal of Advertising, 33 (4): 27–37

EXHIBIT R14.1: MULTI-ETHNIC MODELS AD EXECUTIONS

- More likely to buy online than the general population
- Asian Americans from countries where owing money is seen as taboo are reluctant to buy on credit

Multiculturalism in the Mainstream

Marketers who wish to appeal to different ethnic or cultural markets within their general market advertising instead of, or in addition to, their targeted marketing efforts tend do so in one of two different ways.

We Are The World

Some advertisers feel the best way to appeal to a diverse cross section of the American consumer population is to be all inclusive. These ads, which are hard to miss, usually feature one or more models/spokespersons of every conceivable race or ethnicity, presumably reflecting the actual population in the given marketplace (see Exhibit R14.1). These advertisements are noticeably different from other general market advertisements which will often include almost exclusively Anglo and African American protagonists. In general, this all-inclusive approach may work just fine especially in major cities where people of different cultural backgrounds are more likely to coexist amicably enough. However, the potential danger of using this approach is best illustrated by putting it in an international perspective; this all-inclusive approach would be disastrous in some countries where although many different races and or ethnicities may coexist, they may not only not get along, they may even despise each other. The lesson is clear: whether or not all the relevant races and ethnicities are represented in one's advertisements is not as important as how those different individual

EXHIBIT R14.2: RACIALLY/ETHNICALLY AMBIGUOUS MODEL AD EXECUTIONS

groups feel about being depicted together. In some parts of the U.S. this may be a risky approach because market research is not likely to uncover these intergroup dynamics. Racial or ethnic intolerance is not a socially desirable trait; therefore, if asked, it is doubtful that too many individuals would express intolerance for other races or ethnicities regardless of their actual feelings.

Who Are You?

A more recent and seemingly safer alternative which many advertisers now use is actually so ubiquitous that it has now been ridiculed on national TV. A recent television advertisement for U by Kotex tampons cleverly parodies other commercials in its product class, calling them "obnoxious". In the commercial, a very attractive model dressed in white in an all white background divulges the many advertising tactics used by marketers and at one point states: " . . . You can relate to me because I'm racially ambiguous . . . " Many print and broadcast advertisers now feature models and/or spokespersons whose race or ethnicity is hard to determine (see Exhibit R14.2). Once the accepted standard, it is increasingly rare to see television or print advertisements in which the principal spokesperson is a blue-eyed blonde.

The growing popularity of this approach suggests it is working well. However, it is important to consider how this execution corresponds with empirical research. Studies have shown that when ethnic minorities receive a selling message, they prefer to see models/actors/ or spokespersons that look like them; presumably, if consumers can relate to the faces they see, they are more likely to be persuaded to buy the advertised offering. It should be pointed out then that featuring a racially ambiguous model or spokesperson in one's advertising is not quite the same thing as featuring a model of the same race(s) as one's target market(s). The intent of the former seems to be to *prevent negative feelings* a consumer may feel when receiving a persuasive message from someone outside of their racial/ethnic group; after all, the most accurate way to characterize a racially ambiguous spokesperson is to say they "could pass" for many races/ethnicities, whereas the latter approach attempts to *promote positive feelings* by delivering the same message via someone who is *clearly* a member of the racial/ethnic group being targeted.

Both the 'all inclusive' and the 'racially ambiguous' approaches assume that neither the product nor the message requires any further adaptation in order to appeal to various racial or ethnic target markets.

Regardless of which of these two approaches marketers use when attempting to reach a diverse consumer marketplace through their general market advertising, television may be a different story. When advertisers decide to deliver their selling message via television, they usually assume a network's audience profile will be a good indication of which different ethnic or racial consumer groups will be watching; however, marketers seldom think twice about how well each targeted consumer group is represented in the shows within which they are placing their advertising. Although few would argue that racial/ethnic diversity is a reality of the marketplace, television programming usually fails to reflect the true diversity of the U.S. population. As reported by Entertainment Weekly, Table R14.1 shows a comparison between the number of characters depicted in scripted television series in five major networks (ABC, NBC, CBS, FOX, The CW) during the fall of 2008 and actual U.S. population figures based on analyses of 2007 U.S. Census data.

Considering the amount of news coverage regarding the growth of the Hispanic/Latino market in terms of population as well as political and spending power, it is surprising to see it is by far the most under-represented ethnic group on television. Although they are now the largest minority U.S. population, on television they represent just over 6% of television characters.

If we consider the extent to which so many marketers are relying on product placement rather than traditional TV advertising, these disparities gain a special significance; after all, when a TV character talks about or consumes a branded product

TABLE R14.1: DIVERSITY ON TELEVISION

Race/Ethnicity	U.S. Population	TV AVG	ABC	NBC	CBS	FOX	The CW
White/Anglo	66.2%	74.72%	78.2%	71.0%	**79.3%**	77.7%	*67.4%*
Hispanic/Latino	15.2%	6.38%	**8.3%**	7.5%	8.1%	4.2%	*3.8%*
Black/African American	12.9%	13.92%*	9.4%	11.8%	*9.0%*	12.5%	**26.9%**
Asian	4.5%	4.5%	3.1%	**9.7%**	3.6%	4.2%	*1.9%*

Highest percentage by network for each race/ethnicity is in bold, lowest is in italic.

*This number is somewhat misleading in that the average is significantly affected by the prominent percentage of African American actors featured in The CW programming (26.9%). The average number of black actors featured in all networks excluding The CW is only 10.67%

in a TV show, that character's race/ethnicity may play a part in how much his/her be-havior will influence different members of the consumer viewing audience. There is a distinct possibility that consumers of a different race/ethnicity than the TV character may not be influenced as much as viewers whose race/ethnicity do match that of the TV character.

Targeting Multicultural Markets

When a marketer determines that a product, message, or campaign warrants a tar-geted approach, at least at the local level, there is an abundance of print and broad-cast media choices both in English and in just about every major foreign language necessary. As might be expected, these vary by region and tend to reflect the demo-graphics of the given region. The larger and more established the minority target market, the more likely it is that national or at least regional advertising mediums will be available for marketers wishing to launch broader campaigns.

Cultural differences become increasingly important when a marketer decides to follow a targeted approach. For this, it is essential to have a thorough understanding of the different racial/ethnic groups one wants to target; in fact, the impressive growth of minority-owned research, marketing, and advertising firms suggests it may be necessary to have an insider's perspective.

Two very simple rules which marketers have traditionally broken when they begin to target a new minority group are:

1. Speak and understand the language of your target group; and,
2. Make sure your intended target market can relate to the faces they see in your advertisement.

Excusez-Moi?

Backwards translation is a common tactic used in bilingual research which can be quite useful to ensure that a translated selling message gets across the intended mean-ing. When translating from English to Spanish, for example, one bilingual individual will translate the original English script to Spanish then a different bilingual individ-ual will translate the Spanish translation back to English. The more similar the origi-nal script is to the English translation, the more accurate and proper the Spanish translation. Still, the best advice for any marketer wishing to communicate in a lan-guage other than English is to translate the *idea* behind the selling message rather than the actual words in the message. Very few language combinations can rely on lit-eral verbatim translations. Messages which rely on colloquialisms, humor, or a play on words are notoriously difficult to translate successfully.

Hispanics are the largest but by no means the only cultural group which may re-quire a marketer to deliver his selling message in a language other than English. However, because there are so many different nationalities which comprise the group we refer to as Hispanics/Latinos, it is sometimes challenging to find a word or phrase which has the exact same meaning across the many different versions of Spanish with which these distinct groups may be familiar. Depending on the demographics of the target area or the medium itself (there are many Hispanic newspapers throughout the U.S. which are specifically targeted to Mexicans, Salvadorians, Cubans, etc.), it may be worthwhile to deliver several Spanish language versions of the same selling message. A similar argument could be made for broadcast advertising, which may require not only a slightly different version of the Spanish language script, but possibly a slightly different pronunciation as well to reflect the most common accent and speech characteristics of the targeted group.

Another way in which a marketer can have a language gaffe in its advertising is through the inappropriate use of slang when targeting certain minority groups. In a 2005 McDonald's TV ad campaign for their double cheeseburger targeted at African American consumers, a tagline referring to the sandwich states "I'd hit it." McDonald's marketers thought they were expressing the affirmation "I would eat that" in a very hip fashion, not realizing the expression they chose was more commonly used to convey a desire to have sex with the object to which the expression was directed!

There are many humorous examples of advertising translation gone wrong from the international marketing arena. U.S. marketers who decide they should translate their selling message when targeting U.S. minority groups should go the extra mile to prevent blunders like these:

- When Pepsi entered the Chinese market the translation of their slogan "Pepsi Brings you Back to Life" became: "Pepsi Brings Your Ancestors Back from the Grave."
- When the Dairy Association tried to extend its popular campaign "Got Milk?" to Mexico, their ill-conceived translation actually came across as: "Are you lactating?"
- In Italy, a campaign for "Schweppes Tonic Water" translated the name into a less appealing "Schweppes Toilet Water".
- When Kentucky Fried Chicken entered the Chinese market, they discovered that their slogan "finger lickin' good" was inadvertently interpreted as "eat your fingers off."
- The U.S. slogan for Salem cigarettes, "Salem—Feeling Free," was translated for the Japanese market and read: "When smoking Salem, you feel so refreshed that your mind seems to be free and empty."
- When Parker Pens marketed a ballpoint pen in Mexico they attempted to translate the tag line: "It won't leak in your pocket and embarrass you." Unfortunately, the Spanish translation actually read: "It won't leak in your pocket and make you pregnant."
- When Clairol introduced their "Mist Stick" curling iron in Germany it was brought to their attention that that "mist" is German slang for manure.
- When now defunct Braniff Air Lines translated a tag-line meant to popularize its new seating upholstery, "Fly in Leather," in Spain, it actually read as "Fly Naked."
- The Coors Brewing Spanish translation of its slogan, "Turn It Loose," came across as "Suffer From Diarrhea."

The Man In The Mirror?

Research has shown that when targeting an ethnic consumer group, marketers will benefit if the models or spokespersons featured in the advertisements look like the intended target market consumers. Unlike the tactic of using racially ambiguous models described earlier, when marketers go through the expense of producing distinct advertising for each of the different markets they wish to target, they usually will hire models or spokespersons with which the intended consumer is expected to identify. As simple as this seems, it requires a thorough knowledge of the specific demographics of the different regions where the advertising is planned to appear. The term Hispanic or Latino refers to a wide variety of nationalities, not all of which look exactly the same. This was made clear in the late 1990s, when Coca Cola was advertising heavily in several Hispanic newspapers throughout the U.S. At that time, an overwhelming majority of Hispanics in the Southwest were of Mexican descent; however, these print ads were being created by agencies in Miami and/or New York where the majority of Hispanics were of Cuban or Puerto Rican descent, respectively. As a result of this, most newspaper ads published in the Southwest at that time featured a group of presumed friends in various settings enjoying a Coca-Cola; however, the faces in these ads bore very little resemblance to the people Coca-Cola was attempting to target in that region; Hispanics of Mexican descent.

Is it the Market or the Individual that is Multicultural?

Although the automotive advertising examples given earlier serve as fairly good examples of advertisers looking beyond the obvious in order to connect better with multicultural markets, few marketers are embracing a radically new way of looking at multicultural markets the way that some academic researchers are starting to do so.

Whereas a multicultural market is described as a market where members of several different cultures or subcultures coexist, a multicultural consumer is an individual who embraces and indentifies with more than one culture, usually depending on what the context calls for. The cultural frame switching literature in social psychology has considered how symbols and language can cue either of two distinct cultural identities in bicultural individuals. Cultural frame switching can be described as a specific type of priming, which changes a person's ability to identify, produce or classify an item as a result of a previous encounter with that, or a related item. By activating certain associations in memory, an individual is more likely to think about those associated concepts, ideas, or beliefs and/or to behave in a way that is consistent with those ideas and beliefs, when asked to process information.

One of the earliest studies of cultural frame switching conducted by Ying-Yi Hong and her colleagues in 2000 found that different cultural icons (Great Wall of China vs. American Flag) primed either collectivist or individualistic responses in Chinese-American biculturals. It was hypothesized and confirmed that because China is considered a collectivist society where interdependence and group harmony are highly valued, a Chinese cultural prime would elicit responses in keeping with collectivism and because America is recognized as an individualistic society where independence and self-sufficiency are valued, an American cultural prime would elicit responses in keeping with individualism. Other studies have shown that language can also prime distinct cultural mindsets in bilingual biculturals. Further evidence that bicultural individuals may in effect embrace two distinct identities comes from a recent study of Mexican-American bicultural-bilinguals living in the U.S. conducted by Nairán Ramírez-Esparza and her colleagues in 2006. Their study found that language is capable of cuing either Mexican or American personality characteristics. Subjects who responded to Spanish language personality scales displayed more "Mexican" personality characteristics (as identified in monolingual Mexicans in Mexico) whereas subjects who responded to the same scales written in English displayed more "American" personality characteristics (as identified in monolingual Anglos living in the U.S.)

Language is only one aspect of an individual's culture but it is a defining aspect for bicultural bilinguals. Recent studies suggest that in some cases it is possible that each of a bilingual's two languages can facilitate different types of thoughts and emotions. A 2008 marketing study conducted by Jaime Noriega and Edward Blair found that bilingual Hispanics reacted more positively to a Spanish language print advertisement for a restaurant when the ad mentioned dinner rather than lunch. The explanation for this result was that because subjects were more likely to associate dinner with family, friends, and the home and because Spanish rather than English is more likely to be used with these individuals and in this setting, the Spanish language ad was able to access these types of associations in their subjects' minds more easily than the English version of the advertisement. More recently, a number of studies have shown that both English and Spanish can result in different responses from bilingual Hispanics depending on the context of the advertisement. For a Hispanic bilingual who consumes media in both languages it is also quite possible that an advertisement for a printer, for example, may be more effective and/or efficient when delivered in English, after all, one would assume that English is the language more likely to be spoken at work and whatever associations exist within that mental framework have little to do with family or the home. Indeed, a very recent study of Hispanic bilinguals conducted by Ryall Carroll and David Luna and soon to be published in the *Journal of Advertising* has found that selling messages related to work seem to be more effective when delivered in English.

This research stream suggests that from a marketing standpoint, it may be possible to use the language of the selling message as a prime to engage either of a bicultural bilingual's cultural identities in order to differentially access distinct associations in consumers' minds, something which may ultimately aid in persuasion. And because priming is a general phenomenon, it may also be possible to use other aspects of an advertisement besides language to communicate at a deeper and more meaningful level with one's target market.

In other words, this emerging field of study considers multicultural markets not as distinct groups of homogeneous individuals who are somehow different than their general market counterparts, but rather as groups of individuals who at times will reflect and thereby be motivated by either of the two cultures with which they identify: their American culture or their racial/ethnic/national minority culture. Much of this research is still in its infancy though, so at this time, most marketers still rely on overly simplistic, often arbitrary, and sometimes biased guidelines to determine which language and symbols to use when targeting racial and or ethnic minority consumer markets.

JAIME NORIEGA, PH.D. is an assistant professor of marketing in the College of Commerce, DePaul University. Professor Noriega earned his B.S., M.B.A. and Ph.D. degrees from the University of Houston.

READING
15

Contact and Call Centers

MITCHELL LIEBER, PRESIDENT
Lieber & Associates

What is Customer Contact?

Customer contact is one-to-one individualized communications with a company representative via telephone, web chat or email. When contact is solely by telephone and centralized, the operation is called a call center. Today, many call centers also respond to emails and web chats and are increasingly called *customer contact centers*. This is usually shortened to simply *contact center*. The term *contact center* is used here to refer to both types of operations.

TABLE R15.1: TYPES OF 1:1 CUSTOMER CONTACT

Type of Contact	Description
Inbound telephone calls	Via toll-free or local telephone number
Inbound emails	Via an email address or web form
Inbound web chats	From a company web site
Outbound calls	Dialed manually, by a computer or predictive dialer
Account service	Inbound and outbound calls to service and sell accounts, such as stockbroker clients or business-to-business sales reps with specific account assignments

Customer contact has a variety of business purposes. These include responding to customers with customer service, technical support and order taking. Sales activities are also under this large umbrella. These range from lead generation and lead qualification, to sales cultivation and multi-step sales, to consultative sales, up-selling and cross-selling.

Where Customer Contact Fits In and How it Affects Results

The video and interactive elements of your new campaign really draw people in. The copy sings the right song beautifully. The graphics are on strategy and stunning. The data strategy captures information that will drive sales. The campaign is done!

Not quite. The contact center program needs to be developed.

Companies that give the contact center little attention often sabotage their program's results, for this area can make or break many programs. Here's why. Whether prospects contact your business to order or with questions, via chat or email or phone, one thing is certain for most companies. The most personal and intimate communications a prospect or customer will have with your brand will be at the contact center. It is where the *brand promise* that underlies your advertising comes true or is proved false. Which will it be? The attention you give this area determines the answer.

Will your brand be everything the caller expects? Will reps be accessible, knowledgeable, confident, and customer focused? Or will they be difficult to reach, poorly informed, unsure or indifferent?

Whether 10%, 20% or 50% of your prospects or customers contact you in this personal medium, you want to win them over rather than write them off. Similarly, if you place outbound calls to prospects, you are doing so to win them over.

A Different Type of Channel

There are a number of questions to ask when developing a contact center program. Can the selected organization handle the volume of calls, chats and emails in or out? Will the reps be ready to respond to customers and prospects and do so properly? If the answer is an immediate and unqualified *yes* as it almost always initially is, there's a follow up question. *Who is taking responsibility if that turns out to be inaccurate and sales are lost?* Ask that question, and *yes* may become *maybe*. Dig further, and this may become *maybe, but . . .* or *we didn't know that . . .* or *that will cost $_____ more.* When conducting contact center programs, the devil is nearly always in the details.

Why? Effectiveness in the telephone channel may be trickier than in any other channel, because it is controlled differently.

TABLE R15.2

Channel	Control of Message Delivery	Duplication and Distribution
Web	Agency, copywriter, web designer	Reproduced by computers
Email	Agency, copywriter and designer	Reproduced by computers
Broadcast /Web TV and Radio	Producer, director and scriptwriter	Recording is played
Print Ads	Copywriter and graphic designer	Printing
Direct Mail	Copywriter and graphic designer	Printing
Telephone	Script or call guide writer	Telephone reps
Web Chat / Email Response	Template copywriter	Contact center reps

The contact center is the *only* channel in which individual human beings dynamically interpret and deliver the creative for *each individual impression.*

There is an up-side to this complexity. If a program is carefully designed, it is possible to tailor communications to each prospect or customer, engendering positive feelings about the company's responsiveness. There is a down side as well. A one-size-fits-all approach sticks out like a sore thumb in this most personal of channels, as do sophisticated approaches that fail because they are over-ambitious and implemented poorly or inconsistently. Which occurs is determined by a series of strategic and creative decisions. This is an overview of these decisions, so that you can make choices that help optimize results.

While the gap between quality and poor contact center programs is affected by design and structure, it is also seriously affected by the quality of call center management, organization and staff, and the degree to which they are a match for your program. For example, if a company selects a call center organization that is accustomed to following scripts verbatim, asking them to take a conversational approach following a bullet point outline (called a *call guide*) may not work. It is too different than their management and phone staff's standard operating procedure.

Designing the Contact Center Program

There are key elements that make up each contact center program. Here are the most important ones for the majority of programs.

Purpose of the call or contact: Is it customer service, order-taking, to generate a lead, qualify a lead or close a sale? Do you want to up-sell or cross-sell?

Days and hours of operation: Is it 24×7–×365? Is it 9–5 Monday–Friday? How do the hours affect customers in different time zones? Is it worthwhile for an in-house call center in the central time zone to open an hour earlier to accommodate the east coast, and to stay open two hours later to accommodate those on Mountain and Pacific Time? Will those in Alaska and Hawaii adapt to these hours, or is there a business reason to remain open even later for them?

In-house or outsourced: Will your contact center be in-house, outsourced or in-house with outsourced overflow? If outsourced, who will oversee and manage the outsourcer? Who will work with them to develop training? What arrangements have been made to answer questions as they arise? If in-house, can the call center handle the call types, call volumes and if there are inbound calls or chats, the call or chat arrival pattern? The most extreme arrival pattern is for direct response TV ads, which generate responses in a *spike* pattern. Nearly all calls ring in within 8 minutes of when the ad airs. There are virtually no calls between ads. How will the contact center staff for this?

Management: Who is going to oversee and manage the contact center program at the top level? Who will be at the top of the human chain of command to a small army of telephone reps delivering your company's message one-to-one? Who is going to make sure your company's goals and objectives are being met, initially day-to-day and then probably week-to-week? Will this be someone in corporate marketing, at the ad agency or a call center consultant? In addition to looking at statistics, will the program manager seed lists used for outbound calls (under an unrecognizable name, to receive and evaluate calls)? Will they monitor inbound customer contact? Will they place test calls, chats and emails?

Sourcing inbound calls and contacts: The most expensive part of most inbound telephone programs is making the telephone ring. The cost of the advertising, per call, is larger than the cost of handling it. Tracking the media source of each call is essential to produce reports that inform advertising purchase decisions. Decide whether the media source will be embedded in different phone numbers or extensions assigned to each source, or if the reps simply ask the source and rely on caller recall and a list.

Sales volume per source is the true measure of advertising results. If calls generate leads and a field sales organization is involved, assign a unique identifier number to each lead to track closed sales back to the database record with the source. Similarly, inbound emails that are generated via web forms can be designed to include *tracking URLs* from the original web landing page. Web chats can also be tagged to indicate the web page from which they originate.

Database and calling lists: Nearly all contact center programs involve databases. Inbound lead programs populate a marketing database with leads. Order-taking programs use an enterprise software system to place customer orders, check inventory and provide delivery dates. Customer service and technical support operations use database systems to track issue type, time to resolution and customer information. Each is a very different category of software, but all revolve around databases. All require that decisions be made about the information to capture, the reports required, and the frequency of reports.

In outbound calling, calling lists are generated using specific criteria. A business-to-business win-back program may use RFM (recency, frequency, monetary). Such a program may target customers who are 5–12 months lapsed (recency), ordered more than 4 times a year (frequency) and spent more than $1,000/order (monetary). For large lists, sophisticated multiple-variable predictive modeling may be used to target those most likely to purchase. For small lists, a simple approach may be taken, such as calling every customer who has not ordered within the past 90 days. Calling lists rarely exist in paper form. These are typically electronic lists of prospect or customer records which are selected to receive a call.

Training: Training is a key to success in contact center programs and should address the product or service and its market, as well as the call guide and frequently asked questions. Role-playing and simulated calls are also important components. It's smart to have a product specialist from the company visit the call center (whether in-house or outsourced) to train reps on the product. Reps bond with company representatives and identify with the company as a result of such sessions, which improves how they represent your brand. Imprinted items your company has, such as t-shirts and mugs, are important to bring along and distribute. These help customer contact reps feel that they are an integral part of the company's team and true company representatives.

Scripting, call guides and templates: Some programs require a verbatim script for all or certain parts of calls. However *call guides*, which outline bullet points to guide the conversation, are typically used for business-to-business calls. If reps have proper training and empowerment, call guides also result in more conversational calls on consumer programs. Always have answers to frequently asked questions as part of the call guide or script package. For web chats and emails, commonly used replies should be available as templates, and pasted into messages to facilitate speedy and accurate communications. Outbound sales calls always include objection-responses, which are answers to objections to buying that prospects may raise (however some U.S. states prohibit their use).

System programming: Most contact center programs are set up in computer systems that provide database fields, on-line scripts for reps, and reports. It is wise to develop your requirements for each and to put them in writing. Determine if the contact center will commit to giving your company all of its *must haves* and many of its *would like to haves,* and the cost and time frame for doing so.

Metrics for inbound calls: Contact center programs require constant measurement to stay on course. The most important customer service metrics are *customer satisfaction* and *time to final resolution* per issue. For inbound leads the metrics are the percentage and number *of qualified leads,* based on clear and established lead qualification criteria. For inbound sales the top metrics are the percentage of *closed sales, sales volume per-call* in dollars and sales volume per-hour per-rep. Up-sell and cross-sell close rates and sales volume may also be important.

Speed of answer metrics are commonly used, since a contact center must answer a call before anything else can occur. These are typically the percentage of calls that are *abandoned* before being answered, and the percentage of time that *service level* is met. Service level is a goal that is expressed as % of calls answered within seconds. An example is 80% of calls answered within 40 seconds, or simply 80% in 40. A more sophisticated metric is *tri-level,* which sets speed-of-answer goals for 80%, 99% and 100% of calls. It measures the service delivered to all prospects and customers, rather than just 80%.

Metrics for email and web chat: Email service level goals typically range from a three- hour to a 24- hour turn-around time. Web chat service level goals are similar to those of inbound calls, since they are equally as perishable. The customer service metrics used for inbound calls should also be used for emails and web chats.

Metrics for outbound calls: Outbound calls are most often placed to generate leads or sales. In outbound calling, a presentation to a decision maker is called a *contact.* Since contacts are pre-requisites to generating a lead or making a sale (or for any other goal), they figure prominently into outbound metrics. Results are measured in two ways: as percentages and per hour. A key metric is the *sales conversion* ratio, defined as the percentage of contacts that purchase. For lead generation programs, the percentage of contacts that are qualified leads is key. This might be 4%, or even 12% or 20%. *Per hour* metrics are based on the results produced by one telephone rep on the telephone for one hour. *Sales-per-hour (SPH)* is the key metric. *Contacts-per-hour (CPH), callbacks per hour* and *bad-numbers-per-hour* (disconnected, etc.) are important intermediate metrics.

Outbound calling in consumer and business-to-business: Most outbound consumer calling is to existing customers, recently lapsed customers and inquirers from the past 30–90 days. Such calls require a well-designed, consumer-focused offer to be effective and to deliver a good return on investment. Results are often improved by integrating direct mail and/or email. Cold calling consumers is almost always ill-advised.

Business-to-business calling is heavily focused on the same relationship-based calling programs as consumer calls. Additionally prospecting calls can be effective for niche business-to-business markets, particularly in combination with email and/or direct mail. Such programs are effective when there are a limited number of sources for the product or service you are selling, and it is important to the prospect's business. For example, after-market forklift and clamp truck parts for large fleet owners and repair shops meets both of these requirements. A non-niche market that meets neither requirement is photocopier and laser printer paper for offices, at a price that is 5% less than that of office supply cataloguers.

Monitoring calls and communications: Ultimately, contact centers produce interactions with prospects and customers. These can be counted and the results measured, however the quality of the interactions can only be evaluated by listening to calls (or for emails and web chats, looking at the messages). While this should be done internally by call center supervisors and managers, the owner of the program must also implement a monitoring program. This type of oversight is essential to the success of any contact center program. Contact centers can usually accommodate real time call monitoring from remote locations, and can also provide recordings of calls. Similarly, they can send clients their emails and web chats for review and evaluation.

It is crucial that monitoring employ a set of objective criteria for scoring communications. *Is friendly* is subjective, while *uses customer's name* is objective. Finally, before a monitoring program is implemented, reps must be well trained on these criteria which should be established as rep goals.

Inbound call IVRs and voice recognition: Some inbound call centers use an IVR (interactive voice response) system to accept touch tone data entered by a caller. Others use a voice recognition system to collect caller information on an automated basis. These forms of automation may be used without live reps. However, at most call centers, they are used to route calls to the proper group of reps such as sales or service. When designing such systems, keep in mind that most callers don't feel like they are receiving service until they reach a live person. So when designing these forms of automation, less is more. It is best to get callers to a live person in as few steps and as quickly as possible.

Selecting an Outsourcer

Many contact center programs are handled by outsourcers, because there are insufficient resources to conduct them in-house. When selecting an outsourcer look for (1)overall competence, (2) a match with your program's written requirements and (3) experience handling similar types of programs. All three are essential.

Overall competence is the sum of the competence of management and supervision, of the phone reps and of the operations systems and processes. All are employed to implement your program.

It is necessary to create a set of written requirements for your contact center program, so that there is a clear set of needs against which to score potential vendors. This also forces your organization to distinguish *nice to have* capabilities and characteristics from *must haves*. Attractive and glitzy bells and whistles never substitute for essential functionality that is missing in another area.

The amount of specialization among contact centers may, to someone new to them, seem remarkable. However the goal, process and rep style and skills required varies with the type of program. For inbound programs, handling inquiries to capture basic contact information is different than delivering technical support, and taking credit card orders has its own unique set of skills and processes. Conducting web chats requires a much faster turnaround time than responding to emails. Unlike handling telephone calls, both require the ability to write clearly and well.

Whether outbound or inbound, it is usually wise to primarily consider contact centers that have worked in the program's specific vertical business area such as insurance, infomercials or health care.

Many client companies use geography to determine which outsourcers to consider and choose. This is almost always short-sighted and limiting. Marketers usually visit outsourced contact centers once or twice a year, or at most four times a year during a start-up. Select the contact center on qualifications first, and only consider geography if all other things are equal. Avoiding a poor match between a program and outsourcer is worth an occasional airplane flight or drive. Why? The disastrous results that come from a poor match cost a good deal more in both money and management time than occasional travel.

Special Program Design Concerns

Contact center programs must exist in harmony with a number of business eco-systems. These range from the company's own branding to a particular country or state's regulations. Here are a few of the environmental issues affecting contact center programs.

Branding: Company branding can be incorporated into the call. However, incorporating a slogan or catch phrase usually doesn't work. Here's an example. *This is Theresa Smith calling for GE, we bring good things to life. The reason for my call today . . .* Why doesn't this work? A phone call is a one-to-one personal communications. When was the last time you used a slogan or catch phrase to communicate with someone in a conversation? Slogans are used for crowds via one-way media such as TV, the web and public speeches. Incorporating one into a conversation is out of place and de-personalizes it.

How can branding be incorporated in an appropriate way? The best way is to incorporate the underlying branding principles and to deliver on the brand promise. In other words, *show* that GE brings good things to their life. For example, *if you ever have a problem with this product, just call us at 800-000-0000, or contact us via our web site. We'll solve it for you. This is one of the good things we've incorporated into this product.*

Staff turnover: This is a pivotal concern, and varies widely. If most of the reps who initially learn and do well on your program are transferred or leave six weeks or even six months later, then what? How well will the new reps be trained and how well will they do? Don't assume that the initial staff will be there for any period of time. Ask about and plan for turnover and additional training.

Toll free numbers: We live in an era in which cross-country calls often cost pennies a minute, or are part of a flat rate plan and cost nothing extra. However, toll free numbers continue to be a standard for most inbound calling programs. If the toll free number is a vanity number, which spells out a word or phrase, it is important to also display the numeric digits. Why? Vanity numbers are easier to remember, but can be difficult to dial. Also, the alphabet does not correlate with numbers on some smart phones, such as the Blackberry, making a vanity number impossible to dial! It is often wise to display the hours and days the call center is open along with the phone number.

Communications style differences within the U.S.: Cultural issues often arise when designing and conducting programs. Make sure you understand how your market engages. For example, in the U.S., rapport building and relationships are more important in many Hispanic cultures than they are in Anglo cultures. Similar differences will arise in socio-economic groups, and (in business-to-business calling) in professions and industries, which also have their own cultures. For example, engineers often want detailed information and care little about the duration of a call, email or web chat session if that goal is being met. However, stockbrokers are characteristically very concerned about time and completing calls quickly. In their business, time is money.

International issues: Our world continues to shrink due to instant worldwide communications. However, we still retain distinct ways of doing things. Call guides, scripts and template language often need to be restructured to conform to local cultures. International *free call* numbers are specific to each country, so your program will need separate ones for each, even if it is using a single Pan-European or Central American call center. Laws and regulations are different abroad than in the United States. You may find that the use of credit information will be less restricted but the use of personal information will be more tightly regulated in certain countries. Also, the specifics of laws will differ. Canada's do-not-call law is not identical to the U.S. regulations. To successfully operate call center programs in other countries, it is prudent to have one or more partners who can advise on these types of local issues.

Generational differences: People of different ages communicate differently. Most people born after 1980 will try a web site and web chat before calling, while those born before WWII prefer to speak with live telephone reps instead. Baby boomers are the first significant transitional generation. Some boomers may prefer web chat, but most will prefer the phone call. In fact, a large percentage will not be able to carry on a web chat. Select multiple communications channels that allow easy access for all relevant market segments. Do not choose customer contact channels solely to minimize costs, for this may cause the company to lose customers and sales.

Click-to-call on the web: Commerce today is largely web-focused, and this service moves the contact center to the web. It enables a visitor to a web page to enter their telephone number, click and receive a call from a contact center agent qualified to handle their request. The customer can continue browsing the web site until a telephone rep calls to assist, which usually doesn't take long. The customer avoids waiting on hold and navigating an IVR tree of options.

Off-shore contact centers: Some companies opt to use contact centers in the Caribbean, Philippines, Central America, India and other countries to reduce labor costs. When a sales relationship is not at stake, off-shore call centers can do well. However when a sales relationship is at stake, the labor cost savings can sometimes be surpassed by other costs. These arise due to increased talk time, a larger number of callbacks and even loss of customers. The reasons are that off-shore agents are often not empowered to do more than read a script, and the cultural differences between countries. Plan carefully and thoughtfully if you are considering off-shore for customer service, technical support or sales calls.

Home Agents: One of the growth areas for contact center is the use of home agents. This enables a company to hire qualified staff, reduce expenses for physical space and reduce its carbon footprint. It makes it possible for some who could not commute to a call center to work for one. Some companies have home agents telecommute a majority of the time and come to a physical call center one or two days a week, while others are entirely virtual. Virtual organizations require extra organizational infrastructure including on-line chats, webinars and teleconferences, to successfully communicate company practices with reps and to create a contact center culture.

Speech Analytics: Speech analytics are being used by some large contact centers to identify issues not caught by monitoring. The most common type of speech analytics *listens* to phone calls by transforming speech-to-text, and performs word spotting, looking for particular words or phrases such as *mad, upset, refund or supervisor*, to identify calls with issues. A very sophisticated variation on speech analytics focuses on the tone of voice and emotional state of customers and identifies those who are upset, in real time, so that a supervisor may intervene.

Legal and Regulatory Compliance

Contact centers are a regulated way of doing business, and some ways of doing business via telecommunications are more regulated than others. Responding to incoming customer service emails and web chats in a non-sales situation may be governed by the fewest regulations. Inbound calls, especially when no sales efforts are involved, are minimally regulated. Outbound consumer sales calls are heavily regulated, although fewer rules govern calling one's customers and recent inquirers and most business-to-business outbound sales calls. Unsolicited fax and pre-recorded outbound calls *for sales purposes* are illegal in the U.S. Here is a top level summary of some of the major rules. However a compliance program must be based on more detailed, program-specific and up-to-date regulatory information than can be conveyed here.

Both inbound and outbound calls: For both inbound and outbound calls, call monitoring requires one-party consent (e.g., the phone rep) in most states, and all-party consent in others. The process for paying over the phone, particularly by phone check or periodic credit card charges (sometimes called auto-pay), is prescribed by U.S. law. Contact centers must employ practices to protect prospect and customer information against data breaches, and in the event of a breach must promptly notify those who may be affected

Outbound consumer sales calls: Outbound consumer sales calls are heavily regulated. Every company that places outbound consumer sales calls is required to maintain a company-specific do-not-call list, and to scrub calling lists against it before placing calls. This company specific list is the repository of the telephone numbers of those who have directly asked your company not to call, either on a previous call or via a similar personal communications. During the scrubbing process, those on the calling list who are also on the do-not-call list are *scrubbed* from the calling list.

Additionally, consumer calling lists are subject to scrubbing against the National Do-Not-Call (DNC) Registry, as well as to offer and disclosure laws enacted by the U.S. and many states. There are specific exceptions to National DNC Registry scrubbing for existing customers and recent inquirers. Inquiries must have occurred within the preceding 90 days under U.S. federal law. This is made more complex by a handful of state laws that specify a period that is shorter or even zero days. Also, a few states totally prohibit outbound consumer sales calls.

Companies that only call existing customers, recently lapsed customers and prospects who have inquired within the past 90 days are not required by federal law to scrub against the national Do-Not-Call Registry. Each client company that is required to scrub must pay for its own annual subscription to the registry, even if it sub-contracts the actual scrubbing to its contact center or another vendor. The first five area codes are free. At the time this is being written, the charge for each additional area code is $55 per year up to a maximum of $15,058 per year for all U.S. area codes.

There are a number of additional laws governing outbound consumer sales calls. Examples are those that prohibit the use of objection-responses (sometimes called rebuttals) in certain states, rules that require transmission of specific caller ID information and federal and state laws that restrict calling hours. A handful of states prohibit outbound sales calls on particular holidays. Additionally, federal law prohibits calls to cell phones if a computer dials the number (unless the marketer can prove it has the cell phone owner's specific permission to call).

Business-to-business outbound sales calls: With the exception of *non-durable office or cleaning supplies*, business-to-business sales calls are not included in the most prominent U.S. federal outbound calling regulation, which is scrubbing against the do-not-call registry. State laws vary in this regard.

Canada also has a do-not-call registry and its own set of regulations. These are similar to U.S federal regulations, but are not identical. Similarly, other countries often have regulations as well.

Responsibility for non-compliance: Many companies require the contact center to take responsibility for regulatory compliance, specifying this in writing, as part of the contract. Many have the contact center indemnify the client company for the results of non-compliance due to contact center company negligence. They also have the contact center describe activities that the client must carry out as its partner in compliance. However, when a violation occurs, the government pursues all parties involved and has a history of levying the largest penalties against the culpable party with the deepest pockets. It holds corporations responsible for non-compliance by its subcontractors and independent agents, particularly if a corporation does not take the specific pro-active steps to assure compliance by its agents and their employees outlined in past regulatory actions. Most prominently, the U.S. Federal Trade Commission (FTC) fined DirecTV $5.3 million in 2005, for the actions of independent sales agents selling its satellite TV service. Significantly, in 2009, DirecTV paid a second penalty of $2.31 million for another set of Do-Not-Call and related violations by its telemarketer's sales reps. Its telemarketing firm, a much smaller company, was required to pay a penalty of $115,000 in this 2009 action.

If your company is making outbound consumer sales calls, it is essential to make pro-active efforts to *periodically* confirm that you and your contact center are complying with all applicable federal and state regulations. This should include an audit to determine that both are properly implementing compliance policies and practices, in keeping with regulators' mandates. In fact, this is a prudent measure for all contact center programs.

Also, make sure the contact center has a process in place for keeping all relevant staff informed of changes in federal and state regulations.

Creative Strategy at Work

There are a large number of nuts and bolts in contact center programs. Program managers who strategically select nuts and bolts that are well suited to their program usually experience successful results. Here are a few examples of exceptionally creative approaches to doing so, although please understand that all are based in suitability to the program, which is always the most important factor.

Consumer marketer Zappos puts the right people in its inbound call center: Zappos, the online shoe retailer, has done an exemplary job of creating a service-oriented culture. They begin early and weed out reps who are not fully engaged in Zappos' culture of making customers happy. How? At the conclusion of training, Zappos offers trainees $1,000 . . . to leave the company. Think about the personal and professional qualities of those who choose to leave and those who stay.

JetBlue inbound call center takes off: When JetBlue was a start-up, it wanted to deliver good service by phone but had to do so at a reasonable cost. It decided to use 100% U.S. based home agents, so that it could recruit better quality reps than might do the same work at the same wages at a centralized call center, and to distinguish itself from airlines with overseas call centers.

American Medical Association uses segmentation and conditional close to boost outbound sales: The American Medical Association was selling a directory listing all physicians, their specialties and professional backgrounds to state medical societies, medical libraries, university libraries and others. A direct mail piece was followed by a telephone call. Due to specific modifications, the outbound business-to-business phone campaign produced roughly 400% more sales than in the past.

First, a section early in the script was tailored to each market segment, so state medical societies received a message tailored to them, as did university libraries and other key segments. Second, we discovered that many buyers required approval from a committee or board to purchase, but usually didn't remember to put the purchase on the agenda. Using a *conditional close*, the sales reps told buyers they would be sent an invoice that states the sale is subject to board or committee approval. If approval was received, the organization would pay the invoice and receive the directory. If not approved, they could simply disregard the invoice. The invoice assured that the purchase was on the board or committee agenda, and the purchase was usually approved.

Charity Easter Seals gets a celebrity on the phone for outbound calls: Easter Seals designed an outbound calling program to remind Chicago area supporters about a fund-raising event. The emcee of the event was a famous local TV and radio sportscaster, Jack Brickhouse (now deceased). The phone reps called supporters and said, *I have a message for you from Jack Brickhouse.* They then played a recording Jack Brickhouse had made asking people to come to the event. That evening, many supporters were surely telling their friends, *I received a phone call from Jack Brickhouse today . . .*

Lands' End segments inbound staff to handle calls and web chats: Phone calls and Web chats require an immediate response, while emails require a response within a matter of hours. Contact center reps who can handle both calls and web chats have more skills than those who can only do one or the other, and so command higher wages. The incremental cost of hiring only reps who can handle all forms of customer contact can add up to a great deal of money in a large contact center.

Lands' End was an early adopter of web chat. To deliver speedy service at a reasonable cost, it employed a large rep group that only handled phone calls, and a smaller one that could handle phone calls, emails and web chats. The second group put emails aside for a short time to handle peaks in web chat or phone call traffic. This enabled Lands' End to deliver speedy service at a reasonable cost. How speedy? Lands' End handled 86–90% of calls handled within 20 seconds (about 4 rings), according to Angie Rundle, Supervisor for Internet Sales at the cataloguer.

Contact Center Program Success

So how does one decide what's appropriate and what won't cut it in the contact center? Experience helps a great deal. The best is experience designing, implementing *and measuring* contact center programs. The proof of the effectiveness of strategic and creative choices is usually in the numbers.

Secondarily, rely on your personal experience as a business-to-business prospect or customer, and as a consumer. What engages you in contact center programs? What turns you off? Instead of thinking about them as an abstract mass, put yourself in each of your prospects' or customers' shoes. Would that offer appeal to you? Would you like speaking with that telephone rep? Would you answer the question if it was worded that way? What would make you interested in discussing the product or service? Simply thinking about your program through the filter of the golden rule, *do unto others as you would like done unto you*, will help make your contact center program more customer-focused, successful and profitable.

MITCHELL LIEBER is a frequent speaker on customer contact and president of the consulting firm Lieber & Associates (www.LieberAndAssociates.com). The firm assists companies with call and contact center improvement, strategy, customer experience, management studies, technology and training. Mitchell Lieber pioneered call center innovations in areas of customer experience, call routing, sales, customer centric service and metrics. He was an early predictor of major transformations in mobile marketing, use of the web, call centers overseas, outbound call regulation and call center technology. He is past chair of the Board of Governors of the DMA International ECHO Awards and founder of its ECHO Academy. Mitchell Lieber may be reached at m_lieber@lieberandassociates.com or 773-325-0608.

Marketing Upgrade: Using Web 2.0 to Connect, Build and Sell

STEPHEN K. KOERNIG

Associate Professor of Marketing at DePaul University

NEIL GRANITZ

Professor of Marketing at California State University, Fullerton

Web 2.0 is a second generation of web-based tools, such as social networking sites (e.g. MySpace, Facebook), social sharing sites (e.g. YouTube, Flickr), wikis, and blogs, that has seen explosive growth. A Nielsen study found that over 66% of the worldwide Internet population could be reached through social networks—more than through email, which many view as antiquated. According to the Pew Research Center, adoption and use of Web 2.0 sites is especially high among teens and young adults (a coveted audience by advertisers). Seventy-three percent of American teens use social networking sites, and 45% of 18–29 year olds visit Web 2.0 sites at least once per day. A 2010 eMarketer study indicated that users spend more time on social media than they do on email. Not surprisingly, a recent research study indicates that college students exhibit physical symptoms of withdrawal if they are isolated from social media devices and Web 2.0 sites.

Web 2.0 presents significant opportunities for marketers to connect with customers and build relationships in ways they never have before. Whether you are promoting your company, your personal business, your next career move or a local event, it is critical to understand the value of Web 2.0 to enhance your business or career. This reading will provide you with a better understanding of the new social media landscape, and will present strategies for businesses and individuals to use social media sites to build awareness, increase visibility and engage in conversations with potential and existing customers.

Web 1.0: The Beginning

The advent of the World Wide Web in the early nineties, and the subsequent rapid increase in the adoption and use of the web, was fueled in part by innovations from some (now) well-known companies. America Online (AOL) helped to migrate people onto the web, while Yahoo! and Google made content on the web easily searchable and accessible. The Internet quickly became an integral part of consumers' everyday lives, especially as a significant and influential source of information for consumers about a variety of topics. At the same time, many companies recognized the potential of the web to provide consumers with an almost unlimited amount of information at an extremely low cost, and the number of corporate homepages exploded. In addition to providing information, many organizations also began to use their web sites as a vehicle for consumers to purchase products in addition to (or instead of) their bricks and mortar stores. Companies rushed to develop other business models to take advantage of this emergent technology. Some of the new business models that were tested in the early dot-com days included connect-time revenue splits (AOL, *USA Today*), online auctions (eBay), reverse auctions (FreeMarkets), affiliate/pay-for-performance (Amazon, Barnes & Noble), microcharging (iTunes), and infomediary models (Travelocity, Kelly Blue Book). Thus began the dot-com bubble.

Unfortunately, many of these early business models were not successful. Even though many companies struggled to integrate this new technology into their marketing strategy, thought leaders predicted that after the dot-com shakeout it would not be a matter of whether or not a company used the Internet, but rather how they used it. Currently, companies' use of web sites to provide information and facilitate purchase of products is ubiquitous. Other business models such as auctions and micro-charging have also been quite successful (e.g., Priceline, eBay, iTunes).

Consumer and organizational use of the Internet continues to evolve. The current focus is on collaboration and sharing of content versus passive viewing of content. This new generation of the web has been coined Web 2.0.

Web 2.0: The Present

Tim O'Reilly, an early pioneer of Web 2.0, defines it as follows:

> "Web 2.0 is the network as platform, spanning all connected devices; Web 2.0 applications are those that make the most of the intrinsic advantages of that platform; delivering software as a continually updated service that gets better the more people use it, consuming and remixing data from multiple sources, including individual users, while providing their own data and services in a form that allows remixing by others, creating network effects though an architecture of participation and going beyond the page metaphor of Web 1.0 to deliver rich user experiences" (O'Reilly, 2005).

Web 2.0 developed through the convergence of several existing technologies (see Table R16.1). The concerted use of this technology (and the related tools) has created new "Principles of Web 2.0" (see Table R16.2). Simply stated, Web 2.0 revolves around the social use of the web to create and share information. Collaboration in this creation of new content can take place through many social platforms, including email, chat rooms, message boards, blogs, micro-blogs, podcasts, social networking sites, video/photo sharing sites, wikis, social bookmarking, mashups, news aggregation, and RSS feeds. Harnessing the collective intelligence of the masses through these platforms accelerates and enhances the learning process and the creation of knowledge.

Similar to the dot-com frenzy, many companies are frantically embracing Web 2.0 without a full understanding of how/when/why to use it. One thing is for certain—to remain relevant, companies need to embrace Web 2.0. The question is: Which Web 2.0 tools are appropriate, and how can/should companies use them?

TABLE R16.1: WEB 2.0 TECHNOLOGY TOOLS*

Social Networking Software This software allows users to connect, create, post, and network with other users.	**Examples** Facebook, MySpace, Twitter
Collaboration Tools A wiki is a site that allows users to add and amend content and is used primarily for collaborative authoring; these tools often allow individuals to rate a posted comment or document.	**Examples** Wikipedia, Wikia
Self Expression Tools These tools include blogs, vlogs and podcasts. Blog stands for web log and is a personal diary that is available for the public to read and follow. Several blog search engines allow users to find blogs in the blogosphere (community of all blogs). A vlog is simply the video equivalent of a blog. A podcast is a series of audio or video digital media files which are distributed over the Internet to portable media players and computers; new content is downloaded automatically using RSS (Real Simple Syndication).	**Examples** Blogs: Blogger, WordPress Blog search engines: Technorati, IceRocket Vlogs: FreeVlog, Rocketboom Podcasts: Ask a Ninja, iTunes
Productivity Software These are free web-based software tools that offer a toolbox of capabilities similar to desktop software such as Microsoft Office.	**Examples** Google Docs
Content Tracking Tools A permalink is a URL for a resource that never changes and is always available. Thanks to the permalink, users can keep track of, filter and search a growing amount of Web 2.0 content.	**Examples** Digg, Delicious
Remix and Mashup Tools A remix is the reworking of an original work. A mashup involves the combination of two or more works that may be very different from one another. An application programming interface (API) is often used to accomplish this. Thus, two different web sites are integrated to create a unique third web site.	**Examples** Yahoo Pipes Mashup Search Engine: ProgrammableWeb

* Taken from Granitz and Koernig, *Journal of Marketing Education* (2011)

TABLE R16.2: PRINCIPLES OF WEB 2.0[*]

Web 2.0 is participative; users create value. The traditional view of the web has been one-sided with publishers pushing out content to users; however, low cost tools (access to software, Internet, bandwidth and open source code) allow mass collaboration.	**Example** The California Open-Source Textbook Project offers a new model for creating textbooks by leveraging currently available free content, the expertise of faculty and innovative copyright tools such as Creative Commons.
Web 2.0 is a platform that facilitates the free creation and sharing of information. Organizations offer services (in the form of free software) that attract users to their sites and gives them tools to create their environment. These services allow for a high degree of scalability by allowing individuals to share the information that they have created with an almost unlimited number of people.	**Example** Google delivers free services over the web, such as Google Sites, allowing users to create and edit web pages. Google Sites allows control over who can access and change this content.
Crowdsourcing/Bottom up structure. By users sharing knowledge with the public, the knowledge process is accelerated. Tapscott and Williams (2006) call this "peering": when people self-organize to create knowledge, share experiences or design goods and services.	**Example** In a bid to find mining locations, Goldcorp opened up their databases to scientists, geologists and engineers in the general population.
Success is based on the ability to harness collective intelligence. O'Reilly (2005) refers to the web as a giant global brain.	**Example** Web 2.0 success stories like YouTube, Facebook and MySpace are from organizations that were able to harness collective intelligence.
Web 2.0 is about remix and mashup and creation. End users are rapidly gaining access to content that was once considered proprietary and are exercising the power of creation and distribution.	**Example** The Chicago Police Department employs a web application called "Clearmap" to mash crime data from their online database with Google Maps.

[*] Taken from Granitz and Koernig, *Journal of Marketing Education* (2011)

How is Web 2.0 Different?

Before we get into a discussion of the strategic uses of Web 2.0, a quick discussion of traditional marketing strategy is in order. The marketing "old guard" revolved around the "Four P's": product, price, place (distribution), and promotion. Specifically, promotion includes four main activities including sales promotions, advertising, personal selling, and public relations—all of which an organization can control. However, while an organization has complete control over their public relations strategy, they are at the mercy of independent news sources to spread their message. Possible outcomes of an organization's public relations strategy may be positive publicity, negative publicity, or the very real possibility of no publicity. When positive publicity results from the public relations effort, the organization benefits in two main ways: 1) consumers tend to trust the message compared to a paid advertisement, and 2) the cost for this publicity is negligible, thus resulting in essentially free advertising for the organization. Thus, the primary goal of a public relations campaign is to build positive word-of mouth (WOM) through trusted independent sources. For example, in the pre-Web 2.0 days, restaurant-goers might read a review about a new restaurant in the "Food" section of the *Los Angeles Times* online. The restaurant hopes that the review reports favorably on their food, service and ambience, but they cannot control what is written.

The organization embracing Web 2.0 is faced with challenges similar to their public relations efforts—both are *strategies* over which the company has complete control, but they do not have control over the *outcome* of said efforts. An organization can expect outcomes similar to a PR campaign as a result of their Web 2.0 efforts: positive "buzz", negative buzz, or no buzz. In a Web 2.0 campaign, the buzz is no longer created by independent new sources; rather consumers shape the message and share it among their friends. As a consumer, whom do you trust more? Companies, or people that you regularly interact with? You probably answered the latter! Traditionally, people have shared positive brand experiences with about three people, but share negative experiences with up to 10 people. Thus, in the pre-Web 2.0 era, a positive or negative buzz would build slowly over time. However, Web 2.0 gives consumers the ability to disseminate information instantaneously—to potentially be viewed by millions of people. As such, in an accelerated timeframe, consumer chatter on Web 2.0 sites like Yelp can have a significant impact on the success or failure of your organization. This increases the efficiency of markets where high-quality products are revered and quickly made successful, and low-quality products are besmirched and briskly disregarded.

Web 2.0 developed organically as a means by which people could build and maintain personal relationships, and the "Holy Grail" for Web 2.0 marketers is to tap into these friendship networks to create relationships with consumers and harness their power to spread positive buzz about the brand. The critical issue for organizations is how they can and should tap into this vast potential. Unfortunately, many companies are jumping into the deep end without an understanding of what they want the social media efforts to achieve. In the next section, we offer guidance to help organizations better understand the strategic uses of Web 2.0.

Web 2.0 and Marketing: A Strategic Philosophy

Before launching into the specific marketing strategy elements, we would like to lay out a general philosophy that companies can use when approaching the use of Web 2.0. First, consumers view Web 2.0 as a place where they can meet and connect with others; that is also how companies should see it. It is your chance to mix with consumers and put a face on your business. For example, *A Thousand Words* is a blog written by people who work at Kodak. The byline reads, "We love what we do, and we want to share our stories about imaging and its power to influence our world. We invite you to join our conversation with stories of your own." In this case it is the face of the actual Kodak employees. Second, Web 2.0 is about creating contexts for interaction and engaging a community. It is the next logical step in relationship marketing where companies can create lasting relationships with their constituents. With its Refresh Project, Pepsi is building online community through offline community. They are awarding money to people, businesses, and non-profits that have ideas to positively impact their community. Ideas are submitted by constituents and then voted on by the community. The Refresh Project blog also includes stories of people who have enacted their refresh projects. Third, the purpose of Web 2.0 should be to listen and respond. Companies should draw consumers to their social media sites and listen. If needed, they should respond. Burt's Bees, best known for their beeswax lip balm, had 114,000 members on its Facebook page at a recent count. If one peruses the page, there are positive fans who are loving the products or mentioning negative issues they have with the products; Burt's Bees is responding when necessary. For example, a fan comment of , "I love the toothpaste" gets no response; but the comment, "I am a Burt's Bees advocate, but . . . in the past week, my 15 month old and my friend's baby of the same age had a horrible allergic reaction to the Baby Bees Buttermilk Lotion," gets the response, "We are very sorry to hear of the reaction that your child had with our Baby Bee Buttermilk Lotion," as well as contact info so that the customer can follow-up. Fourth, Social media should not constitute your entire marketing plan; it plays one part of your integrated marketing plan where all the pieces work together to create a positive ROI. Corporations should not use social media for the hard-sell; that is the job of your web site and brick and mortar store. Consumers come to Web 2.0 to connect with friends. This is your chance to be friends with your consumers; friends don't ask friends to buy anything. However, through repeated positive interactions, trust and long-term relationships can develop, which subsequently can lead to sustained sales.

Strategic Marketing Uses of Web 2.0

In this section, examples of successful and unsuccessful Web 2.0 strategies are presented. These are organized around the marketing strategies where Web 2.0 is most advantageous. The outcome of these strategies is reported when it is available; however in some cases the company has not reported the degree of success (or failure) of their Web 2.0 efforts.

Market Research

It is imperative that every company—no matter how large or small—at least dip their toe in the Web 2.0 waters. An excellent entry point for the novice involves monitoring what consumers are saying online about their brand. For an organization completely unfamiliar with Web 2.0, this might require the company's new social media "expert" to first research the use of Web 2.0 by consumers of their product. This will provide the organization with an introduction to some of the specific sites that are currently popular. Additionally, they can search online resources such as Sphinn, Google Knol, or Technorati. A history of these searches can be maintained by bookmarking these articles using Web 2.0 sites such as Delicious, StumbleUpon and Digg.

After building competence with these Web 2.0 sites, the focus should shift to "listening" to customers' (actual, former, and potential) online conversations about your brand. General search engines like Google or Bing are effective at casting a wide net to find these conversations. For a large multinational brand, it might be easy to find conversations about your products; in this case, the difficult task will likely be sifting through all of the clutter to find relevant comments. For example, a search for Starbucks (the coffee brand) might result in a huge number of "hits" that may or may not be related to your search. Instead, you might find results related to news about Starbucks, general corporate information, or even hits related to the character Starbuck from the television series *Battlestar Galactica*![1]. The objective of these searches is to determine where your customers and friends are talking online. Depending on the industry, your customers and friends might be congregating in particular Web 2.0 sites. For example, wine-related blogs such as *Vinography*, *The Wine Blog*, and *Dr. Vono's Wine Blog*, would be good starting points for a wine producer (or seller) to gauge reaction to their products. A perusal of these sites might also provide clues about other Web 2.0 sites that are popular with this audience.

Once a comprehensive search has been conducted (and digested), it is important that the ongoing conversations be monitored. Tools like Google Alerts and Really Simple Syndication (RSS) feeds are useful in this regard. Google Alerts is a free service offered by Google that monitors the web for new content. The user enters search terms and when new content is created on blogs, new sites, etc. matching the search terms, an update is sent via email with the updates. The user can control the frequency of these updates: "once a day", "once a week", or "as it happens". RSS (Really Simple Syndication) feeds give the user a more targeted approach to receive updates about new content, typically from sites that are updated often such as news sites and blogs. By clicking on the RSS icon on a web site, the user subscribes to the site and receives automated updates from it.

Listening to consumers' conversations will result in the following benefits. First, the process of searching Web 2.0 sites will help build knowledge of and comfort with Web 2.0 sites. Second, listening to what your customers are saying is an easy and timely way to collect market research about consumer attitudes, consumer demographics, complaints about your products, new product ideas and uses, and attitudes

---

[1] More on the importance of search terms can be found in the Social Media Marketing Measurement presented later in this chapter.

toward competitors' products. Third, it provides you with an opportunity to participate in the conversation. After finding conversations about your brand on Web 2.0
sites (e.g., blog posts, videos on YouTube, Tweets on Twitter, etc.), you can comment
on the appropriate blog or interact with customers through the social media site. For
example, in New York, Pretzel Crisps launched the billboard ad campaign, "You can
never be too thin". The ad was seen by many as encouraging anorexia and was posted
on the women's blog site, Jezebel, followed by condemning comments and tweets.
The next day, Pretzel Crisps sent out an email to bloggers thanking them for their
feedback, explaining that they thought the word thin was a good way to describe their
product and assuring readers that the ads would be removed.

Ignoring these conversations is dangerous. One of the characteristics of Web 2.0 is
rapid dissemination of information, and if a negative (or positive) buzz is building, it
will build fast. In fact, ignoring Web 2.0 conversations can lead to a public relations
nightmare. For example, in 2009, two Domino's Pizza employees posted a video on
YouTube purportedly showing one of the employees putting a piece of cheese up his
nose (among other, more disgusting, things) and then onto a sandwich being prepared for delivery. Domino's was not actively listening to online conversations about
their brand, and was unaware of this video until advised by a blogger of its existence.
Even after being alerted to the video, Domino's did not immediately respond in an attempt to reduce the damage of the video. In the meantime, bloggers discovered the
exact location of the store by using other businesses shown through the window to
triangulate the location. By the time Domino's reacted to this public relations nightmare, the number of views of the video had surpassed one million in just a few days,
damaging the company's reputation and sales.

Blogging and Targeting Influencers

A web log, or "blog", is a web site which includes written thoughts (about anything
and everything) that may include pictures, sounds, and videos. Many early blogs
functioned as a type of online diary. For example, Stephanie Klein achieved early
fame as a blogger (her blog is called Greek Tragedy) due to her provocative blog
about her personal and professional life (think Sex and the City). She abandoned her
career as an art director for an ad agency in New York to become a full-time blog-
ger/writer after *The New York Times* ran a story about her in the "Sunday Styles" section. Since then, she has continued to blog, and has also parlayed her success as a
blogger into two book deals—both memoirs.

Over time, the blogging community has exploded. An eMarketer study found
that 31% of Americans blog and 89% of them welcome contact from a PR firm.
This growth is due in part to Blogger.com and WordPress.com, the two most commonly used blogging platforms. Both allow any users to set up blog platforms for
free. Blogger has undisclosed millions of users while WordPress boasts over 2 million active blogs. As a result, blogs evolved beyond people's personal musings and
became more focused on particular areas of interest. Some of the more popular
blogging subjects include (but are certainly not limited to) politics, music, travel,
fashion, and food/drink. As blogging increased in popularity, companies realized
the potential for independent bloggers to reach—and influence—large numbers of
people. In 2008, Procter & Gamble identified "mommy bloggers" as an important

and persuasive group of influencers for their product lines (especially their Baby Care and Family Care business segments). To tap into the potential of these influencers, P&G invited 15 mommy bloggers to visit the P&G headquarters in Cincinnati, OH, for an all expense paid trip including airfare, hotel accommodations, tours of the P&G facilities, and group discussions with other mommy bloggers and P&G executives about moms, babies, and P&G products. According to P&G, "We've made it clear that we are not pitching products per se, but exploring areas of common interest, such as baby development and how to help moms in this topsy-turvy time in their lives." Of course, P&G hoped that these influential bloggers would blog about their experience with the company and their products in a positive way—and they did.

A company can also create its own blog. For example, Best Western sponsors a blog, On the Go with Amy, where the author travels the country writing about her experiences. Unlike the above example where an independent blogger promotes the brand (and thus is seen as a credible source), the company-sponsored blog may be seen as a type of advertisement; therefore, it is especially critical that the blog creates value for the consumer. It should deliver fresh and relevant content for your audience that is worth sharing . . . otherwise what is the reason for people to come together and form a community around your brand? For example, on the Best Western blog, Amy visits large cities and small towns in America, reviewing major tourist attractions and off-beat places to visit. A company-sponsored blog is ideal for products with steep learning curves (e.g., high tech products, baby related products, or financial services), when there is a lifestyle associated with brand (e.g., autos, alcohol, or travel) or to promote a social mission (e.g., environmental, homelessness, aid to third world countries).

A major theme of any Web 2.0-oriented strategy should be openness, honesty, and transparency. The company that fails to heed this advice may suffer a backlash from consumers. For example, Wal-Mart's ad agency (Edelman Worldwide) created and paid for a "flog" (fake blog), "Wal-Marting Across America", documenting the adventures of a couple on a cross-country road trip. Along their journey, the couple parked their RV in Wal-Mart parking lots overnight to sleep. They also frequently posted on their blog about Wal-Mart employees that they purportedly spoke with who all voiced their love of working for the company. However, the "couple" were actually professional journalists who were backed and funded by Edelman. This lack of transparency was in violation of the Word of Mouth Marketing Association's Code of Ethics, which Edelman helped to create. Chronicled in a major story in *Business Week*, this added to consumers' pre-existing negative perceptions of Wal-Mart, most likely hurting their sales.

Promotions

Currently, one of the most popular uses of Web 2.0 is for sales promotions. The goal of sales promotions is to increase short-term sales and to get new customers to try the brand—and hopefully become brand loyal. Because of its shortness and immediacy, Twitter, the micro-blogging site, is an ideal tool to use for this. A California pizza chain, Z'Pizza, places ads in local "traditional" media stating that if you followed them on Twitter, you would already know about today's deal. Besides promoting existing specials, there should be online specials to keep consumers following your Twitter account. For example, JetBlue has over 6,000 followers and tweets its online and off-line deals. Naked Pizza, a New Orleans pizza chain hoping to go national, started to track Twitter-inspired sales. In a test, an exclusive Twitter offer brought in 15% of a day's business.

Social networking sites, like Facebook, also provide significant opportunities to increase short-term sales and to foster brand loyalty among current and potential consumers. Sprinkles Cupcakes is an extremely effective example of the successful use of Facebook to promote the brand and to increase consumer engagement with their brand. To rapidly increase its number of Facebook "friends", Sprinkles ran a "BFF Contest". The goal of this contest was to increase the number of friends that Sprinkles had on Facebook to 100,000 (from a little over 30,000). From the start of the promotion until the 100,000th friend (or the contest deadline), anyone who "friended" Sprinkles on Facebook was entered in the contest. The grand prize was a trip for two to Beverly Hills; the location of the first Sprinkles bakery. This promotion helped Sprinkles to quickly meet (and exceed) its goal of 100,000 friends. To keep consumers engaged with the brand, on Facebook and Twitter, Sprinkles posts a secret phrase that customers can "whisper" at a Sprinkles store to receive a free cupcake. Einstein Bros. Bagels also used a Facebook promotion to increase engagement with its customers and to obtain new customers. If a consumer was a "fan" of Einstein Bros. Bagels, they could download one in-store coupon for a free bagel and "schmear" of cream cheese. The promotion was a huge success in terms of getting new fans (from 4,700 at the beginning of the promotion to over 336,000 in three days). Healthy Choice has attempted to exponentially increase the number of people who "like" their brand on Facebook by increasing the value of a coupon as the number of new people joining the page increases during the duration of the promotion. In a little over 24 hours, the number of Healthy Choice fans tripled (to about 53,000 fans); the coupon also grew from 75 cents off to $1.25 off of the next purchase. As the number of fans continued to grow, the coupon morphed into a buy-one-get-one-free offer.

Social media sharing sites, like YouTube, are especially good at increasing engagement among consumers by facilitating the creation of content involving the brand. Procter & Gamble promoted its Crest Whitening Expressions brand through a "catch-phrase" contest. To replace their "Bam!" tagline (made famous by Emeril Lagasse, a celebrity endorser of the brand), Crest asked YouTube users to create and post a video describing their experience with the brand in 10 words or less for the Wintergreen Ice flavor. In a similar vein, Klondike sponsored a "What Would You Do?" contest to reinvigorate the brand with a new audience using their classic tagline. In this contest, consumers created and posted videos on YouTube describing the lengths that they would go for a Klondike bar. Not only do these contests increase engagement with the brand (the Klondike winner actually went to the Arctic to film part of his video), but they also have the potential to be viewed and shared by a large number of other people (e.g., going viral) if the video is funny, cute, or otherwise compelling. Interesting, as of this writing, the winning Klondike video had over 8,600 views on YouTube. However a popular losing entry (submitted by YouTube user "BriTANicK") generated significantly more buzz and has been viewed over 663,000 times.

Ideally, multiple Web 2.0 platforms should be used in the sales promotion. For example, Coca-Cola conducted a nationwide search for three people to serve as ambassadors for the company. Coke fans were involved from the outset by voting on the nine finalists. The three winners traveled to every country in which Coca-Cola products are sold (206) over the course of 365 days. The three contest winners used a variety of social networking sites (including but limited to Facebook, YouTube, Twitter, and Flickr) to document their journey with a focus on finding "what makes people happy" in the various countries they visited.

Customer Service

Customer service is another extremely popular use of Web 2.0. In fact, many social media sites are emerging as new (and more efficient) replacements for email and phone centers. American Airlines asked customers with complaints to email them. There was a 13% increase in email complaints but a 74% increase in downstream traffic to MySpace. Many Web 2.0 sites are ideally suited to serve as quick and inexpensive substitutes for the often-maligned customer service call centers. For example, Frank Eliason, the (now former) Director of Digital Care for Comcast, was instrumental in spearheading the use of Web 2.0 sites to assist customers experiencing problems with their Comcast service. Through the Twitter account @ComcastCares, Frank searched for customers Tweeting about problems and asked "Can I help?" He typically was able to address their problem either on the Twitter site, or for more complex problems he asked the customer to "DM" (direct message; Twitter's version of email) him with their contact information. JetBlue has also embraced Twitter to help assist customers with problems they encounter with the airline, such as flight delays and misplaced baggage. Additionally, they promote new flight routes and special promotions, provide information about airports (e.g. availability of power outlets and access to WiFi), and monitor (and respond to) conversations about JetBlue occurring in real time on Twitter. Many organizations have discovered that an added advantage of solving problems via a Tweet is that customers with similar issues also can see the solution to the problem. In addition, when you publicly solve a problem, you are publicizing good customer service to your constituents.

New Product Development

In a 2006 *Wired* magazine article, Jeff Howe coined the term "crowd-sourcing" to describe the use of customers, potential customers, and other stakeholders as your labor pool to produce your product or service. By its very nature, crowd-sourcing is often perceived to be risky for many companies because the more the product/service is crowd-sourced, the less control the company has over the message and the brand image. However, it is also a very powerful tool to generate new product ideas—and to engage customers with your brand.

Crowd-sourcing can be directly or indirectly used to develop new products. Indirectly, using social media to just listen to customers, for customer service or for product promotions may spur the idea for a new product. For example, Ben & Jerry's started an online "Free Cone Day" to complement their offline Free Cone Day. Facebook users could give their friends a "virtual cone" that would appear on their Facebook wall. This promotion helped bring consumers to their Facebook page, where numerous discussions took place regarding favorite flavors, the availability of flavors, and ideas for new flavors. Other companies have found that changing a package or logo without asking for consumers' opinions first may result in a backlash. In 2009, Tropicana changed their packaging; the longtime symbol of an orange with a straw in it was replaced with a glass of orange juice. Using social media, customer complained. On Facebook, one customer wrote, "My nine-year-old freaked out when he saw the new branding. Yikes! We couldn't force ourselves to buy it." Tropicana promptly reverted to their original packaging. In 2010, Gap changed its logo from the familiar blue background with white lettering to a white background with black letters and a little blue box. On Facebook and Twitter, there was an incredible amount of outcry against the logo. One week later, the company announced (on Facebook) that it would be reverting back to its original logo. Company spokespersons also stated that they should have used social media to involve their consumers in the creation of the new logo. In both cases, consumers rapidly complained that the originals were far superior, and the companies took this information to heart and reverted back to the original designs. Their rapid response likely prevented a long, drawn out battle, which would serve neither company well.

Directly, you can ask customers for ideas for new products. Starbucks offers a site, MyStarbucksIdeas, where users can post their own ideas and vote on the ideas of others. At the time of this writing, the idea of Starbucks offering a birthday brew had received 79,400 votes. Modcloth, a small online clothing retailer, lets consumers "be the buyer". Samples of women's dresses are put on the company web site for 14 days, and during this time consumers can vote for the dress by clicking on a "pick it!" or "skip it!" button. They can also post comments about what they like and don't like about the dress. This provides the company with extremely valuable customer input, which helps them decide which dresses to produce. When a decision is made to manufacture a dress, consumers who voted "pick it!" are sent an email letting them know about their "win", which reminds them about the brand and encourages purchase of the dress.

Sales

For most companies, directly increasing sales should not be a primary goal of the social media marketing strategy. Web 2.0 is about putting a face on business; it's giving consumers someone to trust. It's really about friends connecting with, creating with, and collaborating with each other. People like to talk about brands and identify with them and their fellow users on their Facebook page; however, they might not respond well on sales-oriented company intrusions. Imagine if every time you invited a friend over to dinner he or she tried to sell you something. Would you continue the "friendship" or stop inviting him for dinner?

However, Web 2.0 can be effective in generating sales under the right circumstances. For example, Dell offers consumers refurbished computers at low prices via their @DellOutlook Twitter account. Twitter has been very lucrative for Dell. According to Dell, the @DellOutlook Twitter account has generated revenue of $6.5 million from June 2007 through December 2009. By including links to their products in their Tweets, Dell is also able to track the effectiveness of each Twitter promotion.

An added advantage of drawing customers to the Dell web site via Twitter is that some customers decide to buy a new computer after visiting the Dell Outlet site.

Social Media Marketing Measurement

Although many companies have embraced Web 2.0, a large number of companies have struggled to determine whether or not their social media marketing efforts have been successful. According to eMarketer, as of September 2010, 47 percent of companies worldwide are not able to measure the effectiveness of their Web 2.0 efforts. (Thirty-five percent reported a similar or greater return or value than from other marketing activities.) Of course, measuring the impact of a Web 2.0 campaign may be more (or less) difficult depending on the strategic objectives of the social media marketing efforts. For example, measuring the effectiveness of using Twitter by Dell Outlet to increase sales is relatively easy compared to measuring Jet Blue's use of Twitter to improve customer service and provide customers with information.

In a majority of cases, it is difficult to measure the impact of social media marketing, especially if Web 2.0 is used to increase engagement among consumers with the brand. How do you know if your social media strategy is helping to increase engagement with your brands? If consumers are more engaged with your brands, they likely will be talking more about the brand online. In fact, this should be a primary goal of any Web 2.0 campaign. Thus, measuring the success of a specific Web 2.0 strategy can be done by comparing the online "chatter" before and after the firm's social media marketing efforts. This is actually quite similar to measuring the impact of an ad campaign on increasing brand awareness. For example, the organization measures brand awareness (and or sales) before and after the ad campaign to determine if there are any differences.

The critical issue is how to measure the buzz before and after the social media marketing event. Unlike advertising, there is no consensus on exactly how to do this. An extremely simple method of measuring the impact of your Web 2.0 strategy is to use a general search engine like Google or Bing to compare the number of conversations about your brand before and after your social media campaign. Of course, selecting the "right" search terms may prove to be extremely difficult. For example, do you use the brand name? The corporate name? Brand slogans? All of the above? Even if the "right" search terms are used, for a large multi-national brand, measurement still might prove difficult due to the amount of clutter online. However, for a relatively unknown brand (with little to no online conversation prior to the Web 2.0 campaign), measuring the impact of the social media campaign should be significantly easier.

The quest for an easy, accurate, and customary way to measure the impact of a Web 2.0 strategy has led to the development of public (for sale) and proprietary measurement systems. IBM developed data mining and text analytics software (sold under the SPSS Modeler brand) to help companies monitor and analyze what consumers are saying about their company, brands, products (and those of the competition) on blogs, Twitter, and other searchable Web 2.0 sites. This software uses a sentiment-analysis algorithm to gauge consumer emotions in these conversations; this is a relatively new technology that has yet to fully be developed.

Ad agencies, public relations firms, and other related industries have also rushed to develop tools to measure the outcome of a social media campaign. It is crucial for these organizations to gather this data so that they can demonstrate the impact of their services. For example, the Zócalo Group (a word of mouth and social media marketing agency and a division of Omnicom Group, Inc.), in collaboration with DePaul University marketing faculty, developed the Digital Footprint Index (DFI), which measures the outcome of a social media strategy along three dimensions: *height*, *width*, and *depth*. The *height* deals with the degree to which your brand is being talked about online, and tries to determine the overall volume of all brand mentions across online channels. This is determined by examining the number of blog posts, forum threads, tweets, videos, photos, social networking groups, etc. The *width* involves the degree that your brand conversation is being engaged with and shared by consumers. Different than height, the width is the sum of the engagement metrics for each channel analyzed in the height. Examples include the number of comments, thread replies, video views, photo views, Diggs, Twitter followers, bookmarks, etc. The *depth* tackles the issue of whether or not people are talking about your brand in the way you want them to; this includes the presence of a brand's keywords and messages in Web 2.0 conversations, as well as the tone of the conversation. Are a brand's messages adopted and used by consumers? Are the conversations positive or negative? At present, the height and width are fairly easy to measure using automated programs (assuming there is consensus on the specific sites to include in the search, which is no easy task), but the valence of the message is difficult to measure using people, and almost impossible to measure using automated programs. For example, let's assume that Starbucks conducts an aggressive Web 2.0 campaign promoting a line of 10 new products. In their attempt to measure the impact of this campaign, there may be three blog posts which all mention Starbucks (the coffee). The first blog post is very effusive about Starbucks, and even includes slogans from their new Web 2.0 campaign, but the post is vague as to reasons for this love (or even the products the poster likes). The second blog post is a critical evaluation of the new product releases in the style of *Consumer Reports*. Unfortunately, there is no consensus about the quality of the 10 new drinks—some receive favorable reviews, but others do not. The third post is a very negative one about the use of Web 2.0 to promote these new products. Currently, the only way to evaluate and compare the tone and content of these blog posts involves a subjective classification of the three messages.

In summary, when undertaking any Web 2.0 strategy, it is important that the company designate some measures of the outcome. As the field develops, more accurate, standardized lower cost measurement solutions will become available.

Paid Social Media

While social media web sites offer many "free" ways for organizations to market themselves, the stakeholders of these web sites must make money and offer several "paying" marketing tools that businesses can use to promote their product or service. As the specific properties are often changing their offerings, the discussion will focus on the general major marketing abilities that social media properties offer. To find the various options for each social media web site, one usually just scrolls to the bottom of the site and look for a "business solutions" or "advertising" link.

Banner ads: Banner ads are akin to traditional advertising where the business pays to have their ad appear on a particular page (regardless of the click-throughs). These ads are appropriate when you have to get the word out fast and hit a large general target. As an example, On the YouTube homepage, one might find an ad for the Call for Duty video game.

Targeted advertising: Some social media sites allow advertisers to target ads based upon demographic and personal information submitted to the site by the user. Targeted ads can be very effective in reaching a well-defined but narrow segment. For example, in composing their Facebook profile, a user may have listed that they are a female, aged 20 and like running. As a result, Nike may pay Facebook to place an ad for a female running shoe on this user's site. Furthermore if the user likes the ad, they may click a Like button on the ad and everyone in their network will see the ad and that the user liked it. On LinkedIn, similar targeting can be conducted; Fidelity targets education professionals with special 403k plans.

Content targeting: Some social media sites offer organizations the opportunity to advertise on site pages that match the content of the product or service that the organization is promoting; this is often called content targeting. This type of advertising goes beyond matching search keywords with advertisements; instead it matches the keywords of the search to the contents of Internet web pages, resulting in more useful and relevant search results. For example, on YouTube, a search for "hot dog" might pull up a promoted video by Heinz entitled, 57 Things You Can Eat with Heinz Ketchup.

Promotional search ads: Social media sites, like Twitter and Digg, allow organizations to have their results show up with the organic results searched by the user. Promotional ads work when you have short fast messages to relay. For example, a search on Digg for the latest news will also bring up the headline "Del Taco does Breakfast", with the byline, sponsored by Del Taco. Or under #nowplaying, a popular twitter topic, Virgin America asks passengers in the air to tweet what they are watching.

Paid participation: In this case, the organization can pay the social media site for greater prominence. These ads are useful when corporations do not yet have enough representation on social media sites to automatically appear high in the results. For example, Yelp advertisers can have their advertisement appear above Yelp search results. Businesses that pay Yelp can also prevent the ads of competitive businesses appearing on their page.

Sponsored social media: Even though they don't even know them, many people feel close to celebrities because they can follow their tweets and Facebook fan pages. While this is not a direct service offered by the social media web sites, there are middlemen who represent celebrities and these celebrities can endorse your product on social media sites. Similar to all sponsorships, these ads work best when there is symmetry between the image of the celebrity and the sponsor. For example, Kim Kardashian reportedly gets $10,000 a tweet while promoting brands like Carl's Jr. and T-Mobile Blackberry.

The Future of Web 2.0

The Web 2.0 landscape is constantly evolving (e.g. the lost relevance of once-dominant MySpace and Second Life; the new dominance of Twitter). It is also difficult to predict what the next hot site will be. Indeed, today's "magic bullet" might be irrelevant tomorrow.

At the time of this writing, location-based networks (Foursquare, Loopt, Gowalla) seem to be all the rage. With Foursquare, people can check-in to a location via their mobile phone to earn points and "unlock badges". For example, the first time someone checks into a venue, they receive the "Newbie" badge. A multitude of other badges are available, such as the "Adventurer" badge (for checking into 10 different venues), the "Super User" badge (for 30 check-ins in one month), and the "School Night" badge (for checking into a venue after 3:00 am on a Monday, Tuesday, or Wednesday morning). Additionally, Foursquare taps into the competitive nature of people, and users are motivated to visit various locations to build their collection of badges. For example, the individual who has checked-in three times to the same location in one week earns the "Local" badge. The person who has checked-in the most number of times to a venue unlocks the "Mayor" badge—but they lose it if their number of check-ins is surpassed later by someone else. If an individual is the mayor of 10 or more locations at the same time, they earn the "Super Mayor" badge.

Every time someone checks into a location, an automatic update sharing this location is shown on their news feeds from other social media sites like Facebook and Twitter. This is an extremely effective way to increase consumers' engagement with your brand. Foursquare takes advantage of the sharing aspect of Web 2.0 by repeatedly exposing your brand to the people users are linked with (e.g. their friends, followers, etc.). When a user checks into your location, this may also serve as an implicit endorsement of the brand.

Organizations can also actively encourage users to check-in via Foursquare by providing rewards for visiting their location. For example, the Gap offered 25% off (for one day only) to everyone who checked-in to a Gap store. McDonald's ran a one-day contest and randomly selected people who checked-in to receive a $5 or $10 gift card. Repeated visits can be encouraged by offering rewards to consumers every time they check-in to your location. By offering the "mayor" of your location added benefits, consumers are encouraged to frequently visit the venue (to either topple the current Mayor, or to maintain their Mayor status). Ann Taylor offers a 15% discount to people who check-in five times to the same store, but Mayors receive an ongoing discount of 25%. Domino's (UK) customers who check-in to a restaurant receive free breadsticks; the Mayor of each location also receives a free pizza once per week.

Whatever the next-big-thing is for Web 2.0, one thing is for certain—Web 2.0 is not a silver bullet that will be the salvation of any company using it. However, it can be an important and extremely effective tool in the marketing mix of any company that chooses to use it.

STEPHEN K. KOERNIG is an Associate Professor at DePaul University in Chicago. Steve has won numerous awards for teaching and research and is currently teaching Social Media Marketing, Strategic Marketing Tools, Consumer Behavior, and Services Marketing. Dr. Koernig's academic research focuses on social media marketing, e-commerce, and marketing education. His research has been published in leading academic journals including *Journal of Advertising, Psychology & Marketing, Journal of Marketing Education,* and *Sport Marketing Quarterly*. Steve is an American Marketing Association Doctoral Fellow, and is a member of the American Marketing Association and the Academy of Marketing Science. He received his M.B.A. from DePaul University and has a Ph.D. in marketing from the University of Illinois at Chicago.

NEIL GRANITZ is a Professor of Marketing at California State University, Fullerton. In 1999, he obtained his Ph.D. from Arizona State University. Neil teaches Market Research, Strategic Internet Marketing, and Customer Information Strategy. His research interests include e-commerce, ethics, and marketing education. Dr. Granitz has published articles in several journals including the *Journal of Advertising*, the *Journal of Business Ethics*, and the *Journal of Marketing Education*. While at Cal State Fullerton, he has won the award for *CBE Outstanding Faculty Member*, as well as for *Teaching Innovation*. Prior to pursuing his Ph.D., he was the Domestic and International Director of Market Research for Imasco (Canada's third largest company). Dr. Granitz continues to consult for several companies. In his spare time he reads lots of comic books.

READING
17

Mobile Marketing and the Mobile Decade to Come

MICKEY ALAM KAHN
Editor-in-Chief
www.mobilemarketer.com

How the Mobile Decade Will Change Marketing, Media and Commerce

The nation stands today at a pivotal point where mobile will soon infuse every marketing, media and retail decision just as the Internet did in the last ten years. The Mobile Decade is upon us. Marketers have only to look around this country and see the one thing that consumers today cannot be parted from: their mobile phone. And that device, as the decade wears on, will become the interface between consumer and society.

Are all stakeholders in this economy geared for the major changes down the road? Those who are prepared are already in some version of Mobile 2.0 with their marketing plans. Those who aren't need some more validation before committing time, people and budget to adding mobile to the mix.

Of this all can be certain: mobile will democratize every institution just as the Internet did. It will enhance the value of marketing, content and commerce for some and cut the margins in others. In other words, mobile will level the playing field, empowering consumers even more with information that shifts the balance of power even further away from the marketer. How will this likely play out for marketers as regards brands, agencies, media and retailers?

Brands in the Know

More consumers will rely on their mobile media to tap into news, information, shopping and entertainment. Brands that seek to maintain their edge in this decade will have to roll out 360-degree marketing plans that include mobile advertising on key sites. In addition, they will have to debut mobile-friendly sites and mobile applications to enable an easy, user-friendly two-way communication with their target audience.

Brands will also need a strong Short Message Service (SMS) program to reach out to consumers who choose that medium along with email as their two primary choices for direct marketing. SMS will complement email in loyalty marketing efforts and, equally important, drive traffic to offline channels including retail stores.

Brands cannot afford to be locked out of a mobile relationship with customers and prospects. The alternative is to wish upon themselves the same fate that befell those brands that were stubborn to the attractions—and necessity—of an effective Internet presence in the early- to mid-2000s. Ad agencies, for their part, cannot shelter under lack of education, complexity or inadequacy of metrics any much longer.

Shop Talk

The year 2007 saw the launch of the first web-friendly Apple iPhone. Several upgraded versions and hundreds of thousands of applications later, the market is now crowded with smartphones from Motorola, Samsung, Nokia, Sony Ericsson and, of course, the father of them all, Research In Motion and its BlackBerry models.

Consumer acceptance of smartphones with their own operating systems from Apple's iPhone to Google's Android has been spectacular. Android itself boasts applications in the six figures. Sure, smartphones still accounted for only one-fifth of all mobile subscriptions circa 2010. But, if some researchers are right, the market is only months away from a point where as many smartphones will be in subscriber hands as basic feature phones—in other words, one out of two phones will be web-enabled mobile devices.

That tipping point—when smartphones gain majority acceptance—will become the giant sucking sound of marketing. Advertising agencies cannot afford anymore to ignore this reality—that mobile is rapidly becoming a critical-mass marketing medium, albeit with margins that are nowhere near print or television. Indeed, agencies will have to restructure themselves financially—lean, mean and with the same sheen.

On the creative front, it's time copywriters were taught how to pen copy in 160 characters or six-word headlines on tiny screens. How to be creative and yet get to the point—that's the dilemma copy folks and art directors will have to face. As for the account management teams at agencies? Better get used to pitching mobile to the clients and writing briefs that understand what mobile is all about: relationship marketing.

Mobile will not come at the expense of TV or radio or other older media. But advertisers will soon discover that mobile media are as efficient, if not more, in attracting and retaining customers.

Medium is the Message

Media may have the least time before Mobile 2.0 hits in earnest. If the wired web has cannibalized print media and not returned ad revenues anywhere near old media's, then mobile will simply compound that mess. The media world is about to come to a fork in the road: Either stick to an advertising-supported, free-access model or erect subscription walls to charge consumers for reading on mobile sites and applications.

The history of paid media isn't good. Beyond a few newspapers and magazines that can charge because their content is highly unique, most publications cannot afford to lose traffic over walls that may drive readers elsewhere.

Charging for mobile content will only work if content on the wired web is also gated. Yes, consumers are conditioned to paying for content (such as some apps) on mobile. However, for most consumers, news is not the same thing as content. News has become a commodity. Readers will only pay if the news is viewed as a brand. And that, in this 24-hour news-cycle, is highly improbable. Which leaves the other possibility as the one to bet the house on: advertising-supported media. Publishers will have to work double-duty to ensure that advertisers are offered media plans that include all formats—print, online, broadcast and mobile.

That said, it is a shame to visit sites of noted publishers and see wasted advertising opportunities. Get a big brand to taste mobile. Give a free month-long trial to new advertisers. Let them experience the power of mobile. And work with them to tailor appropriate messages that resonate with an on-the-go mindset. Simply repurposing online ads for mobile won't cut the mustard.

Make the Buy

As for retailers, mobile's benefit is obvious: driving traffic to stores or call centers. Mobile commerce will change the face of retail as we know it.

Now all of these developments hinge on a few factors. First, that wireless carriers will continue to support new web-friendly smartphones with affordable data plans and upgrade networks to handle increased bandwidth demands. Next, that consumers are sufficiently convinced of the wider benefits and security of relating with brands through mobile. Finally, that marketers stretch to acknowledge mobile's strengths.

Either way, welcome to the Mobile Decade. Make it memorable for getting things right at the outset. Consumers want to talk; so listen.

Common-sense Dos and Don'ts of Mobile Marketing

From the noise generated by the myriad mobile conferences, blogs and publications, most brands, advertising agencies and publishers just want to know a couple of things: What's working and what's not working in mobile marketing. Here's a stab at that.

First, it's important to dispel the myth that marketers don't get mobile. They do— ask Colgate-Palmolive, Unilever, Gap, adidas, M&M/Mars, NBC, Kodak, Heineken, ESPN, McDonald's, American Airlines, Sherwin-Williams, Microsoft, AOL, MGM Grand, Johnson & Johnson, Dairy Queen, Jaguar, Skyy Vodka, Ford Motor, The Weather Channel, Discover Card, Procter & Gamble's Gillette, Brita, Jim Beam and Chase.

These aforementioned brands have run mobile campaigns, sites and applications or launched mobile commerce operations. Some of these efforts have morphed into longer-term programs that integrate mobile into overall multichannel outreach initiatives within these Fortune 500 and Fortune 1000 brands.

No doubt mobile will have to work harder to get a larger chunk of marketing budgets. But marketers surely are getting the message that mobile is where they need to be. Consumers—their customers—wouldn't expect any less, not with their newer phone models and better data plans.

Know Your Audience

This leads to the first observation about what's working in mobile marketing: *Understanding the audience and targeting* with appropriate mobile banner and video ads, sites, applications or SMS campaigns—all opted-in, not once but twice by the consumer.

This rule is not exclusive to mobile. A targeted mailer sent to a household has proven to generate sales online, in-store or via telephone. Online banners or emails that sync with the site audience's interests inevitably generate click-throughs and responses to calls to action.

So mobile's not any different. A relevant movie trailer banner ad on an entertainment mobile site will serve both the advertiser and consumer well. Requesting that existing customers opt-in to the marketer's mobile alert programs will also work to great advantage. Ask casino giants such as Harrah's and MGM Grand.

Not surprisingly, it is critical to research the targeted audience's mobile habits. What is it that they consume on the mobile phone? How much time do they spend on mobile? What is it that they would like to initiate elsewhere but complete on mobile or vice-versa?

Visiting a well-thought out mobile site is such a pleasure. Consider *The New York Times'* mobile site at http:/nytimes.com. It is hard to admit this, but the mobile site beats the wired web site simply because the scroll-down interface is easy to navigate and the articles easy to read. The only casualty about the mobile *New York Times* experience is the advertising. While the banner ad units are quite visible, the *Times* needs to work harder on convincing some of its current online advertisers to add mobile to their mix.

It seems almost strange to see a mobile site without ads—not ones that interrupt the experience, but ones that enhance the overall reading experience by offering a window into commercial applications.

At the risk of sounding audacious, perhaps the *Times* should offer sampling opportunities to key advertisers such as Tiffany, Macy's, Cartier and local auto dealers. And if these advertisers don't have a mobile presence, then the *Times* should work with mobile firms to mobilize their client base. Imagine the brownie points scored if mobile gains significant leads and sales for these firms.

Knowing the audience also includes knowledge of their propensity or willingness to receive permission-based communications on their phones. Mobile may not be for everyone, just like the wired Internet isn't.

But it seems quite obvious that marketers offering value through the mobile site, application, banner ad, coupon or text message will find a welcome reception. Training the customer base to expect quality in mobile marketing communications is a corollary to knowing what makes the marketer's target customer tick.

While many industry observers are waiting for a flash of light to let them know mobile is the new tableau for marketing, those already with toes in the water know where the fish are.

Mobile Works for Database and Loyalty Marketing—Absolutely

One of the most astute uses of mobile—besides employing mobile advertising for branding—is the channel's ability to expand a marketer's loyalty program. And the humble foot soldier of loyalty marketing is SMS text messaging. Yes, text messaging is to mobile what email is to the Internet—the choice tool for communicating one-on-one with the customer.

Marketing need not get too complicated if the goal is to convince the targeted consumer to consume the advertiser's product or service over the competitor's. SMS is the easiest way to communicate that message. It takes some legwork to get fully SMS-enabled. The tools required are a common short code, keywords, approval of mobile campaign from wireless carriers and another channel to get the consumer to text in to opt into a program.

Marketers and retailers can use stores, direct mail, television, radio, print, online and billboards to get the consumer to opt-in—not once, but twice—to receiving coupons or alerts from the company.

Once the consumer is signed up, moderate the communications to anywhere from two messages to four messages a month, maximum. And be upfront with the opted-in consumer about the frequency of messages, company privacy policy and option to opt out at any time. Remember, it's a land grab right now. At some point, the consumer will not agree to sign up for any more mobile loyalty programs or alerts. So it is best to start work on incorporating mobile into the company's overall loyalty program.

Legs to Other Channels

Here's another point to remember: mobile's place in the multichannel context. Mobile is not an island unto itself and contrary to what its most ardent fans would like to believe, the channel's best use is in giving legs to other channels.

Mobile has the potential to drive traffic to retail stores, as has been amply proved with campaigns from restaurant chains such as Papa John's, McDonald's, Burger King, Starbucks, Jiffy Lube and countless others with a physical footprint.

The "American Idol" show on television is proof that text messaging can elect winners simply by action of keyword and short code. Shows such as "American Idol" and "Deal or No Deal" are said to generate as much revenues for the programmers from texting as they do from advertising. Maybe it's exaggerating it a bit, but the point is that mobile brings interactivity to TV.

Now here's something that agencies don't want to hear about: actual tracking of brand commercials. Image a keyword and short code on spots—not just at the end of the 30-second spot, but in every frame—that invites the consumer to text in. No, it need not turn into a direct response TV ad, but the texts could give the advertiser an idea of the consumer's engagement with the brand's TV advertising.

Ditto with radio. And it's proved to have worked. Oil change giant Jiffy Lube has gone on the record to acknowledge SMS marketing's role in driving traffic to its locations. In most cases, the SMS call to action was run first on radio spots targeted to drivers in certain areas. What about direct mail and inserts? How about placing targeted keywords and short code on mail and inserts sent to consumers' homes and offices? Ask them to respond via text for prompt fulfillment of the desired call to action. The examples can go on and on. Keep an open mind and a sharp eye on the consumer's needs and market trends.

What Not to Do in Any Circumstances?

It's mostly a bunch of common sense. Don't abuse the privilege. When mobile consumers opt into receiving communications from brands, they are giving access to their most personal medium.

Err on the side of caution when sending text messages—twice a month, instead of four, for example—or make sure that the banner ad doesn't disrupt the viewing experience on mobile.

It's been said before, and bears repeating here: familiarity breeds contempt. Don't inundate the consumer with messages. Space them out and make sure each message is targeted.

Sensitivity is the watchword here. And privacy. In fact, privacy threatens to snowball into one of the biggest issues threatening online and mobile advertising. Privacy advocacy groups and consumer watchdogs are chomping at the bit to restrain marketers from crossing a fine line. They are doing their best to convince the Federal Trade Commission of the need to regulate behavioral and location-based advertising online and on mobile.

These groups' worries, while legitimate, will affect marketing based on data and knowledge of consumer actions, even on an aggregate basis. So give no excuse to these groups or to the FTC or to the various attorneys general nationwide who want to make their name on marketing's back.

Finally, be realistic. Mobile's not a cure for what ails other channels. While it's not even realistic to call it a channel—it's a phone, TV, radio, MP3 player, video player, gaming instrument, camera, computer, email tool, SMS enabler and pathway to the Internet—mobile still works best when matched with other channels.

Mobile thankfully does not enjoy the same degree of hype as the Internet did in the late 1990s. Yes, every agency, conference organizer or publisher has tacked on mobile as the new accessory to their offerings, but the venture-capital money inflow has been measured and realistic.

Those in the field know that mobile victories come hard-fought. It is their job now to communicate that mobile has its advantages and its limitations.

One of the truths is that mobile will not replace other channels, but complement them in a manner that no other channel has.

But mobile requires time to show results, and consumers need time to work out their relationship with the mobile device—is it a phone, entertainment channel, business tool, news source, video, camera, advertising vehicle or shop? All eight, as time and smart mobile marketing campaigns and programs will prove.

MICKEY ALAM KHAN is editor-in-chief of *Mobile Marketer, Mobile Commerce Daily* and *Luxury Daily,* all based in New York. He was previously editor in chief of *eMarketer* and *DM News,* and also served as correspondent for *Advertising Age.* Reach him at mickey@napean.com.

READING
18

DRTV and
Integrated Marketing

TIMOTHY HAWTHORNE
Founder, Chairman and Executive Creative Director
Hawthorne Direct

---

*Direct response television goes hand-in-hand with many other adver-
tising strategies, and should be considered a vital aspect of any company's overall marketing effort.*

In a world where consumers are bombarded by thousands of marketing messages
daily, it's no longer enough to utilize a single selling channel and expect it to perform up to snuff. The question is, how does a marketer approach consumers from
multiple angles in a time/cost-efficient and effective manner? Simple. By using integrated marketing, or the delivery of a consistent message across multiple channels
like retail, television, radio, web, mobile, email, catalog, print and direct mail, among
others.

In this chapter I'll help you understand how the direct response TV (DRTV) channel impacts integrated campaigns, and walk you through the roots of this often-mis-
understood—yet frequently used—marketing medium. I'll show you how the industry has evolved, and compare and contrast it with general advertising. Finally, I'll give
you the lowdown on DRTV's collaborative qualities, and help you maximize your
own integrated ad campaign by tapping into DRTV's unique qualities.

Laying the Groundwork

It may have its roots in Ginsu knives and Pocket Fishermen, but over the last 20 years
DRTV marketing has proven itself as a cost-effective, accountable, measurable and
powerful way to entice customers to place orders over the phone and via the Internet,
or even drive them into retail stores to see and touch the products firsthand.

DRTV is broadly defined as any TV commercial that includes a response mechanism (800 number, URL, SMS code or "push your remote's order button") to generate an immediate response to purchase a product or request more information.

DRTV commercials can be of any length: 15, 30, 60 second "spots" (short form) or 30 minute "infomercials" (long form). They've been around since the dawn of TV and today are a much bigger business than just oft-seen Snuggies, Ab Rockets and Magic Bullets, now accounting for over $100 billion in annual product sales.

Here are just some of the ways that advertisers, both entrepreneurs and big brands, are using DRTV today:

- Drive prospects to the web
- Drive retail sales
- Bypass retail; sell products direct to consumers
- Introduce new products
- Educate about complex product benefits
- Generate leads at low cost
- Extend product lines of existing brands
- Increase product and brand awareness
- Differentiate products from competitors
- Support all other marketing channels

When making the case for DRTV, cost is a key driver. For the cost of 30 seconds of media in prime time network TV (8–11 PM), advertisers can fund dozens of DRTV airings across a broad range of stations. Additionally, the direct response metrics of a long or short form DRTV commercial can be accurately tested with as little as $25,000 in media expenditures. Even if a brand's TV budget has been slashed (as so many have in today's economic environment), for example, it will still be feasible to beef up the campaign with a DRTV-driven marketing effort that produces a measurable return on investment.

None of these facts are news to the ears of seasoned DRTV marketers who already know about the medium's power. Commercial television was launched in the late 1940s and early 1950s by a handful of broadcasters who desperately sought programming to fill their airtime. In those days, a typical television station ran only a few hours of network shows in the morning and then again in the evening.

Around the same time, in Chicago, Philadelphia, and Atlantic City, ad men such as Al Eicoff, and entrepreneurs such as the Popeil and Arnold families recognized the profit potential in this new television medium. They were post-World War II sales, marketing and advertising experts who had already made their names by pitching products on radio, through the mail, in newspapers, or live and in-person at state fairs or on Atlantic City's boardwalk (the latter of which was a favorite haunt decades later for one of DRTV's great pitchmen, the late Billy Mays).

Together, these sales innovators created the first long form TV commercials (what would later be called infomercials). Their television commercials ran anywhere from five to 30 minutes or more and featured evangelistic, often outrageous, product presentations. The same fast-paced sales techniques, honed before thousands of fair-goers and seaside vacationers, provided a new breed of television entertainment that, as it happened, also sold products in the millions.

At the time, there were no toll-free 800 telephone numbers and no credit cards. A "call to action" was intended to persuade viewers to send a check or scurry on down to Walgreens. Families in cities across America huddled around their new Philco TVs, entranced by the exciting demonstration of the latest, one-of-a-kind, "must-have" gadget. It was a time of freedom of expression, prosperity and growth in a new commercial industry—which inevitably would come under regulatory scrutiny that mandated change.

The Golden Age

As the "Golden Age" of television took hold in the mid-1950s, major advertisers began to compete for 60-second time slots that sponsored entertainment programming. Infomercial pioneers were dismayed to find that less and less long form infomercial time was available, and what was still available cost a lot more than in the "good old days."

When the quiz-show scandals of the late 1950s struck, all eyes turned to the rapidly growing television medium, its crass commercialism and apparent ability to corrupt American youth. Television programming and its sponsors had greatly disappointed the American public, whose trusting eyes and ears had once watched and listened and earnestly believed in what appeared on their black-and-white living room Zeniths.

In an effort to stem the tide of public dissent and help salvage commercial television, in 1962 the Federal Communications Commission (FCC) slapped new regulations on the industry. From then on, broadcast television stations were permitted to sell a maximum of 12 to 14 minutes of commercial time per hour, thus ending the initial era of the long form infomercial.

A determined bunch of long form advertisers such as Eicoff and Wunderman adapted to the new FCC regulations by running two-minute direct response spots. Positioned as "key outlet" commercials, they tagged the end of their brief product demonstrations with the names of three to six major retailers that carried the showcased product, thus forcing you to buy the product at retail only.

Meanwhile, in 1968, AT&T introduced the next revolution in direct response television (DRTV)–the WATTS line, or toll-free 800 number. Suddenly, a commercial could run nationwide with a centralized inbound phone reception center taking orders from across the country, an innovation that gave new life to DRTV.

No Smoking

The ban on television cigarette advertising in 1970 created an enormous gap in broadcasters' ad revenues. Television media time became plentiful and inexpensive as broadcast stations hustled to fill the commercial airtime that was once dominated by cigarette advertisers. Short form direct response television commercials filled the gap nicely. Products such as records, books, tools, kitchen gadgets, pest control, and arts and crafts proliferated. Companies like K-Tel and Ronco dominated the DRTV market place. Any mass-market consumer item that could be demonstrated, provide immediate solutions, and sell for $9.95 or less, was a prime candidate for short form DRTV ad campaigns.

But it would still be another two decades before DRTV would gain acceptance in mainstream advertising circles. (In fact, DRTV commercials remained a breed apart from major brand television advertising for most of the first 50 years of TV.) Direct response spots were notorious for being low-budget productions that featured hard-sell, rapid-fire pitches and wildly exaggerated demonstrations and claims made by gregarious hosts relentlessly driving home the sale. As a result, the credibility of DRTV ads left much to be desired among consumers, and deservedly so. Unfulfilled or late orders happened too often, and many of the products that were delivered were of such poor quality that purchasers were left disgruntled and disenchanted with the whole business.

In the early 1970s, Reader's Digest dared to apply classic general television advertising concepts to short form DRTV ads in support of its direct-mail subscription campaign. One of the first direct response integrated marketing campaigns, it was executed with style and substance. Thanks to Reader's Digest, DRTV spot advertising regained some face and, in the process, succeeded in waking up Madison Avenue advertising executives to this "new" mode of advertising that actually provided measurable response and still maintained their Fortune 500 clients' image-enhancing style of traditional high-quality spot ads.

Record and audiotape clubs, book continuity programs, magazines and insurance pioneered the upscale DRTV commercials of the 1970s. Time-Life, Columbia House, Publishers' Clearinghouse, Liberty Mutual Insurance, Rolling Stone, Newsweek, Time and Playboy covered the airwaves. What's more, they weren't restricted to late-night fringe time, lowbrow hours, but appeared throughout the day and occasionally even in prime time.

Earning Respect

Creatively, except for their toll-free number DR ordering component, many of the short form DRTV ads were virtually indistinguishable from general advertising, often shot on 35mm film (providing superior production values), and employing experienced union models and actors in compelling fictional story settings. DRTV was slowly earning a bit more respect from the advertising "establishment" on Madison Avenue.

Meanwhile, from the early 1960s to the early 1980s, all was quiet on the long form front. Only the evangelists for God and nonprofit organizations (WorldVision), not products, could taking advantage of the "Power of the Half Hour"™ on Sunday mornings. Savvy ad agencies spent millions in media time for these causes, which generated donations that well exceeded their media investments. Though officially designated as religious or not-for-profit programming, there's no doubt the evangelists borrowed techniques for closing their "sales" from the best boardwalk pitchmen of the 1950s.

The rebirth of long form advertising was due in part to the advent of upstart, advertiser-supported national cable networks such as The Cable Health Network (now Lifetime), USA Network, and Satellite Program Network (now defunct). In the late 1970s and early 1980s, these fledgling networks were wired into only a small percentage of TV households in the United States and were thus ignored by most major advertisers. Like the pioneering broadcast TV stations 60 years ago, they hungered for ad revenues.

Because they weren't subject to FCC rules regulating broadcast commercial time, these cable networks welcomed the cash-up-front advertising revenues from half-hour commercials in the early 1980s. In 1983, The Sharper Image catalog pioneered the multi-product infomercial on cable, a good three years before the Home Shopping Network launched the same format nationally, 24 hours per day, to great success.

Meanwhile, a few risk-taking broadcast TV stations, still under commercial time regulations, began to air infomercials disguised as TV talk shows and "documentaries" for such products as hair restoration formulas and real estate investment seminars. Most of those infomercial campaigns bear no resemblance to today's programs. They typically ran in a limited number of markets at any one time or had brief runs on cable. It wasn't until the summer of 1984 that infomercials were officially born.

Credit Reagan-era deregulation with helping to spur on that official introduction. In June 1984, the FCC officially removed any TV commercial time constraints. The decision to allow TV stations to self-regulate was well founded, the thinking being that if a station began selling more than 12 to 14 minutes of advertising per hour, viewers simply wouldn't watch the station, which would lower the station's viewership/ratings and their commercial rates. It would not be in the financial interests of broadcasters to increase the amount of commercial time sold.

What wasn't expected from this ruling was how entrepreneurs would use their limited long form experience on cable to conceive a new billion-dollar industry. Annual sales from the long form advertising format have skyrocketed. Infomercials generated approximately $10 million in sales in 1984. Today it's a $30 billion dollar industry.

Introducing the Infomercial

The modern infomercial era really began in the fall of 1984, when Herbalife generated millions of dollars in revenues through its weekly, Sunday-evening motivational pep rallies on USA Network. Since then, the short and long form DRTV industry has grown by leaps and bounds, thrived during several economic downturns and even gained mass acceptance by brand advertisers who have come to love the medium's accountability and direct-to-consumer approach.

Because of the tremendous infomercial industry growth and positive effects of self-regulation instituted by the industry's trade group (Electronic Retailing Association— www. retailing.org), major institutions and Fortune 500 and 1000 corporations are taking advantage of this successful, proven marketing channel. Many well-known retailers, financial institutions, publishers, insurance companies and manufacturers have used infomercials to showcase their products, including (but not limited to):

- ✓ 3M
- ✓ American Airlines
- ✓ Apple
- ✓ AT&T
- ✓ Bank of America
- ✓ Black & Decker
- ✓ Blue Cross Blue Shield
- ✓ Clorox
- ✓ Coca-Cola
- ✓ Estee Lauder
- ✓ Fidelity Investments
- ✓ Fisher Price

✓ Ford
✓ General Motors
✓ McDonald's
✓ Microsoft
✓ P&G
✓ Nissan
✓ Pepsi
✓ Phillips
✓ Sony
✓ Target
✓ Toyota
✓ Wal-Mart
✓ Weight Watchers

The list goes on. In fact, companies of all shapes and sizes are using DRTV to get the word out about their products and services. That's because the medium helps companies tell their story in a format that is not only measurable and accountable, but can perform far better than traditional 15- or 30-second branding spots in recall, intent to purchase, enhanced brand awareness. Using "brandmercials" (a moniker we came up with here at Hawthorne Direct), firms like 3M, Black & Decker, Hoover, PETA, and 1-800 Flowers, among many others, are tapping the power of long form and short form DRTV to tell their story right in the consumer's living room and alongside their other multiple marketing channels. With DRTV, results can be closely tracked, and the selling itself takes place either online, or by phone, at a time that's convenient for the consumer. Who can argue with these benefits? No one.

When brand advertisers jumped into the DRTV pool, something else happened. Their first brandmercials pioneered a wave of upscale production values that worked hard to keep the brand tone intact for Fortune 500 firms. In the late-1990s, Apple Computer was an immediate beneficiary, ringing up $92 million in retail sales on a $3 million DRTV investment. Nissan followed with the most successful DR campaign in company history, and paved the way for others to follow in its footsteps.

When these types of Fortune 500 companies integrate DRTV into the advertising mix, they use a format that lends itself to consumer education on the brand itself, and also on the individual products that the label represents. By telling their stories through these longer-format commercials, these marketers can break through the "blur of image" created by most traditional 15/30 second spots, and delve deeper into the true value that the brand delivers to the consumer.

And, proving many skeptics wrong, DRTV has also demonstrated it can do more than just support brands; it can create them too. Guthy-Renker's ProActiv skin care product started with a million dollar DRTV investment (vs. tens of millions for major brand companies) and is a billion dollar brand today. Other DRTV generated brands include: OrangeGlo, OxiClean, George Foreman Grills, Magic Bullet, Total Gym, Victoria Jackson Cosmetics, Bare Minerals, Little Giant Ladder, Shark Vacuums, Murad Skin Care, Magic Jack, Tempur-Pedic, Rosetta Stone, Zumba, P90X, Select Comfort, Max Clarity, Swivel Sweeper, Provo Craft, Bowflex, Oreck Vacuums, Taebo,

Time Life Music, NutriSystem, Space Bags, Nordic Track, Video Professor, Principal Secret, Youthology and Vonage.

Breaking It Down

Again, what most distinguishes DRTV from brand TV advertising is the presence of an *offer to buy*, or learn more about the product, "now." DRTV commercial "product offers" can be broken down into three types, each of which airs regularly and is used by a wide range of marketers. Here's a breakdown of each type:

- One-Step: As in "it only takes one step to buy this product; use your credit card and call the operator or go online now." The classic one-step DRTV offer dominated the industry for its first 50 years, and remains a DRTV staple today. In many viewers' eyes, the "order now and use your credit card" offer defines the medium. It's usually used to sell such products as exercise equipment, kitchen appliances, cosmetics and diet programs priced less than $99.95. The traditional one-step infomercial sells unique products—often not available at retail stores— directly to television viewers. Because of today's high cost of media airtime, the success rate for testing a one-step offer has fallen from one-out-of-two to one-out-of-twenty. These days, infomercials that employ one-step offers are considered high-risk ventures—that is, if the show itself is the only profit-making element. One-step infomercial marketers have adapted to the increased media costs by attracting customers with the one-step offer while making most of their profits on their Internet orders, retail sales (where most infomercial products will eventually end up) and the "back end." Back-end programs may include continuity programs, outbound telemarketing, direct mail, home shopping appearances, catalogs, and more. In fact, roughly 80 percent of Jordan Whitney's (an industry research company—www.jwgreensheet.com) Top Ten Infomercials each month still feature one-step offers. Obviously, high media costs have not deterred one-step marketers.
- Two-Step: As in "call or go online now for more information." Reacting to the squeeze on one-step offers, advertisers have begun turning toward two-step offers, or "lead generators." Major financial service companies such as Progressive and Geico use the two-step approach to successfully generate leads from infomercial viewers. If your product is priced over $99.95 and your one-step infomercial doesn't work, consider changing your offer to generate a lead. You can't get a more qualified lead than someone who has already watched 2 to 30 minutes of your sales presentation. Jordan Whitney defines approximately 20 percent of its top-ranked infomercials each month as "lead generating," and this percentage continues to grow throughout the industry as a whole.
- Driving Online and Retail: The online and retail-driving DRTV commercials are an interesting hybrid of direct response and image awareness marketing. Ninety-nine percent of a DRTV commercial's viewers will not buy immediately in response to seeing the ad (the average infomercial response rate is between 0.2 percent and 0.4 percent). But these millions of non-purchasing infomercial watchers are primed to purchase the product at retail or online, their preferred buying channels, or are influenced to buy later via print, catalog and direct mail

messaging. Corporations such as 3M, P&G, and Black & Decker, which traditionally marketed strictly through retail, have used infomercials with great success to drive retail sales.

Whether they're looking to sell direct, drive consumers to retail and the web, or build their consumer databases, brand advertisers see DRTV as a viable addition to their arsenals. They're using it to educate their consumers in a meaningful, measurable way, while also reaping the rewards of authenticity that traditional TV branding spots simply can't match.

Unique Attributes

In our new, consumer-driven, fragmented media universe, consumers want more relevant information at more touchpoints. They're no longer prompted to try a new product or check out a new service based on a single contact, and have come to expect a more integrated approach that includes print, TV, radio, web, mobile and other advertising techniques.

The economic downturns of the early 2000s and then in 2008–09, further complicated matters, what with consumers doing more comparison shopping and being more frugal. These consumers track down the best deals, clip or download coupons and wait for discounted offers. They tune out messages that are not relevant to the problems in their lives right now.

They also pay more attention to DRTV, which routinely demonstrates product benefits as solutions to everyday problems. With longer selling messages and prominent value based offers, direct response always speaks the language anxious consumers want to hear. Free premiums and discounts are popular any time; in a troubled economy, they're compelling.

Also persuasive are DRTV's longer-format commercials that "tell" along with the "sell." By taking the time to educate consumers on the benefits and features of a particular product or service, DRTV:

✓ Explains multiple product benefits, thus heightening value
✓ Offers in-depth product demonstrations, thus engaging viewers
✓ Introduces real people and expert testimonials, which builds credibility
✓ Repeats key selling messages, which enhances persuasion
✓ Takes customers through a complete sales story, thus deepening understanding
✓ Differentiates from competitors, which boosts preference
✓ Allows for consideration of the purchase decision, which creates purchase justification

Despite these obvious benefits, the road to widespread DRTV advertiser and consumer acceptance has been fraught with obstacles. Since they began, long form television marketers have had to face down accusations of being "boardwalk pitchmen" of dubious reputation, adjust to regulation, deregulation, and re-regulation by federal agencies, and regain the confidence of a disenchanted TV-viewing audience. Through it all, infomercial advertisers have adapted and thrived and will continue to do so in spite of ongoing challenges, such as those that exist today.

In 1985, for example, an advertiser could purchase cable airtime for as little as $50 per half hour (due to minuscule cable viewership at that time), making it easy to realize a success ratio of $5 in revenue for every media dollar spent. A 10-to-1 ratio was not untypical with a hot show. Media time on the same cable channels currently is going for as much as $30,000 per half hour. The industry wide cost of media time has ballooned an average of 500 percent. These prices reflect phenomenal increases in the number of cable subscribers.

In addition, average production budgets have surged from $30,000 per infomercial in 1985 to anywhere from $200,000 to $800,000 per half-hour show today. Both increases reflect a heated-up competitive marketplace. In 1984, there were five infomercials total on the air; today, five to 10 new programs appear every week.

The Quiet Revolution

While DRTV marketers were battling it out with traditional image/awareness advertisers for TV airtime and respect in the 1990s, a quiet revolution toward brand advertisers and retail-driving infomercials started up and has prevailed every since. Here's a look at how this revolution evolved and grew:

- In 1990, Time-Life Music successfully entered infomercial marketing as the first Fortune 500 Company via their agency, Hawthorne Direct, and Fitness Quest simultaneously launched new products through infomercials and at retail.
- In 1991, infomercial media costs continued to inflate at a frantic pace because of increased competition for limited available time slots ("avails"), while front-end profits and success ratios decreased, and reliance on back-end sales increased. Saturn broadcast the first image-only infomercial (no toll-free number mechanism). Braun, via Hawthorne Direct, produced an infomercial for their Handblender specifically to drive retail sales.
- In 1992, Ross Perot debuted an infomercial designed to educate the nation regarding the details of his United States presidential campaign. Retailers acknowledged the immense impact infomercials have for "as seen on TV" product categories. Juicers sold through infomercials flew off retail shelves. Major advertisers began seriously considering infomercial campaigns: Braun, Redken, GTE and Volvo debuted successful infomercials. Corporate infomercials demonstrated their ability to drive sales at retail while paying for part or all of their TV media airtime with direct response television sales.

DRTV's success has proven that millions of viewers will watch from 2 to 30 minutes of well-produced commercial advertising. At Hawthorne Direct, our internal research shows that consumers are hungry for product information and are growing increasingly skeptical of standard 15–30 second brand advertising.

From my own experience in the industry, I'd say that most brand companies have already embraced the idea that measurable advertising is the way to go, especially in this economy. By 2011, DRTV had evolved to the point where a hybrid DRTV/TRP (Targeted Rating Points—a standard brand media buying methodology) media campaign made sense to many corporate marketing folks, because they could now quantify their TV ad spending both by number of viewers and actual response by those viewers.

Yet $50 billion is still spent every year on general brand TV advertising, with little or no response mechanism. Old habits die hard, and it's no secret that brands and their agencies hate to "ask for the order." Still, DRTV continues to gain traction among those brands, and is particularly attractive to those that are seeking an affordable, accountable advertising mechanism that works well with myriad other mediums.

Why DRTV is so Hard to Ignore

So, what is it about DRTV that makes advertisers swoon and their traditional agencies cringe in fear? In one word, it's the accountability. While the medium comes with many other benefits, one of DRTV's biggest attributes is its ability to accurately and method- ically track exactly where customers are coming from, what they buy (and what they turn down) and how often they come back for more. With this information in hand, advertisers can make quick decisions regarding the best allocation of their marketing dollars—something that traditional TV advertising simply can't match.

DRTV also allows companies to talk directly to their consumers, collect informa- tion from them and educate them in a luxurious amount of time. Using short form and/or long form DRTV commercials combined with other forms of advertising, marketers can not only get their points across, but they can also pound those points home for the TV viewer and web surfer.

Finally, it's hard to ignore DRTV's cost advantages. Spot DR media is regularly purchased as remnant time at 10 to 50 percent off rate card. In the recession-driven soft advertising market of 2008–10, long form DRTV media rates were down between 10 and 20 percent on average, to levels not seen since the turn of the millennium, as TV stations and cable networks responded to deteriorating ad revenues by exchang- ing entertainment programming for paid 30-minute commercial slots. Even today, with people continuing to entertain themselves more at home, TV viewing house- holds and viewing hours are on the rise, always a good sign for DRTV.

Short Form Vs. Long Form

There are two basic DRTV formats: long form, or the 28.5-minute infomercial for- mat, and short form, which comprises any DRTV commercial that is two minutes or less in length (with the most popular being 60, 90 or 120 seconds long). Many long form infomercial products won't succeed in short form because the product requires more than two minutes to fully explain the product features and benefits. Or if your product sale requires creating an emotional bond (via an "improve your relation- ships" self-help course, for example), short form will not cut it.

Think about the classic short form products you've seen over the years and how the products' benefits are quickly understood: classic rock music CDs, the Clint Eastwood movie collection, Ginsu knives, miracle polishers/cleansers, unique tools, Thigh Master, and so on. Most short form products are priced at or below $49.95, and some may even run with a co-existing infomercial campaign.

Short form DRTV spots are placed on TV stations and cable networks by purchas- ing "remnant" time, i.e. media time not already pre-purchased by a brand advertiser. It's "leftover" media time, available at a deep discount, and consequently the time slots rarely can be pinpointed beforehand except in broad dayparts (Morning, Daytime, Late Night). Often, depending on the DRTV short form competition and the strength of the brand advertising market, you will not achieve 100% of your requested time, but rather "clear" only a percentage, from 10% to 90%. Infomercial time slots, on the other hand, are set and secure for at least each upcoming quarter and clear 95 percent of the time.

In general, marketers should use short form when:

- They are selling a less complex product and story
- Their product has a lower price point ($9.95–$49.95) or coupon offer
- They need more targeted media placement
- Their goal is to drive retail, Internet, print, direct mail, radio and/or mobile sales

Long form is more often used when:

- The company has a more complex product and story
- The price point exceeds $49.95
- There is a need for significant differentiation

There are other factors to consider when deciding which format to use, and when to use both in concert with one another, such as:

Product type:
Short Form: Simpler, more impulse items; benefits and features need to be easily understood in 100 seconds.
Long Form: Good for more complex products that require more "consideration."

Product Features and Benefits:
Short Form: Only enough time to focus on five or six major product benefits.
Long Form: Plenty of time to go deep into multiple product features and benefits.

Testimonials:
Short Form: Not much time for "real people" testimonials (good actors are more concise); if strong real people testimonials are available, use very brief sound bites.
Long Form: Enough time for real people testimonials who can tell their product story in depth; more potential for evoking emotion and poignancy.

Call to Action (CTA):
Short Form: Traditionally about 20 seconds to state the offer (800 number could be inserted for virtually the entire spot).
Long Form: Traditionally between 2-1/2 and 3-1/2 minute long CTA's; inserted two to three times in the long form program for a total CTA time of almost 10 minutes (long form CTAs are often cut down and repurposed for 1- and 2-minute short form spots).

Price Point:
Short Form: Lower priced product ($9.95–$49.95), trial offers or lead generators
Long Form: Higher priced product ($49.95–$2,995), blind offers and lead generators

Drive Retail:

Both short form and long form can drive retail, but since short form can play at any time of the day or night it has significantly more reach (number of unique viewers) than long form and works perfectly as a follow-up strategy to a successful long form commercial for driving retail, Internet and other integrated marketing channels.

Strategic Goal:

Within the short form arena there are two distinctly different show types: the one-step offer, and the two-step lead generation approach. Rising media costs over the past 15 years have made it difficult—if not impossible—to get short form DRTV one-step offers to be profitable on immediate sales. But one-step offer short form products are now often run at a loss for months simply to drive the product's retail sales.

Response to DRTV commercials has varied much over the past 25 years, but through it all one constant remains: the success or failure of this type of advertising comes down to the product and the offer. In fact, the product determines which other channels best support short form or long form. For example, an intellectual property DRTV product can hit a home run with radio, whereas a skin product would not. Print supports live seminar DRTV well, but not much else. Online supports it all.

In other words, direct response campaigns are best supported with multi-platform campaigns (TV, radio, Internet, print, mobile). In addition, it has also been shown that long form drives results for short form, which drives online sales. The most successful campaigns know how to harness the power of all media to achieve winning ROI.

Here are a few DRTV "home runs" that have embraced the integrated approach to come out winners:

TABLE R18.1

Product	Total Sales*	Time on the Air
Popeil Showtime Rotisserie	$1.4 Billion+	7 years
George Foreman Grill	$500 Million+	5 years
Jet Stream Oven	$300 Million+	4 years
Magic Bullet Blender	$400 Million+	7 years
Rotozip Tool	$300 Million+	5 years
Swivel Sweeper	$100 Million+	3 years
Juiceman Juicers	$300 Million+	15 years
Miracle Mop	$150 Million+	3 years
Little Giant Ladder	$200 Million+	4 years
Tae Bo Fitness	$600 Million+	2 years
Total Gym	$1 Billion+	14 years
Richard Simmons Deal-A-Meal	$600 Million+	8 years
ProActiv Solution	$2 Billion+	15 years
Carleton Sheets	$1 Billion+	18 years
BowFlex Fitness	$1 Billion+	14 years
Tony Robbins Personal Power	$1 Billion+	15 years

*Figures are anecdotal estimates as of 2010

You probably recognize some or all of these product names, and that's because the companies behind them used (and/or, continue to use) a multi-pronged advertising approach that incorporates DRTV, plus other integrated channels. Not all of them were around for the evolution of Web 2.0 technology, but you can bet they would have <u>all</u> used social networking, online video and mobile advertising to further entrench their messages in their customers' brains.

Powerful Supplements

DRTV effectively supplements a company's existing advertising media mix. Working in concert with your other advertising avenues, DRTV can bolster consumer awareness of your product and provide more information and product benefits than is often possible in other media. By running infomercials on national cable and broadcast television, a product's story and benefits can be shared with millions of additional prospects. Direct sales are made in direct proportion to the number of television viewers. The cost per lead (CPL) or cost per order (CPO) can usually match or beat other direct marketing channels such as direct mail or print ads.

As you plan your infomercial campaign, there are a number of springboards built in to further bolster the success of your product. Back-end direct marketing works off of your infomercial, often resulting in profits that are two to five times those of upfront sales. Continuity programs, upsells, cross sells, list management and more extend profits well beyond your initial expectations. Back-end driven conversions may initially account for 30 to 50 percent of many direct marketers' sales.

Before creating a short form or long form commercial, companies and their DRTV ad agencies should review their customer profile, market research and historical sales results to determine demographic targeting and refine campaign objectives. To structure a productive media test, you'll want to ask yourself a few important questions first. One of the most important queries is: Which of the following do you want your show to achieve? Here are a few of the answers you'll probably come up with:

- ✓ Make a direct sale (one-step offer).
- ✓ Generate a lead (two-step offer).
- ✓ Strengthen customer relationship: increase brand loyalty, develop one-on-one customer database.
- ✓ Influence purchase behavior: enhance product value, move excess inventory, create sales bump with seasonal or event promotion.
- ✓ Reach new prospects: encourage product trial and retention.
- ✓ Launch new product: rapid and inexpensive test marketing.
- ✓ Demonstrate additional product uses: deepen product understanding and education.
- ✓ Build brand awareness; clarify differentiation, enhance image.
- ✓ Sustain and build brand equity: communicate corporate good works, solve a PR problem.
- ✓ Reposition brand: revive a mature product.
- ✓ Seasonal retail sales promotion.
- ✓ Drive retail and Internet sales.
- ✓ A mix of the above.

The infomercial can handle any of the above, based on its half-hour of product story telling time. Short form DRTV is a bit more limiting, but can still help marketers achieve most of these goals much more efficiently than traditional TV advertising.

Dollars and Sense

Infomercial media buying is highly specialized and much different from brand aware-ness spot buying or even short form DRTV spot buying. Image spot campaigns usu-ally have established media budgets. Infomercial media campaigns rarely have budg-ets (other than the initial $20,000 to $50,000 media test). As long as the media buys create profits, infomercial buyers will spend as much as they can.

Brand awareness spot campaigns buy media to obtain a pre-set amount of gross rating points (GRP's = total viewer impressions) and TRP's (targeted rating points = # of rating points among your targeted audience). Traditional infomercial buyers care very little about how many viewers watch. They concentrate on how many pick up the phone, or go to a web site, and order. Image spot buyers purchase airtime to cover six, eight or 13 week "flights," and then take the commercial off the air. Infomercial campaigns can run continuously 52 weeks a year for one, three, five years or more. Spot buyers have difficulty reserving specific 30-second spot periods within any half hour. Infomercial buyers can secure 13-, 26- or 52-week contracts for specific half hours and essentially "own" the time.

Image spot media is planned months ahead, then purchased in 13 week flights all at once, and then left alone to run its course. Infomercial media changes dramatically from week to week based on results, and requires daily cancellation, re-buying, and renegotiation. Image spot campaigns largely have no accountability measurements for success. Infomercial campaigns can measure success or failure within hours of the media run. Image spot campaigns have no need for a historical media database. Infomercial media buyers rely on databases of thousands of previous telecasts and their revenue results to determine future strategy.

Well-Defined Roles

In a DRTV campaign, short form and long form work in tandem with one another. Put simply, short form rounds out and complements the infomercial campaign. Very often, companies will cut 60-, 90- or 120-second commercials out of their infomercial and run a simultaneous short form campaign. Normally, the short form spots are not as profitable as the infomercial, but by reminding viewers of the product (they may have seen previously in the infomercial) in short bursts throughout the day, they can create a synergy with the infomercial to boost profitability.

One other drawback to short form DRTV is that buyers are required to purchase groups of spots (2 to 50) on a weekly basis and measure success primarily on each station's overall results, not individual spot runs. Infomercial buyers can purchase one half hour, or many, on the same station and measure success for each and every individual half hour.

While DRTV airtime rates are clearly lower than the prices for image spots, there are still a few important points for marketers to consider when integrating direct re-sponse TV into their IMC campaigns.

Take media efficiency ratio (MER = total direct sales / media cost), for example.

The universal benchmark used by DRTV marketers to determine if a product is paying out and has a potential future in selling direct to consumers, a "positive" MER always depends on the campaign's breakeven (BE) goal. Some products with high Cost of Goods (COG) may require a high BE MER, say a 2 or 2.5 ($250 product sales to every $100 of media spent). Other products that are looking to drive retail or Internet sales may thrive with a MER as low as .3 or .5 ($50 of direct sales to every $100 of media spent).

But what happens when a product doesn't achieve these minimum MERs? If you're at 75 percent of your goal, you should definitely "tweak" the commercial creative and/or offer. This means looking at making changes in your voiceover talent, music, graphic look, product shots, testimonials and re-editing the show elements to add clarity and improve pacing. Even deeper changes might require you to rewrite the show's opening segment and CTA to make it harder-hitting and the offer more enticing.

If, on the other hand, you're at 50 percent of minimum MER goal or less, you'll need a significant show makeover, which might include: repositioning the product, script rewrite, new product name, on-camera talent, testimonials, set and/or setting. Tests that come in at less than 25 percent of minimum MER goal might benefit from a commercial makeover, but from what I've seen, the chances of success will be very low.

As you've just read, DRTV is a completely different animal than traditional television advertising. It comes with its own set of quirks, but can also offer significant benefits that 15- and 30-second image spots cannot. To most effectively integrate the medium into your marketing mix requires a group of talented, knowledgeable individuals who not only know your product, brand and its idiosyncrasies, but who have their fingers on the pulse of this unique advertising channel.

Collaborative Qualities

DRTV in and of itself is a powerful, highly versatile platform. Pair it with other, equally effective marketing channels, and that strength and versatility increases exponentially. Just as with general TV advertising, ongoing DRTV campaigns lift sales in other channels and can be seamlessly incorporated into a fully integrated marketing plan. With its ability to do the heavy lifting while simultaneously delivering efficiency and effectiveness metrics, DRTV can be utilized in a variety of tactical ways.

The most common tactical use of DRTV by major brands is to create a DRTV commercial that powerfully drives retail store sales, while partially offsetting the cost of media with direct sale revenues, producing MER's of .1 to .3 or more. DRTV campaigns have also launched many CRM initiatives within companies new to one-on-one marketing and previously unaware of the value of a large, dynamic customer database.

Companies often repurpose the DRTV footage for point-of-sale displays and to add "sticky" video assets to their web sites. In fact, DRTV has measurably been proven to outperform general TV advertising in terms of delivering vast amounts of valuable information and lifting overall ROI of advertising budgets. Here's a quick look at how DRTV boosts other sales channels:

✓ 75% of all consumers will not buy products direct over TV but 95% of all TV viewers will watch DRTV commercials.

✓ 47 percent of all consumers bought a DRTV product at retail or online after viewing a DRTV commercial.

✓ Infomercial driven retail sales: 2–5 times the number of direct sales.

✓ Web searches can be boosted by as much as 1,230% and paid click through rates by 58%.

✓ Product storytelling, demonstrations and testimonials benefit all marketing efforts by dramatizing product benefits and consumer preference.

Direct response works particularly well with the new round of advertising options that have taken hold over the last few years. With more companies using social networking, the web, mobile advertising and online video to communicate directly with consumers, it just makes sense that DRTV would serve as the perfect adjunct for these forward-thinking marketing campaigns. Instead of simply slapping a 30-second image spot on the TV airwaves and hoping that customers will respond favorably, companies of all sizes—and from all industries—are taking a more proactive advertising approach using DRTV's greater length and economic media costs.

Online video is a particularly compelling option that works extremely well with DRTV. In fact, we've found that online video helps to create consumer trust and ultimately results in more transactions. And research shows that over 60 percent of DRTV viewers go online to learn more about a product or service before ordering. The boom in online video is happening because "videoactive" web sites (using video intensively on formerly text heavy web pages) educate consumers, entertain them and give consumers an opportunity to opt-in to additional information presented in a highly entertaining video format.

With the use of mobile also on the rise, companies are also seeking out ways to effectively integrate mobile with more traditional channels. This is especially critical for firms looking to hit younger demographic groups, from pre-teen to late-20s, who heavily rely on their mobile phones. Gen X (30–45) and Gen Y (20-somethings) are also good responders to mobile offers, making the case for such campaigns that much more compelling. More and more, the CTAs in DRTV commercials are including SMS codes as a response mechanism alternative to 800 #'s and URLs.

On the Horizon

Developments in and around the DRTV industry reveal an exciting future replete with not only individual successes, but also integrated campaigns that are leveraged across various platforms. Seemingly innocuous announcements (such as Dish's late-2010 revelation that subscribers would soon be able to watch TV content on their iPads, iPhones and iPod Touch devices) actually have substantial impact on the way advertisers and their agencies think, and on the methods they're using to reach current, past and future customers.

Put video-on-demand, interactive program guides and DVRs into the "game changers" category, and toss the Internet and its myriad functionalities into the mix. The end result is a multi-channel advertising world that experts like Backchannel

Media's Michael Kokernak boldly make predictions about. Kokernak envisions a "TV Everywhere" portal that not only gives consumers more choices, but that also provides the following benefits:

✓ Integration with web and devices. Leveraging Internet-enabled technologies such as GPS, video cameras, heart monitors, car diagnostic kits, bathroom scales, etc. will allow the user to combine data beyond mobile phones into a video device.

✓ Customization via advertising and content feeds. Tailoring the user experience will require at least two interdependent feeds, notes Kokernak, kind of like how AdWords assembles advertising results based on a consumer's search request. The television industry, when leveraging multiple devices and a return path clickstream, can create a superior experience to the Internet search.

✓ Path to addressable media. Interlaced bound and unbound content will enable the user to monitor and interact with personally identifiable, and unidentifiable, data sources from a variety of devices wrapped around the core video experience.

✓ A personal level of devices—those that can monitor everything from heart rate to the performance of automobiles—will become commonplace and are a part of the natural evolution of Web 2.0. As consumers multitask, they will seek out privacy-protected devices that can be integrated with "television."

Expect these and other predictions to materialize over coming months and years, as the economy rises from the ashes of the recession and makes its way into "rebound" territory. In periods when we experience lower response rates, it makes sense to maximize the revenue of every call, click and order you get. The industry focus is going to be on hot back-end solutions, such as innovative cross-selling, couponing, retail-driving incentives and new, outside the box approaches to maximize DR revenue.

At Hawthorne Direct, we stay on the cutting edge of the advertising industry, while at the same time employing tried-and-true DRTV methods that deliver consistent results. We use highly innovative upsell techniques and back-end programs, for example, to add significant revenue to the initial DRTV and online sales, and to improve our clients' overall ROI.

As marketers roll out more SMS text codes on their commercials' tag pages to enable growing mobile phone response, and utilize other innovative, integrated advertising methods, we'll be right by their sides. By integrating these and other channel innovations with well-thought-out DRTV campaigns, marketers will be able to gain an edge and approach consumers in the fastest, most efficient and profitable manner possible.

Author of more than 200 published articles, TIM HAWTHORNE is Founder, Chairman and Executive Creative Director of Hawthorne Direct, a full-service DRTV and New Media ad agency founded in 1986. Since then Hawthorne has produced or managed over 800 Direct Response TV campaigns for clients such as 3M, Black & Decker, Braun, Discover Card, Time-Life, Nissan, Lawn Boy, Nikon, Oreck, Bose and Feed the Children. Hawthorne is a co-founder of the Electronic Retailing Association, has delivered over 100 speeches worldwide and is the author of the definitive DRTV book *The Complete Guide to Infomercial Marketing*. A cum laude graduate of Harvard, Hawthorne was honored with the prestigious "Lifetime Achievement Award" by the Electronic Retailing Association (ERA) in 2006.

CASE
1

Allstate Insurance: Building Relationships through Email Campaigns

BLODWEN TARTER
Golden Gate University

MARY CARAVELLA
University of Connecticut

DEBRA ZAHAY
Northern Illinois University

R oberta Borst, Marketing Communications Director for Allstate Insurance, was thinking about the future of the recently launched relationship marketing campaign. Aspen Marketing Services, Allstate's ad agency, had done a terrific job of coming up with an email campaign that would help retain existing customers and open doors for cross-selling new insurance products to them. However, a relationship marketing campaign was new to Allstate. Historically, the company had spent about 30% of its corporate marketing dollars on direct marketing, most of it direct mail. (National general market television accounted for the largest portion of the total corporate marketing expenditures.) These direct mail call-to-action campaigns were intended to generate sales leads primarily for Allstate agents. Of course, Allstate had a web site and previously Allstate had experimented with different kinds of email messages to customers. Individual agents had tried different approaches while the corporate marketing group had also initiated a variety of email campaigns. The results had been sufficiently promising that Allstate corporate marketing wanted to pursue a coordinated email marketing strategy to support the field agents. The email-based relationship marketing campaign was a new venture, both in scope and purpose.

The initial results of the campaign were quite good and the corporate marketing team judged it successful by a number of measures. Now, how could Roberta best sell the agents on the value of continuing this campaign and get their support for enhancing it? What was needed to ensure its continued success? The campaign was just ending its first year and it was time to consider what the next steps should be.

Insurance Industry Overview

The insurance industry exists to protect its customers ("insureds" or "policyholders") from the consequences of risk. The insurer charges a premium for insurance coverage against specified risks, such as an automobile accident or a flood or fire in one's home. In the event that something happens for which the policyholder is covered, the insurance company pays, according to the terms of its contract. By extensive modeling of historical data, insurance companies seek to price coverage in such a way that the insurance company has sufficient reserves to pay out for any damages and still make money. Insurance may be the only product that people buy that they hope they will never use!

In the United States, the $140.1 billion insurance industry[1] is highly fragmented and extremely competitive. Insurance agents and brokers sell a host of insurance products but property and casualty and life insurance account for the bulk of the premiums. In a recent year, 53.4% of premiums were attributable to non-life insurance policies and 46.6% of premiums came from life insurance.[2] Personal property and casualty insurance covers automobiles and personal residences, so-called car insurance and homeowners' policies. Life insurance pays benefits upon the death of the insured.

Insurance companies compete for customers based on coverage (do they offer the kind of insurance needed?), price (are premiums competitive?), service (when a claim is made, how prompt and efficient is the company to process the claim?), and reliability and stability (is the company sufficiently well-managed that it will be able to pay out when claims are made?). Reputation is everything.

A highly regulated industry, insurance companies are subject to state laws and are scrutinized on an ongoing basis by state insurance commissioners. Every state has its own rules and regulations. Agents and brokers must be licensed in every state in which they do business and marketing materials must comply with the varying rules imposed by each state. This regulatory environment makes creating national campaigns more complex for insurance companies than for unregulated businesses.

In the insurance industry, a great deal of effort is spent on first acquiring a customer. If nothing goes awry, the company hopes that customers will simply renew their insurance policies year after year. A satisfied insurance customer is often subject to inertia—once he or she becomes a customer of a specific insurance company, it seems like too much work to move. The customer is also a prime target for cross-selling different products, further tying the customer to the company. Discounts on homeowner policies may be available to those policyholders who also have car insurance with a given company, encouraging customers to buy multiple insurance products from the same company. These bundles of products are lucrative for the insurance company and are the basis for a more in-depth relationship between the

---

[1] *Insurance in the United States: Industry Profile*, Reference Code 0072-2087, Datamonitor, November 2008, p. 3. Accessed via Business Source Complete online database, accession number 35416629. Value as measured by 2007 premiums.

[2] *Insurance in the United States: Industry Profile*, Reference Code 0072-2087, Datamonitor, November 2008, p. 12.

customer and the insurance company. However, as the insurance business becomes increasingly competitive, active customer retention efforts become a higher priority.

Company Background

Allstate is the second-largest US personal lines property and casualty insurer, behind State Farm. The company, originally owned by Sears, was started in 1931, during the Great Depression, as a way for Sears to diversify by selling insurance through its stores. Allstate became a public company in 1993. At that time, Sears divested about 20% of its shares in the company, followed by complete divestiture in 1995. Allstate has continued to grow in size and scope, broadening its product offerings over the years.

The company sells property and casualty and life insurance products in Canada and the US. Allstate Protection, which focuses on the property and casualty lines of insurance, accounts for about 90% of total premiums of Allstate. The Allstate Protection business is somewhat concentrated, with about 40% of its premiums from sales in California, Florida, New York, and Texas. Although customers can purchase some products online, Allstate maintains a network of 12,800 exclusive agencies which sell its Allstate-branded insurance products.[3] Allstate's image is of a reliable, well-established company and the longstanding slogan "You're in good hands with Allstate®" has resonated among generations of Americans. Yet, customers can still be lured away from Allstate by lower rates from discount companies because insurance rates are rising.

Like most insurers, Allstate had taken steps to protect itself from losses due to catastrophic events such as hurricanes, tornadoes, and floods. However, catastrophic losses for Allstate were greater in the first quarter of the current years than all of the previous year. Allstate was also feeling the pain of the weakening US economy. Fewer auto sales meant fewer new auto insurance policies. Rising mortgage defaults and fewer home purchases adversely affected the number of homeowner policies. Investment income, another source of financial strength for insurance companies, was reduced in the face of the turbulent financial markets. Retaining current customers at profitable rates and increasing the number of policies per customer could only help Allstate's bottom line.

Early in the current year, Allstate was grappling with the same issues facing many insurers because of the rise of the Internet. The term "disintermediation" means leaving the middleman out of the picture; the Internet allows people looking for insurance to buy insurance directly over the Internet. Even though most consumers don't actually purchase insurance online, they have the opportunity to instantly compare prices and seek the best deal. Readily available information about prices and coverage could weaken the ties that bind an insurance customer to the insurance company. In response, Allstate developed some new, more competitive products.

These product line extensions were ways Allstate was building its customer acquisition efforts. However, Allstate also wanted to retain current customers buying regular product lines and to keep the new customers initially attracted by lower rates.

---

[3] *The Allstate Corporation,* Hoover's Company Records—In-depth Records, June 5, 2009, accessed via Lexis/Nexis Academic database 11 June 2009.

Historically, many agents had not spent a lot of time between renewals nurturing customers. Allstate corporate recognized that helping agents stay in touch with customers could strengthen ties to Allstate and reduce customer attrition. If customers felt that Allstate cared about them and acted in their best interests they might be less likely to leave for lower rates. So while Roberta wanted to create marketing campaigns that strengthened customers' connections with the Allstate brand, she also wanted the campaigns to help agents stay in touch—reinforcing the key role the agents played in delivering the "You're in Good Hands" brand promise.

The Email Relationship Campaign

Thus, Allstate decided to develop a relationship-building email marketing campaign in order to maximize the lifetime value of current customers, offset attrition and ease the cross-selling process. The company wanted the series of emails not just to "push product" but to create a real dialogue with customers, building an emotional tie that lasted beyond the initial decision to buy or the subsequent decision to renew. Of course, by educating customers to help them avoid problems that caused losses, the company also stood to benefit. Fewer losses meant that Allstate paid less to settle claims and enhanced the company's profitability.

In the words of Allstate's ad agency that developed the program, the initial plan was to "communicate to customers on a monthly basis, provide valuable information without selling, and start to build a relationship beyond insurance." By cultivating the trust of the customer, the ensuing loyalty to Allstate would influence customers to renew their policies. Encouraging policyholders to call their agent with questions would begin a conversation between the policyholder and the agent and help customers become more secure about their Allstate relationship and more invested in it.

How did the Allstate email campaign achieve these objectives?

The company concentrated on three aspects: engaging emails from a recognized sender that encouraged action; using a simple, focused, microsite online that reinforced the message of each email and encouraged educational and fun customer interaction, and by creating an ongoing conversation between the policyholder and Allstate. That dialogue started with emails and the Allstate web site but encouraged personal and direct involvement with the Allstate agent.

A series of monthly emails was sent directly from the agent, a familiar name. Email deliverability was a high priority and Allstate's careful compliance with the CAN-SPAM requirements was expected to avoid messages being caught in spam filters. Once a spam filter blocks an email message there is a high likelihood it would never reach the customer. Responsys, Allstate's email deployment vendor, measured deliverability rates as high as 99% against a benchmark of 85%, suggesting that the Allstate campaign was quite effective in this arena.

The creative execution similarly focused on deliverability and legibility. Designed to be scanned quickly, the HTML text appeared on solid color backgrounds without images that are often blocked by Internet service providers. Carefully crafted messages meant that the email preview pane displayed the key information in full. Allstate knew that it had only seconds to grab the attention of its policyholders to encourage them to read the complete message and then act as requested.

Intriguing subject lines "hooked" customers and drove them to the online microsite to further engage with the company. Subject lines such as "Insurance Facts and Fallacies," "Lower Your Insurance Premiums," "Safe Driving" and "Home Preparedness" led visitors to interactive games, quizzes and surveys designed to entice customer interaction. There, visitors could browse more information on the specific topic as well as read other tips, facts, checklists and vital information. The microsite included valuable downloads like a teen driving contract, a home inventory checklist and car games for road trips. There was also a feedback center where customers could rate each page's content on a 1–5 scale.

Like the emails, the microsite had been designed to be easily scanned and simple to navigate, as well as visually consistent with the emails. From Allstate's perspective, the new microsite page templates made updating fast and easy, so fresh content could be added quickly each month. As customers became accustomed to finding new information on the web site they were more likely to visit again and again, prompted by new emails. Relevant partner offers, such as a discount on a home security system from ADT, made the microsite even more attractive to policyholders. Allstate hoped that the email messages had some pass-along value and that recipients would forward the emails to others who might be interested in the content.

With objectives to build customer trust and loyalty, drive awareness and build good will rather than sell policies, Allstate measured the results of the relationship email campaign primarily by click-through rates (CTR) and participation in the web site-based activities. The results had been impressive with a 165% increase in the email click-through rate from two years ago to one year ago, and a recent average unique click-through rate that was 125% over the email marketing industry average.

As specific examples, the company achieved a 72% email open rate and 13.3% CTR with its ECHO award-winning January "Insurance Quiz." The "Lower Your Insurance Premiums" email produced an email click-through rate four times the financial industry average. July's "Summer Driving" email sweepstakes to win a Rand McNally Road Atlas resulted in entries from 42% of unique visitors to the site. Customers also helped choose where Allstate would give its end-of-year charitable donations—65% of the visitors "voted" online in December of the previous year. For examples of the emails and microsite see Appendix 1.

These results were impressive but left Allstate with the question of where to go next. Click-through rates, although high, had not immediately translated into renewals or incremental policy sales—an overwhelming priority for individual agents. Increases in brand equity had not been measured. Agents were generally supportive of the effort. In fact some customers had called their agents to initiate conversations about existing policies and about new ones. In addition to measurable results, the anecdotal feedback was generally positive. Of course, it didn't hurt that the campaign was funded by corporate marketing, rather than being covered by the regional or individual field agent's budgets.

After the initial launch, it was decided that the emails should be customized for specific areas of the country. Once it was recognized that messages should be geographically targeted, many messages varied by customer location. For instance, an email that suggested ways to prepare for weather disasters could be tailored for tornadoes, floods, or hail, depending upon where the customer lived. This targeting further improved the effectiveness of the messaging, reinforced the corporate/field partnership, and better served the customers receiving the emails.

However, a few agents had been skeptical about the campaign in spite of the fact that the email messages were sent with their names in the "From" line. The agents were more accustomed to direct marketing that specifically called for a renewal or a new sale (e.g. when cross-selling a different insurance product to an existing customer). Other agents simply didn't fully understand how email marketing was supposed to work. So there was still work to be done to deepen appreciation of the value of email marketing in general and about this campaign in particular.

A number of agents asked for suggestions on how to best capitalize on the corporate email marketing efforts to support their own sales efforts. Allstate agents were demographically diverse. Many were unfamiliar with social networking tools and digital marketing. The marketing team helped interested agents integrate their efforts with the overall relationship campaign

Most agents appreciated the corporate efforts to strengthen customer ties to Allstate and to help them build their business. These agents recognized that customer loyalty might make current policyholders more inclined to buy another type of insurance from Allstate and looked forward to the cross-sell opportunities the campaign should open up. But what would the next steps in this effort look like? Should Allstate now include explicit cross-selling messages in the relationship-building campaign or not? The individual agents and the corporate marketing staff were divided among themselves on this question. There was no clear consensus.

So far, the relationship email marketing campaign stood apart in Allstate's corporate and individual agent marketing efforts. There had been an explosion in social media since the campaign began and many consumers reported using Internet search engines rather than calling agents to make decisions on insurance purchases. How could Allstate expand this good start to focus on relationship-building across all sales channels?

Roberta had several ideas for building on this already successful email campaign.

1. **Allstate could continue soft relationship-building email campaigns in order to retain customers.** Creating new and relevant messages that helped build trust in Allstate without explicit selling would be consistent with the campaign just completed. If Roberta went down this path, she would also need to look at how to extend these messages across additional online media.

2. **Allstate could add specific cross-selling messages into the campaign.** Roberta knew that she could analyze the existing customer base to identify who already owned what kind of insurance and what combinations of insurance were most common. For example, were home owners more likely to own automobile insurance and boat insurance? Then Roberta would need to identify to which customers she should offer what additional lines of insurance. Last but not least, once the target was identified, in what ways could she customize the messages to be most effective? How could Allstate transition the messaging from relationship-building, a softer message, to cross-selling, a harder sell? Furthermore, how could Roberta structure a cross-selling campaign in order to measure its effectiveness?

3. **Allstate could develop email campaigns that generated new leads for agents.** People who indicated interest in Allstate insurance but who had not yet purchased a policy needed to be encouraged to apply and then, once approved, to actually buy the insurance. The field agents might welcome this type of assistance, but this was a significant shift away from the original relationship building intent of the email marketing campaign. Where did customer acquisition and lead conversion fit with the email relationship-building campaign?

Of course, there were many ideas floating around. Roberta mentally reviewed her options and reminded herself that she needed to sort through the alternatives and prioritize them. She knew that the company would require full financial justification of the next phase of the campaign. With the recent serious losses, largely due to tornadoes, hurricanes, and hail storms, all marketing expenditures would be scrutinized and evaluated for an adequate return on investment (ROI). Consequently, Roberta might have to collect more data and enhance its analysis to demonstrate the next campaign's value. As she considered how much needed to be done, Roberta directed the agency to provide recommendations for all aspects of the campaign's next phase, from creative to data analysis.

Appendix 1

Samples from the Campaign

EXHIBIT C1.1:
INSURANCE QUIZ, JANUARY

Results

- *Open Rate*   *72%*
- *Click-through Rate*   *13.3%*
- *ECHO Award winner*

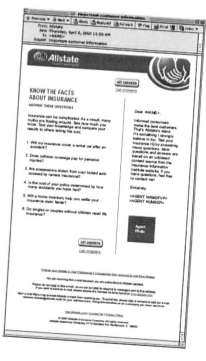

EXHIBIT C1.2: HOW TO LOWER YOUR INSURANCE PREMIUMS, JUNE

Results

- *Delivered*   327,730
- *Bounced*   17,505
- *Open Rate*   64.38%
- *Unique Open Rate*   39.08%
- *Click-through Rate (high)*   22%
- *Unsubscribe*   0.1% (336)

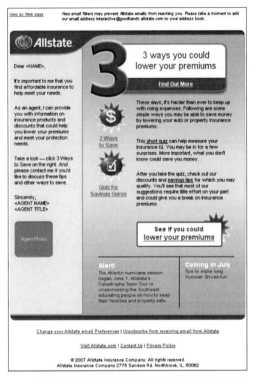

EXHIBIT C1.3: SUMMER DRIVING SWEEPSTAKES JULY

Results

- *Obtained sweepstakes entries from* **42% of unique visitors** *to the site*

EXHIBIT C1.4: ADT PARTNERSHIP OFFER ON MICROSITE

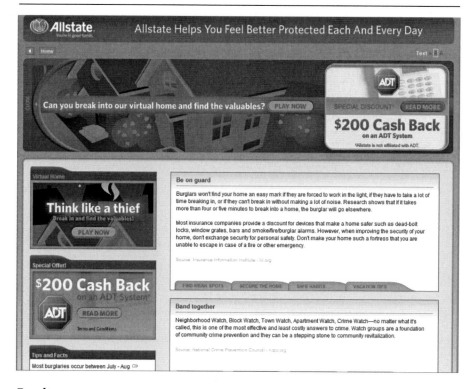

Results

- *Number of leads exceeded ADT's expectations*

Appendix 2

Email Marketing Summary

Advantages: Creates true one to one channel, trackable, measurable, excellent for maintaining and growing a customer relationship using personalized messages

Disadvantages: Difficult to control, driven by end user, limited, not mass, audience

Advantages versus Direct Mail: Faster (3 days vs. 3 weeks), cheaper ($.25 versus a dollar or more), higher response (5% vs. 0.5%).

Response rates (CTR): Vary from 5–10% depending on type of email, audience (list), etc.

Email Uses: Forrester research study of companies doing ecommerce revealed how these firms use email:

- 66% Promotions and discounts
- 48% Newsletters
- 34% New products
- 28% Marketing & advertising
- 24% Alerts and reminders
- 8% Market research

Key email marketing process metrics:

- Bounce rate—undeliverable addresses
- Unsubscribe rate- percent of people who unsubscribe in response to an email
- Open rate—percent of delivered mail that readers open
- Click-through rate number of links clicked or actions taken divided by the number of opened emails
- Example:
  —100 emails sent
   □ 5 are undeliverable so bounce rate is 5%
   □ 5 people unsubscribe so the unsubscribe rate is 5%
  —40 are opened so open rate is 44% (40/90)
  —10 users actually click through on the requested action so the click-through rate is 25% (10/40)

Elements of CAN-SPAM Act compliance:
- Valid 'from' email address, valid reply
- Street address
- Unsubscribe provision
- Label as 'advertising' if the email is unsolicited

How to improve deliverability*

- Use a commercial Email Service Provider with a good reputation with email companies
- Comply with the CAN-SPAM Act (see above)

---

*thanks to Exact Target (www.exacttarget.com) for some of these tips

- Get and confirm permission
- Set content and frequency expectations with customer
- Have a compelling subject line
- Send more relevant content; avoid overly promotional content
- Have an "Address Book" strategy
- Use proper list hygiene
  —Use procedures to remove duplicate addresses from your list
  —Use procedures to screen out addresses on your "do not email" list
  —Check email bounces and correct
- Monitor blacklist reports

Brief Email Marketing Glossary

- **Bounce Rate:** Number of emails undeliverable divided by the number sent
  —**Hard Bounce Rate:** Number of emails undeliverable because of a bad email address divided by the number sent
  —**Soft Bounce Rate:** Number of emails undeliverable for reasons other than a bad email address divided by the number sent
- **Clickstream:** Database created by web site to track user activity on the site
- **Click-Through Rate (CTR):** Number of email offers acted on by clicking a link through to a web page divided by number opened. In online advertising or search marketing, the click-through rate is often instead calculated as the number of users that click on an online ad divided by the total number of exposures. When comparing across media, it is important to understand the calculation being used.
- **Click-to-Purchase Rate:** Number of purchases generated by email campaign divided by number of emails opened
- **Cookies:** Electronic tag on user's computer to enable the web site to recognize that user on their return
- **Dynamic Content:** Changing the email content per user, including personalizing name and other customer information as well as the email content delivered
- **HTML Email:** Emails formatted using the same hypertext markup language used to create web pages. Open rates can only be calculated for HTML emails; rates for text emails and emails opened on many mobile phones cannot be tracked
- **Open Rate:** Number of email offers opened divided by number delivered
  —**Unique Open Rate:** Number of actual people opening offers, divided by number delivered. Accounts for people who look at the email more than once.
- **Permission Email:** solicitations sent with the receiver's prior permission obtained in some manner; recommended email marketing method
- **Spam:** lots of unwanted, unsolicited email, gets its name from the famous Monty Python skit in which spam is mentioned so many times that the word becomes annoying! http://www.detritus.org/spam/ And enjoy the song!

CASE
2

American Cancer Society Chicago Chapter May Walk and Roll Event Marketing Campaign

J. STEVEN KELLY
DePaul University

FRANK K. BRYANT
Cal Poly Pomona

RAYECAROL CAVENDER
Virginia Tech

KATE STEVENSON
DePaul University

REGINE VANHEEMS
Université of Paris I—Sorbonne

The National American Cancer Society

This national organization (www.cancer.org) is well known as the premier association that fights cancer. Through its efforts, the National American Cancer Society (NACS) has been able to channel $3.4 billion into funding for cancer research. The NACS can claim that its efforts have supported every major breakthrough in cancer research. Indeed, the NACS has supported 42 Nobel laureates. The organization's leaders and supporters are proud of the fact that 11 million cancer survivors are "living proof" of the American Cancer Society's progress.

That said, NACS research disclosed that although the American Cancer Society was the most highly recognized health charity brand, many citizens had little understanding about the scope of the organization's programs. Therefore, in a recent year, NACS launched a brand revitalization effort. This campaign positioned the American Cancer Society as "The Official Sponsor of Birthdays." The marketing communications asked the public to imagine a world with more birthdays, and highlighted all of the ways the organization saves lives. These included: helping people stay well through taking steps to prevent cancer or detect it early; helping people get well by guiding them through every step of the cancer experience; finding cures through funding and conducting groundbreaking research; and fighting back by encouraging lawmakers to do their part to defeat cancer and rallying communities to join the fight.

One of their main campaigns for NACS is the American Cancer Society "Relay For Life", its signature fundraising activity. It takes place across the country each year, with many of the local and regional events occurring in the spring. The American Cancer Society's community presence is often best felt through Relay For Life, the largest global grassroots movement and cancer fundraiser that involves more than 3.5 million participants. Relay for Life celebrates people who have battled cancer, remembers loved ones lost, and fights back to end a disease that has taken too much away from too many people. The money raised through Relay has helped the American Cancer Society to play a role in nearly every major cancer breakthrough in recent history.

The new "The Official Sponsor of Birthdays" brand effort included a major national advertising launch during April. It included television programs, e.g. "Good Morning America," the "Today" show, "20/20," "60 Minutes," "The View," "CSI," "Amazing Race," "Dancing with the Stars," as well as shows on cable channels.; in print publications including *Better Homes & Gardens*, *O-The Oprah Magazine*, *Health*, *Family Circle*, *Cooking Light*, *Woman's Day*, *Ladies' Home Journal*, *Prevention* and *Essence*.

The American Cancer Society/Chicago Region

With this background in mind, this case now shifts its focus to one of the major chapters of the American Cancer Society, located in the Chicago region. As the Chicago case opens in fall of the current year, the Vice President of Communications for the Chicago American Cancer Society is fully aware of the national campaigns and programs. That said, his personal responsibility is for the success of the local programs. Like any strategic business unit, the Chicago chapter has financial goals it must meet. Therefore, it is responsible for the marketing of this chapter's own fundraising events as well as assisting with the national programs. Through its 15 community-based regional offices and presence at 50 healthcare partners, the American Cancer Society/Chicago (ACSC) sponsors more than 200 local events— many of them Relay for Life events—each year to raise money. Donors fund $45 million in annual contributions from nearly 400,000 Illinois individuals and companies. To make this happen, ACSC works with nearly 100,000 volunteers.

At this time, the Vice President wants to take a close look at the events referred to as the Walk and Roll fundraisers. These are separate from the other chapter and national ACS office events. In fact, the national events could be said to be competitive to the local events. The local chapter holds five Walk and Roll events in the Chicago area, most in May and one in August (see Table C2.1). Five are in the suburbs, one in the city of Peoria, but the big event is in Chicago the weekend after Mother's Day, usually the second weekend in May. The Vice President wants to focus on this event as a major part of ACSC's fundraising effort. To view the Walk and Roll web site, enter "Walk and Roll" into a search engine.

The results of the previous Spring's events were not up to standard and are outlined here:

TABLE C2.1

Walk & Roll Event	Date	Money Raised Previous Spring
W&R-Elgin	Sat, May 7	$73,628
W&R-Chicago	Sun, May 15	$523,578
W&R-North Shore	Sun, May 15	$42,587
W&R- West Cook (cancelled—participants urged to join W&R Chicago)	Sun, May 15	$9,830
W&R- Lake County	Sun, May 15	$64,795
W&R- Richland County	Sat, May 21	$6,131
W&R-Peoria	Sat, Aug 14	$1,445

This low level of fundraising results was cause for alarm because it fell well below ACSC's goals and previous year's accomplishments. The Vice President felt that his communications team needed to be assembled to review what could be done to turn this situation around.

In fact, in the previous year, more than 6,000 people had gathered for this annual tradition, raising more than $1.1 million to fight cancer. There were 450 teams of participants, 200 in-line skaters, 500 bikers, and 3500 walkers to total 4,200 actual participants. The rest were volunteers who helped participants and manned the route and booths.

The Chicago Walk and Roll event was the ACSC's longest-standing fundraising event in Illinois. It had begun nearly 40 years previous as the Chicago Bike-a-thon and had grown to include walkers, cyclists, and in-line skaters.

The area had a history of supporting ACSC fundraising events. The very first event was the Bike-a-Thon in 1972, operated along the Chicago Lakefront. Later, walking and in-line skating were added to the event. A second event, in 1974, was started in Skokie, a suburb north of Chicago. It had always been much smaller, with perhaps 600 participants and 60 teams. Much more recently, other events were added. Two years ago, one was held in the northwest suburbs, Elgin, with about 400 participants and 40 teams. Then, four other events were established in the previous year, one far north in Lake County with 450 participants, one West in Brookfield Woods with 300 participants, and two outside Chicago in Peoria and Richland County. All of these were operated in May, except the one in Peoria which was in August.

The plan for this coming Spring/Summer was to hold the following Walk and Roll events:

Elgin, Saturday, May 8
Chicago, Sunday May 15
North Shore, Sunday May 15
Lake County, Sunday May 15
Peoria, Saturday, August 14
Richland County, IL, Saturday, May 22

Background on the Fundraising Environment

The ACSC team reminded each other about the charitable donations environment they had been facing. In the U.S., charitable donations fell 3.6% during the first year of the recent recession. That amounted to $303.75 billion given in the previous year, compared to $315 billion in the year prior to that. This was the largest drop in donations since the 1970s, when the country was going through the oil crisis. High unemployment and foreclosures were prevalent during this time, and may have been a contributing factor to this loss. Forty percent of all charitable gifts are given in the last quarter of the year (October through December). One-third of all donations go to religious groups, which are the biggest recipients of donations. The bulk of all donations come from individuals in the form of small gifts. Giving to human services, health, international affairs and environment and animal-related groups all saw increases in the previous year, while donations to education, arts, culture and humanities organizations fell overall.

Statistics found at www.factfinder.census.gov provided some insights into the current Chicago population:

TABLE C2.2

	Estimate
Total Population	2,725,206
Male	1,333,779
Female	1,391,427
Men and Women's Population	
25 to 34 years	453,165
35 to 44 years	415,807
45 to 54 years	356,586
18 years and over	2,065,028
Male	997,859
Female	1,067,169

Also, income figures helped complete the picture of the greater Chicago community and potential participants in the ACSC events.

TABLE C2.3

Income Less than $25,000	610,454
Income of $25,000 to $34,999	269,893
Income of $35,000 to $49,999	389,145
Income of $50,000 to $74,999	559,553
Income of $75,000 to $99,999	409,265
Income of $100,000 to $149,999	438,021
Income of $150,000 to $199,999	172,813
Income of $200,000 or more	181,475
Median household income (dollars)	$60,057
Mean household income (dollars)	$82,320

The participants in the previous Walk and Roll events fell into the following categories. The vast majority of walkers were female, between 30 and 50 years old. Corporate teams brought in young professionals. The average income of participants was consistent with the national average household income. There was some minority engagement through family and friends teams. For the Chicago Walk and Roll, 48% had 606—zip codes (meaning Chicago city residents), with 50% coming in from the suburbs and 2% from out of state.

Competitive Environment

One cause of the poor donation turnout could be addressed by the level of fundraiser run/walk competition that had arisen in the past few years. The citizens of the area had a wealth of opportunities to participate in such events and raise funds for causes. These are just a few of the events scheduled to take place during the general time period that the ACSC sponsors its events:

- Heart Walk—American Heart Assn., September
- JDRF Walk—Juvenile Diabetes, September
- Walk America—March of Dimes, April
- Mother's Day Walk/Run—Breast Cancer Network of Strength, May
- Memory Walk—Alzheimer's Association, August
- Out of the Dark—National Suicide, May
- Light the Night—Leukemia/Lymphoma, September
- NKFI Gift of Life Walk and Family Health Fair—National Kidney Foundation, June
- Bastille Day: 5K Run/Walk—Marcy Home for Boys, July
- Run for Gus, 5K—Young Associate Board, July
- Fight For Air Run/Walk—American Lung Association, September
- AIDS Run & Walk Chicago—AIDS Foundation of Chicago, October
- Susan G. Komen Walk/Race for the Cure—several races and walks in the summer

A point worth noting is that most of these were not events where winning was a goal. Other events in the area, around the same time, did offer athletic competition. The

ACSC team recognized that the amount of preparation required for athletically competitive events did change the perspective of the participant.

The public did seem to want to seek information and involvement in events such as those presented by ACSC. As an example of the popularity of these types of events, a review of key words used for Google search in September showed that the following phrases elicited these numbers:

Cancer walk	246,000
Cure cancer	201,000
Breast cancer walk	165,000
Donate charity	60,500

Current Marketing Program for the Chicago Chapter

The team took a look at the situation they faced in terms of their past communications efforts. Essentially, the ACSC had been adhering to its mission, which it delivered in the message "We save lives by helping people stay well, get well, by finding cures and by fighting back." They had concentrated on these messages because the harsh realities were that on any given day, 170 people in Illinois learned they had cancer, and 70 died from cancer.

Recently, ACSC felt the need to examine the impact of its messaging on the public. The organization undertook brand awareness research to see how they compared to other organizations. In a study done on Illinois residents, for unaided awareness, when thinking about charities that address health problems, the American Cancer Society has the highest overall brand awareness among Illinois residents. This was in comparison to such venerable organizations as American Heart Association, Susan G. Komen Breast Cancer Foundation, American Lung Association, and others. Further, those touched by cancer were more likely to mention American Cancer Society.

When asked what organizations they trusted most for cancer information, the American Cancer Society was rated as "most trusted," even above the respondents' personal physician.

In addition to their messaging toward individuals, the Walk and Roll events offered opportunities for corporations to participate and get involved in the fight against cancer. The NACS gave the IMPACT award to corporations that helped raise awareness and funds to fight cancer. Being involved at this level allowed these corporations to demonstrate sponsorship of the local events, like Walk and Roll. This, of course, showed their customers and employees that they were committed to making an impact on finding a cure for the disease. By sponsoring the events, the companies got brand recognition through Walk and Roll promotional materials, web sites, and thousands of participants wearing apparel with their logos. Also, where appropriate, the companies could give away products at the events, be part of the community, and demonstrate involvement. Finally, it allowed the companies to rally their employees around a worthwhile cause in a family-friendly environment.

The Walk and Roll programs had, in the past, had the following campaign elements:

- Web site—Event information, information on how to raise funds and to donate, stories and testimonials
- Print collateral—Distributed to local storefronts; mailings to past participants
- Past corporate sponsors received materials to mail to their employees
- Kick-off event—Targeted to past teams, top fundraisers and any new prospects secured by committee and staff
- Volunteers—Leveraging personal circles, hanging posters in their communities
- CTA (bus service in Chicago) and Street Pole Banners distributed 30 days out from event
- The local NBC affiliate, Channel 5, was a media sponsor and offered Public Service Announcements 30 days out from event

This was done in the past, but it was obvious that this was not enough to compete with the programs they were facing.

What Did the New Marketing Program Look Like?

The ACSC team recognized in order for the next campaign to meet the target objectives ($2 million in donations, 12,000 participants), it would need to be an integrated, multichannel marketing communications campaign. ACSC would need to grow more volunteers, more participants (walkers and rollers), increase donations, increase corporate teams and sponsorships, gain market share in the Chicagoland walk market (there were a considerable number of events in the summer) and examine what market segments might be included that were not already present.

In order to market the Walk and Roll event, the budget was set at $60,000. ACSC was ready to consider digital and social media options to raise the Walk and Roll event above other charity messages as "the way" to fight back against cancer in Chicagoland.

Noticeably absent from past marketing was any email campaign. The local chapter, despite the years of involvement in these events, had only 5,000 emails of past participants. There was a philosophical reason for this: it was felt that people did not make donations via email. For example, potential participants found out about the web site through print materials, mailers and the like. That point of view might be challenged.

A major consideration that those looking into this program should consider is whether the current Walk and Roll name was still relevant. Also, did this or another name align better with the ACSC brand?

Another question was how does ACSC lean how to "digitize" its marketing communications? It was thought advisable to review what some of the local Chicagoland events calendars might offer in terms of creative program ideas. ACSC was not opposed to joining forces with other media and marketing vehicles. Here are a few:

- http://www.chicagoevents.com/
- http://www.mychicagoathlete.com/
- http://www.cancer.org/docroot/home/index.asp
- http://www.yelp.com/chicago
- http://www.meetup.com/find/us/il/chicago/

- http://www.cararuns.org/
- http://www.americanheart.org/

A competitive analysis would help ACS understand its position with regard to all of these events. There was a need to evaluate top event walks/runs/bike events in Chicago (both athletically competitive and non-competitive). They also needed to evaluate sponsorship benefits to the corporations and consider creating the team programs.

Of course, any multichannel marketing communications program needs to establish a set of metrics to set benchmarks and to track success. What might be done to measure success of the web site? Should a separate micro-site be used (and for what purpose)? What measurements needed to be set up to track success? Should social media be used, and how? A timeline needed to be set up to show what will be done from now, Fall, to the events and beyond. Methods needed to be examined for capturing participant information to help with future programs.

There were other organizations in the Chicago area that might play a part in the program. Corporations have already been mentioned but perhaps the program to reach out to them could be revitalized. In addition, the Chicago Public Schools have over 150 high schools with over 110,000 students. The College and Career Preparation Department of the Chicago Public Schools has requirements for students to complete a minimum of 40 hours of service between 9th and 12th grade; sophomores must complete a minimum of 20 hours of service in order to be promoted to junior status; and students must spend time preparing for and reflecting on the Service Learning experience. Is this something that Walk and Roll could be a part of? Inviting, but it could be more administrative work than the team had time for.

After a great deal of discussion and nail-biting over the past results, the team suggested that they get some outside points of view about marketing the Walk and Roll event. They suggested posing the marketing communications problem to some graduate students at a major local university.

CASE
3

American Standard

MANUAL PONTES
Rowan University

WILLIAM THOMPSON
University of Louisville

FRANK WHITEHOUSE
Lynchburg College

M ary Hickey, the account manager for American Standard at the Carmichael Lynch marketing company, faced some daunting problems as she prepared to meet with American Standard executives at the company's headquarters in Piscataway, New Jersey. Her client was the world's largest producer of plumbing products, such as toilets, lavatories, and bathtubs, with annual worldwide sales of over $1 billion. But the American Standard marketers and Mary realized that there was a gap in the company's marketing strategy that threatened to cut off the company from participation in the hottest part of the market that had the highest profit margins.

To the outsider looking at American Standard's prospects, the problem wasn't evident, Mary noted, as she reviewed the company's materials. American Standard, after all, was a global giant, with 44,000 employees and 106 manufacturing facilities in 35 countries. The three main divisions (air conditioning, plumbing, and automotive products) had leading market shares in their segments. Mary's client, the plumbing products division of American Standard, had the leading market share and a substantial international presence. Indeed, over 65 percent of the division's revenue was generated from outside the United States. But it was in America that American Standard was having problems, and as Mary glanced over consumer survey data, it seemed that at least part of American Standard's problem may have been its very success.

The Plumbing Products Market

American Standard had always been a market share leader in the commercial segment. Its products were often the first choice for office buildings, shopping centers, airports, rest stops, and stadiums. Because of the company's association with toilets in commercial institutions, consumer surveys in the 1990s showed that customers perceived the American Standard (A/S) brand as "boring" and "institutional" with little "emotional" value. The A/S brand name only reinforced the perception of consumers that A/S products were "standard" and functional with little that was aesthetic or pleasing to the eye.

A/S's leading competitor was Kohler. Unlike A/S, Kohler had successfully positioned itself in consumers' minds as the "well-designed" brand. Research showed that Kohler was perceived to be the dominant brand in the high-end consumer market. Indeed, A/S was a distant second to Kohler in sales to the residential market, and its sales and market share were in a downward spiral.

For Mary and the marketers at American Standard, this was clearly an issue that needed to be immediately redressed. In the institutional market that American Standard dominated, plumbing products from the various manufacturers were perceived to be functionally equivalent "commodity products," with less need for design and style. As a result, commercial buyers were extremely price sensitive and profit margins were low

Yet the residential products market, in which American Standard was a secondary player, was forecasted to have faster growth than the commercial market for the foreseeable future. Homeowners were increasingly spending greater amounts of money on bathroom remodeling projects, and the average size and the average number of bathrooms in a new home had steadily increased over the past several decades. Bathrooms were being constructed to cater to individual tastes, and consumers were willing to spend more money for the high-end designs that would fulfill their fantasies. Among residential customers creating their dream bathrooms, American Standard's product image was not especially appealing.

Brand Position

Historically, Kohler had emphasized styling motifs that were distinctive. Kohler's advertising was crafted to evoke an image of sophistication with a European flair. Kohler invoked continental images in the positioning of its upscale lines, such as Kallista, Kohler Germany, and Jacob Delafon (Paris). To combat this, American Standard had developed a new line of products under the Absolut Porcher brand name.

The Absolut Porcher line covered a complete range of bathroom furniture, including commodes, sinks, bathtubs, and fixtures. Design motifs included Scandinavian, French Provincial, Italian and Greek elements, and specific product names (e.g., Sorrento) were applied to invoke the appropriate associations. The Absolut Porcher line was intended to produce the kind of imagery that had, so far, eluded American Standard. Mary was aware that positioning the Absolut Porcher line as a separate upscale brand would be easier if it was not linked to the American Standard name. Doing this, however, would obviate the kind of associations between the two that might assist sales of American Standard's less expensive consumer designs and would definitely require a larger advertising and marketing budget. The retailing environment that had developed in plumbing products might make this more difficult.

Product Distribution

Historically, plumbing products had been sold primarily through independent plumbing supplies dealers who operated at the local level. These independent dealers supplied building contractors and plumbers who were engaged in new residential construction or in the renovation of existing homes. Independent dealers had expanded their reach to include end-users as do-it-yourself projects rose in popularity. These dealers usually carried only one manufacturer's entire line of products, often in a dedicated showroom area. They would provide product literature, design assistance, and product guidance to customers who desired personal service. Many had established relationships with local architects or contractors to assist them in moving product through their showrooms. Few had advertising budgets sufficient to draw residential customers off the streets to investigate plumbing products, unlike the large home superstores such as Home Depot and Lowe's.

The home superstores, which had grown to dominate residential home product sales within the last decade, carried plumbing products as well as a wide variety of other building and home items aimed primarily at the do-it-yourselfer. While most potential customers could find American Standard products on superstore showroom floors, the superstores did not showcase American Standard's entire line. The superstores did not provide dedicated showroom areas or the personal attention and design assistance desired by residential customers pouring thousands of dollars into their bathroom projects. Instead, superstores depended on their own corporate advertising (and that of the national brand manufacturers) to generate store traffic, and displayed competing brands side-by-side.

The home product superstores had become dynamos in their field, which gave them even more power to dictate favorable relationships with their suppliers. While the superstore category grew dramatically during the 1980s and early 1990s, a wave of liquidations and acquisitions had virtually reduced the field to two chains, Home Depot and Lowe's.

Home Depot was expected to have 2,000 stores in the near future and was adding so-called "big-box" stores at the rate of 200 per year. Lowe's, the smaller of the two, was adding about 95 stores per year. For both chains, new stores featured more than 100,000 square feet of retail space. While providing for contractor sales, they catered heavily to residential consumers. Their forté was selling into final consumer demand for repair/replacement items and remodeling. Estimates of share of market for such sales ranged as high as 60 to 70 percent. Gross profit margin for Home Depot was 32 percent while that for Lowe's was 28.3 percent.

Because Home Depot and Lowe's had such huge market share, they could also dictate many aspects of their relationship with the manufacturers. For example, they usually received lower prices from most manufacturers. Also, they would not restock a brand that did not offer superior gross contribution per unit of space per unit of time. Thus manufacturers had to support their products with large advertising budgets, since brands with poor consumer image or little national promotional support could easily lose much of their presence in the distribution channel. The chains, Home Depot most prominently, were even in the position to refuse to carry brands that were available through direct sale from a manufacturer.

However, if American Standard felt itself to be buffeted by the winds of change in the building products industry, the independent plumbing dealers and building supply dealers had felt the dislocations even more. In most areas of the country, they had been largely relegated to cooperating with designers, architects, and upscale homeowners who were designing new homes or vacation homes or performing major renovations on existing structures. In general, these sales were less sensitive to price than those in the superstore channel, but they were much more sensitive to product design and image and the niceties of dealer display and support. But the independent dealers had inadequate marketing budgets and had trouble breaking through the overwhelming presence of the superstores in their own communities to establish that they were a source for plumbing supplies and consumer advice and support.

Decision Problem: The Challenge

In light of the growing portion of revenue that was only available by competing for the residential market, the American Standard marketing team presented these challenging goals to Mary and her colleagues at Carmichael Lynch:

1. Change consumers' perceptions about American Standard
2. Increase sales to residential customers
3. Increase the visibility of the independent plumbing supply distribution channel

As Mary thought about her options, she decided that if she were to fulfill the company's objectives, she had to reposition the American Standard brand among her American consumers. She had to show people that the brand wasn't the white toilets they saw in a highway rest stop, but rather well-designed, beautiful products they would want in their homes. To accomplish that feat, especially after years of persistent consumer beliefs that American Standard was an institutional brand, she had to develop many more contacts between consumers and American Standard's high-end products. She and her account team felt that customers needed additional information and advice before committing to a decision on plumbing fixtures. If she could find the customers as they were contemplating their new bathrooms, introduce American Standard's quality products to them, and then get them into specialty plumbing products showrooms in their communities to see the full American Standard line up-close, she would be better able to persuade them to buy American Standard products.

Mary decided that the campaign had to be targeted toward females between the ages of 25 and 54 who were planning to remodel a bathroom within the next 12 months. Research had shown that females have a greater influence over such household decisions than men do. Now the hard work had to begin. She needed to present a campaign that could find her target audience in time to influence their decisions, present information about the product to them, and help the specialty plumbing product showroom managers and the consumers find each other so the consumers could see American Standard's high-end product line. It was a good strategy, but she wondered about how best to pursue it. If you were Mary's consultant, what would you advise her to do?

FIGURE 1

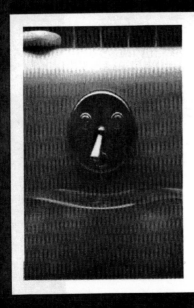

FIGURE 2

You will spend seven years of your life in the bathroom. You will need a good book.

 FREE. For a 32-page guidebook overflowing with terrific bathroom products, ideas and inspiration, send this coupon to: American Standard, P.O. Box 2303, Chatsworth, CA 91313-2303. Or call 1-800-524-9797, ext.740 *American Standard*

Name

Address   City   State

Zip   Phone   740

How soon are you planning to start your project?____ Within 6 months ____ After 6 months

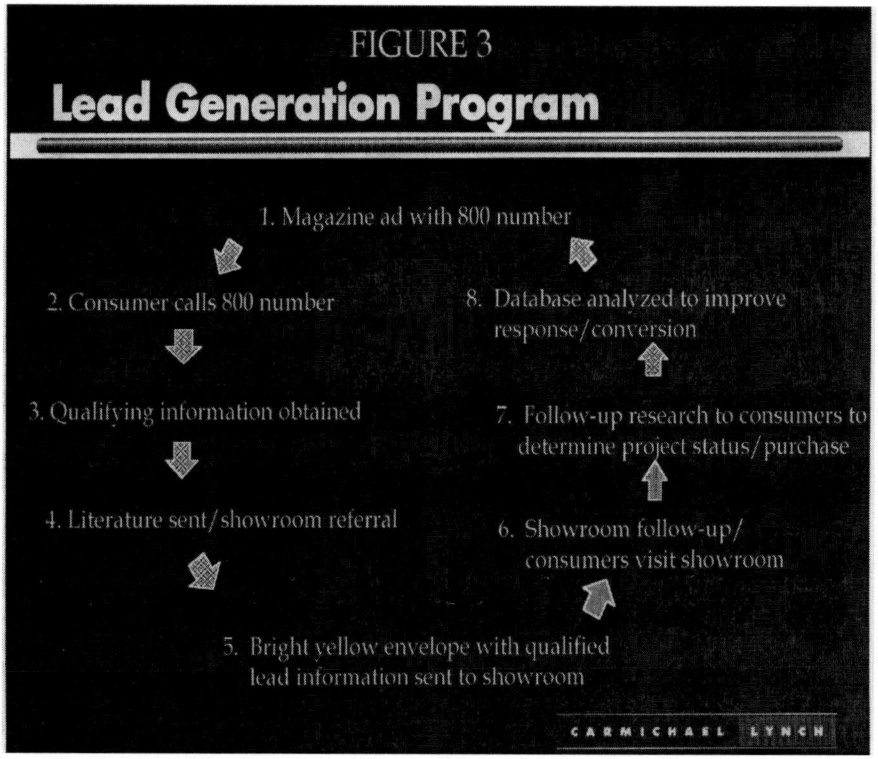

FIGURE 3
Lead Generation Program

1. Magazine ad with 800 number

2. Consumer calls 800 number

8. Database analyzed to improve response/conversion

3. Qualifying information obtained

7. Follow-up research to consumers to determine project status/purchase

4. Literature sent/showroom referral

6. Showroom follow-up/ consumers visit showroom

5. Bright yellow envelope with qualified lead information sent to showroom

CARMICHAEL LYNCH

CASE
4

Amtrak: A Communications Planning Challenge[1]

MARIAN AZZARO
Roosevelt University

This case presents the details of a positioning and communications strategy problem for a very complex consumer service business: Amtrak. The key question facing Amtrak management and its advisors involved identifying the best communications positioning strategy and determining the best way to choose that strategy in order to build the brand and the business.

Background: Business Description

Amtrak is the nation's passenger railroad. Created by an act of Congress in 1971, Amtrak today is still subsidized by the government and almost wholly owned by the U.S. Department of Transportation. Amtrak is a for-profit company, challenged to achieve commercial success while continuing to meet its public service mission. By law, Amtrak is required to provide a national network of passenger rail service. However, many of the mandated routes are not financially viable. As a result, Amtrak stands before Congress every year requesting budget subsidies.

Amtrak today operates a reasonably efficient version of the national route network mandated by Congress. On weekdays Amtrak runs more than 250 trains daily covering more than 22,000 miles of track. In total it provides rail service to more than 500 cities and towns in 46 states nationwide. In general, Amtrak's service is made up of long-distance routes connecting densely populated short-distance service corridors throughout the U.S. Long-distance trains generally operate daily, offering several choices of passenger service class, including first-class sleeping car service, custom class service, and economy service. Corridor services typically run shorter distances with multiple daily frequencies. The premier corridor service offered by Amtrak today is the new Acela high-speed service on the Northeast rail corridor running geographically from Washington, D.C., north to Boston. Acela is the model for development of rail service in other U.S. federally-designated travel corridors.

---

[1]Much of the material for this case is edited from information available on the Amtrak web site, www.amtrak.com. Other specific sources are indicated in the text or the notes that follow.

EXHIBIT C4.1: AMTRAK RIDERSHIP AND REVENUE GROWTH

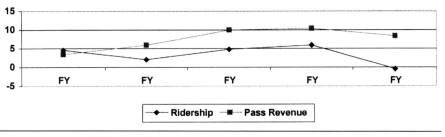

Past 5 Years Percent Change in Ridership and Passenger Revenue

Source: Figures provided by Amtrak

State of the Business

For the past five years Amtrak has successfully grown its passenger business, building revenue by an average of 7.6% per year and building ridership by an average of 3.3% per year (see Exhibit C4.1). For the next five years, Amtrak projects continued growth in passenger revenue at about 4% per year with modest growth in passenger ridership. Much of Amtrak's success can be attributed to its focus on four core strategies:

1. Building public and private partnerships
2. Developing established and new corridor services
3. Revitalizing the Amtrak Brand
4. Delivering improved service quality

Building Public and Private Partnerships

Amtrak began efforts in 1999 to identify commercial and investment partners for strategic business alliances. Today it continues efforts to develop promotional, service development, and investment partnerships. Amtrak envisions such partnerships to be critical to the commercial success of long-distance train service and fundamental to repositioning Amtrak's brand identity.

Developing Established and New Corridor Services

Even as Amtrak launched the Acela high-speed rail service in the Northeast, it was working with other states and business partners to expand improved rail services to other corridors across the country. Amtrak's plan is to leverage expertise and knowledge gained in the Northeast to fast-adapt expansion to the promising corridors of the future:

- The California Corridors, Los Angeles to San Diego and the San Joaquin Valley
- The Midwest Corridor, connecting Ohio, Michigan, Illinois, Wisconsin, Nebraska and Minnesota through Chicago
- The Pacific Northwest Corridor connecting Vancouver, Seattle, and Portland
- The Southeast Corridor between Washington, D.C., and Charlotte, North Carolina

EXHIBIT C4.2: AMTRAK LOGO DEVELOPMENT

Original Logo	New Logos

- The Gulf Coast Corridor between Atlanta and New Orleans
- The Empire Corridor in the state of New York
- The Keystone Corridor in Pennsylvania

Revitalizing the Amtrak Brand and Delivering Improved Service Quality

Amtrak recognizes that its brand encompasses the total experience of train travel, from purchasing the ticket to entering the station to the meals and amenities available during the trip. Proprietary Amtrak research yielded results leading to redefined services, amenities, and offerings; defined service standards to apply throughout the network system; and trained employees delivering the new standards.

In 1999 Amtrak introduced a new brand identity along with its service standards guarantee and the all-new Acela high-speed services to demonstrate its commitment to change (see Exhibit C4.2). The new Amtrak taps into today's consumer values and successfully reflects Amtrak's changing corporate strategies and services.

Cost Management

Most recently, Amtrak has added a fifth core strategy, that of cost management. This strategy is key to Amtrak's chances for success and applies across all of the organization. From train operations to station services to marketing management, all Amtrak employees must seek out and adapt to cost management opportunities. In marketing management, for example, such opportunities will range from buying efficiencies to budget cuts. The Amtrak National Communications plan must reflect this reality.

Traveling Consumers

Amtrak's passengers can be broadly defined as "train interested" travelers. This is a broad sub-group representing about 45% of the total traveling population in the U.S. according to the Yankelovich 2001 *Leisure Monitor*[2]. "Train interested" travelers may or may not have taken a train trip recently, but they have all expressed an interest in doing so within the next two years.

In more specific terms, according to proprietary Amtrak research[3], there are five

---

[2] Yankelovich Partners, Inc., 2001, *The Yankelovich 2001 Leisure MONITOR*, p. 114.
[3] Amtrak 1998 Market Based Network Study.

**EXHIBIT C4.3: AMTRAK CHALLENGES BY
NATIONAL TRAVEL MARKET SEGMENT**

Consumer Segment	Amtrak Challenges	% U.S. Travelers
Business Travelers	Travel time	22%
Young Family Travelers	Travel time, cost, nearby stations	11%
Footloose/Fancy Free	Travel time, station locations, and flexibility	10%
Older Family Vacationers	Cost and convenient station locations	9%
Senior Experientials	Travel time, convenient stations, and comfort	8%

Source: Amtrak Market Based Network Study

market segments of particular interest to Amtrak. Each segment, defined according to life-style and travel purpose, holds some challenge for Amtrak (see Exhibit C4.3). This segmentation scheme works well in that it captures key differences in travel motivation. The needs of consumers differ significantly when traveling for business versus leisure purposes. Needs also differ when traveling alone as adults or traveling with younger or older children. As would be expected, these differences are significant in many ways.

Despite their obvious differences, most of these segments have one important consideration in common: travel time. Travel time can be both good and bad for consumers. They consider it part of the travel experience, and that can be time well spent or time wasted depending on the experience. Travel time for Amtrak can also be good or bad. A trip on Amtrak is all about time because train travel generally takes longer than air travel. Opportunistically, though, time spent traveling on Amtrak can be part of an enriching travel experience, and this is part of the appeal among train-interested traveling consumers.

Demographically, across all of Amtrak, consumers are older and better educated than the U.S. travel market in general (see Exhibit C4.4), but this is somewhat misleading. Amtrak believes that it is not appropriate to consider all products and services as a whole. Instead, the travel experience and the consumer's expectations differ significantly for long-distance leisure versus short-distance regional travel.

Marketing Communications

The marketing budget for Amtrak is planned each year in the late spring/early summer. Budgets are finalized when the business plan is confirmed each year in October. Amtrak marketing expenditures are allocated annually throughout its system supporting the many products and services of Amtrak.

Seasonality for Amtrak is similar to that of the travel industry in general. Summer is the big travel season. Other than the summer season, peaks occur during key holiday seasons such as Thanksgiving through New Year's and spring break. As with the rest of the industry, Amtrak generally experiences high demand during these peak periods and doesn't typically need to advertise or promote to build ridership. Instead, Amtrak plans system-wide fall and spring promotions designed to build ridership in the "shoulder" periods between peak and off-peak times. The fall program each year

EXHIBIT C4.4: AMTRAK NATIONAL TRAVEL MARKET DEMOGRAPHIC PROFILES

	U.S. Market %	Amtrak %	Index
Gender			
Male	50	48	96
Female	50	52	104
Trip Purpose			
Business	33	26	79
Non-business	57	65	114
Both	10	9	90
Age			
18–34	40	29	72
35–54	47	47	100
55–64	10	20	200
65+	2	4	200
Average Age	40 yrs	44 yrs	
Education			
Less Than HS	3	3	100
HS Graduate	24	20	83
Some College	27	24	89
College Graduate	30	33	110
Graduate School	16	20	125
HH Income			
Less than $45K	41	43	105
$45K–$75K	34	33	97
$75K+	25	24	96
Average Income	$59K	$57K	

Source: Amtrak Brand Tracking and Equity Study

is usually some variation of the Amtrak *Explore America* zonal fares. This fall program is usually targeted more to an older adult audience. The spring program is also generally some kind of special fares promotion targeted more to younger adults and traveling families. In recent years, Amtrak has worked to develop and leverage some highly visible partnerships behind its fare promotions (for example, Major League Baseball in the spring).

Product and Service Highlights

In recent years, the two biggest positive news factors for Amtrak have been the introduction of Acela high-speed rail in the Northeast and its system-wide service training and the service guarantee called "The Amtrak Promise."

Acela High-Speed Rail

Inaugurated in November 2000, Acela was heralded by Amtrak as the fastest train in its history. But Acela is not just about speed. Acela is high-service rail with its superior ride quality, world-class service and amenities, and enhanced speed all backed by a customer satisfaction guarantee. Acela is the pride of Amtrak and its model for service standards on all Amtrak trains.

The Amtrak Promise

At the same time, Amtrak began the monumental task of defining and implementing consistent service standards system-wide across the broad range of products and services offered. This effort started with a core team of managers and employees who defined the set of standards and determined the plan for implementation. The first step in implementation was the "Service Success" training program for all employees and managers. The next step was a service rewards and incentives program designed to keep employees on the service track. Finally, Amtrak offered its customer satisfaction guarantee, "The Amtrak Promise," on all trains, at all times.

Other Amtrak Products and Services

Beyond these more recent developments, it is worth noting that Amtrak offers a full range of products and services for traveling consumers.

Amtrak offers coach class, custom class and first-class service on long-distance leisure trains throughout the country. (It is important to note that first-class long-distance travel on Amtrak includes on-board sleeping accommodations and dining car privileges.) Some of the more outstanding and historic Amtrak routes are:

- The Silver Service operating daily along the East Coast between New York, Washington, D.C., and all points in Florida
- The Auto Train carrying passengers and their cars direct, non-stop, and overnight between Washington, D.C. and Orlando, Florida
- The Coast Starlight operating daily along the West Coast with service between Los Angeles and Seattle
- The Sunset Limited, the nation's only coast-to-coast passenger train, operating between Florida and California
- Several spectacular routes running daily out of Chicago: The California Zephyr, The City of New Orleans, The Capitol Limited, The Empire Builder, and The Southwest Chief

Service schedules for many of these long-distance routes afford travelers a one-of-a-kind travel experience unique to train travel: the first-class, overnight excursion. There are several examples throughout the Amtrak route network where first-class passengers can board a train in the late afternoon or evening in one city, enjoy a fine dinner in the dining car, retire to a private sleeping compartment, and wake the next morning arriving fresh and rested in a new city. Examples include Chicago to Denver on The California Zephyr, Washington, D.C., to Chicago on The Capitol Limited, and Chicago to New Orleans on The City of New Orleans.

For consumers who prefer one-stop vacation shopping, Amtrak offers Amtrak Vacations and Amtrak Air Rail. With one phone call to Amtrak Vacations, consumers can book pre-packaged complete vacations or assemble their own vacation plans including the train, car rentals, hotel accommodations, and tour options of interest. Amtrak Air Rail is a one-of-a-kind partnership between Amtrak and United Airlines allowing consumers to travel one-way by train and one-way by plane virtually anywhere in the U.S.

Overall, much is new and exciting about the new Amtrak. Amtrak is actively engaged in redefining and re-establishing its brand equity and succeeding in its efforts. But the network is expansive; Amtrak has 25,000 employees working in more than 500 cities and towns across 46 states. And, Amtrak's business objectives are seemingly at odds, its public service mission often draining profits from commercial successes. This is the continuing challenge of Amtrak's National Communications efforts.

Questions

1. Which Amtrak product or product group represents the greatest potential for building Amtrak's business? State facts to support your recommendation.

2. Which target audience segment represents the greatest growth potential for Amtrak (consider those mentioned in the case and others not mentioned as well)? State the facts that support your recommendation.

3. Thinking about your audience and product focus recommended in 1 and 2 above, what benefit and support would you recommend for Amtrak's marketing communications focus? Explain how your recommended benefit and support fits with the product and the audience segment. Be specific.

CASE
5

Direct Mail Marketing at the Art Institute of Chicago

RALITZA NIKOLAEVA

ISCTE Business School, Lisbon, Portugal

EUNSANG YOON

University of Massachusetts Lowell

ELLA CARTER

Howard University

O ne sunny day in June, Terry Kane[1] joined the Art Institute of Chicago's Department of Development as a Senior Associate Director of Membership Acquisition. She was excited to apply her business experience of direct mail programs to the non-profit sector. Bringing her onboard was part of a restructuring initiative undertaken by the new senior leadership of the museum—dividing the membership team into two key focus areas: Acquisition and Retention. This initiative was in response to the declining membership at the Art Institute of Chicago (AIC), which had significantly decreased in the previous five years. Much of this was due to strategies that focused more on individual event-by-event marketing efforts around exhibitions, and less on comprehensive, long-term membership programs.

Terry was enthusiastic about the task, and the acquisition team immediately began to work on a new strategy. The most immediate issue was the direct mail program. Historically, direct mail marketing had been the primary method for gaining new members and seemed to work well in the past. Therefore, there was a prevailing presumption that direct mail was a necessity for gaining new membership, regardless of the cost. The new team realized that there was no tracking of return on investment (ROI) being done to date. After some research on the outcomes of previous direct mail campaigns, they found that the costs far outweighed the response and revenue. The campaigns during the previous year were exemplary of the gravity of the problem—the average response rate to direct mailings was 0.44% and on average the programs cost 446% more than the revenue they raised.

Since there were no benchmarks against which to measure and evaluate what

---

[1] The personal names in the case have been changed at the request of AIC.

worked and what did not work in the past campaigns, Terry was unsure where to start. Her task was not made easier by the fact that the membership department had never sent out email solicitations before. Coming from a "for-profit" business background, which included work in the member acquisition departments of a credit card company and a commercial real estate company, Terry knew that the biggest advantage of direct mail over advertising was trackability. Therefore, her guiding motivation in the overhaul of the direct marketing campaign of the Art Institute was to maximize its profitability through increases of revenue from membership. What kind of measures would help her to start successfully tracking the profitability of the program?

The City of Chicago and Its Culture

Chicago, Illinois is the third largest city in the U.S. and the largest Midwestern city. Located between the Great Lakes and the Mississippi River watershed, Chicago was incorporated as a city in 1837. It rapidly became a major transportation hub, as well as the business, financial, and cultural capital of the Midwest.

With nearly 3 million people and a very diverse population comprised largely of African-Americans, Germans, Poles, Irish-Americans, Italian-Americans and Swedes, the Chicago arts and entertainment scene is filled with myriad options available to local residents as well as visitors from around the world. The Art Institute of Chicago, the Contemporary Gallery of Art, Art at Navy Pier, Millennium Park, The Chicago Symphony, the Jazz Showcase, the world's second oldest jazz club, and the Chicago Opera Theater represent just a few of the many arts and entertainment options in this exciting city.

Art Chicago™ for nearly 20 years has been one of the leading international contemporary art fairs in the world. Chicago is world-renowned for its amazing collection of museums. Most are open every day, some offer free admission, and many have weekly free days.

Chicago's theater community provides entertainment options such as The Second City and I.O., Steppenwolf Theater Company, the Goodman Theater and the Victory Garden Theater. There is also Broadway-style entertainment at theatres such as *Ford Center for the Performing Arts Oriental Theatre, LaSalle Bank Theatre, Cadillac Palace Theatre, Auditorium Theatre* of Roosevelt University, and *Drury Lane Theatre* Water Tower Place.

For the classical music lover, Chicago offers the famed Ravinia Festival, performances at Symphony Center, The Civic Opera House, and Harris Theater as well as a number of outdoor concerts in Grant Park and Millennium Park. Other live music genres which are part of the city's cultural heritage include blues, gospel, soul, hip-hop and jazz. From the 1980s to the early 1990s, the city was a center for a variety of innovative music genres including industrial, punk, new wave, alternative music and a blossoming independent music culture. Throughout the year, there are a number of festivals including *Lollapalooza*, the *Intonation Music Festival* and the *Pitchfork Music Festival.*

For dance aficionados, Chicago offers performances from well-known groups like The *Joffrey Ballet* and *Chicago Festival Ballet* as well as modern and jazz dance troupes, such as the *Hubbard Street Dance Chicago.*

Chicago Non-Profit Community and Arts Funding

The Chicago non-profit landscape is supported by numerous organizations including The City of Chicago, The Arts & Business Council of Chicago, Prince Charitable Trusts and the Chicago Community Trust, The Wallace Foundation and The Department of Cultural Affairs, to name a few. The City of Chicago provides more than $1 million a year, which is administered through the Cultural Grants Division of the Chicago Department of Cultural Affairs. Grants, issued to Chicago artists and arts organizations through a competitive, peer review process, provide funding for arts activities that reach out to people in every Chicago community. Some of the programs offered through the city are:

- **CityArts I—IV** is a triennial program that provides general operating support to non-profit arts organizations and social service organizations with established arts components.
- **Community Arts Assistance Program** provides support to new and emerging artists and arts organizations projects that address needs in the area of professional, organizational, and artistic development.
- **Neighborhood Arts Program** supports artists who present high quality instructional arts programs benefiting youth, seniors citizens, and people with disabilities in low to moderate income neighborhoods.
- **Cultural Outreach Program** supports nonprofit delegate agencies that offer cultural programming in low-to-moderate income communities.

The Arts & Business Council (A&BC) of Chicago is designed to develop partnerships between the arts and business. This organization provides year-round seminars, symposia, and educational programs that help arts professionals and their board members.

The arts community is also supported by several other non-profit organizations including the Prince Charitable Trusts, which provides support to Chicago organizations with annual budgets over $250,000; the Chinese Fine Arts Society, which promotes Chinese arts and music; and the Center for Intuitive and Outsider Art Intuit, which promotes public awareness and appreciation of intuitive and outsider art.

Customers

Since it was founded in 1879 as a museum and school, the Art Institute of Chicago has collected, conserved, and preserved a collection of more than 5000 years of human creativity representing cultures around the globe (www.artic.edu/). The museum has served the cultural needs of a broad community of visitors from Chicago and around the world, including students, artists, parents, and travelers.

Students

Providing students with educational opportunity is one of the key functions of art museums. This function has clearly been recognized as a key objective of the Art Institute in its mission, i.e. "to assemble a diverse body of intelligent and creative students and faculty in an environment designed to facilitate and encourage the discovery and production of significant ideas and images" (www.artic.edu).

EXHIBIT C5.1: TRENDS OF POPULATION IN THE CITY OF CHICAGO, IL

Year	1990	2000	2010 (estimate)
Population	2,783,726	2,896,016	2,844,623
Age Composition (%)		2000	2006
Under 5 years		7.5	7.3
5–14 years		14.6	12.3
15–17 years		4.1	4.1
18–24 years		11.2	10.7
25–44 years		33.4	30.8
45–64 years		18.9	22.8
65 years and over		10.3	12.0
Median age		31.5	33.6
Median family income		**$42,724**	**$49,113**
(U.S. Total)		**($50,046)**	**($58,526)**

Source: U.S. Census Data from www.census.gov.

Museums in the other metropolitan areas commonly emphasize the importance of students as a target customer group. One example is the Museum of Fine Arts (MFA) in Boston whose mission is declared as "educational obligations to the people of Boston and New England, across the nation and abroad" (www.mfa.org/). Founded in 1876, the MFA has aimed to heighten public appreciation of the visual world by targeting school children and college students as future generation of artists. One of their marketing tools for targeting this group of customers is University Membership, which offers free general admission and reduced-price tickets to special exhibitions for the undergraduate students in the Greater Boston area. Another example is the Museum of Contemporary Art in Los Angeles which runs a program for younger adults, who are invited to various weekend evening events where there is a cash bar along with the opportunity to draw and paint in the galleries (just free-style . . . nothing formal), for helping young people feel comfortable and experience fun (www.moca.org).

Facing a general trend of declining population in this age group, museums need to develop a systematic and creative program to attract them. Demographic data for Chicago area (Exhibit C5.1) suggest a significant decrease of student population. The size of overall population in the City of Chicago has declined from 2.9 million in the 2000 census to approximately 2.8 million in the 2010 census, mainly due to significant decrease of elementary and middle school-age group in recent years (from 14.6 % to approximately 12.3%) and college-age group (from 11.2% to approximately 10.6%) in spite of stable trend of high school-age group (at 4.1%).

Currently, the Art Institute is working on a program to make access easier for Chicago area students. In the current year they have offered free evening hours every Thursday and a discounted membership level for students at the cost of $50.

Artists

Serving as a resource for artists and art students, both those who are already familiar with art and those for whom art is a new experience, is an important activity of many art museums. The School of the Art Institute offers a link between the school art community—students, faculty, and alumni—and the local community of artists by organizing various events and exhibitions. Local artists can be a good resource for co-operative marketing programs of the AIC to increase the general membership by demonstrating their contribution to enriching the cultural reputation of the Chicago community.

Many creative ideas have emerged to enhance the participation of artists in the museum activities. For example, Revolving Museum (RM) of Lowell, MA, has fostered a civic dialogue and a sense of community between artists and the public (www.revolvingmuseum.org/). As an evolving laboratory of creative expression for the local community, especially future generations of artists, RM offers public art, exhibitions and educational programs in cooperation with the local governments, universities and community members. Talented teams of artists, students and community leaders have been encouraged to participate in a number of interactive and multi-cultural art-based urban revitalization programs.

Parents and School Alumni

Attracting the parents and their children to visit museums for educational experience or cultural entertainment during the weekends or holidays, with exhibitions and/or workshops, is an important marketing program for art museums. The Art Institute's Kraft Education Center offers family-friendly spaces as well as exhibitions, games, puzzles, and a children's library. This is accompanied by free admission to the museum for children under 12 (www.artic.edu). Further, the Art Institute offers complimentary memberships for graduation classes of the School of The Art Institute.

Demographic data for Chicago area (Exhibit C5.1) shows that the 25–44 age group has decreased from 33.4% in 2000 to 30.8% in a recent year while the 45–64 age group has increased from 18.9% to 22.8% and the 65+ age group from 10.3% to 12.0%. In response to this population trend, the Art Institute offers a variety of senior programs. Examples of such programs are Art Insights, which brings slide talks to senior centers, senior groups, senior residences, and nursing homes, and "Senior Celebrations," a free, day-long event, which includes a presentation, short talks in the galleries, music, and art demonstrations (www.artic.edu).

Travelers

Travelers also are important customers of the major art museums. Museums in a big city often attract a huge number of non-residents who are attending conferences or traveling for sightseeing. Travelers, however, are not the primary target for membership contributions, because most of them do not visit the city and the museum on a frequent basis. The Art Institute, however, does offer a National Membership level targeted toward the travelers segment.

Community

The Art Institute has a program called Community Associates, which encourages community memberships by providing programs that support and promote adult education in the visual arts. As of the current year, there were 16 groups serving the greater Chicago area and northwest Indiana (www.artic.edu).

In addition to individual members, art museums try to expand the membership with the corporate sponsors making philanthropic donations and sharing the bene-

EXHIBIT C5.2: ORGANIZATIONS IN ARTS, ENTERTAINMENT & RECREATIONAL SECTOR: CITY OF CHICAGO

NAICS Code		# of Establishments	Revenue ($ million)
71	Arts, entertainment & recreational, total	767	1,718
711	Performing arts, Spectator sports & related industries	441	918
712	Museums, historical sites & similar institutions	43	382
71211	Museums	36	382
71212	Historical sites		
71213	Zoos & botanical gardens	4	
71219	Nature parks & others		
713	Amusement, gambling & recreation industries	283	418

Source: Economic Census at www.census.gov.

fits of membership with their employees and their families. Many museums in metropolitan areas, such as the MFA, offer various types of membership targeting local, regional, national and international corporations and institutions such as Institutional Pass Program, Corporate Partners Program as well as the University Membership mentioned above (www.mfa.org/). Currently the Art Institute has a Corporate Partners Program, which includes membership privileges.

Competitors

The Art Institute has a number of other cultural institutions competing for the same base of customers in the Chicago area. The Museum Campus consisting of the Field Museum, Shedd Aquarium, Adler Planetarium and Museum of Science & industry is located on South Lake Shore Drive close to the Art Institute, which is on South Michigan Avenue. Also in close proximity to the Art Institute are the DuSable Museum of African-American History, the Mexican Fine Arts Center Museum, and the Museum of Contemporary Art. In addition to the seasonal sporting events of the Cubs, White Sox, Bulls, and Bears, several public parks such as Millennium Park, Buckingham Fountain in Grant Park and Lincoln Park offer cultural entertainment for residents and visitors. Other performing arts institutions including Symphony Center, the Auditorium Theatre, Steppenwolf Theater Company, Broadway in Chicago and the Second City also are directly or indirectly competing with the Art Institute by offering a variety of cultural entertainment programs.

According to the U.S. Economic Census (Exhibit C5.2), the Arts, Entertainment & Recreational industry (NAICS code = 71) in the City of Chicago consists of 767 organizations generating annual revenue of $1,718 mil. The number of organizations in the performing arts and spectator sports sector (NAICS code = 711) is 441 (or 57.5%) with annual revenue of $918 mil. (or 53.4%). The number of organizations in the amusement, gambling & recreation sector (NAICS code = 713) is 283 (or 36.9%) with annual revenue of $418 mil. (or 24.3%). And the museums sector (NAICS code = 71211) consists of 36 institutions (or 4.7%) with annual revenue of $382 mil. (or 22.2%)

EXHIBIT C5.3: ECONOMIC CENSUS DATA RELATED TO MUSEUM INDUSTRY

NAICS Code		# of Establishments		Revenue ($ million)			
		1997 Census	2005 Census	1997 Census	2000 Est.	2002 Census	2005 Est.
(U.S. Total)							
71	Arts, entertainment & recreational, total	99,099	110,313	104,715	127,394	141,904	165,540
711	Performing arts, Spectator sports & related industries	30,566	37,735	37,619	51,149	58,286	64,891
712	Museums, historical sites & similar institutions	5,580	6,663	6,764	9,350	8.608	10,088
71211	Museums	3,860	4,533	na	na	5,908	na
71212	Historical sites	892	999	na	na	551	na
71213	Zoos & botanical gardens	386	558	na	na	1,789	na
71219	Nature parks & others	442	573	na	na	360	na
713	Amusement, gambling & recreation industries	62,914	65,915	58,463	86,073	75,010	90,561

NAICS Code		# of Establishment		Revenue ($ million)	
		1997 Census	2005 Census	1997 Census	2002 Census
(State of Illinois)					
71	Arts, entertainment & recreational, total	3,832	4,135	4,774	5,738
711	Performing arts, Spectator sports & related industries	1,175	1,331	1,394	1,896
712	Museums, historical sites & similar institutions	156	189	476	527
71211	Museums	101	124	362	371
71212	Historical sites	29	27	5	8
71213	Zoos & botanical gardens	12	16	104	136
71219	Nature parks & others	14	22	3	12
713	Amusement, gambling & recreation industries	2,501	2,615	2,904	3,314

Source: Economic Census at www.census.gov.

The U.S. Census data (Exhibit C5.3) shows that the Arts, Entertainment & Recreational Industry (NAICS code = 71) has continuously grown in the number of organizations by 11.4% from 99,009 a decade ago to 110,313 in a recent year. The Museums Sector (NAICS code = 71211) has grown by 17.4% from 3,860 a decade ago to 4533 in a recent year, while the performing arts and sports sector has grown by 23.5% from 30,566 to 37,735 and the Amusement, Gambling & Recreation Sector has grown by 4.5% from 62,914 to 65,915.

In the State of Illinois containing the City of Chicago, the Arts, Entertainment & Recreational Industry (NAICS code = 71) has grown in the number of organizations by 7.9% from 3,832 to 4,135 and in the amount of annual revenue by 20.2% from $4,774 million to $5,738 million in the same period. The Museums Sector (NAICS code = 71211) has grown in the number of organizations by 22.8% from 101 to 124 and in the amount of annual revenue by 2.5% from $362 million to $371 million, while the performing arts and sports sector has grown in the number of organizations by 13.3% from 1,175 to 1,331 and in the amount of annual revenue by 36% from $1,394 million to $1,896 million, and the Amusement, Gambling & Recreation Sector has grown in the number of organizations by 4.5% from 2,501 to 2,615, and in the amount of annual revenue by 14.1% from $2,904 million to $3,314 million.

Direct Marketing at the Art Institute of Chicago[2]

Terry's task of improving the profitability of member acquisition programs at the Art Institute was not an easy one. Her first step was to examine various aspects of the museum operation and to make an audit of the contributing factors for the dire state of the last year's direct mail acquisition campaigns.

There were some external issues that were undoubtedly contributing to the red ink. Increased postage costs and the increased clutter in the direct mail channel were major factors in the drop of effectiveness of the campaigns. The lack of blockbuster exhibitions in the past year did not present a compelling incentive for new membership. Exhibit C5.4 lists the schedule of exhibitions for previous 12 months.

However, some of the more compelling issues were under the control of the department. If these were addressed properly, they had the potential to significantly improve the profitability of member acquisition. Looking at the old mailings, the new team had no starting point, because there was no control package. Thus, it was impossible to track which parts of the campaigns worked and which did not. One thing that was obvious from the past campaigns, though, was the exhausted prospect lists that the department was using. That was combined with expensive designs and production fees for the mailings. And since there was no cohesive strategy in place for the overall member acquisition program, the department often found itself working under rushed deadlines.

Based on this information, the new Acquisitions team set on a strategy focusing on fixing the controllable factors. The first step was to look at past results and see how they could be improved. The last two campaigns were especially disappointing with an average cost per dollar raised of $9.42. Part of the reason was the high production cost of the campaigns. A meeting with key business partners aimed at reviewing last year's campaigns concluded that they had too many messages, too many inserts, and inconsistent creative solutions. In addition, the mailings contained deeply discounted offers. Exhibit C5.5 shows an example of the previous year's Silk Road campaign. This indicated a need to simplify the mailings and return to basic direct mail components.

---

[2] This section is exclusively based on a presentation by AIC at the Case Writers' Workshop sponsored by the Direct Marketing Educational Foundation in conjunction with the Direct Marketing Association Annual Conference in Chicago, in the current year of the case.

EXHIBIT C5.4: (PY = PAST YEAR, CY = CURRENT YEAR)

Exhibition	Dates
Louis H. Sullivan: A System of Architectural Ornament According with a Philosophy of Man's Powers	December 24, PY–February 18, CY
Chinese Figures: Faithful and Fantastic	December 1, PY–March 4, CY
Young Chicago	November 16, PY–April 29, CY
Renaissance Europe and the Ottoman Empire	October 21, PY–April 2, CY
Eugène Delacroix and North Africa	October 21, PY–April 13, CY
Charles Sheeler: Across Media	October 7, PY–January 7, CY
Photographs by the Score: Personal Visions Twenty-Some Years Apart	October 7, PY–January 14, CY
Focus: Mel Bochner—Language 1966-PY	October 5, PY–January 7, CY
The Silk Road and Beyond: Travel, Trade, and Transformation	September 30, PY–April 22, CY
Unity and Diversity: Art of the Islamic World	September 30, PY–June 30, CY
The Art of Buddhism: Transmission and Transformation	September 30, PY–February 25, CY
Tang China and the Silk Road	September 30, PY–June 30, CY
So the Story Goes: Photographs by Tina Barney, Philip-Lorca diCorcia, Nan Goldin, Sally Mann, and Larry Sultan	September 16–December 3, PY
Julius Shulman: Modernity and the Metropolis	September 2–December 3, PY
The Art of Buddhism: Transmission and Transformation	August 30, PY–July 29, CY
Stories from the Silk Road	August 26, PY–May 28, CY
Harry Callahan: The Photographer at Work	June 24–September 24, PY
José Guadalupe Posada and the Mexican Broadside	June 24, PY–January 21, CY
Douglas Garofalo	June 15–October 8, PY
Faces, Places, and Inner Spaces	June 14, PY–July 8, CY
Learning From Art	June 10, PY–January 7, CY
Drawings in Dialogue: Old Master through Modern	June 3–July 30, PY
Recent Acquisitions of Asian Art	May 27–September 24, PY
Focus: Maureen Gallace	May 25–September 3, PY
Todd Eberle: Architectural Abstractions	May 20–August 20, PY
Utamaro: Aspects of Beauty	May 13–October 22, PY
Zero Gravity: The Art Institute, Renzo Piano, and Building for a New Century	May 9, PY–February 1, CY
Transcending Tradition: The Flowering of a New Artistic Culture in Shanghai	May 6–October 29, PY
Work of Many Hands: The Art of Islamic Bookmaking	May 1–August 28, PY
Casas Grandes and the Ceramic Art of the Ancient Southwest	April 22–August 13, PY
Icons of Divinity from South and Southeast Asia	March 9, PY–June 30, CY
Infinite Shades: Contemporary Chinese Ink	September 22–November 7, CY
Richard Misrach: On the Beach	September 15–November 25, CY
Splendor and Intimacy: Mughal and Rajput Courtly Life, Part 1	August 4–November 3, CY
The Capital of the 19th Century: Paris in Maps	August 1–December 3, CY
The "Gates of Paradise": Lorenzo Ghiberti's Renaissance Masterpiece	July 28–October 14, CY

EXHIBIT C5.4: CONTINUED

Xefirotarch	July 11–October 28, CY
Poetry of Friendship: Surimono and the Cultural Salons of Japan	July 7–September 16, CY
Japanese Art of the 1960s: The Struggle with Tradition	June 30–September 16, CY
Jeff Wall	June 29–September 23, CY
Postwar Works on Paper	June 25–August 5, CY
Focus: Jana Gunstheimer	June 7–August 26, CY
On the Scene: Kota Ezawa, Sarah Hobbs, Angela Strassheim	May 19–September 3, CY
Society for Contemporary Art: Acquisition Selection CY	May 7–July 30, CY
The Earth As It Was: Photographs by Ansel Adams, Eliot Porter, and William Clift	May 5–September 3, CY
Typing for Tomorrow: Modernism and Typography in the Collection of the Ryerson and Burnham Libraries	May 1–July 31, CY
France in the 18th Century: The Allure of China and Persia	April 21–October 1, CY
Japonisme: The Impact of Japanese Prints in 19th-Century Europe	April 21–October 1, CY
A World of Things by Kamisaka Sekka (1866–1942)	April 14–July 1, CY
The Practice of Tea from the Edo Period to Today	April 14–July 1, CY
18th-Century Masters of Ink: Shohaku and Rosetsu	April 7–June 24, CY
Perpetual Glory: Medieval Islamic Ceramics from the Harvey B. Plotnick Collection	March 31–October 28, CY
Image/Text: Youth Interprets the News	March 17–April 29, CY
Louis H. Sullivan: A System of Architectural Ornament	March 4–June 8, CY
When Color Was New	February 24–April 29, CY
Cézanne to Picasso: Ambroise Vollard, Patron of the Avant-Garde	February 17–May 12, CY
Focus: Kasmalieva and Djumaliev	February 1–May 6, CY
Far from Home: Photography, Travel, and Inspiration	January 20–May 6, CY
Foreign Faces in Japanese Prints	January 20–April 8, CY
Western Viewers, Eastern Subjects: Scenes of Empire	January 2–May 1, CY

Source: www.artic.edu

Another important step towards minimizing costs and evenly spreading the department's workload was to design a timeframe for the implementation of each step of the campaign process, in order to meet the final mailing dates. This included adequate time for planning the campaign, for producing the copy and the design to be delivered to the print house, and from there to the mail house, which was ultimately responsible for the actual mailing of the packages.

Even as there seemed to be a number of problems with past campaigns, it was clear that they could not be addressed all at once. Since there was no existing control package, it was essential to prioritize what tests should be done first. There were three general areas that could be tested in the Art Institute's direct mail campaign—the offer, the creative design, and the message. It was decided that the offer and the creative design would be tested at a later stage since they required some additional

EXHIBIT C5.5: PREVIOUS YEAR'S SILK ROAD DIRECT MAIL CAMPAIGN

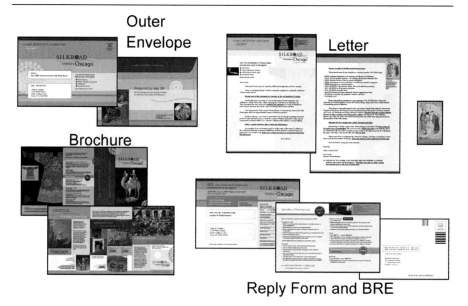

Outer Envelope

Letter

Brochure

Reply Form and BRE

preparation. For example, in order to test the effect of different offers, they needed to establish a base of response to "no offer". For the creative design, they needed to look at industry's best practices and find cost-efficient solutions to establish a baseline. Consequently, the consensus fell on testing three distinct messages—advertising of exhibitions as a driving force of Art Institute membership, emphasizing member benefits such as free passes and reciprocity programs, or building on the civic pride of Chicagoans as supporters of one of the best art museums in the world.

That set the stage for the creation of the copy and the design of the mailings. In order to cut costs, these functions were performed in-house. The packages included letter copy that conveyed the tone of voice of the President of the Art Institute. For consistency purposes, the copy incorporated taglines that carried through each of the three message tests throughout the packages. Since the purpose of the campaign was to test the three alternative messages and to decrease the production costs from previous campaigns, it incorporated a simple design based on the direct mail industry's best practices. Exhibit C5.6 shows a copy of the three different brochures used for the different messages. In addition, the package contained the President's letter, a reply form with a return envelope, and a list of membership levels and benefits. Exhibit C5.7 shows the different membership levels.

While the in-house simplified design would decrease costs, it was imperative to improve the targeting of the mailings in order to increase response rates. Improved targeting leads to a better revenue stream and has the potential to save costs by printing smaller amounts of mailing packages and ultimately achieving greater efficiency. For this reason, list hygiene is essential. Improving the quality of mailing lists utilized

EXHIBIT C5.6: EXHIBITION BROCHURE, BENEFITS BROCHURE AND CIVIC PRIDE BROCHURE

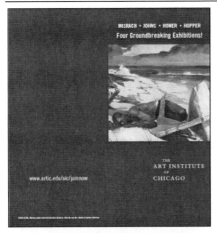

EXHIBIT C5.7

MEMBERSHIP BENEFITS

	INDIVIDUAL	FAMILY	MUSEUM ASSOCIATE	ALLIANCE	ALLIANCE COUNCIL	ALLIANCE ROUNDTABLE	SUSTAINING FELLOW
	$70	$90	$150	$250	$500	$1,000	$1,500+
Number of Guests	1	1+*	5	5	5	7	7
Private Viewings			1	3	3	3+	3+
Reciprocal Membership							
Insider Tour							
Complimentary Individual Gift Membership							
First Look at Special Exhibitions							
Recognition in Annual Report							
Invitation to A. James Speyer Lecture							
Curator Luncheons							
Art Walk of Private Collections							

* one adult and all children under 18

by the Art Institute was of utmost importance toward the goal of achieving profitability with the campaigns. Terry's decision was to concentrate on lapsed members and ticket buyers, and to discontinue using commercially available magazine lists and the Chicago Cultural Cooperative lists, as these had become depleted. Instead, she added new prospects through purchased Prizm Code lists recommended by recent membership analysis. Prizm is a geodemographic segmentation system developed by Nielsen Claritas that divides US households into 66 segments and allows marketers household-level precision targeting in direct marketing initiatives (www.claritas.com/MyBestSegments/Defaults.jsp).

With these preparations set in place, the team was ready to test the first of the overhauled campaigns. The department budgeted for the following costs (assuming a minimum production run of 100,000 mailing packages):

Printing	$0.11/piece
List rental[3]	$23,200
Mailhouse	$0.07/piece
Postage	$0.12/piece

If they mail 200,000 packages, at what response rate would they break even? Was this a realistic assumption? In addition, Terry was wondering what else could be done to bring down the cost of the campaigns and increase their efficiency. Or, if there is a limit in reducing the costs, are there any ways to increase the response rate, given costs? Should she request a supportive, interactive communications program to increase the efficiency of the direct mail campaign?

---

[3] This list was to be used in all of the 4 direct mail campaigns in the fiscal year.

CASE
6

The Chicago Girl Scouts

GREG BALEJA

Alma College

THOMAS A. TULLY

University of Dubuque

BENJAMIN WEEKS

St. Xavier University

Gwen Ferguson, Volunteer Personnel Manager for Girl Scouts of Chicago, returned to her office high above Union Station in downtown Chicago and replayed the meeting she had just had with her boss, Chicago Council Executive Director Brooke Wiseman. The topic had been a familiar one: *How can Girl Scouts of Chicago recruit adequate numbers of replacements for the 25% of adult leaders who leave scouting each year?*

The Chicago area had tens of thousands of Girl Scout alumnae from the 80+ years Girl Scouting had been part of the Chicago scene, yet each year it became harder and harder to find suitable volunteers. Worse, participation rates among girls age five to seventeen had been dropping steadily, attributed in part to lack of adult volunteer leaders. Girl Scouts of Chicago had tried a variety of methods to entice new volunteers to become part of Girl Scouting, but results had been disappointing.

Was there anything she could do, Gwen wondered, to attract an adequate number of qualified volunteers necessary to maintain or to build Chicagoland Girl Scouting, or was the Girl Scout movement, like others, the inevitable victim of the changing American socio-economic scene? The Board of Directors was meeting in two weeks, and Brooke wanted to present a new recruitment plan to them at that time. With a glance at the late afternoon Chicago skyline, Gwen began to outline a plan.

Background

Girl Scouting in the United States traced its origins to Sir Robert Baden-Powell, the Englishman who founded the Boy Scout movement in 1908. A year later, after some girls appeared at a Boy Scout rally, Baden-Powell concluded that girls should have their own separate organization and he created the Girl Guides. In 1910, he retired from the British army and devoted his life to developing both the Boy Scout and the Girl Guide programs.

Juliette Gordon Low, founder of Girl Scouts of the U.S.A., was born and raised in Savannah, Georgia. In 1886, she married a wealthy Englishman, William Mackay Low, and moved to England. William Low died in 1905 and Juliette drifted for several years in search of some direction for her life. In 1911, she met Baden-Powell, who encouraged her interest in his new youth movements. A year later, Juliette returned to America and organized the first American Girl Guide troops in Savannah. She recruited 18 girls to form the first two troops on March 12, 1912. Her niece, Daisy Gordon, was the first registered American Girl Guide. In 1913, Low changed the name from Girl Guides to Girl Scouts.

In recent years, Girl Scouts of the U.S.A. had involved almost 2.6 million girls between the ages of five and seventeen and over 800,000 adult members, including volunteer leaders, consultants, board members, and staff specialists.

Girl Scouts of the U.S.A. directs and coordinates Girl Scouting in the United States. Through U.S.A Girl Scouts Overseas, it also serves over 23,000 American girls living with their families in 81 different countries. The national office, located in New York City, writes handbooks, provides training for adult staff and volunteers, charters local councils, maintains membership files, and provides liaison with outside agencies. Nearly half (47 percent) of the funding for national operations comes from the $6 membership dues, which are required of each child and adult member. An additional 28 percent comes from the sale of uniforms and equipment.

A national Board of Directors is chosen for three-year terms by delegates to a triennial National Council meeting. The board's function is to manage the affairs of Girl Scouts of the U.S.A. between meetings of the National Council. Of the 54 directors chosen at a typical conference, 47 were women and 7 were men. Thirty-four of the directors were former Girl Scouts and 24 had served as presidents of local Girl Scout councils. Twenty-four percent of the directors were African-Americans and 17 percent were Hispanic. American Indians and Asian-Americans constituted 7 and 6 percent, respectively.

Below the national organization are 321 local Girl Scout councils chartered by Girl Scouts of the U.S.A. Each council has a volunteer board of directors that establishes policies and long range goals, manages the councils' real and personal property, raises money, promotes the Scouting program, and represents Girl Scouting in the community. Each council is responsible for securing its own funding to carry out operations. The typical council relies heavily on product sales, especially cookies, to generate revenue. Approximately 57 percent of each council's income comes from product sales, with local United Ways and various program fees each accounting for an additional 12 percent. Gifts, investments, and other sources make up another 19 percent. Girls and their leaders typically take part in Girl Scouting through organized groups called troops. A troop is usually a group of between 10 and 30 girls led by at least one volunteer adult troop leader and one or more assistant troop leaders. In recent years the number of troops hovered around 220,000, with locations throughout the United States and the 81 countries where U.S.A Girl Scouts Overseas operated.

Girls Scouts are organized into five program levels. The average troop has from 10 to 12 girls, ranging from a minimum of 5 to a maximum of 30. There are strict ratios as to the number of girls to leaders and there must be a minimum of two leaders per troop.

The lowest level, called Daisy Girl Scouts, involves girls aged five and six, usually kindergartners and first graders. Their troops meet at least once every two weeks to learn songs and crafts, to take day trips, and to participate in community service projects. Brownie Girl Scouts are six to eight years old and gather together as often as once a week or as seldom as once a month. Brownies have more opportunities to develop their own interests and skills than Daisies do, and occasionally go on local overnights. They are also eligible to take part in the annual cookie sale. The third level of Girl Scouting, called Junior Girl Scouts, involves girls between the ages of eight and eleven. At this level the girls take a more active role in planning and executing their activities. Cadette Girl Scouts are between the ages of eleven and fourteen, and frequently move into council-wide or even national and international activities. The final level, called Senior Girl Scouts, has members between fourteen and seventeen years of age.

The Chicago Girl Scout Council

Girl Scouts of Chicago was chartered in 1920 to provide a program for girls in Chicago, Norridge, Harwood Heights, and Norwood Park, Illinois. In recent years, the Chicago Council was serving over 13,000 girls between the ages of five and seventeen years, most of whom were organized into 804 troops (see Exhibit C6.1). Almost 50 percent of all members were living at the low or moderate income level.

At the same time, about 2,000 adults were involved in Girl Scouting in Chicago, about 1,400 of whom were serving as either troop leaders or assistant leaders. African-American adults represented 29 percent of the total, while Caucasians were 65 percent, Hispanics 5 percent, and all others 1 percent. Although the 2,000 adults actually represented a net increase of 28 over decade-ago levels, the 1,400 leaders and assistant leaders represented a drop of 56 from the number participating a decade previous, and a drop of 154 from five-year-ago levels.

The Chicago Council had a full-time staff of 36, supplemented by part-time staff aides who worked in the Council's outreach programs. Meeting locations for the troops included churches, schools, Park District facilities, libraries, and police departments.

EXHIBIT C6.1: CHICAGO COUNCIL
GIRL SCOUTS: TROOPS AND MEMBERS[1]

Type of Troop	Number of Troops	Number of Girls Enrolled
Daisy	75	814
Brownie	340	6,225
Junior	254	3,522
Cadette	106	949
Senior	29	250
Totals	**804**[2]	**11,760**[3]

Source: Girl Scouts of Chicago Most Recent Year End Membership Report
[1] As of September in the year of the case
[2] Plus 8 Shelters and 31 Activity Centers
[3] Plus 1,626 girls in Shelters, Activity Centers, or in individual programs

Chicago girls participating in Girl Scout activities dropped from a high a decade previous of 19,576 to 13,386 by the end of the year of the case, a decline of 6,190, or 32 percent. Caucasian girls represented 36 percent of total membership in the previous decade and climbed to 41 percent by the end of the year of the case, but total numbers dropped by 1,543, a decline of 22 percent. African-Americans constituted 51 percent of all Girl Scouts in Chicago ten years earlier, but in the year of the case that number had dropped to 45 percent. Total numbers slid substantially, however, dropping from 10,102 to 6,020, a net loss of 4,082, or 40 percent. Hispanic girls were 12 percent of the total both a decade earlier and in the year of the case, but actual numbers declined from 2,273 to 1,660, a 27 percent drop. Numbers of Asian-American and other ethnic groups rose only slightly during the ten-year period, from 210 to 292, representing an increase from 1 percent of total membership to 2 percent.

Retention of Girl Scouts in the Chicago Council averaged 45.25 percent in the 12 previous years, ranging from lows of 40 percent earlier in the decade to highs of 53 percent in the two most recent years. What's more, retention rates varied considerably by type of troop. Daisy troops had the lowest retention rate at 9 percent, followed by Brownies at 50 percent. Juniors retained 64 percent of their members, while Cadettes and Seniors had retention rates of 83 percent and 72 percent, respectively. Of the 5,492 new Scouts recruited in the past year, 62 percent came in at the Brownie level, while another 22 percent entered as Juniors. Twelve percent of new Scouts were Daisies. Most of the remaining 4 percent entered as Cadettes.

Although the number of existing troops had stabilized recently, the mix was altering. Thirteen more Brownie troops were established—bringing the total to 340 for an increase of 4 percent—to accommodate an 11 percent growth in Brownie membership. Ten fewer Junior troops reflected a 4 percent drop caused by a 3 percent decline in Junior Scouts. At the Cadette level one more troop was organized, while at the Senior level four troops were dropped, a decline of 12 percent in the face of a 6 percent drop in the number of Senior Scouts. Despite a 21 percent increase in the number of Daisy Scouts in the previous year, no additional Daisy troops were formed. On the adult side, 23 fewer leaders were available in the previous year and there were 56 fewer assistant leaders. The declines in numbers were 4 percent and 7 percent, respectively.

Because of a shortage of volunteers in some areas of the city, not all of the girls were able to participate in troops, and a variety of alternative outreach programs staffed by paid part-time workers were developed. In the current year these programs included:

- Shelter Troops, designed for homeless girls, their siblings, and parents, served 149 girls in eight shelters throughout Chicago
- Neighborhood Activity Centers provided after-school and summer programs for 1,410 girls at 31 neighborhood sites
- Chicago Housing Authority Troops, centered in public housing developments, served approximately 600 girls
- Juvenile Detention Center programs delivered activities to 50 incarcerated girls

It cost the Chicago Council approximately $175 per year to serve each girl within the council. Currently, Girl Scouts of Chicago had income of more than $2 million per year, 10.9 percent of which came from United Way. Although United Way was an im-

EXHIBIT C6.2: SEVEN TRUTHS ABOUT BEING A GIRL SCOUT LEADER

1. You don't need a special skill or talent to be a leader, just a sincerity and willingness to work with girls. We provide you with free training, resources, and an abundance of support services to help organize your troop.
2. Girl Scout troops are community-based. That means you can meet right in your neighborhood at the park district, the community center, the school, or even at your church.
3. Let's face it. There are only 24 hours in a day, 7 days in a week. And we realize you have busy, full lives. Girl Scout leaders can set their own hours for meetings. Your troop can meet weekly or twice a month. You can meet on Saturdays, Sundays, or on weekdays.
4. Being a parent is not a prerequisite for being a Girl Scout leader. You must be 19 years of age and older. Our leaders are retirees, college students, senior citizens, and part-time and full- time workers, and they have jobs in a wide range of professions.
5. Don't worry, we won't send you up a creek without a paddle. Going camping is not a requirement. But most girls enjoy it, and if you like the outdoors we will train you. And anyway, today Girl Scouting is about more than camping. Girl Scouts perform community service, mentor with successful business women, go on field trips to places of interest, and participate in events that are fun and educational.
6. The annual membership fee is only $6 per year. Troops participate in the cookie sale, collect meeting dues, and hold special troop/neighborhood events as a way to raise funds for their activities. Additionally some financial assistance is available to troops.
7. Girl Scouting is for today's girl. Our program is designed to meet the changing needs and challenges of today's world. Girls can explore aviation, literacy, computers, math and science, business, finance, and the arts.

Source: Girl Scouts of Chicago Recruiting Brochure, Chicago, Illinois

portant source of funding, income from that source had been declining in recent years. Given the reduction in United Way's contributions each year, the Council was looking for new, creative, and non-traditional ways to improve its fund raising. Other income generators included cookie sales, gifts, contributions, bequests, public and private grants, inkind donations, and special events.

The Ideal Adult Leader

There is a commonly held belief in Girl Scouting that "if you have the adult leaders, the girls will follow." According to Chicago Girl Scout Council leaders, the ideal adult volunteer leader is female and is usually the mother of one of the girls in the troop. There was some concern expressed that non-mothers were self-selecting out of Girl Scouting. "If they don't have a daughter, there was the FALSE assumption on their part that they would not qualify as a leader," according to one Chicago Council executive. Males can only serve as a co-leader with another female leader. Most of the Council's volunteer adult leaders were employed full-time outside the home. (See Exhibit C6.2, "Seven Truths About Being a Girl Scout Leader.")

The Chicago Council wanted to target the following groups for potential adult leaders:

- African-American women
- Former Girl Scouts, especially those who were involved as Brownies and Juniors

- College-aged women
- Senior citizens

The Girl Scouts specifically sought caring individuals who could work well with children. They also wanted leaders who were willing to work with girls to make a difference in their lives. Extensive training was offered to supplement any shortcomings for potential leaders. References were checked for all volunteers, and random criminal background checks were done on the applicants. (One in five applicants were checked.)

Although most Girl Scout volunteers were recruited because of their daughters' involvement with scouting, the Girl Scouts of Chicago attempted to recruit leaders in other ways. One of the most successful methods for recruiting new leaders was the "Self-Replacement Program." Under this program, the current troop leader was responsible for finding her own replacement prior to her resignation as leader. Staff members of the Chicago Council were also very heavily involved in the recruiting process. They recruited at school through Parent-Teacher Associations (PTAs), churches, and volunteer recruiting fairs. They also made extensive use of flyers. Public service announcements (PSAs), press releases, and live radio interviews were also used. In addition, the Council solicited the help of businesses to find new adult leaders. Specifically, the Council used promotional pieces in corporation newsletters, placed promotional recruiting posters in corporate offices, tried cold calling, and posted recruiting flyers in retail stores. None of these latter four methods worked very well.

Only limited research, such as exit interviews, was conducted to determine why current leaders were resigning. However, some generally accepted assumptions for the resignations included:

- The leader's daughter had completed her tenure in Girl Scouting and it was someone else's turn to serve as leader
- Burnout
- Job pressures

In the Chicago Council, the majority of the girls and the troops were made up of individuals under the age of eleven, correlating to the Daisy, Brownie, and Junior levels. After the Junior level, there was a marked drop-off in participation. It was assumed that this drop-off was caused by an increase in the availability of school-related activities. The Council was also experiencing great difficulty in recruiting adult leaders for the Cadette and Senior troops. This was due in part to the belief among adult volunteers that it was much easier to work with younger girls than with older girls.

The Chicago Council had the names of approximately 1,000 Girl Scout alumnae in their database. In most cases, the database only included the names and addresses of these individuals. Most of these people were self-identified as Girl Scout alumnae in response to articles in newspapers or they were recruited at PTA meetings. Expanding this database could potentially help the Council overcome a variety of problems.

Volunteerism in the United States

A study by the Independent Sector found that in the previous decade, Americans donated 9.7 billion hours worth an estimated $112 billion to non-profits each year. That

EXHIBIT C6.3: PERCENTAGES OF ADULT POPULATION DOING VOLUNTEER WORK IN A RECENT PERIOD

Age	Percentage of Population Volunteering	Educational Attainment	Percentage of Population Volunteering
Total	48.8%	Elementary school	18.7%
		Some high school	26.1%
18–24 years old	38.4%	High school graduate	43.1%
25–34 years old	50.8%	Technical, trade, business school	51.2%
35–44 years old	55.0%	Some college	56.3%
45–54 years old	55.3%	College graduate	70.7%
55–64 years old	47.9%	**Household Income**	
65–74 years old	44.7%	Under $10,000	34.7%
75 years old and older	33.7%	$10,000–$19,999	34.3%
Sex		$20,000–$29,999	41.2%
Male	45.1%	$30,000–$39,999	48.0%
Female	52.2%	$40,000–$49,999	52.7%
Race/Hispanic Origin		$50,000–$59,999	64.1%
White	51.9%	$60,000–$74,999	56.4%
Black	35.3%	$75,000–$99,999	64.8%
Hispanic	40.4%	$100,000 or more	69.4%

This exhibit was adapted from Exhibit 613 of *The Statistical Abstract of the United States* published by the Department of Commerce.

same organization reported that volunteerism in the United States was declining, to less than 50 percent participation. (Abraham Spencer, "Litigation's Stranglehold on Charities," *The Public Interest*, Spring 1997, p. 96.) However, a follow-up study by the Independent Sector showed that the number of volunteers was increasing slightly in the United States for the first time in nearly a decade. That same study indicated that 60 percent of the volunteers came from churches, 20 percent from the workplace, and 14 percent from schools or colleges. (John Fialka, "Many Americans Quietly Serve as Volunteers Even as Summit Stresses Need for Many More," *The Wall Street Journal*, April 23, 1997, p. A20.) See Exhibit C6.3 for statistics on adult volunteers in the United States.

As a result, many experts believed that volunteerism was alive and well in the United States, despite the longer work hours of individuals and the increasing number of married women in the workplace. According to *The Economist*, "Toqueville pointed out in the 1830s that the tenuousness and distance of government in America required men to do many community jobs for themselves, and, although government seems to have become all embracing, creeping into every fissure of life, many Americans still like to think that they can help the community by their own effort when the need arises." ("The Worker and the Volunteer," *The Economist*, April 26, 1997, p. 28.)

Most individuals volunteer because they were asked (a friend at work asks you to participate in a walkathon for a charity), an opportunity arose through an organization of which they were a member (a service club might volunteer at a soup kitchen on Thanksgiving), or a family member or friend would receive a benefit (grandmother would baby-sit for her daughter). (Michael Gerson, "Do Do-Gooders Do Much Good?" *U.S. News and World Report*, April 28, 1997, p. 26.) Other studies have indicated that individuals volunteer to satisfy achievement, affiliation, and power needs, as well as to meet new people. Some believe it is easier to obtain a leadership position in a volunteer organization than at work. As a result, it is important for the non-profit organization to recognize the contribution of its volunteers. For example, at one Girl Scout council, troop members placed signs in the yards of leaders that recognized their contributions. (Beverly Geber, "Managing Volunteers," *Training*, June 1992, p. 21.)

Often prospective volunteers use the excuse that they are too busy. Because of the "time crunch" in today's society, it is more difficult to recruit effective volunteers. Many corporations have expanded geographically and have given managers more responsibility. With the advances in transportation and mass communication, individuals are able to cover more territory. As a result, individuals have less time for philanthropic activities. "Therefore, when recruiting a person to volunteer for your organization, be aware that you are not asking for their spare time, you are requesting to be made a priority." (G. Douglass Alexander, "'Too Busy'—Not a Priority," *Fund Raising Management*, January 1997, p. 46.) Some experts suggest that organizations provide staff assistance to support the volunteers, offer job descriptions that specify expectations, and make requests for the number of hours required of the volunteer. (Alexander, "'Too Busy'—Not a Priority," p. 46.)

There are many benefits to employees (and the corporation) from volunteering. Employees who get involved in volunteer work acquire a feeling of elation that affects their lives and jobs. They are ten times more likely to perceive themselves in better health than the non-helper employee. This altruistic feeling could also soften the impact of work problems and infuse them with job enthusiasm and confidence. (Margaret Finney, "Operations that Build Smiles, Confidence, Skills and Community Goodwill," *HR Magazine*, April 1997, p. 110.)

One of the problems facing the Girl Scouts and other volunteer organizations has been the increase in the participation of women in the workforce, resulting in a reduced volunteer base. There are a number of reasons for this trend. First, although the divorce rate in the United States has declined recently, many women are now the head of a household and have to work full-time to provide for the economic welfare of their family. Second, many married women are now working outside of the home because of economic pressures and the desire to provide a higher standard of living for their families. Third, the women's movement has encouraged many women to seek employment opportunities as a means of satisfying their personal needs and sense of self-worth. Many women are now going into professions in which they were under represented such as medicine, law, and business. (See Exhibits C6.4 through C6.7.)

As a result of the aforementioned trends, the nature of volunteerism has changed over the years. Prior to the 1970s, most volunteers were women who were staying home to raise children. Non-profits welcomed these individuals with open arms. These women were unable to transform their skills learned as a manager of the house-

EXHIBIT C6.4: FEMALE LABOR FORCE, WITH PROJECTIONS: 1980 TO 2005 (MILLIONS)

	1980	1990	1995	1996	2000 (proj.)	2005 (proj.)
Total Female	45.5	56.8	60.9	61.9	65.8	70.3
16–19 years	4.4	3.7	3.7	3.8	4.0	4.2
20–24 years	7.3	6.8	6.3	6.3	6.5	7.1
25–34 years	12.2	16.1	15.5	15.4	14.3	14.2
35–44 years	8.6	14.7	16.6	17.0	17.8	17.1
45–54 years	7.0	9.1	11.8	12.4	14.8	17.1
55–64 years	4.7	4.9	5.4	5.5	6.6	8.6
65 years and over	1.1	1.5	1.6	1.6	1.8	1.8

EXHIBIT C6.5: FEMALE LABOR FORCE PARTICIPATION RATES, WITH PROJECTIONS: 1980 TO 2005 (PERCENT)

	1980	1990	1995	1996	2000 (proj.)	2005 (proj.)
Total	51.5%	57.5%	58.9%	59.3%	60.6%	61.7%
16–19 years	52.9%	51.6%	52.2%	51.3%	51.2%	50.7%
20–24 years	68.9%	71.3%	70.3%	71.3%	70.5%	70.7%
25–34 years	65.5%	73.5%	74.9%	75.2%	75.3%	76.4%
35–44 years	65.5%	76.4%	77.2%	77.5%	78.7%	80.0%
45–54 years	59.9%	71.2%	74.4%	75.4%	78.2%	80.7%
55–64 years	41.3%	45.2%	49.2%	49.6%	53.4%	56.6%
65 years and over	8.1%	8.6%	8.8%	8.6%	9.5%	10.2%

Exhibits C5.4 and C5.5 were adapted from Exhibit 620 of *The Statistical Abstract of the United States 1997* published by the Department of Commerce.

hold to those needed by the corporation. This situation changed drastically in the 1970s because of the women's movement and economic necessity. According to Deborah Walsh of the United Way in Hartford, Connecticut, "It was very scary. We couldn't get people to drive for Meals on Wheels." As a result, the makeup of the volunteer pool has changed dramatically as most are full-time employees. (Beverly Geber, "Managing Volunteers," *Training*, June 1992, p. 21.)

Volunteer organizations that have traditionally relied upon the stay-at-home mom no longer have an "unlimited" pool of volunteers to call upon. Many women who would have participated in the Girl Scouts, the PTA, and local community organizations, are now working in full-time jobs that take up many hours, reducing the time available for volunteerism of any kind. As a result, it is more difficult for volunteer organizations to staff their organization with the type of individual willing and able to perform the required tasks.

EXHIBIT C6.6: LABOR FORCE PARTICIPATION RATE OF MARRIED WOMEN CONSIDERING PRESENCE AND AGE OF CHILDREN: 1960 TO 1996

	1960	1970	1980	1985	1990	1993	1994	1995	1996
Children under 6	18.6	30.3	45.1	53.4	58.9	59.6	61.7	63.5	62.7
Children 6 to 17	39.0	49.2	61.7	67.8	73.6	74.9	76.0	76.2	76.7

This exhibit was adapted from Exhibit 631 of *The Statistical Abstract of the United States 1997* published by the Department of Commerce.

EXHIBIT C6.7: LABOR FORCE PARTICIPATION RATE OF MARRIED WOMEN BY AGE: 1960 TO 1996

	1960	1970	1980	1985	1990	1993	1994	1995	1996
Total	31.9	40.5	49.8	53.8	58.4	59.4	60.7	61.0	61.2
16–19 years	27.2	37.8	49.3	49.6	49.5	49.8	48.9	51.6	48.6
20–24 years	31.7	47.9	61.4	65.7	66.1	65.1	65.8	64.7	66.0
25–34 years	28.8	38.8	58.8	65.8	69.6	70.6	71.6	72.0	71.7
35–44 years	37.2	46.8	61.8	68.1	74.0	74.7	75.8	75.7	75.8
45–64 years	36.0	44.0	46.9	49.4	56.5	59.9	61.9	62.7	63.7
65 and over	6.7	7.3	7.3	6.6	8.5	7.6	9.4	9.1	9.0

This exhibit was adapted from Exhibit 629 of *The Statistical Abstract of the United States 1997* published by the Department of Commerce.

Prior to the increase of women in the workplace, many volunteers were women who used volunteering as an occasion to socialize. However, the new female volunteer is usually part of a two-income family and might volunteer in order to network professionally. Although women tend to volunteer more than men, the gap is closing. A poll of its members by the Junior League of Indianapolis found that 65 percent of its members worked full or part-time. (Maureen Dobie, "Volunteer Structure Shifts to Accommodate Working Women," *Indianapolis Business Journal*, September 20, 1993, p. 98.)

In a consultant's report for the Girl Scouts of the U.S.A., the questions were asked: "Who is the potential volunteer? And, how must she be reached?" It was found that the potential volunteer is a former Girl Scout with a daughter in scouting, works full-time, and is between 30 and 45 years of age. She can most likely be reached by stressing the importance of building a relationship with her daughter and her daughter's friends.

Other findings were:

• Seventy-eight percent of Girl Scout volunteers have a daughter who is a Girl Scout
• Seventy-four percent of the Girl Scout volunteers work and of those that work, approximately 68 percent have full-time jobs

- Fifty percent of the Girl Scout volunteers work in either blue-collar (29 percent) or technical business (21 percent) occupations.
- Seventy-nine percent of the Girl Scout volunteers are between the ages of 25 and 35.

The main reasons why Girls Scout volunteers like the Girl Scouts are that they enjoy helping others, they want to build relationships with their daughters, they like Girl Scout activities/organization, and they enjoy giving back to their community.

One of the major problems of the Girl Scouts of Chicago was the need for more volunteers, particularly in the African-American community. Twenty-nine percent of the volunteers and forty-five percent of the girls were African-American. The Girl Scout Council of Chicago had a total of more than 2,100 adult volunteers, with an annual turnover rate of 25 percent per year. They needed an additional 250 to 500 African-American volunteers. Although most of the women volunteers were mothers with a daughter in the troop, when the daughter left scouting, the mother often followed.

The Girl Scout Council of Chicago had established several programs aimed at older girls who might want to become leaders and to increase the leadership pool. The Leader-in-Training program helped Senior Girl Scouts ". . . acquire the skills and confidence necessary to guide a group of younger girls and hold future leadership positions within and outside of Girl Scouting." There were three parts to the program: an 8- to 10-hour Leader-in-Training course, 3 to 5 hours of observations of troop participation, and a minimum of 25 hours in an internship program working with a troop. In the Chicago district, approximately ten girls per year complete this course.

A second leadership opportunity is the Senior Girl Scout Troop Assistant. An extension of the Leader-in-Training program, the girls must work with a particular troop for at least one full year, exercising leadership skills, speaking in public, and gaining a greater understanding of Girl Scouting. A final program, the Counselor-in-Training, enabled the individual to work with younger girls in a camp setting and learn how to manage a camp. This program was discontinued because the Girl Scouts had temporarily discontinued the summer resident camp.

Many volunteer organizations use generally accepted human resource techniques for recruiting volunteers. At an Easter Seals Rehabilitation Center, volunteers undergo an extensive interview process to ascertain their interests, background, and experience, as well as a background check. At a Girl Scout council in Orange County, California, prospective troop leaders sign a "volunteer agreement": " . . . a volunteer might volunteer to be a Brownie troop leader during that time and to perform the list of tasks typically required for that position." (Beverly Geber, "Managing Volunteers," *Training,* June 1992, p. 21.) Of course, the recruiting, screening, training, and supervising of volunteers can be expensive in certain types of organizations. For example, this process costs the Big Brother/Big Sisters $1,000 for each volunteer. (Michael Gerson, "Do Do-Gooders Do Much Good?" *U.S. News and World Report,* April 28, 1997, p. 26.)

In Great Britain, non-profits are using national newspaper, magazine, and radio advertising, as well as targeting human resource managers. According to a director of the Samaritans, "We go to professional bodies, to synagogues and, increasingly, to employers. I still feel a bit sheepish about pushing ourselves, but there is certainly a lot of benefit to be gained from the intensive training course we run—and the skills we teach must pay off for employers, too." (Jilly Welch, "Charities Face Battle to Recruit Volunteers," *People Management*, March 6. 1997, p. 12.)

A major problem of many volunteer organizations is in attracting low-income volunteers. These individuals often do not have the disposable income necessary to pay for out-of-pocket expenses such as meals and transportation. One expert suggests that non-profits establish "volunteer reimbursement accounts" that would help those individuals who want to volunteer, but lack the required financial resources. (Glenice B. Pearson, "Is it Time for a Paradigm Shift on Volunteers?" *Fund Raising Management*, August 1996, p. 12.)

A recent trend has been for colleges to offer courses with a service component. For example, San Francisco State University offered 50 courses in 1997–98 in which students volunteered for four hours per week. Supporters believe that such offerings enable students to transfer their classroom learning to the real world. On the other hand, critics question the quality of both the education and the community service in these courses. (Ben Gose, "Many Colleges Move to Link Courses with Volunteerism," *The Chronicle of Higher Education*, November 14, 1997, p. A45.)

Another potential source of volunteers is senior citizens. As early as 1981, the Girl Scouts had been recruiting older Americans to serve as troop leaders, offering these individuals the opportunity to perform a wide range of jobs in the organization and giving married couples the option to work together. In an article aimed at individuals over the age of 65, the national president of the Girl Scouts stated: "The expertise and skill retirees have practiced for decades are vital to an organization like the Girl Scouts—where volunteers are policy-makers, not simply workers." ("Girl Scouting for Retirees," *Modern Maturity*, August-September 1981, p. 12.)

Decision Problem: The Dilemma

Girl Scouts of Chicago was critically short of adult leaders in general and African-American leaders in particular. The annual turnover rate for volunteer adult leaders averaged 25 percent, which meant that the Council had to replace approximately 500 to 600 adult leaders per year in order to maintain Girl Scouting at current levels. In addition, they wanted to increase the percentage of African-American leaders to better mirror the demographics of their market. As a stop gap, the Council had been using part-time paid staff if no local adult volunteers were available, but this was not an acceptable long-term solution to the problem. "I'm confident that potential volunteer leaders are out there in substantial numbers," thought Gwen. "But how do I find them, how do I recruit them, and how do I keep them?"

CASE
7

Coldwell Banker—
Virginia Beach

Lisa D. Spiller
Christopher Newport University

Carol Scovotti
University of Wisconsin-Whitewater

The Memorial Day weekend was just a few days away, which meant that the summer residential selling season was in full swing. However, as Mark Sarrett, General Manager of Coldwell Banker Professional, Realtors® (CBPRO) made his way down the hall in the company's Virginia Beach office, he noticed the network of glass-walled conference rooms were void of activity. A few years ago, those rooms as well as conference rooms in the 12 other offices of the CBPRO franchise, had been bustling with buyers, sellers, and agents closing deals on homes and condominiums. These days only one or two of the rooms were occupied at any given time. "This market correction is killing us," he thought to himself. "Inventory is up, sales are down, and our agents are off doing their own thing without understanding how their actions affect the overall company. There has to be something we can do to pick up more market share."

Mark had overall profit and loss responsibilities for the franchise's 13 offices in the greater Hampton Roads, Virginia and northeastern, North Carolina markets. A certified public accountant by training, he had spent 18 of the last 19 years in commercial real estate. The past year and a half with CBPRO on the residential side had been a

---

EXHIBIT C7.1: MARK SARRETT

new world for Mark. The sales process for residential real estate was different than selling commercial property and although he was well liked and respected by associates, a few questioned the value of his marketing initiatives for the residential marketplace. "That's not the way you sell a house" was a common response to many of Mark's franchise-wide marketing ideas.

All players in today's residential real estate industry faced a host of challenges resulting from the recent market correction, rise in advertising rates for traditional media, and growth of Internet applications. One of the biggest difficulties was the nature of durable goods; when customers bought their homes, they effectively took themselves out of the market and destroyed (or extensively delayed) future demand. In addition, Mark was concerned about confusion emanating from the company name. While Coldwell Banker was an internationally recognized brand, many prospective customers in the franchise's service area were not aware of its market presence. His most difficult challenges were the lack of accountability of advertising dollars spent and the struggle to get corporate leaders to view marketing expenditures as an investment rather than an expense.

Mark reached the break room at the end of the hall. As he filled his coffee cup, he thought, "There has to be a better way to market residential real estate. Right now we're eighth in sales and seventh in offers under contract in our service area. That's not good enough. In the next couple years, I think we can be third. The question is how to get there? How do we increase our listings? Do we need more sales associates? How do we attract more buyers more quickly for the listings we have? Do we change our media strategy? How do we get independent agents who are paid on commissions to function together as a team?" As he pondered these questions, he returned to his office with a hot cup of coffee—on a quest to put the bustle back into those empty conference rooms.

The Company

Colbert Coldwell founded a real estate company in 1906 as part of the efforts to rebuild San Francisco after the city was devastated by the earthquake that year. In 1914, Coldwell invited Benjamin A. Banker to become his partner, creating the organization now known as Coldwell Banker Real Estate Corporation. The company currently had 3,800 independently owned and operated residential and commercial real estate offices with over 126,000 sales associates in 35 countries.

Coldwell Banker was renowned for several "industry firsts." It was the first real estate firm to attain a nationwide presence; the first national real estate brand with a web site; one of the first with an interactive online property search tool, Personal Retriever®, where visitors were guided through the listings by its trademark character, *Rusty the Retriever*, and the first national real estate organization to offer online seller proposals. In addition, the company had received awards for Coldwell Banker Concierge® Service, a program that helps homeowners find local contractors for home repair and renovation. Coldwell Banker Mortgage and a host of other services provided buyers and sellers with the help they needed to complete a home sales transaction.

Nationally, Coldwell Banker Real Estate Corporation was widely recognized as one of the premier real estate organizations. Recent research indicated that the

EXHIBIT C7.2: RUSTY THE RETRIEVER

**EXHIBIT C7.2:
RUSTY THE RETRIEVER**

brand had over 90 percent recognition among recent home buyers and sellers. Brand recognition was perpetuated with national television campaigns, the web site (www.coldwellbanker.com) that hosted 250,000 visitors a day, and public relations efforts that promoted Coldwell Banker in broadcast, print, and electronic media. The goal of the corporation was to provide its franchise operations and their agents with the tools and support needed to develop profitable relationships with their customers. Through its "Celebrating 100 Years with 100 Homes" campaign, Coldwell Banker gave back to communities across the country by sponsoring the construction of 100 new Habitat for Humanity homes.

Coldwell Banker Professional, Realtors® (CBPRO)

EXHIBIT C7.3: CBPRO'S TERRITORY IN VIRGINIA

CBPRO had been an independent franchisor of the Coldwell Banker brand since 2001, created through the merger of six independent real estate firms across Hampton Roads, Virginia. Since then, the company had grown to 13 offices with 299 agents. Its geographic area now started at Richmond and extended south to northeastern North Carolina and the top of the Outer Banks. While only a few years in existence, CBPRO ranked first in the service industry and second overall in a recent Virginia Chamber of Commerce "Fantastic 50," which rewards the companies in Virginia for the highest growth.

Management believed that success resulted from the empowerment of its sales associates. To live up to its mission, "to be the premier real estate firm in the markets we serve, providing the highest quality service in an uncompromising professional and ethical environment that will empower our agents to grow professionally and personally," the company provided proprietary services in addition to those available through corporate. Customers (buyers and sellers) would find special offers on the CBPRO web site (www.cb-pro.com). For sales associates, CBPRO offered creative and production services for the marketing materials needed throughout the sales process.

Since its inception, CBPRO's growth had been formidable. In the first three years, record breaking years for the sale of residential real estate, its sales rose 2,848 percent. The following year, sales grew another 53 percent. Like the industry in general, sales flattened in the next year, down 2.5 percent. Exhibit C7.4 indicates that the most recent year's settled sales were down 10.7 percent while Exhibit C7.5 suggests that a rebound would be forthcoming with sales under contract up 16.4 percent from the previous year.

EXHIBIT C7.4: REIN CUMULATIVE STANDINGS REPORT— SETTLED SALES IN CBPRO AREA

Through 4/30 of most recent year—Dollar Figures in Thousands

	Company	Current Year	Previous Year	% Change
1	William E Wood	$618,218	$663,387	- 6.8
2	Rose & Womble	434,006	463,959	- 6.5
3	Long & Foster	347,326	359,531	- 3.4
4	Prudential Decker	265,573	239,077	11.1
5	Re/Max Allegiance	192,244	221,143	- 13.1
6	Wainwright	155,128	170,511	- 9.0
7	GSH Real Estate	137,707	153,879	- 10.5
8	**CBPRO**	**114,722**	**128,488**	**- 10.7**
9	Nancy Chandler	109,698	89,104	23.1
10	RE/Max Alliance	88,659	88,574	0.1
	All Others	515,617	511,268	0.1

EXHIBIT C7.5: REIN CUMULATIVE STANDINGS REPORT— UNDER CONTRACT SALES IN CBPRO AREA

Through 4/30 of most recent year—Dollar Figures in Thousands

	Company	Current Year	Previous Year	% Change
1	William E Wood	$824,254	$800,472	2.9
2	Rose & Womble	585,791	583,685	0.4
3	Long & Foster	421,191	449,175	-6.2
4	Prudential Decker	324,256	302,863	7.1
5	Re/Max Allegiance	223,894	256,068	-12.6
6	Wainwright	197,675	194,781	1.5
7	**CBPRO**	**180,752**	**155,320**	**16.4**
8	GSH Real Estate	176,045	190,159	-7.4
9	Nancy Chandler	130,906	130,470	0.3
10	C21 Nachman	111,738	103,582	7.9
	All Others	742,595	682,919	8.7

The Residential Real Estate Industry

The residential real estate industry has a significant impact on the overall GDP of the country. In good times it fuels consumer confidence and spending, causing the economy to grow. In bad times, it prompts the economy to plummet into a recession. The housing market at the time of this case could be classified as "extremely volatile," with a major fluctuation arguably capable of causing a wide-scale recession.

In the first half of the decade, the country had seen a surge of new and existing home sales. Homeowners came to expect their property values to increase at least five percent a year. After the stock market bubble burst at the beginning of the decade, housing appeared to be a "can't lose" investment. The Federal Reserve's ongoing reductions of interest rates were designed to stimulate the economy. They also made mortgages (seemingly) more affordable and prompted the creation of offerings like interest only and sub-prime loans. A recap of mortgage rates is found in Exhibit C7.6. As a result, a host of new buyers entered the marketplace, purchasing new and existing residences with little to no money down and bad credit ratings. While the cost of the "dream home" rose, buyers felt it was still affordable because of the historically low interests rates and special mortgage offerings.

However, as interest rates rose, so too did mortgage rates. The sub-prime loans with special one-percent introductory rates, lenders' willingness to loan up to 100 percent of the appraised home's value, and the lack of concern about credit ratings had caused consumers who extended themselves to be in jeopardy of losing their homes. Many could no longer afford the cost of maintaining their adjustable mortgages. An estimated one in eight sub-prime loan holders was currently behind on their payments, and in many cases, homes were worth less than the loan amounts. Consumers in the worst shape were those who purchased at the end of the bubble when prices were at their highest and now needed to sell. Today's buyer wasn't willing to pay what homes sold for two or three years ago.

The pace of housing starts was also down 33 percent from its peak in January of the previous year. The slowdown in residential investments was considered to be one of the reasons for the lackluster 2.6 percent growth in GDP in that year. Currently, lenders were tightening their standards on mortgage approvals, which was affecting home sales. Sales of existing homes had reached their slowest pace since June of four years prior, and unsold inventory continued to rise. This combination was a recipe for weaker prices as seen by the reduction in the median home prices experienced in the two previous years.

What all these factors meant for the future of the residential real estate industry was subject to debate. According to economists at the National Association of Realtors, the current Pending Home Sales Index suggested sales would continue to decline but should stabilize and level off by the end of the current year. Other economists were not so optimistic. Given that Americans had $20 trillion in housing wealth, they suggested a 10 percent price reduction would cause consumer spending to decline and send the economy into recession.

Local Competition

Primary competitors in the Hampton Roads market include the following companies:

- William E. Woods and Associates
- Long and Foster Realtors
- Re/Max
- Rose & Womble Realty Company
- Prudential Decker Realty
- Wainwright Real Estate
- GSH Real Estate

EXHIBIT C7.6: MORTGAGE RATES & MEDIAN HOME PRICES IN THE LAST FOUR YEARS

Mortgage Rates	3 Yrs. Ago	2 Yrs. Ago	1 Yr. Ago	Current Rates
30-year fixed	6.28%	5.62%	6.67%	6.37%
15-year fixed	5.63%	5.52%	6.26%	6.06%
1-year ARM	3.98%	4.26%	5.68%	5.64%
Median Home Price	$215,700	$226,100	$243,200	$220,900

Sources: Freddie Mac and National Association of Realtors

EXHIBIT R7.7: COMPETITION FOR CBPRO

GSH Real Estate

As the real estate industry continued to evolve in the Hampton Roads area, so did the number of competitors. The leading real estate company in this area was William E. Wood and Associates, with a sales volume exceeding $2.45 billion and a sales force of over 800 full-time agents. It began more than 35 years ago and currently had more than 20 locations in Virginia and North Carolina.

Rose & Womble Realty Company was the next largest real estate company in the area, conducting business solely in Southern Virginia and Northern North Carolina. It was established in 1998 with a merger of two of the top real estate companies in the region and was now the 36th largest independent realty company in the nation. Long and Foster Realtors was the third top contender with strong visibility and a solid reputation in the area.

Other leading competitors ahead of CBPRO included Prudential Decker Realty, RE/MAX Allegiance, Wainwright Real Estate, and GSH Real Estate. Each of these competitors offered a number of locations with many real estate agents offering quality real estate services in the Hampton Roads area.

The Residential Real Estate Agent

The job of the real estate agent is to match customers with their desired residences. As the intermediary between buyer and seller, the agent works with his or her client from search or sale initiation through closing and beyond. Agents help buyers find and purchase residences as well as help existing property owners advertise and sell their homes. In some cases, an agent may represent both buyer and seller simultaneously.

Whether it's across town or across the country, moving is one of the most stressful activities a person undertakes. When a real estate agent works with a prospective buyer, s/he must first understand the customer's lifestyle preferences, neighborhood/community needs and desires, and budgetary guidelines. A buyer's representative should be familiar with an area's available housing inventory, knowledgeable about the community, including neighborhood composition, services, schools, and property taxes, as well as the price and features of recently completed residential transactions in the area. The buyer's agent uses this knowledge base to find appropriate properties, set appointments for showing, visit properties with customers, and follow up with the seller agents with whom appointments were arranged.

When buyers find a property they want to purchase, the agent completes the formal paperwork and submits the offer to the seller or his/her representative. The agent serves as the intermediary throughout the negotiation to the conclusion of the deal. Once an offer has been accepted, the buyer's agent helps the buyer arrange for property inspection, title search, financing, and other services that may be needed to complete the transaction.

When the agent works on behalf of the seller, s/he needs to discover the selling points and potential drawbacks of the residence, determine the appropriate target market, and how to position the home for sale. The seller's agent should also understand local market conditions and available inventory movement to determine a competitive price. S/he completes all the necessary paperwork to list the home and gathers the data included on the Multiple Listings Service (MLS) database. The MLS is the shared database accessed by realtor subscribers nationwide and serves as the central information resource for available and recently sold property. The seller is also responsible for all advertising and promotion, arranging showing and hosting open houses to sell the home. When a buyer extends an offer, the seller's agent works with the homeowner to negotiate a deal acceptable to all parties. S/he represents the seller through to the closing of the transaction.

Regardless of whether agents represent buyers or sellers, an agent's success depends on his/her understanding of people and their needs. They are inquisitive, good listeners capable of asking pertinent questions and able to integrate what they learn about their customers with their community and inventory knowledge, to negotiate deals that satisfy their customers' needs. They are knowledgeable and capable of handling the legalities and logistics of property transfers. In essence, they create and manage the conduit between residential buyers and sellers needed to complete property transactions.

The relationship between prospect and agent begins with the initial contact. This contact may result from the prospect contacting the agent directly or the company through phone, Internet, or stopping by the office. However, agents also solicit clients, either directly or through referrals. Thus, the residential real estate agent is also responsible for prospecting new business.

Technically, an agent is an employee of the real estate company to which s/he is affiliated. However, the agent functions as an independent service provider. Typically, the company provides the marketing services and tools needed for real estate sales. In many cases the agent pays a set fee for those services. The company also provides the agent with an office or desk, but again, the agent pays a fee to "rent" the space. CBPRO agents were provided with office space and basic promotional materials at no charge. Agents choose to work for a real estate company to offset the burdens of educational requirements, financial accounts, licenses and infrastructure needed to operate a real estate company as well as take advantage of the benefits of strong brand recognition and the results of advertising campaigns.

A residential real estate agent is paid a commission on properties bought and/or sold. Arrangements vary by company and individual. No standard fees exist as that would be considered a violation of federal antitrust laws. However, like every industry, there are traditions. The typical commission paid to full service real estate companies on the sale of homes is six percent of the purchase price, with half going to the buyer agency and half staying with the selling agency. The amount of commission maintained by the real estate firm is dependent on the level of support services provided and level of production of the agent. Some firms split commissions evenly between firm and salesperson. At CBPRO, new agents were paid 50 percent of the commission received by the firm. However, firms that offer less support may offer agents up to 90 percent of the commission received. In those cases, the agents are responsible for paying all operational and marketing expenses.

Given the nature of the agent/company relationship, it is not surprising that agents change affiliations relatively frequently. If successful agents find the arrangements with their existing employer unsatisfactory, there are plenty of competitors in the marketplace where they can negotiate a better deal. At CBPRO, productivity was rewarded. The more an agent sold, the greater the percentage of commission the agent kept without incurring additional marketing costs.

The Residential Real Estate Customer and CBPRO

According to a recent National Association of Realtors Profile of Home Buyers and Sellers, the typical homebuyer was 41 years old, earned $71,800, and purchased a home costing $243,000 that was slightly larger than 1,800 square feet. These residential consumers searched eight weeks and visited nine homes prior to making a purchase decision. U.S. Census Bureau data indicates that married couples had the highest tendency to own homes. Over 84 percent of all married couples in the U.S. were homeowners. The percentage of single males or females owning one-person households was significantly lower. However, a recent trend in home ownership was emerging in that 24.8 percent of Americans aged 25 years or younger were homeowners in a recent year, up from just 14.9 percent a decade before. This trend may be due in part to increased higher education rates and the availability of mortgages with low interest rates. Another trend thought to influence home ownership among young adults was

EXHIBIT C7.8: CBPRO SALES & LIST PRICE ANALYSIS REPORT— JANUARY–APRIL OF CURRENT YEAR

Sale Price ($)	Listings Taken– Closed	% of Business	% of AGC	Buyer Controlled –Closed	% of Business	% of AGC	Number of Listings	% of Inventory
0–99,999	11	4.48	2.34	11	3.68	1.66	20	4.03
100,000– 249,999	115	46.76	41.38	154	51.50	44.16	150	30.24
250,000– 499,999	101	41.04	59.46	112	37.45	51.38	263	53.04
500,000– 999,999	19	7.72	20.06	22	7.35	17.90	48	9.68
1 million– 1,999,999	0	0	0	0	0	0	12	2.41
2 million– 3,999,999	0	0	0	0	0	0	1	0.20
4 million +	0	0	0	0	0	0	2	0.40

AGC = Adjusted Gross Commission
Source: Company

the increase in the number of younger real estate agents: A record 150,000 members of the National Association of Realtors were now under 30 years old.

CBPRO targeted repeat homebuyers, age 35 to 54, who were more economically affluent. Unlike competitors in the area, CBPRO customers tended to be more sophisticated, hi-tech savvy, led busy lives, more highly educated, and more actively involved in civic and community activities. Exhibit C7.8 indicates the prices of the homes bought and sold through CBPRO between January and April of the current year, as well as the inventory of listings it maintained at that time.

Decision Problem: The Challenge

In light of the increasingly competitive U.S. real estate industry, coupled with residential real estate fluctuating with national economic conditions, and the narrowly defined CBPRO target customer, CBPRO faced several distinct challenges. Mark clearly understood the need to create a synergy among the 13 CBPRO offices to demonstrate and enhance its market presence and increase the use of measurable marketing activities to justify the dollars spent. However, he also realized that getting his agents to buy into that concept would be a formidable task.

Upon joining the company, Mark spearheaded efforts to create a uniform image for the entire organization. Mark worked with the marketing support staff at franchise headquarters to create a logo, business card and newspaper ad formats, as well as signage, web site, direct mail, even apparel design. Successful integrated marketing communications campaigns require a strong and consistent message regardless of the

EXHIBIT C7.9: TYPICAL NEWSPAPER AD CREATED
BY AN INDIVIDUAL OFFICE

customer touch point. He was confident a uniform image would help CBPRO build the brand recognition across the region it needed to continue to grow.

However, since residential real estate agents function as independent businesses, agents working in the 13 offices often designed and created their own promotional materials. Mark had tried to convince the managers and agents of the advantage of a unified effort and promote more cooperative advertising among offices, but had been unsuccessful thus far. Exhibits C7.9 and C7.10 demonstrate the discrepancy between ads created and run by an individual office versus one designed by the franchise.

EXHIBIT C7.10: TYPICAL NEWSPAPER AD CREATED BY FRANCHISE HEADQUARTERS

Decision 1—Improving and Unifying the CBPRO Brand Locally

Mark began identifying specific issues he needed to address to get his agents "on board" to enhance the effectiveness of their branded marketing efforts. He thought his first task was to identify and document consumer perception about the brand. Were residential consumers aware that Coldwell Banker was a leading real estate company? What first came to the consumer's mind when *Coldwell Banker* was mentioned? What could be done to improve the current level of visibility and market presence of CBPRO in its local market?

Once he understood consumer perceptions about the brand, he saw his second task as involving agent perceptions about the value of advertising cooperatives to

EXHIBIT C7.10: TYPICAL NEWSPAPER AD CREATED
BY FRANCHISE HEADQUARTERS (continued)

EXHIBIT C7.11: COLDWELL BANKER FOR SALE SIGN

promote the brand. How could he get the offices and agents to portray a more unified branding effort? He wondered what the role of *Rusty the Retriever* should be? How would greater use of this trademark character influence consumer behavior?

As Mark thought more deeply about his company's situation, he began reviewing and evaluating the current market situation and the arsenal of both national Coldwell Banker and local CBPRO marketing activities. CBPRO paid a national franchise fee (NAF) to its parent company, Coldwell Banker Real Estate Corporation. In the previous year, the parent company had aired a national television campaign that was broadcast across all major networks and cable stations. In addition, it ran public relations efforts that resulted in over 552 million media impressions with an equivalent advertising value of over $30 million. Online and traditional media campaigns focused on promoting the Coldwell Banker brand and **coldwellbanker.com** as the destination to find out about open houses. The online "Open House" promotions on msn.com and MY Yahoo resulted in more than 300,000 people visiting the corporate web site in just two days.

Beyond the national advertising campaign provided by Coldwell Banker, local CBPRO marketing activities included newspaper advertising, such as regular newspaper listings of properties for sale in the real estate sections and newspaper inserts; word-of-mouth and personal referrals; open house promotions; and the many marketing tools available via the CBPRO in-house marketing support agency, CB Net. This service provided creative and production services for the specialized marketing materials sales agents might use to promote themselves as a resource and obtain new clients or sell the properties they currently had listed. The materials that CB Net produced included business cards, postcards, flyers, brochures, direct mail packages, promotional items, apparel, and signage. It also offered personal web site design services.

Strong brand awareness and image advertising campaigns had been implemented at the national level. However, the biggest challenge for CBPRO was leveraging that national brand awareness at the local level to drive consumer behavior to increase residential listings and sales. What were the most effective direct/interactive marketing strategies for CBPRO in penetrating the residential consumer market? Considering how consumers shop for real estate, *how could CBPRO impact this trend and gain additional residential listings and clients?*

Decision 2—Driving More Business with its Web Site and IMC Campaign

Mark was convinced that the Internet was the single most important tool for successfully competing in the residential real estate market and he had plenty of statistics to back this up.

Mark was concerned about the expense and effectiveness of the traditional home listings placed in local newspapers. Old-fashioned listings just didn't deliver anymore. Given the target market CBPRO was trying to attract, he was convinced a strong CBPRO web site was the way to grow market share. Results from previous research supported his feelings:

- Over 20 million people browsed real estate listings each month. In the past six years, real estate companies had increased their Internet presence through search engine marketing by 83 percent.
- According to a recent National Association of Realtors (NAR) study, 75 percent of the people searching for homes on the Internet were considered "serious" buyers with nearly half of those searching already pre-qualified for a mortgage loan. Of those who found the information they were looking for via the Internet, 33 percent requested more information from a realtor.
- In the previous year, approximately 24 percent of actual home buyers had used the Internet as part of their home search efforts. This was up from 15 percent two years before that, and only 2 percent a decade previous.
- Individuals who utilized Internet searches were more likely to use an agent to complete the home purchase than were non-Internet users (81 percent and 63 percent respectively.)
- The typical buyer searched homes for approximately eight weeks prior to purchasing a home, and most reported they found at least one home they wanted to view through an online listing.

However, as important as the Internet was today, the CBPRO web site could not be effective without an integrated marketing campaign to drive customer and/or potential client traffic to the company web site, and ultimately increase CBPRO sales and listings. Mark knew that he needed to come up with a *big idea* to project throughout online and offline channels. He thought that idea involved an integrated marketing communications (IMC) campaign.

He thought about what had to be considered; analysis of the current CBPRO marketing mix; determination of the most effective marketing and media plan with justification for each medium recommended and the overall strategy behind media utilization; as well as strategic decisions regarding CBPRO offers, positioning, message and media channels, testing, list rental, budget, and ROI projections. *What should be included? What should be omitted?*

Given an overall objective to drive brand awareness and consumer demand for CBPRO residential services, he knew it was important to stay open to any approach, provided it was logical, within budget (Mark allocated $120,000 for the brand building budget), and results were measurable. The traditional newspaper real estate listing ads were to be excluded from the IMC campaign. Replacing newspaper listings was probably too extreme in the eyes of the agents and office managers at this time. However, augmenting them with a branding campaign could be the first step to eventually eliminating them, provided the branding campaign delivers results.

There were lots of local media options that could be used. *The Virginia Pilot* and *Daily Press* were the two main newspapers CBPRO used on a regular basis. They could be used to help build the brand. In addition, a variety of local publications served the marketplace. Exhibit C7.12 provides current print publication advertising rates. Another media avenue was radio. Mark contemplated using radio ads as there were a number of local stations with listening audiences that effectively reach the CBPRO target market Exhibit C7.13 lists local radio station advertising rates. Outdoor advertising was another medium that could be investigated. Based on the

EXHIBIT C7.12: PRINT PUBLICATION MEDIA RATES

(Rates are based on standard, non-contracted, single full-page, 126 inch, 4-color ad)

Publication	Day Published	Cost per inch	Cost per ad
Yorktown Crier	Thursday	$ 9.30	$ 1,171.80
Gloucester Gazette	Thursday	$ 8.50	$ 1,071.00
VA Gazette	Thursday	$ 9.00	$ 1,134.00
Smithfield Times	Wednesday Saturday	$ 15.30	$ 1,927.80
Norfolk Compass	Sunday	$ 27.00	$ 3,402.00
VA Beach Beacon	Thursday Sunday Combo rate	$ 49.00 64.00 90.00	$ 6,174.00 8,064.00 11,340.00
Chesapeake Clipper	Friday Sunday Combo rate	$ 23.00 29.00 42.00	$ 2,898.00 3,654.00 5,292.00
The Suffolk Sun	Thursday Sunday Combo rate	$ 17.00 22.00 32.00	$ 2,142.00 2,772.00 4,032.00
The VA Pilot	Mon–Wed Thurs–Sat Sunday	$ 112.00 118.00 151.00	$ 14,448.00 15,222.00 19,479.00
Daily Press	Mon–Thurs Fri & Sat Sunday	$ 54.20 57.10 68.65	$ 6,829.20 7,194.60 8,649.90
Oyster Pointer	Monthly	$ 16.39	$ 2,065.00

EXHIBIT C7.13: RADIO & BILLBOARD MEDIA RATES

Radio Station	Format	Cost per 60 second spot—Morning Drive Time
WPTE-FM The Point 94.9	Modern Adult Rock	$ 175.00
WVBW-FM The Wave 92.9	Adult Contemporary	$ 150.00
WGH-FM Eagle 97.3	Country Variety	$ 200.00
WAFX-FM The Fox 106.9	Classic Hits	$ 160.00
WPYA-FM BOB-FM 93.7	Adult Hits	$ 225.00
WTYD-FM The Tide 92.3	Williamsburg	$ 75.00
WBQK-FM Wbach 107.9	Classical	$ 45.00

information provided by the CBPRO marketing department, the cost of one outdoor board on a highway location would be $6,500 per month. Creative and production of all advertisements in the campaign could be handled by CB Net so it wouldn't come out of the media budget.

In addition to newspaper, radio and billboard ads, Mark also thought that direct mail might be a powerful medium to promote the brand and drive prospective buyers and sellers to the CBPRO web site. But who should be targeted and what should be the message? He made a mental note, "check NextMark.com for available lists and rental costs." While CB Net could handle traditional postcards and mailings, he had seen innovative direct mail pieces involving enlarged and see-through postcards (cost of production and mailing each postcard—$2.00) as well as tube mailings (cost of production and mailing each tube—$2.70) at last year's Direct Marketing Association Conference. Should he use traditional postcards that cost around $0.55 to create, produce and mail or should he go with one of these more eye-catching options that could generate three to six times more response?

What should he keep? What should he eliminate? How can he get the agents onboard with this company-wide IMC campaign? Given the above budget, what kind of response rates would be needed to "break-even" on such an IMC campaign? If CBPRO allocated 0.4 percent of the agency commissions maintained to this campaign, how many homes would need to be sold?

In addition to the IMC campaign, he wondered what should be done to improve the CBPRO web site. How can the web site be made more attractive and user-friendly? What additional links or applications should be included to become the "go to" site for the area's upscale residential prospects?

Summary

Mark stared out his office window at the beautiful shores of Virginia Beach. The company had come a long way since its inception in 2001 and with sales-under-contract figures up, perhaps the market correction was nearing its end. Yet his head was filled with questions and concerns. The main challenges were formidable—developing the strategy to increase and enhance corporate brand image, establish itself as the leading real estate agency for the area's upscale residential customers, and increase sales and listings. What made accomplishing those objectives especially tricky was that he not only had to accomplish these objectives with customers, he also had to convince CBPRO agents and office managers that a more unified branding effort was best for all involved. "I have to sell our associates as well as our customers," he thought to himself. Customers were changing the way they bought their homes, and Mark wanted CBPRO to be considered the de facto choice by upscale buyers and sellers in the area. As he packed his briefcase and prepared to leave the office to watch his son's baseball game, he knew that these issues couldn't wait. Something had to be done now.

CASE
8

Domino's Pizza: Growing Sales With Technology

MATTHEW H. SAUBER
Eastern Michigan University

DAVID A. MAROLD
Eastern Michigan University

ALICIA ANDERSON
Eastern Michigan University

Since 2007, Domino's customers have been able to visit its web site and browse the menu to build their own pizza and add sides such as Buffalo Chicken Wings or Chocolate Lava Crunch Cakes. Customers can watch the simulated image of the pizza they are ordering. The image changes as they select a different pie size, choose a sauce and add pepperoni, black olives and other toppings. They can also watch the price when the order changes and ingredients get added or removed and when they apply a coupon.

Domino's web site also allows customers to track orders with updates. Once the order is placed, a "pizza tracker" communicates with customers in real time and through a bar graph when their order is being processed, baked, checked and sent out for delivery. Over twenty-five percent of all Domino's orders are placed online through the company web site, which is great for impulse purchases according to Dennis Maloney, Domino's VP of Multi-Media Marketing. The CEO, Patrick Doyle, explains that when customers order pizza online " . . . it enhances the ticket, as we can remind them [via pop-up windows] that we sell drinks, chicken wings and chocolate cake too," (Change at Domino's, 2010; Domino's Pizza Investor Presentation, 2010).

Domino's online presence extends well beyond its own web site. The company understands the critical importance of reaching out to its target market using social media. To stay in touch with its customers, Domino's uses major social media such as Facebook, MySpace, Twitter, and YouTube. Through its corporate account, for example, Domino's monitors Twitter feeds around the clock to hear from followers about its brand, products, and services. The company methodically uses social media to review, respond, and react to what fans and followers post. A company representative, for example, responds with instructions on how to ask for a refund if a customer is dissatisfied with the product. Domino's also uses Facebook to make special offers, news, and reminders to place an order. "Digital media affords you the opportunity to go much more in-depth and be much more transparent with your message," says Russell Weiner, Chief Marketing Officer. "We want people to know that we have nothing to hide and that we have a better pizza." (Change at Domino's, 2010).

Company Background

In 2010 Domino's Pizza celebrated its golden anniversary by opening its 9000th store globally. The company has come a long way since its humble beginning. In 1960, brothers Tom and Jim Monaghan borrowed $500 to purchase DomiNicks, a local pizzeria in Ypsilanti, Michigan (Boyer (2007). Eight months later, Jim Monaghan traded his share of the restaurant for a Volkswagen Beetle. In 1965, Tom renamed the business "Domino's Pizza, Inc." (Our Heritage, 2008).

The restaurant had minimum seating, making delivery essential for success. Initially, Tom Monaghan hired laid off factory workers as drivers, compensating them based on commission. With an efficiency focus, the menu was reduced from subs and small pizzas to only offering "regular pizza". The business concept took off, leading to expansion through franchising and the first franchise store opened in 1967 (Domino's Pizza, Inc., 2008).

Expansion

The company continued with its expansion, overcoming challenges including a fire destroying company headquarters in 1968 and a legal battle headed by Domino's Sugar over trademark infringement (Amstar Corporation, 1980). Originally, Monaghan added dots to the logo for each new franchise opened. With the aggressive expansion rate the idea became impractical. There were 200 franchises in operation by 1978. Domino's opened its 1,000 stores five years later. In 1983, Domino's opened its first international store in Winnipeg, Canada (Exhibit C8.1). This paved the way for a global expansion of 1,000 pizzerias overseas—in Europe, Australia, South America, Africa, and Asia—by 1995. In 1997, Domino's opened its 1,500th overseas location (Domino's Pizza Investor Presentation, 2010).

After 38 years of ownership, Tom Monaghan announced his retirement and sold Domino's Pizza to Bain Capital, Inc. in 1998 (Domino's Founder to Retire . . . , 1998). A year later, the company named David A. Brandon Chairman and Chief Executive Officer (Domino's Pizza, Inc., 2008). The company went public in 2004.

Domino's marked the opening of its 8,000th and 9,000th franchise stores in 2006 and 2010 respectively (Domino's Open 9,000th Store, 2010). The company has franchised stores in all 50 U.S. states and 62 foreign countries (Domino's Pizza Investor Presentation, 2010).

As of January 3, 2010, the company reported 8,999 stores in operation worldwide, of which 4,072 were international and 4,927 were domestic stores. Of the domestics stores 466 were company owned and 4,461 were franchise stores (Exhibit C8.2).

Domino's same store sales grew 1.4% domestically and 3.9% internationally in the 2009 4th quarter. The growth rate was smaller (.5%) for domestic stores and more robust (4.3%) for international stores for 2009 as a whole (Exhibit C8.3).

EXHIBIT C8.1: DOMINO'S MILESTONES

1960	Tom Monaghan and his brother, James, purchased "DomiNick's," a pizza store in Ypsilanti, Mich. Monaghan borrowed $500 to buy the store.
1965	Tom Monaghan, renamed the business "Domino's Pizza, Inc."
1967	The first Domino's Pizza franchise store opened in Ypsilanti, Michigan
1968	First Domino's store outside of Michigan opened in Burlington, Vermont
1978	The 200th Domino's store opened.
1983	Domino's first international store opened in Winnipeg, Canada. The 1,000th Domino's store opened. The first Domino's store opened on the Australian continent, in Queensland, Australia.
1985	The first Domino's store opened in the United Kingdom, in Luten, England. The first Domino's store opened on the continent of Asia, in Minato, Japan.
1988	The first Domino's store opened on the South American continent, in Bogota, Columbia.
1989	Domino's opened its 5,000th store.
1990	Domino's Pizza signed its 1,000th franchise agreement.
1995	Domino's Pizza International opened its 1,000th store. First store opens on African continent, in Cairo, Egypt.
1996	Domino's launched its first web site (www.dominos.com).
1997	Domino's Pizza opened its 1,500th store outside the United States
1998	Domino's launched HeatWave®, a hot bag using patented technology that keeps pizza oven-hot to the customer's door. Domino's Pizza opened its 6,000th store in San Francisco, California. Tom Monaghan announced retirement and sold 93% of the company to Bain Capital, Inc.
1999	David A. Brandon was named Chairman and Chief Executive Officer of Domino's Pizza.
2000	Domino's Pizza International opened its 2,000th store outside the United States.
2003	Domino's became the "Official Pizza of NASCAR." Domino's was named Chain of the Year by *Pizza Today*. Domino's introduced it Pulse Point of Sale, a touch screen ordering, system.
2005	Domino's Pizza Australia opened its 400th store in Aspley, Brisbane. Domino's Pizza United Kingdom opened its 400th store in Wadsley Bridge, Sheffield.
2006	Domino's opened its 8,000th store by simultaneous opening the 5,000th U.S. store in Huntley, Illinois and the 3,000th international store in Panama City, Panama.
2007	Domino's rolled out online and mobile ordering in the United States.
2009	Domino's ranked No. 1 in customer satisfaction per the annual American Customer Satisfaction Index (ACSI). Domino's introduced Pizza Tracker.
2010	Domino's changed its pizza recipe "from the crust up". J. Patrick Doyle became Domino's Chief Executive Officer Domino's opened its 9000th store in New Delhi India Domino's ranked No. 1 in Keys Brand taste test

EXHIBIT C8.2: DOMINO'S PIZZA STORES WORDWIDE
AS OF JANUARY OF THE CURRENT YEAR

	Domestic Company-Owned Stores	Domestic Franchise Stores	Total Domestic Stores	International Stores	Total
Store counts:					
Store count at September 6, Previous Year	481	4,456	4,937	3,949	8,886
Openings	–	49	49	140	189
Closings	(14)	(45)	(59)	(17)	(76)
Transfers	(1)	1	–	–	–
Store count at January 3, Current Year	466	4,461	4,927	4,072	8,999
Fourth quarter Previous Year net growth	(15)	5	(10)	123	113
Net Growth Previous Fiscal Year	(23)	(97)	(120)	346	226

Source: Domino's Pizza, Inc., www.dominos.com

Although Domino's does not provide quarter or annual sales forecast, the management believes that the following year-over-year growth rates are achievable over the long term:

Domestic same-store sales: 1%–3%
International same-store sales: 3%–5%
Net units store growth   200–300
Global retail sales growth   4%–6%

International Growth

Domino's received 40 percent of sales from the company's international division in 2009. The proportion was expected to grow and surpass the domestic sales in the next three to five years according to the company (Domino's Pizza Investor Presentation, 2010). The company reports many years of same-store sales growth in its international operations. The key growth areas are the top ten markets (Exhibit C8.4) where Domino's has used master franchises—well-financed local businesses with the rights to own, operate many stores and franchise branches as chains. Domino's Pizza Enterprises, for example, owns and operates stores in Australia, New Zealand, France, Belgium, and the Netherlands. The master franchises for the UK and Ireland are publicly traded as Domino's Pizza UK & IRL (Litterick , 2010).

EXHIBIT C8.3: DOMINO'S DOMESTIC AND GLOBAL SALES (PREVIOUS FISCAL YEAR)

	Fourth Quarter	Fiscal Year
Same store sales growth: (versus prior year period)		
Domestic Company-owned stores	+0.9%	(0.9)%
Domestic franchise stores	+1.5%	+0.6%
Domestic stores	+1.4%	+0.5%
International stores	+3.9%	+4.3%
Global retail sales growth: (versus prior year period)		
Domestic stores	+7.4%	+1.3%
International stores +28.1% +3.3%		
Total	+16.4%	+2.2%
Total (on a 52-week basis)	+7.8%	(0.3)%
Global retail sales growth: (versus prior year period, excluding foreign currency impact)		
Domestic stores	+7.4%	+1.3%
International stores	+21.6%	+14.4%
Total	+13.5%	+7.1%
Total (on a 52-week basis)	+4.9%	+4.6%

Source: Domino's Pizza, Inc., www.dominos.com

EXHIBIT C8.4: DOMINO'S TOP 10 INTERNATIONAL MARKETS

- Mexico*
- United Kingdom*
- Australia*
- South Korea
- Canada
- India*
- Japan
- France
- Taiwan
- Turkey

*These indicate publicly traded companies in their home countries

Source: 2010 Chain of the Year, *Pizza Today*, June 2010, www.pizzatoday.com

EXHIBIT C8.5: U.S. MARKET SHARE

- ■ Independents
- ■ PizzaHut
- ■ Domino's
- ■ PapaJohn's
- ■ Little Caesars
- ■ Other Top Chains

Source: Pizza Power: Report 2009, *PMQ Pizza Magazine,* September 2009.

Industry Overview

Categorically, Domino's Pizza belongs to the Quick-Service-Restaurant (QSR) industry. The QSR industry consists of restaurants with fast food service and limited menus of moderately priced and cooked to order items. The U.S. QSR pizza category is highly competitive, large, and fragmented. With sales of $33.5 billion in the twelve months ended November 2009, the U.S. QSR pizza category is the second largest category within the $230.1 billion U.S. QSR sector. The pizza category is primarily comprised of delivery, dine-in, and carryout (Domino's Annual Report, 2010). Approximately *three billion* pizzas are sold in the U.S. each year (Bloomenfield and Associates, 2010). On average, each man, woman, and child in America eats 46 slices, (23 pounds), of pizza per year (Package Fact, 2010).

About 59 percent of pizza outlets in the United States are independently owned. They control 51 percent of the industry sales (Exhibit C8.5). A recent survey reports that 54% of consumers prefer independent stores to chains (2010 Chain of the Year, 2010). The Big Four—Pizza Hut (14.46%), Domino's (8.29%), Papa John's (5.55%), and Little Caesars (2.88%)—as a collective unit, have kept steady sales and market share during the recession.

Pizza Hut

Pizza Hut is a division of Yum! Brands, Inc., the world's largest restaurant company in terms of system restaurants with more than 37,000 restaurants in over 110 countries and territories and more than 1 million associates. Yum! is ranked No. 239 on the Fortune 500 List, with nearly $11 billion in revenue in 2009 (Yum! Brand Annual Report, 2009).

Pizza Hut, based in Dallas, Texas, is America's first national pizza chain, established in 1958. It is the world's largest pizza chain with more than 7,500 restaurants in the United States and over 5,600 restaurants in 97 countries and territories around the world. Pizza Hut became the first national chain to offer pizza delivery on the Internet in 1994. It offered online ordering in all its U.S. locations in 2007 and mobile ordering, through text messaging and web-enabled cell phones, in 2008. Specializing in Pan Pizza, Thin 'N Crispy® Pizza, Hand-Tossed Style Pizza and Stuffed Crust Pizza, Pizza Hut was celebrated as America's Favorite Pizza in 2007.

Faced with 9% decline in same-store sales in 2009, Pizza Hut responded by cutting its pizza prices and rolling out a "$10 any way you want it" promotion that resulted in a dramatic improvement in sales. The company's long term strategy is to transform the brand from "pizza" to "pizza, pasta and wings." They are focusing on improving the speed of their service and have added a new mobile application ahead of their major competitors (2009 Yum! . . . , 2009).

Papa John's

Since opening its first pizzerias in 1985, Papa John's has grown to be the third largest U.S. pizza chain. Headquartered in Louisville, Kentucky, the company had 3,469 restaurants in operations, as of December 2009, of which 614 were corporate owned and 2,167 were franchised restaurants operating in all 50 states and 688 restaurants in 29 countries (Papa John's Annual Report, 2009). Papa John's international development pipeline projects the opening of 1200 new restaurants in the next eight years. Their sales were down 2.3% in the 12 months ended March 31, 2010 (Standard & Poor's Stock Report, 2010).

Papa John's long-term business goal is to build the strongest brand loyalty of all pizza restaurants. The company's key strategies are based on a menu of high-quality pizza along with side items, efficient operating and distribution systems, team member training and development, national and local marketing, developing and maintaining a strong franchise system, and international operations (Domino's Annual Report, 2010).

Papa John's "traditional" domestic restaurants are delivery and carryout operations that serves defined trade areas. As such, Papa John's is the closest competitor to Domino's.

Papa John's advertising slogan and brand promise is, "Better Ingredients. Better Pizza." Domestic Papa John's restaurants offer a menu of high-quality pizza along with side items, including breadsticks, cheese sticks, chicken strips and wings, dessert items and canned or bottled beverages. Papa John's traditional crust pizza is prepared using fresh dough (never frozen). Papa John's pizzas are made from a proprietary blend of wheat flour, cheese made from 100% real mozzarella, fresh-packed pizza sauce made from vine-ripened tomatoes (not from concentrate) and a proprietary mix of savory spices, and a choice of high-quality meat (100% beef, pork and chicken with no fillers) and vegetable toppings.

In 2001, Papa John's became the first national pizza company to offer online ordering and was the first pizza company to surpass $1 billion in online sales and now has recently surpassed $2 billion in sales (Domino's Annual Report, 2010). In addition to placing orders online at papajohns.com, customers can place order via text messaging and mobile web capabilities of cell phones.

Domino's

Based in Ann Arbor, Michigan, Domino's Pizza is the number one pizza delivery chain in the United States. The company pioneered the pizza delivery business and has built the brand into one of the most widely recognized consumer brands in the world. The Domino's Pizza® brand was named a Megabrand by Advertising Age magazine in 2009. Domino's was also ranked number one in customer satisfaction in a survey of consumers of the U.S. largest limited service restaurants, according to the annual American Customer Satisfaction Index (ACSI).

Domino's operated a network of over 9000 franchised and company-owned stores in all 50 states and 62 international markets. The company had global retail sales of over $5.6 billion in 2009, comprised of $3.1 billion domestic sales and over $2.5 billion international sales (Horovitz, 2010).

Domino's business model emphasizes on-time delivery of quality pizza. The model entails: (1) delivery-oriented store design with low capital requirements, (2) a concentrated menu of pizza and complimentary side items, (3) a network of committed owner-operator franchisees and (4) a vertically integrated supply-chain system. Revenues are largely driven from sales through company-owned stores and at franchise levels, comprised of royalty payments and supply-chain revenues.

Domino's operates primarily within the U.S. pizza delivery market. Its $10.3 billion of sales accounted for approximately 31% of total U.S. QSR pizza delivery sales in the twelve months ended November 2009. Domino's and its top two competitors account for approximately 45% of the U.S. pizza delivery market—based on reported consumer spending—with the remaining 55% market share attributable to regional chains and individual establishments (Horovitz, 2010).

Domino's also competes in the carryout market, which together with pizza delivery comprise the largest components of the U.S. QSR pizza industry. The U.S. carryout pizza market had $13.8 billion of sales in the twelve months ended November 2009. Although Domino's primary focus is on pizza delivery, it is also favorably positioned to compete in the carryout segment given its strong brand identity, convenient store locations, and affordable menu offerings (Domino's Annual Report, 2010).

Domestically, Domino's competes against regional and local pizzerias as well as the national chains of Pizza Hut ® and Papa John's. These companies generally compete on the basis of product quality, location, image, service and price. They also compete on a broader scale with quick service and other international, national, regional and local restaurants. In addition, the overall food service industry and the QSR sector in particular are intensely competitive with respect to product quality, price, service, convenience and concept. The industry is often affected by changes in consumer tastes, economic conditions, demographic trends and consumer disposable income (Horovitz, 2010).

According to Dennis Maloney, Domino's Vice President of Multi-Media Marketing, "the recessionary economic climate has contributed to less delivery and more carryout and home cooked and frozen food, substituting for some QSR purchases." (Phone Interview with Dennis Maloney, 2011).

Competitive Analysis Summary

Pizza Hut is the number one pizza chain in the world. It competes in delivery, carryout and sit-down segments of QSR. The recession of 2009 took its toll on Pizza Hut as its sit-down restaurants were hit harder than other segments. Pizza Hut responded by cutting its pizza prices and rolling out a "$10 any way you want it" promotion. It is transitioning itself to be known for pizza, pasta and wings. It also sees itself as a leader in technology and was the first to introduce an application for iPhone.

Papa John's grown to be the third largest U.S. pizza chain in the 25 years since it was established. It competes in the delivery and carryout segments and as such it is the closest competitor to Domino's. Papa John's advertising slogan and brand promise is: "Better Ingredients. Better Pizza." It is generally agreed that it lives up to its quality promise. In 2001, Papa John's also focused on technology and it became the first national pizza chain to offer online ordering and was the first pizza company to surpass $1 billion in online sales and recently surpassed $2 billion in sales. In addition to placing orders online at papajohns.com, customers can place their order via text messaging and mobile web devices.

Domino's is No. 1 in delivery and No. 2 in the overall pizza chain sales after Pizza Hut. Domino's is striving to be No.1 in technology and to improve the perception of the taste of its pizza and the value it provides to consumers. Domino's Pulse system is arguably the best system in the industry and a demonstration of its leadership in Point of Purchase Database Marketing. The launch of the new pizza recipe and a new menu with 80% changed items between 2008 and 2010 have contributed to sales increases and changing perceptions. Evidence of the industry recognition of the change at Domino's is that in June, 2010, Domino's was named "2010 Chain of the Year" by *Pizza Today*.

Customer Profile

Although pizza is a favorite meal for all Americans, young and old, and more than 95% of population eats pizza, there are variations in consumption based on age, household size, and income. Mintel surveys reports that 21% of people in the 18-24 age category purchase pizza more than three times a month, compared to only 7% of those aged over 65 (Pizza Power Report, 2009).

Among households with children, 20% purchase pizza more than 3 times a month, compared to 12% of those households with no children. Research also indicates that households with annual income of $100,000 and beyond are more likely to prefer pizza from independent, local pizzerias, while households with children are more likely to visit a pizza chain (Corporate Porfile, 2010).

Buying Behavior

U.S. consumer pizza-buying behavior was negatively impacted in 2009 because of the difficult economic environment. As such, consumers reduced their discretionary spending during 2009 in response to increased unemployment and adverse economic conditions. As a result, the QSR Pizza industry sales were approximately 1.0% lower in 2009 compared to 2008. Cost-conscious consumers are opting for less-expensive pizza choices at QSRs and the low-end of the market appears to be saturated. Thus, pizza chains aiming for higher growth are targeting consumers from high-income households (Corporate Profile, 2010)

Other buying trends indicate that consumers are shifting dining-out occasions toward breakfast and lunch and away from dinner in recent years. Consumers are also being attracted to alternative dinner meals from non-pizza QSR chains, including the ones focusing on fresh sandwiches. Many casual diners began using other restaurants that emphasize carryout and curbside meals.

Value consciousness is perhaps the biggest trend among QSR customers. Consumers look for value meals at nearly every QSR outlets, big chains, and small independents. A recent survey by the National Restaurant Association (NRA) reported that 75% of consumers would patronize full-service restaurants more often if they offered discounts for frequent dining or for dining on slow days of the week. The NRA survey also reported that 44% of consumers are more likely to make a restaurant choice based on the restaurant's energy and water conservation practices. Some QSR chains are showing leadership in green initiatives by conserving energy and reducing water use (Corporate Profile, 2010).

Focus on healthy food, for adults and children, is a trend that will stay here. Seventy-six percent of those who were surveyed by the NRA reported that they are trying to eat healthier meals in restaurants compared to two years ago. Forty-five percent said they would frequent quick-serve restaurants more often if the restaurant offered an expanded menu of healthy items for children. Large chains have answered the call by adding salads, flatbreads, whole-wheat crusts, salad-topped pizza, locally grown produce, and organic items to their menus in order to appeal to health conscious consumers (Corporate Profile, 2010).

In its report, "A look into the Future of Eating," the NPD group has forecasted that healthy foods, especially the ones labeled "organic," will be among the fastest growing consumption trends in the next decade. On the other hand, Mintel's research reports that 84% of surveyed consumers consider pizza as indulgence and they do not care if it is healthy or not (Corporate Profile, 2010).

Domino's SWOT Analysis

Strengths

- *Cost-efficient store model* is characterized by a delivery and carry-out oriented store design, low capital requirements, and a focused menu of quality, affordable pizza, and other complementary items. At the store level, the simplicity and efficiency of operations provide advantages over competitors who, in many cases, also focus on dine-in.
- *Strong brand awareness.* The Domino's Pizza® brand is one of the most widely recognized consumer brands in the world. Consumers associate the brand with the timely delivery of affordable pizza and other complementary items.
- *Domino's PULSE™ point-of-sale system.* Domino's PULSE™, the proprietary point-of-sale system, is installed in every company-owned store in the United States and substantially in all of the domestic franchise stores. Features of Domino's PULSE™ point-of-sale system include:
  —Ability to implement centralized promotional activities throughout the marketing mix, including couponing and flyers as well as communicating back to the consumers in the manner they communicated;
  —Touch screen ordering, which improves accuracy and facilitates more efficient order taking;

—A delivery driver routing system, which improves delivery efficiency;

—Improved administrative and reporting capabilities, which enable store managers to better focus on store operations and customer satisfaction;

—Enhanced online ordering capability, including Pizza Tracker, which was introduced in 2007 and Pizza Builder, which was introduced in 2008;

- *Successful new pizza recipe* with subsequent successful taste tasting and higher sales results

Weaknesses

- Perception by many that Domino's pizza ranks near the bottom on taste;
- Because Domino's business model is heavily dependent upon deliveries, there are areas of the country that it is difficult for the company to expand to and serve;
- Extended menu that may reduce effectiveness of delivery and great service that Domino's is renowned for.

Opportunities

- Great prospects for international expansion in densely populated parts of the world;
- Opportunity to differentiate the brand in terms of health, nutrition, and environmental sustainability;
- Opportunity for growth domestically upon economic recovery in the United States;
- Opportunity for expansion by acquiring local and independent pizza stores

Threats

- Lingering economic doldrums hamper profitability and growth;
- Stronger competition from pizza chains, independents, and take-and-bake options as well as OSR categories other than pizza;
- Healthy eating trend and organic food consumption

Domino's Growth Strategy

Growth is Domino's top business mandate domestically and internationally. The company uses two primary strategies, menu and technology, to grow domestically.

Menu-based Growth Strategy

Domino's has expanded its menu significantly since 2008. To attract the lunch crowd, it added the Oven-Baked Sandwiches line in 2008 in direct competition with Subway. The company also rolled out several BreadBowl Pasta varieties in response to the pasta line from Pizza Hut.

Domino's also expanded its pizza line by launching the American Legends—a line of six specialty pizza varieties featuring 40 percent more cheese than its regular pizza, cheesy crust, and premium toppings—in 2009. The addition of the American Legends was to strike a balance in Domino's pizza offerings to premium oriented customers according to the CEO, Patrick Doyle.

In January 2010, Domino's launched a new pizza recipe to change its reputation from what was one of the bottom of the barrel. It even ran a "self-flogging" advertising campaign that showed that customers commented on Domino's Pizza crust tasting like cardboard and its sauce like ketchup. The new recipe has been credited for Domino's sales rebound in 2010 (Horovitz, 2010).

Starting from scratch, Domino's changed "part of core," beginning with crust up. In the new crust it added butter, garlic, and parsley. The new cheese was shredded instead of diced mozzarella, with a hint of provolone. And the new sauce was made sweeter, with a red pepper kick.

Domino's communicated the arrival of the new pizza to its customers on every box it delivered:

"DOMINIO'S NEW PIZZA. 50 YEARS IN THE MAKING

Our hand-tossed pizza is new. It's not a slightly-altered version of the old pizza. It's not the same old product in a fancy wrapper. It's completely new pizza from the crust up. And we're pretty doggone proud of it. Because while it doesn't take long for you to get one, it's taken us 50 years to create a pizza of this perfectitude. Fifty years worth of listening to feedback, tasting cheeses, crafting sauces and trying every possible combination of combinations we could think of. So what's new about it? For starters, everything: our cheese made with 100% real mozzarella and flavored with just a hint of provolone. Our sauce with a dose of spicy red pepper to put a spring in your step. And our garlic-seasoned crust with a rich, buttery taste. Now you may be wondering, is it really different? Will it be as good as they say? Is 'perfectitude' actually a word? Well, there's only one way to find out. Take a bite. Then if someone asks if we actually abandoned our old recipe and completely revamped our pizza, you can tell'em . . . Oh yes we did."

In a national taste test, sponsored by Domino's and appeared on their web site, three out of five people preferred the taste of Domino's pepperoni pizza, sausage pizza, and extra cheese pizza over Papa John's and Pizza Hut's. Domino's used social media to announce the new arrival by means of its "Pizza Turnaround" documentary on YouTube, showing how they listened to customers who complained about the "old" recipe and how they developed the "new" recipe.

The company's 2010 first–quarter financial results indicate that the new recipe is a hit with the customer. Domino's domestic same-store sales grew a staggering 14.3 percent in the first quarter, while international same-store comparables were up 4.2 percent (2010 Chain of the Year, 2010).

Technology-Based Growth Strategy

Domino's has developed a reputation for innovation in business processes. It pioneered the corrugated cardboard boxes and 3-D car-top signs that are synonymous with the pizza industry. The company strengthened their efficiency with the time saving invention of the Spoodle, a combination of a spoon and ladle. To ensure that customers received the best pizza, the Domino's HeatWave Hot Bag was introduced. This technology utilizes electro-magnetic energy and 3M Thinsulate Insulation to deliver pizza hot and without excess moisture (Corporate Profile, 2010). To improve their daily operations, the Domino's Pulse point of sale system was introduced in 2003

EXHIBIT C8.6: DOMINO'S DIGITAL PIONEERING

1996	Launched its first web site, www.dominos.com
1998	First ordering through interactive television
1999	Direct ordering through Quickorder.com
2004	Launched its dedicated web site for digital marketing
2006	Received Revolution Award as the Best Online Retailer
2007	Launched mobile commerce by introducing SMS pizza ordering service

(Domino's Pizza . . . , 2003). The touch-screen ordering system significantly improved the accuracy and efficiency of order taking.

Early Adoption of Online Technology

Dominos Pizza has led the restaurant industry as an early adapter of online technology to reach customers. It utilized Internet marketing as early as 1996 by launching its web site www.dominos.com (Making Pizza since 1960 . . . , 2010). The first ordering method deviating from the standard call-and-place norm began two years later through a television set (Exhibit C8.6). In 1998, Domino's launched this new ordering method with Open, the "world's first interactive TV platform" in the United Kingdom (Strategic Play . . . , 2005). In the following year, Domino's began a partnership with Quickorder.com, allowing customers to place a delivery or pick-up order directly through the Internet. The user's order was automatically routed to the closest store's point-of-sale system, with a confirmation email sent to the customer (Connor, 2000).

Domino's hired AKQA, an innovative agency with a focus on digital marketing, to create a functional web site to stimulate online ordering in 2004 (Agency of the Year . . . , 2004). The agency's successful feat won Domino's Pizza recognition in the digital marketing world by 2006, with a nomination for a Revolution Award as the Best Online Retailer (Revolution Award . . . , 2006). In July 2007, Domino's began their exploration of the mobile commerce by introducing a SMS pizza ordering service (Domino's Pizza . . . ., 2007). To place an order, the customer was required to set up an account online with a keyword attached to their favorite orders and the delivery address. An option for credit card or cash upon delivery allowed the consumer payment flexibility. To place the order for delivery through their mobile phone, the customers sent their chosen word in a text message to 61212 (Domino's Pizza UK, 2007).

Improvements followed the establishment of e-commerce and m-commerce sales channels. Mobile ordering advanced to an application accessible with web-enabled phones at the end of 2007. The expanded sales channel allowed customers more spontaneity in ordering, choosing their desired pizza and side items from the mobile screen. The option of entering an online ordering ID and Password was available to accelerate repeat ordering transactions (Ross, 2007).

In 2007, Domino's reconfigured its online ordering application to include the Pizza Tracker. This monitoring system allowed the customer to view the progressive action of the pizza creation process in real time, from order placement to leaving the store for delivery. Traditional ordering advanced as well with the Pizza Tracker technology. This system was made available to customers who used smart phones to order. Once the order was placed, the customer could monitor it through the Pizza Tracker icon on the Domino's web site (Domino's Launches . . . , 2008).

The "Build Your Own Pizza" feature began to enhance the Internet user's experience in 2008, allowing the customer to create a progressive photo of their pizza with chosen toppings. The ordering system enhancement was combined with other features to assist the store operations. The improved point of sale system provided the restaurant with delivery route maps and optimal scheduling assistance (Jargon, 2009).

In 2008, Domino's entered another television-based sales outlet, TiVo. After viewing a Domino's Pizza commercial, TiVo users can click on the "I want it" to place an order for pick-up or delivery. They can use the Pizza Tracker to watch the progress of their pizza on their TV screen (Liddle, 2008).

Domino's aggressive mobile commerce expansion occurred in 2009. The company entered into a partnership with Air2Web to provide an opt-in mobile coupon service, tailored to the customer's ordering history (Butcher, 2009). In August 2009, a new version of the mobile web site was released, specially designed for iPhone, Android, and Palm Pre users. This mobile site mirrored the web platform by providing the Pizza Tracker with menu visualization, order graphics, and ability to browse and apply available coupons that the customer used (Domino's Pizza Launches . . . , 2009).

New Media Strategy

Although television accounts for more than 90% of Domino's media spending, the company is increasingly utilizing new media, such as online advertising, email, mobile, search, and social networking, to connect with its younger customers. Domino's recently tripled its online advertising spending to promote its new menu and delivery service across a broad range of sites such as Amazon, Ask, Facebook, MySpace, Yahoo, College Humor, and Yellow Pages as well as sites from local newspapers.

Email marketing at Domino's ranges from a variety of special deals, promotional offers, and coupons to new menu item introduction and menu suggestion for special occasions (e.g., lunch, family gathering, gift) to just a simple reminder to order from Domino's. Established customers typically receive weekly email with promotional deals and suggestions.

Domino's search marketing was catching up with its archrival, Pizza Hut. It demonstrated a strong showing in organic search—a testimony to the company's effective advertising and strong web site experience—as opposed to paid search where Pizza Hut made a bigger commitment.

Mobile is one of the fastest growing elements of new media that all the three pizza chains are paying attention to. Although, mobile marketing at Domino's is a small proportion compared to online marketing via the Internet, the company reports that it is growing at an average rate of 20% per month. The growth rate dovetails mobile commerce, the fast growing area of retail purchases in the United States. Shoppers were expected to order $2.2 billion worth of merchandise using cell phones in 2010, $1 billion more than 2009 and five times more than 2008, according to ABI Research Inc., a New York technology research firm. To respond to the rapid growth in mobile shopping, 30% of retailers have installed mobile-commerce web site (Mattioli, 2010).

Domino's has taken a different approach toward its mobile media. Instead of developing smart phone application to provide access to mobile ordering, Domino's has decided to streamline its web site for mobile access. The advantage of the site is that it requires few clicks for mobile ordering and no downloading or registration for access. By visiting http://www.dominos.com, customers can create order by tapping "Express Ordering" or "Create Your Own Pizza," examining the menu, special offers and coupons, and using the Pizza Tracker upon placing order.

Domino's social media strategy is a broad ranging program that encompasses Facebook, Twitter, and YouTube. Domino's engagement in social media was hastened in April 2009 when a prank video, posted on YouTube, showed two employees were abusing and mishandling the food they were preparing in a franchise kitchen. The video quickly spread all over the Internet and received more than a million views in less than 24 hours on YouTube. Domino's President properly responded and discredited the prank in another video posted on YouTube. The company also set up a Twitter account, shortly after the incident, and started answering the questions addressed to Domino's.

Domino's continued using social media to announce the arrival of its new-recipe pizza by its "Pizza Turnaround" documentary on YouTube. They also showed the success of their taste test by beating Papa John's and Pizza Hut on a "Celebrate" page. And they had a "Stop Puffery" campaign, also on Twitter, which made fun of Papa John's (Domino's Pizza Rewards . . . , 2010).

Domino's integrated its social media campaign on Facebook by encouraging consumers to try its new-recipe pizza. An interactive contest, "Taste Bud Bounty Hunters", rewarded Facebook users with free food for getting their friends to try the new pizza recipe. On the web site, pizzaholdouts.com, photos were displayed of the top bounty hunter contestants and those pizza holdouts with "wanted taste buds".

Challenges Ahead

As a $5.6 billion company with 170,000 employees and over 9000 stores in 62 countries, Domino's Pizza Inc. is readying to celebrate its 50th anniversary. Basking in the company's success, the management is realistically thoughtful about the list of challenges ahead. On the top of that list are the state of the economy and the maturity of the U.S. pizza market. The question before the management is whether the same-store growth performance is domestically sustainable and achievable in the near future. Per company reports, the U.S. sales rose slightly, from $3 billion to $3.1 billion in 2009. It is expected that quick-service restaurants fare slightly better than full-service restaurants in the coming year, according to the National Restaurant Association. Because of the lingering slowdown in the economy, however, the average amount spent per order won't increase appreciably as consumers continue to hold tight to their wallets.

The international growth is one area that management is hopeful about. Currently over 40% of the company revenues are from the international operation. The proportion is expected to pass 50% in the next three to five years.

The success of Domino's new recipe has created momentum for the brand whose maintenance is subject to proper marketing strategy and execution. Since 2008, Domino's significantly expanded its menu to include multi-variety Oven-Baked Sandwiches, BreadBowl Pasta, and the American Legends line of specialty pizza. While the additions contribute to higher sales and growth at store level, they may complicate order processing, preparation, and delivery as well. Whether the expanded menu would slow down Domino's fast delivery and great service when the economic recovery begins and business picks up remains to be seen.

Case Discussion Questions

1. Discuss Domino's point-of-sale (POS) ordering system. What are the advantages of the new system, for Domino's, its franchisees, and its customers?

2. Analyze the pizza home delivery market. What are the market size and growth? Who are the major competitors? What are Domino's competitive advantages and disadvantages? Evaluate Domino's growth potential in the pizza home delivery market.

3. With the advent of online and mobile ordering, the rivalry among Domino's, Pizza Hut, and Papa John's has been heightened in the past three years. Each company claims that its online/mobile ordering system is as easy to use as blinking. You can engage in online shopping and purchasing by browsing the menu, ordering a pizza, and tracking your pizza in real time from order to delivery on their web site. You can also search for deals, valuable information on nutrition, health, and environment. So, what else can you do on these web sites? Check it for yourself by visiting Domino's, www.dominos.com, Pizza Hut, www.pizzahut.com, and Papa John's, www.papajohns.com. Browse the menu, go over menu items, and decide on a meal from different types of pizzas, side items, and drinks. Check out the listing of various toppings that are offered. Examine the nutritional value of the menu items. After choosing your meal, try to place an order by clicking on the order tab. How many steps you have to go through before completing your order? What information do you have to have to decide on delivery versus carryout? After you place your order, can you track it online from submission to delivery? What other communication / information do you receive after the completion of the delivery? Evaluate your experience with each web site you visited. Which site is easier to use? Which site is user-friendlier? Is ordering pizza online better or worse than ordering pizza over the phone? Why?

4. Domino's recently announced the launch of a new version of its mobile ordering web site, http://mobile.dominos.com. The enhanced version is optimized to access Google's Android operating system, used by iPhone, Palm Pre

and others. Discuss the enhancements of the new ordering site and its marketing implications.

5. What types of data does Domino's collect when it transacts with customers online? Identify at least *five* different ways that Domino's can use customer data to increase sales and market share.

6. Discuss Domino's recent marketing activities using social media. Compare Domino's social-media strategies vis-à-vis those of Pizza Hut and Papa John's. Address Domino's advantages and shortcomings in using social media. How do you think Domino's can leverage social media to better connect with its customers and advance its brand?

References

2009 Yum! Brands Annual Customer Mania Report, 2009.

2010 Chain of the Year, Pizza Today, June 2010, www.pizzatoday.com.

"Agency of the Year: Digital Agency of the Year—Best of the Rest". Dow Jones. 15, December 2004.

"AMSTAR CORPORATION, Plaintiff-Appellee, v. DOMINO'S PIZZA, INC. and Atlanta Pizza, Inc., Pizza Enterprises, Inc. and Pizza Services, Inc., Hanna Creative Enterprises, Inc., Defendants-Appellants.". United States Court of Appeals for the Fifth Circuit. 2 May 1980. http://altlaw.org/v1/cases/525090.

Blumenfeld and Associates, 2010.

Boyer, Peter J. (19 February 2007). "The Deliverer". The New Yorker. http://www.newyorker.com/reporting/2007/02/19/070219fa_fact_boyer.

Butcher, Dan. "Domino's Pizza Exec: Mobile Commerce Growing at Astounding Rate". The Mobile Marketer. 4, September 2009. http://www.mobilemarketer.com/cms/news/commerce/4102.print.

"Change at Domino's." nyse magaine.com, 2010. http://www.nysemagazine.com/dominos.

Connor, Deni. "QuickOrder Brings Domino's Pizza to You in 30 minutes or Less". Network World. 6, March 2000.

"Corporate Profile". Domino's Investor Relations, 2010. http://phx.corporate-ir.net/phoenix.zhtml?c=135383&p=irol-homeprofile.

Domino's 2010 Annual Report, 2010.

"Domino's Founder to Retire, Sell Stake". Los Angeles Time. 26 September 1998. http://articles.latimes.com/1998/sep/26/business/fi-26500.

"Domino's Launches Revolutionary Customer Tool: Pizza Tracker™; Industry-Leading Technology Allows Customers to Follow Progress of their Order Online—Even if they Order by Phone". PR Newswire (U.S.) 30, January 2008.

"Domino's opens 9000th store". Nation's Restaurant News. 11, March 2010. http://www.nrn.com/breakingNews.aspx?id=380448&menu_id=1368

"Domino's Pizza & Breakaway Roll Out of New Pulse POS System". Pizza Marketplace. 5, February 2003. http://www.pizzamarketplace.com/article.php?id=2277.

"Domino's Pizza Enables Ordering by SMS". New Media Age. 26, July 2007.

"Domino's Pizza, Inc." Datamonitor Company Profiles. Datamonitor. 12 November 2008. http://www.datamonitor.com/store/Product/dominos_pizza_inc?productid=1744376E-79E5-49F9-9298-F128768A73E5.

Domino's Pizza, Inc. (2008). "David A. Brandon Biography". Press release. http://phx.corporate-ir.net/phoenix.zhtml?c=135383&p=irol-govBio&ID=115901.

Domino's Pizza Invester Presentation, January 2010. http://phx.corporate-ir.net/External.File?item=UGFyZW50SUQ9MjY5Mjh8Q2hpbGRJRRD0tMXxUeXBlPTM=&t=1

"Domino's Launches Revolutionary Customer Tool: Pizza Tracker™; Industry-Leading Technology Allows Customers to Follow Progress of their Order Online—Even if they Order by Phone". PR Newswire (U.S.) 30, January 2008.

Domino's Pizza Rewards the 'Taste Bud Bounty Hunters'. Restaurant News.Com. 11, May 2010. http://www.restaurantnews.com/dominos-pizza-rewards-the-taste-bud-bounty-hunters/

Domino's Pizza UK (2007). "Domino's Pizza Launches UK's First Ever Text Message Pizza Order Service". Press Release. http://www.dominos.uk.com/media_centre/pdf/Text%20Ordering.pdf.

Horovitz, Bruce (May 5, 2010) "New pizza recipe did wonders for Domino's sales". USA Today. http://www.usatoday.com/money/industries/food/2010-05-05-dominos05_ST_N.htm Retrieved 2010-06-18

Jargon, Julie. " Business Technology: Domino's IT Staff Delivers Slick Site, Ordering System—-Pizza Chain Rolls Out Point-of-Sale System in U.S. Stores to Woo Customers, Streamline Online Orders". Wall Street Journal. 24, November 2009.

Liddle, A. "Domino's Pioneers 'Couch Commerce,' Expands its Ordering Options with New TiVo Partnership." Nation's Restaurant News. 1, December 2008.

Litterick, David (February 23, 2008). "Colin Halpern sells £4 m slice of Domino's Pizza". The Daily Telegraph. http://www.telegraph.co.uk/money/main.jhtml?xml=/money/2008/02/23/cndomino123.xml.

"Making Pizza Since 1960. . . . ". Domino's Pizza Inc.. http://www.dominosbiz.com/Biz-Public-EN/Site+Content/Secondary/About+Dominos/History/.

Mattioli, Dana (June 11, 2010). "Retailers Answer Call of Smartphones". The Wall Street Journal. http://online.wsj.com/article/SB10001424052748704749904575292

"Our Heritage". Domino's Pizza, Inc.. 2008. http://www.dominos.com/Public-EN/Site%2BContent/Secondary/Inside%2BDominos/Our%2BHeritage/.

Packaged Facts, New York, 2010.

Papa John's 2009 Annual Report, 2009.

Phone interview with Dennis Maloney, Domino's Multi-Media Marketing Vice President, 2011.

"Pizza Power Report, 2009". PMQ Pizza Magazine, September 2009, www.pmq.com

"Revolution Awards 2006: Is Your Work in the Running?". Revolution. 28, February 2006.

Ross, J. "Domino's, Papa John's Look to Build Clientele Via Text Message Ordering". Nation's Restaurant News. 10, December 2007.

Standard & Poor's May 15, 2010 stock report, 2010.

"Strategic Play—Domino's Pizza: Speedy Delivery". New Media Age. 14, April 2005.

Yum! Brands 2009 Annual Report, 2009.

CASE
9

Häagen-Dazs®
Loves Honey Bees

BLODWEN TARTER
Golden Gate University

JACK SAUNDERS
Golden Gate University

It was mid-summer when Katty Pien, director of the Häagen-Dazs ice cream brand in the United States, sat down to prepare for an important meeting. In a few weeks, the Häagen-Dazs team and its advertising and public relations agencies would start planning the marketing campaign for the next calendar year.

But first, Ms. Pien wanted to review the current Häagen-Dazs Loves Honey Bees (HD_HB) campaign and, quite frankly, to enjoy its run-away success. She thought back to the launch on the previous February. That was the day the company released a press announcement earmarking $250,000 in research grants to scientists studying honey bee Colony Collapse Disorder (CCD) and sustainable pollination at Pennsylvania State University and the University of California at Davis. It was the first of many moves to raise awareness of a serious environmental problem and to link the Häagen-Dazs brand with its solution.

About one-quarter of the country's winged farm workers, the common honey bee, had died the previous winter from an as-yet poorly understood malady. But this much was known: it was taking down whole hives, virtually overnight. Häagen-Dazs had a direct stake in this crisis. More than forty percent of the super-premium ice cream maker's line depends on ingredients that honey bees pollinate. But this was not just a potential strategic supply chain crisis for Häagen-Dazs. Preliminary research determined that the problem was even more far-reaching. Fully one-third of the U.S. food supply was at peril.

Häagen-Dazs had the opportunity to do something that might save the company while helping out the food chain in general. If successful, Häagen-Dazs would emerge not only with its supply chain security restored, but also with a new and timely brand association in "the green space" of sustainability and environmentally conscious business practices.

Of course, the underlying goal was to increase sales of Häagen-Dazs ice cream in an intensely competitive marketplace, but the fundamental opportunity could hold even greater consequence for future profitability. Here was the chance to marry the brand's heretofore understated reputation for all-natural ingredients with the emerging and high-profile ethic of environmental sustainability. Such a brand identity could have extraordinary value as a strategic differentiator if the consumer segment favoring all-natural ingredients also valued companies demonstrably committed to sustainable agricultural practices.

Ben & Jerry's®, a respected competitor in the super-premium ice cream category, had for years claimed a praiseworthy pro-environment corporate attitude. But the Vermont-born firm had been sold to European conglomerate Unilever, and the new parent had done little in years to capitalize on the founders' environmental beliefs. So Häagen-Dazs, even without first-mover advantage, was in a good position to trump Ben and Jerry's with an environmental intervention that was eminently concrete and practical. Häagen-Dazs would set out to bring what could honestly be construed as "health care" to the littlest farm workers in an hour of crisis.

In spite of initial skepticism within the company, HD_HB was succeeding on all fronts when Ms. Pien began to assess progress in July and to consider the brand's moves for the coming year. Sales of Häagen-Dazs ice cream were up in a category that, historically, showed no/low growth. The media and the consumers loved the support that Häagen-Dazs was providing to bee scientists. A few months in the marketplace had given the marketers the information they needed. Nearly 850 separate stories in print, TV, radio, and online described some aspect of the campaign—in its first week. Clearly, news professionals rated the initiative as something consumers would surely want to know about. Just one hundred days into the campaign, the story had racked up almost 188 million media impressions, using standard reach and effectiveness calculations.

The company had received numerous letters, emails, and phone calls from groups and individuals proposing alliances. Some were artists and entertainers, thinking about performances themed to the honey bee plight. Environmental grassroots groups and sustainability enthusiasts signed on with support. Even supermarket retailers were expressing interest in partnering on the campaign.

So planning for the coming year would begin with the sweet hint of success in the air. But first, Ms. Pien reviewed the familiar terrain of the past year. Where were they now and how did they get there?

Ice Cream Industry Background

Häagen-Dazs may love honey bees, but everyone loves ice cream. At least, according to Mintel, more than 90% of United States households do. The love of ice cream crosses demographic categories: people of all ages, ethnic groups, and both genders eat ice cream regularly. On average, ice-cream eating households consume a little less than three quarts (or six pints) per month. Ice cream consumption on a per capita basis is reported to have been steady from in the mid-2000s. Given the high penetration among possible consumers and the amount consumed per person, the ice cream market is described as stable, growing primarily as the population grows.[1] Not only

---

[1] *Mintel Ice Cream and Frozen Novelties- US- June 2007* "Household Usage" section. Accessed online.

does everyone love ice cream, ice cream is big business. IBISWorld estimated that, in the United States, the ice cream and frozen dessert category would exceed $9 billion in sales for at-home consumption in a recent year and require more than 7 billion pounds of milk for its manufacture, about 8% of the total U.S. production of milk.[2] Including away-from-home consumption in ice cream shops, restaurants and other retail sales outlets brought the total to more than $21 billion.[3]

However, consumption is seasonal. Ice cream is the quintessential warm weather treat, with sales markedly lower in the cold months of the year. In spite of efforts to counter this trend by introducing seasonal flavors, such as peppermint and eggnog, the pattern of consumption remains consistent. Because of this seasonality, promotional efforts for the category are heaviest in the spring and summer.

With the growing problem of childhood obesity and increased concern about nutrition and eating healthy, food manufacturers of traditional ice cream have another reason to worry. Hence, the industry is developing healthier versions of ice cream—light/low fat ice cream, sherbet, no sugar added ice cream, fruit sorbet, fat free ice cream and non-dairy ice cream—as well as offering frozen yogurt and soy-based confections. In recent years, the industry also has jumped on the organic foods bandwagon. *Dairy Foods* reported the introduction of 31 new organic ice cream products in a recent year, increasing to 49 in the next year.[4] This health concern contrasts with the seemingly contradictory trend towards indulgent consumption: "I'm worth it so I will eat super-premium ice cream." The majority (79%) of ice-cream eaters still report eating regular, premium or superpremium ice cream rather than the healthier alternatives.[5] Super-premium ice cream, generally defined as 18–22 percent butterfat,[6] is the ultimate in the indulgent category, and Häagen-Dazs occupies a prime position in that category.

Within the super-premium category, Häagen-Dazs competes head-on with Ben and Jerry's. According to Information Resources, Inc., Häagen-Dazs has a 6.6% market share of the total ice cream market while Ben and Jerry's has a 5.9% share.[7] Other super-premium brands are local or regional with substantially smaller market presence.

Consumers tend to have one or two favorite brands but will eat another brand in a pinch. Given this brand loyalty and the stagnant growth of overall ice cream consumption, any increase in market share is most likely to come from convincing ice cream eaters to switch brands. To entice consumers to choose their brand, ice cream manufacturers typically rely upon a limited set of methods. New products, whether

---

[2] *IBISWorld Industry Report, Ice Cream Production in the US: 31152*, 13 February 2008, p. 13.

[3] http://www.idfa.org/facts/icmonth/page2.cfm accessed 20 May 2008.

[4] "New Products and Marketing, Dairy Market Trends: Ice Cream's Bright Spots: Wellness, FroYo, Novelties and Private Label," *Dairy Foods*, March 2008, p. 44.

[5] *Mintel Ice Cream and Frozen Novelties- US- June 2007*, "Household usage" section.

[6] David Landau, spokesperson for the International Ice Cream Association, quoted in "Adult Appeal," Julie Cook, *Dairy Field*, October 2002. Accessed online http://findarticles.com/p/articles/mi_qa3846/is_200210/ai_n9103025

[7] Information Resources, Inc., based on 52-week sales for period ending 4 November 2007 as cited in "Private Label Drives Ice Cream," *Dairy Foods*. January 2008. Vol. 109, Issue 1, p. 70, 72.

new flavors or new formulations, are common. Price promotions and coupons are also popular. National advertising is rarely used, in part because local and regional brands have relatively small marketing budgets, and in part because national advertising is inefficient for those companies. Public relations efforts tend to focus on new product introductions and flavor sampling, or to be opportunistic. For instance, if there is a major fire, the first-responder firefighters are likely to be served donated ice cream. The margins on ice cream are thin, often less than 10%, so creative and cost-effective promotions are required.[8] Ice cream manufacturers must not only convince consumers to switch brands but they must also persuade their retail channels to allocate space—at the expense of other brands. Frozen food case space is very expensive in supermarkets, and manufacturers typically pay meaningful slotting fees for this category.[9]

The ice cream company and the retailer need to be very confident that they can sell more of brand X to justify the additional slotting fees and the cost of adding a new product to an already crowded freezer case. It is more difficult and expensive to expand shelf space for frozen foods than for other food categories. In most cases, physical expansion is not a realistic option, so other products must be displaced.

While more than 60% of the nation's ice cream is sold in supermarkets, convenience stores are growing in importance, especially for the smaller-sized packages. Ice cream parlors also are important outlets for reaching consumers, but they tend to be single brand outlets; whether national brands such as Häagen-Dazs or Baskin-Robbins® or local brands.[10]

Häagen-Dazs Background: Positioning and Target Consumers

For Häagen-Dazs, arguably the first super-premium ice cream and one of the best-known brands, distinctiveness is key. Founded in 1961 by New York dairyman Reuben Mattus, Häagen-Dazs has always distinguished itself by its exceptional craftsmanship, high quality standards and all-natural ingredients. Dreyer's Grand Ice Cream, the company that manufactures Häagen-Dazs in the United States, also sells the premium Dreyer's and Edy's® ice cream, The Skinny Cow® low fat ice cream, Nestlé® Drumstick® line of novelties, Dreyer's Fruit Bars—even Frosty Paws® ice cream for dogs. Häagen-Dazs stands alone atop this pyramid of tasty delights.

Häagen-Dazs adheres to a simple rule: absolutely nothing that is not found in the well-stocked household pantry may be used in the making of its ice cream. For exam-

---

[8] Mark Scott, "Ice Cream Wars: Nestle vs. Unilever," *Business Week Online*, 27 August 2007, p. 12.

[9] According to an FTC study, slotting fees for ice cream range from $2,680 to $12,682 per UPC per store, averaging $10,625 per UPC per store among the admittedly small sample of retail grocers. See Table 5, page 39, *Slotting Allowances in the Retail Grocery Industry: Selected Studies in Five Product Categories*, an FTC Staff Study, November 2003 accessed at http://www.ftc.gov/os/2003/11/slottingallowancerpt031114.pdf 9 June 2008.

[10] *IBISWorld Industry Report, Ice Cream Production in the US: 31152*, 13 February 2008, p. 9–10.

ple, artificial flavorings and preservatives are out under this rule as are fructose and gums. These are not "unnatural" ingredients but they are rarely found in the typical home cupboard.

Other ingredients, called "inclusions" in the trade, are selected only after exacting searches. Reuben Mattus took six years to find a suitable strawberry for Häagen-Dazs ice cream. Two particular strains, Hood and Totem strawberries, grown in Oregon, are prized for their deep red color and exceptional sweetness. They cost more, but Häagen-Dazs knows that the quality makes these strawberries worth it.

The Häagen-Dazs target consumer is best defined by attitude, rather than by demographic characteristics. The ice cream enthusiast is an ardent fan and consistent consumer of ice cream, seeking out and trying new flavors regularly. This aficionado has high standards and is willing to pay more for the best-tasting ice cream. Other target consumers are those who may not eat ice cream regularly or as frequently, but when they do, they want the very best and they are willing to spend more money for it. At $4.39 a pint, Häagen-Dazs is priced about three times higher than the average regular ice cream, which costs approximately $5.00 for a three-pint (1.5 quart) carton. Häagen-Dazs' convenient pint package allows retailers to put more flavors into the available space while consumers can think of their Häagen-Dazs purchase as an affordable, but special, treat.

More than seventy flavors make up the complete line of Häagen-Dazs branded ice cream. Consistent with the overall industry trend, vanilla flavors are the best-sellers. Recently, Häagen-Dazs had introduced the Reserve Series, its most upscale offering for ice cream aficionados, featuring exotic, gourmet flavors. Beginning with six unusual flavors, including Lehua Honey and Sweet Cream, it later added Fleur de Sel Caramel.[11]

The Idea for the Upcoming Year

Each summer, Häagen-Dazs invites proposals for the following year's marketing campaign. At the current year's "pitch" meeting for the brand's upcoming year plan, the brand management team considered a number of ideas presented by the advertising agency Goodby, Silverstein, and Partners, and the public relations firm Ketchum Public Relations. As usual, the quest was for a theme that underscored the quality message, something that would make the brand, and the company behind the brand, attractive to the upscale customer, a food and fashion enthusiast, not overly concerned about price but highly keen to enjoy the very best.

Some annual campaigns have taken a "democratic" turn, inviting consumers to propose new flavors in a contest format. A couple of years earlier, Häagen-Dazs and the Food Network created a Scoop! Ice Cream Flavor Contest. The finalists were flown to the Häagen-Dazs test kitchens where batches of their flavors were created. The grand prize winner saw her creation—Sticky Toffee Pudding—join the line of Häagen-Dazs flavors. A subsequent flavor contest, in partnership with *Gourmet* magazine, resulted in the Caramelized Pear and Toasted Pecan flavor, also added to the Häagen-Dazs line.

---

[11] "Häagen-Dazs Reserve: For Ice Cream Connoisseurs Only," *Frozen Food Age*, January 2008, Vol. 56 Issue 6, p.10.

For the upcoming year, a Goodby representative floated a new idea. What about "something linked to the environment?" Specifically, what about the honey bee crisis? Honey bees suggested nature, environmental balance, health and happiness. This seemed to work with the all-natural ingredients fetish. The only trouble was: What could Häagen-Dazs do? Häagen-Dazs had no particular expertise in apiary science. Nor did anyone, even the scientists, really know what the honey bee crisis was.

It was simply known by then that the U.S. honey bee population had declined by 25% over the past winter, and that agricultural interests (some of them, anyway) were on the verge of panic. Almonds, for example, a $1.9 billion crop and the country's most important horticultural export, depend entirely on honey bees for pollinating the almond trees.[12] And these hard-working insects were suddenly disappearing. In the worst case, almond growers faced potential ruin. Goodby had no concrete idea how Häagen-Dazs might frame the issue to advantage, only a notion that this could underscore the brand's distinctive all-natural, quality positioning. Dori Bailey, director of consumer communications for all of the brands Dreyer's manufactures, had been casting about for ways to enter "the green space." She was at the time inventorying corporate steps on energy conservation, recycling, green facilities upgrades, etc. But so was every public relations office in the country. This was a different idea, dovetailing perfectly with the Häagen-Dazs all-natural positioning. It was a true fit as honey bees were crucial to the growth of the nuts, berries, and fruits on which Häagen-Dazs depended.

The Honey Bee Crisis

There were risks. For example, what if CCD were found to be caused by pesticides? Häagen-Dazs is not an organic brand. The cost of an entirely organic dairy product would force an increase of already premium prices at retail. The brand could not insist that its suppliers eschew pesticides, only that the "inclusions" pass standard USDA testing for health and safety. Could Häagen-Dazs take on the entire agricultural industry?

Ketchum PR suggested Häagen-Dazs form an advisory panel of bee experts, naming it the Häagen-Dazs Bee Board. Meeting with these leaders in apiary science, the team gained some comfort. Pesticides had been around for hundreds of years. There had been isolated cases of bee die-offs as more potent chemicals came into the fields, but after adjustments, the honey bees, until very recently, had done fine with the commonly prescribed doses.

But now, something had changed. Bees were deserting their hives—simply disappearing and presumably dying. Dubbed Colony Collapse Disorder, the cause was unknown. Malnutrition? Mites? Physical stress? Toxic chemicals? Disease? Some lethal combination of threats that separately didn't pose a problem?

According to the USDA more than 90 crops depend upon bees for pollination including apples, almonds, blueberries, cherries, and pears. That meant one-third of the United States food supply was at risk, worth $15 billion.[13] Bee-pollinated fruits

---

[12] "Record almond crop forecast," *Sacramento Bee*, 8 May 2008, p. D1. Accessed online at http://www.sacbee.com/agriculture/story/921571.html.

[13] *USDA Colony Collapse Disorder Action Plan*, 20 June 2007, accessed at http://www.ars. usda.gov/is/br/ccd/ccd_actionplan.pdf 9 June 2008.

and nuts are essential ingredients in more than 40% of Häagen-Dazs flavors, meaning the brand faced a unique strategic supply chain challenge. Typically, a business that foresees supply trouble will search for substitute materials or alternative suppliers, perhaps suppliers unaffected by a regional problem. For Häagen-Dazs, there would be no substitute ingredients. And CCD was not an isolated problem—it was appearing across the continental United States, and in parts of Canada and Europe.

But the problem also offered a unique opportunity to tie Häagen-Dazs to a cause and a legitimate focus on the environment. It required no stretch of the imagination, only some straight-forward explanation, to show how important this issue was to the future of Häagen-Dazs and how logical it was for the brand to promote awareness of CCD. No "greenwashing" here!

The Plan and Implementation

From the vague idea of "something to do with the environment", the honey bee campaign began to take shape. The Bee Board helped Häagen-Dazs understand the science of bees and the mysteries of the CCD problem. From there, the creative ideas flew fast and furious. Eventually, the team settled on a blend of traditional and non-traditional media with emphasis on community involvement. Part of the goal was to enlist everyone to help the honey bees. Häagen-Dazs wanted to raise awareness of the problem and suggest meaningful actions for people to take—while associating Häagen-Dazs with the all-natural ingredients that honey bees help create.

This integrated marketing campaign used virtually all types of marketing communications. Häagen-Dazs launched with the announcement of its $250,000 contribution to the two leading bee science centers in the country. UC Davis used a portion of the donation to fund a fellowship for a bee scientist specifically researching honey bee biology and health. A 30-second television commercial showed the tragically failed courtship of a bee and a flower set to an original operatic score. First aired on national TV, it continued to reach numerous viewers when posted on the YouTube web site.

National Geographic carried an advertorial depicting the potential impact of honey bee declines on crops across the country. Co-sponsored by the National Geographic Society, a map of the United States showed the 35 states in which key food crops were known to be at risk. An ad printed on special flower seed-impregnated recycled linen paper was inserted into selected issues of *Newsweek* delivered to subscribers. Tear out the ad, plant the paper and watch the bee-friendly garden grow! To encourage even more people to plant bee-friendly gardens which serve as critical food sources for honey bees and other native bees, Häagen-Dazs organized a one million seed giveaway to community groups, garden clubs, parent-teacher associations and schools. If all the seeds were planted, bee habitat would increase substantially.

To use the product itself to carry the honey bee message, a cute HD_HB logo was added to the package of each ice cream flavor identified as bee-dependent. Häagen-Dazs promised to contribute a portion of the profits from the sale of cartons of bee-dependent ice cream to bee research. Buying ice cream, often considered a selfish activity, now served the greater good. While Häagen-Dazs didn't hold a flavor contest for the year the bee campaign was introduced, neither did it abandon the new flavor idea. The schedule called for introducing the new flavor Vanilla Honey Bee simultaneously with the program launch in February. Community tasting events featuring local beekeepers highlighted the new flavor and the work Häagen-Dazs was doing on behalf of the bees.

Häagen-Dazs devoted much of its resources to building the www.helpthehoneybees.com web site. Virtually every Häagen-Dazs message would include the URL of the web site where visitors could read about the CCD problem, the progress in finding a solution, and discover more ways to help. Links to the bee research institutes at UC Davis and Penn State made it easier for people to donate money directly to the research efforts. You could create your own honey bee avatar to email to friends, along with a more serious message about the honey bee crisis.

The team wanted every person in the company to be involved and committed to the cause. Engaging Dreyer's employees started with mailing a packet of seeds and a letter inviting employees to "educate your neighbors, schools, and community groups about the severe situation the honey bees and our food supply are facing," to plant a garden of bee-friendly plants, and to encourage other cause-related non-profit events with a donation of Häagen-Dazs ice cream. Dori Bailey even verified that the plants surrounding Dreyer's corporate headquarters and the production facilities that manufactured Häagen-Dazs were bee-friendly. Furthermore, the Häagen-Dazs team was delighted that Nestlé, the global food company that owns Dreyer's, supported the campaign's premise.

Convincing the sales force that HD_HB would help them sell more ice cream proved to be a more challenging task. After all, Häagen-Dazs was venturing into environmental territory that had been Ben & Jerry's domain for many years. The sales people were, at best, skeptical about the honey bee angle, an issue that few people had even heard of at the time this campaign was being formulated.

Feedback on the HD_HB campaign— "A Genuine and Authentic Cause"

The Häagen-Dazs internal team was pleased to report that overall sales were up. Based on retailer response, the sales force had high hopes that this growth would continue. Anecdotal evidence suggested that long-sought inroads were being made among certain retailers. A Whole Foods store manager read about the HD_HB campaign in *National Geographic* and created a freezer case wrap featuring Häagen-Dazs and the "Help the Honey Bees" message. Whole Foods was a perfect fit with the Häagen-Dazs brand and this grassroots support was promising.

Consumer response was even more exciting. The Häagen-Dazs team could not keep track of the number of times and places in which the campaign was mentioned online. A Google search in early June showed over 26,000 results for "haagen dazs honey bees" while the same search on Yahoo yielded 50,000 results.[14] Independently-created videos, reiterating the need to help the honey bees, were posted on YouTube in response to the Help the Honey Bees commercial. A Dane started a Facebook group to "helpthehoneybees" and linked to the official web site. A few commentators

---

[14] Search conducted by the first author 9 June 2008 at www.google.com and www.yahoo.com.

questioned the importance of the issue or the motives of the company for highlighting the plight of the honey bees but the vast majority were positive, even enthusiastic, about Häagen-Dazs' actions. Sure, Häagen-Dazs would benefit from the exposure but this issue was serious and solving the CCD problem would benefit everyone.

The beekeeping and scientific community wholeheartedly supported the program. Without exception, they were grateful for the exposure of the problem and did not begrudge Häagen-Dazs any benefit the brand derived from the campaign. Links from the www.helpthehoneybees.com web site led to more than 100 gifts directed to the research teams at Penn State and UC Davis. A Brooklyn, NY beekeeper requested 100,000 seeds to distribute at his local farmer's market, then wrote his own press release promoting the seed giveaway and a flyer explaining the campaign. As these groups experienced the positive impact of the Häagen-Dazs name recognition, they considered more and different actions for the cause partnership.

Equally empowering, employees at all levels of Dreyer's embraced the cause. A Dreyer's employee worked with his children's elementary school in San Leandro, CA to develop a curriculum that included class presentations and a "Honey Bee Day" for planting seeds (accompanied, of course, by donated Häagen-Dazs ice cream). More than 500 students, staff, and teachers participated.

An incidental, but nonetheless gratifying outcome for the Häagen-Dazs team, was the favorable acknowledgement of the campaign by fellow marketing and public relations professionals. The San Francisco American Marketing Association chapter awarded its annual Excellence in Marketing Award for large companies to Dreyer's for the Häagen-Dazs Loves Honey Bees campaign. Advertising pundits reviewed the TV commercials, dedicated web site, and unique print ads in the trade press—and gave the team kudos for the concept, the execution, and the company's commitment to a "genuine and authentic cause."[15]

The Next Steps: The Remainder of Year One and Decisions for Year Two

New ideas were cropping up daily and new partners, both formal and informal, were taking up the issue. With all of this hoopla and increasing momentum, what should Dreyer's do? Now and in the year to come? What would the agencies suggest? What ideas did the company team have? There were so many possibilities for the Häagen-Dazs brand. How would they choose among them?

For the remainder of Year One, should Dreyer's modify the Häagen-Dazs campaign or let it run as planned? The scheduled TV and print advertising had been completed, but the team wondered if more appearances of the operatic TV commercial would be useful. Should they focus on leveraging the now-attentive interest of retailers? How could they capitalize on the sales force's newly developed enthusiasm—and how could they sustain that enthusiasm? What should they do about the continuing overtures from performing artists, documentary producers, and authors?

Of greater import, the team had to decide what they should do for Year Two.

---

[15] Barbara Lippert, "Häagen-Dazs Tries Beekeeping," *Adweek*, 5 May 2008, Volume 49, Issue 15, p. 30.

Should Häagen-Dazs continue to ride the wave of the heightened focus on sustainability and environmental consciousness? The campaign had momentum now. But what if people grew tired of the theme and enthusiasm waned? If the researchers could not quickly identify the cause of CCD would people grow skeptical that it could be solved and lose interest?

If the Year Two campaign continued with the HD_HB theme, should the company pull back from paid media and concentrate even more on word-of-mouth? Advertising can be expensive but the company controls the message—what is said, when, where, and by whom. Word-of-mouth and viral marketing can spread like wildfire and cost little in terms of cash outlay. However, the consumer takes control of the message, rather than the company. The reach and frequency, as well as the content and context, of the message are unpredictable. How should the Häagen-Dazs team allocate their marketing communications mix?

A new Häagen-Dazs flavor had been introduced annually for several years—and might now constitute a tradition. Is another new bee-related flavor needed? Could one be developed that would be appropriately connected to the honey bee theme?

The company knew that it wanted more people and companies to join with it to raise awareness and to stimulate constructive action towards unraveling the mystery of CCD and sustainable pollination. Häagen-Dazs had no monopoly on the issue which had truly far-reaching implications. How could they inspire even greater grassroots involvement to fund CCD research and to create more nectar-laden gardens to help honey bees survive and thrive? What about starting a non-profit through which donations could be collected and directed to further honey bee research? Could they continue to give away Häagen-Dazs branded seeds to local groups or would people tire of that approach? Perhaps a number of high-quality seed, plant or even garden supply catalog companies would be receptive to linking their name to the Häagen-Dazs brand. Might they join forces with one or more of the many farming cooperatives with crops at risk? How could Dreyer's retain the acknowledged authenticity of the HD_HB campaign and still further the Häagen-Dazs brand?

Katty Pien wondered what alternatives she and her colleagues would focus on and, ultimately, what theme and specific campaign elements they would they recommend to senior management for Häagen-Dazs in Year Two.

All trademarks are the property of their respective owners. Häagen-Dazs is a trademark of General Mills, licensed to Nestlé for use in the United States. The Skinny Cow, Frosty Paws, Nestlé Drumstick, and Edy's are trademarks owned by Société des Produits Nestlé S.A., Vevey, Switzerland. Ben and Jerry's is a trademark of Ben and Jerry's Homemade Holdings Inc.

Appendix 1

Most Popular Ice Cream Flavors by Percentage

Ice Cream Flavor Percentage

Vanilla 26.0
Chocolate 12.9
Neapolitan 4.8
Strawberry 4.3
Cookie N' Cream 4.0
Chocolate Chip 3.8
Butter-Pecan 3.2
Chocolate Mint 3.2
Vanilla and Chocolate 1.9
Rocky Road 1.6

Source: International Dairy Foods Association. *IBISWorld Industry Report, Ice Cream Production in the US: 31152,* 13 February 2008, p. 9

Appendix 2

The HD_HB Campaign

The Campaign Logo

The Package Logo

Häagen-Dazs loves Honey Bees

Source: helpthehoneybees.com

Appendix 3

Related Web Sites

www.haagen-dazs.com
www.helpthehoneybees.com
www.dreyersinc.com
www.benandjerrys.com

CASE
10

Hallmark Gold Crown Card Program

Member Relations Challenges in a Relationship Industry

CARLA JOHNSON
St. Mary's College

MONLE LEE
Indiana University

SUSAN SEYMOUR
Webster University

During a focus group discussion, a Hallmark Gold Crown Card program member described herself as "one of the last nice people left in this world" because she regularly remembers others with greeting card messages. Indeed, the company's philosophy is to create "products that help people capture their emotions and share them with one another" and seek "to honor and serve what is universal to the human heart: the need to love and be loved, to be understood and to understand, to sustain hope, to celebrate, to laugh, to heal."[1] Hallmark is in a rare business: "We help bring people together, make them happy, and give them ways to show how much they care."

Operating under its philosophy to "bring people together," Hallmark launched *The Very Best* direct marketing program and the *Gold Crown Card* consumer loyalty program, responding to challenges to its retail stores posed by alternative channels of greeting card distribution and aggressive, competitive card discounts. Three years later, the loyalty program had enrolled 17 million permanent card members. Hallmark Gold Crown Card manager Elizabeth Murphy felt that the program was "nearing that point where we're not fighting that hard for enrollment." Instead, she found herself faced with new issues: how to maintain the loyalty program's freshness, to keep its members involved, and to reactivate members who were currently inactive.

---

[1] Hallmark Homepage: http://www.hallmark.com/ourcompany_bin/ourcompany.asp.

Cindy Jeffries, Manager of Advertising–Hallmark Brand, described the customer life cycle as "acquire, assimilate, cultivate, and reactivate." Since the Gold Crown Card program was now in the final, cultivation and reactivation stage of this cycle, its initiatives had to deal with problems peculiar to this phase. As Jeffries put it, how do you make a program "build and grow once you've reached critical mass?"

Industry Background

Greeting cards evolved from the Victorian picture postcard fad. The birth of the modern-day greeting card industry and the history of Hallmark Cards, Inc., are synonymous. Messages of congratulations and good cheer have been exchanged for centuries, but not until recent times have they taken the form of greeting cards. More than anyone else, Joyce C. Hall, founder of Hallmark, is regarded as the architect of the modern-day greeting card industry. Hall founded Hall Brothers in 1910 when he arrived in Kansas City, Missouri, to expand his postcard wholesaling business. The "Hallmark" brand name first appeared in 1928. Today, Hallmark is a multibillion-dollar corporation, a worldwide organization with international headquarters in Kansas City.

Consumers recognize the symbolic and tangible benefits of greeting cards as: 1) a means to express feelings; 2) a reflection of caring by virtue of the effort involved in getting, signing, and sending; 3) a physical item to be saved; 4) a way to add to a special occasion.

Since the greeting card industry was built on relationships, it was appropriate for Hallmark to bring card buyers together in a continuity program that felt like a "club," which members said was the case with the Gold Crown Card program. Customer relationships, Jeffries said, "are evolutionary, not an event." According to the Greeting Card Association (GCA) Industry Fact Sheet, the near-universal desire to nurture relationships among women, who purchased approximately 85 to 90 percent of all greeting cards, had led consumers to purchase over 6.6 billion greeting cards yearly, with over $7 billion in annual retail sales. The size of the industry testified to the fact that relationships continue to be one of the most important aspects of people's lives. Greeting cards allowed people to fulfill a basic need to stay in touch and connected with others.

The GCA Industry Fact Sheet estimated that there were more than 1,500 greeting card publishers in the U.S. serving the average person, who purchased 30 cards per year, eight of which were birthday cards. In 1942, the first year of the GCA's existence, total greeting card sales were $43 million (wholesale). U.S. retail sales reached $2.1 billion less than 40 years later, and continued to climb dramatically in the decades to follow.

According to the GCA, everyday cards for occasions that occur evenly throughout the year, like birthdays and anniversaries, represented 49 percent of the category dollars. Seasonal cards made up 51 percent of total category dollars and included major and minor holidays. Christmas (47 percent), Valentine's Day (16 percent), Mother's Day (13 percent), Easter (8 percent), and Father's Day (7 percent) represented over 90 percent of seasonal dollar volume. However, consumers have felt somewhat less inclined to purchase cards during holidays than in the past.

Over the past decade, seasonal card unit volume had declined while everyday unit volume had remained flat.

Greeting cards were sold through various channels of distribution, such as card/specialty (card shops), department stores, drug stores, general merchandise stores, and food stores. Over 50 percent of all cards were purchased in mass channels, and this proportion had been growing for more than a decade. Fueling this growth were time deprivation (the need for convenience and one-stop shopping), perceived price/value associated with mass channels, and an increasing number of mass channel stores with increased card selection.

Prices had increased faster than the rate of inflation over the past 15 years. However, as consumers had resisted higher prices, greeting card price increases had begun to slow, approaching key thresholds ($2 and $3 at retail).

Brands and Products

Over three-quarters of greeting card buyers preferred Hallmark. They saw Hallmark's personality as wholesome, caring, traditional, tasteful, dependable, and friendly, consistent with the brand's long-time slogan, "When you care enough to send the very best." Hallmark's Claire Brand characterized her company's strengths as "emotion, creativity, and relationships."

Through decades of consumer marketing and advertising, Hallmark had created one of the strongest brands in the U.S. National print ads started in 1928 and, in 1938, Hallmark sponsored a national radio program. Since 1951, the award-winning dramatic series "Hallmark Hall of Fame" had addressed social issues and employed legendary talent, greatly enhancing consumer awareness and associating Hallmark with quality. Ongoing television advertising had played an increased role since the late 1970s.

Hallmark marketed products under the flagship "Hallmark" brand, Hallmark Gold Crown, the Ambassador brand, and Expressions From Hallmark brand. Other card and product lines included Hallmark Connections™ technology-based products, Hallmark Keepsake Ornaments, Party Express party products, and Shoebox Greetings humor cards. In addition, the company provided greeting cards and specialty items for a diverse range of consumers through its Ethnic Personal Expression products, which included the Mahogany line for African-Americans, Tree of Life for Jewish consumers, and Primor for American Hispanics. The Hallmark Business Expressions™ line targeted corporations and other business organizations.

Competition in the Greeting Card Industry

Consumers purchased over 6.6 billion greeting cards in a recent year—representing over $7 billion in retail sales. There were two major players in the industry: Hallmark Cards, Inc., and American Greetings Corporation. Hallmark was the undisputed industry leader with $3.6 billion in sales and a 44 percent share of domestic greeting card sales. American Greetings was the number two player with $1.7 billion in sales, a 6.7 percent annual growth rate, and a 30 percent share of domestic greeting card sales. The two major brands had been gaining share over the past five years at the expense of smaller brands, including number three Gibson Greetings (with a 5 percent

EXHIBIT C10.1: ANNUAL SALES AND MARKET SHARE IN GREETING CARD INDUSTRY

Company	Sales	Market Share
Hallmark	$3.6 billion	44%
American Greetings	$1.7 billion	30%
Gibson Greetings	$546 million	10%

annual growth rate expected in the coming years). These three competitors made up about 80 percent of industry sales.

Hallmark and American Greetings had distinctly different marketing philosophies. Hallmark employed a consumer-focused "pull" strategy for its primary brands (Hallmark and Expressions From Hallmark) that featured strong consumer advertising and communications. The consumer preference strategy had the added benefit of making Hallmark-branded products more attractive for retailers who value strong brands. On the other hand, American Greetings had a trade-focused "push" strategy, offering lucrative trade terms of sale (price discounts) rather than consumer advertising. In fact, one of their messages to the trade was that "brands don't matter" to the consumer. To avoid direct competition with its two major competitors, number three Gibson aimed to be the leading discount brand ("Premium products at less than premium price"). The company concentrated on licensing, although Hallmark had rights to 16 of the top 19 licensed properties. Gibson's products were sold mostly in food and deep discount stores. The remainder of the greeting card industry was made up of scores of small greeting card companies with a total dollar market share of about 20 percent. They primarily targeted a specific segment of the population or reflected a distinct "niche" design style.

Situation Analysis

During the past decade, the overall industry had remained relatively flat in terms of unit sales while growing in dollar volume due to increasing greeting card prices. With Hallmark's leadership, card price increases had begun to slow in the past two years as consumers resisted higher card prices and as many card prices approached key price thresholds ($2 and $3 at retail).

According to Elizabeth Murphy of Hallmark, greeting card specialty retailers faced two key challenges in the early 1990s. First, greeting cards were sold in a rapidly increasing number of retail and non-retail outlets, including mail order catalogs and even car washes and gas stations. Mass retailers, such as food, chain drug, and discount department stores, were expanding their greeting card departments as a result of the category's strong profit contribution. Although an outlet might also offer limited sections of other, smaller "niche" brands, primarily there was only one major brand per outlet. Therefore, consumer brand purchase might be based on whatever brand the consumer's favorite store carried, and the consumer might settle on the cards available at the most convenient store at any given time.

Second, in response to escalating negative consumer price perceptions, many mass retailers (especially deep-discount department and drug stores as well as mail order channels) had begun to advertise aggressive discounts on greeting cards. Additionally, a new channel of distribution—the deep-discount card shop—was launched and began expanding rapidly within key greeting card markets.

As a result, the card specialty channel began to lose market share to competitive channels of distribution, especially among the industry's heaviest users. According to research, over 50 percent of all greeting cards were purchased in mass channels, and this proportion had been growing throughout the past decade. Increasingly busy consumers perceived these alternative channels of distribution as not only satisfactory but also more convenient than the traditional card specialty stores primarily located in malls and strip centers.

The Very Best

To combat the market share shift from specialty card stores to deep-discount stores, Hallmark had launched *The Very Best* direct marketing program on behalf of the Hallmark specialty retail network, comprised mostly of independently owned card shops. A quarterly newsletter was sent to consumers who identified themselves on promotional name generation forms as heavy greeting card users who purchased the majority of their cards in specialty stores. The program also featured special offers, gifts, and informational mailings intended to drive traffic to participating stores. As a result, Hallmark's card specialty stores regained market share that had been lost to mass channels of distribution.

The Gold Crown Program

After two years of existence, *The Very Best* program was becoming less effective as its novelty started to diminish. At the same time, the following opportunities emerged: 1) the widespread dispersal of a POS (Point of Sale) system designed to collect more detailed consumer-level sales data enabled Hallmark to begin defining—and rewarding—shoppers using actual versus self-reported purchase data; and 2) approximately 5,000 card specialty stores had attained Hallmark Gold Crown status by meeting or exceeding sales and service benchmarks that had, historically, been a trade versus consumer distinction. As a result, Hallmark initiated a major, long-term consumer advertising campaign to market the Hallmark Gold Crown Store retail brand.

The Hallmark Gold Crown program worked this way:

1. Members enrolled at any Hallmark Gold Crown store by supplying their name, address, phone number, and birth date. They could begin earning points immediately using a temporary membership card included in the enrollment materials. Once members earned at least 100 points, they were issued a personalized plastic membership card.
2. Members earned points for every dollar they spent on greeting cards and related products at Hallmark Gold Crown stores, plus additional points for every card they bought. Members could also take advantage of periodic bonus offers, which awarded extra points for shopping during a specific time period, purchasing specific types of products, or reaching target spending levels.

3. Points converted to certificates redeemable at Hallmark Gold Crown stores for regularly priced Hallmark products. Certificates were sent in quarterly statement mailings, which also included point statements, newsletters, and information about upcoming bonus offers.

Currently, Gold Crown Card purchases represented over 30 percent of Hallmark Gold Crown Store transactions and 40 percent of Hallmark Gold Crown Store dollar sales. Once they became members, customers visited the store more often and purchased more greeting cards than they did before, leading to significant card specialty market share increases among participating households. Gold Crown Card members spent over 50 percent more per trip than other shoppers.

Customer Demographics

According to *American Demographics,* "Women don't need much prompting to buy more cards."[2] However, women "are a complex segment that can't be marketed to as a single unit," says Judith Langer, a market research company president. "They're a growing segment. Both the number of working women and their purchasing power are increasing."[3]

While women constituted as many as 90 percent of card buyers, *American Demographics* segmented card buyers by age: "Empty-nesters aged 55 and older spend 27 percent more than the average household on cards . . . Couples aged 35 to 54 who don't have kids at home spend 6 percent more than expected. Most of these people have children and grandchildren who live elsewhere, which is probably why they are in the market for lots of cards. . . . couples with any children under age 18 living at home are only average in their card-buying behavior."[4] In general, men and children didn't buy cards. The least card-conscious demographic, singles under age 35, spent 21 percent less than their household share on greeting cards, according to A. C. Nielsen.

In an attempt to appeal to these "reluctant young adults," American Greetings targeted the "technologically gifted" through interactive kiosks. But targeting women was far more common among greeting card manufacturers.

Elizabeth Murphy saw the Gold Crown program member in more personal terms, "defined more by attitude or role. These women have stretched wallets, stretched schedules. More of them are working. They value connecting with family and friends. They're relationship-oriented people who keep emotional ties with those in their lives." She described Gold Crown program members as "busy, vital women with a lot going on, yet who find it important to find time to be 'one of the last nice people left in the world' through sending cards."

Murphy employed "club style" communication with her members. The effort to foster a sense of belonging to a club seemed to be successful: in focus groups conducted by Hallmark, Gold Crown card members often referred to being part of the Gold Crown "club." Focus groups provided consumer feedback, allowing Murphy to "listen" to her members.

---

[2] Marcia Mogelonsky, "Say It with Cards," *American Demographics,* February 1996.

[3] Gerry Myers, "Reaching the Professional Woman," *DM News,* March 28, 1994, p. 50.

[4] Marcia Mogelonsky, "Say It with Cards," *American Demographics,* February 1996.

The Problem Solvers

One of the first companies to offer employee coffee breaks in 1935, Hallmark had twice ranked in the top ten among 100 Best Companies to Work for in America, and also was in *Fortune* magazine's 100 Best in America. The company had been named to *Working Mother* magazine's Top 25 Companies for Women for twelve consecutive years, and appeared on the magazine's list of 100 best companies. It also received the *Personnel Journal* Optimas award for a proactive approach to employees' quality of life. Hallmark had a creative staff of 740 artists, designers, stylists, writers, editors, and photographers, one of the largest creative staffs in the world.

Elizabeth Murphy exemplified the loyalty that characterized Hallmark employees. Recruited "straight from" her undergraduate marketing degree, Murphy had been at Hallmark ever since. She started in product development, and now devoted 100 percent of her time to the Gold Crown Card. She works closely with the database, research, and production managers, as well as Cindy Jeffries, Manager of Advertising– Hallmark Brand. Jeffries, a double major in business and communication at Southwest Missouri State University, spent over seven years working for a Kansas City retailer before coming to Hallmark in the late 1980s. An advertising specialist, Jeffries worked "with all the media (from TV to print to database) to create an integrated communication message." The importance of integrated marketing communication at Hallmark was evident in the focus on listening to the consumer and, wherever possible, creating a dialogue with the consumer.

Current Approaches to the Problem

Hallmark was challenged to keep the Gold Crown Card program exciting and relevant, especially among members who had been enrolled since the launch of the program, who also tended to be the highest spenders. To maintain the Gold Crown Card program's freshness, to keep members involved, and to reactivate currently inactive members, Hallmark took the following actions.

To combat "loyalty fatigue," Hallmark launched a *Preferred* membership level to demonstrate appreciation to the best customers, roughly 10 percent of the database. Due to significant similarities between the Gold Crown Card *Preferred* membership level and *The Very Best* direct marketing program, *The Very Best* was transitioned into the Gold Crown Card program when the *Preferred* membership debuted. *Preferred* members enjoyed special benefits, such as a richer reward structure, exclusive mailings, special gifts and offers, and priority customer service.

The focus for the first few years of the Gold Crown Card program had been membership growth. In fact, the 15 million members acquired in the first three years exceeded expectations. Over two-thirds of members had used their card at least once in the last year. As the program matured, focus shifted to maximizing the productivity of the membership base. Reactivation efforts focused on predictive modeling to better target inactive members. The model was based on recency, frequency, and monetary value information available in the Gold Crown Card database. Data was gathered from all Hallmark Gold Crown stores. From this information, Hallmark calculated membership profitability and projected future purchase behavior.

EXHIBIT C10.2: TYPES OF SECONDARY DATA

Internal	External
* Customer name and location	* Census data
* Sales invoices/information	* Profiling customers
* Amount spent	* Industry product sales and market share
* Customer complaints	* Demographic data
* Service records	* Consumer behavior data
* Promotion history	* Lifestyle data

Internal Data

The following basic data was received from Hallmark Gold Crown stores for each Gold Crown Card transaction: the date, the store number, the dollar amount, the number of cards purchased, and any bonus offers to which the member responded. Additionally, over half of the stores identified which Hallmark stock keeping units (SKUs) were purchased in the transaction. Stores had to be equipped with POS registers in order to record the SKU numbers.

Data was accessed on a daily basis. Standard reporting occurred on a weekly basis. These reports included weekly, yearly, and program-to-date program stats, e.g., how many members used their card, what their average spending had been, dollar volumes, transaction volumes, etc. This information was used to determine which members should receive upcoming mailings, what bonus offers should be targeted to them, and so on. Membership segmentation had been an ongoing process dependent upon the database. "I want to see what they [members] like and give them more of what they like," Elizabeth Murphy explained. The "passionate ornament collectors," those with product affinities, and the "brand loyal" were segmented.

External Data

Elizabeth Murphy categorized behavioral data as "by far the most useful predictor of profitability and responsiveness, so we don't keep much external data at all. In terms of demographic information, our internal database has pretty much just the bare minimum we need to communicate with our members and reward them."

Use of Database Segmentation in Direct Mailings

Overall, member segmentation incorporated internal and external factors on the database, but was based primarily on dollars and product affinities. However, for more targeted mailings, Murphy relied on other attributes: "For instance, for our in-activity mailings, we rely heavily on recency/frequency. For our seasonal mailings, we rely on seasonality. For product-specific mailings (e.g., ornaments), we rely on product information. The one variable that we don't really use is ethnicity, since we do not capture this on the database. Although, long term we see an opportunity to identify members who have purchased our ethnic product lines and market to them more specifically."

Direct Mailings

Direct mail was Hallmark's primary channel of communication with its Gold Crown Card members. Standard mailings included an initial mail-in enrollment form distributed by retailers; periodic Point Statement mailings, which included reward certificates and information about special offers; Preferred Member Status mailings, if a customer had achieved that status, which included a Preferred Member newsletter; a "Welcome" packet, which included the Gold Crown Card and a Member Guide; and the Hallmark Gold Crown catalog mailed to customers of participating stores (in order to participate, the retailer paid a per-catalog price for each catalog mailed on behalf of the store to its Gold Crown Card members).

Two special mailings had been tested recently to try to reactivate inactive members. These reactivation mailings included an Inactive Member Holiday Postcard and an Inactive Member Holiday Statement. A special holiday mailing was also sent to Preferred Members.

Decisions

At Hallmark, in the company's tradition of observing the seasonal holiday, offices were decorated for Easter. In the spirit of springtime freshness and renewal, Elizabeth Murphy turned to decisions she had to make about the Gold Crown Card program. The Christmas holiday mailings to one million preferred members, the inactive member postcard to 10,000, and the inactive member holiday statement to 773,000 resulted in a 7 percent response rate from preferred and 1 percent from inactive members. The cost of reactivation and retention mailings was $350 per thousand package cost.[5] With this and the program's goals in mind, she found herself faced with the following strategic and creative decisions.

Direct Mail

Are the direct mail pieces effective in terms of the offer? In terms of relevance to the audience segments? In maintaining member relationships and building a member "community?" Should future packages be designed utilizing new customer knowledge available from the database?

Segmentation

Ten million cardholders used the card in the most recent year. Almost all of these cardholders could be considered "heavy users" within the greeting card category. The company had also identified 1.5 million super-heavy users—the Preferred customers. To what extent should specific marketing efforts be directed at heavy and super-heavy users? A database consultant said of *The Very Best* customers, "The customer should not be bombarded with marketing programs. . . . Spend our marketing dollars on the middle three quintiles; encourage them to move up, to get into Gold Heaven." Should this approach also apply to the Gold Crown Card members? Could the database be

---

[5] Figures for cost of mailings and response rates are estimated from direct marketing industry research and in no way reflect the actual Hallmark figures.

segmented further? If so, what information, in addition to the purchase data collected in the POS database, might be necessary to identify additional segments?

Loyalty

The Gold Crown Card program based loyalty primarily on "promotional currency" in which members earned points, bonus points, and reward certificates to apply toward future purchases. Is this too "mercenary" for such an emotional product category? Many loyalty programs have two main components: reward and recognition. How could Hallmark incorporate recognition into the program?

Reactivation

Five million cardholders did not use their cards in the previous year. Should the company continue to commit resources—time, talent, dollars—to reactivate these members since they did not contribute to profits? Based on the type of information available in the database, what could the company learn about its active versus inactive members? In addition to information already housed on the database, what other types of information might the company need to gather in order to better target the different categories of members?

Hallmark believed it should give its best offers to its best customers. To what extent should price incentives be used to reactivate members? What other incentives might it offer inactive members while still reserving its best offers for its best customers? What type of offer would be most meaningful to the "fallen away?"

Murphy was ever mindful that the decisions she made involved her program's long-term relationship with its members, nice people who regularly remember others and "Care enough to send the very best."

CASE
11

ING Direct Cafés

STACY NEIER
Loyola University

BLODWEN TARTER
Golden Gate University

DEBRA ZAHAY
Northern Illinois University

Juan ordered his usual small cup of Peet's coffee at the ING Direct Café in Chicago, close to Loyola University, from which he was about to graduate. Jessica, his friend since they met in their freshman dorm, joined him for her standard cappuccino. They were there for the inexpensive, savory coffee, free Internet access, and a low-cost pastry, whiling away time before their next class. Ostensibly, they were brainstorming about a final project for their direct marketing class; one of the last assignments due before graduation.

The two friends also were enjoying one of their last visits to a place they had frequented in recent years. As Juan waited in line, he looked out over the sleek and cheerful setting. To his right were tables and chairs, where café customers with laptop computers lingered over coffee and skimmed the *Wall Street Journal* and London *Financial Times*, financial newspapers provided for café visitors free of charge. Nearby, a bookshelf exhibited copies of *The Orange Code*, by the CEO of ING Direct USA. The decor was minimal, accented with ING Direct's trademark color, orange. Several computer kiosks were available for those who wanted to sign up immediately for ING Direct accounts. To Juan's left was a large room with classroom seating where several of his classes had met, and where he had attended an ING seminar on how to manage personal finances. There was another area set aside for private meetings with ING's prospective customers.

Not surprisingly, Juan and Jessica were chatting about their post-graduation futures, procrastinating on the project. It was easy to be distracted. The café was filled with other students and flat screen televisions broadcasting news and updates on the financial markets. Caffeine was flowing fast and furious, fueling debates about the various job offers everyone was hoping for, and a few had received, as well as the merits of graduate school versus a "real job." Juan wondered if ING Direct actually made money on the café, since most people were not opening accounts or checking their online bank accounts.

But now it was time to get down to business and focus on that team project. What would Juan and Jessica do for their direct marketing class? They looked through their class notes and, staring into space, tossed around a number of ideas; none of which really appealed to either of them. Surely, the ING Direct Café could provide some inspiration?

Jessica's face brightened as she paged through the photos she had posted online of their spring break trip to New York City. Of course, they had been serious tourists: visiting the Metropolitan Museum of Art, walking through Central Park, staring at the constellations painted on the ceiling of Grand Central Station. But they also had visited a more familiar place, the New York ING café, at 58th and Third Avenue. When they arrived on a Friday morning, it had been quieter than their Chicago experience. Sure, there were several people there. The coffee was just as good—and a great value in a very expensive city. Getting strong, flavorful coffee for $2 proved to be surprisingly welcome. It entitled them to 45 minutes of free Internet time on one of the 11 terminals arranged around the side and end of the second-floor loft. The couches were comfortable, the large screen monitors on both floors were filled with the changing financial and world news, and the view of the passersby was intriguing. Frankly, it was bit of an oasis in the hustle and bustle of New York City.

There were a number of events scheduled in the early evening for the coming week that sounded interesting, although they were scheduled to take place after Juan and Jessica returned home from New York. Neither Juan nor Jessica had been paying much attention to the financial topics for which the Chicago café had been hosting workshops. In New York, being away from their normal environment and thinking about graduation made them reflect more about their financial futures. After all, they hoped for jobs with salaries, health insurance, 401Ks, and some income to save or invest—and they knew they would soon have to begin repaying their student loans. Maybe it was about time to pay attention to the messages quietly pervading the ING Direct cafés. Maybe one of them should open a savings account or a free checking account? Maybe they should learn more about ING Direct's online services now, so they could be ready when those regular paychecks began to arrive.

These musings gave Jessica an idea about an even more immediate need . . . that direct marketing project. Why not evaluate ING Direct's marketing approach and the role of its much-used cafés? After all, neither Juan nor Jessica had yet become ING Direct customers for anything other than coffee and pastry. (Well, Juan had bought an ING-orange colored environmentally-correct coffee cup in the Chicago café, which he used every day for his coffee there.) Did that mean that Juan and Jessica weren't the target market for ING Direct or that the messages weren't effective, or what? Jessica turned to Juan and suggested that they explore the topic and see what they could learn. The idea certainly had its appeal: they both liked the ING Direct café, they knew plenty of students who used it, they could work with something they knew—and the café staff was both friendly and helpful.

Where should they start? It seemed like a good idea first to fill in the gaps in their understanding of online banking, which was ING Direct's main offer, and then to review ING Direct's current marketing practices.

Online Banking Overview

Online banking started in 1995, shortly after the introduction of the first graphical user interface browser, Mosaic, and the commercial introduction of the World Wide Web. Innovative banks quickly realized that entering the online banking arena early might result in larger market share and a well-deserved reputation for being cutting-edge while serving the needs of technically-savvy customers, both individual consumers and businesses. Internet banking had subsequently evolved into a service online that provided most banking transactions at the time customers wanted it, conveniently at any place with Internet access. Over time, this meant personal computers, smart phone, or internet-enabled personal digital assistants (PDAs) could be used as well.

At first, online banking had grown slowly, as people needed to first adopt the Internet and then become comfortable with the idea of conducting banking electronically. Concerns about data security and a general preference for having a more personal experience when it came to money needed to be overcome. Now, however, online banking was a well-established practice. According to Comscore, more than 58 million people had visited online banking sites in the previous year.[1] The Pew Internet *Usage Over Time Report* detailed impressive growth.[2]

TABLE C11.1

DATE	% of US Internet Users who "do online banking"
March 2000	17%
June 2003	34%
November 2004	44%
April 2009	57%

Juan and Jessica were surprised to learn that Gen X was the most likely group to bank online with 67% of that group banking online.[3] They had assumed that Gen Y, their age group, would be the heaviest users of *anything* online. What was going on here?

They also found it intriguing that there were several different approaches to online banking. The most common approach was for an existing bank, often with many physical branch locations, to simply add an electronic component for serving its customers. Customers could visit a local branch, call a central service group and get assistance on the phone, or go online to open accounts, get information, and do a wide variety of banking activities: check balances, pay bills, transfer funds, etc. The specifics varied by bank.

---

[1] comScore, Inc. *The 2010 State of Online Banking Report*, 10 May 2010, accessed 24 May 2010 at http://www.comscore.com/Press_Events/Presentations_Whitepapers/2010/The_2010_State_of_Online_Banking_Report/(language)/eng-US

[2] Pew Internet *Usage Over Time*, 15 July 2009, Excel spreadsheet at http://www.pewinternet.org/Static-Pages/Trend-Data/Usage-Over-Time.aspx accessed 24 May 2010

[3] Pew Internet *Generations Online in 2009*, 28 January 2009, http://www.pewinternet.org/Reports/2009/Generations-Online-in-2009.aspx accessed 24 May 2010

In contrast, there were now a small number of "online only" banks. These banks had little or no physical presence and depended almost entirely upon the Internet, postal mail, and the telephone to deliver services and build relationships. A number of these "pure-play" banks sprang into being in the early days of the World Wide Web, but most had now gone out of business. Only a few remained and they were definitely a minority. ING Direct was one of these unique "online only" banks, but with a difference. It had a different philosophy. ING had neither traditional bank branches nor typical cyber cafes.

ING Direct USA Overview

In 1997, Arkahdi Kuhlmann led the opening of ING Direct in Canada with a single product: a savings account. A unit of Internationale Nederlanden Group (or ING Groep N.V.), ING Direct, a "branchless bank," was founded on the principles described in *The Orange Code* (See Appendix A.) By 2000, the Canadian operation was profitable: it had $2.75 billion in assets and 300,000 customers.[4] This success in Canada meant ING Direct was ready to expand to the United States. By 2002, ING Direct in the US was profitable (two years ahead of plan) and had over $8 billion in assets.[5] In 2004, it was the 42nd-largest bank in the US as defined by deposits ($19 billion) with 1.5 million customers.[6] Jessica and Juan learned that, at the end of 2008, ING Direct was ranked 17th in the US with $71.8 billion in deposits.[7] In May 2010, the company web site reported 7.5 million customers in the US.[8] The direct-to-consumer banking model had quickly become a star entity of the ING Group parent company.

1. No product proliferation: limited offerings, simple for the customer and the bank
2. Value for money proposition
3. Superior customer service
4. Low cost delivery: efficient back office for high volume and direct ("branchless") service delivery

Initially entering the US with just two products, high-interest savings accounts and certificates of deposit, the ING Direct offering had now expanded to include

---

[4] Silcoff, Sean. "Dutch (re)tread: Maverick Arkadi Kuhlmann built ING Direct and rattled the big Canadian banks. Now he wants to do the same in the US, if only his bosses would let him. *Canadian Business*, 21 August 2000, volume 73, Issue 15, page 42. Accessed via ProQuest 29 April 2010.

[5] Billis, Steve. "Online Banking: Good Start for ING Direct, But Can it Last?; With a handful of Internet cafes tossed in, the company is pushing standard thrift banking products in cyberspace." *Bank Technology News*. June 2002, Volume 15, Issue 6, page 37, accessed via ProQuest 29 April 2010.

[6] Swibel, Matthew. "Where Money Doesn't Talk." *Forbes*. 24 May 2004, Volume 173, Issue 11, page 176. Accessed via ProQuest 29 April 2010.

[7] Reported by the website Online Financial Innovations at http://www.onlinebankingreport.com/resources/100.html as of 30 May 2010. Source credited: American Banker.

[8] http://home.ingdirect.com/about/about.asp accessed 30 May 2010.

residential mortgages, checking accounts, and online brokerage. The focus on efficiency and simplicity remained unchanged and ING Direct continued to acquire new customers.

The company had a simple and efficient web site, www.ingdirect.com. It attracted prospects via a variety of integrated marketing techniques. Direct mail, online banner advertising and paid search marketing played important roles, with easily measurable outcomes. Television commercials and event sponsorships created awareness. Outdoor advertising rounded out the menu. Jessica and Juan found that they could review many examples on the ING Direct web site itself and on video-sharing sites such as YouTube. ING Direct even had sponsored a Direct Marketing Educational Foundation collegiate ECHO competition several years ago, asking students to create a compelling direct marketing campaign for the bank focused on acquiring mortgage or savings account customers.

Existing customers were asked to opt-in to receive email messages regularly, and ING Direct reported that 25% of its customers had done so.[9] ING Direct encouraged the use of Twitter and Facebook for its customers and prospects, attempting to leverage the evolving marketing capabilities of social networking and micro-blogging.

ING Direct Cafés

ING Direct's stated purpose on its web site was to "bring Americans back to savings." Kuhlmann also sought to keep banking as "simple as having a cup of coffee," and realized that not everyone was comfortable sharing personal details online to open an account. Accordingly, a limited number of ING Direct cafés were created. Instead of reading about ING Direct's value propositions online, the café employees shared the benefits of being an "orange saver" in person. Over time, cafés were opened in prime locations in New York, Los Angeles, Chicago, St. Cloud (Minnesota), Wilmington (Delaware), Honolulu, and Philadelphia.

In-store signage communicated the ING Direct message of seeking financial independence. Brochures described the Declaration of Financial Independence which café customers were encouraged to sign, either physically on an in-café copy or virtually online. From time to time, the Financial Independence microsite was highlighted at the cash registers along with other specials.

At one point, a popular Chicago café promotion to inspire customers to "be orange" offered a free beverage for anyone who entered the café wearing orange on Fridays. This offer was available both for those customers who were ING Direct account holders and for those who were just visiting the café. Later, the promotion was changed to a Friday special for Electric Orange Checking account holders, where account holders showed their debit cards to receive a complimentary beverage of choice. Eventually, the café switched to daily specials available only to account holders.

The cafés also actively hosted in-café seminars related to savings and financial independence. The events were communicated through in-store signage and links within the ING Direct café web pages. Attendees were encouraged to RSVP through a

---

[9] Engen, John. "Web Banking: Europe's ING Direct Bucks US Tradition," *Bank Technology News*, December 2005, volume 18, issue 12, page 38 accessed via ProQuest 29 April 2010.

link on the web site and then to check in at a welcome table staffed by café employees. Often, a complimentary gift was offered to attendees. Gifts had included a copy of *The Orange Code* book and complimentary drink vouchers for future café visits.

The café staff often sent out invitations to events via email to its community, but this personalized email invitation effort was not necessarily directed at account holders. For example, the Café coordinator of the event might send an e-mail to a faculty member of a nearby campus inviting them to forward the invitation to interested students.

Based on an informal survey conducted among their friends and acquaintances who had become ING Direct customers, Jessica and Juan learned that opening an account through the ING Direct web site was quite easy. At their local ING Direct café, opening an account took no more than 30 minutes with the assistance of a café staff member. The staff member escorted the prospective customer into a private, glass-enclosed space where the staff member input standard information into a desktop computer and explained the new account features and benefits. Or, café staff used an orange laptop to bring the account opening process direct to the café floor. Once a customer had opted-in to receive email, email offers with promotions for complementary products were received approximately once a month.

The Decision Problem

This brought Jessica and Juan back to their original musings. How could they use the ING Direct café for their current direct marketing assignment?

While they admired ING Direct's success and they loved the comfort and convenience of their local ING Direct café, they felt that there were some missed opportunities for increasing the number of people to whom the local café and the parent company could market the ING Direct products, and with whom relationships could be built. After all, they were regular café visitors but they had not yet become customers. Nor did they feel that they were individually targeted with appropriate messages outside of the café itself. How could ING Direct use the café retail environment and the café community to build its database and to acquire new customers?

As Jessica and Juan thought about the situation further, they wondered more fundamentally how the cafés fit into the overall ING Direct strategy. Were the cafés really useful to reinforce the brand? How could ING Direct better integrate its online presence and current marketing practices with its cafés for customer acquisition and building customer relationships? What could ING Direct do to better leverage the ING Direct cafés across the country?

With another cup of coffee in hand, Jessica and Juan sat down to brainstorm possibilities and to develop a thorough recommendation of what ING Direct should do.

Appendix A _____

The Declaration of Financial Independence[10]

We will spend less than we earn. Saving a little out of every dollar we bring home is the foundation of independence. Without it, we can't build equity in our home, we can't invest for the future, and we can't be ready for challenging times. We promise to pay ourselves first, always.

We will use our home as a savings account. Besides shelter and comfort for our family, the role of a house in our financial life is to build equity. We will have a healthy down payment when we buy. We'll choose the mortgage that lets us pay down the principal fastest. And then we'll leave that equity safe where it is instead of spending it on things that don't last.

We will take care of our money. It's not enough to have money in a bank. We will put it where it will grow. We'll keep track of it. And we'll check every account we have every year to protect ourselves against fraud or escheatment.

We will defend our credit worthiness. Good credit is going to be precious in the years to come. We will pay our bills on time. We'll borrow only when we need to and in amounts we can comfortably pay back. And then we'll do just that.

We will ignore unsolicited credit card marketing. We decide when we need a credit card, not some marketer. And mostly, we probably don't need another one at all. We won't even open those solicitations. We'll shred them.

We will know the cost of borrowing. The interest lenders charge us is real money, too. When we buy a mortgage or finance a purchase, we'll figure out what that interest is really going to cost in dollars, add it to the purchase price, and ask ourselves if it's still worth it.

We will invest for the long term. Futures are built out of patience and prudence, not luck. We will not put off being a saver because we think there's a lottery win in our future, in Vegas or on Wall Street.

We will take care of the things we have. We work hard for our money, and it's disrespectful to waste it—or the planet—by treating our possessions as disposable.

We will remember what matters. We are not the things we own. If we have to spend and spend on bigger, more impressive things to keep up with our friends, then they are not our friends at all.

We will be heard. Our representatives in government and the corporations we deal with need to know that we are paying attention. If we're silent, we're accepting the status quo, and the business practices that got our country into this situation will continue. We are not going to accept that.

_____

[10] Found at http://wethesavers.ingdirect.com/save-money-declaration/ accessed 30 May 2010.

CASE
12

J. Jill: Transforming the Customer Experience

J. Steven Kelly
DePaul University

Francey Smith
DePaul University

Régine Vanheems
Université of Paris I—Sorbonne

Introduction to J. Jill

Walter Erickson, Senior Vice-President of J. Jill, was preparing his team to go to senior management to ask for an innovative new approach to their way of doing business. Leaders at the Quincy, MA headquarters of the J. Jill Group were facing some challenges, and Mr. Erickson felt that it was time for innovation.

The image that J. Jill promotes is high-quality women's apparel, accessories and footwear characterized by natural fibers and fit for the woman whose lifestyle requires versatility in her wardrobe. According to the corporate mission statement, "Our mission is to build J. Jill into a premier national brand for women age 35 and older." At the time of the development of this case, J. Jill had developed from an operation that was catalog-only to a multichannel retailer involving the Internet (www.jjill.com), J. Jill catalog and J. Jill retail stores. It had developed marketing programs targeting women who were aged 35-55 years old, affluent, and who wore what they described as "sophisticated casual lifestyle clothing with a unique, artistic expression."

J. Jill's net sales at the end of the past fiscal year were near $350 million, with net income of approximately $18 million. It employed approximately 1,100 employees. Since 2000 J. Jill's stock price changes have been positive and kept ahead of the stock market average.

Originally a direct marketer via catalogs, it had been mailing 26 different catalog editions per year since 1996. By the end of the present year the total mailings would be over 77 million total sent to customers in domestic markets. J. Jill opened its first store in the fall of 1999 and at present had 88 stores in over 30 states. It launched its first web site that same quarter. With its stores, Internet presence, catalogs and phone center, it had opened all possible touch points to its customers and was truly a multi-channel operator.

J. Jill's promotional support has been creative and on target. For instance, recently J. Jill developed an exciting promotional program involving the singer/songwriter Alice Peacock along with a multi-faceted marketing campaign called the "Rewards Shoppers" program. The promotion, co-sponsored with Cotton Incorporated (an association of cotton producers), featured a gift-with-purchase promotion with the sale of two or more cotton items and a grand prize sweepstakes. To highlight this promotion, Peacock was hired to do a five-city music tour and in-store public appearances in a month-long campaign in early summer of the current year. Cotton items were represented by the Seal of Cotton® trademark in J. Jill's stores, catalogs and web site to promote J. Jill's support of cotton as the ideal fabric for summer apparel. Use of all three channels was considered an advantage in reaching their audience. Peacock was considered an excellent spokesperson for J. Jill because, as described by USA Today, she possessed a "warm heart, an engaged mind, and a probing conscience... (and) a sweetly sassy vocal style that invites comparisons to Shawn Colvin and Sheryl Crow." Her musical style blends folk, rock and pop. She participated in meet-and-greets with customers in J. Jill stores in Boston, San Francisco, Chicago, Denver and Minneapolis. The campaign had the objective for both J. Jill and Cotton Incorporated to look forward to breaking the mold of the tried-and-true public appearance by focusing instead on a new concept: gathering a group of like-minded women who share an appreciation for stylish, comfortable and casual living, a love of music by independent female singers and a sense of confidence. The campaign was further enhanced by private concerts, co-sponsored and promoted by local radio stations in each city, which followed the in-store gatherings.

Recognizing the value of retail stores in its revenue generation, J. Jill had taken on a dramatic policy of growing stores at the rate of about 35 per year. This could have been too much since the firm had reported a third-quarter loss of $2.9 million compared to a $3.6 million profit of a year ago. Total sales for the quarter had risen 2.9%, but the sales from the direct division had fallen 17% compared to a growth in the retail stores sales of 36%. More expensive store operations (compared to catalog and web sales) meant that margins went from 38% to 30%. Selling and general administration expenses went from 30% to 35% of sales. The operation was originally built on a catalog-only business model, and according to Gordon Cooke, President and CEO, the catalog alone could no longer support what they had been doing. It was expected that the major growth would come from stores, so there was now need for a change in merchandising and in the way J. Jill sourced and flowed products. He added this would require shifts in merchandising and execution from new core competencies and expertise.

Competitive Analysis

On top of the less-than-glowing financial news for J. Jill, the firm was in a highly competitive industry. J. Jill was confronted with a myriad of competitors for the women's apparel dollar through stores, mail order catalogs and the Internet. Needless to say, there are dozens of ways to shop available to the 35–55 affluent women who shop at J. Jill, ranging from strictly online and catalog operations to women's apparel specialty stores to full-service department stores. To refine the focus for this case, we will rely on a report from CIBC World Markets ("Baby Boomer-ang . . . ") that focused on specialty women's apparel retailers who target the Baby Boomers. Although the report states that Neiman Marcus, Bloomingdales and many other local department stores and specialty stores might capture customer attention, it highlights that over 50% of the 35–55 year-old customer with an annual income averaging $75K shop at the following stores or direct outlets: Chico's, Coldwater Creek, Talbots, J. Jill and Christopher & Banks. Obviously, the marketing team needed to attend to what these companies were doing in a market important to J. Jill.

Chico's

The CIBC report indicates that they expect Chico's to have the best chance at a major market-share gain over the next year or so. Chico's sells exclusively designed private label women's clothing and related accessories. The organization is a vertical operation, which means it controls design, manufacturing, distribution, and retail, which in turn allows greater control over margins. The company operates 571 women's specialty stores, including stores in 46 states, the District of Columbia, the Virgin Islands, and Puerto Rico, operating under the name Chico's or White House | Black Market. The Company owns 410 Chico's front-line stores, 23 Chico's outlet stores, and 126 White House | Black Market stores. The average Chico's customer is 53 years old. The operation grew from less than $80 million in annual sales five years earlier to more than $530 million this past fiscal year.

Chico's reported October sales of $68M, but direct sales were only about 3% of total on catalogs of about 35 million mailings. Chico's does not do email campaigns. J.Jill does twice the catalog mailings and is involved in email campaigns. Chico's "Passport Club" is its loyalty program, where club members receive a 5% discount for life based on a $500 initial purchase at Chico's. This Passport Club is key to getting customer information. It is used as a sales promotion tool as well as a method of cementing relationships with customers.

J. Jill perceives Chico's primarily as a retailer. Although Chico's sends catalogs to Passport Club members, the main purpose is to drive traffic to their stores and not to create mail order sales.

Talbots

Talbots was founded in 1947 near Boston. During the following year the company launched its direct mail business by distributing 3,000 black-and-white flyers to names obtained from *The New Yorker* magazine. Today, Talbots is a leading national specialty retailer, cataloger and e-tailer of classic apparel, shoes and accessories. Presently, Talbots operates about 900 stores throughout the U.S., Canada and the United Kingdom. Like J. Jill, Talbots distributes a variety of catalog editions (26) with a catalog operation circulating approximately 48 million catalogs worldwide in a recent year. Talbots online shopping site is located at www.talbots.com. Each of its three sales channels (web, catalog and store) offers classic, high-quality merchandise. Talbots has been especially mindful of its responsibility to the communities where it resides. Its over 10,000 employees are involved in community service, and it offers scholarships. It also has two telemarketing centers to handle customer calls. Talbots has managed its multichannel operation successfully by offering the same merchandise and services online as it does through its store and catalogs. Online shoppers can return purchases to any Talbot store or distribution center (Talbots web site, www.talbots.com). Talbots gets over 80% of its business from retail operations, while the remainder comes from mail order catalogs. Recently, Talbots has also created stores for men to go after some of the $50 billion a year that men pay for clothing. In addition, they have opened stores for kids, petites, accessories and shoes.

The Senior Vice-President sees Talbots and J. Jill as going after the same shopper, although the Talbots shopper leans more to classic lines rather than the trendier styles at J. Jill

Coldwater Creek

Coldwater Creek is publicly traded and expects to develop to 500 stores soon. Like J. Jill, Coldwater started out as a catalog-only operation. Coldwater Creek stores sell clothing, jewelry, accessories, shoes and gifts. Their catalog sales at the time of this case development were about $400 million. This upscale women's apparel retailer headquartered in Sandpoint, Idaho, reported a first-quarter net income increase of 35.4% in a recent year. The company announced net income of $1.9 million from $1.4 million in the year-ago period. Net sales increased 8.4% to $115.2 million from $106.2 million. At the end of the fiscal quarter, the retailer operated 44 full-line retail stores, up from 30 stores at the end of the previous fiscal quarter. Founded in 1984 as a catalog retailer, Coldwater Creek opened its first brick and mortar store in 1999. The company decided opening stores was the best way to build the brand because about 92% of sales within the $84 billion women's apparel market occur in brick-and-mortar locations.

Coldwater and J. Jill seem to have parallel business models. Starting out as catalog only, they have moved rapidly into stores after 1999 (same brick-and-mortar time frame as J. Jill).

In summary, Chico's, Coldwater Creek, Talbots and even store-only Christopher and Banks seemed to be making forward strides at the time of this writing. It was clear that J. Jill had to address some issues in order to transform the customer experience to help J. Jill make major inroads into these competitors' market share.

The Marketing Issues

Of course, simultaneously operating retail, web, and catalog channel operation created issues. The major question at J. Jill was whether the direct (online and catalog) and store operations should be merged or run separately. Needless to say, the cost of combining marketing, operations, sales and service into one system would be significant. If the divisions stayed separate, the direct marketer did not have to collect sales taxes in states where they had no store presence. The issue of developing a tax collecting and remittance system alone would take months. Moreover, delivering consistency to customers across channels while shopping would not be easy, and it would require resources and investment in appropriate technology. The implementation of "hassle-free multichannel retailing"—including participating in the same loyalty program across channels, ordering online for payment and store pick-up and returning online purchases to physical stores—would need organizational learning and time.

On the other hand, it was thought that there would be synergies that could not be obtained by running separately. A variety of synergy benefits related to reduced costs and an improved differentiation could probably be derived from interrelationships across tangible and intangible assets of the company. The synergy among channels should come from their common use of infrastructures, the implementation of common marketing policies and operations, and finally the share of their customers.

For this reason, a fundamental question became how to remove the "wall" between J. Jill's marketing and operating divisions so that it could enhance long-term customer loyalty. Financial executives were concerned about the cost involved in bringing their channels together compared to the payoff in revenue from the hoped-for enhanced customer satisfaction.

For instance, presently J. Jill's customers could not take returns of catalog purchases to the stores. Finally, there were unresolved questions about whether retail stores would "steal or cannibalize" sales from the catalog channel and whether cross channel promotions would be possible without a combined system.

The Senior Vice-President was intuitively convinced that synchronizing the channels could be a competitive edge for the company and that it would not necessarily mean "cannibalization" across channels. A cross-integration could undoubtedly be a way to improve the management of the relationship of the firm with its current customers. Creating a link among the touchpoints (store, web, catalog, and phone center) should allow the firm to understand its customers better and then develop products and services that meet their needs more accurately. It should also be an opportunity to interact more often with them and with a higher contact quality. As a consequence the company should be prepared to steadily increase the service value it delivers to its customers.

Linking channels would probably also help the firm increase the share of wallet of its present customers. The issue of developing strong relationships with the customers and enhancing their trust in the company through multiple touchpoints could certainly be an efficient means to develop cross-selling and up-selling and could be one of the most important components of an innovative new approach of doing business. Furthermore, the merger of the touchpoints should be an efficient strategy for retaining customers who value the resulting purchasing convenience. Creating some added value or new services outputs could give them fewer reasons or opportunities to switch to competitors and be more loyal. For instance, it is commonly thought that the use of the Internet or even of the catalog before purchasing easily provides extensive information while being at home, which should lead to less dissatisfaction.

The Senior Vice-President also thought that multichannel integration could provide opportunities to personalize the offer and to customize the services— that could lead to a "one-to-one" approach—what is certainly the basis for competition and competitive differentiation today. It could create "lock-in effects" as well. The company could develop services, customize communication media as well as delivery channels based on its customers' needs and service expectations.

On the other hand, the absence of consistency across channels or even conflicts among them could lead to customers' dissatisfaction and could cause a deterioration of J. Jill's image in the long range. In this case, being a multichannel operator could be a disadvantage compared to competitors with fewer channels. For example, if a customer surfs on the Internet to get information about a particular product and does not find it when visiting the store for purchase, he could actually be disappointed.

That said, the Senior Vice-President was unsure as to how to manage a multichannel company, did not exactly know how to provide added value and wasn't sure what to favor while creating consistency among channels. He would have to think it over with his management team.

Single View

The Senior Vice-President believed that in order for J. Jill to advance, he must convince senior management that the multiple channels had to be joined into one. He envisioned that J. Jill needed to develop a customer-centric organization that would create a single view of the J. Jill customer.

What did this single view mean? Data capture was essential. Presently, the retail customer information was not available to the catalog side and vice versa. Customers could be regular catalog buyers and also shop in the stores, but retail would not be aware of this. Retail customers could receive catalogs, but the frequency of their receipt (periodically or monthly or more) was not related to their *total* J. Jill experience (this is referred to as a "corporate buyer" as opposed to a buyer in a specific channel like direct or retail).

J Jill could not see their most valued customers, from a corporate standpoint, by looking at either their retail or direct databases. The J. Jill card, a proprietary card formed in partnership with a major bank, did allow J. Jill to know about the users' shopping patterns at both the store and catalog when the customer charged their purchases to the J.Jill card. However, only 30% of retail purchases came through the card, so 70% of purchases were made by shoppers that J. Jill could not track. For instance, did they receive catalogs and did they buy direct (catalog or online)?

Since it was presently impossible to identify the most valued customers, the Senior Vice-President had asked his team to do some benchmarking to collect data about multichannel retailers operating in other areas. The idea was to find an alternative way of doing business.

The resulting information was very interesting: in numerous studies, multichannel shoppers (MS) were considered the most valued customers. For instance, a study showed that over 60% of retailers claimed that their MS were more profitable than customers who used only one channel. Some earlier studies conducted by Mc Kinsey in 2000 and by Double Click in 2003 had also concluded that multichannel shoppers had a significant tendency to spend more than one-channel shoppers. Then customers who shopped across multiple channels are supposed to provide more revenues and higher share of wallet than those who shopped in one channel only. For instance, his team took the example of Staples, which noticed that customers who shopped in the store and in the catalog spent twice as much as those who shopped in the store only and those who shopped using the store, the catalog and online channels spent nearly four times as much as store-only shoppers. Even if these results were particularly interesting, the Senior Vice-President was actually not able to confirm this tendency in J. Jill since its most valued customers could not be identified. It was then not possible to understand them and make retention efforts accordingly.

Another issue was the challenge in preparing the catalog circulation plan without knowing the profile of the store-only customer. As J. Jill opened stores, catalog shoppers could be going into stores to purchase, thereby reducing or eliminating their direct purchases. If the catalog database had one million names and 30% were now buying from a store, their productivity on the catalog list would go down and if that shopper, for instance, did not buy from the catalog channel in more than one year, she would be dropped from the catalog customer database. Yet, that dropped catalog customer might be buying from a corporate standpoint, and J. Jill would not know that. That original catalog customer would receive fewer, and eventually, no catalogs.

More generally, miscellaneous questions were raised about the way the company might use its available channels to both promote and develop sales in each of them reciprocally. The opportunities could be numerous. However the lack of experience in this new business made it difficult to analyze and evaluate their possible mutual contribution (in term of image, sales, and added value . . .).

If J. Jill had a single view of its customers across all channels they would be able to: apply the data for catalog circulation; prospect for both retail and catalog customers; and apply customer's ZIP codes for retail site selection.

Prospecting for new customers for the stores is always a challenge. If a retailer has advertising dollars, valued for lower CPM (cost per thousand) than direct methods, then traditional media can be used to drive new traffic. Having a database of catalog shoppers may not be enough. The retailer's own database would give a profile of the core customer, and then they could go to "cooperative" list owners like Abacus (now a Double Click subsidiary) and Z-24 from Experian to find potential shoppers. However, these catalog shoppers may not be potential retail shoppers because it is known that catalog shoppers tend to be older than retail shoppers. So, do those names make the best customers to "drive" into the stores? Another important issue with rented lists like this is that the response rate is seldom over 2.5% and often it is below 1%. A lot of names would have to be rented to drive significant numbers to the new store locations.

On the contrary, the store should perhaps offer a way of collecting new names that could be future potential customers for the Internet or the catalog. When prospecting becomes difficult and expensive, stores could be used to bring new customers to catalogs or the Internet. Likewise, it could be interesting for the company that got new customers through expensive stores' operations to foster their switch to relatively inexpensive means of selling like the online channel, at least for some purchases. It may be a means to avoid a decrease in the margins caused by the development of stores.

Without the single view, there are retail site location analysis issues. As J. Jill began an aggressive store development campaign, as any operation would, it employed experts—in this case, retail development experts. Those professionals used standard retail site location techniques, which did not take advantage of catalog information. J. Jill had a proprietary card that its patrons used but since only about 30% of sales were generated through them, a good share of customer information was not available for store sites.

Another interesting aspect about developing a single view is that it would allow

EXHIBIT C12.1: THE CRM PROCESS

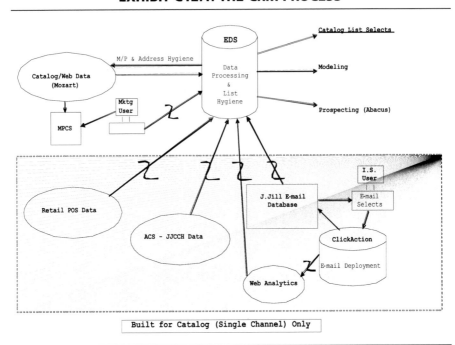

NOTE: The squiggly Z symbol on the lines connecting to the EDS database means there is "disjoint" or disconnect.

the analysis of customers' moves between and among channels in a dynamic way. As a matter of fact, if the Senior Vice-President decided to allow customers to use whatever channel or combination of channels they wanted to, the company would be able to track those customers' choices and moves between and among channels and evaluate the impact of those moves on the company's share of wallet. A common database makes it possible to measure the profitability of customer flow across channels. The purpose, of course, is to foster the most profitable flows and to implement an efficient customer flow strategy.

The Senior Vice-President felt that a single view set-up of the J. Jill customers would allow a number of important advantages. He felt that he had to make a compelling argument to senior management for why the additional cost was necessary. Exhibit C12.1 shows the database system as it now stands. It does not represent what would be considered the single view.

Several questions remain:

1. How does the Senior Vice-President make the case to implement the single view approach?
2. If you were designing the single view system, what customer data capture would be needed from the various channels and how would it change how each channel operates?

3. How would marketing under the new system change for catalog, online, and retail?
4. How can the company improve its Customer Relationship Management thanks to this single view?
5. What measures could be used to value the customer (quantifying current profitability as well as future potential value)
6. Give some examples of direct marketing actions that will probably increase the future customers' potential value.
7. How can the company manage to reinforce mutual contribution between the channels?

CASE
13

Kiln Creek Golf Club & Resort: On Par for An Integrated Marketing Communications Campaign to Acquire New Members

LISA D. SPILLER

Christopher Newport University

CAROL SCOVOTTI

University of Wisconsin-Whitewater

Jamie Connors arrived early at the golf course to play a quick nine holes before work. It was a pristine April morning—warm and sunny. The well-manicured greens sparkled as the rising sun reflected off the morning dew. He was confident that an early round would help him clear his head before tackling the mounting marketing issues affecting Kiln Creek Golf Club & Resort (hereafter referred to as KCGC&R or 'the Club'). The annual meeting with the board of directors and the Club's membership was fast approaching.

As usual, Jamie played very well. Then again, great rounds were *par for the course* for the head golf pro of the facility. He birdied the ninth hole and headed back to his office in the clubhouse. Along the way, he saw the first group of the day preparing to tee off on the first hole. He recognized two of the foursome as members who play a few times a week. "Looking good, Jamie," one of the members cheerfully exclaimed as he pointed to the lush fairway that lay before him. Jamie smiled and agreed with great pride. After all, this course was his baby. As he thanked the golfers and wished them luck, he thought of the irony of the marketing challenges he faced. The Club had a challenging, picturesque 18-hole golf course with driving range, practice putting green, chipping green, tennis courts, swimming pool, clubhouse, gourmet restaurant,

---

Some of the data provided by the company has been disguised and is not useful for research purposes. The authors would like to thank Jamie Conners for his help in this project.

day spa and inn nestled within a planned community with nearly 3,000 private homes, townhomes, condominiums and apartments. Running a facility of this quality was a golf pro's dream. Despite the quality of the facilities and its convenient location for almost 15,000 nearby residents, club memberships were down. Even with its "open to the public" policy, fewer non-members were playing individual rounds of golf. Jamie was confident that if he could persuade golfers to try the course, the experience would cause them to come back again. The problem was drawing them into the facility.

A Rochester, New York native, Jamie has considered golf both his passion and profession for his entire life. In college, he discovered he had a talent for teaching and coaching. Now a 22-year member of the PGA, Jamie's career had progressed from golf coach for a Florida-based university, to teaching pro at a country club in New York, and instructor at both ESPN Golf and Golf Digest Schools.

The opportunity at KCGC&R was his first in the leadership role. When he arrived three years ago, Jamie saw the entire resort as a diamond in the rough. Everything needed work, but he was confident that with the proper vision and management, the Club could become a thriving facility within the community. He established three priorities that the board of directors accepted. First, the entire golf program from the course itself to the clubhouse, pro shop, and cart garage, needed work. Second, all the other services and facilities needed to be upgraded and/or integrated to enhance the value of membership. Third was marketing. Jamie believed that he had to have a strong product before marketing it.

It took two years, but the first and second priorities were well on their way to being addressed. As the members on the first tee observed, the course was in great shape. The same went for the tennis courts, restaurants, pool, and day spa. What was missing were people. Despite the growing popularity of golf in the area and around the country, memberships and use of KCGC&R facilities continued to wane. Something had to be done to get this facility back on track. It was time to address Jamie's third priority—marketing. The board had been patient, but he was concerned that patience was wearing thin.

Kiln Creek Golf Club & Resort

The Kiln Creek Golf Club & Resort was established in 1991 to provide residents throughout the Hampton Roads, VA area with a recreational club with state-of-the-art amenities. The facility contained a professionally rated 18-hole golf course, pool, fitness center, tennis courts, and a day spa. The club also had a restaurant and lounge for dining and socializing with friends and neighbors as well as rooms for hosting catered events.

The Club was located in the middle of the Virginia Peninsula in Newport News, Virginia, just 30 minutes from the beach and 20 minutes from historic Williamsburg. The Newport News/ Williamsburg International Airport was just minutes away by car, making the facility an easy-to-reach destination.

In addition to all its recreational facilities, KCGC&R included a beautifully remodeled Inn and tastefully decorated restaurant, banquet and meeting rooms. It offered

"Stay-and-Play" get-away packages and hosted numerous weddings and other special parties, events and gatherings.

Since its inception, KCGC&R had hosted more than 5,000 functions. Its banquet and event facilities boasted a Grand Foyer and breathtaking views from the ballroom. Whether a meal with a couple of friends or a party for 350 people, the Club strived to provide patrons with a stress-free, memorable experience.

The facility included:

- 18 Hole, Par 72 Championship Golf Course
- Full Service Golf Pro Shop
- PGA Professional Staff
- Meeting and Banquet Facilities
- Manchester Grill—a casual dining restaurant serving breakfast, lunch and dinner
- 14-Room Hotel overlooking the Golf Course
- Outdoor Swimming Pool
- Outdoor Tennis Facility
- Day Spa
- Fitness Center

KCGC&R initiation and monthly membership fees differed according to the membership category. Membership packages varied based on the number of people joining, facilities that could be used, and where the member resided. The Club offered specific membership packages for individuals and families, residents and non-residents of the Kiln Creek community, as well as specially priced packages for other membership categories. Exhibit C13.1 details the various categories along with their associated rates and fees.

EXHIBIT C13.1: KCGC&R MEMBERSHIP CATEGORIES AND RATES

Membership Category	Initiation Fee	Monthly Dues	Food & Non-Alcoholic Beverage Minimum
Full Family Golf	$2000	$262	$30
Single Golf	$2000	$223	$30
Senior Golf Family	$2000	$223	$30
Active Military Family	$1000	$223	$30
Weekday Membership Single	$900	$168	$30
Swim/Tennis/Social	$500	$95	$30
Non-Resident Membership	$500	$65	-None-
Junior Sports	$100	$70	-None-
Corporate Membership	$5000	$620	$120

Additional services and amenities for Club members, guests and non-members included golf carts, driving range balls, locker rental and club storage. Exhibit C13.2 lists these services and amenities along with their respective fees.

EXHIBIT C13.2: ADDITIONAL KCGC&R SERVICES

18 Holes Guest Play	Monday-Thursday	Friday	Saturday-Sunday
Guest of Member	$37	$40	$48
Non-Member Public	$45	$52	$59
Cart Fees	18 holes—$17.00	9 holes—$9.00	
Driving Range Balls	Member—Free	Non-Member—$7.00	
USGA Handicap Service		$30 annually per member	
Club Cleaning & Storage		$100 annually per member	
Locker Rental		$100 annually per member	
Locker Rental and Club Storage Combined		$150 annually per member	

The products and services offered by the KCGC&R Pro Shop were consistent with other pro shops in the area and included a wide variety of clubs, accessories and clothing. The professionally trained staff at the Pro Shop offered many services to assist golfers in improving their games. In addition to private lessons, golf clinics, and junior golf camps, golf professionals offered club-fitting services. The typical $60 fee was waived with the purchase of a set of golf clubs. The Club also offered several unique packages for members that organized group golf events. Exhibit C13.3 details three available packages.

Although the Club had a variety of recreational facilities, it was first and foremost a golf resort. According to *Golf Digest*, the resort's 6,972 yard, par 72, 18-hole course was rated as one of the five best courses in Virginia. *Tee Time Magazine* recognized the course as one offering the best par 4 holes in the Mid-Atlantic region. The club had hosted the Executive Women's Golf Association two years previous, and held both amateur and professional golf tournaments on a regular basis.

The Golf Industry

Golf is referred to as the "unofficial" sport of the business world (Golf, 2005) and, up until the most recent recession, had been a thriving industry. Recent U.S. Census indicated that there were approximately 12,000 public, semi-private, and private courses across the country with combined annual revenue of about $21 billion. About 25 percent of these courses were owned by non-profit entities such as municipalities, while the vast majority were for-profit facilities. Greens fees represented the largest single source of revenue for private and semi-private courses (about 33 percent), with cart fees, golf lessons, handicapping fees, initiation fees, and pro shop product sales accounting for the remaining 67 percent (First Research, 2010). Greens fees accounted for more than 60 percent of public course revenue.

While facilities and amenities varied significantly within the industry, there were three general categories of golf courses. 'Private' referred to facilities for the exclusive use of members, and typically offered extensive ancillary facilities. 'Semi-private' offered facilities used by members as well as the general public. KCGC&R was considered a semi-private facility. Depending on the available facilities of the club, members

EXHIBIT C13.3: KCGC&R OUTING PACKAGES

Caddy Package:
- Available weekdays anytime
- 18 holes of golf with cart
- Custom-made golf cart signs with player names
- On-course contests
- Unlimited use of practice facility one hour prior to start of event
- Cash only Beverage Service on course
- Post tournament scoring by professional staff
- Par Buffet

Amateur Package:
- Available weekdays anytime, weekends after 1 p.m.
- 18 holes of golf with cart
- Custom-made golf cart signs with player names
- Professionally staffed bag drop
- On-course contests
- Unlimited use of practice facility one hour prior to start of event
- Cash or Master Bill Beverage Service on course
- Post tournament scoring by professional staff
- Create your own menu

Pro Package:
- Available any day at any time
- 18 holes of golf with cart
- Custom-made golf cart signs with player names
- Professionally staffed bag drop
- On-course contests
- Unlimited use of practice facility one hour prior to start of event
- Cash or Master Bill Beverage Service on course
- $4.00 per player in merchandise gift certificates
- "Beat the Pro" Contest (winner receives one complimentary weekend stay at the Club)
- Unique menu customized by the resort's Executive Chef

had access to amenities based on membership type, while the public typically paid a higher fee and could only play golf. 'Public' courses were open to anyone and generally focused strictly on golf. Over the past 50 years, the number of private clubs had decreased substantially, down from 62 percent of all courses in the 1950s to only 27 percent in 2005 (Fore, 2008).

According to the National Golf Foundation (2010) the number of rounds played in the previous three years decreased 0.1 percent, 1.8 percent, and 0.6 percent respectively. This decrease was attributed to both the economic recession and the decrease in the number of "core golfers" who played eight or more rounds per year. Ten years previous, core golfers were estimated at 17.7 million. Four years previous, that figure decreased to 15 million. The main reasons why people left the sport included the amount of time it took to complete a round, rising costs, and pursuit of other interests.

EXHIBIT C13.4: TOP U.S. MARKETS FOR GOLF

Rank	Designated Market Area (DMA)	% of Households that Play Golf	Index (Base = 100)
1	Green Bay—Appleton, WI	25.5	151
2	Grand Rapids-Kalamazoo—Battle Creek, MI	24.0	142
3	Minneapolis—St. Paul, MN	23.7	140
4	Sioux City, IA	23.7	140
5	Palm Springs, CA	23.4	138
6	Ft. Myers—Naples, FL	23.3	138
7	Lansing, MI	23.2	137
8	Traverse City—Cadillac, MI	23.2	137
9	Mankato, MN	22.9	136
10	Wausau—Rhinelander, WI	22.8	135
127	Norfolk, Portsmouth, Newport News, VA	15.2	90
210	Greenwood—Greenville, MS	7.5	44

The decrease in the number of core golfers and rounds played caused 39 of the nearly 4,400 private golf clubs and 800 of the 7,600 semi-private and public courses across the U.S. to shut down between over the previous two years. Another 389 were forced to open their doors to the public (Brinkley, 2010). Median gross golf fee revenue was nearly flat at -0.2 percent nationally in September of the previous year, compared to the year before that. To slow this decrease, some courses had reduced the minimum number of golfers for group rates as well as decreased prices on golf outing/lunch combinations (Schmidt, 2009).

EXHIBIT C13.5: SELECT DEMOGRAPHIC DATA— U.S. GOLFERS & HAMPTON ROADS DMA

Demographic	U.S. Golfer	Hampton Roads DMA
Median Adult Age	50.4 years	48.3 years
Marital Status		
Single Male	21.9%	21.5%
Single Female	9.4%	23.7%
Married	69.4%	54.8%
Home Ownership		
Owner	79.0%	65.1%
Renter	21.0%	34.9%
Median Income	$70,638	$50,430
Credit Card Usage		
Travel/Entertainment	22.4%	13.6%
Bank Card	86.8%	80.6%
Gas/Department Stores	27.0%	20.3%
No Credit Cards Used	9.3%	16.0%

**EXHIBIT C13.6: COMPARISON OF TOP 5 LIFESTYLES—
U.S. GOLFERS & HAMPTON ROADS DMA**

Lifestyles	U.S. Golfers			Hampton Roads, VA DMA		
	%	Index	Rank	%	Index	Rank
Snow Skiing	16.1	230	1	5.9	84	67
Tennis	13.9	224	2	6.5	105	27
Wines	34.5	184	3	19.1	102	37
Stock/Bonds Investments	34.9	175	4	22.0	111	12
Boating/Sailing	17.1	175	5	12.4	122	2
Real Estate Investments	16.0	172	8	11.1	119	3
NASCAR	18.0	148	22	15.1	123	1
Our Nation's Heritage	9.5	142	26	7.9	118	5
Bible/Devotional Reading	24.8	107	72	27.3	118	4

Golfer Demographics & The Newport News Area

There were an estimated 19 million-plus U.S. households where one or more members played golf (SRDS, 2008). As seen in Exhibit C13.4, of the top 10 golf markets, eight were located in the Midwest. The Norfolk, Portsmouth, Newport News (also known as Hampton Roads) designated market area (DMA) ranked 137th out of 210 markets nationwide in golf play.

There are discernable differences between the demographic and lifestyle indicators of the typical U.S. golfer and the residents of Hampton Roads. Exhibit C13.5 compares key demographic data of the golfing population versus all residents of the Hampton Roads DMA while Exhibit C13.6 denotes lifestyle differences.[1]

Local Competition

Southeastern Virginia had a multitude of private, semi-private, and public golf courses. Within a 25-mile radius, there were five private clubs KCGC&R considered its primary competition. James River Country Club was a private, full-service country club situated on the James River in Newport News. It too offered an 18-hole golf course with picturesque river views. It also housed a world-renowned golf museum in its clubhouse. Membership in this club was quite exclusive and the application process included submitting two letters of recommendation or sponsorship from current members.

Kingsmill Resort & Spa was also located along the James River in nearby Williamsburg. It offered three championship golf courses designed by Pete Dye, Arnold Palmer, Tom Clark and two-time U.S. Golf Open champion Curtis Strange. Renowned for great golf, Kingsmill positioned itself as a full-service resort, offering 425 posh guest rooms and suites, a restaurant, and an elaborate spa. It focused its marketing efforts on attracting conferences that included group golfing packages.

---

[1] Psychographic data reflects 73 distinct activities measured in the *Lifestyle Market Analyst Report* published annually by Standard Rate and Data Services.

Also in Williamsburg were Ford's Colony Country Club and Golden Horseshoe Golf Club. Located on a hill of 3,000 acres of beautiful countryside in Williamsburg, Ford Colony had two golf courses, restaurants and a full-service pro shop. Golden Horseshoe Golf Club offered 45 unique holes of golf. It was one of the top 75 golf resorts around the world, with a rating of 4.5 stars by *Golf Digest*. It also had a full-service pro shop and offered memberships to those who resided within a 75-mile radius. The initiation fee was $5,000 with annual family dues of $4,320 or annual individual dues of $2,895.

Cypress Creek was located in Smithfield, across the James River from Newport News and Williamsburg. It offered an 18-hole golf course also designed by Tom Clark and Curtis Strange. In addition to competition provided by the area country club and resorts, there were a number of public golf courses in the area that offered golfers the opportunity to pay on a daily basis to enjoy either nine or 18 holes of golf. These courses did not require membership.

Previous KCGC&R Marketing Efforts & Challenges

Promoting and building the golf program continued to be the main focus for Jamie and his staff. Ideally, Jamie hoped to attract new members to KCGC&R who would utilize all of the Club's amenities. New member acquisition might be a bit challenging due to the poor economy and all of the local competitors that were vying for golfers. However, Jamie felt strongly that if people came and played the KCGC&R course a few times, they would fall in love with it and join the Club.

Jamie and his assistant, Tyler, had been discussing their marketing strategies. They reviewed the following key facts about KCGC&R:

Reputation and Member Retention

The Club had an excellent reputation among its highly satisfied members. Its annual membership retention rate was approximately 80 percent. In addition to the normal attrition due to the Hampton Roads area military relocations, the sluggish economy had negatively affected its rate of obtaining new members. Most golfers seemed satisfied to use a "pay as you play" approach to golfing—as opposed to joining a golf club or resort and paying both initiation fees and monthly membership dues.

Target Customer

While the KCGC&R customer could conceivably be anyone in the vicinity, the demographic profile of an existing member was a professional between the ages of 30 and 60, with an interest in golf. Interestingly, only three percent of the current members resided in the Kiln Creek community. Despite the high moving rate in the area caused by a significant military population, Jamie thought that the Kiln Creek residential community held an untapped base of prospects.

Unique Selling Point

KCGC&R currently promoted itself as a country club experience. Its positioning statement, *"The country club lifestyle is within your grasp,"* implied that KCGC&R provided members with country club living at a more affordable price. Initiation and dues comparisons with the nearby country and golf clubs suggested that KCG&R was a good value for the money.

Previous Recent Marketing Activities

In the past year, KCGC&R had purchased an advertising schedule on Cox Cable Television that ran for 16 weeks, reaching approximately 12,000 households. The budget for this television campaign that promoted the temporary elimination of the new member initiation fee was $5,000. By its conclusion, the campaign had generated more than 30 inquiries, with 20 new golfers playing the course, and a total of five new KCGC&R memberships.

The club also had a member referral program and had relied on its staff to promote memberships on a person-to-person basis, but these activities had not been overly effective. Otherwise, KCGC&R had not been proactive in promoting the Club to attract new members. Jamie and Tyler needed to address this immediately.

Although the Club had not been proactive in membership marketing, Jamie had tried several promotions to generate awareness and entice people to come and play the course. He placed a small-space advertisement in a neighborhood publication with a circulation of 1,200, targeting Chamber of Commerce members in the surrounding area and emphasizing "Resort Golf without the Resort Fees." The ad offered a special 18-hole golf game rate of $30 for golf during the week and $40 for the weekend (golf cart included) to attract newcomers to try the course. This ad cost $600, garnered a 9 percent response rate, and worked well to generate 108 new golfers to try the course.

Another promotion to generate play was a special game rate offer of $35 for 18 holes (golf cart included), extended to 7,500 members of the Virginia State Golf Association. The cost of this promotion was $900, and it achieved a 2.5 percent response rate, and again was effective in getting new golfers to visit KCGC&R.

A final promotion to generate golfers involved an advertisement offering a golf school with a well-known golf professional at a nominal fee of $20 per two-hour lecture. It was exposed to approximately 18,000 individuals. More than 400 golfers signed up for the school and each was offered a free round of golf at KCGC&R at the conclusion of the lecture. All participants were also invited to sign up for a one and one-half day golf clinic—with 56 golfers accepting and participating. At the conclusion of the golf clinic, these golfers were given a golf card entitling each to return for three free rounds of golf with up to three additional golfers at a special discount rate of $25 each. The cost of this promotion was $7,200, and it achieved a 2.3 percent response rate. Again, it was effective in getting prospective golfers to visit the KCGC&R facility.

With the exception of the television campaign, marketing efforts to date had focused on getting people to try the course. What Jamie discovered through these efforts was that conversion to membership didn't happen naturally. He wondered if conversion had to be its own effort, or if it could be integrated into the campaigns and media he was already using.

KCGC&R Location: The Villages of Kiln Creek

When Jamie first came to KCGC&R, he recognized that its location was both a significant problem and an opportunity. The Club was nestled in an upscale planned community comprised of 31 distinct neighborhoods or villages, and 2,918 residences.

The Kiln Creek community was beautifully landscaped, and featured miles of winding bike and jogging paths, social and recreational activities, and an active homeowners association.

With so many residents, strong support of the neighborhood Club could be expected. However to date, less than three percent of the homeowners (70 families) were currently members of the Club. Although KCGC&R was available to the residents, it was not affiliated with the Villages of Kiln Creek and was not automatically included as an amenity for its residents. Interestingly though, the Kiln Creek Neighborhood Owners Association promoted KCGC&R as an amenity available to residents, on its web site.

While the Club had an excellent reputation among its highly satisfied members, it had a distant relationship with the homeowners' association. Part of this strained relationship was due to strong petitions from the Neighborhood Homeowner's Association for the Club to curtail its interests in rezoning and developing a parcel of land previously used for golf, into a residential area. Since 1998, the Homeowner's Association bylaws no longer allowed additional villages within Kiln Creek, and this potential new residential development would not be directly affiliated with the currently established Kiln Creek Villages. Therefore, the new residents would not be subject to the Kiln Creek covenants, rules and restrictions nor would they pay annual assessments like the current residents did.

The land rezoning issue was only part of the discourse between the Club Owner and the Homeowner's Association Board. Jamie had been informed that the officers of the Homeowner's Association Board had made it difficult for the owner to promote the Club for years.

This strained relationship was not good for anyone—the Club or the residents. Prior to the current Club ownership, the previous owners had allowed the golf course to become an eyesore for the neighborhood, which led to a poor golf course reputation. Much had changed in the past decade and the current owner/entrepreneur invested heavily in the KCGC&R and revitalized the golf course. It was now in everyone's interest to move forward and encourage the thousands of Kiln Creek residents to support their local neighborhood club facility.

Where to begin? Jamie thought current Kiln Creek residents who were club members might help the Club establish relationships with other residents. Given the persuasive power of word-of-mouth marketing, he was confident that an innovative referral program would work. How should such a program be structured? How should he reward members for their participation? Also, given the limited number of resident members, even stellar results from such a program wouldn't boost overall membership that much. More would need to be done. He considered various options.

Decision 1—Improve & Build the Relationship with Residents of the Kiln Creek Villages & its Homeowners Association

KCGC&R needed to remediate its relationship with the homeowner's association to attract residents to the Club. Jamie knew he must create an attractive offer for the residents of Kiln Creek, but with 31 separate neighborhoods (known as villages) with condominiums, apartments, townhouses and single family homes for diverse demographics, he was not sure of the structure of the offer. Also, should he develop more than one offer? How should the community be segmented? What should be included in the offer(s) for Kiln Creek residents given that they already had a park, tennis courts, clubhouse, and pool facilities as amenities of ownership?

If he decided to go this route, he would also have to determine a promotional strategy including creative approach and media mix. How might sales promotion, perhaps special events, fit into the overall strategy? Jamie's career experiences taught him that whatever strategic direction he and his staff chose, success would depend on consideration of each and every detail.

Decision 2—Acquire More Members beyond Kiln Creek with an IMC Campaign

The Villages of Kiln Creek was an obvious starting point. Where else should Jamie focus his marketing efforts? KCGC&R might benefit from an integrated marketing communications membership drive. Jamie thought he might rent some lists to target specific prospects to get them to come to KCGC&R and play a round of golf. But, what lists should he rent? What demographic profile should he target? As the area's Lifestyle Market Analysis report indicated, golf is not a top draw in Newport News. What should his offer be in this campaign? He also questioned whether a campaign could both attract players and convert members. Marketing efforts to date were good at the former but not the latter.

Another consideration that crossed his mind was targeting businesses to purchase corporate memberships. The facilities were perfect for small business meetings tied into rounds of golf. That would boost the banquet and perhaps the Inn business. Then again, he didn't know if that was trying to accomplish too many things at once.

Summary

So many possible directions! Jamie knew the tasks before him were formidable. The poor economy and the continuing battle with the homeowner's association weren't helping matters. The trick was finding the option(s) that best fit his $20,000 a year marketing budget and the know-how of his staff. The board of directors and members meeting was fast approaching. He wanted recommendations he could confidently present that successfully addressed the issues at hand.

Jamie parked his golf cart and headed to his office. Time to grab a quick shower and then get to work. That beautiful course needed more traffic and he was committed to generating it.

Case Questions

1. How should Jamie prioritize his prospecting strategies? Who should be his target market?
2. What media mix should Jamie utilize given his $20,000 marketing budget and the desired prospective customer segments which he was interested in attracting to the Club? How should he allocate this budget between prospect generation and member conversion?
3. What type(s) of special events could Jamie plan at the Club to promote a stronger relationship with the residents of the Kiln Creek villages? How might these be structured to be effective in generating both golfers and new members?
4. How would you suggest obtaining information to help build the KCGC&R prospect database? Should Jamie investigate renting lists of prospective golfers? If so, what segmentation profile should he pursue? What lists and list selects would be potentially effective?

References

Brinkley, Christina, 2010. Admitting Jeans to the Club, *Wall Street Journal*, May 27.

First Research, 2010, Golf Course Industry Profile including Statistics, Trends and Analysis from First Research, February 22, 2010. http://www.first research.com/industry-research/Golf-Courses.html. Retrieved March 22, 2010.

Fore, 2008. View Beyond the Verandah, *Golf Advisory Associates.*

Golf, 2005, http://www.spiritus-temporis.com/golf/social-aspects-of-golf.html, Retrieved March 23, 2010.

Golflink,com, 2009, "How Many People Play Golf in the USA?" http://www.golflink.com/facts_6246_many-people-play-golf-usa.html

IBIS World USA, 2010, Golf Courses & Country Club Industry Research in the U.S. by IBIS World Industry and Company Research Reports and Information, January 13, 2010, http://www.ibisworld.com/industry/default.aspx?indid=1652. Retrieved March 22, 2010.

National Golf Foundation, 2009. National Rounds Played Report, https://ngf.org/cgi/research.asp Retrieved June 1, 2010.

PGA/NGCOA, 2009, *PGA PerformanceTrak News*, October 29, 2009. Retrieved March 23, 2010.

Schmidt, Edward Jr. 2009. Sour Economy No Game-Breaker for Golf, *Meeting News, 33* (4), March 9, 30.

C A S E
14

Lane Bryant

EVE CAUDILL RAPP
Winona State University

LOUELLA BENSON GARCIA
Pepperdine University

Introduction

Spring was just breaking in Chicago: the sky was a deep azure blue and the sun glistened off the windows on fashionable Michigan Avenue. But Marisa Ness, account supervisor at Columbian Advertising Agency (CAA), didn't notice the gorgeous day outside her office window. Deep in thought, she jumped when the telephone rang. She listened intently as Lane Bryant's vice president of marketing expanded on issues concerning Lane Bryant's forthcoming direct marketing campaign. It was important that Marisa understood exactly what her client needed. CAA and The Limited had worked together for four years, but it wasn't until just recently that CAA had been given the opportunity to help with the Limited's Lane Bryant.

Thirty minutes later, as her administrative assistant finished making dinner arrangements, Marisa convened a late Friday afternoon meeting with her project team. "Forget any weekend plans," she warned her team. "With the high level of attention this project has gotten, it's extremely important that each phase of this direct marketing campaign is successful. And you know what that means . . . testing! We have to come up with a plan to test each part of the campaign we've developed, and the client expects a full report early Monday morning." Pausing for a moment, Marisa added, "Of course, that's in addition to making the final decisions for this campaign."

The Issue

Top management at Lane Bryant had engaged Marisa Ness and her colleagues at CAA when analysis showed that sales figures from their Gold cardholders (their premier customers) were trending down. Decreasing credit card volume and lackluster sales volume figures indicated these customers were not visiting the plus-size fashion stores or purchasing their products. It appeared they had abandoned Lane Bryant. In addition, research indicated that long-term prospects also appeared dim. Something had to be done, and CAA was hired to assist Lane Bryant in its campaign to convince customers to return to Lane Bryant stores.

Although Lane Bryant management didn't know why their premium customers were no longer purchasing the Lane Bryant brand, the company did know who these customers were, and this knowledge should prove useful in the campaign to win them back. Fortunately, the company had amassed a huge portfolio of information on its customers: names, addresses, and purchasing history. Owning this information was not enough, however. The information could tell Lane Bryant management "who" their customers were, but it couldn't tell them why the customers had left and how to bring them back. Lane Bryant desperately needed to know what would motivate these customers to take a second look. But how? It knew it had to change, but once it did how could it communicate its new image? After all, if the customers weren't coming into the stores, how could the company show them the new and improved fashions for the upcoming season?

A number of focus groups were conducted, which yielded some surprising results—Lane Bryant's best customers felt they had been forgotten! A central theme coming out of the focus groups was that these customers thought of Lane Bryant as "a friend who hasn't been there for me." Furthermore, these customers began to see shopping at Lane Bryant not as an uplifting experience, but as "stressful."

Two additional themes emerged from the research. First, as management had already suspected, the Lane Bryant stores needed an image upgrade. Currently, the stores carried a limited product selection, which was not merchandised with optimal appeal. The clothes were not geared to the cutting edge of fashion. Instead, they tended toward being old-fashioned and "dowdy." And clothes were not sold as separates, but as "sets." This merchandising mix conflicted with the needs of the target market, who wanted to feel attractive in their clothes. And they wanted information on how to look attractive in a variety of situations, including both social and professional. There were, however, differences among these plus-size consumers—differences both in terms of body type and fashion needs, which Lane Bryant acknowledged it had to address.

Lane Bryant management suggested some changes in the merchandising. One suggestion included selling separates rather than sets so that customers had the freedom to choose tops and bottoms in different sizes. A second suggestion was to offer fabrics not traditionally sold to large-sized women, which would allow these women to be in style. And finally, management suggested adding a Lane Bryant brand to their mix of merchandise.

The second theme that emerged from research was the need for a coordinated direct marketing campaign that would deliver targeted information to a younger, more active group of plus-size consumers. CAA was hired to develop this campaign and was assessing several direct marketing strategies. The goal of the campaign was to communicate the exciting changes occurring in the Lane Bryant stores, changes that would satisfy the plus-size consumer's need to look and feel attractive.

In developing these direct marketing strategies, Marisa and her colleagues at CAA had to satisfy several criteria, which had been outlined by Lane Bryant management at the beginning of the project:

- Create awareness of store merchandise
- Create a dialogue allowing Lane Bryant to treat customers as friends
- Build and maintain the relationship with best customers

- Increase credit card activation, usage, and loyalty
- Generate incremental sales

Although a number of strategies had been developed, the direct marketing campaign had not yet been finalized: decisions still had to be made regarding which of the strategies should be used, and some of the strategies still had specific issues to resolve. In addition, a plan for testing the components of the campaign had to be developed.

Background

Although lagging behind the rest of the industry in offering fashion-forward options to plus-size women, Lane Bryant finally began the road back to recapturing its disillusioned customers. It began to restructure internally; it redesigned stores and worked to bring more fashionably palatable merchandise to its clientele.

The Limited, Inc.

Founded in 1963 by Chairman Leslie H. Wexner, The Limited, Inc., had more than 5,400 stores, including The Limited Stores, Express, Lerner New York, Henri Bendel, Structure, Limited Too, Galyan's Trading Company, and Lane Bryant, as well as majority shares of Bath & Body Works, Victoria's Secret Stores, Victoria's Secret Catalogue, and Abercrombie & Fitch.

In the prior ten-year period, The Limited's net sales and gross income had increased in nine years out of ten. Operating income had increased each year until about three years ago, and then decreased. Operating income as a percentage of sales steadily decreased from 11.5 percent to 5.2 percent in the most recent year.

The Limited's "mall strategy" involved analyzing the structure of the mall in terms of the "fit" of stores and the customers these stores targeted. The anchor stores in a particular mall were important to this strategy. The Limited looked at the anchor stores to assess the "walk-by" traffic and then fit their line of stores between the two anchors, which would take advantage of the synergy generated by the other stores in the mall. Often The Limited stores would be placed in proximity; for example, Bath & Body Works, The Limited, and Structure (Now Express Men) stores are often seen near each other. Following its parent company's strategy, Lane Bryant relied on walk-by traffic in malls to generate sales. It did not advertise locations or product mix selections through the mass media.

Lane Bryant

Lane Bryant was a specialty retailer for women who wore plus sizes (typically sizes 14 to 28). The stores carried fashions, intimate apparel, hosiery, and accessories. Lane Bryant operated no outlet malls and was not affiliated with the Lane Bryant catalog company.

The Limited acquired Lane Bryant in 1982 and by 1989 had expanded it from 200 stores to 720 stores. In 1990, the New York headquarters were moved to The Limited's headquarters in Columbus, Ohio. Chairman Leslie Wexner called the move a signal as to the importance of Lane Bryant to future growth, although financial analysts cited the chain as "the most challenged" of The Limited's divisions because of its balance of fashion-forward apparel with basic merchandise. Kenneth Gilman, executive vice president and CFO, agreed the merchandising and marketing did not have the right focus.

In 1992, Lane Bryant closed its Fifth Avenue flagship, which was 22,000 square feet and the chain's largest. Within the next five years Lane Bryant closed 40 of its unprofitable stores, but opened 19 and remodeled 50. The new and remodeled format was about 10 percent larger (regular stores were about 4,900 square feet), with interior tones of sage green, off-white, and khaki (rather than the prior black and gold theme).

Increased Retailer Competition

Two factors led to The Limited, Inc.'s, recent concern for Lane Bryant stores: increased retailer competition and decreased sales. Competition in the retail industry was already rising when Lane Bryant approached CAA. While Lane Bryant continued to offer basic merchandise (such as tunics, leggings, and oversized cotton/polyester knits), designer plus-size clothing entered the scene to cater to the evolving needs of plus-size women. Emanuel Ungaro and Gianni Versace were among the first high-fashion designers to ride this trend. Contemporary lines were also targeting this market, such as Anne Klein and Dana Buchman, who began designing more fashionable clothing. Marshall Field's, (now Macy's) Neiman Marcus, and Saks Fifth Avenue were examples of high-end department stores that began to offer plus-size clothing.

Discount store retailers also began offering sportswear and other clothing lines, some of which was private label, to customers previously ignored. Federated Department Stores' chain of plus-size stores, Bullock's Woman, had been launched in 1988 with a 3,100-square-foot store in Las Vegas, along with ten additional stores on the West Coast. Other growing chains for large-size women were the moderately priced Clothes for Eve and Woman's World, and the more pricey Forgotten Woman. Not to be left out were local, independent retailers that opened across the country, as well as catalog companies such as Lane Bryant (not affiliated with Lane Bryant stores).

Home shopping also took off. For example, television actress Delta Burke began a fashion firm that included sportswear, evening wear, accessories, and lingerie, which soon reached an annual wholesale volume of $21 million. She took her career wear, sexy dresses, and denim apparel to QVC, and home shoppers responded.

The Customer

Fashion writer Ann D'Innocenzio cited a "backlash against anything that seems politically correct or that smacks of Puritanism . . . as a boon to the plus-size business." Valerie Steele, museum chief curator of the Fashion Institute of Technology, echoed this opportunity for the plus-size industry: "For so long, there were so many rules for plus-size women—you couldn't wear sleeveless, or bare backs. Now, there's this attitude that you can still wear really nice clothes, and that is encouraging. The industry is responding to people's desire."

For many plus-size women, shopping for clothes historically had not been a pleasant experience. Marshall Field's and other leading retailers finally began using mannequins to showcase plus-size clothing in the early 1990s. Prior to 1994, this clothing had been positioned in the back of the store.

In an interview with *Women's Wear Daily* magazine, the Lane Bryant vice president of marketing explained that Lane Bryant was "as much at fault as the rest of the industry in not bringing the large-size customer fashion merchandise. We underestimated her sophistication. If flannel was the fabric for fall, we weren't sure. If the skinny-knit mock turtleneck was the top of the season, we didn't offer it."

The Work Begins

As the blue sky deepened outside the conference room windows, Marisa updated her team members on her most recent conversation with Lane Bryant. "Lane Bryant loves the customer profiles we've developed where we have given each woman a name, personality, and lifestyle and the life-size diary that describes her relationship with Lane Bryant and how they can communicate with her. Lane Bryant is also very happy with how we're positioning the company as a fashion-forward retailer for plus-size women, which supports the affirmation and celebration of plus-size women and their individuality. Furthermore, it has tentatively agreed to our proposed campaign theme that Lane Bryant is like a friend—it cares and is 'there' for its customers."

As her team members began to prepare to present the various parts of the direct marketing campaign, Marisa reminded her team members of one concern the client had continually voiced to her in conversations over the past few weeks: expenses had to be kept low. "Remember this program has to be self-sufficient—it has to pay for itself. That means that total costs have to be carefully monitored and we have to factor in all the different costs generated by each part of the campaign while taking into account response rates. Furthermore, the program has to fit short-term goals (profitability) while focusing on long-term relationships with key target customers. And that is why testing is so important."

Before they started, Marisa quickly summarized what should be included in the campaign. "As you know, our research uncovered different customer purchasing patterns and profitability levels among customers, which we used to form four segments: Top Performers, Actives, new Gold Cardholders, and Inactives. We've developed this campaign with these four segments in mind. As we discuss the issues associated with each component and each group, begin to formulate testing strategies and we'll discuss your ideas for testing tomorrow morning." As Marisa walked back to her seat she quickly evaluated the presentation lineup and changed speakers, "I'm changing the order of presentations—Henry, you present first with information on the Gold Cardholder Strategies followed by Maggie who will present additional information on Gold Cardholder and Top Performer Customer Strategies. The remaining team members follow in the order I've already laid out."

Henry and the rest of the project team presented the different components of the direct marketing campaign they had developed for Lane Bryant for the next two hours. The following is a summary of these presentations as well as the disagreements that arose over some of the components. Remember, as a member of CAA's advertising team, you are required to develop a testing plan for each component of this campaign as well as choose what you believe to be the best solutions to the disagreements. As Marisa already told the group, you need to be prepared to discuss your ideas at the scheduled breakfast meeting tomorrow morning starting at 8:00 A.M. (sorry, no weekend plans for you either).

Strategies for New Gold Cardholders

The management at Lane Bryant was particularly concerned about the declining sales from their most profitable customer group—Gold cardholders. These cardholders were the top 10 percent of current credit card customers who made five or more purchases and spent $1,000+ in a 12-month period. Research had shown that increased competition, both from other retailers and from designer brands, and a lack of customer knowledge regarding new product lines, contributed to this decline. These customers were particularly sensitive to the perception that Lane Bryant was a "friend who hadn't been there for them."

Welcome Kit

A Welcome Kit was a direct marketing package that was designed to begin communication with new Gold cardholders. The Welcome Kit had been developed as a way to deliver a credit card to these new cardholders and included the new credit card along with a brochure explaining the benefits associated with the card. When presented with this strategy, team members disagreed on two issues. First, it was suggested that both a letter and a brochure accompany the credit card rather than just a brochure. "Bring the pros and cons to our meeting tomorrow," Marisa stated, attempting to speed up the presentations.

The second issue involved the brochure itself. Some members disagreed with the friendly tone of the copy, which read "Enclosed is your Gold Card that brings you even more great benefits—enjoy, because you deserve it!," and pushed for a more formal tone. They noted the wording seemed to contrast with the premium quality of the brochure. Marisa explained the general strategy behind the brochure, "We wanted to initiate a 'one-to-one' relationship with Lane Bryant's best customers and tried to develop a package that would make them feel special and motivate them to take a second look at Lane Bryant. That's also why we chose four-color photographs featuring models wearing never-before-seen fashions." She paused to show a copy of the brochure and then continued, "We expect these customers will love it; they'll begin to see Lane Bryant as a quality company that is 'cutting edge,' a company that can help them out with all their fashion needs. Furthermore, Gold cardholder customers have to receive additional perks that less profitable customers don't receive—to show appreciation for their business."

Strategies for New Gold Cardholders and Top Performers

First Thursdays

The team members, still disagreeing on some of the particulars of the Welcome Kit communication strategy, agreed that a testing plan had to be formulated to help them come to a decision. Attention turned to the First Thursday strategy. This strategy was still in the preliminary stages of development; so far they knew that premium customers would be offered an incentive to visit stores on the first Thursday of each month. Team members asked about the goal of this strategy and what incentives would be motivating enough to get cardholders to visit a mall on a Thursday. Marisa explained, "We're looking at achieving several goals with this strategy. Obviously, one goal is to reward Lane Bryant's most valued customers by offering them a discount. A second goal is to get these customers into Lane Bryant stores; once these customers are in the stores, they'll see all the exciting new fashions being offered. And, a third goal is to try to build store traffic on a day other than a weekend . . . to shift demand to a less busy day."

Marisa continued, "There are so many different types of incentives. Part of our goal this weekend is to decide which one to use. Offering a discount may be a viable choice or perhaps a free gift would motivate special customers to visit Lane Bryant stores. If we go with a discount, we then have to choose the amount to offer—do we offer 10 percent, 15 percent, or more; if we offer a free gift, what gift will be offered and should it change each month? Or should we go with something else? What do you think?" A heated discussion ensued as team members debated back and forth the viability of different incentive offers. During this discussion it was pointed out that a decision also had to be made regarding the promotional vehicle used to inform customers about First Thursdays. A number of promotional tools were listed, including postcards, inserts, and bag stuffers. Someone mentioned the use of stickers placed on the front of customers' gold cards that would serve to inform customer about the program and then later to remind them to visit Lane Bryant every month.

Newsletters

A newsletter was suggested as another direct marketing vehicle that could be used to promote a quality image to customers and provide an incentive for them to visit Lane Bryant stores. "I believe a newsletter would be a good way to continue that long-term relationship the company so badly needs," Marisa explained when the viability of this strategy was questioned. "What we need to do here, however, is decide just what will be included in the newsletter and how often it should be sent." She proceeded to list some of the ideas developed during previous brainstorming sessions: buyer profiles; beautiful plus-size models, dressed perhaps in negligees (to enhance the idea that plus sizes are attractive); fashion and lifestyle editorials; beauty tips; internal Lane Bryant offers such as sweepstakes; added-value offers from outside partners; and special events information, such as sweepstakes, mall tours, etc. She continued, "We've already decided that the newsletter will include quality fashion photography of the new season's collection. Can you think of additional ideas we can take to the Lane Bryant meeting on Monday? Remember, we want to focus on building confidence in their customers. Rather than focusing on 'slimming down,' the newsletter needs to show plus-size women how to 'flatter their own shape.'"

It was agreed that although team members really liked the newsletter concept, Lane Bryant management would most likely question the effectiveness of this strategy on store traffic. "Remember, the overall goal of this campaign is to ultimately increase sales and profitability at Lane Bryant stores," Marisa reminded those present. "Although the newsletter is meant to change current perceptions of customers, it ultimately has to drive them into stores to purchase products—so how are we going to track the impact of this vehicle on customer sales?" Noting the importance of proving to Lane Bryant the effectiveness of each component of this direct marketing campaign, Marisa asked several team members to come up with solutions to these questions. She then turned to the question of who else might receive the newsletter.

Premium customers would be the first to receive the newsletter, titled *First Look*, but the group was indecisive as to the viability of other customer segments receiving the newsletter. Some thought that if this newsletter were successful then a second newsletter could be developed to target the base card customers—those cardholders who did not spend as much as the Gold cardholders. Several suggestions were made: the name could be different, perhaps *Real Style* rather than *First Look*; the format could be shorter, perhaps one page with a lesser offer than that given to premium customers. And there still was the question of how to track whether or not the newsletter was actually motivating these customers to purchase products.

Strategies for Inactives

Postcards

Evening had become night when the presentations turned to providing incentives to inactive customers to get them interested again in Lane Bryant. It was thought that postcards might be effective—they were relatively inexpensive to send and could include an incentive for these former customers to reactivate their cards and purchase products. This strategy was in its beginning stages of development and a number of decisions had to be made: the message, the timing, the number of postcards, the incentive, and a tracking measurement.

Several message ideas were offered. Some team members liked a "Miss You" type of message, which would remind inactives about Lane Bryant; others liked a "Thank You" type of message, which would both remind former customers of their past purchases and encourage renewed purchasing. "The postcard should feature photographs of models wearing Lane Bryant fashions," one team member offered. "It should include an incentive such as a gift or a gift certificate." Offered another, "Perhaps a discount would be best." "Postcards are a great idea . . . why can't we send them to some of the other customers groups also?" queried a third.

Strategies for All Customer Groups

Mailings

Lane Bryant needed a vehicle to offer credit card lines to various member groups and the CAA team thought that direct mail packages should be developed, packages that would encourage recipients to open the envelopes and then motivate them to visit a Lane Bryant store. But what would entice recipients? A heated debate again ensued around the conference room table: "How about four-color"; What's wrong with two-color photography or perhaps black and white"; "Let's offer a pre-approved credit offer letter and outer envelope"; "I like that but let's also use photography and a focus on fashion with that credit card offer"; "An offer letter signed by top management could communicate special attention to special cardholders"; "If we use a credit card offer we have to decide on a annual percentage rate (APR)"; "Do we offer a low APR . . ."; "Or, would a discount of 10 percent or 15 percent be better?" Ideas were flowing so fast that Marisa had trouble capturing them all on paper.

Continuity Programs

Coffee and dessert were served as the group settled in to talk about the continuity option. Mindful that Lane Bryant had unsuccessfully tried to launch three previous rebate continuity programs, group members knew it would be difficult to sell this option to Lane Bryant management. All seemed to agree that a conservative, yet creative strategy would be the safest route to take and, most importantly, it had to have realistic predetermined spending levels. Agreement was harder to get on what merchandise to use and on which customer groups to focus.

New Account Nurturing Program

A separate program was advanced that focused on new account cardholders. It would initiate immediate contact with new base cardholders. Again, several options were bandied about. Suggestions included a solo mailing of the newsletter, which would begin a relationship with the new cardholder; a welcome letter from the President, to be included with the newsletter; a $5 certificate, to stimulate an immediate store visit; and perhaps a follow-up postcard mailed sometime after other communication vehicles. The team agreed to postpone some of these decisions until later.

Sweepstakes Programs

The team started winding down as the last presenter unveiled the final option—sweepstakes! CAA had been working on this strategy for several months and only minor decisions now had to be made. Proposed were two different sweepstakes, one titled "The Paris Sweepstakes" and the second titled "Seaside Serenity." The Paris Sweepstakes offered as the grand prize a nine-day, first-class, escorted tour of Paris and the Champagne and Normandy regions of France. In addition, Lane Bryant provided 10 first-place prizes—$250 gift certificates, 25 second-place prizes—$100 gift certificates and 250 third-place prizes—Lane Bryant chemise nightgowns. The Seaside Serenity Sweepstakes was a Mother's Day promotion run prior to Mother's Day and offered as the grand prize a four-night spa package for two at the famous Don CeSar Resort in St. Petersburg Beach, Florida. An additional prize was a terry cloth robe and white cotton nightgown for one winner per store.

The only decision that needed to be made was how Lane Bryant should promote these sweepstakes. Team members were divided. Knowing that this decision was the last before they left for the evening, however, they kept their suggestions short. One camp opted for in-store materials, including counter cards and perhaps a continuously looped video featuring the two destinations and Lane Bryant fashions. The second camp thought the promotional material should be included in other communication vehicles; most thought the newsletter would be the best vehicle in which to place an entry form and perhaps a feature on the sweepstakes.

It was nearing 10:00 P.M. as group members gathered their information to carry home. Marisa, pleased with the progress the team had made, complimented her team members on their hard work. "We'll all meet back here at 8:00 A.M. tomorrow morning, and we'll discuss testing methods and lay out more ideas on some of these direct marketing strategies." What would you advise?

CASE
15

Scratch-off Summer Games at Lettuce Entertain You in Chicago

JAN OWENS,

Carthage College

RALITZA NIKOLAEVA

ISCTE Business School

NEIL YOUNKIN

Saint Xavier University

ELLA CARTER

Howard University

S ummertime, and the living' is easy. Those who experience Chicago's summer can definitely attest to this. After the bitter Chicago winter, summer is the longed-for season when everyone tries to spend as much time outside as possible. For this, the city provides plenty of outdoor entertainment. Music lovers can enjoy events such as: the Chicago Blues Festival, the largest one of its kind in the world; the Annual Chicago Gospel Music Festival; the Country Music Festival; or "Viva! Chicago"—the annual Latin Music Festival. For those who like to combine food and music, there's the Taste of Chicago. And for those who consider food less important, there is Bike Chicago—an event promoting the benefits of bicycling. Of course, this is also the season of barbeques, vacations, and general summer fun.

Yes, summer fun in Chicago is great . . . unless you are a restaurateur like Rich Melman—one of the founders of Lettuce Entertain You Enterprises (LEYE). The problem faced by LEYE is that casual, outdoor summer fun rarely translates into eating out at an upscale restaurant. Hence LEYE has had to resort to special promotions to draw customers to their bouquet of upscale restaurants in the Chicago area. One of their latest successful summer promotions had been a scratch off game that rewarded customers for visiting their locations. The objectives behind the promotion were to drive consumers to visit and dine in the restaurants and to also get customers to try different restaurants within the corporate umbrella, that is—to increase their overall frequency of visits to LEYE properties. The promotion had been successful in past years, but LEYE executives questioned whether it could continue its success. More

EXHIBIT C15.1: HOME WEB PAGE OF THE ORIGINAL R.J.GRUNTS

importantly, could it be successful in bringing in new customers? Could other promotional tactics yield better results in attracting new customers and encouraging repeat behavior in current customers?

The History of Lettuce Entertain You

Lettuce Entertain You Enterprises began in 1971 when Rich Melman and Jerry Orzoff opened a Lincoln Park restaurant called R.J. Grunts. During their partnership, Rich would come up with the culinary ideas while Jerry helped to keep Rich on track.

The two opened R.J. Grunts in 1971 with an initial investment of $17,000. The name, R.J. Grunts, combined their first initials with a word that described the noise made by a girlfriend of Jerry's while she ate. The restaurant was a true innovator in terms of the salad bar it offered. Before Grunts, salad bars only offered a few kinds of greens and dressings. The R.J. Grunts salad bar, on the other hand, had 40 or 50 items including fare such as egg and potato salad and chopped liver, as well as other non-traditional dishes. Rich's girlfriend, who later became his wife, suggested that the new company be named Lettuce Entertain You in honor of the Grunts' salad bar. The quirky character of the original joint is still evident today in its web page (Exhibit C15.1).

Starting in 1973, new restaurant concepts were created including Fritz That's It, The Great Gritzbe's Flying Food Show, Jonathan Livingston Seafood and Lawrence of Oregano. The quirky names indicated their off-beat casual restaurant style. Rich has since stated that the "one thing I regret today is the silly names, because people didn't take us seriously."

Rich then moved in the direction of restaurants that offered fine cuisine. LEYE reopened the famous Pump Room in Chicago in 1976. Due to the success of the Pump Room, Lettuce Entertain You continued to expand their fine dining restaurant concepts. As a result, LEYE is now one of the most diverse restaurant operations in the U.S.

EXHIBIT C15.2: LEYE'S MOST POPULAR CHICAGO AREA RESTAURANTS AND THEIR FORMATS

Antico Posto	Italian Cafe & Wine Bar
Ben Pao	Contemporary Asian Restaurant
Big Bowl	Fresh Chinese and Thai
Brasserie JO	Everyday French
Cafe Ba-Ba-Reeba!	Tapas and Paella
Community Canteen	A Market Inspired Cafe Combined with Take-Away and Catering Services
Di Pescara	Fresh Seafood, Italian and Steaks
Don & Charlie's	Championship Dining & American Cuisine
Everest	Personalized French Cuisine
foodlife	At Water Tower Place—a collection of kitchens
Frankie's 5th Floor Pizzeria	Classic & Sardinian Pizzas, Seasonal Antipasti & Fresh Salads
Hub 51	Modern American Food in a Hip, Casual Environment
Joe's	Seafood, Prime Steak & Stone Crab
L. Woods	Tap and Pine Lodge
L2O	A Modern Seafood Restaurant
Magic Pan Crepe Stand	Dessert and Entrée Crepes
Mity Nice Grill	Good Food Served Right!
Mon Ami Gabi	A Classic French Bistro
Nacional 27	Modern Latin Restaurant, Ceviche Bar & Salsa Club
Petterino's	In the Heart of the Theatre District
Scoozi!	Comfortable Italian
Tru	Progressive French
Vong's Thai Kitchen	Today's Thai!
Wildfire	Steaks, Chops & Seafood
Wow Bao	Hot Asian Steamed Buns

Today LEYE continues to create innovative, successful high quality restaurants. Co-founder Rich Melman now serves as chairman. The other co-founder, Jerry Orzoff, who played a crucial role during the early days of the venture, died in 1981 at the age of 45.

To date LEYE has opened more than 150 restaurants. Its portfolio includes 80 establishments in 11 states with several more in the works (Exhibit C15.2 provides a sample of LEYE's most popular restaurants in the Chicago area and their formats). Although marketable concepts like The Corner Bakery and Maggiano's have been sold off, the restaurants continue to embrace a diverse style of cuisine. LEYE is privately owned, but by a rough estimate annual sales amount to $325 million. In addition, LEYE has around 6,000 employees. The company tries to create a family atmosphere for its workers and even provides 401(K) plans.

Through the company's growth Rich has formulated a business philosophy based on the importance of partners. The strategy is to share responsibilities and profits with them and expand the business together. The organization has over 50 working partners, most of whom have come up through the organization.

Rich truly understands the essence of marketing which is differentiation. He says,

"I'm always looking for holes in the marketplace and for things we can do differently or better or both." Rich is not content to leave things as they are and is constantly open to embracing innovative ideas and challenges. "We've had the ability to give people what they want almost before they know they want it. You can call it trendsetting. I prefer to call it the ability to listen to people." LEYE is always varying or innovating its menu items. Rich and LEYE's test kitchen personnel taste new foods on a daily basis.

In summary, Rich states, "We're a very disciplined organization. We run restaurants well. People think of us as creative . . . and I do believe we possess creativity . . . but more importantly, we play good solid ball. Our costs are good. We surround ourselves with good people and we train well . . . not a lot of fancy stuff, just the basics. And, we work very hard." They have to, because the competition is tough.

The Competitive Environment of the Chicago Restaurant Scene and Its Loyalty Programs

Many Chicago area restaurants have started loyalty programs. Most are based on some formula of points awarded per dollar spent at the restaurants. Most have no registration fee to join and offer some form of promotional discounts for participating in the program, e.g. gift certificates, discounted food, or complimentary menu items.

An important difference among the loyalty programs is the variety of dining options offered to participating diners. The loyalty programs of the single-brand restaurant chains reward dining purchases within a relatively narrow restaurant and menu format. These include fast food restaurant chains such as Arby's and Cousin's, where convenience is as much a part of the chains' success as is the food, and mid-priced chains such as Red Lobster or Texas-based EZ Brick Oven and Grill. In contrast, a few restaurant groups, such as the LEYE or the Levy Restaurants, offer a wider variety of restaurant formats that could address different dining needs of its membership, such as fine dining, café-style dining, or different ethnic cuisines.

The level of complexity of the rewards programs generally depends on the format of the restaurant. Fast food restaurants with limited menus (Cousin's Subs; Arby's; Starbucks) keep track of customer purchases with a simple card that gets punched for every major item (e.g. sandwich or coffee) ordered. The reward is a bonus item from the menu after a specified number of purchases. The advantages of such programs are that they are simple to administer, require relatively little investment in information systems that track customer loyalty, and do not have to "pay up" if the customer loses the membership card that records purchases. There is much to admire in a simple program, as Red Lobster discovered when its Passion Points program encountered technical difficulties. While it promises a points-for-sales program in the future, Red Lobster's current "Fresh Catch Club" program largely offers chances to win sweepstakes prizes, such as free dinner delivered to the winner's home or a vacation to a destination associated with good seafood. Indeed, many loyalty programs in this price range focus on using the Internet to offer discounts and coupons, and communicate with members about new menu items or public relations messages.

The loyalty programs of mid-tier restaurants are quite varied in their complexity and generosity with rewards. TGI Friday's "Give Me More Stripes" program is perhaps the most extensive in its awards and requires customer involvement in this price range. Customers must go online to register, which results in an immediate contact point with the customer. New members get a free appetizer or dessert and a one-time pass to the head of the waiting line, and are continually sent coupon offers, invitations to food tasting events, and other premiums. A database tracks customer spending and awards a coupon worth $8 for every $100 spent. In a different reward mode, Rock Bottom Brewery tracks customer visits and offers rewards of premiums such as mugs, T-shirts, etc., and stresses promotional events.

In contrast, chains like Qdoba or Olive Garden are relatively stingy in their offers. Qdoba offers a free basket of chips and salsa for enrolling, and then rewards points on the order of each sandwich (not including sides or drinks,) with points expiring every year. Olive Garden and Applebee's, like many in this price range, emphasize direct marketing relationships through the Internet rather than loyalty programs.

In contrast, the few loyalty programs at fine dining establishments with higher price points tend to be the most complex. The typical customer at these restaurants is more adventurous and sophisticated in culinary tastes and spends more on dining out than the average customer. As such, many restaurants in this price range prefer to maintain an email contact list that announces special events (e.g. wine tastings; special cuisine nights) or standard promotional schedules (e.g. small plates at Morton's Steak Houses in the bar). For those restaurants that offer a loyalty program, dedicated systems track customer purchases, maintain interactive customer point accounts, and develop special incentives that are more active and tailored to specific locations. The support systems may be maintained by third party providers, but the strategy of the programs requires active development, participation and assessment by restaurant management. Examples of these programs include the LEYE and Levy Restaurants based in the Chicago area. In part, these restaurant groups can keep finicky customers happy by offering a range of dining options. These customers want more for their dining loyalty than a fast, cheap burrito, and a loyalty program at this level requires options that meet a customer's various dining requirements.

Exhibit C15.3 summarizes the loyalty programs of the closest competitors to the dining experiences required by the LEYE customers. The following discussion explains some of these differences, and competitive advantages and disadvantages of each. Note that in every case, the menu must have enough variety to satisfy someone who dines out frequently throughout the year. This could be satisfied by one restaurant format with a wide menu, or a number of restaurants in the program, each with its own positioning and menu offering.

Lettuce Entertain You. The LEYE program is relatively unique in that it requires a membership fee that is credited to the loyalty account after customers dine at the restaurants ($25 for Illinois residents, refunded to the account after three dining visits; $10 for diners who are not Illinois residents, refunded after one dining visit). With a choice of over 70 restaurants in Illinois, Minnesota, Las Vegas, California, Arizona, and Washington, D.C., the group can attract diners with a range of offerings, particularly in the Chicago and Minneapolis areas. The restaurants range from the culinary stars of Chicago (e.g. Tru and Everest) to ethnic cafes (e.g. Big Bowl, Maggiano's and

EXHIBIT C15.3: COMPARISON OF DINING PROGRAMS

Restaurant/ Criteria	Lettuce Entertain You	Levy "Levy Preferred"	Park Grill "PC Card"	TGI Friday "Give Me More Stripes"	Open Table	AA Dining Advantage Dining Program
Fee	$10/$20 refundable	No	No	No	No	No
Point Accumulation	$1 = 1 pt. up to $1000 $1 = 1.25 pts 1K–5K $1 = 1.5 pts over 5K	$1 = 1 pt. Over $2000: upgrade to 1.25 pts. Following year	$1–1 pt.	$1 = 1 pt.	1 reservation = 100 pts.	$1 = 3 pts. Over 10 visits: $1 = 5 pts.
Point Spend Conversion Credit	350 pts = $25	250 pts = $25	300 = $25	100 pts = $8	1000 pts = $20	Direct conversion to airline miles
Restaurant Distribution	Chicago, Minneapolis, Las Vegas, Arizona, Washington D.C.	Chicago, Orlando, Deer Valley, UT	One location, Millennium Park, Chicago	Nationwide	Nationwide, Canada, United Kingdom	Nationwide
Restaurant Type	Casual upscale cafes to fine dining; wide variety of ethnic cuisines	A few upscale cafes and restaurants, many sports venues	375-seat indoor/ outdoor restaurant and casual cafe	Casual dining; single format	Wide variety of participating restaurants	Wide variety of participating restaurants and bars
Extra Perks	Complimentary promotional items on certain evenings	Invitations to special events, wine tastings, cooking classes	Coupons and discounts; priority seating	Immediate complimentary menu item; Coupons, etc.		
Extra earning opps	Double point dates		Double points dates		1000-pt reservation opps	Various bonus opportunities
Other Conversions	Free signature dish; Wine selection; Spa day; Travel Package	Chef's dinner; Airline Ticket; Travel Packages				
Other	Pts expire; Home delivery of menu items	Pts do not expire, but dining certificate does	Adjacent to major public park and entertainment venues	Email sign-up only	Pts. Forfeited for no-shows; expire if inactive 12 mos.	

Nacional 27) to more traditional American fare (e.g. Shaw's Crab House and Wildfire.) The Las Vegas, Arizona and D.C. markets offer opportunities for Illinois and Minnesota residents when they travel to popular destinations, meanwhile establishing beachheads for the development of more restaurants in those towns.

The program itself is quite complex. Diners are rewarded with a $25 gift card for every $350 they spend on a dollar-per-point basis, but customers that qualify for Silver or Gold levels earn more points per dollar, achieving rewards more quickly. There are also options for double point nights or specific items. In addition, patrons can cash in points for non-food rewards that reflect the more sophisticated lifestyles of this customer segment. They include 12 wines selected by celebrity wine master Alpana Singh, a spa day at the Elizabeth Arden salon, and a vacation at the Ritz Carlton Laguna Niguel. Points expire, but not those awarded for gift cards. Tapping the customers' desire for good food without fuss, LEYE also offers home delivery of its menu items via Peapod (www.peapod.com) delivery service. The program does not award points for Saturday evenings or specified holidays when the restaurants are typically busy.

Levy Preferred Frequent Dining Program. The Levy Restaurants have 78 restaurant venues, but are much less versatile for a frequent diner than LEYE. Levy has some noteworthy Chicago restaurants across a variety of formats (Spiaggia, Café Spiaggia, and Bistro 110) and locations (Chicago; Disney World in Orlando) but most of its outlets are in sports arenas, stadiums, convention centers, and company cafeterias. Only the dozen or so restaurants in Chicago, Orlando, and Deer Valley, UT are eligible for the dining program. This limits the ability of the program to offer a very wide variety of dining options. In its favor, Levy rewards a $25 gift card for every $250 in purchases, and promotion to the Gold Level, resulting in earning 1.25 points for every dollar spent over $2000. Reward certificates may also be redeemed for items such as a round trip airline ticket, a chef's dinner for four at any of the restaurants, or a vacation in Orlando. The certificates expire after one year, although the unredeemed points do not.

Park Grill. The Park Grill is located at the entrance to Millennium Park in Chicago, and offers both indoor and outdoor dining. Thus, while much more limited than the range of offerings of LEYE or Levy, the American menu indoors and the ethnic and American grill at the outdoor café offer a variety that can attract local residents, museum-goers, concert-goers, and others in the populous neighborhood. Park Grill also operates the other concessions in the Park, and will produce picnic bags for a gourmet picnic. The basic loyalty redemption rate is a $25 credit on the Park Grill card for every $300 spent. Members enjoy priority seating, coupons and promotions sent via email, and opportunities for double points.

Two program types not affiliated with a specific restaurant group have the potential to win customer loyalty, but could work in complementary ways with restaurant loyalty programs. Open Table (www.opentable.com) awards 100 points for every reservation made through its online network of nation-wide members, but there are opportunities for 1000-point reservations in slack periods or time slots, depending on the location. The member restaurant variety is vast, with formats from the ultra-luxurious to the neighborhood café (but not fast food chains.) Restaurants pay a service fee for the booking, but this may be evaluated as a reasonable marketing expense depending on the client restaurant, its promotional alternatives, and whether it is in a tourist area. There is no charge for customers to join, and rewards begin with a $20 dining credit for an Open Table participating restaurant, and redemption tiers of 1% at 5000 and 10,000 point levels. However, customers forfeit all points if a reservation is not kept or properly canceled, and points expire if the account is inactive for more than 12 months.

Second, many *airlines* have a loyalty program that awards airline miles if the customer registers a credit card, uses the airlines site to book a restaurant, club, or nightspot, and that card is used. The registered card does not have to be an airlines-affiliated credit card. For example, American Airlines awards three points for each dollar spent if the customer uses it 10 times during the year at participating venues, and five points per dollar thereafter. A criticism of the plan is that customers have become very annoyed at the lack of availability to cash in reward points as airlines cut back on the number of flights and planes become more crowded with paying customers. One assumes that there is a charge to participating restaurants, but it is not clear at this time. Also: the roster of participating restaurants is much more limited than the list from Open Table.

In sum, the Lettuce Entertain You group offers a competitive loyalty program that is well designed for its target market. Because customer accounts are kept online and available for customer viewing, customers can be actively involved in tracking points for redemption. The fact that LEYE offers a wide variety of dining options encourages customers to dine at its restaurants without becoming bored thus meeting the need for different dining situations.

Customer Segments

Many companies use various methods to segment and identify potential customers. Some use demographic, others use psychographic and behavioral segmentation tools, but most use a combination of these variables to identify and profile customer groups. Two of the more common marketing tools include VALS™, which was developed by SRI Consulting Business Intelligence (http://www.strategicbusiness insights.com/) and Prizm® NE, which was developed by Nielsen Claritas. In the VALS™ systems, consumers are segmented into eight groups on the basis of personality traits that define consumer behavior. The Prizm® system combines consumer and behavior segmentation to assist in identifying 66 demographically and behaviorally distinct segments (www.claritas.com).

Although many companies use the previously mentioned tools, LEYE uses Equifax Intelligence to segment and describe its customer base. According to Equifax Niche 2.0, customers are clustered based on information at the household level rather than using a geo-demographic information system like Prizm™. Each niche represents a stage in life. According to Michael Lynch, Director of Loyalty Marketing and Market Research for LEYE, "About 80% of Lettuce Frequent Diner Club members fell within eight of the 108 Equifax Superniches™." The order of prominence among our

EXHIBIT C15.4: LEYE FREQUENT DINER CLUB SEGMENTS

Niche	Super Niche	Median Income	Median Age of Head	Demographic Profile	Interests
I. IRA SPENDERS	I1	$79,000	69	Homeowners, few kids, credit card owners, mail buyers, mail responders, professional, post-graduate degree	Tennis, snow ski, health magazines, catalog orders by phone, computers, video camera, fund raising, foreign travel, wines, antiques
D. DIAMONDS-TO-GO	D1	$82,000	45	Homeowners, professional, few mail buyers, few mail responders, credit cards, kids	Videogames, late night talk shows, snow skiing, running, computers, tennis, computer magazines, camping, household pets, country music
	D2	$82,000	64	Homeowners, professional, mail buyers, mail responders, credit card owners, retired	Grandchildren, auto tools, foreign travel, cook for fun, stocks/bonds, truck owner, own one car, domestic wine, civic activity
C. CASH-TO-CARRY	C2	$81,000	45	Homeowners, professional, few mail buyers, mail responders, credit card owners, few kids	Pay TV, Public TV donor, lottery user, motorcycles, snow skiing, home remodeling, cable TV, running, hunting, frequent flyer
	C3	$81,000	67	Homeowners, professional, mail buyers, mail responders, credit card owners, retired	Grandchildren, camping equipment, volunteer work, civic activity, stock/bonds, fund raising, new age music, foreign travel, knitting/needlework
B. BIG SPENDER PARENTS	B1	$81,000	44	Homeowners, professional, post graduate degree, credit card owners, high home value, kids, mail buyers, mail responders	Racquetball, gardening, magazines, volunteer work, fund raising, foreign travel, reader, audio equipment, jewelry
C. CASH-TO-CARRY	C1	$81,000	46	Homeowners, professional, mail buyers, mail responders, credit card owners, few kids	New age music, equity loans, running, camping, lottery user, computers, real estate, household pets, volunteer work, auto tools
E. EASY STREET	E1	$81,000	65	Homeowners, credit card owners, mail buyers, mail responders, white collar, some college, kids	Videogames, auto do-it-for-me, snow skiing, daily paper reader, computers, running, tennis, household pets, camping, coupon user

Frequent Diner Club members is listed in Exhibit C15.4 from most prominent to least prominent.

According to Lynch, "When looking at the total population of diners at Lettuce Entertain You restaurants, the majority are either under the age of 35 or over the age of 55. The consistent demographic is that they either have no kids at home or the kids are old enough to care for themselves. He further states that "About 25% of our revenue comes from banquets, parties, or corporate events. About 70% is dine-in and 5% is either carryout or delivery. We find that the Frequent Diners who live within 5 miles of the restaurants visit most often. Results from marketing campaigns show that we are far more successful in trying to get a guest to try a new restaurant with a different cuisine that is located close to their homes than we are in getting the guest to try a restaurant with cuisine that is similar to their favorite that is further from their home. They are very loyal to their favorite restaurant and it is unusual to find a Frequent Diner Club member who regularly visits a number of different restaurants. Our members under the age of 35 tend to be more adventurous than our members over the age of 50. However, our guests are extremely predictable. Their visitation patterns are set and rarely change. A guest who visits on the second Tuesday of the month and spends $80 per visit will continue to visit on the second Tuesday of the month and spend about $80."

LEYE's Summer Blues

While the management of LEYE was happy with their loyalty program, it needed a boost during the slow summer months. That was the idea behind the scratch-off game, which let customers win extra bonus points. Since the goal of the new promotional offer was both to increase visits of existing customers and to attract new customers, it was aimed at both loyalty card holders and non-loyal customers.

The promotion consisted of a scratch-off direct mail coupon redeemable for different amounts. The amount was revealed once the server scratched off the coupon and was redeemable on the spot. The reward for frequent diners was extra points and for non-loyal customers it offered a different amount of dollars off the restaurant bill. There were three segments that LEYE wanted to target with this offer: LEYE frequent diners; participants from previous campaigns, but not frequent card holders (LEYE prospects); and brand new customers. The direct mail strategy was based on the following lists: 60,000 postal and email records of existing frequent diners, 50,000 postal and email records of prospects from previous campaigns, and 100,000 postal addresses of consumers with a history of dining out.

The problem with many direct mail programs is that lists get exhausted. For LEYE, this was not the first time that they were using the promotional scratch-off game. From past years they knew that participants keep on using the program year after year—they had more than 40% response rate. They also knew that the best customers live in close proximity to the restaurants, that frequent dining is a lifestyle choice and that it requires a certain level of affluence since the average bill at LEYE restaurants was around $70. The problem was that they were mailing to the same zip codes using the same selects over the years. When the lists are exhausted, there is less probability of attracting new prospects and ultimately the direct mail campaign becomes less efficient. Therefore, the question for LEYE was how they could find new prospects for a seemingly successful direct mail program.

For some time LEYE had been using the services of an agency—Diamond Marketing Solutions (DMS). DMS was behind the scratch-off promotion game as well. As they are a veteran direct marketing agency, they were well aware of the problem of exhausted lists. Hence they were looking at new ways to segment the market.

Cathy Thurman was the experienced database expert behind the effort of finding fresh segments for the LEYE summer program. She started from the traditional data mining position of a comprehensive analysis of the respondents from past years (both frequent diners and occasional customers) to understand their demographics and lifestyle. That yielded the following zip code segments:

- The traditional $70,000+ income, 35+ age
- $70,000+ income, 35+ age in high density responding zip codes
- $70,000+ income, 30+ age for new movers in combination of old and new performing zip codes
- A new segment—$70,000+ income, 30–34 age, no kids, included rentals in urban zip codes

However, from past experience, Cathy knew that this was a standard way to segment the market that would hardly increase the effectiveness of the scratch off promotional program over the past year.

The next task was to create super niche clusters based on the "birds of a feather" concept by looking at behavioral segmentation. The idea behind such segmentation is that people who share similar behavior also communicate to each other. Thus, a targeted communication strategy has the benefit not only of reaching the right people, but also of spreading more quickly among them.

The way this is done in practice is by creating clusters of similar households based on demographic characteristics. More particularly, household data are aggregated in "block groups," each of which consists of 10 households. While the data are not household-specific, they work on the assumption that similar people congregate and live near each other and therefore a household would exhibit similar lifestyle characteristics as their neighbors. Thus, every household is given a SuperNiche code, which helps with the understanding of the psychographic profiles of people based on their shared behavior.

With this idea in mind, Cathy selected specific clusters based on their match to the LEYE's loyalty customers. These were the IRA Spenders, Diamonds to Go, Cash to Carry, Big Spender Parents, and Easy Street. However, she was looking for something more. The above segments were tried and they were yielding good, but not spectacular results. And then she got the "a-ha" idea that the scratch-off game should appeal to gamers and gamblers—people who get excited by the winning factor. Thus, they decided to test a new segment—Gamers and Gamblers. The segment was constructed on the premise that the scratch-off game is similar to lotteries and has a gambling element. It had the following characteristics: $70,000+ income, 35+ age, in specific zip codes based on the best ROI of the previous year's summer effort. With these specifications DMS obtained a list of gaming and gamblers, which was compiled from multiple sources including casinos, lotteries and self-reported surveys.

After the segment selection, DMS was ready to go with the execution. The campaign was to be carried out through direct mail mainly and email as a support function to remind customers to come to the restaurants and use their rewards. Would this new segment deliver the superior results Cathy was looking for? The promotion started with a budget of $200,000 and total mailings to 210,000 households. In order to know how successful the campaign is, DMS measures results on: response rate by household, number of coupons redeemed, ROI on marketing costs, and number of new participants in the program over the previous year. Cathy's hope was that the new strategy would exceed the previous year's results, which attracted 13,534 households who redeemed 21,478 coupons and added 4126 new participants to the loyalty program.

Cathy pondered whether the scratch-off cards were the best promotional tactic for LEYE's core and prospect target markets. LEYE has a wide range of restaurants—should she investigate which restaurants received the most scratch card redemptions? Further, which are the tactics that would be most effective with different target groups? Are there other variables that should be considered when developing future promotional campaigns? All of these questions can be summed up by: Should different promotional tactics address different marketing objectives?

Cathy decided that these questions were too complicated for late-day decision-making, and decided that a nice glass of wine at the bar at a nearby LEYE restaurant, observing the post-workday crowd, might provide some inspiration. She got her coat.

Case Discussion Questions

1. LEYE's customers could dine out in venues that are more convenient (quicker) and less expensive. Why do they choose LEYE restaurants?

2. Evaluate the scratch-off card promotion. Why might this form of promotion be "good, but not spectacular" in attracting LEYE's target market segments?

3. Would the targeted Gamers and Gamblers segment be very different from LEYE's traditional target segments?

4. Evaluate the "Gamers and Gamblers" campaign. Describe how this campaign is supposed to "work" in attracting new customers. How would (or could) Cathy know if this program was effective? (Discuss how effectiveness is being measured. What are the minimum response and redemption rates that the new program should achieve in order to be deemed more effective compared to the old segmentation strategy?)

5. Would the scratch-off card be appropriate for all of the LEYE venues, i.e. consistent with strategy? Could Cathy expect that it would be more effective in increasing business at certain venues?

6. What are some other ideas that Cathy could suggest to LEYE that would increase restaurant patronage? Clearly identify the target group, the tactic proposed, and how it could be evaluated.

7. What are some recent dining trends that LEYE could consider when designing future promotions or menus?

8. Should LEYE consider teaming up with OpenTable.com or the airlines' points programs as marketing venues? What are some of the issues LEYE should consider?

C A S E
16

McDonald Garden Center

CAROL SCOVOTTI

University of Wisconsin-Whitewater

LISA D. SPILLER

Christopher Newport University

It was a wintry morning, and Pat Overton, Marketing Director for McDonald Garden Center (MGC), had arrived early to review the coming year's marketing plan. There were several nagging concerns she just couldn't get out of her mind. "So much to do, so little time," she thought to herself. "You'd think that after 37 years in this business, I'd have seen it all. We offer the best products and personalized service. Our prices are competitive with other specialty garden centers. Yet each year, we lose more customers to the big box stores. This job just isn't getting any easier."

She sat back in her chair and surveyed the greenhouse adjacent to her office. Rows of dirt-filled trays were coming to life with tender, green seedlings. It wouldn't be long before those seedlings would start sprouting the fresh buds of spring. With the first flowers came the customers. It was her job to see that those customers kept coming.

Pat couldn't stop thinking about the decisions that had to be made . . . allocating the media mix . . . the future of the rewards program . . . growing the customer base. She decided to take a walk through the network of greenhouses and clear her mind before meeting with her promotions coordinator, Sherry Connell, and the team of associates that assist with marketing activities. Decisions would have to be made soon to be ready for the spring selling season.

The Company

MGC was founded in 1945 as a single retail garden center in Hampton, Virginia. Today it serves the entire Hampton Roads area from its original store as well as two additional retail locations. The Virginia Beach store on Independence Boulevard at Haygood is near a high-income neighborhood on a busy thoroughfare with high visibility. The Chesapeake location is on Portsmouth Boulevard on the west side of the city. Although this area is still somewhat rural, city expansion is moving in that direction. (See Exhibit C16.1 for a map of the area.)

Each retail location operates as a strategic business unit and profit center (also see Exhibit C16.1). Its web site, www.mcdonaldgardencenter.com, serves as an information

EXHIBIT C16.1: ORGANIZATIONAL STRUCTURE OF MCDONALD NURSERIES CORPORATION AND HAMPTON ROADS MAP

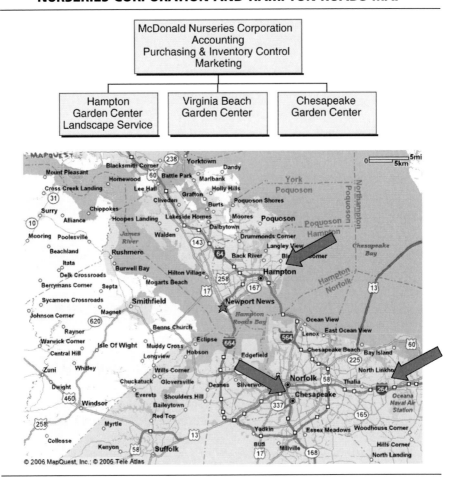

and communication resource for the organization, offering advice, promoting workshops and seminars, and highlighting products. Given the perishability of the plants, there is no option to purchase products online.

The company is owned and operated by Eddie Anderson, a man with a passion for gardening who's dedicated to his customers and staff. Eddie and his crew strive to make MGC the premier garden center in Hampton Roads, offering a wide variety of high quality products and services that enhance the lifestyle of customers for all seasons. MGC focuses on providing customers with the most informative, enjoyable, and successful shopping and gardening experiences possible.

Pat Overton describes herself as being "older than dirt" when it comes to marketing the garden center. Sherry and the staff refer to her as a guru. She's been in the industry since long before many of them were born. Eddie calls Pat and Sherry the dynamic duo and respects their zeal to know who the customers are and what they need. In this industry, strong customer relationships are critical to staying in business.

The MGC Retail Customer

MGC serves both commercial and residential customers. The commercial business serves landscapers and is managed by a separate group from the Hampton location. The typical retail customer is female, 35 to 65 years of age, with a mid-to-upper income. Customers are well educated, married with families, and own their homes. They also tend to be active (busy), civic-minded individuals who enjoy outdoor living and take great pride in their homes and gardens. MGC customers admit they willingly pay more for products because of the added value from the personalized service they receive.

Within the retail side of the business, MGC segments its residential customers by the types of products purchased. These sub-segments include:

- **Collectibles**—Collectors of unique items like Department 56 Villages and Snowbabies.
- **Outdoor Living**—Purchasers of patio furniture, fountains, statues and other outdoor decorations.
- **Indoor Plants**—Purchasers of houseplants and potted items.
- **Color Plants**—Purchasers of annuals and perennials for outdoor gardens, typically do-it-yourselfers.
- **Seed and Mulch**—Typically men who purchase lawn seed, fertilizer, peat moss, mulch, garden rock, etc., for home use.
- **Outdoor Tree and Shrubs**—Purchasers of various sized trees, bushes and shrubs for home use.

Products and Services

The diverse needs of the multiple retail segments MGC serves require an equally diverse line of products and services. In addition to indoor and outdoor plants, MGC also sells gifts and collectibles, seed, mulch and lawn care products, as well as an expansive selection of Christmas products and services. It produces many of the plants it sells to insure their hardiness. Services range from delivery, gift cards and garden advice to landscape design and installation, including tree planting and fountain set-up. Eddie sums up the philosophy of the company in one simple statement; "We know gardening and we share what we know."

Plants are an investment in the garden and home. Purchasing the best quality plants insures this investment. Plant production requires substantial resources—large areas protected from the elements, skilled staff, and lots of water. Despite substantial overhead costs, MGC prices are competitive with other garden centers and specialty stores in the area. However, its prices are usually higher than those of the big box retailers like Lowe's, The Home Depot, and Wal-Mart. Pat laments that maintaining the balance among price, variety, and service becomes more difficult as the big box stores increase their garden products offerings.

EXHIBIT C16.2: RECENT YEAR MARKET SIZE AND SECTOR SALES

All Gardening Product Sales	Four Years Ago	Three Years Ago	Two Years Ago	One Years Ago	Last Year
	$26.5	27.8	29.2	30.6	32.1
—Seeds and plants	8.3	n/a	n/a	n/a	10.1
—Lawnmowers and power tools	7.2	n/a	n/a	n/a	8.7
—Buildings and leisure equipment	5.9	n/a	n/a	n/a	7.4
—Chemicals, lawn care and fertilizer	3.7	n/a	n/a	n/a	4.1
—Hand tools and implements	1.4	n/a	n/a	n/a	1.8

The Gardening Products Industry

In the most recent past year, an estimated 84 million U.S. households participated in some form of do-it-yourself indoor or outdoor lawn and garden activity. This represented about 80 percent of all American households. As seen in Exhibit C16.2, Americans spent $32.1 billion on gardening products that year. The increase in new home sales was presumed to be a major reason for the growth in sales over the past five years.

Garden seeds and plants was the largest sector within the industry. Hand tools and implements such as trowels, shovels and spades, while the lowest in sales revenue, also experienced substantial growth. Much of the sales of garden and leisure equipment were attributed to the purchase of outdoor lawn furniture as homeowners sought to create beautiful outdoor environments to use and enjoy. Garden chemicals and fertilizers showed the slowest growth, in part, because of an overall market trend towards more organic ways to cultivate plants and lawns.

According to Euromonitor International, retail sales of garden products in the U.S. were forecast to grow to $40.8 billion within the next five years. Steady growth was expected over that period, with overall annual sales increasing by approximately five percent a year. The seeds and plants sector was expected to remain the largest, with sales reaching $12.9 billion in the next five years. The buildings and leisure equipment category was expected to reach $9.9 billion, with growth coming from the purchase of luxury garden accents like high-end barbeques, fountains, sculptures, and accessories. Both power and hand tool sales were expected to grow at their current rates. Only chemicals and fertilizer sales were projected to flatten, increasing only about 1.7 percent over the next five years.

Nationally, over half of all garden products were sold between April and June, typically in springtime. However, climatic spring occurs at different times of the year depending on geographic location. The country is divided into eight climate zones, signifying the necessary plant hardiness and the start of the growing season. Exhibit

EXHIBIT C16.3: INDUSTRY SALES BY MONTH & CLIMATE ZONE MAP

Month	Percent of Sales	Month	Percent of Sales
January	0.7	July	6.3
February	0.7	August	5.1
March	4.1	September	6.7
April	14.7	October	6.3
May	29.1	November	4.9
June	12.8	December	7.7

Source: National Gardening Association

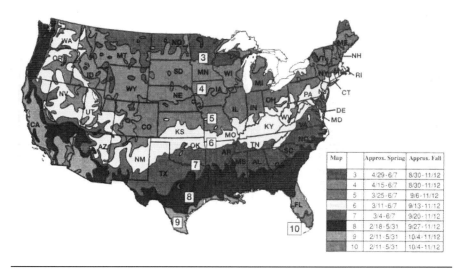

Map	Approx. Spring	Approx. Fall
3	4/29 - 6/7	8/30 - 11/12
4	4/15 - 6/7	8/30 - 11/12
5	3/25 - 6/7	9/6 - 11/12
6	3/11 - 6/7	9/13 - 11/12
7	3/4 - 6/7	9/20 - 11/12
8	2/18 - 5/31	9/27 - 11/12
9	2/11 - 5/31	10/4 - 11/12
10	2/11 - 5/31	10/4 - 11/12

C16.3 indicates the sale of gardening products on a monthly basis and the various climate zones.

Retail Outlets for Gardening Products

Homeowners shop for gardening products at a variety of retail outlets. Discount stores and home centers topped the list with The Home Depot achieving a 24 percent market share in the previous year. Wal-Mart was second (18 percent) and Lowe's was third (10.5 percent). These three retailers accounted for over half of all residential gardening products sold in the U.S. Price, variety, and location were the primary reasons consumers shopped at these stores.

Garden supply stores accounted for 21 percent of sales that same year, down from 23 percent in the previous year. This category of retail outlet included specialty garden retailers, including the small, independent local or regional chains like MGC. Customers who enjoy close, personal relationships and advice from more knowledgeable horticulturalists tend to shop at the smaller, locally owned garden centers. However, the composition of this category could possibly change. Rumor had it that The Home Depot planned to open Landscape Supply stores, the first nationwide lawn and garden chain aimed at lawn care and garden professionals. This move was expected to cause more wholesale sales to shift in the gardening supply store category but could make it more difficult for specialty garden retailers to hold market share. With census data indicating that Hampton Roads accounted for 0.5 percent of all households and with the greater propensity of Southerners to use landscapers, the area appeared to be a prime candidate for one of the new Landscape Supply stores.

The Typical Gardener

The breadth of what is classified as gardening is extensive. For some, gardening means having a few potted plants on an apartment balcony. For others, it means various sized plant and vegetable beds. Some of the most extravagant gardens are extensive spaces filled with plants, ponds, and furnishings.

The National Gardening Association estimates that, on average, U.S. households spent $449 on gardening products in the most recent year. This was up slightly from the previous year where the expenditures averaged $440 but down from the year before that, where the typical household spent $466. While practically all American homeowners purchase gardening products, the ones who purchase more than the national average tend to be 45 years of age or older, college graduates with an annual income of at least $50,000. Households in the Midwest and South tend to spend more on gardening activities than those in other parts of the country. The typical buyer is married and lives in a two-person household where both are either employed full-time or retired. Despite industry-wide efforts to involve more children in gardening, those who spend the most on gardening products tend to have no children living at home. Men purchase more lawn seed, fertilizer, power tools and mulch while women purchase more plants, lawn decorations and hand tools.

The Professional Landscaping Business

While the purchase of gardening products has increased over the past several years, so too has residential use of professional landscape and lawn care services. In the previous year, 17.4 million households nationwide spent an average of $556 with service providers in lieu of doing the work themselves. Exhibit C16.4 indicates residential use of these services. The typical residential user of landscaping service is 50 years of age or older, has a college degree, and an annual household income of over $75,000. Research suggests that as homeowners get older and make more income, they are more likely to use professional landscaping companies to handle their lawn and garden maintenance needs.

The residential use of professional landscaping services differs by region of the country. Homeowners living in Southern states tend to rely on landscape professionals more so than elsewhere in the country. An estimated 24 percent of Southern households, including those in Hampton Roads, use outside service providers compared with 16 percent nationwide. This trend is of particular concern to MGC because as the income of area residents rises, so too does the likelihood they will hire

EXHIBIT C16.4: RESIDENTIAL USE OF PROFESSIONAL LANDSCAPING COMPANIES

	Five Years Ago	Four Years Ago	Three Years Ago	Two Years Ago	One Year Ago
Households that Use (in %)	14	15	16	17	16
Households that Use (in Millions)	14.9	16.3	17.8	19.4	17.4
Average Spent per Household ($)	540	543	547	550	556
Total Spent per Year ($ Billions)	9.0	9.7	10.4	10.7	9.8

Source: National Gardening Association

professional landscapers rather than do the work themselves. How that would impacts retail gardening product sales remained to be seen.

Special Events Marketing and Pre-Rewards Program

MGC strives to portray itself as the area's premier, full-service garden specialist, having the most knowledgeable staff that offers sound advice, quality plants, and "no questions asked" guarantees. Pat, Sherry and the marketing staff run several special events each year to highlight seasonal items and activities, as well as drive customers to its retail locations. Some of its big events include:

- **Outdoor Show**—Here customers can discover new products and services presented by local businesses, seeing everything from stir-fry cooking to elegant floral arrangements in a garden setting. This March event features over 80 vendor exhibits, displays, demonstrations, free seminars, activities, and a Kids' Corner.
- **A Butterfly Affair**—This annual event is held each May and includes live-action displays featuring crawling caterpillars and flying butterflies and the plants that attract them. Seminars and "how-to" classes by a butterfly specialist inform attendees of the butterfly life cycle and how to attract them to their yards.
- **Crepe Myrtle Festival**—This is one of MGC's oldest promotional events. "Myrtle Money" is distributed to customers who purchase products between May and July, redeemable at the festival in mid-July. The event features exhibits, booths, and refreshments.
- **Garden Fiesta**—This festival celebrates the spirit and color of the Southwest, complete with Mexican music, sombreros, piñatas and fiesta balloons. The event is held in June and features seminars, "how-to" demonstrations, and activities for children.
- **Designer Days**—Consumers have the opportunity to make their garden visions come to life in August with access to landscape designers, "how-to" seminars,

EXHIBIT C16.5: MEDIA BUDGET ALLOCATION— PRE- AND POST- REWARDS CARD LAUNCH

Media Type	Percent of Budget: Pre-Rewards Program Launch	Percent of Budget: Post Rewards Program Launch
Newspaper	65	45
Broadcast (Television and Radio)	20	30
Direct Mail (including Newsletters)	10	22
Other	5	3
Total Budget	100	100

Source: Company

and speakers. A "visions" contest awards the creativity of several consumer do-it-yourself garden projects.

- **Grass Roots and the American Red Cross**—This cause-related event is held every Labor Day weekend. The focus is on fall lawn care, with educational programs and putt-putt golf for customers. A portion of weekend's net sales benefits the American Red Cross.
- **Holiday Open House**—This November event features ideas, products, gifts, and time-saving decorating tips for the holiday season.

In addition to these annual events, MGC offers over 50 customer educational seminars throughout the year at each store. It distributes its *Greenleaves* newsletter to approximately 20,000 customers on its mailing list. In years past, most of its marketing budget was spent on promoting the annual events. Getting people to come to an event was thought to drive customer retail traffic to the stores.

As popular as the events were, MGC felt the growing pressures from the big box stores. The Home Depot, Wal-Mart, and Lowe's used low price as a strategic weapon. MGC's marketing budget at that time was 3.5 percent of annual sales. Exhibit C16.5 shows the percent of budget for the media mix before the *Garden Rewards* program was introduced.

The "Garden Rewards" Program

One day about four years previous, as Pat and Sherry strolled through the bodacious gardens of the Hampton store, they realized the company's existing marketing activities wouldn't continue to deliver the results achieved prior to the entry of the mass merchandisers. Pat lamented, "We just can't beat their prices."

Sherry noted, "And the cost of media keeps going up. Cable TV has created so many viewing options for prospective customers, we can't afford to buy time on all those different stations to reach them. Who's to say they're even seeing our commercials?"

Television wasn't the only problematic medium. With more than 33 radio stations in the Hampton Roads area, it was especially difficult to select and expensive to buy enough ad time to reach prospective customers. The power of newspaper advertising was also diminishing as readership rates decreased due to people's busy schedules. As Pat and Sherry reviewed the media mix, they realized that most of their marketing activities were not measurable. They were "mass marketing" to the entire geographic market in hopes of reaching a select group of prospects. The media delivered impressions . . . but no one was sure of the response or the return on the promotional dollars.

Pat and Sherry were sure that the "80/20 Principle" applied to the company's customer base, but they had no way to identify or communicate with that most valued 20 percent. After extensive research, they determined a loyalty program would help the company establish stronger relationships with its best customers. A customer loyalty program would enable them to know the value of each customer and tailor product and service offerings that fit their gardening activities.

While a rewards program appeared to be a sound idea, it wasn't without its challenges. Over the past few decades, several retailers have tried a variety of incentives to build customer loyalty. Results have been mixed. Those able to impact loyalty the most seemed to make their programs the focal point of all promotional efforts. For Pat and Sherry to make their program work, all existing marketing activities would have to be integrated to reflect the importance of the new program. That meant MGC's newsletter, collectibles program, Golden Gardeners program for senior citizens, business partner programs, coupons, and all future advertisements would have to be changed. A "Privacy Policy" would need to be established to let customers know of the company's commitment to protecting information about them. Despite the implementation complexities, Pat and Sherry decided to establish such a program.

"Garden Rewards" had launched nearly four years ago. Membership was free to anyone willing to sign up. Benefits included members-only price discounts, participation in special events, and various program partnership opportunities. Pat and Sherry thought the cornerstone incentive would be the annual rewards attained by accumulating points. Exhibit C16.6 shows the *Garden Rewards* card, list of benefits, and reward point awards.

Just prior to launch, all MGC employees were trained to get everybody "on board" with the program, and change their mass media mentality to a one-on-one marketing mindset. The overall goals of the initiative were to identify current customers and their needs to serve them better. All customers were encouraged to become cardholders. Initial benchmarks were purposely set high—30 percent of all transactions would be recorded in the customer database through card use within the first two weeks of the program launch, and 60 percent of all transactions within the following six weeks.

Within six weeks of the launch, 15,375 customers signed up and used their card at least once. Over 42 percent had used their cards two or more times. The data also revealed findings Pat never expected. For example, the maximum number of times a single card was used in the first six weeks was 26! About seven percent of the cardholders had spent over $1,000 with their Garden Rewards card in the first six weeks of launching the program.

Within six months of the launch, 32,000 Garden Rewards cards had been issued. Over 28,000 cards had been used once and 15,173 cards were used two or more times. One card had been used a whopping 67 times! Was this an anomaly? Not really. During that six-month timeframe, a water-gardening customer used her card 55

EXHIBIT C16.6: GARDEN REWARDS CARD
AND PROMOTIONAL MATERIALS

active membership **benefits**

- **Special member discounts on selected plants and garden products**
  ~ Special garden rewards prices on plants and products just for card members.

- **Special member discounts on McDonald Garden Center brand items**
  ~ Extra savings on Lawn Food, Green Leaf Plant Food & more.

- **Special savings on new or exclusive introductions**
  ~ When new plants arrive, members will get early choices and extra savings.

- **Golden Gardeners Day**
  ~ Every Tuesday, members over 60 automatically receive 10% off reg price

- **Greenleaves newsletter subscription for active members**
  ~ The best gardening news for Hampton Roads, mailed to your home — with valuable coupons!

- **FREE local delivery on purchases over $500**

- **FREE registration to seminars and workshops**
  ~ Sign up in advance without a registration fee.

- **FREE pH soil testing**
  ~ Bring a soil sample and we will test the acidity so you know your planting needs.

- **Special Member Days**
  ~ Special preferred member appreciation days with exclusive opportunities.

- **Lost Key program**
  ~ Your key tag assures keys can be dropped in any mail box, return postage guaranteed.

- **Advance notice of selected special events & programs**
  ~ Notification of special customer previews & programs.

- **No annual membership fee**
  ~ Good year after year.
  ~ Not a credit card.

garden reward points

Earn garden reward points on all purchases throughout the year.

Reward Points & Annual Awards

500 to 999 points = $10 gift card

1000 to 1999 points = $25 gift card

2000 to 2999 points = $75 gift card

3000 points and up = $150 gift card

~ Earn one point for every $1 purchase of goods.

~ Use of each card or tag contributes to your total purchases and earns you extra garden reward points throughout the year.

~ Reward points are accrued within each calendar year.

~ Check your point progress on our website: www.mcdonaldgardencenter.com

- Points will be awarded annually; point rewards are awarded by mail before the end of the first quarter.
- All information involving use of this card will be kept confidential and used exclusively to provide you with our special values.
- We reserve the right to change or discontinue the program, card or benefits at any time.
- Returned items will show as adjusted (deducted) points. Points are non-transferrable.

**EXHIBIT C16.7: AVERAGE TRANSACTION AMOUNTS—
GARDEN REWARDS MEMBERS VS. UNIDENTIFIED CUSTOMERS**

Retail Location	Average Transaction: Without Garden Rewards Card	Average Transaction: With Garden Rewards Card
Hampton	$35.15	$44.12
Chesapeake	$33.34	$42.52
Virginia Beach	$38.98	$48.40

Source: Company

times. In addition, overall transaction amounts were found to be higher among card-holders compared to the unidentified customers. (See Exhibit C16.7.)

The Garden Rewards program enabled MGC to divert much of its marketing budget to more targeted media, and in doing so, increase overall profitability. Although the number of retail transactions was down in the first year of the loyalty program as compared to the previous year, average revenue per transaction was up between $9 and $10. While the company continues to allocate 3.5 percent of sales to its marketing budget, the net effect has been a two percent increase in gross margin for the year.

The new focus on the loyalty program caused Pat and Sherry to also allocate more of the budget for broadcast media. Television spots would now focus on the benefits of membership in the loyalty program and invite prospects to visit one of the stores to sign up. The last column in Exhibit C16.5 indicates today's budget allocation figures by media.

Decision #1: Keeping the Offer Fresh

In the time since the launch of Garden Rewards program, over 96,000 customers had obtained and used the card. However, the number of active customers remained at about the same level it did six months after the launch of the program. The challenge Pat and Sherry faced was continuing to identify new ways to keep the Garden Rewards program fresh and persuade more customers to use it. The persistent question at every brainstorming session was "What more can we offer these people? What will entice the different customer segments to shop more frequently and spend more at our stores?"

Popular benefits previously introduced included:

- Two-for-one admission tickets for many of the area's educational and historical museums, including The Chrysler Museum, Endview Plantation, Lee Hall Mansion, Mariner's Museum, Norfolk Botanical Gardens and Virginia Air & Space Center.
- Free local delivery of MGC purchases over $500.
- Bonus points on random days or for the purchase of specific products.
- Advanced notices via email for special events and promotions.

- Free pH soil testing service.
- Lost key program. (MGC supplies its *Garden Rewards* members with a coded key chain. Lost keys could be dropped into any mailbox by the finder, with MGC paying the postage for returning the keys to the owner.)

Sherry assembled ideas for five different postcard mailings planned for the coming year or two and presented them to Pat. The projected costs as well as sample pieces are found in Exhibit C16.8.

Decision #2—Cleaning and Expanding the Customer Base

MGC's database currently held 96,000 records with approximately 12,000 new customers signing up each year. However, only 32,000 were considered active, earning at least 50 reward points in a given year. The longer the company maintained the database, the greater the challenge of keeping customer records current. Knowing that 20 percent of Americans move each year, Pat feared the database had records of people who no longer lived at the addresses on file. With a high percentage of military personnel living in the area, many who had moved might no longer be in the state.

Both Pat and Sherry agreed the records in the database had to be checked for currency and cleaned. The question was how? Once the outdated records were removed, how many "actives" would remain? They also struggled with determining the "right" definition of "active." Fearing the worst, they knew that in addition to efforts to retain existing customers, they would have to do something to attract new ones.

After much research and work with a list broker, they identified several list rental possibilities. But which ones would maximize response for a new customer offer? Exhibit C16.9 provides details regarding several lists Pat and Sherry are considering. Each list also had options for additional segmentation selections to pinpoint who they thought would be the most likely customers. Lists could be further segmented by zip code (for an additional $5 per thousand), gender ($6 per thousand extra), state ($8 per thousand extra), income ($10 per thousand extra), education ($7 per thousand extra) and/or marital status ($8 per thousand extra).

In addition to list selection, they also needed to determine an attractive offer. Sherry created two postcard offers to increase membership in the Garden Rewards program, one for free garden gloves, the other for a free geranium plant. (See Exhibit C16.10.) Each offer was determined by looking at product inventory, availability, quantity, cost, season, and broad market appeal. Before making a final decision on the offer, Pat proposed a 500-piece test mailing of both to measure response rates. Each mail piece would cost $0.93 to produce at such limited quantities and $0.39 to mail First Class. Garden glove fulfillment costs were estimated at $4.00 while the geranium plant fulfillment cost was $5.00.

Summary of the Decisions

Pat returned to her office refreshed. Walking through the gardens always helped her clear her head. She sat down, opened her notebook, and made a list of the questions to cover with Sherry and the marketing staff during the upcoming meeting.

EXHIBIT C16.8: SAMPLES OF POSSIBLE UPCOMING POSTCARD MAILINGS WITH ASSOCIATED COSTS

Offer	Potential Segment	Quantity Mailed	Cost per Piece		
			Printing	*Postage*	*Redemption*
Cone-Crazy	Top 600 GR Members	600	$0.50	$0.37	$2.50
Garden		350	$0.50	$0.37	$2.50
Center of the Year	Top 350 GR Members				
Halloween		500	$0.50	$0.37	$5.00
Happy Birthday	Top 500 GR Members GR customers who spent > $500 in the previous year	413	$0.84	$0.39	$2.50
Roses	Top 2000 GR Members	2,000	$0.50	$0.37	$6.25

GR = *Garden Rewards*
Source: Company

EXHIBIT C16.9: LIST RENTAL OPTIONS

List	Description	Base Price	Minimum Quantity
American Gardener Magazine	Members of the American Horticultural Society. Avid and master gardeners, professional horticulturalists.	$100/M	5,000
American Private Golf Club Members	Serious golfers who play at private country clubs. Compiled from membership lists and prize recipients at golf events.	$95/M	5,000
Backyard Garden Design	Passionate, creative home gardeners. Subscribe to multiple home and garden publications	$85/M	5,000
Gardening Enthusiasts	Consumers with a love for gardening and a green thumb to prove it. From seeds to soil, these gardening buffs are open to offers that will help them enhance their gardens	$70/M	5,000
Hobby Enthusiast Network	Hobbyists with interests ranging from gambling to gardening.	$70/M	5,000
Hispanic Hearth & Home	Individuals who want to improve, decorate, and landscape their property.	$85/M	5,000
Martha Stewart Living Gardening Enhanced	Affluent, paid subscribers who have expressed an interest in gardening. Upscale, well-educated women who love to garden and have the discretionary income to purchase garden products and services.	$105/M	7,500
New Homeowners	Compiled from public sources including county deed records. Updated monthly.	$64/M	5,000

Source: NextMark, Inc.

- What should we do to keep the *Garden Rewards* program fresh and enticing to get members to continue shopping at our stores?
- What level of response can we expect when targeting such small segments of customers like Sherry recommends? What will it cost us to generate that response?
- Of the five postcards Sherry recommended, are there one or two offers that look the most promising? Given the costs and quantities, what response rates are needed for the mailing to breakeven?

EXHIBIT C16.10: SAMPLES OF POTENTIAL POSTCARDS FOR CUSTOMER ACQUISITION PROGRAM

Source: Company

Some of the data provided by the company has been disguised and is not useful for research purposes. The authors would like to thank Pat Overton and Sherry Connell of McDonald Garden Center for their help in this project.

- How should we go about cleaning the database and how many active records are likely to remain once the old ones are deleted?
- How should the *Garden Rewards* program database be segmented? Should we be treating customer segments differently?
- Which of the lists identified look most promising for generating new *Garden Rewards* program members?
- Have we extinguished all the possibilities with what we have in house? How might we prospect for new customers using our current customer database?
- If we do use one or more of these outside lists, should we add additional selects?
- Can we estimate which of the two offers Sherry created for new customer acquisition has the best chance of success? What are the response rates needed to breakeven with each of these options?
- Numbers aside, what do we expect the qualitative impact to be if we go with either of these offers?
- Given the highly competitive environment, are our growth aspirations realistic?

As Pat reviewed her list of questions, she realized the decisions she and her staff were about to make would impact the company for years to come. Just then, Sherry poked her head into the office. "You ready for us?" Sherry asked. Pat replied, "Sure. Let's do it."

Bibliography

Enright, Michael and Heath McDonald, (1997). "The Melbourne Garden Nursery Industry: A Qualitative Review of Marketing and New Product Development Orientation in a Retail Environment," *Journal of Product and Brand Management,* 6 (3), 175—188.

Florkowski, W. and G. Landry, (2000). "An Economic Profile of the Professional Turfgrass and Landscape Industry in Georgia," *The Georgia Agricultural Experiment Stations: University of Georgia,* December.

"Garden Market Forecast: Retail Consumer Behavior," (2003). Unity Marketing, Stevens, PA. www.retailindustry.about.com.

"Garden Market Research," (2006). *National Gardening Association.* www.gardenresearch.com.

"Gardening Products in the USA—October 2005, (2005). Euromonitor International.

Jerardo, Alberto, (2005). "Floriculture and Nursery Crops Outlook," *Electronic Outlook Report from the Economic Research Service,* United States Department of Agriculture, September. www.ers.usda.gov.

Mosquera, Gabrielle, (2003). "Gardeners," *Target Magazine,* May, 26 (5), 65—66.

NextMark List Research Systems. (2006). NextMark, Inc., Hanover NH., www.nextmark.com.

"Population by State," (2006) United States Census Bureau. www.census.gov.

CASE
17

Nonna's Italian Restaurant

LISA D. SPILLER
Christopher Newport University

CAROL SCOVOTTI
University of Wisconsin-Whitewater

It was a dreary Saturday morning in May. Anna Russo Coggeshall watched as a long awaited delivery of fresh produce arrived at the new location of Nonna's Italian Restaurant. The co-owner scrutinized several cases of broccoli rabe while her brother and business partner, Cris Russo, moved about the still unfamiliar kitchen. In addition to preparing for the usual lunch and dinner crowds, a large private event was scheduled for the restaurant's outdoor patio later that evening. With the growing chance of rain, it didn't look good for an outdoor party. As she examined the shipment, Anna chastised herself. "Never agree to serve a dish for a catering client with hard to find ingredients, especially when it has to come from a supplier the family hasn't used before." The broccoli rabe, available only from a distributor new to Anna and Cris, arrived two days late. She wanted to fulfill a special request from a customer who booked a birthday party for 60 people at the restaurant's outdoor patio that evening. "At least we can cordon off some space in the restaurant if the weather is too bad," she thought to herself. "The one thing you can count on is things never going according to plan."

Like the rest of the country, Hampton Roads was feeling the impact of the economic recession. In the harsh business climate, area restaurants and catering businesses were even hungrier than usual for customers. Everyone in the business knew their continued operation depended on keeping customers walking through the doors. Parties of 60 people were becoming few and far between. To renege on a promise, even one as simple as getting a favorite vegetable, could have dire consequences. After all, this wasn't just one dinner affected by a late delivery, it was 60. In Anna's mind, that was 60 potential customers. While good customer experiences take time, money, and effort to disseminate, and even longer to register in the minds of customers, she knew that news of an unsatisfied customer's experience spreads like a virus, potentially driving the few remaining customers away to the competition.

Some of the data provided by the company has been disguised and is not useful for research purposes. The authors would like to thank Anna Russo Coggeshall for her help in this project.

EXHIBIT C17.1: ANNA RUSSO COGGESHALL AND CRIS RUSSO— OWNERS OF NONNA'S ITALINA RESTAURANT

Luckily the batch of vegetables was perfect so the special request could be fulfilled. Anna motioned her approval to Cris, who scooped up the thirteenth-hour arrival, whisking off the boxes of broccoli rabe for last minute preparation. One crisis avoided. However, Anna knew it would take more than last minute vegetable arrivals to get the business through the tough economic times that lay ahead.

The Family Tradition Continues . . . Sort Of

Anna and Cris came from a long line of family restaurateurs so they knew the importance of reputation, loyalty, and quality. Anna's Pizza, a family owned pizzeria and Italian restaurant franchise, was started by their grandfather more than 40 years ago. Cristoforo Russo emigrated from Sicily in the early 1960s. He believed the "American Dream" was his for the taking with lots of hard work, passion for food, and talent for cooking. He named his first restaurant after his mother, sister and daughter: Anna. The first Anna's Pizza and Italian Restaurant opened in New York City, but within a few years of arriving in America, Cristoforo moved his family and business to what he saw as an up and coming area in southern Virginia. In the 20 years that followed, he opened multiple Anna's Pizza restaurants across Hampton Roads, which he sold to his children and other relatives who relocated to the area. One of his restaurants was purchased by his son Joseph, the father of Anna and Cris.

From the moment Joseph's children could walk, they were involved with their father's restaurant. Joseph knew that one day it would be his turn to continue the

EXHIBIT C17.2: NONNA'S MENU

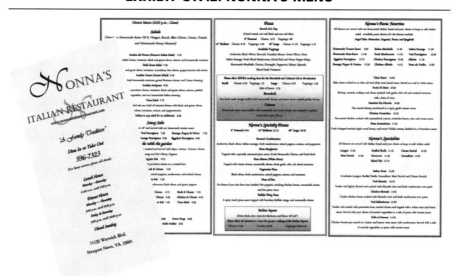

Anna's Pizza family franchise tradition so he trained his four children in the business as his father had trained him. However, as the third generation of Russos entered adulthood, Anna and Cris had other ideas. Although the siblings wanted to honor everything their grandfather and father had worked so hard to achieve, they felt the Anna's Pizza concept needed a makeover. The traditional small pizzeria with laminated tables in a strip mall wasn't for them. Instead, they wanted to branch away and create a more upscale, reasonably priced, dine-in Italian restaurant. In addition to the upscale dine-in format, they envisioned their restaurant to have the capacity to handle large parties and events. At the ages of 25 and 24 respectively, Anna and Cris found a small, but suitable location in a strip mall with capacity to seat 70 people. While it wasn't ideal for their catering plans, it was a good test site to see how their upscale concept would work.

Like their father and grandfather, Anna and Cris made all their food from scratch using only fresh ingredients. They revived old family recipes created by their great-grandmother (the family matriarch Anna) for dipping oil, salad dressing, and tomato sauce. Customers loved the unique sauces so much that it didn't take long for demand for these specialty products to grow. Anna and Cris saw their new restaurant concept taking on a dimension never before tried by the family—a line of packaged gourmet products.

One of the first obstacles the duo faced was what to call their new restaurant. They wanted a strong name that would honor their family and connect the new restaurant with their grandfather's well-known business, but without calling it "Anna." After considerable debate and a bit of family conflict, they named their restaurant "Nonna's", the Italian word for grandmother. The name quickly became a great conversation starter among their patrons. Customers often inquired about its origin, which gave Anna, Cris, or their employees an opportunity to explain the family background in the restaurant industry. It also gave them the opportunity to casually promote the specialty oil, dressing and tomato sauce they had developed from great-grandmother's recipes. The sibling partners found the name and the story served as a source of credibility that most young entrepreneurs would otherwise have to work long and hard to create. Given the economic climate, they would need all the advantages they could muster.

The Restaurant Industry in Crisis

In harsh economic times, the restaurant industry is not for the weak of heart . . . or stomach. Total sales across all formats of full service restaurants in the U.S. were an estimated $181 billion in a recent year. According to the National Restaurant Association, sales were projected to decline in the following year by 2.5 percent. When money gets tight, people stop eating in restaurants. A study of American consumers by Nielsen found that 52 percent of Americans were going to casual dining establishments less often than the prior year and 66 percent no longer frequented fine dining restaurants. When Americans did go to restaurants, they stopped bringing their children. That meant smaller average check amounts. According to a study released by the NPD Group/Crest, adults-only parties had increased two percent in the previous year, while parties with children had decreased three percent in the same timeframe.

The result of fewer people patronizing restaurants less often and spending less money prompted restaurateurs to significantly reduce their staffing levels. Casual and fine dining establishments were the categories hardest hit in the recession. More than 70 percent of all casual dining restaurants were forced to reduce their staff while more than 80 percent of upscale casual/fine dining restaurants made personnel cuts over the past year (Lebhar-Friedman Inc.).

Anna and Cris had opened Nonna's almost two years ago in June, just prior to the economic downturn. However, their lifetime of experience and Anna's education in direct marketing caused the duo to realize they had to become innovative with their marketing. What they needed was "shark marketing on a minnow's budget." Database-driven direct marketing was the answer.

Database-Driven Direct Marketing

During the first 18 months of Nonna's business operation, Anna got to know her regular patrons. In addition to maintaining a record of the likes and dislikes of her regular customers, she created a "comment card" that customers completed, providing feedback on their dining experiences. Along with their comments, Anna asked for contact information—specifically, name, postal and email addresses. She created a rewards program of sorts where, on a monthly basis, she would treat one of the respondents from the prior month to a free meal. The comment cards provided valuable customer input that she used to establish a database for Nonna's and the possibility of a free meal enticed patrons to complete them. Armed with their new customer database, Anna and Cris were able to promote their specials and offers to their regular customers in a cost efficient and effective manner.

As their business grew, the need for larger space became evident. The upscale dine-in concept coupled with the delicious fare drew in customers to the extent where there were wait times of over an hour. The demand for the packaged specialty products was more than their little kitchen could withstand. Plus, Anna and Cris still didn't have the facilities they wanted for their catering business. In just under two years in business, and amid an economic downturn, the twosome found themselves in need of more space.

Location, Location, Location

Successful restaurants are found in locations that cater to the needs and desired experiences of its customers. Unlike Anna's Pizza where customers either picked up orders to go or ate quickly at small tables inside the pizzeria, Nonna's was more of a dining destination. In addition to finding a building with the desired amenities in the right price range with all the utilities required of the business, site selection experts suggest restaurants in the midscale casual category should be located in a mixed use area that has residential dwellings, colleges, universities and/or business parks. Convenient access, ample parking, visibility from a main thoroughfare and opportunity for adequate signage are also important site selection criteria (Nation's Restaurant News, 2006; White 2008). Anna and Cris also wanted it to be close to their strip mall location so current customers wouldn't have far to travel.

Within months of deciding to move to larger space, Anna and Cris found what they considered to be the perfect location. The stand alone building had the capacity to seat 250 people, with a private dining room that could seat 35 and an outdoor patio for up to 60 people. The kitchen was substantially larger so it could accommodate the production of the gourmet specialty products as well as the meals for the restaurant. It was in a mixed use area with a high school, grade school and large church just one block away. Within a mile radius, there was a state university, regional medical center, and several popular museums and civic centers. A large technology park housing hundreds of businesses was less than three miles away. Unlike the old location that was hidden in the back of a strip mall, the new location offered excellent visibility from a major boulevard with the capability of large signage that could be seen from the street. Best of all, it was less than a mile away from the former location so there would be minimal loss of neighborhood clientele.

Shortly after the opening of the new location, Anna and Cris held a special "invitation only" dinner for their regular customers. A professionally designed invitation was created and mailed to 130 of their regular customers. Exhibit C17.4 displays the direct mail package for this special event. This direct mail promotion garnered a 31 percent response rate, filling the new large restaurant on the day of their special event. When the invited guests responded, they were encouraged to bring their friends to the event and share the special experience. Anna and Cris used this opportunity to expand the Nonna's database with the new patrons while strengthening relationships with their existing customers.

EXHIBIT C17.3: NONNA'S ITALIAN RESTAURANT

EXHIBIT C17.4: NONNA'S DIRECT MAIL INVITATION PACKAGE

Competition

Nonna's has several direct competitors serving Italian cuisine within a 10 mile radius. In addition to outlets for major and mid-size chains like Olive Garden, Romano's Macaroni Grill, and Fazoli's, three independently owned restaurants operate in the area; Anna's Pizza and Italian Restaurant, Joe and Mimma's Italian Restaurant, and Azure's Italian Restaurant. With their multi-million dollar advertising budgets funding prime time television commercials that claim, "When you're here, you're family," the large chains capture a significant portion of local market share. Their buying power enables them to maintain low prices. Anna and Cris knew that trying to compete head to head with these giants in the mainstream media was impossible. Where they could compete was on the quality of their products. Nonna's commitment to only serving homemade foods with fresh ingredients differentiated them from the large chains that use pre-packaged ingredients. The difference in taste between Nonna's and the large chains was indisputable to the discriminating palate.

Anna and Cris found their fiercest competition to be the nearby small independent restaurants. The owners of Joe and Mimma's as well as Azure's are cousins of Anna and Cris and offer similar family recipes. The Anna's Pizza and Italian Restaurant up the road is the only family franchise that Cristoforo sold to an entrepreneur who was not in the Russo family. All used a combination of fresh and pre-packaged ingredients.

There are positive and negative factors associated with competition among family businesses. On the positive side, being close to other family restaurants lends both recognition and credibility to all associated with the family enterprise. When patrons of Anna's Pizza and Italian Restaurant discovered that Anna and Cris are third generation Russos, they were more willing to try Nonna's. Many became loyal customers. Another competitive edge was that the other competing Italian restaurants used the pizzeria format, while Nonna's was a full-service Italian restaurant that featured a full bar, banquet room and outside patio.

EXHIBIT C17.5: NONNA'S PROMOTIONAL OFFERS

Offer	Quantity Mailed	Quantity Redeemed	Response Rate	Cost per Piece		
				Printing	Postage	Redemption Costs
Valentine's Day Special	300	175	58%	$0.88	$0.42	$20.00
Family Feast Day Special	600	225	38%	$088	$0.42	$25.00
Discount Offer	2,000	1,200	60%	$0.88	$0.42	$10.00 (Ave.)
Cooperative Mailings						
Buy One/Get One Free	3,600	100	2.8%	—	—	$12.00 (Ave.)
$ 5.00 Off	250	20	8%	—	—	$5.00

Source: Company

On the negative side, competing with family relatives is emotionally difficult and can generate conflict. While Anna and Cris wanted their family members to be successful with their business ventures, they knew that any customer dining down the street was not in their restaurant. Some who frequent multiple Russo establishments have mentioned the higher prices charged at Nonna's as a reason for not patronizing and of course the relatives/owners have been quick to point out that the young entrepreneurs charge the highest prices in the area. Nonna's prices are between 10 and 20 percent higher than the nearby family competition. Despite the continual pressure, Anna and Cris have decided not to compromise the quality and taste of Nonna's products to lower their prices or make a larger profit on their products. They see having fresh, made from scratch food as a competitive advantage and use it as a unique selling point (USP) when compared with its local competitors. The quality and taste of food is often noticed at first bite. Nonna's distinct building design, along with its many services sets it apart from both the large chains and nearby independent restaurants.

Promotional Activities

Along with many intrinsic and extrinsic rewards of owning and operating a family restaurant, the business poses many challenges. One of the biggest on-going challenges is effective marketing. Since they first opened the restaurant's doors nearly two years ago, Anna and Cris have tried a variety of special direct response promotions to drive customer traffic to the restaurant and increase customer patronage. As detailed in Exhibit C17.5, some of these offers have been more effective than others in attracting customers to Nonna's.

To date, Anna and Cris have spent more than $30,000 on direct response promotions to market their restaurant. Marketing efforts have included the creation of Nonna's web site, brochures, menus, signage on the restaurant building and road, cooperative mailing coupons, direct mail and flyers, ads placed in the Yellow Pages phone book and the Yellow Book. In addition, Nonna's has incurred public relations expenses in the form of product and gift certificate donations to local school and community groups. Since its establishment, Nonna's has offered regular discounts on the purchase of food items to students and service men and women with proper identification.

When Nonna's first opened, Anna and Cris invested a lot of time and resources to try to attract customers to their new restaurant. They soon discovered that "Free" and "1/2 off" direct mail offers did not generate the type of business or clientele that they desired. In fact, the "free" direct mailers had a negative effect on the business and its image. Anna and Cris participated in two different cooperative mailings and found that although these direct mail formats were less costly than sending stand-alone direct mail to prospective customers, they were not effective in generating loyal customers. These cooperative formats included:

- **Money Clip**—The coupons placed in this medium seemed to produce coupon-reliant customers who would only visit the restaurant when they had a coupon in hand. Although Anna placed monthly ads in this booklet for an entire year, it did not create loyal customers for Nonna's. The coupons featured the following offers:
  —**Buy one Dinner get second of equal or lesser value for free**
  —**Buy one Dinner get second of equal or lesser value for 1/2 off**
  —**Buy one Large Pizza get a second pizza for 1/2 off**
  —**Receive $3.00 off on one large pizza**

- **Val Pack**—Advertising in this monthly coupon mail pack was another method that was ineffective in generating regular customers. This medium was utilized for two consecutive months; however, it garnered negative feedback and was discontinued. The coupons used included the following offers:
  —**Buy any 2 dinners and 2 beverages and get $5.00 off your ticket price**
  —**Buy any 2 lunches and 2 beverages and get $2.00 off your ticket price**

Beyond cooperative advertising, other methods and mediums used by Nonna's to promote the restaurant included:

- **Discount Mailers**—Discount postcards offering a 10 percent discount on the next purchase were distributed to the local neighborhoods surrounding Nonna's. These postcards were effective in generating awareness of a "new neighbor" and garnered a number of loyal customers. See Exhibit C17.6 for Nonna's discount postcard.
- **Special Invitation Dinner Events**—Postcards, shown in Exhibit C17.7, were mailed to select loyal customers from Nonna's customer database for two unique special dinner events—a Valentine's Day Dinner and a Seafood Feast. The first event was a family style dinner night at discounted price. The second was a five course meal at a discounted price. Both of these special events were very well received and generated great business.
- **Our Town Mailers**—This direct mailer is distributed monthly to new residents within specified ZIP code areas. The mailer can be used to generate a database, based on the customers who redeem the direct mail offer. However, this method has not generated good repeat business and will be discontinued at the conclusion of the one-year contract.

EXHIBIT C17.6: NONNA'S DISCOUNT OFFER POSTCARD MAILER

Nonna's Italian Restaurant
11006 Warwick Blvd, Suite 446B
Newport News, VA 23601

PRST-STD
U.S. POSTAGE
PAID
CITY, ST
PERMIT NO.

Present this postcard and receive
10% OFF
your next purchase

(Not valid with any other specials or discounts)

Call today for reservations
or visit our website   ▶ ▶ ▶   (757) 596-7323
www.nonnasitalianrestaurant.com

EXHIBIT C17.7: NONNA'S DIRECT MAIL SPECIAL EVENT POSTCARDS

- **Raffle Donations**—Nonna's has donated many gift certificates and coupons to local schools. The gift certificates were good for specific money values, free pizzas, and free dinners depending on the needs of the school or local business that were given the donations. Nonna's continues to donate gift certificates and discount flyers because this is inexpensive advertising in comparison to other methods and is excellent public relations; however, these donations seldom produce regular customers.
- **School Fundraising**—Nonna's has sold pizzas at a very low cost to a local Parent/Teacher Association (PTA) so that the PTA could sell pizzas as a fundraiser. With the pizzas, Nonna's also gave discount flyers. The donations to the PTA for its fundraiser did not generate any foot traffic into the restaurant. Nonna's participated in the PTA fundraisers three times and lost more money by reducing its pizza prices than was generated via return customers.
- **Web Site**—Nonna's web site has generated a lot of business. Nonna's dine in, carry out and catering business has benefited from the web site. The web site gives customers the in-house and carry out menu, catering tray menu, wine menu, pictures of the restaurant, driving directions to Nonna's, family and business history, and any features or specials that are being offered. The web site has been a great marketing tool for the restaurant.
- **Yellow Pages**—The Verizon Yellow Pages phone book and Internet advertising did not prove to be beneficial for the monthly cost that was incurred. The listing of Nonna's Italian Restaurant was incorrect for the year and a half that it was posted and the Yellow Pages refused to provide corrections. This method not only drained

EXHIBIT C17.8: NONNA'S FREE ITALIAN KNOTS COUPON

more than $3,000 of Nonna's marketing budget, it generated no business because the address and name of the restaurant were listed incorrectly.

- **Wednesday Pizza Specials**—Every Wednesday is Nonna's pizza special day. All large pizzas are discounted by $3.00 and all medium pizzas are discounted by $1.50. This has helped to generate repeat and new business inside the restaurant because most of the customers who like pizza visit Nonna's on Wednesdays to take advantage of the special pizza price, but also patronize the restaurant on other week days for pasta entrées and subs.
- **In-house coupons**—The owners and servers regularly distribute in-house or "bounce back" coupons to customers with their guest receipts. By personally showing customers that their business was appreciated, the customers often visit Nonna's more than once per week. Not only do these coupons effectively serve to thank and reward the customer, they also strengthened customer relationships and aroused customer curiosity. Customers do not know if and when the next "thank you" coupon is going to be presented with their guest check, therefore, these coupons offer an added element of fun that may contribute to regular customers coming in more frequently.

While Anna and Cris have experimented with a variety of different marketing activities, they have realized that the most effective marketing has come from their satisfied customers. Happy customers visit the restaurant often and tell their friends about Nonna's. This repeat business and word-of-mouth advertising has really helped to build Nonna's business. To capitalize on this phenomenon, Anna and Cris have continued to give in-house "bounce back" coupons to regular restaurant customers when they receive their guest receipts. An example of this is the "free garlic knots appetizer" offer featured in Exhibit C17.8.

Anna projects that the response rate or redemption on this thank you "bounce back" offer thus far is approximately 85 percent. Moreover, happy customers have not only returned to dine in the restaurant, but they are utilizing Nonna's special catering services as well.

Direct & Interactive Marketing Applications— The Three Case Challenges.

Case Challenge #1: Increase Guest Traffic to Nonna's Italian Restaurant

Nonna's is targeting anyone who seeks delicious, homemade Italian food at a great price. Prospective customers include anyone looking for a great place for a first date, a family gathering or any other occasion that would leave you wanting a fine dining experience at a casual cost. The customers may reside in the area or be attracted to the area by the schools, museums, and shops in the area.

Nonna's will target organizations and business clients of all ages who are craving a taste of Italy. For business-to-business (B2B) customers, Nonna's can provide food and a small meeting space for businesses and organizations to hold a comfortable business lunch meeting, interview or company gathering. Prospective B2B customers are wide open and include the following:

1. **Churches and Clubs**—Groups and organizations that would like to host small gatherings can utilize Nonna's private banquet room or outside patio to host their meeting or function.
2. **Local Businesses (Banks, Attorneys, Accounting firms, etc.)**—Individual businesses looking for a restaurant to have business lunch meetings, or conduct interviews can enjoy a quiet atmosphere without spending a lot of money. The tall booths of the restaurant provide desired privacy for such events.
3. **Local Schools and School Groups**—Nonna's is also an inviting place to enjoy a great meal and hang out with friends or have a group study session. The restaurant booths offer privacy for teachers or other school groups that want to discuss any school related issues over a meal. The patio and banquet room are also great for privacy while dining.

The variety of final consumers that Nonna's can serve is limited only by your imagination. Any individual who is hungry and wants a great place to enjoy fresh, made from scratch meals is a prospective customer for Nonna's. Individuals and their friends and family who are looking for delicious food served in a family oriented restaurant, at a reasonable cost can find it at Nonna's

Case Challenge #2: Increase Nonna's Catering Business

Catering for Nonna's includes any party booked for more than 20 people inside the restaurant, any large orders of food that require delivery and set up at a specific location or large orders that are placed in advance for pick-up by the customer. Most of Nonna's catering business has been generated by Nonna's web site, its catering brochure, and of course, word-of-mouth referrals from satisfied customers.

- **Web Site**—Nonna's web ssite has aided in the booking of many parties and large orders. Many people have seen the catering and the "Party Trays to Go" menus and have decided to let Nonna's do the cooking.
- **Catering Brochure**—Nonna's had a separate catering brochure created to give it a more professional look and hopefully a competitive edge compared to most local restaurants that provide catering services. As shown in Exhibit C17.9, the

EXHIBIT C17.9: NONNA'S CATERING BROCHURE

brochure includes a picture of Cristoforo and Josephine Russo, the original owners and founders of Anna's Pizza, and brief history of the family business.

- **Word of Mouth**—Word of mouth promotion has been the single most effective mechanism in building Nonna's catering business. Most of the parties and events that Nonna's has catered, both on-site and off-site, have been secured from customers telling other potential customers about Nonna's great food and service and recommendations to let Nonna's do the cooking and the catering.

Nonna's offers the following three forms of catering services—dine-in parties, casual catering and formal catering. Each form of catering offers a customized menu to be selected and specified by the customer. Let's now examine Nonna's special services in greater detail.

a. **Dine-In Parties**. The restaurant has a 250-seat capacity if an organization wanted to reserve the entire restaurant. However, the banquet room and patio are perfect spaces for much smaller dine-in parties. The menu may be customized to the specifications of dine-in parties if desired. Nonna's is able to offer buffet dinners as well.

b. **Casual Catering**. These casual off-site catering services are ideal for business meetings, lunches, holiday parties and much more. The menu may be customized and food will be delivered piping hot on time for these special engagements.

c. **Formal Catering**. These formal off-site catering services may be for up to 500 people. Weddings, showers, and a wide range of other formal events provide the venue. Nonna's provides the meal, complete with all inclusive set-up service, servers, utensils, and supplies needed to make these formal events a tasty success.

EXHIBIT C17.10: NONNA'S CATERING HISTORY

Size of Party	NPBT (%)	Type of Party	Event Type
40	14.5	Buffet	Graduation
50	14.5	Buffet	Bridal Shower
50	22.5	Delivery	Funeral
100	23.5	Delivery	Unknown
45	22.5	Delivery/Set Up	Rehearsal Dinner
167	26.0	Delivery/Set Up	District PTA Meeting
200	26.0	Delivery/Set Up	Christmas Party
35	0	Dine In/Full Menu	Church Function/ NO SHOW
40	16.5	Dine In/Full Menu	Car Club Meeting
40	16.5	Dine In/Full Menu	Church Function
20	20.0	Dine In/Set Menu	Garden Club Luncheon
25	20.0	Dine In/Set Menu	Birthday Party
40	20.0	Dine In/Set Menu	Engagement Party
200	22.0	Dine In/Set Menu	Fraternity Party
25	23.5	Pick Up	Engagement Dinner
30	23.5	Pick Up	Office Luncheon
75	23.5	Pick Up	Valentine's Dinner

To date, Nonna's has serviced more than 30 catered events, both in the restaurant and at off-site locations. Nonna's catering services have ranged from parties of 12 people to 250 people. Exhibit C17.10 provides an overview of Nonna's previous catering jobs, including the net profit before taxes (NBIT) for 17 scheduled catered events. Note that NBIT was calculated by analyzing the cost of producing the food, as well as all of the variable and fixed costs associated with running the business. Marketing costs are attributed as a percent of total marketing expenditures.

Note that Nonna's has catered four large events for more than 150 people. The catering business has grown slowly, but steadily. The pace has been consistent which has given Anna and Cris the time and ability to learn how they need to more effectively and efficiently market and manage that part of their business.

Anna is currently working on a specific catering menu that will be created similar to most catering menus found at hotel banquet facilities. The menu will be set on a cost per person scale and sectioned into types of food to be served. For example there will be set cost per person for set hors d'oeuvres, salads or soups, dinners and desserts. Once the menu is complete, more time and money will be put towards increasing the catering sector of the restaurant.

Case Challenge #3: Generate Sales for Nonna's Homemade Tomato Sauce, Dressing and Dipping Oil Products

After having many customers rave and inquire about purchasing Nonna's made from scratch garlic and olive oil dipping sauce, homemade Italian oil and vinaigrette, and Italian pasta sauces, Anna and Cris saw an market opportunity. Anna and Cris realized they needed to begin marketing Nonna's popular gourmet products since

EXHIBIT C17.11: NONNA'S SPECIALTY DIPPING OIL, DRESSING AND TOMATO SAUCE

demand for them has continuously grown. However, in these first two years of restaurant operation, Anna and Cris have had few resources and even less time to dedicate to marketing its new line of products. Therefore, Anna and Cris would like to expand its business and name recognition by serving customers who desire the fresh taste of "made from scratch" sauce, salad dressing and dipping oil at home, yet do not have the time to prepare the food.

The challenges of marketing these products have stumped both Anna and Cris. Until they can figure out how to market their products outside of the restaurant they have been bottling the dressings and putting them on display inside the restaurant. The displays have prompted customers to buy the items that their taste buds have fallen in love with while dining at Nonna's. Exhibit C17.11 features Nonna's specialty product line.

Some of the challenges that Anna and Cris have run into include finding a starting

EXHIBIT C17.12: NONNA'S SPECIALTY PRODUCT COSTS AND PRICES

Product	Retail Price	Packaging	Ingredients/Processing
Dipping Sauce	$9.00	$3.50	$2.00
Italian Dressing	$8.00	$3.50	$1.50
Tomato Sauce —16 oz container	$8.25	$0.75	$5.25
—32 oz container	$10.25	$1.50	$7.00

point for the bottling process. Not knowing what is required by the FDA and any other food associations has stumped the owners. Until they can determine how to mass produce and effectively market the products, they will continue to successfully sell the products at the restaurant to their regular customers who purchase the items for themselves and for gifts. Exhibit C17.12 details the current costs and prices of Nonna's specialty product line.

Anna and Cris are highly motivated to sell their specialty products both locally and regionally. Prospective customers include both final (B2C) and organizational (B2B) consumers. These products could be distributed to grocery stores for retail sale, as well as distributed via direct marketing mediums, including Nonna's web site and direct mail. The postcard introducing Nonna's specialty products is featured in Exhibit 13, however, Anna and Cris have yet to embark in mailing these cards because they aren't sure "who" should be targeted for the initial mailing.

Future Challenges & Opportunities

Determining and utilizing the most effective promotional mix to market Nonna's is an on-going challenge and opportunity for the young entrepreneurs. Nonna's Italian Restaurant is still new and the lack of funds for adequate marketing is an on-going concern. The owners have yet to utilize new high-tech digital formats for marketing beyond their web site.

Anna and Cris have realized that the business will continue to grow larger than the two of them can handle alone, which has led to many managerial challenges and opportunities. One of the biggest challenges has been running the restaurant's day-to-day business operations, while taking the time to market their catering and specialty foods product line. Anna and Chris see many opportunities for Nonna's Italian Restaurant to grow in both brand recognition and profitability. Unfortunately, the lack of time and resources may slow down Nonna's growth exponentially.

The owners would like to package and distribute their popular dipping oil, dressing and sauces, but to date, have not been able to find the time and funds to dedicate to making that widespread marketing a reality. Anna and Cris feel that if they can create great brand recognition for Nonna's, the products will sell well outside of the restaurant. The challenge is bottling the products and selling them throughout the local and regional markets. With so many different opportunities tied up in their new restaurant, the ultimate question for these young entrepreneurs is . . . where and how

**EXHIBIT C17.13: NONNA'S SPECIALTY DIPPING OIL,
DRESSING AND TOMATO SAUCE**

NOW you can enjoy our Specialty Items at home

*N*ONNA'S
ITALIAN RESTAURANT

Homemade Products at GREAT Prices!!!

*N*ONNA'S
ITALIAN RESTAURANT

Call today for reservations
or visit our website   ▶ ▶ ▶   (757) 596-7323
www.nonnasitalianrestaurant.com

Nonna's Italian Restaurant
11006 Warwick Blvd, Suite 446B
Newport News, VA 23601

PRST-STD
U.S. POSTAGE
PAID
CITY, ST
PERMIT NO.

EXHIBIT C17.14: NONNA'S MULTIDIMENTIONAL MARKETING MODEL

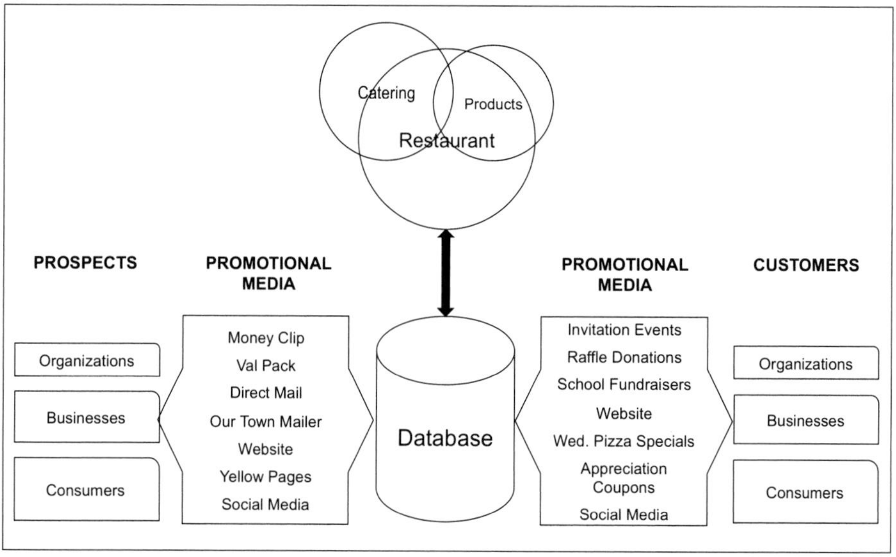

to begin? How should they prioritize their market opportunities? Who should they target and why? What would you recommend?

Case Questions:

1. What other forms of direct and interactive marketing would help Nonna's?
2. What type(s) of special events might help boost Nonna's business?
3. How would you suggest obtaining information to help build Nonna's customer database? (This is especially important for marketing Nonna's catering services and its specialty product line.)

References

Anonymous (2006). "Finding the Perfect Spot: Site Selection Crucial to Any and Every Franchise," *Nations Restaurant News,* Dec. 11, 30–31, 53.

Labhar-Friedman Inc. (2009). "Outlook 2009," *Nation's Restaurant News,* Jan. 5, 29.

Nielsen (2009). "Americans Who Are Going Out Less Often, 2009," *Research Alert,* 27 (4), Mar. 6, 25.

White, Geneva (2008). "Location, Location, Location," *Nation's Restaurant News,* June 14, S10–11.

CASE
18

Peninsula Society for the Prevention of Cruelty to Animals (PSPCA)

LISA D. SPILLER
Christopher Newport University

CAROL SCOVOTTI
University of Wisconsin-Whitewater

In 1866, New York resident Henry Bergh decided he could no longer sit idly by and watch a street merchant beat his defenseless horse. On that day, the first Society for the Prevention of Cruelty to Animals (SPCA) was born. Named the ASPCA, or the American Society for the Prevention of Cruelty to Animals, this organization became the first of its kind to exist for the sole purpose of helping make the world a better, safer place for tens of millions of companion pets.

Since that time, hundreds of SPCAs and Humane Societies have been formed across the United States to serve their community's needy and homeless animals. While the primary goal of these organizations is to find new homes for their homeless pets, they also provide humane education to their community's pet owners, provide low-cost medical services to indigent families, and care for sick and injured stray animals. SPCAs also have the difficult responsibility of euthanizing animals that are not adopted. In a recent year, approximately 50 percent of sheltered animals, totaling more than four million animals, were euthanized because people opted to buy pets rather than adopt and because people allowed their pets to breed.

SPCAs generally have small staffs and largely rely on volunteers and private donations to operate. Given that these organizations must raise their own money, they often lack the funds necessary to employ skilled employees or to even engage in the most basic business practices. Modern-day tactics such as direct and interactive marketing are often overlooked or are simply not considered due to a lack of time or money. This was the case for the Peninsula SPCA located in Newport News, Virginia.

Some of the data provided by the company has been disguised and is not useful for research purposes. The authors would like to thank Vicki Rowland for her help in this project.

EXHIBIT C18.1: PSPCA TWO-YEAR MARKETING PLAN

PSCPA Two-Year Marketing Plan

Goal 1: Increase Adoptions	Estimated cost	Estimated Income
Objective A: Increase Exposure	$12,000	$6,000
Objective B: Increase Media Contact	$600	$ –
Objective C: Create Marketing Materials	$1,500	$ –
Objective D: Increase Contact with Municipal Partners	$ –	$ –
Goal 2: Increase Donations		
Objective A: Create Direct Mail Donations	$30,000	$70,000
Objective B: Create Event Donations	$45,000	$157,000
Objective C: Increase Bequests	$ –	$ –
Objective D: Create Grant Income	$ –	$ –
Objective E: Create Product Line	$12,000	$17,000
Subtotal	$101,100	$250,000
Labor	$45,000	
Total Cost/Income	$146,100	$250,000

Net Income $103,900

Peninsula SPCA

Founded in 1967, the Peninsula SPCA (PSPCA) became the only shelter in a four-city region to provide sheltering and adoption services. For over 35 years, the PSPCA provided these services to the best of its ability; however, its adoption rate never exceeded 30 percent. As the nation's best shelters evolved and began attaining adoption rates of 50 percent or more, mounting community demands pressured the PSPCA to reorganize and begin integrating modern-day business practices.

In 2004, a new volunteer Board of Directors was elected to achieve this goal. At that time, there was no marketing plan, no marketing strategy, and no employees were focused on marketing or fundraising. The only marketing activity that the PSPCA engaged in was direct mail, and even this activity was outsourced to a vendor that charged 35 percent for cookie-cutter solicitations. For an organization that relied on donations to exist, this required a prompt overhaul of massive proportions. The first item of business was to form a task force of a few Board members with the sole job of focusing on marketing initiatives. This small group concentrated on creating the PSPCA's first-ever marketing plan and establishing a budget for marketing activities. The next challenge was to create a marketing manager's position and fill that position with someone to handle the marketing duties.

The job went to Vicki Rowland, a 24-year-old college graduate with a love of animals and a keen understanding of direct and interactive marketing. One warm and sunny day in June, Vicki joined the PSPCA as its new Marketing Manager. After all of the introductions and a brief tour, Vicki sat in her office and stared at the current marketing plan. "Where to begin?" She thought to herself. As Exhibit C18.1 shows, the marketing plan had two goals: to increase animal adoptions and to increase funds raised.

The 'Increase Funds Raised' goal was largely driven by direct marketing principles and will be the focus of the rest of this case. This overall goal was broken down into multiple objectives and numerous supporting strategies, which included creating both a direct mail program and special fundraising events. As Vicki began to get organized, she knew that since the heart of direct and interactive marketing is a customer or client database, her initial efforts should be focused on creating the PSPCA's first real customer database. Vicki quickly organized a team of volunteers to assist her in the tasks associated with database development.

The Database

Vicki investigated several database software solutions and evaluated each on the same criteria: ability to synchronize with the PSPCA's sheltering software, importing/exporting functionality, reporting tools, and price. Ultimately, WiseGuys™, by Database Marketing Solutions, Inc., was selected as it was "user-friendly" and able to be customized to meet PSPCA's needs.

The next task was to import existing donor names and addresses from Excel into the new database. Vicki established source codes and match codes for each unique customer record, which would allow the PSPCA team to analyze which sources provide the most responsive and profitable donors. The next step was to determine appropriate customer segmentation criteria, which would enable messages to be tailored and targeted to each unique segment. Vicki realized she needed additional information in order to create a sound segmentation strategy. She obtained a team of volunteer market researchers from the marketing department of her Alma Mater and began surveying more than 15 of the top SPCAs across the country to learn how they segmented their databases. The results showed that most SPCAs were not segmenting their databases—a result of a lack of time and inability to integrate current marketing practices. Of the few SPCAs that did, the following segments were identified: Donors, Potential Donors, and Volunteers. Exhibit C18.2 provides additional detail about these segments.

The final step in the database development process was to establish ways to generate leads and train volunteers to enter new data. Data entry took much longer than Vicki envisioned, but it was well worth the effort. Vicki created processes to capture new names of people adopting, visiting the PSPCA, and/or participating in a fundraising event. With the database foundation established, it was time to begin executing the marketing plan.

The Marketing Plan

Direct Mail Program

Research revealed that the optimal frequency of direct mail solicitations was four to six times per year. Therefore, the direct mail plan was built around executing four direct mail solicitations per year.

As Exhibit C18.3 reveals, the first solicitation focused on the transformational changes taking place at the PSPCA. It included a callout box that highlighted the work local vets were donating to the PSPCA—a fact that was not known in the com-

EXHIBIT C18.2: DATABASE MARKET SEGMENTATION

A. Donors

1. Cat People—people who specifically love cats.
   Gift History
       a. High—donation $500 plus
       b. Medium—donation $100-$500
       c. Low—donation $items-$100
2. Dog People—people who specifically love dogs.
   Gift History
       a. High—donation $500 plus
       b. Medium—donation $100-$500
       c. Low—donation $items-$100
3. Animal Lovers—people who do not have an animal preference.
   Gift History
       a. High—donation $500 plus
       b. Medium—donation $100-$500
       c. Low—donation $items-$100

B. Potential Donors

1. Cat Adopters—people who have adopted a cat from the SPCA.
       a. Newborns—first six months of adoption
       b. Infants—after six months to one year of adoption
2. Dog Adopters—people who have adopted a dog from the SPCA.
       a. Newborns—first six months of adoption
       b. Infants—after six months to one year of adoption
3. Animal Adopters—people who have other pets from the SPCA.
       a. Newborns—first six months of adoption
       b. Infants—after six months to one year of adoption
4. Participators—participants of raffles, fundraising events, and/or the Petting Zoo.

C. Volunteers

munity and that would inspire confidence in the PSPCA's operations. Another callout box was included that highlighted the story of a rescued dog—the purpose of this callout box was to test how many people would visit the PSPCA's web site to read his rescue story.

This direct mail campaign was distributed to more than 7,000 past donors and cost $2,500. It yielded a 7.1 percent response rate and raised $19,415, which translates into a 677 percent return on investment. This was considered an excellent response that validated the profitability of the direct mail strategy. Vicki was very pleased but wondered, "What more could be done to increase the response rate?"

The results of the subsequent direct mail campaigns can be seen in Exhibit C18.4. Notice the varying response rates on each of the direct mail campaigns.

As Exhibit C18.5 illustrates, direct mail solicitations are not created equal and there are many factors that contribute to their success. The dip in January could have been caused by seasonal fluctuations in donation activity. Or it could have been

EXHIBIT C18.3: INITIAL PSPCA DIRECT MAIL PIECE

Helping discarded dogs like him...
...is what we do.

This dog was found in the middle of the road, skeletal and missing most of his coat. Read his SPCA rescue story at peninsulaspca.com!

Dear SPCA Supporter:

Each day, 10,000 humans are born in the United States. By comparison, 70,000 puppies and kittens are born each day. Since there will never be 70,000 new homes available each day, millions of healthy animals will face early deaths as a form of animal control. Others will be left to fend for themselves against automobiles, inhabitable weather, neglect and cruelty.

At the Peninsula SPCA, we are working very hard to change these statistics on the Virginia Peninsula.

Over the last few years, we have overhauled our management and Board of Directors, replaced outdated financial systems, scrutinized our expenses, improved our relationship with our municipal partners, and examined every aspect of our operations. The transformation continues, and we vow to leave no stone unturned! As a result of this tireless effort, we have proudly established an unshakable foundation for our future.

Now, we need your help!

We are creating an aggressive strategic plan to realize our mission of finding a good home for every adoptable pet. This will be impossible to achieve without your support! The suggested donations below illustrate how your money could be used TODAY to improve the quality of life for our animals. If you will donate to our animals today, we pledge to you that 100% of your contribution (yes, every penny!) will go towards helping the precious animals in our care.

On behalf of all of our animals, I thank you for your generosity and support.

Sincerely,

Doug

G. Douglas Bevelacqua
President, Peninsula SPCA Board of Directors

P.S. We are now on the web! Please visit us at *www.peninsulaspca.com!*

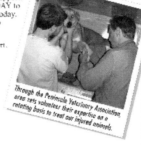

Through the Peninsula Veterinary Association, area vets volunteer their expertise on a rotating basis to treat our injured animals.

PENINSULA SPCA

Your donation will go directly toward improving the lives of the animals in our care. See what your donation could provide:

❏ $15 keeps one homeless animal free of fleas and ticks for one month.

❏ $25 provides antibiotics for one injured animal.

❏ $50 provides complete grooming for one severely neglected pet.

❏ $75 spays or neuters one underprivileged pet.

❏ $100 provides all vaccinations, flea & worm treatments, and a microchip for one homeless pet.

❏   I want to help more!

Name: _____

Address: _____

City, St., Zip

Yes, I want to receive email updates from the SPCA!

email: _____

Visa   Master Card   Discover   (circle one)

Card # _____ Exp. Date: _____

Signature:

EXHIBIT C18.4: DIRECT MAIL CAMPAIGNS
RESPONSE RATE ANALYSIS

Date	Mailing	Number Mailed	Response Rate	Funds Raised	Cost	Net Income	ROI
April Year 1	Helping Discarded Pets is What We Do	7,389	7.10%	$19,415	$2,500	$16,915	677%
Sept. Year 1	Operation: On The Run & Having Fun!	7,390	7.24%	$21,089	$2,500	$18,589	744%
Jan. Year 2	Together, We Changed Lives	8,794	4.97%	$14,759	$3,300	$11,459	347%
June Year 2	PVA/SPCA Clinic Fund	46,000	0.80%	$22,885	$24,000	($1,115)	–5%
	(SPCA Donors)	8,806	2.77%	$13,860	$4,594	$9,266	202%
	(Pet Owner Prospects)	37,194	0.34%	$9,025	$19,406	($10,381)	–53%
Sept. Year 1	Never Again (Disaster Planning)	9,548	4.16%	$16,985	$3,000	$13,985	466%
Dec. Year 2	Holiday Appeal	9,548	6.00%	$27,500	$3,000	$24,500	817%

caused by a more complicated reason such as lack of communication with donors other than solicitations, poor messaging, or a combination of political or market factors. Vicki didn't know for sure. She thought that more time was needed to confirm or rule out the timing or seasonal possibilities. She also thought focus groups or short surveys might shed some light on the significant variation in direct mail results. However, surveys and focus groups take time. In the meantime Vicki had to make decisions about future marketing efforts.

The dip in June is likely to be attributable to an attempt to cultivate new donors. In an effort to expand its donor base, Vicki reached out to the veterinary community to solicit its clients. Since clients of vet clinics own pets, Vicki and her PSPCA team speculated that they would be sympathetic towards the PSPCA's mission and willing to support it financially. Several veterinarians in the area provided Vicki with their customer lists, which the PSPCA mailed, requesting a donation. She knew that prospect solicitations often lose money in the short run; however, the lifetime value of each donor far exceeds the initial gift, so effective prospecting can be a lucrative long-term investment. In this instance, a 0.34 percent response was achieved . . . 112 new donors. Vicki and the team saw this effort as a means of generating awareness and "planting seeds for the future" rather than an unsuccessful direct mail effort.

Overall, the PSPCA direct mail campaigns were highly effective, both in strengthening relationships with its donor base and generating funds for the shelter. However, Vicki and her team were not focused solely on direct mail campaigns to generate both awareness and funds for the PSPCA, they were also busy planning special events.

Special Fundraising Events

Before Vicki was hired, the only fundraising event the PSPCA sponsored was an annual golf tournament. Results had diminished over the years as past participants moved, had lifestyle changes, or just lost interest. Part of Vicki's charge within the new marketing plan was to create and implement profitable fundraising events. The question she faced: What kind of events to run? To determine the most successful

**EXHIBIT C18.5: GRAPHICAL ILLUSTRATION OF
TOTAL INCOME AND NET INCOME**

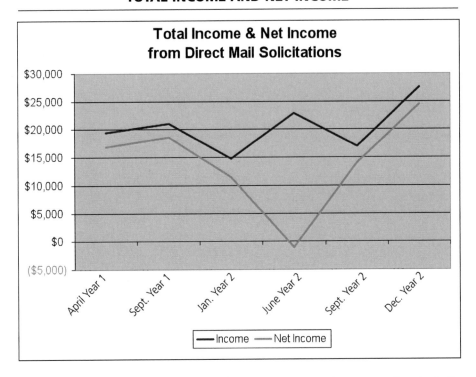

fundraising events, Vicki again surveyed top SPCAs across the country. Results indicated the flagship fundraiser of most SPCAs was a pledge walk, with top SPCAs earning between $100,000 and $200,000 each year on that event alone.

The premise of the pledge walk is basic: get individuals to register and raise money from their friends and family. Participants have many ways to raise money: ask in person, mail requests, hold their own mini-fundraisers at work/school/church, etc. Participants can also easily create an interactive, personal fundraising web page that allows participants to email their requests, complete with a picture of their pet. Team formation is encouraged and prizes are awarded for top individual and team fundraisers.

So, how could this simple idea yield hundreds of thousands of dollars? The answer is simple: it's a direct marketing extravaganza. Rather than using a mass request to ask thousands of people for money, a pledge walk provides a fun way for individuals to make requests on behalf of the PSPCA. The beauty of this approach is that each request is a highly targeted, one-on-one plea to the hottest leads of all—friends and family. In addition to requesting donations, registered individuals also ask for their friends and family to register themselves, thus exponentially expanding the PSPCA team's reach.

The PSPCA launched its first dog walk, "Paws for a Cause Dog Walk & Festival," with great anticipation. Following the advice of the Tampa Bay SPCA, the majority of

Vicki and her team's energy was focused on recruiting walkers to fundraise on its behalf. Additionally, Vicki approached many local businesses to sponsor the event and donate via in kind contributions so that 100 percent of pledges raised from the walkers would benefit the animals. With the help of everyone at the PSPCA and many volunteers, a massive festival was put together to draw non-participants to witness the walk, which included local rescue groups, pet-related vendors, canine games and contests, and canine demonstrations. Exhibit C18.6 presents the direct mail piece promoting this event.

The event was a resounding success and raised more than $77,000. Since only $15,000 was raised in company sponsorships, the remaining $62,000 came from the direct marketing engine comprised of hundreds of motivated individuals making targeted, individualized requests on piping hot leads. Vicki again was extremely pleased with these results and quickly began planning what she would do differently for next year's dog walk and festival.

The Outcome—Year One

As the successes and disappointments of the PSPCA's marketing efforts illustrate, direct marketing is not a success-only journey, and the PSPCA team learned several important lessons along the way. Since it is every marketer's goal to maximize profit on every activity, it is important to recognize the role that measuring and analyzing results play in ensuring that tactics that are effective are repeated and tactics that are not effective are eliminated. It is also vital to recognize the importance of performing solid research to avoid investing in activities that are likely to fail.

At the end of its first year, Vicki and the PSPCA team had raised more than $165,000 from marketing activities and projected raising over $250,000 in the second year. Just as importantly, however, the team's marketing efforts began the critical task of forming thousands of relationships with community members—people that might well become future donors, future volunteers, and hopefully, future families for the homeless animals of the Virginia Peninsula.

The Case Challenges—Year Two and Beyond

Given the successes enjoyed during the first year, Vicki was highly motivated to tackle year two. She revised the PSPCA marketing plan and began to plan more direct mail campaigns and special events. But first, Vicki focused her efforts on a few of the other critical marketing objectives: the development of the PSPCA's new tag line, product line, web site updates and on-line store. Exhibit C18.7 shows the portion of the PSPCA marketing plan pertaining to the "Funds Raised" goal. It also details the related strategies for each of the marketing objectives.

Along with the creation of the new PSPCA tag line, *"Think. Adopt. Love."* Vicki realized she needed to order new PSPCA merchandise to promote the new slogan.

**EXHIBIT C18.6: PAWS FOR A CAUSE
DOG WALK & FESTIVAL DIRECT MAIL PIECE**

PAWS FOR A CAUSE
DOG WALK & FESTIVAL

Come join us for a fun-packed day to raise money for our animals!

Riverview Park, Newport News

**Sunday, May 20
12:00 - 4:00 pm**

EVENTS WILL INCLUDE:

- Demonstrations including the Great American Disc Dog Show
- Police & bomb dog demonstration
- Dog trick workshop
- Tail wagging & dog costume contests
- Avenue of Heroes (local rescue groups)
- Woofstock stage featuring music & entertainment
- Raffle & prizes
- Food & exhibitors

PRE-REGISTER TO BEGIN COLLECTING PLEDGES NOW!

Benefits of pre-registration include:

- Exclusive event t-shirt
- Goody bags
- Prizes for top fundraisers in both individual & team categories
- Pledge packet
- Free personal web page
- Monthly fundraising tips & event updates

PENINSULA SPCA
peninsulaspca.com

Sponsored in part by:

EXHIBIT C18.7: PSPCA MARKETING PLAN—GOAL 2

Marketing Plan Goal 2—Objectives & Strategies

Goal 2: Increase Donations

Objective A: Increase Direct Mail Donations

Strategies:

1. Analyze last two years' direct mail results	$ –	$ –
2. Plan/Execute upcoming year direct mail plan	$12,000	$50,000
3. Increase size of database	$18,000	$20,000

Objective B: Increase Event Donations

Strategies:

1. 2nd Annual Paws for a Cause Dog Walk & Festival	$15,000	$80,000
2. 4th Annual All Fore Animals Golf Tournament	$10,000	$25,000
3. 1st Annual Fur Ball	$20,000	$50,000
4. Write playbooks for all events	$ –	$ –
5. Collect lessons learned for each event	$ –	$ –
6. Research other shelters for income ideas	$ –	$ –
7. Fine Arts Shop & Hausers Fundraisers	$ –	$2,000

Objective C: Increase Bequests

Strategies:

1. Research how other shelters secure bequests	$ –	$ –
2. Plan/Execute bequest plan	$ –	$ –

Objective D: Create Grant Income

Strategies:

1. Create a list of grants the SPCA is eligible for	$ –	$ –
2. Get grant-writing tips from city contacts	$ –	$ –
3. Recruit volunteer grant writers	$ –	$ –
4. Partner with CNU grant writing classes	$ –	$ –
5. Apply for grants	$ –	$ –

Objective E: Develop Product Line

Strategies:

1. Research other shelters' product lines	$ –	$ –
2. Design product line	$10,000	$15,000
3. Establish inventory tracking system	$ –	$ –
4. Establish display in lobby	$2,000	$ –
5. Establish online store	$ –	$2,000

The merchandise included T-shirts, sweatshirts, and hats in a variety of attractive colors. In addition to being displayed in the front reception area at the PSPCA, the merchandise was promoted at all off-site PSPCA events and activities. The staff proudly wore the new apparel with the new tag line to further integrate the brand image and promote animal adoptions. Sales of merchandise were steadily increasing. Vicki was pleased that the staff and volunteers seemed so in tune with the new PSPCA look and slogan. Of course, Vicki quickly updated the PSPCA web site with its new tag line and began investigating the creation of an online store to further promote the new apparel. With the merchandise displayed and the web site updated, Vicki began to focus on planning the next direct mail campaign and special event.

With the holidays approaching, Vicki's thoughts turned toward a combined appreciation and holiday greeting direct mail campaign. "What a perfect time to thank our donors and volunteers for all they have given us during this past year. Let's host an open house and invite everyone to visit the shelter, enjoy refreshments and a tour of our recent shelter renovations, and view our new PSPCA apparel—which would make great holiday gifts," she exclaimed. The idea was quickly accepted and endorsed by Vicki's Executive Director and the entire PSPCA board. The enthusiasm was contagious and everyone quickly got busy planning for the event. The holiday direct mail piece served as an invitation to the open house, a holiday greeting, and a fundraising effort all in one. Exhibit C18.8 shows this holiday direct mail piece.

The results of the holiday direct mail appeal (previously shown in Exhibit C18.4) were quite impressive. The holiday mailer garnered a six percent response rate, $27,500 in donations, and more than 500 visitors to the shelter for the Open House. Many of the PSPCA friends at the Open House were eager to hear more about the plans for PSPCA's first annual Fur Ball. When Dr. and Mrs. Boxx asked Vicki about the event, Vicki was happy to share details. "The Fur Ball will be a black-tie event which will be held at a local ballroom. Everyone will be able to enjoy an evening filled with cocktails, fine dining, and live music. This event will also feature both silent and live auctions to benefit our animals. But, the real unique feature of this event is that our guests will be welcome to bring their canine and feline companions to the ball and we'll have a dedicated portion of the evening for our guests to show off their furry friends." Everyone thought it sounded divine! Vicki was so enthused she could hardly wait to get back to preparing for the Fur Ball. Exhibit C18.9 presents the PSPCA Fur Ball invitation.

This inaugural event was a success. Everyone had a wonderful time and established donors brought new donors with them to the event. Vicki was especially glad to see the PSPCA database grow. With three flagship special events held in a one-year span of time, Vicki was both exhausted and totally enthused. A review of the special events shows that the initial dog walk and festival incurred the largest expense, but also generated the most revenue for the PSPCA. See Exhibit C18.10 for a summary of the funds generated via the three special events.

As Vicki began to analyze the outcomes of the direct mail campaigns and special events, she thought, "I know that there is much more we should be doing . . . but what? How can we improve on the foundation we've just established? Act I went well. What do we do for Act II?"

Vicki began to make some notes of the marketing challenges she must tackle and

EXHIBIT C18.8: PSPCA HOLIDAY DIRECT MAIL CAMPAIGN

Until he extends the circle of his compassion to all living things, man will not himself find peace.

– Dr. Albert Schweitzer, Nobel Peace Prize 1952

Dear Friend of the SPCA:

Peace. With the holiday season upon us, we hear a lot about peace. We wish it for others, we seek it for ourselves and everything from greeting cards to store displays proclaims its presence. Yet it remains elusive. Maybe Dr. Schweitzer was right.

As a friend of the Peninsula SPCA, you are part of a circle of compassion that has touched thousands of lives during the past year. We hope the support you have given---by making a donation, adopting a dog or cat, or volunteering with us—has provided you with a measure of peace and goodwill.

Together, this is what we have accomplished just this year:

- Found homes for more than 3,000 animals
- Reunited over 1,300 lost pets with their families
- Performed nearly 800 spay/neuter surgeries in our new on-site vet clinic

As the new executive director of the Peninsula SPCA, I am pleased to invite you to visit our "new" shelter, which has undergone extensive renovations in the past several months. The result is a more comfortable environment for the animals in our care and a more welcoming atmosphere for our public.

We welcome you to come to our open house complete with guided tours and refreshments. You also can see our new SPCA apparel for holiday giving!

In the meantime, we are turning to you and counting on your compassion for help, so that we can do even more for the Peninsula's homeless animals in 2008. Your tax-deductible contribution is needed now more than ever before. With your added support, we can realize our vision of saving the lives of all the healthy cats and dogs in our region.

Dr. Schweitzer also wrote that "compassion can only attain its full breadth and depth if it embraces all living creatures and does not limit itself to mankind."

Thank you for helping us embrace our homeless animals.

May peace be with you and your family (both two- and four-legged) during this holiday season.

Gratefully yours,

Home for the Holidays

Recently, we received a letter from a seven-year-old girl named Lexi Solomon, whose parents had adopted two kittens, Mataaka and Buttons. Concerned about the other homeless animals in our shelter, Lexi made a very thoughtful gift in support of our cats and dogs. Her letter below expresses her compassion and love for our homeless animals.

Read more of our success stories online!

Ritchie L. Geisel, MBA
Executive Director

Doug Bevelacqua, M.Ed., NCC
Chair

PENINSULA SPCA

P.S. Remember, mark your calendars now for Saturday, December 15th for our open house celebration!

EXHIBIT C18.9: PSPCA HOLIDAY DIRECT MAIL CAMPAIGN

Name: _____ Company: _____ Phone: _____

Address: _____ Email: _____

Fur Ball

Attendees: Qty: □ Sorry, I am unable to attend the event,
□ $125 per guest   _____   please accept my contribution of: $_____
□ $65 per pet   _____

*Please write the names of those attending (pets and people) on reverse.

Please choose an entrée(s):   Qty:
□ Roast sirloin of beef au jus with a bordelaise sauce   _____
□ Pan seared chicken breast with a rosemary veloute sauce   _____
□ Oven roasted tomato stuffed with barley and grilled vegetables _____
□ Herb crusted tilapia with a sun dried tomato cream sauce   _____

Method of Payment: □ Cash   □ Check

Card #: _____ exp date: _____ Total Payment: $_____
        □ Visa   □ Mastercard   □ Discover

For telephone reservations, please call 757.595.1392.
Thank You for supporting the animals!

the strategic decisions that must be made in order to continue moving the PSPCA on an upward path.

Decision #1—Cleaning and Expanding the Customer/Donor Database

A big concern was maintaining the integrity of the newly created database. People move. Lifestyles and interests change. How and when should the database be updated? Were there other ways to segment customers to make correspondence with them even more personalized and relevant? Should there be more information the PSPCA should track in its database? She even wondered about the effectiveness of tracking the age of a customer's pet as many seek a "replacement companion" upon the death of a household animal.

Decision #2—Establishing Effective Prospecting Strategies

Another major issue that had to be addressed was prospecting for new donors. The immediate fundraising results from the lists provided by local veterinarians were dismal, but Vicki expected prospecting would take time. Vicki knew that her Executive Director was very supportive of investigating future list rental strategies. Vicki recalled a recent conversation: "Vicki, I'm prepared to allocate an additional $5,000 to your marketing budget for next year to support list rental strategies if you believe they will generate long-term donors and a solid return on our investment over time."

EXHIBIT C18.10: SPECIAL EVENTS SUMMARY

Event	Paws for A Cause Dog Walk & Festival	Fur Ball	Paws for A Cause Dog Walk & Festival
Date	May 20, Year 2	April 4, Current Year	May 18, Current Year
Number of Participants/Guests	392	169	380
Sponsorship Income	$10,850	$20,250	$6,775
Total Funds Raised	$66,510	$44,894	$49,597
Total Expenses	$15,049	$ 2,979	$ 8,254
Net Income	$62,311	$41,915	$48,118

Vicki's questions were: "Will it be worth it? How long will it take to cultivate new donors? Where could she find appropriate lists? Should she change her fundraising approach to new prospects? What should be the offer and primary message to prospective donors? How should she test the lists to get the most out of her prospecting efforts?

Decision #3—Direct Mail Fundraising Campaign Analysis

Most of the PSPCA direct mail campaigns generated funds beyond the costs incurred in their execution, however, Vicki was troubled by the fact that some were more profitable than others. "Why did some direct mail campaigns generate a larger response rate than others? How can I analyze each campaign to better understand the mindset of our donors? Are our fundraising appeals hitting the right emotional chords? How can I improve each direct mail package? Should I be communicating with our donors more often or less often?" Vicki had lots of questions for which she desired answers.

Decision #4—Special Event Planning

Planning each special event takes time and resources, but the residual effect is worth it. The Dog Walk & Festival and the Fur Ball were excellent events that generated both awareness and funds to support the PSPCA mission and cultivated friends for the shelter. Vicki knew that she would recommend continuing these events on an annual basis. However, she was always searching for other creative ideas for special events. "What other types of events might be effective? Should I be planning more events each year? Should I survey our donors and volunteers for ideas?" These were just a few of the questions Vicki posed to herself.

Decision #5—Animal Adoptions

While the focus of this case and much of Vicki's time has been dedicated to the goal of raising funds to support the PSPCA, she was also mindful of the shelter's mission—to find a loving home for each animal brought to the shelter. Vicki realized that the two goals were not isolated—and in fact, generating community awareness of the shelter, raising funds, cultivating PSPCA friends, and promoting PSPCA special events were certainly having a positive impact on animal adoptions. But, Vicki wanted to do more. She thought to herself. "How can the PSPCA influence or change the mindsets of residents in the community to think about adopting an animal from our shelter prior to visiting a local pet store? What types of marketing activities can we conduct to attract potential adopters to visit the shelter?" Vicki also wanted to do more to promote the sale of the new PSPCA apparel. She wondered how the new "Think. Adopt. Love." tag line could add value to the promotion of the new merchandise while getting the adoption message out to the greater community. "How can we use the new tag line to increase our animal adoptions?" Vicki thought she might generate more possibilities if she took a stroll through the shelter and visited some of her favorite furry friends.

Vicki returned to her office with a smile on her face. "Animals are the best medicine to cheer a person. What awesome companions they make! The animals in our shelter deserve to become pets of loving families. I have to work harder to help make that happen!" With those thoughts and the images of the faces of those cute puppies and cuddly kittens Vicki had just visited in mind, Vicki was rejuvenated and was ready to begin tackling her strategic decisions with even more passion and determination.

CASE
19

Primetime Developmental Playthings, Inc.

HARLAN SPOTTS
Western New England College
GREG BALEJA
Alma College

It was 2:00 p.m. on a sunny November afternoon. Laura Thomas and Mary Fischer were sitting in the conference room at the corporate headquarters of Primetime Developmental Playthings (PDP), Inc. As marketing directors, Laura and Mary were working to develop the new marketing plan for the company. It was necessary to devise a strategy to establish a corporate identity for PDP, stimulate consumer demand for PDP products, and maintain retailer loyalty through building consumer store traffic.

Laura and Mary looked around the conference room. Toys from the various PDP product lines filled the walls and corners of the room, which had recently become more crowded with the addition of two new product lines to the current product mix. As they contemplated the future strategy of the firm, Laura and Mary knew they had to get to work. Carson Scott, president of PDP, had asked Laura and Mary to have a draft of their plan on his desk within the next week. Time was an important factor since the company needed to develop a new database structure and put it in operation early next year. The new database was integral for developing new relationship marketing strategies in the future.

Laura and Mary had spent weeks reviewing the various company documents spread before them on the table. The first step required them to clearly define their target market and set marketing objectives. The next step in the process was to develop the marketing strategy they would propose to Carson Scott within the week.

Industry Overview

The United States shipped over 2 billion toys annually and was the largest market for toys in the world. There were over 120,000 individual stockkeeping units (SKUs), with approximately 6,000 new toys introduced every year according to the Toy Manufacturers of America (TMA). Retail sales were estimated currently at $20 billion annually, an increase of 7 percent over the previous year. Manufacturer sales were estimated at approximately two-thirds of retail sales ($13+ billion), up 3 percent over the previous year.

Industry sales were fueled by large annual sales increases in dolls (12.1 percent), ride-ons (10.4 percent), and games and puzzles (7.5 percent). Some categories, however, had not fared so well, with video games (–19.5 percent) and male action toys (–14.1 percent) posting the largest declines (see Exhibit C19.1). Other categories of toys (games, pre-school, infant, and activity toys) exhibited relatively stable sales patterns or intensely hot selling periods due to technological innovations (flying toys, drawing toys, radio-controlled vehicles, toys licensed from popular movies and television shows)—all according to TMA.

As with many industries, toy industry sales suffered from severe seasonality. Almost two-thirds of industry sales occurred between October and December. As one would suspect, the holiday season drove this massive buying trend.

Toy manufacturers attracted consumers through product differentiation. Some toys exhibited fad life cycles, being highly promotional and trendy. In contrast, there were many traditional toys that constituted the backbone of the industry. Given the competitive and volatile nature of the industry, companies started up and went out of business often. Recently, many companies had merged as industry leaders tried to solidify their market positions and competitors worked to achieve differential advantage. Some of the larger past acquisitions included Hasbro's purchase of Tonka in 1991 and Mattel's purchase of Fisher-Price in 1993. In November of 1996, Mattel announced their purchase of Tyco for $175 million. At that time, this acquisition solidified Mattel's number-one position within the industry.

The toy industry could be split into two primary segments, mass and specialty toy markets. While both sectors of the industry produced toys for infants and children, they were drastically different in terms of industry structure, product offerings, and marketing activities.

The Mass Market Sector

This sector was dominant, accounting for approximately 80 percent of industry sales. While there were many toy manufacturers, Mattel and Hasbro dominated in terms of market share and influence. Sales for these two companies have been $3.6 and $2.9 billion, respectively, in a recent year. These larger manufacturers marketed many well-known brands, including Barbie, Tonka, Lego, GI Joe, and Hot Wheels.

Toys produced for this sector were aggressively marketed and distributed through mass merchandising retail chain stores (i.e., Toys 'R Us, Wal-Mart). They also were supported by large expenditures in national television advertising and consumer/trade promotions (see Exhibit C19.2). Mattel and Hasbro were both among *Advertising Age*'s Top 100 Advertisers, each having spent in excess of $260 million in the U.S. in a recent year. This was a highly competitive industry with dominance of retail shelf space being of prime importance.

According to S&P Industry Surveys, some trends affecting the industry included:

- Increased competition for retail shelf space as mass market toy retailers close stores and cut back on the number of SKUs in inventory

EXHIBIT C19.1: TMA CATEGORY SALES RESULTS

Estimated Manufacturers' Shipments by Product Category
Dollars (First Billing Value[1]) and Units Current Year vs. Previous Year
Volumes have been projected to reflect total industry levels (estimated volumes in millions)

		DOLLARS			UNITS		
	Prior	Current Year	% Current Year	Prior Change	Current Year	% Current Year	Change
I.	**INFANT/PRE-SCHOOL**	**$1,345**	**$1,391**	**3.4**	**201**	**207**	**3.0**
	Infant Toys*	462	480		73	76	
	Pre-School Musical Toys	61	63		10	11	
	Pre-School Blocks/Accessories	24	27		4	5	
	Pre-School Villages/Scenery Sets*	105	125		9	10	
	Pre-School Talking/Sound Toys	64	62		8	8	
	Pre-School Learning Toys	50	57		7	8	
	Pre-School Tub Toys	14	16		3	4	
	Pre-School Role Playing Toys*	170	170		27	25	
	Pre-School Push/Pull Toys*	27	25		4	4	
	Pre-School Vehicles*	161	180		23	26	
	Pre-School Remaining	207	186		33	30	
II.	**DOLLS**	**$1,691**	**$1,896**	**12.1**	**221**	**241**	**9.0**
	Large Dolls	331	341		26	27	
	Large Doll Accessories	46	49		11	12	
	Fashion Dolls/Clothes/Accessories*	693	855		97	113	
	Mini Dolls*	220	273		51	55	
	Mini Doll Accessories	90	70		9	7	
	Soft Dolls	31	30		6	6	
	Remaining Dolls/Accessories***	160	170		12	13	
	Doll Houses/Furniture*	120	108		9	8	
III.	**PLUSH**	**$921**	**$914**	**−0.8**	**123**	**123**	**0.0**
	Musical/Electronic Plush/Accessories	120	125		8	9	
	Traditional Plush**	782	767		112	110	
	Puppets**	19	22		3	4	
IV.	**MALE ACTION TOYS**	**$926**	**$795**	**−14.1**	**165**	**145**	**−12.1**
	Action Figures	687	592		139	122	
	Action Figure Accessories*	180	154		21	19	
	Male Role Playing	59	49		5	4	
V.	**VEHICLES**	**$1,198**	**$1,213**	**1.3**	**238**	**231**	**−2.9**
	Radio Controlled Vehicles*	250	289		10	11	
	Remote Controlled Vehicles**	34	38		4	5	
	Battery Operated Vehicles	43	36		6	5	
	Other Powered Vehicles	24	22		7	7	

[1]First Billing Value: first price paid for an item in the U.S.

(Continued)

EXHIBIT C19.1: TMA CATEGORY SALES RESULTS (Continued)

Prior	DOLLARS Prior Year	Current Year	% Change	UNITS Prior Year	Current Year	% Change
Boats/Aircraft—Powered	24	24		4	4	
Mini Vehicles	282	261		147	138	
Non-Powered Cars	46	45		9	9	
Non-Powered Aircraft/Boats	34	34		10	10	
Non-Powered Trucks*	156	144		17	16	
Vehicle Accessories	88	95		10	10	
Electric/Battery Car Sets/Accessories	42	44		2	3	
Electric Train Sets/Accessories**	175	181		12	13	
VI. RIDE-ONS	**$722**	**$797**	**10.4**	**31**	**35**	**12.9**
Metal Tricycles	22	21		1	1	
Plastic Tricycles	35	33		2	2	
Other Pedal Ride-Ons	35	34		1	1	
Non-Pedal Ride-Ons	79	91		3	4	
Battery Operated Ride-Ons & Accessories*	172	191		2	2	
Stationary/Rocking/Spring Horses	14	15		1	1	
Riding Sports***	331	370		19	22	
All Other Riding Vehicles	34	42		2	2	
VII. GAMES/PUZZLES	**$1,220**	**$1,312**	**7.5**	**222**	**230**	**3.6**
Card Games*	87	94		34	36	
Dice Games	17	19		5	5	
Word Games	30	30		4	4	
Puzzle Games	18	19		5	5	
Standard Games	35	37		9	10	
Travel Games	35	36		8	9	
Children's Board Games	94	100		13	14	
Pre-School Games	40	66		7	9	
Family Board Games	87	111		8	10	
Adult Board Games	90	97		7	8	
Children's Action Games	182	173		27	25	
Family Action Games*	19	21		2	2	
Strategy Games*	55	56		6	6	
Electronic Handheld/Tabletop Games***	260	271		20	21	
Cardboard Puzzles*	135	144		58	57	
Wood/Plastic/Other Puzzles*	36	38		9	9	
VIII. ACTIVITY TOYS	**$1,821**	**$1,827**	**0.3**	**560**	**573**	**2.3**
Building Sets	366	345		41	39	
Scientific Toys**	55	57		7	8	
Fashion Accessories**	108	95		41	36	
Powered Appliances	21	22		1	1	
Non-Powered Appliances	98	77		5	4	
All Other Household/Food Toys	75	73		19	18	

EXHIBIT C19.1: TMA CATEGORY SALES RESULTS (Continued)

	DOLLARS			UNITS		
Prior	Current Year	% Year	Prior Change	Current Year	% Year	Change
Reusable Compounds*	78	96		25	29	
Mechanical Design	120	122		15	15	
Traditional Kits/Supplies**	196	203		58	60	
Sculpture Kits/Supples	17	17		4	4	
Crayons/Markers/Chalk Etc.**	255	270		182	193	
Crayons/Markers/Chalk Sets & Supplies**	108	116		35	37	
Paint Sets/Supplies**	143	152		83	86	
Sewing, Yarn, String Kits/Supplies	21	22		7	7	
Model Kits/Accessories	123	125		26	26	
All Other Activity Toys**	37	35		11	10	
IX. ALL OTHER TOYS	$3,199	$3,289	2.8	1,049	1,040	−0.9
Water/Pool/Sand Toys**	296	323		67	74	
Audio/Visual Toys	186	191		24	24	
Children's Furniture*	102	109		9	10	
Electronic Learning Aids Hardware	225	263		7	8	
Electronic Learning Aids Software	15	18		2	3	
Sports Activities*	485	507		92	95	
Musical Instruments*	*35	36		2	3	
Pre-School Playground Equipment	127	175		3	4	
Guns/Weapons & Accessories**	187	175		58	51	
Swingsets/Gym Sets & Accessories**	89	96		3	3	
Trading Cards & Accessories**	954	887		561	536	
Mini Figures/Scene Sets*	66	72		15	16	
Miscellaneous Toys***	432	452		206	213	
TOTAL TOY INDUSTRY	$13,043	$13,434	3.0	2,810	2,825	0.5
VIDEO GAMES	$3,148	$2,533	−19.5	67	58	−13.4
TV Video Hardware*	700	638		6	4	
TV Video Software*	1,671	1,302		36	33	
TV Video Accessories*	217	173		9	9	
Portable Video Hardware*	251	213		3	3	
Portable Video Software*	250	169		9	6	
Portable Video Accessories*	59	38		4	3	
TOTAL INDUSTRY WITH VIDEO GAMES	$16,191	$15,967	−1.4	2,877	2,883	0.2

- Number of companies responding = 74
- Figures include imports
- All sales are on a GROSS basis
- Data are compiled through a process which includes a polling of major U.S. toy and game manufacturers, and a comparison of trends with the U.S. Toy Market Index (TMI) and Toy Retail Sales Tracking Service (TRSTS)

*Previous Year Figures Revised
**Limited Sample
***Both Previous Year Figures Revised and Limited Sample

EXHIBIT C19.2: TOY INDUSTRY ADVERTISING EXPENDITURES

	4 Years Ago	3 Years Ago	2 Years Ago	Prior Year	Current Year
Spot TV	$200,268,400	$254,297,400	$267,728,200	$261,132,300	$231,087,800
Network TV	153,035,500	208,497,900	220,508,000	241,601,300	219,015,500
Cable TV Networks	42,840,900	78,503,800	128,620,900	142,513,800	157,133,500
Syndicated TV	93,631,400	102,432,400	117,175,400	190,895,800	194,141,500
Magazines	44,292,100	65,097,700	51,973,700	57,530,400	83,378,700
Newspapers including Sunday Magazines	3,556,000	5,755,600	3,002,900	6,045,800	4,503,500
Outdoor	21,600	62,200	92,100	130,000	83,300
Network Radio	809,400	743,600	18,200	377,600	953,000
National Spot Radio	2,014,900	1,424,900	1,250,900	2,035,500	4,431,600
TOTAL	$540,470,200	$716,815,500	$790,370,300	$902,262,500	$896,670,300

Source: Competitive Media Reporting and Publishers Information Bureau

- Continued industry growth through the marketing of licensed products with tie-ins to televisions shows and movies
- Collectible toys having a major influence on the industry, with Barbie and Matchbox leading the way
- Major manufacturers moving in the direction of multimedia and CD-ROM technology, taking advantage of the increased penetration of personal home computers
- Decreasing resin costs for plastic products over the last year, relieving some of the pressure on profit margins

The Specialty Sector

This sector of the industry was almost the exact opposite of the mass market. It was small, accounting for approximately 20 percent of industry sales according to *Playthings,* and the companies competing in this sector were, for the most part, privately owned. Annual market growth had been steady at 5 percent.

While there were hundreds of companies that manufactured specialty and educational toys, no one company appeared to have the market dominance of a Mattel or Hasbro. It was very likely that a small, privately owned company with a few employees could dominate a product category, but not the overall market. Some of the more well-known names in this sector included Brio, Educational Insights, LearningCurve, Primetime Developmental Playthings, and Playmobile.

Manufacturers in this sector almost exclusively distributed their products through specialty toy retailers. Recently, some of the larger manufacturers, such as Playmobile, had been testing the mass merchandising market. Marketing activities in the specialty arena were reflective of industry size and retail structure. Most companies did not engage in national television advertising or consumer promotions. Trade promotions were limited, with many manufacturers restricting their purchasing requirements to favorable payment terms. Some manufacturers used price-off promotions, but these were usually small (less than 20 percent) and occurred only one time during the year (usually prior to Christmas holidays). From a marketing perspective, this sector of the industry was much less sophisticated than the mass market.

Retail Market Structure

The two primary distribution channels consisted of manufacturer direct to retailer and manufacturer to wholesaler to retailer (TMA). A very small number of companies, such as Discovery Toys, sold direct to consumers. There were over 70,000 retailers across both sectors selling toys and games (TMA). This number included many different types of retailers, from the large mass merchandisers carrying toys as a sideline, to the large, "toys only" merchandisers, to the small, independent toy retailers.

Mass Merchandisers

The mass merchandiser was typified by the "category killer" outlet such as Toys 'R Us, and discount department stores such as Kmart and Wal-Mart. These retailers competed on both selection and price. They carried mainstream toys, both traditional and fad, in inventory and were supported by millions of advertising dollars. Many of the toys carried in these stores were based on popular movie and television programs through tie-in licensing agreements (i.e., *Batman, Star Wars, Star Trek, The Simpsons, Space Jam*). These stores often carried many nationally advertised products and loss leaders to stimulate store traffic. Margins for advertised toys ranged from 15 to 25 percent, while non-advertised toys had margins ranging from 35 to 40 percent (TMA).

Specialty Retailers

The specialty store retailers supported the specialty toy manufacturers. There were approximately 15,000 specialty and educational toy retailers in the United States. The majority of specialty retailers were small, with one to five locations. Recently, a number of chains had begun to expand within the U.S. market, growing rapidly in size. While the total number of retailers had remained constant over the last six years, there did appear to be a high level of turnover with enough new stores opening up to replace the existing stores going out of business.

These retailers actively avoided carrying mass market merchandise because they could not compete in the rough-and-tumble, price-oriented segment of the industry. Instead, they sought to obtain a competitive advantage by providing high-quality developmental and educational toys that made parents feel good about the products they purchased for their children.

While specialty retailers tended to sell higher priced toys, they provided unique product offerings and services to consumers not available from mass merchandisers. Specialty toy retailers were interested in getting to know their customers and determining their need for specific and unique toys. They would even special order specific items for consumers if a particular toy was not in stock. This type of service was in stark contrast to the mass merchandiser, where self-service was standard operating procedure and sales clerks knew relatively little about the products stocked in the store. This resulted in a much more impersonal store experience for the consumer.

Primetime Developmental Playthings: Company Overview

The headquarters for Primetime Developmental Playthings was a renovated loft located in the former warehouse district of Cleveland, Ohio. It was a young, fast-growing company that had increased from 10 to 52 employees in the previous two years. The facilities were rustic, utilizing the open office concept with a corporate culture best described as "West Coast Casual."

PDP was a concept-, rather than an item-, driven company. Its mission could be described as " . . . providing the highest quality toy brands that stimulate children's natural creativity and encourage development backed by a lifetime guarantee." It was a business centered around PDP's relationship with its customers. Thus, all products produced and marketed needed to fit within the overall concept of the company. One of PDP's goals among retailers was to become a leading supplier of toys in the specialty segment of the industry. Among consumers, PDP wanted to have the same name recognition for toys that the "Good Housekeeping Seal of Approval" had for consumer products.

The products that PDP manufactured were sold through specialty toy stores across the country. Independent sales representatives or sales representative organizations sold PDP products to specialty toy store retailers on a commission basis. PDP had no direct control over the sales organizations. All consumer sales went through the retailer; there were no direct sales to consumers.

Founder and president of the company, Carson Scott, had started PDP about three years ago. The company grew out of a struggling retail venture owned by a French company, Best Start Eduplaytion Centers (BSEC). Best Start was a retail specialty toy chain with stores in France, Britain, and Germany, and had opened a chain of U.S. stores based in New Jersey about a decade previous. The chain experienced a number of problems and Scott was brought into the operation to decide whether BSEC should keep, reorganize, or close the retail chain in the United States.

The decision was made to close the U.S. operations of Best Start and Scott jumped from retail to manufacturing with the establishment of Primetime Developmental Playthings, Inc. PDP was started with one product line, Puff N' Chuff Railroad, which was manufactured by a small company in North Carolina. At this time, PDP contracted with a distributor to handle the warehousing and logistics of the Puff N' Chuff product line.

After 18 months of operation, PDP established a customer service department to interface with retailers and customers at the corporate headquarters in Cleveland. In addition to customer service, PDP hired one sales manager to oversee the selling of

PDP products. The distributor maintained the warehousing of products and the independent sales agents were responsible for selling PDP products to retailers.

The distributor's warehouse was located in Bayonne, New Jersey. Another change also took place at this time with the manufacturing of PDP products shifting from North Carolina to Mexico. As with many manufacturers, cost was a consideration in this decision; however, there were also a number of product quality improvements that resulted from the change.

Laura Thomas was the sixth employee hired by PDP. Mary Fischer was the seventh, hired approximately six months after Laura. They had seen rapid expansion in three years' time. PDP's sales went from under $2 million in its first year to over $10 million in its third year of operation (see Exhibit C19.3). The product line grew from one brand to the current eight. Laura Thomas was the marketing director for Puff N' Chuff Railroad, Kinectics Construction Sets, and NuScience Exploration Sets, as well as the new Bake-it Clay Sculpting product line. Mary Fischer, also a marketing director, oversaw the other product lines, including L'Enfant, Primetime Primers, Felt N' Safari and the newly acquired Castlewood line. (see Exhibit C14.4 for details). Each product line had an individual marketing assistant.

PDP had been successful and was working to capitalize on the rapid growth of the company to continue the trend. The company had expanded internationally and now had its products distributed in ten countries around the world.

Product Concept

PDP had a philosophy represented by the corporate name, Primetime Developmental Playthings. The product line was designed to provide *developmentally* appropriate toy products to children in their *prime* developing years, from birth to age 15. "Primetime Developmental Playthings' success is not that they just make a good product," said Mary Fischer. "What sets PDP apart from other toy manufacturers is its concept orientation, not a compilation of products with no inter-relationship between the product lines. In PDP, no product stands apart by itself, it is all part of a larger whole. It is a great product design and a great concept for parent-child interaction, the real 'primetime'!"

The product development team at PDP worked with child development experts at a large, public university on the West Coast in the creation of new product lines. These experts reviewed all of the product lines to make sure they were developmentally appropriate. They also created the child development pamphlets included with many of the products to explain to parents exactly what stage their child was in and how the toy could help to enhance certain age-appropriate developmental skills. See Exhibit C19.4 for a complete description of the PDP product line.

While the product line was well developed, Laura and Mary were not satisfied with the level of consumer and retailer understanding of PDP's overarching concept. They knew that any marketing plan must have some product line objectives beyond just sales quotas. In fact, distribution was an area of major importance. While PDP products were distributed in over 3,500 specialty toy stores, not all of the stores carried the complete PDP line. Thus, it would be advantageous to both increase retail penetration and the number of stores carrying all of PDP's products. Within the next two

EXHIBIT C19.3: PRIMETIME DEVELOPMENTAL PLAYTHINGS PERFORMANCE

Figures cited in millions of dollars (000)

	Year 1	Year 2	Year 3	Projected Year 4
Sales Revenues	$1,495.00	$4,562.00	$9,758.00	$12,525.00
Promotional Allowances	14.95	45.62	97.58	125.25
Cost of Goods Sold	807.30	2463.48	4976.58	6262.50
Gross Margin	$672.75	$2052.90	$4683.84	$6012.00
Advertising and Promotion Expense	44.85	136.86	487.90	751.50
Sales Expense	29.90	114.05	195.16	187.87
Administrative Overhead	448.50	1391.41	3122.56	4008.00
Net Profit	$149.50	$410.58	$878.22	$1064.63

Numbers are for instructional purposes only and not actual figures.

years, PDP would like a 12.5 percent increase in retail penetration and a doubling of the number of stores carrying the full product line from the current 25 percent.

Retailer Perspective

In discussions about PDP's objectives, Laura related to Mary experiences from her most recent retail store visits. It was clear that there were some difficulties in working with the specialty retailer. While PDP products received good reviews, Laura detected an undercurrent of dissatisfaction with some retailers.

One serious problem PDP faced at both the independent and chain specialty retailers was the merchandising of the various PDP product lines in different areas of the store instead of all together. This merchandising tendency potentially diluted the PDP image and inhibited the cross-sell/upsell strategy. Retailers indicated that they had their own product mix to worry about and did not necessarily see any unique relationship among PDP products. In fact, many specialty toy stores merchandised their product assortments by age group. One specialty toy store in Oregon maintained a web page structured in the same manner as the PDP product line concept.

Retailers were also not satisfied with the sales representatives of PDP always trying to push the bulky displays for PDP products on them. As it was, retailers threw out many of the merchandise displays given to them by manufacturers, instead opting to design their own merchandising plans. This concerned Laura and Mary since the displays were expensive to produce and important for emphasizing the holistic product line concept.

The difficulty with the displays was compounded by the amount of merchandise required to completely fill the unit. The display was designed to have the retailer carry the whole PDP product line. Some retailers wanted to pick and choose products specific for their target markets. The display did not allow for this flexibility. The unit

EXHIBIT C19.4: PRIMETIME DEVELOPMENTAL PLAYTHINGS, INC.

Description of Product Lines

Product	Age	Description
L'Enfant	Birth to 1	This is a complete line of infant toys designed to stimulate the variety of awakening senses experienced by newborns. The first year of life is a powerful year of learning. All products in this line help the infant explore the senses. Included in this line are rattles, teething rings, quilts, mobiles, music boxes, and soft playthings. All products are made in bright and contrasting colors and a variety of shapes.
Primetime Primers	1 to 5	During this time children are beginning to actively explore their environment. They are working through a variety of psychological states as they take command of their bodies. Later during this stage, a lot of emotional and intellectual development takes place. Products in this line include the basic wooden building block sets in a variety of colors, puppet play sets, clay sculpture, wooden pull toys, and a variety of wooden puzzles.
Felt N' Safari	3 to 6	This product line consists of felt playsets with a variety of jungle and zoo motifs to stimulate children's curiosity and learning about animals and rainforests. Playsets are made for both table play and refrigerator play with self-adhesive magnets.
Puff N' Chuff Railroad	4 to 8	This railroad set is very similar to other wooden train sets on the market, such as Brio, Thomas the Tank Engine, and T.C. Timber. Puff N' Chuff includes a variety of characters based on a popular series of children's books. In addition to the wooden train track and trains, buildings and people are available to create complete play towns. The basic set has been immensely popular. Future product introductions will include self-propelled trains using either spring-loaded or AA battery power.
Castlewood	6 to 9	This recently acquired product line allows children to create a medieval castle and town from pre-cut and decorated wooden parts. Consists of a variety of sets that include towers, dungeons, knights, and much more. Each set comes with an informational booklet that provides a variety of interesting facts and details about this fascinating time period.
Bake-it Clay Sculpting	8 to 12	A more advanced art and sculpting kit using a new kitchen oven-firing clay for the budding sculptor in the house hold. Comes with a booklet with step-by-step, illustrated instructions. Also included are finishing paints and glaze for the artistic finishing touches.
Kinectics Construction Sets	8 to 12	This product line contains a number of sets that are a cross between KNEC and LEGOs. The sets provide children in this age range with imaginative play, but at the same time incorporate a number of activities that allow for the learning of basic principles of physics. Includes the use of levers, motion, and sound.
NUScience Exploration Kit	11 to 16	A new and unique product to market, these sets provide children with the basic tools and instruction booklets for conducting science experiments at home. The concept draws upon many household items that can be used to simply and easily demonstrate basic scientific principles. Experiments include biology, chemistry, and physics.

design was also tied into the minimum order requirement for PDP products, which was set at $5,000. This was a large investment for small specialty retailers who might want to only carry the Puff N' Chuff Railroad to round out their wooden train lines, which also included TC Timber and Brio.

In response to the high order size requirements, some small retailers were banding together to purchase PDP products. One retailer placed the order, which was then distributed to the other retailers involved upon arrival. This greatly concerned Laura and Mary, since this activity split up the whole PDP product line across stores. Further, there were some retailers who sold PDP products and never saw a sales representative. This was a lost opportunity to educate retailers on the PDP product line concept.

Marketing Activities

Primetime Developmental Playthings engaged in various activities to market their products, including some trade and consumer promotion, advertising, and direct marketing activities. All promotional activities were directed toward parents—PDP did not target any of its promotions toward children.

Trade Promotion

These activities were fairly limited. PDP on rare occasion would discount the wholesale price of their product to the retailer for special promotions. It was more likely that retailers would receive favorable payment terms that allowed them to pay for the merchandise after it had been sold, a standard industry practice. This was especially beneficial to retailers during the Christmas season.

PDP also provided retailers with cooperative advertising support, usually in the form of displays, flip charts, take-ones, and shelf liners to promote the product line concept at the point of purchase. Laura reiterated that while point-of-purchase materials were made available, retailers did not necessarily merchandise the PDP products as a "system." In fact, it was quite common to walk into a specialty retailer, such as FAO Schwarz, and see PDP products merchandised in different parts of the store. This reinforced Laura's conclusion that not all retailers understood the PDP concept. Any strategy would need to take this issue into consideration.

Retailers were also encouraged to hold PDP "Plaything Playtimes" to enhance store traffic. This was an event held at the retail store providing customers with a chance to actually play with a variety of toys from the PDP product line. PDP supported these events with coloring sheets and other promotional items that children could take home with them. An attempt was made to have a sales or marketing representative from PDP in the retail store to provide additional support. The current staffing levels were making it increasingly difficult for PDP to handle these events.

Consumer Promotions

Consumer promotions were used sparingly. The few promotions used by PDP were restricted to couponing and sweepstake offers to current customers. The problematic issue that Laura and Mary faced was how to implement a promotion to stimulate add-on sales within a product line, and/or cross-selling between product lines without giving away margin on sales that would normally occur anyway. (Since these two promotions were a foundation of PDP's direct marketing strategy, they will be discussed in more detail below.) In discussions with retailers, Laura found they were very hesitant to be involved in price discounting and coupon promotions. These were mainstream tactics for the mass merchandising sector and not part of how specialty stores conducted business. Specialty retailers strongly felt they could not compete on price and therefore were reluctant to reduce profit margins, even if PDP was paying for it.

Direct Marketing Activities

The Primetime Club—The major vehicle for PDP consumer promotions were the direct marketing activities associated with the "*Primetime Club.*" *Primetime Club* was a program developed so that PDP could talk with its customers. The club informed members of new PDP products and provided them with helpful developmental tips and information. The ultimate goal of this program was to move customers through the PDP product line as their child grew, and to provide these customers with the ultimate in customer service.

The *Primetime Club* program was initiated by a consumer purchase. Inside each toy package was a warranty card (see Exhibit C19.5). The warranty card collected a variety of data about the consumer, including postal and email addresses, names of children, birthdays, and an inventory of PDP products currently owned. While all products had a lifetime warranty, PDP encouraged the return of the warranty card through the use of a sweepstakes promotion. Unique to the industry, PDP entered all customers who returned warranty cards into a sweepstakes to win free products. This sweepstakes was held six times a year.

Once the warranty card was recorded at PDP, customers then received an invitation to join the *Primetime Club* (see Exhibit C19.6). PDP uses this as an opportunity to collect and verify any information provided in the returned warranty card. Customers were encouraged to join the club by completing the registration card (see Exhibit C19.7). Once the registration card had been recorded at PDP, the customer received a third mailing asking for verification of the information provided. In return the customer received the following benefits: 1) inclusion in the sweepstakes drawing, 2) free gifts for their children, and 3) *Development Dollar$*.

**Development Dollar$**—*Development Dollar$* were personalized coupons for discounts on the purchase of specific PDP products at participating specialty retailers. The information and *Development Dollar$* each parent received depended on the age of the child and the previous buying history of the parent.

Development Dollar$* posed a number of implementation challenges. The logistics of personalization were demanding due to the need for tracking customer purchases. Laura and Mary knew that the challenges created by this program needed to be addressed immediately to avoid any problems that might arise in the future. Also, given the retailers' reluctance to engage in consumer promotions, PDP needed to spend extra time educating and convincing retailers of the benefit of using the *Development Dollar$. Retailers were not quite sure what to do with the coupons and were wary

EXHIBIT C19.5: WARRANTY CARD

L'Enfant
Lifetime Warranty Registration Card

Fill out this warranty card to be automatically entered in a sweepstakes to win $500 worth of L'Enfant toys. Drawings are held six times a year, so be sure to register.

Parent's Last Name   MI   Parent's First Name

Street Address   State   Zip Code

Email Address

Bar Code of Product Purchased

Last Name (1st Child)   MI   First Name   Sex   Mo Day Year

Last Name (2nd Child)   MI   First Name   Sex   Mo Day Year

Please check all of the toys that each child currently owns: _____
                                1st Child   2nd Child
L'Enfant   _____   _____
Castlewood   _____   _____
Primetime Primer   _____   _____
Felt N' Safari   _____   _____
Puff N' Chuff Railroad   _____   _____
Bake-it Clay Set   _____   _____
Kinetics Const. Sets.   _____   _____
NUScience Exploration Kit_____   _____

about whether or not they would get their money back from PDP. The *Development Dollar$* program was strictly voluntary on the part of retailers.

The PDP Database—In addition to these challenges, the database used for the direct marketing activities was in need of restructuring. It was definitely in the early stages of development, with most of the information in the database collected from the warranty cards. The database currently had approximately 20,000 to 25,000 names and addresses, with the expectation of increasing to over 60,000 addresses within the next year. Since PDP was a relatively new company, the majority of names in the database represented customers who purchased, or received as a gift, Puff N' Chuff Railroad products, the first product line.

EXHIBIT C19.6: INVITATION TO JOIN THE PRIMETIME CLUB

(On PDP Letterhead)

Dear Mr. _____ :

   I would like to take this opportunity to invite you to join a wonderful organization—PDP's Primetime Club. This organization is devoted to informing parents of new PDP products and providing them with helpful developmental tips and information as their children grow and develop.

   If you become a member of the Primetime Club, you will receive the following benefits:

1. Inclusion in the sweepstakes drawing for a $1,000 Savings Bond,
2. Free gifts for your children, and
3. Free Development Dollar$—Development Dollar$ are personalized coupons for discounts on the purchase of specific PDP products at participating speciality retail stores.

   In order for you to join the Primetime Club, please complete the attached Registration Card. All we ask is that you correct the information that appears on the card. The information contained on the card is based on the information provided on the Warranty Card you recently sent to us. This is a chance for us to verify our records.

   Please drop the completed Registration Card in the mail as soon as possible. Thank you, and I hope that your child is enjoying their new PDP toys.

Sincerely,

Carson Scott

PDP would like to more effectively utilize its database to expand its cross-sell/upsell strategy. Managing the size of the database was critical and PDP would like it to grow, but only to the extent that the information can be used. Dave Hudson, advertising and direct marketing director, pointed out that a common problem firms encounter in setting up a database is collecting too much information that will never be used. An additional issue that PDP needed to address was how to integrate the Castlewood database acquired in the recent purchase of Nature's Way Toys, Inc., into the current information system.

This database operation was critical to PDP's strategy. It was important for them to not only communicate with their customers, but also to figure out how this tool could provide value-added services to specialty retailers. The database generated through the *Primetime Club* could form a powerful bridge between the retailer, the consumer, and PDP. With the impending foray into database marketing, it was extremely important to Carson Scott that PDP be able to calculate the "lifetime value" of a PDP customer, although he was not quite sure how this could be done. Laura, Mary, and Dave all agreed on the importance of being able to calculate the value of a customer who first purchased a PDP product for a child who was two years old, as compared to the customer who first purchased when the child was ten years old.

EXHIBIT C19.7: PRIMETIME CLUB REGISTRATION CARD

Primetime Club Registration & Sweepstakes Entry Card

Complete the information requested and you will receive the following benefits:

1. Inclusion in the sweepstakes drawing for a $1,000 Savings Bond,
2. Free gifts for your children, and
3. Development Dollar$.

Information Currently on File		List any corrections below
Parent's Name	N. Marcus	_____
Street Address	100 N. Macy St.	_____
City, State, Zip	Anytown, US 10000–0001	_____
Email Address	Marcus@osu.edu	_____
1st Child's Name	Katie	_____
1st Child's Birthday	08/11/07	_____
2nd Child's Name	Matthew	_____
2nd Child's Birthday	10/2/09	_____

___ **All of the information above is correct.**

Would you be so kind as to tell us approximately how many toys you currently own from each of the product lines listed below:

_____ L' Enfant	_____ Castlewood
_____ Primetime Primers	_____ Bake-it Clay Sculpting
_____ Felt N' Safari	_____ Kinectics Construction Sets
_____ Puff N' Chuff Railroad Kits	_____ NUScience Exploration Kits

The Internet

PDP maintained a presence on the Internet through its own web site, which was promoted to parents in all correspondence. This site contained the complete product line catalog. Aside from allowing parents to examine PDP products, it provided an additional instrument for collecting data from those customers "surfing the Net." Web site visitors were encouraged to correspond with PDP through online discussion groups.

The web site had an additional helpful feature called the "Store Finder." The Store Finder allowed a consumer to find the closest specialty retailer carrying the PDP product of interest. This service made shopping easier for consumers. At the same time, it was a vehicle that helped generate store traffic for the specialty toy retailers that stocked PDP products. Only stores that agreed to accept *Development Dollar$* were included in the Store Finder listing. Still, not every store wanted to be involved with the *Development Dollar$* promotion. This was a perplexing issue for Laura and Mary.

Advertising

This part of the communications program played a minimal role in the marketing activities of PDP. Approximately 3 percent of sales were spent on placing ads in print media promoting PDP and some of its brands to both retailers and consumers. Further, included in the product packaging was a "mini-catalog" that provided consumers with information about complementary products within the product lines they had just purchased. At this point in time catalogs cross-selling other product lines were not included inside the package.

Laura and Mary knew that a major objective was the establishment of PDP's corporate identity. Manufacturers often use media advertising to create an image in the minds of consumers. Was an expanded advertising program the answer?

Consumer Profiles

A wide variety of people purchased toys. The toy industry had been affected by major demographic trends, with Baby Boomers and the "boomlet" having an impact on growth. Toys were purchased by parents for their children or as gifts to other children. The first child would often receive more toys than the second or third children. Many families had two wage earners, resulting in more discretionary income to spend on toys.

Children and teenagers purchased toys for themselves, as well as for gifts to give to other children. It was estimated that children annually spent $1.9 billion of their own money on toys and games (TMA). Grandparents were another major force among consumers buying toys. Spending on toys within this population was large, estimated at approximately 14 percent of retail sales.

The TMA reported that 55 percent of the retail sales reflected a planned purchase on the part of consumers. These consumers were pulled into the retailer after having been exposed to millions of dollars in television advertising to stimulate store visits. Consumer purchases were usually made after comparison shopping, with selections made at the store with the widest variety at the lowest prices (TMA).

There was, however, a difference between those who shopped at the mass market toy retailer as opposed to those shopping at specialty toy retailers. Generally, the primary target market was adults, predominantly women, in their mid 30s, with a relatively high level of education (all had graduated high school with a majority having been to college). Households were small, two to three children usually close together in age (one to three years' separation). Almost all had higher than average incomes, usually from one spouse working full-time. These people had the money to afford higher-priced toys, and higher levels of education made them more concerned about what their children playing with. These parents wanted their children to grow up to be future presidents, not "vidiots."

The reality was that most customers were small families with one or two children, often more affluent. However, demographic background varied by product line. From the data at hand, Laura and Mary knew that many consumers purchased products in the L'Enfant line as baby gifts. Consumers purchasing Puff N' Chuff Railroad products came from the broader market due to the appeal of a popular children's storybook series. These consumers tended not to shop at specialty toy stores exclusively. Within the Kinectics product line, children tended to be older, from more upscale families, and had more influence over the purchase of specific items.

Decision Time

The afternoon sun was waning. Laura and Mary sat in the crowded conference room mulling over the myriad issues they needed to address during the development of their marketing plan. The particularly problematic issue was how to increase consumer awareness for the corporate name (PDP), and support their retailer network by increasing store traffic on the limited budget available to them. One of PDP's concerns was that most of its customers were more familiar with the various brand names (Puff N' Chuff Railroad, L'Enfant, etc.) than they were with PDP.

It was apparent that many of PDP's competitors took advantage of the brand equity that was built up over time through the use of mass media advertising. Further, retailers were often more supportive of manufacturers that developed this brand awareness since it translated into increased store traffic and sales. How might PDP develop this level of awareness? Laura and Mary knew that any strategy must strive to achieve the objective of developing corporate identity and/or equity.

At the same time, PDP was not only competing with other specialty toys, but also with mass market toys. Specialty toy stores prided themselves on the extra service and support they gave to their customers in order to differentiate themselves from the mass merchandisers in the industry. With their limited resources, how could PDP help these small, specialty retailers compete? Herein lay the dilemma. PDP wanted to support the retailer, but the specialty toy retailer did not necessarily support PDP to the same degree. It was a basic divergence of objectives. PDP wanted to sell the company and its system, and use its products to generate store traffic. Specialty retailers wanted increased traffic, but were simply interested in selling any product within their store that fits their consumer's needs, which might not necessarily be PDP products. How could PDP profitably maintain consumer loyalty once they get into the store?

CASE
20

The Red Bell

DIRK BALDWIN

University of Wisconsin–Parkside

HARLAN SPOTTS

Western New England College

Linda Rosenthal looked up at the ringing bell announcing the arrival of a customer at her specialty toy and educational products store, The Red Bell. "Good Morning! May I help you?" Linda asked, as she cheerfully greeted her first customer of the day. "Why yes, you may be able to," the woman replied. "I received this flyer in the mail" she said, showing Linda a multicolored brochure of children's toys. "I am looking for a different kind of toy to give my grandson for his birthday and thought that these looked interesting."

Linda examined the flyer. "We carry a complete line of Playmobil products right over here. How old is your grandson?" "He is six years old," the woman replied. "Playmobil has a new western play set," Linda continued, as she explained the product features.

Fifteen minutes later . . . "Thank you very much for your help," the woman said, as she wrote out a check to cover the cost of her purchases. "You're very welcome," Linda replied. "Let me know how your grandson likes the new western play set."

Linda took a moment to record the purchase in the journal she kept next to her cash register. Picking up her packages, the woman turned to leave, then stopped and asked, "Do you have a catalog? Your store seems to have such interesting toys." "Yes, we do," Linda replied. Handing the woman a Red Bell catalog she said, "Here you are. Have a nice day."

As the woman left, Linda Rosenthal turned her gaze toward the busy thoroughfare outside her store. The late morning sun of mid-summer filtered through the front windows as she contemplated the future of her business.

Introduction

The Red Bell was a specialty toy and educational products store located in Racine, Wisconsin. A second store was located in the neighboring city of Kenosha. Specialty toys such as Playmobil, Brio, Breyer Horses, and others made up half of the product assortment carried by the two stores. The other half consisted of educational supplies, mostly sold to elementary and secondary teachers at public and private schools for use in their classrooms.

January through June were slow times for the Red Bell. Late July and August were busy, as teachers purchased supplies for the next school year and Christmas items purchased at the February toy show began to arrive. Business slowed down again during September and October, the calm before the storm so to speak. More product shipments arrived during this time for the Christmas season. Later in the fall parents begin shopping for Christmas gifts.

As Linda walked back to the sales desk she knew that the time was long past due for both operational and marketing strategy changes. The Red Bell operated like stores had over two decades ago. While the cash register was automated, the tracking of product sales was done almost completely by hand. General product assortment information was captured in a handwritten journal beside the cash register. This system limited the amount of information that could be collected. Further, Linda's ability to generate useable information for marketing-related decisions was hampered.

The bell jingled as the front door to the store opened, breaking Linda's concentration. Julie, Linda's full-time employee, was here. "Good," thought Linda, as her stomach made her aware that lunch time was approaching. "After lunch I can get to work on the marketing communications program for the next year. The current promotion activities are just not delivering the results that I need."

Industry Overview

The United States shipped over 2 billion toys in a recent year and was the largest market for toys in the world. There were over 120,000 individual stockkeeping units (SKUs), with approximately 6,000 new toys introduced every year, according to the Toy Manufacturers of America (TMA). It was estimated that the toy industry reached $20 billion in retail sales in that same year (the TMA estimate was based on an average 33 percent gross margin). This was a 7 percent increase over the previous year (TMA). Manufacturers' sales for the year were estimated at $13.43 billion, up 3 percent over the previous year.

As with many industries, there is severe seasonality associated with the sales of toys. Almost two-thirds of industry sales occur between October and December. As one would suspect, the holiday season drives this massive buying trend.

The toy industry is characterized by product differentiation in order to attract consumers to products. Some toys exhibit fad life cycles, being highly promotional and trendy (flying toys, drawing toys, radio-controlled vehicles, and toys licensed from popular movies and television shows). In contrast, there are many traditional toys that constitute the backbone of the industry (dolls, games, pre-school, infant, and activity toys). Given the competitive and volatile nature of the industry, companies start up and go out of business often. There have also been numerous mergers as industry leaders solidify their market positions and competitors try to achieve differential advantage (TMA).

There are two primary segments, the mass and specialty toy markets. While both sectors of the industry produce toys for infants and children, they are drastically different in terms of industry structure, product offerings, and other marketing activities.

The Mass Market Sector

This sector dominated the industry, accounting for approximately 80 percent of industry sales. While there were many toy manufacturers, two dominated the industry in terms of market share and influence. Mattel and Hasbro were the industry giants. Sales for these two companies were $3.6 and $2.9 billion, respectively, in a recent year.

Toys produced for this sector were aggressively marketed and distributed through mass merchandising retail chain stores (i.e., Kmart, Toys 'R Us, Wal-Mart). Mattel and Hasbro were both in *Advertising Age*'s Top 100 Advertisers in that same recent year, each spending in excess of $260 million in the U.S. This was a highly competitive industry with dominance of retail shelf space being of prime importance.

Other trends affecting the industry, according to S&P Surveys, included:

- Increased competition for retail shelf space as mass market toy retailers closed stores and cut back on the number of SKUs in inventory
- Continued growth in the industry through the marketing of licensed products with tie-ins to televisions shows and movies
- Collectible toys having a major influence on the industry, with Barbie and Matchbox leading the way
- Many of the major manufacturers moving in the direction of multimedia and CD-ROM technology, taking advantage of the increased penetration of personal home computers
- Decreasing resin costs for plastic products over the last year, relieving some of the pressure on profit margins

The Specialty Sector

This sector of the industry was almost the exact opposite of the mass market. It was small, accounting for approximately 20 percent of industry sales according to *Playthings*, and the companies competing in this sector were, for the most part, privately owned.

While there were hundreds of companies that manufactured specialty and educational toys, no one company appeared to have the market dominance of a Mattel or Hasbro. It was very likely that a small, privately owned company with few employees might dominate a product category, but not the overall market. Some of the better-known names in this sector included Brio, Educational Insights, LearningCurve Toys, and Playmobil.

Manufacturers in this sector traditionally distributed their products through specialty toy retailers, exclusively. Recently, Playmobil decided to test the mass market. Marketing activities in the specialty arena were reflective of industry size and retail structure. Most companies did not engage in national television advertising or consumer promotions. Trade promotions were limited, with many manufacturers restricting their activities to favorable payment terms and cooperative advertising dollars. Some price-off promotions were encouraged by manufacturers, but these were usually small (20 percent or less) and occurred at only one time during the year, prior to Christmas holidays.

From a marketing perspective, this sector of the industry was much less sophisticated. One area of increased interest among retailers was the development of information databases to increase efficiency of store operations and marketing.

Retail Market Structure

The two primary distribution channels consisted of manufacturer direct to retailer and manufacturer to wholesaler to retailer (TMA). A very small number of companies sold direct to consumers. There were approximately 74,000 retailers selling toys and games (TMA). This number included many different types of retailers, from the large mass merchandisers carrying toys as a sideline, to the large, "toys only" merchandisers, to the small, independent toy retailers.

Mass Merchandisers

The mass merchandiser is typified by the "category killer" outlet such as Toys 'R Us, and the discount department stores such as Kmart and Wal-Mart. These retailers competed on both selection and price. The products carried in inventory were mainstream toys, both traditional and fad, which were supported by millions of marketing dollars. Many of the toys carried in these stores were based on popular movie and television programs through tie-in licensing agreements (i.e., *Star Wars, Star Trek, The Simpsons, Space Jam*). These stores carried many nationally advertised products and loss leaders to stimulate store traffic. Margins for advertised toys ranged from 15 to 25 percent while non-advertised toys had margins ranging from 35 to 40 percent (TMA).

Specialty Retailers

The specialty store retailers supported the specialty toy manufacturers. According to *EdPlay* trade journal, there were approximately 6,700 specialty and educational toy retailers in the United States. The majority of specialty retailers were small, with one to five locations. Recently, a number of chains had begun to expand within the U.S. market, growing rather rapidly in size. While the total number of retailers had remained fairly constant over the last six years, there did appear to be a high level of turnover with enough new stores opening up to replace the established stores going out of business.

These retailers actively avoided carrying mass market merchandise because they knew that they could not compete in such a price-oriented segment of the industry. Instead, they sought to obtain a competitive advantage by providing high quality developmental and educational toys that made parents feel good about the products they purchased for their children.

While specialty retailers tended to sell higher priced toys, they provided unique product offerings and services to consumers that were not available from mass merchandisers. Specialty toy retailers were interested in getting to know their customers and determining their needs for specific and unique toys. Then, once needs had been determined, the specialty retailer could recommend the appropriate toys for a child of a particular age. These retailers would even special-order specific items for customers if a particular toy was not in stock. This type of service was in stark contrast to the mass merchandiser, where self-service was standard operating procedure and sales clerks know relatively little about the products stocked in the store. This resulted in a much more impersonal store experience for the consumer.

Overview of the Red Bell

The Red Bell was a small, family-owned and operated business located in southeast Wisconsin. The main, and first, store was located in a small business district approximately three miles from downtown Racine, a small city of approximately 85,000 people (see Exhibit C20.1 for household estimates). This location was on a busy thoroughfare that connected the downtown with the expanding, western regions of the city. A second, newer store was located ten miles away in the neighboring city of Kenosha, population 80,000. The Red Bell's mission was "To be a major independent distributor of specialty toys, games, puzzles and teaching resource materials in southeastern Wisconsin and northeastern Illinois with an emphasis on customer service, product quality, and educational value of the product."

The Red Bell product mix consisted of approximately 5,000 items supplied by over 200 vendors. Started in 1978, the Red Bell has experienced steady growth over the last few years. Both sales and profits had increased. While the stores had been doing well, Linda felt they could do even better with a more focused marketing effort.

History of the Red Bell

The Red Bell was established in 1978 and operated by two previous owners before Linda and her husband purchased the business in 1990. At that time it was very small, consisting of just 600 square feet of retail space. With the goal of aggressively marketing the store and its products, Linda moved the store to a new location, more than doubling the space to 1,400 square feet. Business grew fast from the beginning, with sales revenues increasing from $40,000 in 1990 to $140,000 in 1992.

Given the number of customers from Kenosha frequenting the Racine location, the neighboring city was targeted as an area for expansion in early 1992. However, two competitors opened stores in Kenosha that year, delaying the opening of the second Red Bell store. These competitors quickly went out of business. Thus, in 1993, the Red Bell opened its new Kenosha store and that year achieved $45,000 in sales.

By 1994, sales at the Racine store were rapidly growing beyond the space currently available. This was due, in part, to the introduction of high quality specialty toys to serve the parent market as a supplement to the educational resources carried for local teachers. An additional 2,100 square feet was added to the current Red Bell location by leasing an adjacent store front. A passageway was cut through the wall separating the two stores to make one store with two rooms. As product lines continued to be added to the product mix, sales for the Red Bell grew to $275,000 that year.

The Kenosha store also was growing rapidly. In 1995, a new commercial development provided the opportunity to double the size of this store to 4,000 square feet. This would mean relocation from the downtown business district to the north side of the city, closer to the local university. This new facility allowed Linda to remain open longer each day, and seven days a week.

EXHIBIT C20.1: CENSUS ESTIMATES OF HOUSEHOLDS
FOR KENOSHA AND RACINE COUNTIES*

	Kenosha	Racine
Total Resident Population (1996)	139,938	182,892
Percent College Graduates (1996)	12.7	16.5
Per Capita Personal Income (1993)	$18,695	$21,000
Retail Sales (1992)	$968,114,000	$1,290,366,000
Total Households (1990)	47011	63,788
Married Couple Households with children		
under 18 years (1990)	13,141	18,086
Male Householder with children under 18 years (1990)	736	989
Female Householder with children under 18 years (1990)	3,038	4,884
Educational attainment of households of		
persons age 25 and over (1990)		
Some College, no degree	14,760	20,276
Associate Degree	6,174	7,134
Bachelor's Degree	6,969	12,740
Graduate or Professional Degree	3,281	5,459
Household Occupations (1990)		
Executive, Administrative and Managerial	12,245	19,301
Technical and Sales	8,632	113,363
Age of Householder by Household Income in 1989		
25 to 34 years of age		
$25,000 to $34,999	2,467	3,037
$35,000 to $49,999	2,583	3,449
$50,000 to $74,999	1,320	1,941
$75,000 and over	38	436
35 to 44 years of age		
$25,000 to $34,999	1,836	2,347
$35,000 to $49,999	2,734	4,284
$50,000 to $74,999	2,432	3,524
$75,000 and over	836	1,305
45 to 54 years of age		
$25,000 to $34,999	1,203	1,175
$35,000 to $49,999	1,790	2,650
$50,000 to $74,999	1,969	2,821
$75,000 and over	9,61	1,614

* Data abstracted from U.S. Census 1996 County Summaries and 1990 Census

Operations

Linda Rosenthal had primary responsibility for developing store strategies and managing the daily operations of both stores. The Racine store was the main location, with Linda spending most of her time there. There was a manager responsible for the daily operations of the Kenosha store. Each location had one full-time and three part-time employees.

In addition to store operations, Linda made several trips each year with her daughter to purchase store stock. At least one trip per year was made to New York City to attend the annual toy fair. In addition to these buying trips, Linda, her husband, and daughter made at least 13 trips each year to regional conventions and shows both to sell toys and promote the store.

Pricing policies for the Red Bell were based on standard mark-ups determined by the manufacturer. Overall, Linda attempted to achieve some specific objectives with respect to gross and net profit margins. Specifically, an average gross margin of 51.5 percent and net profit margin of 18.9 percent were maintained.

Linda had been increasingly dissatisfied with the performance of her promotional dollars. She advertised the Red Bell in both the Racine and Kenosha newspapers, but had difficulty targeting her message since certain more affluent sections of the city had low newspaper penetration. Being located in a small city with a population of people who commuted for work to either Chicago or Milwaukee was a special challenge. Many of these people were not long-term residents of Racine or Kenosha and did not read the local newspaper, instead preferring newspapers such as the *Chicago Tribune* or *Milwaukee Journal Sentinel*. These large newspapers had a prohibitive cost per thousand advertising rate for a small retailer such as the Red Bell and were an extremely inefficient way for Linda to reach this market segment.

As for other promotional activities, Linda would often buy ad space in special sections or inserts in the local newspaper to increase her visibility. Cable television had been another media vehicle used, since Linda could obtain prerecorded commercials with a Red Bell overlay from manufacturers such as Educational Insights (see Exhibit C20.2 for the current marketing communications plan). There was a Red Bell catalog of educational supplies that was sent to all Red Bell customers who were school teachers (see Exhibit C20.3). Smaller catalogs of specific toy products were also produced by using cooperative advertising dollars from manufacturers such as LearningCurve and Educational Insights (see Exhibit C20.4). However, none of these media allowed Linda to establish the kind of customer relationships needed for success in this industry. Specialty toy stores needed a loyal clientele who visited often. At the same time, new customers were needed to expand the customer base.

The Parent Market

The parent market was where the real growth of the business had been and was expected to be in the future. The Racine store had a current parent/educator market sales ratio of 50/50, while Kenosha was at 15/85. These numbers were on target for Racine, but were way below target for Kenosha. The number of families moving into Kenosha from Illinois was increasing at a very rapid pace.

Generally, there was a difference between people who shopped at mass merchandisers and specialty toy stores. Consumer research revealed that Red Bell customers

EXHIBIT C20.2: MARKETING COMMUNICATIONS PLAN

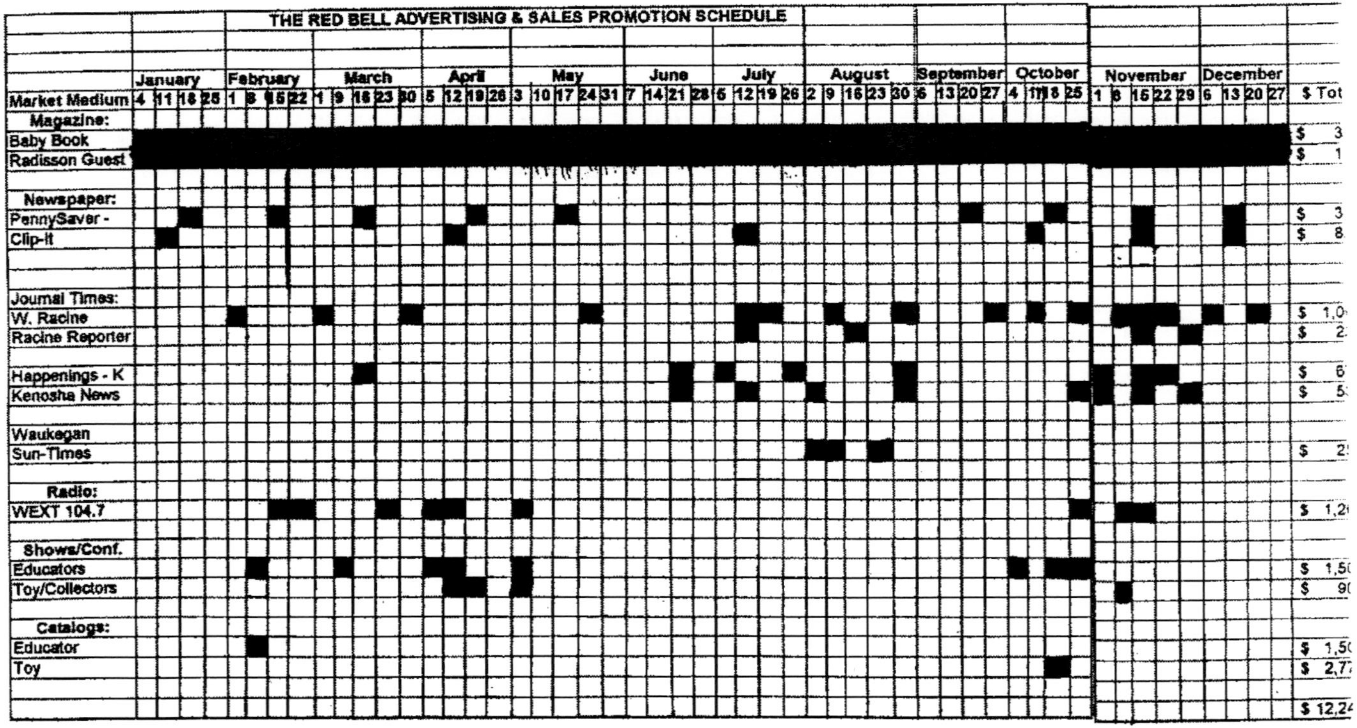

THE RED BELL ADVERTISING & SALES PROMOTION SCHEDULE

Market Medium	January 4 11 18 25	February 1 8 15 22	March 1 8 15 22	April 5 12 19 26	May 3 10 17 24 31	June 7 14 21 28	July 5 12 19 26	August 2 9 16 23 30	September 6 13 20 27	October 4 11 18 25	November 1 8 15 22 29	December 6 13 20 27	$ Tot
Magazine:													
Baby Book													$ 3
Radisson Guest													$ 1
Newspaper:													
PennySaver -													$ 3
Clip-It													$ 8
Journal Times:													
W. Racine													$ 1,0
Racine Reporter													$ 2
Happenings - K													$ 6
Kenosha News													$ 5
Waukegan													
Sun-Times													$ 2
Radio:													
WEXT 104.7													$ 1,2
Shows/Conf.													
Educators													$ 1,5
Toy/Collectors													$ 9(
Catalogs:													
Educator													$ 1,5(
Toy													$ 2,7,
													$ 12,24

EXHIBIT C20.3: COOPERATIVE ADVERTISING CATALOG

EXHIBIT C20.4: COOPERATIVE ADVERTISING CATALOG

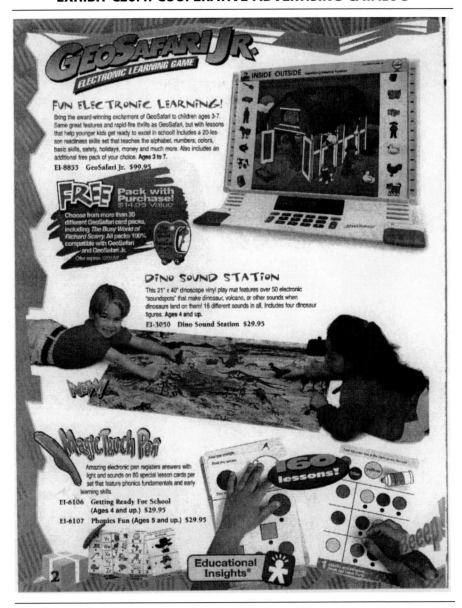

tended to be local, coming from regions close to the respective Racine and Kenosha locations. They were women, 31 to 50 years old. Average household size was four to six members, with household incomes ranging from $25,000 to $50,000. These households also had above-average levels of education.

Understanding consumer behavior was very important. Almost 80 percent of customers visited the store once a month, but did not necessarily buy. The Red Bell benefited from being the only specialty toy and educational supply store in the Racine/Kenosha area, with 40 percent of consumers shopping the store for this reason. These customers also shopped other toy stores (Wal-Mart, Toys 'R Us, etc.) in the area for mainstream toys.

During the week, the store was busiest between 1:00 P.M. and 5:00 P.M., with 65 percent of customers visiting the store during this time period. Store visits were spread evenly across the six-day week from Monday through Saturday. Customer traffic was marginally heavier on Tuesdays, Fridays, and Saturdays.

The methods of payment customers used for purchase were checks, cash, or charges. Customers were most likely to use checks (48 percent) rather than cash (38 percent) or credit cards (14 percent). Credit card usage increased as the total amount of the purchase increased.

It is important to understand the buying patterns and motivations of consumers for shopping at the Red Bell. This was an intriguing aspect of consumer behavior since, on average, specialty toy stores tended to have higher prices than mass merchandisers. Observational studies revealed three distinct shopping patterns for customers visiting the store. Shopping scripts changed depending on whether or not the shopper had made the purchase decision prior to entering the store, and whether or not children accompanied them to the store.

For those shoppers who had made the purchase decision prior to entering the store, they walked directly to the area of the store displaying the item(s) for which they were looking. Depending on the degree to which the decision had been made, shoppers spent varying amounts of time examining the product offerings. After examining the item(s) for correct selection, shoppers then took these items to the sales counter for purchase. The items were paid for and the shopper left the store.

For those shoppers who had not made the product purchase decision prior to entering the store, the shopping script was different. When these shoppers walked into the store, they browsed. Beginning at the front of the store, shoppers took their time examining the various educational toys on display. Working their way through the store, shoppers ended up in the educational book section located at the rear of the store. During the process of browsing, if the shopper had a specific toy or book for which they might be looking, they would often stop and ask the sales clerk for assistance. The salesperson then worked to determine the shopper's needs, showing them the products about which they inquired as well as other, related products. While browsing, shoppers usually picked up the toy box and examined the contents and price. Usually, shoppers would browse through the store, even after they had made their desired product selection. Depending on whether or not a purchase was being made, the shopper would either proceed to the sales counter or leave the store.

The script for shoppers entering the store with children was a variant of the previous two scripts. Upon entering the store, the parents and children separated. Children proceeded to a play area equipped with toys sold in the store while the parents either browsed or found the products for which they were looking. If a purchase was made, it was usually done without the children. Children were left to play as long as possible, and were only gathered together when it came time for the family to leave the store.

Consumers used a distinct decision-making process (see Exhibit C20.5) when purchasing specialty toys and educational supplies. There was a strong belief among consumers that toys purchased in the Red Bell had a higher educational value than those purchased in mass merchandisers. Further, parents felt better about themselves when they purchased toys they thought were enhancing the developmental abilities of their children. Exhibit C20.6 contains a means-end chain evaluating the attributes, consequences, and values of specialty toys for children.

The Educator Market

Teachers from public and private schools had provided a solid customer base for the Red Bell since its beginning as an educational supply store. While Linda would have liked to achieve a 50/50 parent-to-teacher customer ratio, she realized that substantial opportunity for market penetration still existed within the educator market.

EXHIBIT C20.5: DECISION-MAKING MODEL FOR SPECIALTY TOYS

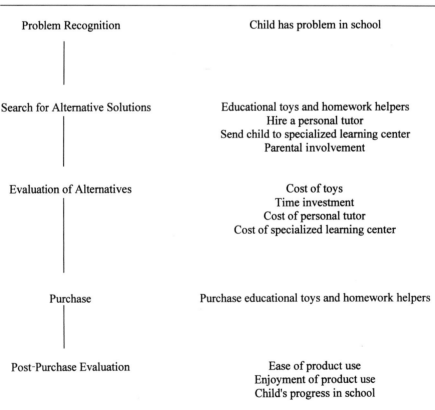

Problem Recognition	Child has problem in school
Search for Alternative Solutions	Educational toys and homework helpers Hire a personal tutor Send child to specialized learning center Parental involvement
Evaluation of Alternatives	Cost of toys Time investment Cost of personal tutor Cost of specialized learning center
Purchase	Purchase educational toys and homework helpers
Post-Purchase Evaluation	Ease of product use Enjoyment of product use Child's progress in school

EXHIBIT C20.6: MEANS-END CHAIN ANALYSIS

Attributes	*Consequences*	*Values*
Age appropriate characteristics	Child Comprehension	Task Accomplishment Self-Esteem
Enhances creativity	Stimulates Growth and Imagination	Perform at Peak Level
Toys maintain value and are collectible	Creates Hobbies and Interests	Personal Enjoyment

Teachers who shopped at the Red Bell were primarily from elementary and middle schools located in the Racine, Kenosha, and northern Illinois region. General school supplies could be found at many different stores, including Kmart, Target, Office Max, Office Depot, and Shopko. The Red Bell provided specialized educational products that teachers used to teach students in the classrooms, including workbooks, posters, charts, and flashcards.

Buyer behavior for the educator market was very different from the parent market. Eighty percent of total segment purchases occurred in July and August. This was similar to the Christmas season for the parent market. Products primarily purchased at the beginning of the year include opening thematics (e.g., apples, oceans, etc.), room decor (trimmer, banners, and posters), job assignment products, incentive materials (stickers and charts), record books, and planners. After school began, the teachers came back for specific products to reinforce classroom learning. These might include books on math, language arts, and reading. Also, many seasonal products such as stickers were sold.

There were two distinct shopping scripts for educators. Teachers looking for specific products for the beginning of the school year or to replace classroom materials had a very focused buying script. They entered the Red Bell and walked through the toy section at the front of the store to the educational supply section at the back of the store. These shoppers were single-focused and did not stop to browse the toy section. They found the items they needed, purchased them, and left.

Teachers who were looking for resources to support a new teaching idea were somewhat different. Usually they knew what it was they were trying to do in the classroom, but did not know exactly what they needed. It was "I'll know it when I see it" behavior. Sometimes the Red Bell did not have the products available for a teacher to develop an idea. In these situations Linda would special order the product(s) to satisfy the teacher's need, which was a service not provided by other retailers in the area.

The special order process would usually satisfy only about 90 percent of these teachers, since many exhibited an "I need it yesterday" attitude. Because of the last-minute shopping behavior exhibited by some teachers, they ran the risk of encountering stock-outs from either the wholesaler or manufacturer.

In general, customers from the educator market were very demanding and sometimes difficult to please. They were, however, a valued part of the Red Bell's customer base and every effort was made to maintain and grow this source of revenue. Even though they were demanding, teachers exhibited very predictable buying patterns, were repeat customers, and were easily reached.

Linda did not currently have a specific communication campaign to reach this segment. Many teachers found out about the Red Bell by word-of-mouth or local newspaper ads. Linda would personally visit some of the local schools to deliver catalogs and occasionally deliver flyers promoting the store. The Red Bell could benefit, however, from a planned effort to cultivate this market.

Competition

The Red Bell faced competition from two distinct types of competitors: 1) the traditional toy outlet and 2) other independent specialty toy and educational resource retailers. The traditional toy outlets included Toys 'R Us, Kmart, Target, Shopko, and KB toy and hobby store. These stores carried mass marketed toys and competed primarily on price.

For competition from other retailers like the Red Bell, the closest is Teach N Toys with four locations in the Milwaukee area, approximately 30 minutes to the north of Racine. Other stores of similar design include Highsmith DBA, The Education Station, and The Learning Shop. The first two were located in the Madison area, approximately two hours to the northwest of Racine, while the latter chain was located in the Appleton, LaCrosse, and Madison areas. There were no direct competitors to the Red Bell in the Racine, Kenosha, and northeastern Illinois regions. However, some of the other specialty toy stores maintained a presence on the Internet and in direct mail catalogs.

Summary

Linda realized the urgent need for an information system to improve the operational efficiency and marketing effectiveness of the Red Bell. She had to sort out the requirements of the system before it could be acquired and marketing communication strategy developed.

Ideally Linda wanted to track customer behavior at the transaction level. Having taken a course in management information systems at a local university, she knew that tracking customers would require some type of database. Could she target her customers in a way that would stimulate a closer relationship? Also, would this relationship marketing strategy be appropriate for both the teacher and parent market segments? How would she start generating lists? What would a marketing communications strategy based on database marketing techniques look like?

Linda knew that competitors were moving into direct marketing, but was not sure whether it was an appropriate strategy for her business. In general, Linda needs to determine the uses for the new information system, the data to be stored, and the steps necessary to acquire the information system and generate the database.

CASE
21

Saint Laurie
Merchant Tailors

TANYA BENDER HENDERSON
Howard University

SUSAN K. JONES
Ferris State University

GARY KASKOWITZ
Moravian College

BETTY PARKER
Western Michigan University

On a sunny day in August, Andrew (Andy) Kozinn and his colleagues bustle around their fabric-packed, fifth-floor showroom above Manhattan's lively Koreatown neighborhood. Although the distance is only 1.3 miles, Andy's current workspace seems a world away from the elegant Park Avenue storefront where his Saint Laurie custom suit business used to reside.

Andy Kozinn represents the third generation of family ownership for Saint Laurie, which was started by his grandfather in 1913. Andy's son, Jacob (Jake), also is actively involved in the business as a clothing and costume designer—and as the chief strategist for Saint Laurie's online lead generation efforts.

The men's clothing business has undergone dramatic changes over the past decade or so, sparked by the business casual movement as well as other social and attitudinal changes. As Andy candidly admits, the swiftness of these changes and some business miscalculations almost put Saint Laurie out of business. But with some timely adjustments—and valuable help from Jake—Andy now has Saint Laurie back in the black with good prospects for the future.

A Visit to Saint Laurie

Exiting the New York Subway at Herald Square—the stop for the venerable Macy's department store—a Saint Laurie visitor heads two blocks south to 32nd Street and encounters the exotic sights and enticing restaurant aromas of Koreatown (known by the locals as K-Town). An elevator in an unassuming building at 22 West 32nd Street whisks prospective suit buyers to the fifth floor. Upon opening the decorative wrought iron elevator door, Saint Laurie Merchant Tailors appears. The showroom is deep and narrow; filled with table after table of sumptuous fabrics, sample suits and jackets, incredibly lovely and unique silk ties, and Saint Laurie's own cufflinks and accessories. Behind the scenes at the same location is the firm's turnkey clothing manufacturing business.

Andy Kozinn himself is likely to greet you as you enter the showroom, wearing his trademark wide braces (suspenders), round horn rim glasses, custom shirt and well-cut slacks. A 1974 graduate of Northwestern University's Medill School of Journalism, Andy makes a colorful interview subject.

From Park Avenue to K-Town

From 1913 to 1984, Saint Laurie was located in a loft on Manhattan's Fifth Avenue. Then from 1984 to 1997, the company had its own building at Broadway and 20th. In the summer of 1997, Andy Kozinn opened the doors of his elegant midtown Manhattan store at Park Avenue and 51st Street—directly across from the celebrated Waldorf-Astoria Hotel.

"It was 'Wall Street North'—near Chase Bank and UBS," Andy recalls. "I thought we would have walk-in traffic from all the right people." Unfortunately, that didn't happen. Looking back, Andy realizes there were ominous signs of what was to come in the menswear business. "I remember a day when a group of young guys came to check out the store and they didn't have their suit jackets on. At least they had ties on—today they wouldn't even have that!"

A fan of classic movies, Andy had a flashback that day to a scene from the 1961 film "Breakfast at Tiffany's," based on the Truman Capote novel. At one point the hero of the movie, played by George Peppard, hurries outside to run after Audrey Hepburn's character, the infamous Holly Golightly. But not before stopping to put on his suit jacket! No self-respecting gentleman would be seen on New York streets in those days without his jacket and tie!

Business at the stylish new store just never took off, according to Andy. It seems his long-term customers perceived that prices would rise when he moved from the lower-rent district in Lower Manhattan to swanky Park and 51st. And business dress requirements were changing rapidly in the late 1990s—indeed, after 1999, men's suit sales in the U.S.A. went down 30%; and after the dot.com bust and 9/11/2001 they were ultimately down a whopping 50%.

After the 9/11 terrorist attacks on the World Trade Center and the resulting loss of thousands of lives, most Manhattan businesses experienced lower sales and lower traffic. Layer on the move to business casual, and Andy Kozinn found himself nearly drowning in red ink.

One day when it was apparent that the store on Park Avenue wasn't working, Andy found himself groping for a way to salvage the business. He was taking a breather, sitting outside at a coffee shop on 51st Street. "A homeless person came by and said to me, 'Buddy, it can't be that bad!'—imagine the look I must have had on my face. Momentum is an amazing thing. We went down, down, down," Andy recalls. "I don't believe you should fight it spending money during a downturn. People weren't ready to acknowledge that suits were over. You can't fight a fashion trend. You just hunker down, lay off, cut costs. We saw New York City go through a terrible recession, but now it has really bounced back."

Even so, it took Andy many months to figure out how to re-build Saint Laurie where it is today—on the fifth floor in lively K-Town.

The Evolution of the Men's Clothing Business

The changes Saint Laurie has confronted in recent years have to do with a more casual atmosphere in business—first exemplified by the "computer geeks" of Silicon Valley—and the overall shift toward business casual. A business built on suits as working attire for the white-collar work force, Saint Laurie (like the men's suit business in general) lost half its volume post-9/11/2001.

Andy Kozinn notes, "9/11 got us back to a more sober way of looking at the world. In the immediate shock from 9/11 people weren't buying anything. The positive change had to do with values—people were less frivolous about how they appeared. This seems like ancient history now. It's a fact that the 'New Economy' is not suits, but casual attire. The 'Old Economy' is suits."

Even though the dot.com bust and 9/11 brought the business crisis to a head for Saint Laurie, upon reflection Andy knows that the seeds of change were being sown much earlier. Indeed, in some creative businesses, people stopped dressing up as early as the 1960s. Andy recounts, "A cartoon from 1969 shows two ad agency guys talking. One guy says 'What are you going to do on vacation?' The other guy says, "What I never get to do—wear a suit!" The 1970s brought pastel polyester leisure suits onto the scene, even for work in some cases, but the Reagan-era 1980s represented the *Dress for Success* decade, as exemplified by John T. Molloy's conservative how-to-dress books for both men and women.

Then in the early 1990s, Andy Kozinn started seeing people wearing nothing but black—every day—near his then-headquarters in Lower Manhattan. At the time, he says, "I thought it was a downtown phenomenon—everyone downtown was dressed in black—but in Midtown people still dressed like *mensches*." (Mensch is a Yiddish word referring to an individual with admirable characteristics and fundamental decency.)

According to Andy, casual Friday came about because "people were working so hard that they had done their 40-hour week by Thursday—so business casual on Friday was a relief. But middle-aged guys don't look good in business casual. They are *schlemiels* (dolts or bunglers, in Yiddish) in their khakis and shirts that don't hide the pot belly. Is that what they went to college for? To look like a blue-collar worker?"

To Andy, a suit is more than a business uniform. He says, "The suit was equated with a uniform—but ironically business casual did not turn out to be a liberating experience for people. It came with its own set of rules so that ultimately there is more conformity in business casual than there ever was with suits. Some companies began to actually require business casual, with people ridiculing fellow workers who showed up for work in something more formal. As it turns out, business casual is just another kind of 'business uniform,' with everyone in khakis and a blue shirt."

Andy says he never saw the change coming with lawyers, accounting firms, and IBM. "I was just floored when they all went business casual in response to the casual atmosphere in Silicon Valley and the overall shift to less formal attire. I used to ask people how they dressed for work. One customer who worked for Arthur Andersen said that he conformed to 'the way the client dresses.' Suits to visit clients wearing suits, and business casual to visit clients wearing slacks and shirts. Arthur Andersen changed to full-time business casual a year or so before they went under. To me that indicates a culture of conformity that is unhealthy for a CPA firm. It seems to me that someone from the outside, like an auditor, ought to be independent in how they dress—just as they should be independent in how they assess the client's business.

"Another example is the Janus Funds. I was an investor and read the annual report where the pictures indicated that every fund manager dressed identically—the same as the CEO—and all those funds had equally mediocre performance because everyone was thinking the same way." Andy believes there could have been different personalities for different funds, perhaps manifested in part by different approaches to clothing on the part of the fund managers.

Saint Laurie's New Niche in Custom Clothing

While men's suit-wearing habits were changing rapidly in the United States, Saint Laurie also had to deal with global dynamics in the clothing business.

When the Iron Curtain fell, the market was flooded with inexpensive "custom" suits made in Poland and Hungary. According to Andy, these "cheap suits" stalled the custom suit business in the United States because "they weren't presented as 'cheap suits,' but rather as $800 suits for $300. It's why some people still have a fairly negative view of custom suits. It takes so long to get them while today's customer wants everything instantly. The influx of Eastern European suits set the custom suit business back about 10 years."

As it turned out, however, these Eastern European suits couldn't touch Saint Laurie in terms of quality and uniqueness. Andy adds, "Some companies in our field went out of business at the time we were struggling, so now what we're doing is more special."

Hong Kong tailors have long been famous for creating inexpensive custom suits, but Andy says they "lack taste and finesse." He admits that the Italians are the deans of the custom suit industry—they have the good taste and sophistication to relate to the ultimate purchaser—but at a price that currently is prohibitive for most buyers. "Italy is getting clobbered because of the strong Euro," he explains. British tailors also have a long history of "bespoke" (custom) suit making, but Andy says "there are hardly any British tailors left."

When the business was on Park Avenue, Andy Kozinn had correctly foreseen a future for Saint Laurie in custom tailoring. "The store at 51st and Park was mostly custom suits, although we offered some that were ready-made. We were already getting into just-in-time manufacturing. 'No inventory' was going to be the future. My wife, Carey Graeber, helped get us grants to develop systems for made-to-measure clothing."

Since Saint Laurie was able to offer finely made and distinctive suits for those who appreciate them, Andy says that in the long run, "It turns out business casual was the best thing for us. The worst thing for us was the proliferation of cheap 'custom' suits."

Indeed, the tide has turned and Saint Laurie's elegant and distinctive suits are again seen as prestigious. "Senior managers are wanting to separate from the troops," Andy says. What's more, he notes, "Sport coats and slacks came back in business casual, and shirts became important. Now we find a guy will spend $200 on a custom shirt, whereas before the business casual movement, the shirt business had been flat."

What's more, Saint Laurie has been able to attract younger customers—people with a long period of buying ahead of them. "The old joke is that with every funeral, Brooks Brothers loses another customer, but our business is really growing with guys in their 30s. Younger people understand that something made for them is a service, not a product. They happily pay for personal trainers, psychologists, nutritionists, career coaches and other services whereas the older generation's philosophy was to 'tough it out' and not ask for help."

The biggest advocate for the "New Saint Laurie" in K-Town has been 20-something Jake Kozinn, who studied clothing design in school and also is an avid computer buff. "Jake didn't like being as "front and center" at 51st Street and Park," Andy explains. "He thought custom suit customers might not like people looking in on them while they were measured and fitted. Moving upstairs actually became a more comfortable fit for our customers—also, it was not too posh an environment. People don't care about the environment except that it should be efficient, easy, and comfortable. Jake thought we should make Saint Laurie a 'find'—something people felt proud of discovering. For most people when they find that special tailor or barber they keep it a secret. It's a private thing that they might share in hush-hush tones with a few friends."

Saint Laurie and Technology: From Body Scanners to the Web

Andy Kozinn has always been interested in technology, whether it relates to the suit business or business in general. "In the late 1990s I went to Germany to check out the body scanners they were using there for custom suit design. There are very few good tailors left in Europe, so the scanner helps manufacturers." Andy bought a body scanner in 2000, for use in his New York business.

The Saint Laurie web site at www.saintlaurie.com quotes NY1 technology reporter Adam Balkin's report about the Vitus 3-D scanner, which creates a perfect 3-D image of the person it's scanning.

As Balkin wrote, "'Over about seven seconds, it scans your body,' says Jacob Kozinn. 'Thirty seconds later I have a picture in gray-scale of your body on the screen that I can rotate and take cross-sections of and take measurements anywhere I want on your body, and it's all very accurate. Normally if you left after ordering a suit, we have twelve measurements to interpret your body. Now when you leave we have your body, so we know every base is covered. To scan your body, you stand between four towers and lasers scan your body and pinpoint specific spots on your body. Next to the lasers there are little tiny cameras that take pictures along the way. The image is then passed along to a computer, where exact measurements from any number of points can be calculated.'"

As numerically accurate as the body scan may be, Andy and Jake soon learned that it could not completely take the place of the tailor-customer relationship. Tailoring is as much an art as it is a science. As Andy explains, "Elements that are important in custom suit making include fitting, construction, design, fabric and fabric knowledge, tailoring, and customer relations skills. Saint Laurie has the people to be good in all these areas. It's a team effort to make the business work." What's more, even if a body scan is done, the tailor has to be able to communicate well with the customer about how the clothing will fit. Fit is a very individual choice. Some customers want to look like they are almost "poured into" a suit, while others prefer something looser. "Some tailors are both without ears," Andy jokes. He attributes a good part of his success to careful listening and providing customers with exactly what they want and need in terms of a suit's look and feel.

About the time Andy was investigating body scanner technology, he and Jake decided to launch the first web site for Saint Laurie. The father-and-son duo soon learned that just as they successfully combined the "art" of tailoring with the "science" of the body scanner, their online efforts required both technical expertise and an ability to interpret the qualitative aspects of web site development and promotion.

Introducing www.saintlaurie.com

Recalling their lesson from customer reactions to the overly upscale Park Avenue store, Andy and Jake built a web site that was what Andy calls a "dark and simple" approach. "We're trying to reach a mature audience in a mature industry," he explains. "It's a very foolish thing to think that web sites for all types of businesses in all industries should be the same. A law firm's web site should not look the same as someone selling computers. There's a subtle message that the typeface, graphics and colors of a web site sends."

With its warm, textured suiting fabric backgrounds and basic design, the web site is nowhere near as slick looking as it could be. The idea is that discovering Saint Laurie on the web is similar to discovering it in K-Town—a personal 'find' for customers to share with just a few friends. Andy's wife Carey adds, "Saint Laurie's web site has to be tactile . . . almost romantic. You don't want customers and prospects to think, "Oh, that's where they place their energies—on creating this web site, not on serving me."

Of course, creating a site is just the beginning. Every company with a web presence has to find the best way to attract prospects and customers to the site and keep them coming back. For Saint Laurie initially, the main method of attracting web traffic was the use of Google sponsored search. "General advertising was so wasteful for us," Andy notes. "We received a steady stream of customers from Google." Andy reports that for every one dollar invested in Google sponsored search, the firm was bringing in five dollars of incremental, new business—not to mention the long-term value of those new customers.

"With Google we just bought certain words that produced click-throughs for us," Andy continues. "Google has a methodology for seeing which words work best." Sponsored search is a very dynamic environment, so Jake took charge of staying up with what was working and how to make sure Saint Laurie remained at the top of the sponsored search list for the firm's chosen key words and/or word combinations.

After discovering Saint Laurie via Google, people tended to send an email to Andy saying something like "put me on your mailing list." Andy took a proactive stance with those leads. "I responded to them and asked them, 'Are you in the market for something?'" Andy kept up the email dialogue with the prospect, answering their questions with more questions until they either "got exasperated," as he says with a smile, or gave him a specific area of product interest.

Andy says that much of the new business that Google brought to Saint Laurie was still from people in the greater New York City area. However, with people traveling regularly to New York once again, Andy adds, "for someone to visit us from Cincinnati, Pittsburgh, or even Los Angeles or Chicago was not such a big deal. Our customers do have to come here at least to have initial measurements done. We got two to three new customers a week here in the showroom, attributable to Google. It turns out the scanner wasn't our 'technology key to success' after all . . . the web was."

Once Saint Laurie started using Google, men in the age range of late 20s to early 40s began discovering the firm in the online search for something special. "Younger men wanted to get linen suits for a whole bridal party," for example. "For weddings we got a lot of business." Saint Laurie is happy to serve the specific needs of diverse clientele, as well. Andy explains, "For instance, one of our customers is a Buddhist. We must wait on him barefoot, and then he blesses our feet." That type of service is not likely to be readily available in the men's clothing section of the average mainline department store.

Customer Relationship Management at Saint Laurie

Andy Kozinn is a big advocate of using direct mail to keep his list of customers informed about new products, sales, and special events at Saint Laurie. The company's post cards often feature advertising ephemera (defined by www.dictionary.com as "printed matter of passing interest"). As Andy explains, "We used eBay to get old ephemera about tailoring. These pieces of art are in the public domain and can be used in our direct mail and in-store advertising." Saint Laurie promotions also feature photos of Andy's grandfather, the founder of Saint Laurie, as well as photos of the company's tailors and seamstresses from generations past. "We call people on their birthdays, too," Andy adds.

While Saint Laurie does not allow customers to negotiate on price, the company does have periodic sales, which are featured on the postcard mailers. Andy considers Saint Laurie's prices reasonable for what the customer gets. As he says, "In the old days when a guy paid $32 for a suit he might be making $21 a week." So he believes that $1500 for a Saint Laurie suit, for his type of customer, is not an outlandish amount to pay.

After a customer has been to the Saint Laurie showroom once, Andy notes, "I can do follow-up business without them coming here." Customers can be sent fabric samples and make their selections for suits, slacks, sport coats and custom shirts, knowing that Saint Laurie already has their measurements. As for selling directly on the web, Andy hasn't tried that except for cufflinks, belts and other accessories. "It hasn't been that successful," he admits.

Innovations from the Fourth Generation of Saint Laurie

Andy exhibits obvious pride in his talented designer son, Jake. "Jake has enthusiasm and youth, and now he has introduced his own line as a designer. The business is revived when a new generation comes in." Jake's designs are for younger customers who want a suit they can wear to work and then out to the club in the evening.

Jake also spearheads Saint Laurie's successful costume business, working with some of the nation's top theatrical clothing designers. The firm does about five productions a year, spread among movies, television and Broadway shows and outfitting actors including Liam Neeson, Al Pacino, John Goodman, and Steve Buscemi.

EXHIBIT C21.1: WEB SITE SCREEN CAPTURE
FROM THE TIME THE CASE
WAS WRITTEN: www.saintlaurie.com

Saint Laurie's web site uses tweed and pinstripe "fabric" as background and highlights the firm's proprietors, prices and services.

Looking Ahead for Saint Laurie

With 20% sales growth in each of the previous two years and a strong source of leads coming in from the web, Andy Kozinn seemed upbeat about the near future for his business. But then all of a sudden, some of the bigger players in the custom suit field discovered what it took to gain high rankings on Google and other search engines. Almost overnight, they outbid Saint Laurie to the point where the firm's sponsored search efforts were stymied. Thus Saint Laurie was on the lookout for new ways to attract customers in a cost-effective manner—be it online or offline.

As a veteran of a number of changes in the men's clothing business and the economy, Andy remains constantly alert to deal with whatever situations develop. And with Jake Kozinn providing fresh ideas and youthful energy, the future looks promising for Saint Laurie Merchant Tailors, no matter what challenges lie ahead.

Custom Suits Versus Made-to-Measure

Although Andy Kozinn uses the term "custom suit" quite often in discussing his product, the more correct term for what Saint Laurie creates is "made to measure." As Andy explains, "'Custom'" sounds better than 'made to measure,' but true custom tailoring is actually a poorer way of getting clothing made." As he describes it, custom clothing is made "from scratch"—reinventing the wheel every time—which often produces a poorer product that is not very stylish.

"Ready-made clothing designers have to stay innovative," Andy explains. "Custom tailors who just measure someone for a suit are not always thinking about what will look best on someone who is hard to fit. Made-to-measure clothing allows the tailor to correct the areas where a fashionable style is wrong for the individual customer, without starting from scratch. While custom clothing is better than ready-made in most ways, it can be worse in one way: the styling. To me, quality is not just about fabric workmanship and fit, it's also about style. Many custom tailors don't have good taste so they put together what the customer seems to want, or they don't have design skills.

"A made-to-measure firm has designers who provide very good style while still being able to adapt to fit preference and body style." Made-to-measure is an offshoot of ready-to-wear manufacturers with fashion-conscious designers, whereas custom suit places may make the same basic suit for years. On the other hand, according to Andy, not all made-to-measure is "created equal." As he explains, "Department store tailors who say they are doing made-to-measure are not at the same skill level you have at a custom tailor like Saint Laurie."

According to Andy, for over 100 years, "made to measure" has been recognized as the best way to tailor suits specifically for a customer. For example, the famous upscale suit maker, Oxxford, is a made-to-measure company, not a custom suit maker. Oxxford made-to-measure suits sell in the $3000 to $4000 range.

The old-fashioned tailor often had to do as many as 10 fittings to get the "from scratch" garment right. Instead, Saint Laurie keeps an inventory of sample garments customers can try on and use for feedback about cut and fit. Andy says, "Most of our customers are short on time—if they don't have multiple fittings, they're happy."

**EXHIBIT C21.2: GOOGLE SCREEN CAPTURE SHOWING
SAINT LAURIE COMING UP #1 FOR "CUSTOM SUITS"**

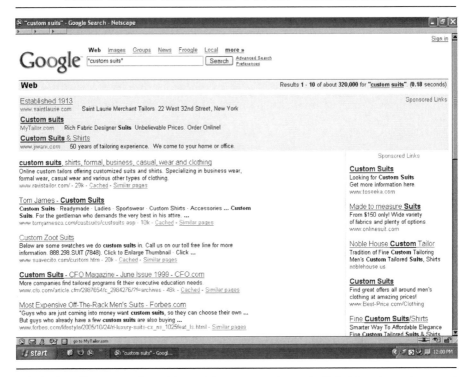

When they first started working with sponsored search, Saint Laurie endeavored to make sure that when prospects and customers put terms like "custom suits" into Google, www.saintlaurie.com came out on top in sponsored links.

Men's Fashion through the Ages

Men's clothing has been adjusted and refined over time, in response to the needs of the wearer. The loose robes worn by men before the Renaissance were originally designed more to conceal than enhance. This gave way to more constructed clothing, meant to accentuate the contours of the man. This was a vast change from clothing of utility in the Middle Ages—and thus men's fashion was born.

It was during the Renaissance period that the pattern maker (cutter) and the tailor joined the ranks of other skilled craftsmen of the era. Until this time, most of the focus on clothing design was on the weaver of the cloth, and most clothing was made in the home. But as societies shifted from the rural agrarian lifestyle toward the formation of towns, cities and eventually states, the services of the tailor were needed and fashion took hold.

Italy, Spain and France emerged as the fashion centers of the world, and the dress of the man became synonymous with power. This was marked by notables such as the

French King Louis XIV (1643-1715). The well dressed from across Europe and the world traveled to Paris for the "must have" items of the season. By the mid 17th century, the coat, vest and breeches had almost replaced the doublet, hose and cloak as the standard masculine costume worn since the 1500s, and the men's suit—the mainstay of men's wardrobes—was born.

The English Effect

It was during this time that the English began to move from the embroidered ornamentation of menswear toward more conservative styling, no doubt a result of the effect of wars and conflict. By the 18th century, styles worn by the gentry and mercantile class were easily distinguishable from those of the court circle, but by the early 1900s their dress was nearly the same. The tailors of London became leaders in the fashion world. The blending of the subtle styles preferred by the landed gentry, sportsmen and bourgeois businessman characterized the English menswear style, a style concerned more with the fit of clothing rather than its adornment.

Clothing was mainly made from woolen fabrics during this period and techniques for "molding" the cloth close to the body without exactly duplicating the true form of the wearer were developed over many years of experimentation. A new aesthetic of dress was created by the English tailor, and the modern tailor's art was born. The concept was to mimic the body while "improving and idealizing" it at the same time—while favoring discretion, simplicity and the perfection of cut.

American Evolution

In the U.S., despite the influence of its British origins, styles began to change. Revolutionary leaders discouraged Americans from embracing the styles worn by their British forefathers, thus becoming less dependent on importing clothing. The brocade jacket and lace shirt of George Washington gave way to the plain blue coat, drab colored waistcoat and green velveteen breeches worn by Thomas Jefferson at his inauguration in 1801.

In the 1800s, U.S. industrial development saw American manufactured cloth as an innovation over the homespun. As hand tailoring gave way to sewing machines, fashion moved toward clothing that fit lifestyles more so than conventions of style. New York City emerged as a center for clothing production after 1815. Ready-made clothing was offered at a cheaper price and hand tailoring became an emblem of class and refinement.

The 20th century saw the introduction of the first mass-produced suit, the "sack suit"—an almost shapeless coat without a waist seam. The polo coat and the button-down collar were introduced by Brooks Brothers around 1910. The first sports jacket was produced in the 1920s, the baggy pant was introduced, and flannel became the fabric of choice.

Depression-era Influences

After the stock market crash of 1929, the fashion industry followed the sentiment of the economic world and saw cutbacks in the manufacture and purchase of men's clothing. To lift the spirits of the wearer, men's suits were restructured to create an image of a wider torso and shoulders and the double-breasted suit grew in popularity. Suits took on the more stable and conservative hues of charcoal, steel, slate, navy and midnight blue, and these colors have remained the mainstay of the corporate world to this day.

As the country began to rebound, the "Zoot Suit" of the 1940s brought more flair to men's style and featured a long, full-cut look. More leisure time saw the emergence of the casual shirt. For the first time, the young began to dictate fashion trends and their parents followed. These young men went off to war, returning to create a dress code for their new business and industrial jobs. The new business suit consisting of a narrow- breasted, single-breasted coat—sometimes with a velvet collar—was worn in the mid-fifties with pastel-colored shirts rather than the starched and stark white that had been the uniform in the past.

Late 20th-Century Menswear

In the 1960s, the suit became more streamlined and tight-fitting with narrow pants. It was worn by the gents with long sideburns and sometimes hair over their collars. Leisure wear took on a decidedly more "feminine" look that would have made men's Victorian forefathers proud—paisley shirts in bright fluorescent colors with puffy sleeves and bell-bottomed velvet pants. The 1970s followed suit with polyester bell bottoms and the bright floral "body shirt" worn by both males and females. As more women began to enter the workforce during this era, the business suit became the uniform for all.

Sometimes called the "ugly eighties," the business world saw the birth of the "power suit" and major designers orchestrated the movement of fashion into the conservative "preppie" look—the oxford cloth button down shirt of the 1920s returned as did the baggy pant as corporate wear. Casual wear also took the preppie turn, however, mixing T-shirts with dinner jackets and loafers with no socks. The 1990s saw a return to the traditional, the vintage second hand store became the rage and the businessman no longer saw the need to follow a standard uniform, often wearing suits in a wide range of cuts, colors and patterns.

Men's fashion in the new millennium can be best described as a combination of all fashion eras.

Search Engine Optimization and Sponsored Search

Search engine optimization (SEO) focuses on e-marketing activities such as the design of web pages and the selection of keywords that will yield high rankings for a web site that is relevant to the word or phrase being searched. A well-optimized site has been designed so that search engine spiders can easily find the page and include it in the search engine database. The earlier the web site appears in the search engine's page ranking, the more likely it is that a consumer seeking information will see and

EXHIBIT C21.3: GOOGLE SCREEN CAPTURE SHOWING OTHER FIRMS COMING UP #1 FOR "CUSTOM SUITS"

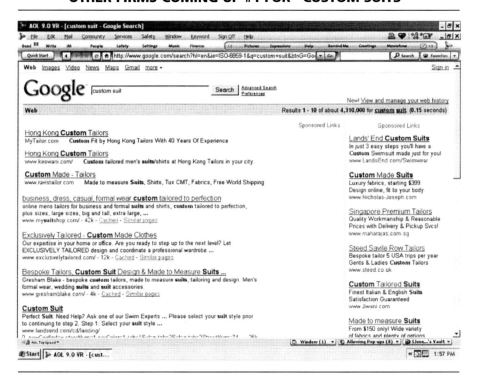

After two years of dominance for the key words "custom suit" in Goodgle, Saint Laurie was overtaken in the bidding by other, larger companies.

click on the link, as compared with competitive web sites that may appear lower in the rankings.

Keywords and Phrases

Marketers may rely on "natural" or "organic" search listings that enable consumers to find their web site. Natural searches utilize web site design techniques such as metatags (relevant words in HTML programming code that describe the web page contents), which generate the page ranking according to search engine criteria. Some search engines such as Google have developed ranking schemes that rely on the number of pages that link to the web page or term being searched.

Marketers may also utilize "paid" or "sponsored" keyword search to help drive online traffic to their site. Sponsored search involves the purchase of keywords and phrases from search engines. The search words may be relevant brand names or trademarks, such as "Microsoft" or "Whopper". They may also be generic keywords, such as "software" or "hamburger" or phrases such "two all-beef patties." Search engines often provide buyer assistance on suitable, popular keywords or phrases.

Sponsored links are noted in blue and appear at the top or far right side of the page to distinguish them from natural online rankings. When the consumer clicks on the sponsored link, they will be connected to the desired web site's "landing page."

Marketing Strategy and Growth Issues for Saint Laurie

The United States Small Business Administration defines a small business as "one that is independently owned and operated and which is not dominant in its field of operation." While there is some disagreement as to what exactly is a small business, nearly every measure would classify Saint Laurie as a small business.

Many small businesses in general, and service providers in particular, are very proficient at their respective specialty (e.g., accounting, physical therapist, counseling, coaching) yet they often do not use strategic marketing planning when they conduct their businesses. This is especially true for small, local businesses that see their competitive advantage in serving a niche market while trying to maintain current customers and do not necessarily have a cohesive strategic plan for attaining new customers. It is not uncommon for small businesses to define their business in terms of the products that they sell rather than the value a customer gains by using the product (e.g., a movie theatre might state its business purpose as "showing movies" rather than "providing entertainment.").

The marketing practices used by any business can generally be classified as being either strategically directed or tactically directed. In order to be classified as a strategically directed firm, a business should have a cohesive marketing theme for all of its marketing endeavors. This overriding theme provides the organization with direction for coordinated business decisions in marketing. Successful strategic marketing decisions require a thorough understanding of the environment in which a business operates, as well as a complete understanding of all competitors to the organization and the capabilities and weaknesses of the organization itself.

In essence, an organization that has a strategic-marketing focus addresses the "what to do" questions. The answers to these questions drive all of the tactics and steps an organization conducts in fulfilling this marketing strategy. Examples of a strategic-marketing focus would be whether all members of the organization can articulate and understand the positioning of the organization (e.g., unique selling proposition), does the organization make effective use of databases and tracking to identify customers and effective promotions, and does the organization make use of education, joint-venturing, or other strategies in a coordinated manner? In addition, an effective marketing strategy would make use of testing and tracking all marketing campaigns, and carefully manage its brand and perception of brand among its customers/clients.

By contrast, an organization that is primarily tactically directed in its marketing efforts tends to have a shorter-term focus to its marketing efforts. The decisions for product, promotional, or branding campaigns also tend to be made in a reactive manner. These organizations often apply little forethought as to whether or not a particular marketing endeavor fits with the overall business strategy and very little, if any, testing or follow-up is initiated when a marketing campaign is conducted.

Organizations with a tactically driven marketing strategy tend to focus on individual marketing elements (e.g., a single brochure, mail-out campaign, web site, etc.) and not an overall theme where the elements are all parts of the same structure. In essence, organizations that have a strategic-marketing focus tend to be proactive and coordinated in their marketing efforts, while tactically driven organizations tend to be reactive and disconnected in their marketing efforts.

CASE
22

Powered by SRAM

DAVID ARON

DePaul University

WILLIAM KEEP

Quinnipiac University

Eric Schutt, special events director for SRAM, scanned his office one last time, looking for any other files, reports, or shrink-wrapped packages of promotional handouts that he might need in Las Vegas. Eric was preparing to represent the bicycle component manufacturer at the Interbike Show, the largest bicycle industry trade show in the United States. Eric would be pitching SRAM's "comfort platform" series of bicycle components, including the integrated accessory handlebar add-on called SmartBar®, to anyone in the industry who would listen: manufacturers, retailers, and biking enthusiasts. There were many other goals set forth by the executives at SRAM, and Interbike was the best place to get a feel for the product and competitive environment in the world of cycling. At this international trade show, Eric hoped to gauge the viability of SRAM's marketing initiatives.

The bicycle industry is a complicated one. Actually, the manufacturing process is fairly straightforward: the manufacturers, based on suggestions from key retailers, and using components from companies like SRAM and its larger, more influential rival Shimano, build bikes and send them to retailers around the world. The retailers sell bikes to customers, whose interest levels range from casual to fanatical. The process is clear enough, but the layers and directions of communication among the players in this industry represented a constant source of uncertainty and frustration for Eric. Eric knew his basic objective: to put SRAM components on the bicycles made by Trek, Giant, Pacific, and the other manufacturers. How to make this happen was the far more complicated issue.

There were other challenging issues facing Eric and SRAM as well. The bicycle industry was stagnant in the United States and the future wasn't promising. The number of biking enthusiasts was dwindling in the U.S.A., where bicycles are not woven into the culture as they are in Europe and Asia, and the aging baby-boomer generation seemed not to like how bicycle seats feel on their expanding behinds. Nature was taking its course, and that was not helping SRAM or the rest of the parties involved in manufacturing, accessorizing, or selling bicycles.

To make matters even more complicated, every customer and member of the value chain that Eric wanted to reach seemed either to be busy listening to someone else or out riding their bikes—away from the mass media.

Company Background

SRAM is pronounced just the way it is spelled, and the company's Internet site (www.sram.com) provides help for those who might think that SRAM is simply Mars spelled backward:

"SRAM is the conglomeration of our founders' names, Scott, Ray and Sam. The initials provided a simple way to come up with a corporate name that could be trade-marked and directly translated into languages other than English. It is not pronounced S-RAM, SchRAM, or SkRAM. Just SRAM."

SRAM Corporation came into being in Chicago in 1987 when six employees set up shop. Even now, as the company had grown to become a widely-recognized and international presence, SRAM remained a privately held company.

SRAM found early success in 1988 when it introduced the Grip Shift®, a road bike gear shifter that allowed the cyclist to shift more easily, using the bike's handlebars. This innovation, reminiscent of the gear-shift procedure found on motorcycles, was met with enthusiasm but at a surprising cost to SRAM: the product was better known than its manufacturer. Just as consumers might not realize that a company named Kimberly-Clarke makes Kleenex® or that 3M manufactures Scotch Tape®, cyclists came to believe that the useful new accessories on their bikes were made not by SRAM, but by a company called . . . Grip Shift. While the executives at SRAM would never want to trade the revenue that the Grip Shift® brought to SRAM, the fact that the name SRAM was subordinate to the name of their product could have negative consequences as the company attempted to introduce new products to the industry. As SRAM grew, it did manufacture a variety of bicycle components, including brakes, levers, shifters, derailleur, hubs, chains, and the SmartBar®, one of SRAM's most recent innovations.

Marketing to SRAM's Customers

SRAM's customers represented all the different slots in the channel of distribution, from the manufacturers to the retailers to the cyclist preparing for his next race to the customer simply browsing the floor of the bike shop. A difficulty for SRAM and the other component manufacturers was that customers tended to depend heavily on the advice of the retailer, or the retailer's sales rep working on the showroom floor. The retailers, in turn, acted as most retailers do: they looked for items that they knew they could sell in the least amount of time. To meet customers' needs, the manufacturers also depended on the retailers to serve as their eyes and ears. The nature of the process seemed to almost exclude the component makers, like SRAM. This confounded the introduction of a new product even further.

The bicycle market could be separated into a variety of categories. One approach looked at the types of products sold. According to estimates, about half (48 percent) of all bikes sold annually were mountain bikes. The rugged, wide-wheeled mountain bike was a remnant of the 1980s. Then, and now, mountain bike owners exemplified what might be called "SUV syndrome," like the owners of sports utility vehicles who rarely, if ever, drove their vehicles through the rugged terrain featured in the advertisements. Similarly, mountain-bike owners rarely left the streets of their neighborhoods.

The second most popular style of bicycle was called the hybrid, a scaled-down mountain bike with many characteristics of the road bike. The hybrid represented almost one-fourth of the bicycles sold, with the balance of bicycle sales falling into the following categories: youth (14 percent), BMX (10 percent), cruiser (2 percent), and road (2 percent). Bicycles were available in each category from a variety of manufacturers at a variety of price ranges. Most adult buyers would purchase a mountain bike or a hybrid.

There were groups of customers that were of particular importance to SRAM and the other members of the value chain. One such group was made up of people who worked on the sales floor of bike shops or in the store's repair shop. Often, these bike shop employees were working at the shop mainly for the employee discount that the store offers. Yet it was these bike shop employees that wielded substantial influence over the purchasing decisions of the customer.

Another group seen as vital to Eric and SRAM were highly brand-loyal biking enthusiasts that Eric has dubbed "SRAMbassadors." SRAMbassadors represented the audience targeted by the grassroots marketing and sponsorship programs that Eric had initiated, programs that involved rider and event sponsorships and appearances at "Demo Days," events such as health fairs, carnivals, even regattas. SRAMbassadors tended to live up to their name, generating favorable word-of-mouth about SRAM and its products at events and through chat rooms and online communities. The SRAMbassadors knew Eric by name and he treated them with reverence, as satellite executives of the company.

Eric also worked with the riders he sponsored, what he called his SRAM Factory Team. While not SRAM zealots to the same degree as the SRAMbassadors, the Factory Team represented SRAM by wearing the SRAM logo in competition. Event and rider sponsorships represented an important part of SRAM's marketing program and some of their most visible efforts.

SRAM's marketing program involved several elements, all executed at a low cost and all meant to pursue the elusive bicycle customer. Eric aggressively distributed flyers, water bottles, post cards, T-shirts, and promotional CDs at every opportunity. He worked with retailers to set up point-of-purchase (POP) displays involving window clings, hanging signs, and countertop displays made specifically for the SmartBar®. Outside of the store, SRAM was active as an advocate of building and maintaining bicycle trail networks. SRAM's online presence, seen on the World Wide Web at www.sram.com, was meant to inform, entertain, and generate a relationship with their technologically savvy customers.

The Bicycle Channel of Distribution

Despite the fact that consumers ultimately chose the bicycle with the options they wanted, manufacturers and dealers chose which options to make available on the showroom floor, in what quantities, and at what locations. This decision-making process within the channel of distribution further complicated product positioning.

**EXHIBIT C22.1: MARKET SHARE OF BICYCLE MANUFACTURER
LIKELY TO OFFER THE SMARTBAR**

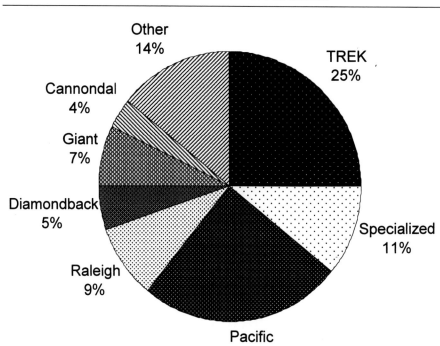

One of Eric's goals at Interbike was to make both manufacturers and retailers see value in putting the SmartBar® on their bicycles. Just eight companies manufactured the bulk of bicycles likely to feature the SmartBar®. The market shares shown in Exhibit C22.1 reflected Eric's best guess as to the relative importance of the manufacturers SRAM would want to target. Trek and Pacific were the largest, together selling 1.4 million bikes in the previous year. In that year, the top four manufacturers controlled 70 percent of a 2.8 million unit market. Some manufacturers offered multiple brand names. For example, Pacific offered the brand names of Schwinn and GT.

The structure of the retail environment further complicated the buying process. While a large number of bicycles were sold through mass merchandisers, high-end bicycles tended to be sold by a relatively small number of bicycle specialty shops. These specialty shops were owned and managed by experienced bicyclists who worked hard to make their shops market leaders within their geographic areas. In other words, in order for the bicycle-shopping consumer to try a new component like the SmartBar®, these retailers needed to show models featuring this component on their shop floors. If these important retailers were not interested in the component, the consumer simply was not likely to see SmartBar® as an option.

Thus SRAM faced a challenging channel of distribution. The traditional market approach had been one of channel "push" rather than consumer "pull." Component manufacturers had relied mostly on direct selling supported by mailings and appearances at trade shows and bicycle events to convince manufacturers and retailers to offer a specific component on some models. Eric realized that success on the consumer end would eventually bring more orders, perhaps expanding demand for the SmartBar® to additional models. Up to this point, however, SRAM's marketing efforts and corresponding marketing expenditures had been overwhelmingly directed toward buyers at key manufacturers and owners of leading specialty bicycle shops, not at the end users.

The Competition

As the bicycle industry's channel of distribution suggests, relationships are vital and the components industry was a competitive one. SRAM was a key player, but was a distant second in terms of sales to their Japanese rival, Shimano. Shimano was a formidable competitor. SRAM had, in fact, been third in the industry until 1997 when the company purchased Sachs, which had been ranked second. While SRAM continued to focus its efforts on bike components, Shimano was more diversified, making a variety of products ranging from bicycle accessories to fishing reels to golf clubs.

Shimano held the largest market share of all bicycle components sold in the United States and was generally considered to be a firm that offered a quality product. SRAM, a much smaller company, was an up-and-coming competitor with a reputation built more on innovation. SRAM had tried to distinguish itself from its larger rival with speed in bringing products to market. With products such as the SmartBar®, SRAM strived to be first to market. This came at a cost. While the larger Shimano was known to be methodical, it was also regarded as "quality-centric," often allowing SRAM to gain a first-mover advantage. But this advantage could be tenuous. SRAM had experienced reliability and durability problems with its components in the past, while Shimano banked on its size and its strong reputation as well as SRAM's willingness to, essentially, test the market for the market leader. Retailers seemed to favor Shimano due to its size and customer recognition.

A third component manufacturer, SunRace, was gaining popularity in the shadow of Shimano and SRAM. SunRace also made a variety of bicycle accessories including their JuJu® twist shifter. The JuJu® had been rated high in quality and durability, and while slightly more difficult to use than SRAM's shifters, it compared favorably to SRAM's product at a lower price.

Recently SRAM purchased RockShox®, a well-regarded manufacturer of suspension systems, to continue building a company that offered leading bicycle components. Eric was confident that increasing its product line of quality shifters, brakes, chains, suspension units, and comfort add-ons would allow SRAM to more successfully compete with Shimano. Nonetheless, when a SRAM representative called on a buyer from Trek, or one of the other large bicycle manufacturers, she faced the challenge of building business for each of SRAM's product categories, plus trying to induce them to offer the SmartBar® on some models.

Price was a key factor, and not only in the eyes of the cyclist. Shimano and SRAM had been long engaged in a legal battle regarding Shimano's predatory pricing activity. In December 2000, a jury in California found that Shimano was selling shifters at a price below their cost and awarded SRAM $9 million. Litigation was currently underway in Europe, where SRAM's German office had filed a similar dumping charge against Shimano. The stakes were higher in Europe, where bicycling was far more important, both as a mode of transportation and as part of the lifestyle, than it is in the United States. An important question was whether the constant and costly legal wrangling took a greater toll on the rule-bending giant Shimano or the smaller, faster SRAM.

Positioning the Product

For all of the technological elegance and user benefits of the SmartBar®, Eric had told others at SRAM that the product was "suffering from a weird upward, backward, sideways flow of information." The enthusiasts that Eric stayed in close contact with and that SRAM sponsored actually did not seek the comfort features such as the SmartBar®.

The SmartBar® was one of a number of "comfort add-ons" that represented a new trend in bicycling. These add-ons often employed visible technology that allowed the consumer to see and feel the effects of technology-based components. SRAM's own promotional material describes SmartBar® as:

> " . . . the most radical new design in handlebars in decades. Ergonomically-designed, the SmartBar® handlebar allows the rider to easily reach customized accessories such as its headlights (which are controlled from the handlebar), racks, rearview mirrors and an integrated on-board wireless computer which measures ride time, distance, speed, etc. The SmartBar® also features a 'Flip-Flop' stem that allows the rider to adjust the bar's height and reach, as well as rise and angle."

In addition to the multi-functional SmartBar®, other new advances include power-assist drive systems, ergonomically designed brake levers, shifters requiring little effort with highly visible gear indicators, and suspension (i.e., shock absorbers) for forks, frames, and seats. Since many of these advancements were new, the markets for individual add-ons had yet to be fully developed. The proliferation of options was fragmenting the traditional bicycle market. Component manufacturers like SRAM did not yet know how many potential customers there were for each of these various product enhancements.

The SmartBar® would be added to bicycles originally priced in the $400 to $1,000 range, and Eric feared that consumers purchasing lower priced bicycles would likely be unwilling to pay the extra $150 to $200 for the SmartBar®. Those buying bikes priced at $1,000+ were generally not looking for comfort, but rather performance-enhancing options. A mountain bike or a performance bike would basically lose its identity if it included the SmartBar®.

Eric's thoughts still came back to the basic fact that bicycle dealers would want the bicycles on their showroom floors to have options that customers wanted and were willing to pay for. The SmartBar® and other comfort add-ons created a special problem because there was little known about the evolving comfort market. Thus Eric faced a dilemma. Continuing to push the SmartBar® to manufacturers and retailers could be difficult because these channel partners were not yet convinced of consumer acceptance. Alternatively, if SRAM could demonstrate consumer demand of sufficient magnitude, manufacturers and retailers would be convinced that they needed to adopt the SmartBar® for some of their models. But going direct to the consumer was new for SRAM and other component manufacturers. These companies were not experienced with marketing efforts designed to "pull" the product through the channel using consumer demand.

Eric knew that the SmartBar® had consumer appeal, yet at this point not a single OEM (original equipment manufacturer) bike had SmartBar® included on it in the U.S. market. Efforts directed toward the retailer might generate a call to the manufacturer's rep, yet that rep would also be listening to Shimano. Shimano's FlightDeck was a somewhat integrated computer initially released for road bikes. The FlightDeck was connected to the bicycle's shifters, so the computer knew what gear the bike was in. FlightDeck had been well received by OEMs and cyclists, but was initially released only to a small market: road bikes. Shimano had subsequently expanded FlightDeck to work with other bike styles, but its complexity and cost had limited its success.

Who Would Buy the SmartBar®?

If one goal was to establish the level of consumer demand, then the natural question was: Which consumers were likely to value the benefits offered by the SmartBar®? The answer to this question was difficult. On the one hand, Eric has considered any consumer to be a potential buyer. The SmartBar® and other comfort add-ons could be ideal for most buyers of mountain bikes and hybrids since the majority did not actually go off-road. But which buying segments were most likely to adopt first? Researching a new-to-the-world consumer product is not easy.

Eric expected that taking a bicycle featuring a SmartBar® directly to consumers could help establish interest and provide valuable feedback. Market surveys designed to measure consumer demand could also be developed. Survey research alone, however, might not accurately measure new product sales. It is one thing for a consumer to indicate an intent to buy in a survey response and quite another for them to make a purchase.

On the other hand, initial consumer comments collected by Eric had been very favorable. Bicycles featuring the SmartBar® had been taken to various locations around the country and consumers had raved over its convenience and comfort. In addition to offering added functionality and comfort, the SmartBar® also had an attractive high-tech appearance. As a result, some early adopters had purchased the product, but as an add-on. Eric had data collected from a small sample of these early adopters. A buyer database was created from information cards returned to SRAM in exchange for a small gift. While not a random sample of all SmartBar® buyers, the data available on approximately 100 buyers provided some interesting insights.

Exhibit C22.2 shows the age breakdown for those SmartBar® buyers who returned buyer information cards. This product was clearly purchased for comfort by older consumers. In fact, 57 percent of all buyers were ages 46 and up, with another 20 percent between the ages of 36 and 45. Only 14 percent of these SmartBar® buyers were aged 35 or less with only 3 percent aged 25 or less. In addition, Exhibit C22.3 shows that these buyers were primarily intermediate-level bicycle riders. Only 21 percent

EXHIBIT C22.2: AGE OF SᴍᴀʀᴛBᴀʀ® BUYERS

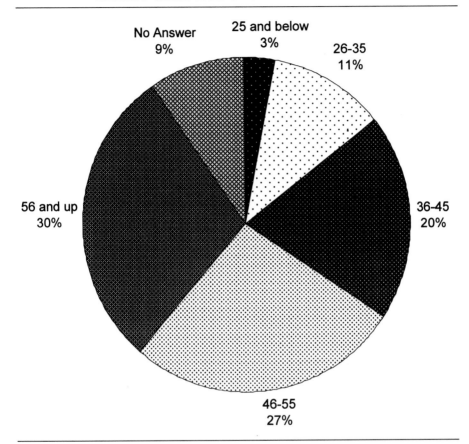

considered their bicycle riding ability to be at the advanced or professional level. This sample suggested that indeed the SmartBar® was a comfort add-on, apparently for those riders of a comfort-seeking age. The average price further suggested that these consumers had above-average income. Eric saw the data as valuable but wondered to what degree it accurately represented the potential SmartBar® market.

In addition to who buys a SmartBar®, when they buy is also important. To offer the product as an after-market add-on meant using a different channel of distribution, one involving component wholesalers, and a higher selling price. In the after-market the consumer would have already purchased a bicycle complete with handlebars and shifters only to spend another $200 to replace them with the SmartBar®. While this type of upgrade seemed doable, the perception within SRAM management was that only a small percentage of consumers would follow this route. That means the most likely time of purchase would be when buying a new bicycle with the SmartBar® as an OEM component. Eric's nagging questions remained: How could this be accomplished and at what cost?

EXHIBIT C22.3: SELF-REPORTED SKILL LEVEL OF BICYCLE BUYERS

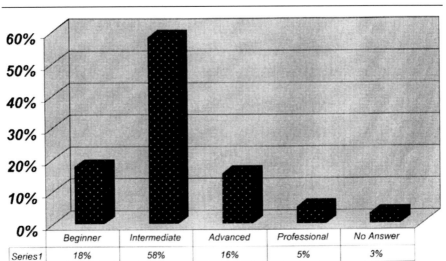

	Beginner	Intermediate	Advanced	Professional	No Answer
Series1	18%	58%	16%	5%	3%

Skill Level

Developing a Marketing Program for the Comfort Bike Segment

Eric's unstated goal at Interbike was to find industry support for what he believed to be true: SRAM's salvation resided in the comfort bike segment. "Our riders are getting older," Eric acknowledged. Therein lay the conflict that continued to plague Eric and SRAM. They had a product perfectly suited for this segment, the SmartBar®, and were even researching a prototypical architecture for a high-end comfort bike, yet the fact remained that SRAM did not make bicycles.

Eric had been losing sleep over this issue. Continuing to market the SmartBar® to manufacturers was not a problem. SRAM sales representatives would be calling on buyers for all the major manufacturers at the conference and thereafter on a regular basis. Yet SRAM's commission structure encouraged SRAM representatives to push the company's full range of components. This meant that they might or might not get much time to spend with manufacturer buyers solely to sell the SmartBar®. SRAM would also continue direct marketing efforts toward important specialty retailers. These retailers were well-known to the company and would be contacted on a regular basis. And yet, to Eric's dismay, all of these past efforts had failed to put the SmartBar® on the retail shop floor.

In the weeks leading up to the conference, Eric had been considering a direct mail campaign directed at consumers. The idea is to attract likely buyers to try the SmartBar® at a specialty retailer near them. If Eric could convince those at SRAM to take this path it would be the first time ever that the company tried to pull a bicycle component through the channel by going directly to the consumer's mailbox.

In recent months, most of Eric's time had been spent on this project. Using the unlimited energies of a marketing intern from a nearby university, Eric had attempted to analyze the consumer markets around the most important specialty bicycle retailers in the country. With an off-the-shelf GIS system, the marketing intern had pinpointed important demographics for the zip codes surrounding each specialty retail outlet. Eric told the intern to focus on age, household (i.e., HH) income, and population. The age breaks available on the GIS system were broader than those in the current buyer database, making comparisons imperfect but still relevant. Eric and his intern realized that comparing databases that do not match perfectly is more the rule than the exception.

Exhibit C22.4 provides basic demographic information for the zip code areas served by the 27 key specialty bicycle retailers throughout the country. The information provided includes retailer name, number of outlets, state, household income, population, and the population percentages for three age categories. The income and population data are aggregated at the zip code level with forecasts for the year 2005 based on earlier U.S. census data. About half of the retailers had more than one location. In these cases the data was first aggregated for each zip code area where the chain retailer had a store and then averaged across all zip codes served by the retailer.

The overall plan was to send a direct mail piece to likely buyers in a small sample of zip code areas. Potential buyers would be invited to come into the specialty retailer near them (i.e., an outlet of one of the 27 key retailers) to try a new bicycle featuring the SmartBar® and receive a small gift. An interested consumer could then special-order a bicycle with this option, thereby helping to demonstrate to manufacturers the demand for the product. The direct mail campaign allowed SRAM to market directly to the consumer, increasing brand awareness that could benefit the company in other product areas. One list vendor indicated that prescreens for health and previous purchases would probably result in lists equal to about one-third of the total number of adults available in each zip code area.

Selling the plan inside SRAM had not been easy. Resources and time were scarce. A budget of between $15,000 and $20,000 had been established. Eric wanted to carefully choose the sample zip codes. Yet unanswered questions included:

- How many zip codes can be sampled?
- What criteria should be used?
- What geographic areas should be considered?
- What response rate will be needed to succeed?
- What should the free gift be?
- What should be the mix between chain retailers and single-outlet retailers?
- In the case of chain retailers, does only one outlet need be chosen or should it be more than one?
- Who should choose the outlet, the chain retailer or SRAM?

The one sure thing was that in order for this campaign to be a success SRAM needed to sell at least 180 bicycles featuring the SmartBar®. Could they do it?

EXHIBIT C22.4: TOP BICYCLE RETAIL SHOPS IN THE U.S.

	Bicycle Retailer	# of Stores	State	Est. HH Income 2005	Est. Pop 2005	% Ages 25–44	% Ages 45–54	% Ages 55 and up
1	Albuquerque Cycles	3	NM	$ 69,114	40089	0.288	0.152	0.226
2	Belmont Wheelworks	2	MA	$ 97,877	23771	0.330	0.155	0.258
3	The Bike Rack	1	IL	$ 163,472	19418	0.224	0.168	0.223
4	Brands Cycling and Fitness	1	NY	$ 109,911	32252	0.254	0.164	0.288
5	Carl Hart	1	NY	$ 70,658	12647	0.300	0.156	0.174
6	Criterium	1	CO	$ 33,318	15742	0.305	0.131	0.191
7	Cycle Loft	1	MA	$ 112,121	24860	0.305	0.146	0.267
8	Danzizen & Quigley	1	NJ	$ 171,774	30607	0.248	0.172	0.276
9	Eddy's Bike Shop	4	OH	$ 93,978	26664	0.256	0.155	0.292
10	Erik's—Burnsville	8	MN	$ 85,558	29212	0.317	0.148	0.203
11	Frenchie's Cyleworld	1	NY	$ 130,903	61964	0.275	0.166	0.254
12	Gregg's Bellvue Cycle	3	WA	$ 122,817	36038	0.329	0.171	0.278
13	Helen's Cycles	5	CA	$ 104,243	33909	0.302	0.172	0.261
14	I. Martin Imports	1	CA	$ 73,517	24795	0.278	0.193	0.395
15	Kozy's	3	IL	$ 113,730	48803	0.389	0.185	0.232
16	Landis Cyclery	4	AZ	$ 141,334	29319	0.276	0.170	0.261
17	Landry's—HQ	5	MA	$ 99,844	23302	0.271	0.161	0.270
18	Mill Race Cyclery	1	IL	$ 101,391	24005	0.243	0.165	0.237
19	Missing Link	1	CA	$ 42,015	22757	0.321	0.089	0.285
20	Penn Cycles—Bloomington	5	MN	$ 94,645	26481	0.329	0.155	0.233
21	Richardson's Bicycle Mart	2	TX	$ 103,276	34202	0.249	0.171	0.305
22	Roy's Sheepshead Cyclery	1	NY	$ 47,979	73970	0.259	0.140	0.356
23	Supergo Bike Shop	5	AZ	$ 83,578	43057	0.272	0.159	0.301
24	Turin of Denver	1	CO	$ 41,800	15834	0.447	0.176	0.239
25	Wheatridge Cyclery	1	CO	$ 57,891	23462	0.282	0.138	0.284
26	Wheel & Sprocket (HQ)	6	WI	$ 118,861	18490	0.240	0.165	0.266
27	Zanes	1	CT	$ 94,697	27370	0.271	0.175	0.291

CASE
23

Home Equity Loans in Texas: The Wells Fargo Experience

MARY ALICE SHAVER
Michigan State University

CAROL ANN HACKLEY
University of the Pacific

Home equity loans have become an important part of the bank consumer credit business, reaching new popularity with both customers and bankers at the end of the 20th century. Two factors were primary contributors to this: 1) Mortgage interest rates plummeted to levels of 4 to 6 percent in the early 2000s—the lowest rates in nearly 30 years, and 2) with the removal of federal tax credit for consumer debt, home equity loans remained as one of few deductible areas. Further, this money could be used for any expense—car loans, weddings, college tuition, and vacations—in many states. Finally, although interest was payable monthly, the principal of most loans could be deferred for up to ten years. All of these factors were appealing to consumers.

For Wells Fargo, applications were up in most locations, as customers vied for these popular loan packages. The exception was in Texas, where, since 1837, laws had prevented any borrowing against homestead property value, except for actual home improvement loans. The Texas state legislature debated the home equity issue for over five years. Finally, the Texas House and Senate passed a home equity law, which left the issue up to a vote of the electorate. The bill was complicated: Unlike other states, where home equity loans provided customers with what was essentially a book of checks to be written at the whim of the consumer, the Texas law provided for actual loans only. Other restrictions included a 12-day waiting period after the initial consumer application or the receipt of home equity disclosure, whichever was last, before the lender could confirm the loan. In addition, loans had to be signed in a title company (or branch) or in an attorney's office rather than at the consumer's home. Furthermore, there was an 80 percent cap on loans. In other words, loans could be made only if owners had a full 20 percent of equity in their homes. Under this proposal, lenders could lose the entire amount of the loan if they violated any of the restrictions during the loan process. An official at Wells Fargo termed the Texas restrictions as "Draconian."

The vote on the legislation was slated for November. Draconian provisions or not, the passage of this bill would open up the state of Texas to enormous revenue opportunities for banks that were able to take advantage of this market. But everything had to be in place by November, to move into instant action if the bill passed in the general election.

The national market for home equity loans was estimated to be $150 billion in lendable equity opportunities. Of this multi-billion figure, 6 to 10 percent was loaned annually, either in refinancing or new home equity loans. The potential of the market in Texas was estimated by Wells Fargo to be $10 billion over the first 24 months of the program.

Home Equity Loan Background

Home equity loans are perceived as a way for homeowners to raise cash for many needs, using the money that they have accrued in their homes as equity or collateral. In many states, the money is available if the owner has only 5 or 10 percent equity or value in the home. Some banks in other states had introduced home equity packages that allowed homeowners to actually borrow more money than the home was worth—up to 125 percent of the home value. Many home equity loans were not restricted as to use or time of use by the loan recipient, and all carried tax-deduction privileges. For the consumer, the loans provided a way of getting ready cash to pay big bills, while having a delayed principal pay-off period and getting a welcome tax deduction. For loans that provided what amounted to an open checkbook, customers could "borrow" money without having to discuss the need with anyone at the bank and with no delay, as easily as writing a check. For the lenders, it provided an incentive for customers to choose the bank for the initial home mortgage, an additional value-added service, and yet one more revenue-producing asset. The home equity loan truly seemed to be a win-win situation for all of those involved. But it was a win-win situation that excluded the population-heavy state of Texas with all its potential home equity loan customers.

Company Background

Wells Fargo Bank, N.A., is the primary subsidiary of Wells Fargo & Company, founded in 1852. Wells Fargo has projected a strong Western image since the days when its stagecoaches traveled across the West to deliver mail and cash. The Wells Fargo traditions are service, convenience, and value. At the time the home equity situation was heating up in Texas, Wells Fargo & Company had assets of $94.8 billion.

Until its merger with Norwest Bank, Wells Fargo had 1,865 branches in ten western states. While California had the most (1,072), Texas ranked third with 177 Wells Fargo branches. Before the merger, Wells Fargo had done nearly 50 percent of its business outside of California, operating in nine adjacent states from Texas to Washington.

In the late 1970s, Crocker Bank was the first to enter the home equity loan business. The Crocker Bank was later acquired by Wells Fargo, giving the company the opportunity to enter the home equity market.

Wells Fargo also had acquired First Interstate Bank, headquartered in Los Angeles.

At the time of that merger, First Interstate did not have a strong brand presence in Texas, although it had branches in the major cities of Dallas-Fort Worth, Houston, and Austin. Despite the fact that some First Interstate customers defected after the merger, Wells Fargo saw the acquisition as a new opportunity to build business and gain a presence in the banking world of this important state. In its new advertising campaign, Wells Fargo focused on stability and its long history to suggest trustworthiness to its new customer base.

Texas Home Equity Loan Opportunities

With the introduction of the Texas home equity legislation, Wells Fargo was ready to make a move into that lucrative market. With just five months until the November election, the strategy had to be to learn as much about the market and the consumers as quickly as possible. Texas was viewed as having great potential consumer demand for home equity borrowing. A successful bank would have to recognize this grass roots demand and capitalize on it.

Decisions had to be made swiftly in a number of areas, including consumer research, assessing the place of Wells Fargo in the consumer mind a year after the Norwest merger, budgeting for the campaign, determining the appropriate level of spending necessary to gain a top market share, designing advertising, working against the competition, lobbying public officials, and positioning Wells Fargo as a leader in the home equity line of business. Without knowing whether the law would pass or not, Wells Fargo had to build an infrastructure for the home equity loan business so it would be ready to compete and to lead the market.

Consumer research focused on brand name recognition and awareness of home equity loans. Research revealed low awareness and uncertainty and fear of losing homes due to borrowing against them. Wells Fargo was seen as the bank that merged with First Interstate, but it had a favorable image associated with the values of the Old West. One strategic advantage for Wells Fargo was that consumers were neutral toward First Interstate, so there was no usurper image to overcome.

From their consumer research, Wells Fargo profiled the target customer as "a Texas homeowner who is looking to a trusted financial services provider for information about home equity loans, and who values excellent service and has demonstrated creditworthiness."

The Direct Mail Campaign

The decision was made to implement two direct mail home equity loan components. The first, labeled "Stampede," was sent on October 22. According to the strategy statement, this mailing was consistent with the overall plan to roll out to all Wells Fargo customers across the state, as well as to non-customers in the Dallas-Fort Worth MSA. On November 20, if the law had passed, a second mail initiative, termed "Dust," was to be sent to non-customer homeowners in the Houston MSA. The goal was to profitably originate business through education on the new law, maintenance of strong customer focus, and low cost/expeditious production. Because Wells Fargo only had a 6 percent share of deposits, it had to go outside the customer base with direct mail.

EXHIBIT C23.1

WELLS FARGO BANK

Yours free —

answers to
your questions
about Home
Equity Loans.

Wells Fargo Bank
Texas Home Equity DM
Non-Cust "Promotional"
WFO-00-003,10/7/97

Dear Prospect,

On November 4, a referendum which amends the Texas constitution to allow home equity lending, goes before voters. If the referendum is approved, Texas homeowners will, for the first time, have the opportunity to borrow against the equity in their homes.

What will this mean for you? It may mean that you have a new financial tool available to help with expenses such as a new car or truck, tuition, home improvement, bill consolidation, large purchases, medical expenses or investment opportunities.

To help you understand what home equity loans are and how they will work in Texas, we've prepared a booklet that can answer your questions.

The Wells Fargo Bank Consumer Guide to Home Equity Loans provides the answers to Texas homeowners' most frequently asked questions. This booklet explains:
- the advantages home equity loans may provide and what they are generally used for
- the tax deductibility of home equity loan interest (consult your financial advisor)
- how to estimate the available equity in your home
- what to expect during the loan application process and more

You're invited to accept this Guide with our compliments — and without any obligation.
Wells Fargo Bank is a recognized leader in the home equity loan industry. In fact, Wells Fargo was America's first home equity lender. And we want to be sure that Texas homeowners have access to the resources they need to make informed decisions about home equity loans.

To request your complimentary *Guide,* call us at 1-800-872-8228. Our home equity representatives are ready to answer any questions you have. You can also complete and mail the request form below, or fax it to 1-800-511-1998.

We appreciate the opportunity to be of service to you.

Sincerely,

Chip Carlisle

Chip Carlisle
President, Wells Fargo Bank (Texas)

P.S.   To request your complimentary *Consumer Guide to Home Equity Loans,* or for more information, call 1-800-872-8228 — 24 hours a day, 7 days a week. We'll be happy to assist you.

Request for More Information

Get the facts on
home equity loans.
Request your
complimentary
booklet today.

(Please correct name/address if necessary.)

Wells Fargo Bank
Texas Home Equity DM
Non-Cust "Promotional"
WFO-00-003,10/7

Reservation No. 12345678901 1234
Expiration Date: 11/30

Phone No. (____) _____

Best Time to Call: ☐ Morning ☐ Afternoon ☐ Evening

Call 1-800-872-8228 now to request your complimentary *Consumer Guide to Home Equity Loans.* Wells Fargo Bank representatives are available to answer your questions. Or complete and return this request form.

Call 1-800-872-8228

24 hours a day, 7 days a week.

MAIL TO:
WELLS FARGO BANK, P.O. BOX 3310, PUEBLO, CO 81005-3310
FAX TO: 1-800-511-1998

It was critical that the next mailings:

- Gather information on purchase behavior, customer attributes, credit attributes, and home values for future targeting models
- Gain early market share
- Test the right factors to influence profitability of the coming year's efforts
- Test vendors' account processing capabilities

The Mailing Plan

"Stampede" was a combination Wells Fargo Bank customer cross-sell and prospect extract mailing. The plan was to target approximately 142,000 homeowners for the new Texas home equity loan. The "Stampede" mailing base included 39,000 customers and 103,000 prospects. Because of the pending election on the proposed law, the mailing was necessarily a two-step pre-qualified mailing. Because "Stampede" was delivered before the November 4 election, the customer first received an offer for a "Consumer Guide to Home Equity Loans." This was part of the brand name building and customer education component. After the election, if the law passed, the fulfillment stage was to be enacted. In this second step, the customer received a pre-qualified offer. Because the names had been prescreened, all respondents to stage one received the pre-qualified offer. No additional screening was done between the two stages.

The November mailing, "Dust," to 50,000 was a traditional pre-qualified mailing to non-customer prospects in the Houston area.

Several different letters were sent. The first solicited responses requesting the Guide; the second accompanied the Guide and invited recipients to call for additional information. Another mailing targeted pre-qualified homeowners and stressed both the low 7.99 annual percentage rate (APR) and the after-tax translation of that rate to as low as 5.75 percent.

The October program was expected to generate 752 accounts with $16.9 million in commitments (an average of $22,473 per loan). The November program was expected to generate 149 accounts and $3.3 million in commitments. The projected difference in the two campaigns was due to the smaller mailing in "Dust" and, more important, to the fact that past experience and focus group research showed that customers are expected to respond at much higher rate than non-customers. To qualify for the loans, customers and prospects needed to have an annual income of over $30,000 and a clean credit rating. The average projected home equity loan was $22,500 for both "Stampede" and "Dust."

Wells Fargo believed that the response rate for the first "Stampede" mailing would be very high, due to the fact that the product was new to the market and that the mailing offered information. The response rate was estimated at 8 percent of the 142,000 contacted, or just over 11,000. For the second mailing, the fulfillment stage, a higher than typical response rate of 20 percent was also anticipated, due to what was seen as pent-up demand in the Texas market. The conversion rate of respondents to final loans was forecast at 33 percent, a lower than typical equity conversion, due to three factors: lack of equity in existing homes, newness of the product offered, and rate shopping. The average loan amount of $22,500 was also seen as lower than the rest of the franchise, due to lower home values in the market and to the large non-customer population.

The initial "Stampede" mail drop occurred on October 22. The "Stampede" information offer expired on November 30. With the successful passage of the home equity loan legislation, the second phase of the "Stampede" mail plan was implemented. The fulfillment offer, sent to all those who had responded to the original "Stampede" information mailing, expired the next January 15.

In accord with the plan, the "Dust" mailing sent to non-customer home owners in the Houston area was dropped on November 20. "Dust" consisted of both information and an offer with an expiration date of January 5 of the coming year.

Wells Fargo allowed a several weeks' grace period to responders for both campaigns. Further, because the Texas Home Equity referendum did not go into effect until January 1, the required home equity disclosure that had been included in the fall pre-registered mailings had to be re-mailed to customers after January 1. Wells Fargo allowed five days for receipt of the disclosure by the customer. Due to the 12-day waiting period, the earliest date to close a loan was January 17.

A telemarketing campaign was initiated once the law had passed on November 4. Of the approximately 192,000 direct mail pieces mailed, Wells Fargo had telephone numbers for 150,000 for outbound follow-up telemarketing purposes.

The Marketing Strategy

The marketing strategy for the home equity loan mailings was to:

- Develop an understanding of mailing home equity loan offers to Texas
- Gain early market share
- Test telemarketing for servicing non-customer prospects
- Explore early closing strategy through outbound telemarketing follow-up to customer applications
- Build an understanding of response behavior

The creative design for "Stampede" was a simple clean look. The offer consisted of a one-page letter with an attached perforated response certificate. A legal disclosure covering the proposed law, the "Terms and Conditions," and the government monitoring information was clearly printed on the reverse side of the letter. The logo read, "Wells Fargo Bank" to clearly define that Wells Fargo was a bank. A similar simple design was used for the "Dust" mailing.

Three versions—one for Wells Fargo customers and a split run for non-customers in each market—were designed. The woodcut stagecoach logo of Wells Fargo was screened in the background of the letter.

In addition, other advertising was implemented. Teaser 60-second TV spots stated, "If you have questions about Home Equity in Texas, Wells Fargo has the answers. Kids, college, car, vacations." A tag line was "For all your reasons why." The pre-election teaser ads also offered a free guide to home equity loans.

The Time Line for the Start-up Campaign

The Wells Fargo start-up and ready-to-go campaign began in June with a staff of two and followed this time line:

July
• Consumer insight research initiated
• Advertising agency hired

August
• Wells Fargo position decided
• Call center hired
• Budget recommendations made
• Marketing plan finalized
• Decision made to go "heavy direct"
• Decision made to develop an online call center

September
• Advertising campaign development initiated
• Product definition finalized
• Training for October 20 launch of teaser campaign begun at bank branches and operation centers

October
• Mailings of "Stampede" sent
• Advertising campaign implemented
• Wells Fargo helped fund Texas Bank Association lobbying effort of state leaders
• Ads projected image of Wells Fargo as "first home equity leader"

Wells Fargo's projected target share of the market was 10 percent or $1 billion with $24 million in net income from new home equity loans in 24 months.

The Bank spent $1 million in up-front costs associated with advertising and preliminary infrastructure associated with call center development and training of 700 people in four weeks.

Results of the Campaign

By October 20, phones were ringing. Although home equity loans could not be finalized until mid-January, there were approximately 4,000 applications in by January 1. In ten weeks, Wells Fargo had 20,000 calls concerning home equity loans. The first people were hungry for credit.

Unfortunately, the quality of the applications was not as high as anticipated. Once approval could be given, the rate of completion was 35 percent. Many of the applications that were below the Wells Fargo cut-off were referred to the Associates Home Equity Loan Service that accepted these applications on a referral commission basis.

For the Texas campaign, there were two goals: to meet the objectives set for volume of loans granted and for market share. Although the market share goals were met initially—Wells Fargo attained an initial number one or number two market share—the target volume of loans was not met. By January, the total volume was lower than expected: Only 50 to 60 percent of the predicted dollar/volume goal was met. Further, the market was softer than anticipated. Market acceptance of the home equity packages was also lower than projected. The direct mail campaign was not as successful as had been hoped in driving the customers into the branch banks to finalize loans. The challenge

EXHIBIT C23.2

Right now, Wells Fargo home equity loan rates are as low as 7.99% APR!*

Wells Fargo Bank
NW, SW, RM Home Equity - M2
8356 - Pre-Qualified Prospect
Western Control

HOME EQUITY LOAN
You're pre-qualified
for up to
$100,000

Hurry! Offer expires June 15
Call **1-800-605-8686**

Dear Prospect,

Congratulations!

Your outstanding financial record has pre-qualified you for a home equity loan up to $100,000. It lets you use the equity you've already earned — so you can make any dream a reality.

Get an after-tax rate as low as 5.75% APR.†

Home equity loan interest is usually tax-deductible — and that means a lot. Just ask your tax advisor. You could enjoy significant savings. And with a Wells Fargo home equity loan, you'll save in lots of other ways too:

- **There are absolutely no points or fees.**
- **And you can choose your own term — from five to thirty years — for the low monthly payment you want.**

You can even choose an EquityLine® of credit. If you don't need a home equity loan right now, EquityLine lets you easily access up to 100% of your available equity — *any time you need it.*

Wells Fargo is America's first home equity lender, with a tradition of personalized service since 1852.

We can help you do more for yourself and your family now. *For instant approval of your home equity loan or EquityLine, call 1-800-605-8686, 24 hours a day, 7 days a week.* You can also mail or fax the attached Certificate, or bring it to your local branch. We look forward to hearing from you soon.

Sincerely,

Colin Walsh
Vice President/US Equity, Wells Fargo Bank

P.S. You're pre-qualified for up to $100,000 — and you have your choice of a Wells Fargo home equity loan or EquityLine of credit! Whatever your financial needs, call Wells Fargo at **1-800-605-8686** for instant loan or line approval today.

*7.99% Annual Percentage Rate (APR) as of April 13, 1998 based on loan amount of $50,000, a 5-year term and automatic payment from a Wells Fargo Bank checking account. For example, a 5-year loan of $30,000 at 7.99% APR would be repayable in 60 monthly installments of $1,013.58 each. Your actual rate may be different. Call us for EquityLine rates and rates for other loan amounts and terms. Rates subject to change without notice. †After-tax equivalent rate assumes a 28% tax bracket.

052-3

became how to maintain the momentum, while targeting more narrowly to those potential customers who would both qualify for and finalize loans.

At this point, the ad campaign expenditures and exposures were reduced. Ads for the home equity program, particularly the expensive broadcast commercials, were adjusted downward.

It was just at this time, as Wells Fargo geared down to contain costs, that other banks in the market became more competitive in the home equity business. The major competitors—Nations Bank (which originally had said it was not entering the home equity market in Texas), the Texas Commerce Bank, and the United Bank of

EXHIBIT C23.3

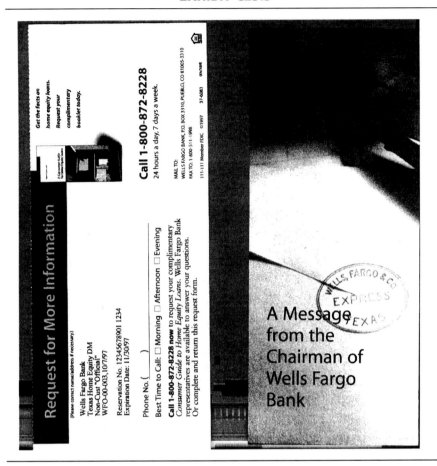

Texas—were advertising rates of .25 to .50 lower. The public perception was that Wells Fargo charged too much. Eventually, Wells Fargo dropped from first or second in market share to third or fourth as the other competing banks grabbed the top end of the market. However, although the volume of loans dropped off, the approval rate for loans rose to 50 percent as the market matured.

Factors in Wells Fargo Failing to Meet Projected Goals

This was a situation in which decisions about start-up plans and costs, advertising spending levels, and the anticipated demand curve needed to be made before even knowing whether the product was going to be marketable. To be competitive in this lucrative market, Wells Fargo needed to move immediately after the May legislative decision and to invest heavily well in advance of the November referendum election.

Although projections as to total market viability could be made using experience from other states, population/home ownership figures, and bank deposit levels, no firm data on demand existed for Texas, which had never allowed home equity loans for any use but remodeling. Other factors contributed to the failure to meet volume goals:

- Start-up costs to establish the working infrastructure were high. In June, Wells Fargo had one person on the Texas Home Equity account. In the next four months, over $1 million had been spent on research, advertising, call center development, and the hiring and training of 700 people.
- With the necessary heavy expenditures for the aggressive campaign, the cost for each loan application was approximately $200.
- Research showed Wells Fargo had little brand awareness, which had to be overcome with advertising through both broadcast and direct mail.
- Many initial applications did not meet the minimum income or equity standards set by the bank.
- Market acceptance of the home equity product was lower than anticipated.
- Competing banks entered the market aggressively, once the referendum had passed, with loan rates fractionally lower than Wells Fargo. This led to a public perception of Wells Fargo being expensive.

The Aftermath

Valuable lessons were learned in the Texas campaign, however. The aggressive advertising did work to pre-empt the competition in the beginning. More important, the components that worked were introduced into other Wells Fargo market states. The marketing group was successful in using the strategy in Seattle, Phoenix, Denver, and in all nine states in the Wells Fargo region outside California. Profits missed in Texas were made up in the more mature markets.

The marketing group was effective in reorganizing home equity loans as a solid line of business for Wells Fargo. The U.S. expansion of the home equity effort was launched in March. It was so successful that, by August of that year, home equity generated as much business as it had in the entire previous year.

Questions

1. How could the direct mail campaign have been conceived to be more effective in generating branch bank traffic for home equity loans in Texas?
2. How could the direct mail pieces have been improved for quality consumer response?
3. How could synergy between the efforts in television advertising, direct mail, and telemarketing effort have been increased?
4. How could Wells Fargo have reduced its risks with this Texas home equity loan start-up, when the time frame was so tight and there were so many unknowns?
5. What lessons were learned in Texas that enabled Wells Fargo to be more successful in subsequent home equity campaigns?

INDEX